Handbook for Measurement and Evaluation in Early Childhood Education

Jossey-Bass Publishers

San Francisco • Washington • London • 1980

HANDBOOK FOR MEASUREMENT AND EVALUATION
IN EARLY CHILDHOOD EDUCATION
Issues, Measures, and Methods
        by William L. Goodwin and Laura A. Driscoll

Copyright © 1980 by: Jossey-Bass Inc., Publishers
                      433 California Street
                      San Francisco, California 94104
                             &
                      Jossey-Bass Limited
                      28 Banner Street
                      London EC1Y 8QE

Library of Congress Cataloging in Publication Data

Goodwin, William Lawrence, 1935–
    Handbook for measurement and evaluation in early
childhood education.

    Bibliography: p. 556
    Includes index.
    1. Child development—Evaluation. 2. Ability—
Testing.   I. Driscoll, Laura A., joint author.
II. Title.
LB1115.G635   372.1'2'6   79–88768
ISBN 0–87589–440–2

Manufactured in the United States of America

JACKET DESIGN BY WILLI BAUM

FIRST EDITION

Code 8001

The Jossey-Bass
Social and Behavioral Science Series

Preface

This handbook focuses on three topics that have, until now, been considered separately: early childhood education, measurement, and evaluation. Although this may seem to be an unusual combination, the uniqueness and strength of the handbook rests upon this merger. The result is a vital contribution to the field, for approaches and procedures are systematically presented for finding out what works in early childhood education by the judicious use of measurement and evaluation.

There is an important, multifaceted need for this handbook. First, it contains vital guidelines and information for concerned professionals in the field. Practitioners in early childhood education need to be aware of how measurement and evaluation can improve their efforts to nurture and support the development of young children. Directors of early childhood education programs have similar information needs and, increasingly, are asked to understand the evaluation of both programs and persons. Similarly, preparers and supervisors of teachers, inservice instructors, measurement and evaluation consultants, and professors teaching graduate-level courses can all benefit from the handbook's coverage.

Second, the reference list reflects a comprehensive survey of the literature on early childhood education, measurement, and evaluation. The compilation of this exhaustive list was necessary to achieve the assembly of ideas and techniques presented in the handbook, and the references will serve as an up-to-date resource for professionals desiring to delve even more deeply into the hundreds of topics addressed.

Third, for the first time, a single source is available that provides material in both introductory and more advanced form to be of maximum value to students as well as to professionals.

Chapter One examines the present, yet ever-changing, status of early childhood education. This initial chapter focuses primarily on issues involving the use of measurement and evaluation within the field and also considers probable future trends.

Next, a seven-chapter block is devoted to measurement in early childhood education. Chapter Two defines basic measurement terms and concepts and describes general types of measure and measurement methodology, particularly as they relate to early childhood education. Included are basic statistical concepts, such as the normal curve and measures of relationship, as well as material to permit the reasoned interpretation of scores. Different types of standardized tests are delineated, as are teacher-constructed or teacher-initiated measures, such as work samples. Chapter Three discusses the key measurement concepts of validity, reliability, and usability and provides a system for evaluating measures. Although some material in Chapters Two and Three may already be familiar to readers, we have found that many professionals in early childhood education appreciate an integrated and straightforward treatment of these central concepts. Chapter Four looks in detail at a measurement methodology particularly appropriate for early childhood education—observation. Developing and implementing an observation system is considered, and a few existing prototypic systems are described.

Chapters Five through Eight examine early childhood education measures in the cognitive, affective, and psychomotor domains. Treatment of the three domains in separate chapters should not be interpreted to mean that human behavior or its measurement divides neatly into three mutually exclusive areas. The overlap between the domains and their obvious and subtle interactions are real and substantial. Cognitive measures considered in Chapter Five are intelligence tests and instruction-related, readiness, and achievement tests. Chapter Six contains developmental and handicapped screening surveys, language and bilingual tests, and creativity measures. Affective measures for young children are highlighted in Chapter Seven, including measures of personality, self-concept, social skills and competencies, and attitudes and preferences. Chapter Eight, psychomotor-domain measures, considers a number of areas related to children's physical attributes and performance. Each chapter contains actual measures illustrative of each type.

The final four-chapter block focuses principally on evaluation in early childhood education. Chapter Nine contains several conceptual frameworks for conducting the evaluation of early childhood education programs, with explicit suggestions for application and use. Chapter Ten examines the evaluation of children, parent involvement, and program staff, with sufficient information to permit the reader to implement suggested evaluation procedures. Chapter

Eleven presents several evaluation case studies that serve to illustrate the application of both evaluation and measurement to the field and that also serve to highlight important outcomes from the evaluations. Finally, Chapter Twelve considers contributions from a variety of sources, such as academic disciplines and various "schools of thought" on both evaluation and education. Adjunct to the entire book, but especially to Chapters Five through Eight, is an appendix in which many source books of early childhood measures are described. For the more relevant sources, detailed illustrations of their use are included.

In total, then, this handbook covers a wide range of vital material relevant to the field of early childhood education, and concomitantly it develops in the reader considerable sophistication about measurement and evaluation. Further, the coverage reflects our belief that sage use of measurement and evaluation can greatly benefit early childhood education and, in turn, young children themselves.

Many persons have contributed to the writing of this book, but we have chosen to thank them personally rather than list them here. However, special mention is due to Gene Glass for his extensive editing of Chapter One and to Jean Hughes for her helpful critique of Chapter Eight. The wizardly performance of Victoria Bergquist on the typewriter and in spotting so many of our mental lapses is most appreciatively acknowledged.

Jamestown, Colorado   William L. Goodwin
December 1979   Laura A. Driscoll

Contents

Chun, Cobb, and French's Measures for Psychological
Assessment • *Clarke's* Physical and Motor Tests in the
Medford Boys' Growth Study • *Coller's* The Assessment
of "Self-Concept" in Early Childhood Education •
Comrey, Backer, and Glaser's A Sourcebook for Mental
Health Measures • Educational Testing Service's Head
Start Test Collection • *Goolsby and Darby's* Bibliography of
Instrumentation Methodology and Procedures for
Measurement in Early Childhood Learning • *Hoepfner
and Others'* Tests of Higher-Order Cognitive, Affective,
and Interpersonal Skills • *Lake, Miles, and Earle's*
Measuring Human Behavior • *Mardell and Goldenberg's*
Learning Disabilities/Early Childhood Research Project •
Robinson and Shaver's Measures of Social Psychological
Attitudes • *Shaw and Wright's* Scales for the Measurement
of Attitudes • *Stott and Ball's* Infant and Preschool
Mental Tests: Review and Evaluation • *Straus'* Family
Measurement Techniques • *Thomas'* Psychological
Assessment Instruments for Use with Human Infants •
Wylie's The Self-Concept • *Concluding Remarks*

The Authors

WILLIAM L. GOODWIN is professor of education at the University of Colorado. He teaches courses in early childhood education, educational psychology, measurement, and research methodology at the Denver Campus and is affiliated with the Laboratory of Educational Research at the Boulder Campus. Goodwin was awarded the B.S. degree in education from the University of Nebraska (1957). After three years of service in the Marine Corps, he was awarded the M.Ed. degree in guidance and counseling from the University of Illinois (1961). He then taught high school social studies in Madison, Wisconsin, and in 1965 was awarded the Ph.D. degree in educational psychology from the Laboratory of Experimental Design, University of Wisconsin at Madison, with emphasis on learning, research design, and measurement. He continued for one year there as research associate at the Research and Development Center for Cognitive Learning. From 1966 to 1969, Goodwin was assistant professor at Bucknell University and director of three Title III Elementary and Secondary Education Act projects. The following year, he was a postdoctoral fellow in early childhood education at the Laboratory of Human Development, Harvard University. In 1970, he joined the faculty of the University of Colorado. His prior publications include several textbooks and numerous articles in educational and psychological journals.

LAURA A. DRISCOLL is assistant professor at the University of Colorado Health Sciences Center in Denver, where she serves as evaluator on several special projects and teaches courses in research and evaluation methodology and statistics. Driscoll was awarded the B.A. degree in history and English (1971) and a M.A.T. in education and history (1973), both from the University of Santa Clara. From 1973 through 1975, she served as assistant director of the University of Colorado Protocol Materials Development Project. In 1977, she was awarded her Ph.D. degree in research methodology, evaluation, and measurement through the Laboratory of Educational Research at the University of Colorado, Boulder. Her previous publications have appeared in the National Society for the Study of Education Yearbook, the American Educational Research Journal, and various journals in the field of nursing.

To our parents:
William and Eileen Goodwin
Gerald and Frances Driscoll

Handbook
for Measurement
and Evaluation
in Early Childhood
Education

Issues, Measures, and Methods

Chapter 1

Status of Measurement
and Evaluation

The title of this book contains three elements that require definition: measurement, evaluation, and early childhood education. Preliminary definitions will help establish the specific connotations intended by the authors as the terms are used throughout the book and will set the boundaries for the content of the book.

Measurement is the process of determining, via observation or testing, an individual's behaviors or traits, a program's characteristics, or the characteristics of some other entity, and then assigning a number, score, or rating to that determination. Measurement involves scales, numbers, constructs, validity, and reliability. Humans have been measuring since the start of civilization. More recently, Thorndike (1918) spurred the development of educational measurement by proposing that anything that exists, exists in some amount and therefore can be measured. In the past six decades, measurement, both formal and informal, has become very much a part of the American educational scene, although its influence has waxed and waned. A multitude of individual behaviors and traits germane to the process of education have been measured— subject matter achievement, "readiness," IQ, creativity, language, motivation, curiosity, conceptual tempo, attentiveness, attitudes, interests, values, physical skills, and coordination, to name a few. These measures of persons can, in some contexts, also be considered measures of programs. Measures unique to programs exist as well—for example, effectiveness, environmental setting, and side effects. As implied by this definition and as will be made clear in later chapters, measurement devices include many things other than paper-and-pencil tests.

Evaluation is the process of judging the worth of something—often in terms of its costs, adequacy, or effectiveness. Much meaningful evaluation is comparative, although some judgments are made according to a selected standard or criterion. Thus, one could evaluate Program A by comparing its outcomes with those of Program B, or appraise the adequacy of a student's past learning for the purpose of assigning more advanced material, or judge the effectiveness of the Head Start Program in attaining its objectives. Evaluation can be applied to any activity, person, product, or program and normally terminates once a judgment is made. Thus, evaluation involves values, measurement, criteria, bias control, cost analysis, and needs. Based on evaluation outcomes, decisions are made or other actions taken. Because evaluative judgments are usually (and advisably) data-based, measurement is included in the evaluation process as a functional subcomponent. The credibility of an evaluation, therefore, rests quite directly on the quality of the measures used.

Early childhood education, as it is used in this book, focuses on children when they are in more or less "formal" educational settings—not just school or preschool settings but any that have educational objectives or some clearly identifiable educational components. Such educational objectives and components are broadly conceived to include academic or academic-related performance, affective behavior, psychomotor skills, and other developmentally appropriate behaviors. Excluded, for the most part, are settings whose orientations are primarily caretaking, such as a daycare center with no educational components, or clinical, such as a psychological clinic to which children are referred for a variety of "problem" behaviors. The clinical domain, though important, has been addressed elsewhere (for example, see Palmer, 1970).

Emphasis in this book is on children from two to eight years old. Thus, for the most part, measures and evaluations centering exclusively on infants are not included. Mention will be made, however, of a few prominent infant measures and also of selected intervention efforts with infants that have resulted in longitudinal data on children in the "early childhood" (two to eight years) age range. This limited attention to infant programs appears warranted at this time because relatively few have explicitly articulated educational objectives. Within the targeted age range of two to eight years, we have been partial to the narrower bracket of about three to six years. Limited attention to the two-to-three age group reflects the scarcity of both educational programs and measures for this population. At the other end of the age bracket, six to eight, reduced attention is warranted by the fact that many existing publications focus on measures for elementary school children. Nevertheless, several primary school measures and evaluations are included and discussed, particularly those that link rather directly to related (or nearly identical) measures or evaluations for the three-to-six age group.

Status of Early Childhood Education

Measurement and evaluation in early childhood education are related to the status of the field itself. Rather than present a complete history of the field, we will emphasize recent events and trends.

In the United States in the 1960s, a convergence of academic and sociopolitical forces created fertile conditions for a revitalization of interest in early childhood education. From the academic world came a succession of influential statements asserting the importance of early experience. Bruner highlighted the role of education in children's intellectual development by stating (or possibly overstating), "Any subject can be taught effectively in some intellectually honest form to any child at any stage of development" (1960, p. 33). Hunt (1961) challenged the idea that intelligence is fixed at birth and claimed that an enriched environment, particularly in early childhood, could make a significant difference in rate and level of intellectual development. Bloom (1964) concluded that intellectual development occurs at an accelerated rate in the early years of life and, therefore, that environment is most critical then. Interest in children's mental development was further stimulated by a growing recognition of Piaget's work. All of these writings emphasized the importance of the early years as the foundation for later competence and development. (Note, however, recent views, such as those set forth in Clarke and Clarke, 1976, that question the belief that experience in early years sets irreversible trends and that the early age period is therefore more critical developmentally than later age periods.)

Various sociopolitical forces also generated interest in early childhood education—and undoubtedly served as the greater prods to action. The violence and unrest in many urban areas were thought to be rooted in the poverty-disadvantage cycle—a frustrating, devastating treadmill, which particularly trapped young, poor Blacks and other ethnic minorities (National Advisory Commission on Civil Disorders, 1968). Many minority children entered school behind in achievement and fell further behind each year. Such situations led, in part, to the federal War on Poverty as well as attempts to equalize educational opportunity through such efforts as Title I of the Elementary and Secondary Education Act of 1965, Head Start, Home Start, and school integration. Concurrently, the rising divorce rate and increasing number of women entering the work force accentuated the need for childcare. The women's liberation movement placed childcare high on its list of demands. Another sociopolitical force not to be overlooked might be termed the *Sputnik counterreaction*. After the jolt provided by Sputnik in 1957 and an early wave of criticism of American education, there seemed to be in the early 1960s a reaffirmation of public support for education.

One outcome of these converging influences was a gradual increase in preschool enrollment, especially among children of the middle class, and an increase in daycare services for both lower- and middle-class children. A more dramatic outcome, already alluded to, was the initiation of a large number of new educational programs for children in the preschool or early school years.

For the most part, these programs had a "compensatory" flavor; focusing primarily on children from poor families, they were designed to ameliorate the disadvantages such children experience in school.

Over a decade of experience has accrued with these new programs. The early enthusiasm dimmed somewhat as program outcomes frequently fell short of expectations. But much was learned during the decade. Evans (1975) noted six principal outcomes of the early intervention movement:

1. Lowered expectations about the effects of early education on children. In general, significant performance gains by participating children were very difficult to establish and, if established, were even more difficult to maintain over a sustained time period.
2. Increased appreciation of home-related factors. Experiences with many of the early childhood programs gave renewed support to the importance of such factors as parental involvement and support and also nutrition.
3. Heightened sensitivity to cultural differences. Given the target groups for many of the early childhood education programs, it was predictable that a greater awareness of minority-group characteristics would emerge. Cole and Bruner (1971) made a strong argument that *culturally different* was a preferable and more accurate term than *culturally deprived* or *culturally disadvantaged*. (We address this point more extensively later in the chapter.)
4. Increased development of curriculum models. Considerable activity was undertaken to translate and operationalize various learning theories into programs for young children. A good example was Follow Through, with its twenty-two different models.
5. Increased interest in master plans or blueprints for early childhood development. This outcome was manifested locally by attempts to coordinate childcare within the community and also to implement developmental daycare, an expanded concept of care with diagnostic, social, medical, nutritional, and educational components. In some states (such as California), state agencies or task forces sketched out plans for statewide early childhood education; such plans often met mixed public reactions.
6. Greater evaluation imperative. Competent evaluation is needed to determine the worth of various educational programs for young children. (In a certain sense, this outcome continues to be more a wish than reality, as indicated in the next section of this chapter. Nevertheless, the writing of this book is a clear indication of our support of Evans' evaluation imperative.)

Evans did not expect the experiences of the 1965–1975 period to lead to any reduction in support of, or need for, early childhood education. Nevertheless, there were events during the period that undermined the base of support for such programs; several of them are presented in the course of this book. Two of the more salient challenges came from Jensen and from Moore and Moore (also see Rohwer, 1971). Jensen's controversial article "How Much Can We Boost IQ and Scholastic Achievement" (1969) concluded, among other things, that large-scale compensatory programs had failed to increase significantly measured

IQ or scholastic performance of school-disadvantaged children. Moore and Moore (1975) argued at length that the home is a much better place than a preschool for a child's early education. In fact, they felt that most children under age eight have not attained an "integrated maturity level" necessary for success in school without risk. In some respects, the Moores' position seems an extreme elaboration of the Gesellian school readiness concept (Ilg and Ames, 1972); certainly, it was a challenge to California's Early Childhood Education plan.

At the same time, other writers were also expressing their (generally more positive) views on the early childhood education movement. Sigel (1973) argued that the expectations for early childhood education programs were largely unrealistic and grandiose. He suggested that such programs were probably effective but that relevant data and suitable analysis were needed to document their impact. Goodlad, Klein, and Novotney (1973) strongly supported the idea of publicly funded preschools with voluntary admission at age four. White and his colleagues (1973a, b, c, d) conducted a comprehensive review of federal programs for young children. Their recommendations, in general, can be viewed as suggestions on how to improve daycare, preschool, and early elementary education projects. In no sense did they suggest a dismantling of such programs, although they did raise several concerns (considered subsequently). Even Moore and Moore allowed that "There are exceptions to our home-care thesis, of course—glaring ones. And they include, perhaps, as many as 20 to 25 percent of our children. The *handicapped* child—blind, crippled, spastic, or deaf, who deserves the best clinical help we can find. The *disadvantaged* child, the prisoner of the ghetto or the mountain hollow, whose life must be enriched. The *deprived* child, whether he lives in a tenement or a mansion, whose parents are indifferent to, or overly indulgent, or ignorant of his needs. The *normal* child whose mother is forced by stark financial need to work for a living outside the home. Many, if not all, of these children should be given out-of-home care in environments that substitute for homes as closely as possible" (Moore and Moore, 1975, pp. 3–4).

Early childhood education is a relatively stable field with a large constituency. Even with the reduction in three- to five-year-olds in the U.S. population from 1965 (12,549,000) to 1976 (9,726,000), there was an annual increase in the number of such children enrolled in educational settings each year from 1965 (3,407,000) to 1975 (4,958,000), with only a small decline in 1976 (4,790,000) (Snapper and others, 1975; U.S. Bureau of the Census, 1977). Thus, nearly half of all three-to-five-year-olds are currently enrolled. There is no apparent reduction in "compensatory" preschool programs, although public funds are growing scarce. Programs and provisions for handicapped young children are multiplying. Women continue to enter the labor force at an increasing rate, and the rate for married women with children under six years old has shown a sharper increase in the 1970s than has that for married women with no, or older, children (U.S. Bureau of the Census, 1977). Thus, we anticipate no reduction in the number of young children who will need care or preschool programs of some type; in fact, a small gradual increase seems likely in the future.

What types of experience these programs will provide, and through what delivery systems, are less easy to predict. We feel there is a trend toward preschool programs with clearly identifiable educational components, which, however, embrace more than just preparation for the traditional subject areas of reading, language, and arithmetic. At the daycare level serving children in the first three years of life, we see some increase in the number of programs purporting to nurture development of children. However, White and his colleagues have pointed out that our present knowledge of daycare effects is limited and that "there is virtually no way at present to know what must be added to such basic care so as to positively affect children's development generally" (1973d, p. 30). With time, we expect some developmental-educational guidelines to become clearer for this young age group. Likewise, we expect to see changes in program delivery. With the present push for more and more meaningful parent involvement, it is not immediately clear what modifications in delivery systems might occur. Further, action by the federal government might have profound effects on daycare (Zigler and Hunsinger, 1977).

It is unclear what role public schools will play in determining the content of, and delivery system utilized in, early childhood education. The American Federation of Teachers is actively seeking to extend public schools to include three-, four-, and five-year-olds. Such an extension would provide many jobs for teachers. But this proposal has met vigorous opposition. Developmental psychologists and daycare spokesmen suggest that public schools are not oriented to take on such a task, that the task itself is far from well-defined, and that the schools are unable to deal with their current problems, let alone assume new responsibilities (Divoky, 1976). Obviously, the eventual outcome of such an issue (which is quite unpredictable now) could have profound effects on the field of early childhood education.

In summary, we envision an increasing number of preschoolers being exposed to educational programs and, by degrees, this educational trend appearing also in daycare settings. The number of children in early childhood education should remain at least at the present level or continue to gradually increase. But the field is clearly still emerging, still taking shape. With all of its direct and indirect links to the rest of society, early childhood education is bound to undergo significant changes in this period of social change. During this period, we envision an increasing need for measurement and evaluation in early childhood education so that, despite what changes occur, programs can be increasingly responsive to public concerns about resource expenditures and, more important, increasingly adept at nurturing young children's development.

Issues Surrounding Measurement and Evaluation

Many of the issues being debated in the field of early childhood education have some bearing on measurement and evaluation. Evans (1975) clustered general early childhood issues using a simple, familiar scheme:

- *What?*: Exactly what should constitute proper education for a young child? Should it be preparation for basic academic skills, or a series of planned experiences of social interaction with others, or simply a setting in which exploration and curiosity are made easy, or just what?

- *How?:* Overlapping with the previous "what" question is the question of how educational activities should be conducted—that is, what delivery methods and techniques should be used. Should activities be conducted with rote, drill-like precision or with little structure, at a fast, intense pace or one that is learner-determined, or in exactly what fashion?
- *Where?:* In what settings should educational experiences for young children take place? Should they take place in the home, or in small homelike groups, or in centers, or in preschools? The importance of this question for many people was alluded to in the previous section.
- *Who?:* What persons should "deliver" educational services to young children? Should they be fully certified teachers, paraprofessionals, the child's own parents, public or private agencies, or public schools? "Who" can also be extended to ask which children should be involved. Should participants include all children, or only those from less affluent socioeconomic environments, or only the handicapped?
- *When?:* At what age should early childhood education commence? Should it begin at age five years, four, two, at six months, at birth, or even (indirectly, through the mother) prior to birth?

These general issues are considerably more complicated than they appear at first glance. Certainly, the few short alternative answers provided are far from exhaustive, given that the response to any what, how, where, who, or when question can nearly always be challenged by a "Why?" Further, many persons in the field could not easily or definitively answer such questions without first being given much information about the specific children intended as participants. That is, different answers apply for different children. Also, many of the questions interact in very complex ways. This interaction was noted for the "what" and "how" questions but functions between nearly every pair (such as "where" and "when" or "what" and "when") and even between larger combinations (for example, "what," "how," and "who"). This discussion may remind some of the well-known Abbott and Costello routine, "Who's on first?" However, these general early childhood education issues are substantially more complex than that routine and not nearly as humorous. The issues are both important and serious, and they have far-reaching implications.

No attempt will be made here to deal with these critical general issues, as they are beyond the scope of this book. They are mentioned only to denote the complex context within which measurement and evaluation issues arise. Here we will concentrate on those issues directly related to measurement and evaluation in early childhood education. Whenever possible, we will direct the reader to other chapters in this book where a given issue receives considerable attention or has substantial relevance.

The issues have been grouped into two sections: those involving individuals and those involving programs. In several senses, the sections are interconnected. The latter section builds on the first in that the evaluation of persons is often a core component of program evaluation. Both sections, and particularly the latter, draw upon and extend an earlier work (Goodwin, 1974). Following these two sections, an important overriding issue is addressed—the influence that measurement and evaluation have with early childhood educators.

Issues Involving Individuals. Five issues are commonly raised concerning measurement and evaluation of individuals in early childhood education. The first four focus on young children, while the fifth concerns adults working in early childhood education settings.

Issue 1: Should Young Children Be Measured? This issue is basic and, if the answer is no, precludes all remaining issues. The issue, when it arises, usually reflects a concern that the very act of measuring young children is deleterious—either harmful or traumatic or both. To our knowledge, however, this concern has never been substantiated. The more common presumption is that educators working with young children are generally careful not to do them any harm. (A quite different question involves the use of measurement data once generated; see Issues 3 and 4.)

This issue has at times appeared in cases where measurement is conceived of narrowly, specifically as paper-and-pencil tests. Some adults working with small children, say five years old or younger, shudder at the vision of their charges sitting down, crayon or pencil in hand, to take a test. Some elementary school teachers feel the same. These same adults often heartily endorse procedures such as careful, systematic observation of children or diagnostic procedures to ascertain developmental status, strengths, weaknesses, or the like. The issue for them, it seems, is not whether measurement should take place but rather the particular form that it takes. In actuality, as will become apparent in later chapters, paper-and-pencil tests are infrequently developed for young children, although they are available for kindergartners and, on an increasing but still limited basis, for even younger children. Individually administered tests, whereby an examiner records a single child's response or performance, are the most commonly used type of test for children four years of age and younger.

In reality, the first issue has not occupied center stage. Even writers most critical of existing procedures (for example, Hein, 1975; and Macdonald, 1974) offer alternatives rather than calling for an abstention from the measurement of young children. The importance of this issue could change rapidly depending on the general societal outlook on measurement and testing. The question is emerging whether testing serves the public interest (Jones, 1976), and recent challenges to large testing companies have been made, such as Nader's criticism of Educational Testing Service (Moore, 1976b, which incidentally the company has rebutted, see Moore, 1976a).

Issue 2: Is Measurement Possible with Young Children? This issue is a familiar one to anyone who has studied the history of tests and measures and may be an excruciating one for anyone who has personally attempted to develop a creditable measure for young children. No one asks the question whether measurement is easy with young children; the answer is an obvious and resounding no. In general, the younger the child, the greater the measurement problems. Further, measurement of affect is normally more difficult than measurement of cognition. Thus, although measurement with young children is possible, it becomes increasingly difficult the younger the child and the more one is interested in affective domain measures. For example, in the section "Source Books of Early Childhood Measures" (following Chapter Twelve), the Center for the Study of Evaluation (CSE) Preschool/Kindergarten and Elementary School Test Evaluations are described; an analysis of the test ratings therein via the scheme used by Haney and Cohen (1978) supports the greater difficulty of measuring young children and, particularly, for affective constructs. Definite statements about psychomotor domain measures for young children are also difficult given that domain's less advanced stage of development. It should be noted, in passing, that although measures are frequently grouped into domains for convenience, as we have done in later chapters, there is a growing awareness that such a distinction for a given measure is more a matter of degree than kind.

The measurement difficulties just indicated figure importantly in evaluating programs available for young children. As White summarized, "Existing instruments are, relatively, most adequate for assessing effects on children of early school; next most adequate in assessing preschool effects; and least well developed for the assessment of daycare effects in the 0–3 age range" (White and others, 1973a, p. 259). Subsequent materials presented by him make it clear that the issue is not whether measurement is possible. Instead, the issue appears to be the quality of the measures that are used. (In Chapter Three, attention is directed toward the validity, reliability, and usability of measures in early childhood education.)

Issue 3: Are Measuring Instruments Used Appropriately with Young Children? This is a broad issue. One aspect of it is so current and pervasive—the fairness of the measures for specific individuals and groups—that it is considered separately as Issue 4. The important aspect examined here involves the range or types of measure available for young children. Other important but lesser aspects of the measure appropriateness issue will be presented in Chapter Three.

The IQ test has played a dominant role in early childhood education (for example, see Anastasi, 1976; Anderson and Messick, 1974; or White and others, 1973a). There are good reasons for its central role: the venerable and established position of the IQ test within psychology, its considerable predictive validity even as early as age four (Cronbach, 1970), and its general respectability on many criteria for judging measures. At the same time, the IQ test has been increasingly criticized for its limitations and, particularly, its misuses (see Issue 4).

In the early primary grades, subject-matter achievement tests have become widely used, no doubt because they, too, meet well the established criteria for measures. However, achievement tests have increasingly come under fire themselves. For example, Hein (1975) considers achievement tests unsuited for open education. (For a more complete discussion of open education, see the last section in Chapter Twelve.) More generally, the Representative Assembly of the

National Education Association has encouraged a national moratorium on standardized testing, including intelligence, aptitude, and achievement tests, "until completion of a critical appraisal, review, and revision of current testing programs" (National Education Association, 1972). Several other organizations have issued related proclamations (Oakland and Laosa, 1977). Although standardized achievements tests have many staunch supporters in our society, the initiatives just mentioned and others (see Houts, 1977; Perrone, 1977) reflect a growing dissatisfaction with the use of such tests in American schools.

The fairness issue aside, dissatisfaction exists largely because of the limited range of creditable measures available for use. An important attempt to surmount this problem is reported in Anderson and Messick (1974). In early 1973, a panel of experts in child development and in testing was assembled by the Office of Child Development to attempt to define *social competence* in young children. The task was not easily accomplished, and a large integrative effort was required after the panel had disbanded. However, pertinent to Issue 3, the panelists agreed that social competence was something more than general intelligence. It then became necessary to determine what constituted that "something more" in order to foster and evaluate children's development.

Enroute to specification of numerous measures that collectively would make up social competence in the young child, the panel had to address several problems. They are reworded and listed here simply as an amplification of the difficulties inherent in the "appropriateness" issue (Anderson and Messick, 1974, pp. 287–288):

1. Distinguishing between child behaviors valued widely by many groups in numerous situations and behaviors not necessarily universally appreciated or appropriate in only a limited number of situations.
2. Distinguishing between capability and performance (as when a child knows a response but fails to make it or makes a low-level response) and also between maximal and typical performance.
3. Interpreting the different meanings of variables at different levels of intensity or in their negative and positive ranges (for example, determining the optimal position on a continuum from extroversion to introversion).
4. Separating positive components of social competence that should be fostered from negative ones that serve as obstacles to development, learning, and adjustment (for example, anxiety, hostility, and aggression).
5. Specifying with precision developmental trends of different variables.
6. Regarding and assessing social competence in dynamic, longitudinal terms rather than static ones.
7. Explicating the relationships between program goals or social competencies sought for children and program goals established for parents.

The conference then presented twenty-nine elements of social competence, indicating that the list was probably incomplete but nonetheless a creditable first effort. The elements are presented in Table 1 in clusters. The wording

Table 1. Proposed Elements of Social Competence in Young Children

Cognitive Competence
- Language skills
- Categorizing skills
- Memory skills
- Critical thinking skills
- Creative thinking skills
- Problem-solving skills
- Quantitative and relational concepts, understandings, and skills
- General knowledge for functioning in and out of school
- Flexibility in appropriately using information-processing strategies
- Proficiency in using human and material resources for learning and problem solving

Psychomotor Competence
- Perceptual skills
- Fine motor dexterity
- Gross motor skills
- Perceptual-motor skills (coordinates visual, auditory, and motor behavior)

Motivational Competence
- Curiosity and exploratory behavior
- Control of attention (controls appropriately the direction, duration, and intensity of attention)
- Competence motivation (shows desire to improve or master skills and to seek new learning)

Personal Care Competence
- Habits of personal maintenance and care

Affective Competence
- Concept of self as an initiating and controlling agent.
- Differentiated self-concept and consolidation of identity
- Realistic appraisal of self, with feelings of personal worth
- Differentiation of feelings and appreciation of their manifestations and implications
- Sensitivity and understanding in social relationships
- Positive and affectionate personal relationships
- Role perception and appreciation (understands role expectations and their situational nature)
- Appropriate regulation of antisocial behavior
- Morality and prosocial behavior (is cooperative, helpful, fair)
- Positive attitudes toward learning and school experiences
- Enjoyment of humor, play, and fantasy

Source: Based on Anderson and Messick, 1974, pp. 289–292.

of the elements is most often directly from Anderson and Messick, but we have reordered the twenty-nine elements somewhat and grouped them by general type of competence. Note that in Table 1 and throughout the book we make reference to the cognitive, affective, and psychomotor domains defined and elaborated by Bloom, 1956; Krathwohl, Bloom, and Masia, 1964; and Harrow, 1972, respectively.

Table 1 reveals a major effort to move away from reliance on a single competency or a few competencies in evaluating young children. The problem is that for these multiple competencies to be assessed, measures would have to be developed for each. Such an effort would represent a Herculean task. Nonetheless, progress in such a direction would do much for measurement and evaluation in early childhood education and would be a major step toward a positive resolution of Issue 3. Anderson and Messick (1974) took a broad-base view of the measures that would be needed, including ratings, records, tests (or other performance measures), social indicators, and observations. We believe such a view is appropriate and that it, also, is likely to help resolve the third issue. Currently, the Administration for Children, Youth, and Families (the former Office of Child Development) has funded Mediax Associates, Inc. to monitor the adaptation of existing measures and the development of new measures appropriate for children ages three to seven.

Issue 4: Are Measuring Instruments Used with Young Children Fair? This issue frequently is discussed as *test bias.* A test is biased if its results contain systematic error due to factors irrelevant to what the test is supposed to be measuring. Many contend that IQ tests, and even achievement tests, are unfair to ethnic minorities (Samuda, 1975). At times the issue has been broadened to include other tests—primarily cognitive and school-related—and other groups, such as children with low socioeconomic status (SES) from impoverished homes and neighborhoods, regardless of ethnic background. (As it turns out, large proportions of children from certain ethnic minorities, such as Blacks, Chicanos, Native American Indians, and Puerto Ricans, have low SES.) The issue is certainly not a new one, as it has surfaced several times this century; however, given school integration endeavors (whether court ordered or not) and the increasing assertiveness of minority groups, its societal implications now are particularly intense.

The many criticisms that have been directed at standardized assessment practices have recently been summarized by Laosa (1977, pp. 10–11):

1. Standardized tests are biased and unfair to persons from cultural and socioeconomic minorities since most tests reflect largely white, middle-class values and attitudes, and they do not reflect the experiences and the linguistic, cognitive, and other cultural styles and values of minority group persons.
2. Standardized measurement procedures have fostered undemocratic attitudes by their use to form homogeneous classroom groups which severely limit educational, vocational, economic, and other societal opportunities.

3. Sometimes assessments are conducted incompetently by persons who do not understand the culture and language of minority group children and who thus are unable to elicit a level of performance which accurately reflects the child's underlying competence.
4. Testing practices foster expectations that may be damaging by contributing to the self-fulfilling prophecy which ensures low-level achievement for persons who score low on tests.
5. Standardized measurements rigidly shape school curricula and restrict educational change.
6. Norm-referenced measures are not useful for instructional purposes.
7. The limited scope of many standardized tests appraises only a part of the changes in children that schools should be interested in producing.
8. Standardized testing practices foster a view of human beings as having only innate and fixed abilities and characteristics.
9. Certain uses of tests represent an invasion of privacy.

The many diverse facets of the complicated issue of test fairness or bias have been extensively addressed elsewhere (for example, see Flaugher, 1978; Hobbs, 1975; Hobbs and others, 1975; Oakland, 1977; and Phillips, 1973). Rather than attempt to repeat those comprehensive treatments, we will instead focus briefly on the question of the fairness of IQ tests.

Clearly, one major misuse of IQ tests, which has generally worked to the detriment of poor and minority children, is the practice of using IQ test scores to label children permanently. All too often, an IQ score is used to categorize a child as a slow learner, disabled, or unsuited for further schooling; after that, little attempt is made to provide a rich educational environment since "it won't do any good anyway." This unfortunate practice results from erroneously assuming (1) that an IQ test score is fixed and unchangeable, and (2) that a specific IQ test is equally appropriate for measuring children from all types of environment.

Regarding the first assumption, IQ test scores do exhibit considerable stability in correlational studies, and this stability provides actuarial data appropriate for group predictions. However, large and dramatic shifts in an individual's measured IQ are well documented (for example, Honzik, 1973; and Moriarty, 1966). The assumption that an individual's measured IQ is fixed is clearly wrong. This belief evokes the long-standing controversy over the relative effects of heredity and environment on intelligence—the issue of nature versus nurture. Early in this chapter, we touched on this issue in our discussion of the status of the field of early childhood education. It is sufficient to note here that the Hunt and Bloom pronouncements, so influential in revitalizing interest in early childhood education, clearly emphasized environment.

The second erroneous assumption—that the same IQ test should be suitable for measuring children from different backgrounds—lies near the heart of Issue 4. Some persons making this assumption take the position that the IQ test is not unfair because it does not know the ethnic or environmental background of the child being tested; further, it is accurately predicting success in our society. Such a view would hold that it is irrelevant to know that a child from a poor home did poorly on an IQ test primarily because of lack of parental encouragement to develop verbal abilities and to reason critically. Since abstract thinking and critical reasoning are indispensable for success in modern life, the test score earned is appropriately predictive.

We believe that such a position begs the question with regard to this fourth issue. It seems to presume that IQ tests serve only an actuarial, group prediction purpose. In fact, it is apparent that IQ test scores are used to make many immediate decisions about individual children. Such decisions can be significant, such as placement in a particular group or "track" in school or even assignment to a special school or setting (for example, a class for "gifted" students, a class for educable mentally retarded students, and so on). It is difficult, in such a context, to view the IQ test as equally fair for all children. As a case in point, Mercer (1973, 1974) found that a disproportionately large percentage of children classified as mentally retarded came from minority groups and that the community agency serving as the "primary labeler" was the public school system. Another relevant but complicating observation is that children from certain identifiable American subcultures, such as Chinese, Japanese, and Jewish, seem to do particularly well in school and on IQ and school-related tests, suggesting that their home environments might be optimal for success at school (White and others, 1973a). Several court cases in this decade have led to state laws and regulations prohibiting special education placement solely on the basis of an IQ score or a single professional's recommendation; two other requirements frequently instituted are (1) considering the child's school performance, developmental history, and cultural background, and (2) testing by a psychologist fluent in the child's home language (Zettel and Abeson, 1978).

Issue 4 asks whether tests used with young children are fair. Clearly, the answer must be, "Not in all cases." What, then, can be done to make tests more fair? Answering this question—and thus helping to resolve Issue 4—appears very difficult. Prohibiting the use of standardized tests, a "solution" we saw advocated in the discussion of Issue 3, seems extreme and unproductive. If followed, it would be all too likely to lead to new and serious injustices, as human judgment would be exercised without the tempering influence of "objective" data that such tests provide. Other procedures already alluded to are likely to partially alleviate unfairness, such as having the test given by a skilled person fluent in the child's preferred language.

An extensive attempt to resolve this issue has been made for several decades via conscientious efforts to design culture-fair instruments. In general, results of such efforts have been disappointing. "The attempted solutions usually took the form of motor or performance scales, tests that avoided as much as possible dealing with the vocabulary and linguistic factors that are so manifestly different among children from different milieus. We now know enough (1) to believe that performance tests cannot be proxies for verbal tests in an estimate of a unitary general intelligence, but rather get at abilities that are significantly differentiated from and independent of verbal abilities, and (2) to believe that cultural differences are not just language differences, but involve attitudes and approaches to problem solving that may as easily manifest themselves in motor as in performance tests. Our lack of success in developing a culture-fair IQ test, despite serious efforts, has precipitated some pessimism about our ability to solve the problem" (White and others, 1973a, p. 313). In fact, mounting evidence suggests that performance tests may be more culturally loaded than language tests (Anastasi, 1976).

At the present time, we quite agree with Anastasi's estimate of the situation with regard to culture-fair tests.

> It is unlikely, moreover, that any test can be equally "fair" to more than one cultural group, especially if the cultures are quite dissimilar. While reducing cultural differentials in test performance, cross-cultural tests cannot completely eliminate such differentials. Every test tends to favor persons from the culture in which it was developed. The mere use of paper and pencil or the presentation of abstract tasks having no immediate practical significance will favor some cultural groups and handicap others. Emotional and motivational factors likewise influence test performance. Among the many relevant conditions differing from culture to culture may be mentioned the intrinsic interest of the test content, rapport with the examiner, drive to do well on a test, desire to excel others, and past habits of solving problems individually or cooperatively. . . .
>
> Each culture and subculture encourages and fosters certain abilities and ways of behaving, and discourages or suppresses others. It is therefore to be expected that, on tests developed within the majority American culture, for example, persons reared in that culture will generally excel. . . . Cultural differences become cultural handicaps when the individual moves out of the culture or subculture in which he was reared and endeavors to function, compete, or succeed within another culture [Anastasi, 1976, pp. 345–346].

A number of other solutions have recently been proposed. In sharp contrast to the culture-fair development efforts are the attempts to create culture-specific tests—that is, tests designed specifically for each prominent subcultural group. One interesting example is the Black Intelligence Test of Cultural Homogeneity (or BITCH), consisting of one hundred multiple-choice vocabulary items for adolescents and adults concerning the Black subculture (Williams, 1972; also note critical reviews of BITCH by Cronbach, 1978, and Krauskopf, 1978). A second example is the Enchilada Test, thirty-one multiple-choice knowledge items focusing on childhood experiences in a Chicano barrio (Ortiz and Ball, 1972). Other proposed solutions, drawn from Goodwin (1978b) and especially Oakland and Matuszek (1977), include:

1. Involving minority group members as full partners in efforts to develop new tests.
2. Insisting on proportional representation of minorities in norm samples.
3. Adapting both test language (that is, translating English) and content for specific minority groups (also see Chapter Six).
4. Estimating and correcting (statistically) for test bias.
5. Using criterion-referenced measures when appropriate.

Although these procedures represent only partial solutions to Issue 4, and at times create other pitfalls, collectively they advance the interest of fairness.

We believe that charges of unfairness against a particular test most likely occur and are warranted when a test score is inappropriately interpreted as definitive. Treating a test score as absolute reflects a basic misunderstanding of tests. There is some hope that such basic misunderstandings might become less common as a result of vigorous educational efforts, such as instruction of test-score users in appropriate interpretation. Unfortunately, we do not perceive such efforts as extensively under way, despite early warnings and recommendations such as the "Guidelines for Testing Minority Group Children" (Society for the Psychological Study of Social Issues, 1964) and the "Standards for Educational and Psychological Tests" (American Psychological Association, 1974).

Any proposed educational remedy should be buttressed by protections for individual children. Mercer (1974, pp. 132–138) proposed five interrelated rights of children with regard to psychological assessment procedures, and we have added one more.

Right 1: To be evaluated within a culturally appropriate normative framework. Essentially, this right would protect children from being evaluated on a single normative framework if it was based on a cultural value system significantly different from their own. As Mercer stated it, classification as abnormal should not occur simply because children "have been socialized into a non-Anglo cultural tradition." This right speaks to two requirements: (1) using appropriate norms and (2) considering cultural background when interpreting test performance.

Right 2: To be accorded ethnic identity and respect. Mercer viewed most current school practices, including assessment, as "Anglocentric." This right would ensure that schools and other agencies recognize in their assessment practices the value and integrity of different cultural traditions. It requires that schools adopt a pluralistic, multicultural approach to assessment as well as the culturally appropriate view of performance suggested by the first right.

Right 3: To be evaluated as a multidimensional human being. A given child's retardation is often school-specific; that is, the child violates the norms of a teacher from a different cultural milieu, is referred for psychological evaluation, and does poorly on the narrow range of behaviors sampled by an IQ test. The same child, in nonacademic settings and roles, frequently displays adequate competencies and considerable adaptive behavior. This third guarantee would significantly reduce the emphasis placed on school-related behaviors, such as performance on an IQ test, in reaching classification decisions about children. Rather, evaluation would increasingly also focus on the child's adaptive behavior in out-of-school settings. This right further implies multiple-factor assessment rather than reliance on any single test score or measure.

Right 4: To be free of labels. The practice of labeling individuals is widespread, and it has unfortunate consequences. Bradley and Caldwell (1974) indicated the extraordinary hazards associated with the labeling of preschoolers because "problems of reliability and validity (all types) are much greater with the very young child" (1974, p. 13). Mercer spoke only of the necessity of avoiding stigmatizing labels (possibly because of her preoccupation with retardation), but we consider the use of any labels questionable. As noted elsewhere (Goodwin and Klausmeier, 1975), three especially unfortunate effects frequently accompany labeling. First, the label placed on a child may imply that a real, unchanging, and pervasive characteristic has been identified—clearly, such is often not the case. Second, a label can be doggedly and uncomfortably tenacious, following the child for years. Third, the connotations that accrue to many labels are often misleading in the case of the individual and can set up inappropriate expectations; this process can be especially harmful if the labels are negative ones. It is easy to build a case against labeling children; emphasis might better be placed on the need for more complete description and on understanding individual children.

Right 5: To be fully educated. According to Mercer, many children and parents of children in programs for the mentally retarded complain that the programs are repetitious and not challenging. Children relegated to such programs or other low-expectation "tracks" could end up being educated significantly below their potential. Mercer indicated that most children in such predicaments escape the "retarded" or "slow learner" labels once they leave school and begin to function in adult roles. The right to be fully educated, however, calls for a more complete, more challenging, and more rewarding education, increasing the quality of life both in school and in subsequent years.

Right 6: To be fully informed about the results of psychological evaluations and about any information recorded and filed therefrom. This right, which is entrusted to the child's parent or guardian, is added to Mercer's list both because it is in keeping with the Family Educational Rights and Privacy Act of 1974 and because it is necessary to reduce the likelihood that individual students will become victims of the very psychological evaluations intended to help them.

The fairness issue must be continually addressed, although it is unlikely ever to be fully resolved. It has been suggested that "testing is as American as apple pie" (Cooley and Lohnes, 1976), and the authors of that statement observe that there is nothing wrong with either as long as appetite is controlled by reason. With respect to the fairness issue, our impression is that the societal appetite for testing has exceeded reason—with serious consequences for millions of children.

Issue 5: Should Adults Working in Early Childhood Education Be Measured and Evaluated? To what extent should measurement and evaluation be used in selecting early childhood program personnel and in judging the adequacy of their later performance? This familiar issue is not unique to early childhood education; it arises in educational settings of all kinds. In a sense, the four issues already considered for young children could be readdressed for adults working in early childhood education settings. No doubt these issues would be resolved more quickly and decisively for the adults than for their young charges—largely because of the generally accepted practices of personnel selection and employee evaluation, in some form.

Lest the reader get the idea that this is an open-and-shut issue, we hasten to note that much controversy accompanies both the purpose and the process of such evaluation efforts. In the public elementary schools, the evaluative process for the past several decades has typically consisted of principal or supervisor visitation, observation, and rating of teachers (Tomblin, 1976). However, some alternatives have appeared, such as self-evaluation, peer evaluation (a teacher is evaluated by other teachers), and cooperative appraisal (a teacher sets goals in consultation with the principal and subsequent performance is judged by both of them). For about a decade, considerable controversy has surrounded the proposed use of student test scores as a means to evaluate teacher performance; this proposal usually occurs in the context of discussions about accountability. Student evaluation of courses—utilized increasingly in higher education—is unusual at this level, although it has occurred recently on a scattered basis.

At the early education level, including preschools, no tradition of formal staff evaluation exists. Licensing requirements influence the initial selection of personnel, but evaluation of on-the-job performance is highly variable and generally informal. Certainly, there has been no call to involve children so young in the evaluative process. Often, staff evaluation is implicit, with directors or head teachers making judgments about the quality of their employees' work, but without any formal or elaborate system of data collection and analysis. Books available on how to conduct early childhood education programs generally give only limited attention to staff evaluation itself (for example, see Almy, 1975; Brophy, Good, and Nedler, 1975; Decker and Decker, 1976; and Stevens and King, 1976), although some (such as Robison, 1977) consider it more fully. Such books typically advocate self-evaluation procedures.

Virtually no one advocates "no evaluation" of staff in early childhood education settings. Further, a trend toward more comprehensive staff evaluation at this level may be emerging, in part because of the continuing societal emphasis on accountability and the increasing difficulty of supporting the rising and substantial personnel costs of such programs. Our own convictions are that staff evaluation can lead to stronger and more viable programs for young children, and therefore we believe that the answer to Issue 5 should be "definitely yes." Further, and in accord with Anderson's and Messick's plea for a wide range of measures for assessing young children's social competence, we advocate a broad-base approach to measuring adults' performance in, and contributions to, such settings. To this end, the process of staff evaluation in early childhood education is considered at length in Chapter Ten.

Issues Involving Programs. New issues come into play when one examines the operation of the measurement and evaluation processes with regard to programs. Since programs involve persons, the five issues already presented are also relevant to program evaluation. Ten additional issues are now considered.

Issue 6: Is Evaluation Worth its Cost in Time and Money? This issue is frequently raised. If program directors perceive that the resources available for their programs are limited, they may be reluctant to make evaluation a high-priority use for those resources. In essence, the issue is whether a program can afford the funds and the personnel for evaluation. Stated differently, is the typical evaluation of enough value to justify its costs in time and money?

Two points are especially pertinent to the case for evaluation. First, in many situations, a program hoping for at least moderate longevity can ill afford not to evaluate. Second, great variability is possible in the complexity and cost of evaluation activities. Both points require elaboration.

With regard to the first point, a program must include evaluation when it is required by the funding agency. Further, many projects find they must demonstrate their value, in the absolute sense or relative to other programs; evaluation helps address such matters. Also, evaluation can serve to reduce project costs, actually saving more than is spent on the evaluation itself. Such savings can occur at any stage of the project's life but seem more likely when the evaluation is planned prior to the start of the program and focuses on the intended objectives.

This before-the-fact cost saving is illustrated well by an evaluation strategy titled "the cheapy competitor" (Scriven, 1972). The evaluator serves as the devil's advocate for his employing client, conjuring up a program or product that seems to have as high a probability of achieving the same objectives as the client's program or product and at less cost. The client, then, must examine and defend his intended activities against the less expensive alternative. A prime example of a cheapy competitor was demonstrated by a consumer research group's finding that a solution of Tide cleaned rugs better than any of the foam-type rug cleaners being tested—and cost only one tenth as much. Since evaluators seem reasonably adept at suggesting cheapy competitors that are judged by experts to have substantial potential, the strategy might well be used more frequently. In general, evaluation can result in considerable resource savings. Scriven, a philosopher of science and an active evaluation consultant, recently advertised a "cost-free" evaluation procedure in which the program client has no risk; that is, the savings made possible by the evaluation should exceed the actual costs of the evaluation. Scriven (1974) has elaborated a rationale for this cost-free evaluation.

With regard to the second point, evaluation need be neither complex nor costly in terms of money or time. Certainly, some evaluations are complex and costly; several evaluations contained in Chapter Eleven deserve such descriptors. Yet complexity and cost are not a requirement; many evaluations are relatively simple and inexpensive. For example, consider an evaluation conducted to determine how well students learned from audiotapes played aboard a school bus (Goodwin and Sanders, 1971). Five cartridge tape players and individual audio headsets were installed on a school bus serving a rural, mountainous district where students spent considerable time each day enroute to and from school. Each student could select any of the five programs according to interest and needs. As the audio-bus program was developed, several questions were answered using evaluative techniques. In this case, the question was whether listening to a tape aboard the bus would lead to more or less learning by lower elementary school students than hearing the same tape in the classroom.

A formative evaluation (see Chapter Nine) was designed and subsequently conducted in a single morning. Students were randomly assigned to one of three groups. Group 1 was "taken for a ride" and heard a twenty-minute tape on the bus. Group 2 listened to the same tape in a regular classroom. Group 3 students heard no tape and either remained in their usual classes or took recess. All three groups received their treatments simultaneously; then all students returned to their usual classrooms and took a short multiple-choice test on the taped material. The two groups hearing the tape significantly outperformed Group 3 but did not perform very differently from each other. Although this brief study did not represent the entire evaluation design, it did permit judging rationally certain aspects of the audio-bus program. Subsequent studies provided replication and controlled for novelty. This example demonstrates that some evaluation activities can be conducted quickly and inexpensively, and that the evaluation design need not be complex.

Evaluations sometimes can be designed to operate at reduced costs without impairing the quality of the findings. One procedure used is to test only a sample of children within a program, or to give each child a sample of items or subtests rather than a full test battery. With sufficient students involved, this procedure reduces costs and yet still allows a suitable program evaluation. (It also lessens concerns mentioned under Issue 1, as children are tested less.)

Issue 7: Is Evaluation Fair to Fledgling Programs? Program staff may resist evaluation of a program that has just gotten under way. First, they consider it unfair to expect the new program, with its growing pains and frequent disruption of the status quo, to compare favorably with long-standing established programs, particularly if only program outcomes are evaluated. Second, they believe that early evaluation could straitjacket a program, tunneling staff interest inordinately toward evaluation requirements (see Issue 11) and, concurrently, dulling staff to opportunities that arise for creative redirection of the program. This second concern—that evaluation would stifle program creativity or cause a program to prematurely redirect its efforts—was of special interest to directors of innovative programs funded under Title III (now Title IV-C) of the Elementary and Secondary Education Act (ESEA) of 1965 (Miller, 1967). Several such programs involved early childhood education.

As an illustration of this second concern, consider the concept of early returns. In laboratory studies, early returns refer to the performance of the initial group of subjects undergoing the experimental conditions. Researchers may be unduly influenced by such early returns, to the point of changing their procedures or even forming new expectations that might function to shape subsequent experimental results (Rosenthal, 1966). It is possible that early evaluation returns in field studies might have analogous effects on the staff of young early childhood education programs. If program staff were too responsive to such early evaluation returns, a restrictive and inappropriately narrow approach to program development might ensue. For example, early returns might cause Program B to make extensive changes to improve its outcomes relative to Program A. However, it is possible that an unaltered Program B might have been more effective in the long run. The overhaul of Program B could result in considerable confusion and disruption, as time for personnel retraining or other ordinarily preparatory activities would be severely limited, and such disruption could further reduce B's effectiveness. Of course, the alterations might permit Program B to outperform A. Regardless, it is improper for summative evaluations (see Chapter Nine) to change programs in the very process of evaluating them.

Granting the legitimate concern over evaluation of new programs, we feel that this issue needs to be qualified and viewed from a more balanced perspective. Note, for example, that the fairness of comparing a new program with an established one is debatable. True, the program of longer standing has tradition and set procedures working in its favor, but the new program typically has the novelty effect facilitating its efforts. In a given situation, the novelty effect might be greater than, less than, or counterbalanced with, the disruption effect generated by new program procedures (Bracht and Glass, 1968). It is therefore an oversimplification to argue that a new program not be evaluated because it is "struggling" or not yet reaching its full potential.

It is important to realize that evaluation can serve more roles than assessing overall program worth, comparing programs to determine which is most effective, or speaking to fund-no fund decisions. An evaluation plan may focus on program process rather than outcomes and therefore be appropriate for new programs. For example, in the audio-bus evaluation described under Issue 6, emphasis was on internal program improvement, sometimes labeled *formative evaluation*. Even when an evaluation is summative in nature and fund-no fund or go-no go decisions must eventuate, certain procedures can reduce the concerns reflected in Issue 7. For instance, sheltered implementation or warm-up periods can be instituted before a program is evaluated. Or, to minimize the effect of early returns, a moratorium can be instituted to prevent the release of volatile comparative data from early evaluations until programs are well into their implementation phases.

In the latter chapters of this book, a wide variety of available evaluation designs and procedures are presented. Evaluation designs can be flexible and innovative themselves, a point developed more fully under other issues. Finally, evaluations can be designed to reduce any direct intervention in, or interaction with, the program (such as evaluating intended objectives apart from their implementation or by using regularly given tests or other unobtrusive measures as principal data).

Issue 8: Is Evaluation Necessary If One Can "Sense" Program Effectiveness? Many people have confidence in their intuition about the value of program processes or outcomes and therefore see no need for formal evaluations. In contemporary slang, they have "gut-level" feelings or receive "vibes" that tell them exactly how effective a program is. Curiously, this absolute confidence in one's perceptual abilities and affective sensors is often unshakable. As a case in point, an outside independent evaluator was commissioned to determine a fair payment under a performance contract between several school districts and a commercial organization guaranteeing pupil gains of one year or more on standardized reading comprehension tests (Goodwin, 1971). No payment was to be made for students gaining less than a year over the course of the school year. The evaluator presented a design calling for extensive testing and identification procedures to determine eligible students, and for the establishment of a randomized control group before the program commenced. Such events would delay the start of the program for two weeks. A research office spokesman from one of the school districts insisted that such elaborate procedures and delay were unnecessary because his past experiences and intuition would permit him to determine how effective the program was. Over his protests, the formal evaluation design was implemented—and later proved his intuition dramatically wrong.

Issue 8 is relatively easy to resolve. There is no compelling evidence for any consistent accuracy in inituitive judgments. Predictive statements about probable program outcomes, whether issued prior to, during, or even after program operation, are notoriously unreliable. Gut-level feelings about the worth of programs should not be ignored. However, systematic evaluation is needed to substantiate such feelings so that they might, on occasion, assist in determining the causes of program effects or similar matters.

Issue 9: Are Most Evaluations Merely Whitewashes? If evaluation is seen to result almost always in a positive view of the program considered, is it really necessary or is it little more than frosting on the program cake? Campbell (1969) ironically offered sound advice for the program administrator who must conduct an evaluation but cannot allow the program to appear a failure or even to be seen in a negative light. For instance, he identified grateful testimonials from program participants as a highly dependable way to assure a favorable evaluation. In a similar vein, he suggested that a positive outcome is likely if the program director confounds selection with treatment by choosing persons for the program who are more able and more likely to profit from the experience.

The counterposition on this issue is easily stated and defended. It is simply not true that evaluation inevitably results in program praise or exoneration. Negative evaluations have been submitted in a significant number of cases, and in other cases separate evaluations have resulted in conflicting assessments of the same program (see Chapter Eleven). There is no denying that political and ethical issues get tightly intertwined with many evaluations and that some evaluations can turn out to be whitewashes (Brickell, 1976; and House, 1972). Still, evaluation as a process should not be condemned or considered superfluous because of such possibilities. Some partial safeguards are available to increase the "honesty" of data collection and reporting and to reduce contaminating biases. Examples are using more than one independent evaluator, employing the adversary model of evaluation (Chapter Twelve), or implementing single-blind testing conditions, in which the tester is unaware whether or not the person being evaluated was a program participant.

Issue 10: Should Evaluation Compare Programs With Different Goals? A standard objection to evaluation is that since Program A has different goals from Program B it is not sensible to compare their outcomes or, in general, to evaluate them on a single set of criteria.

We believe, however, that it is legitimate and meaningful to compare programs that do not have identical goals. Such evaluations could compare programs in three areas: on goals specific to Program A, on goals specific to Program B, and on goals common to both A and B. For example, goals for students in Program A might be to develop internal locus of control, to initiate conversations with adults, and to improve performance in prereading skills, language, and personal maintenance skills. Program B's major goals might be to develop problem-solving skills, to persist on academic-type tasks, and to improve performance in prereading skills, language, and mathematics activities. By comparing Programs A and B in all of these separate areas, their differential performance could be measured and interpreted. One would expect Program A students to do better on the measures of internal control, initiation of conversations with adults, and personal maintenance skills, and Program B students to outperform Program A students on the measures of problem solving, persistence, and mathematics. However, such expectations require verification. Comparative performance on the common goals involving prereading skills and language could also be assessed and would be of direct interest to both programs as well as to others.

The programs might also be compared on goals supplied by other potential consumers; program staff may be totally unaware of such goals. Thus, a program with the expressed goal of improving children's language skills might be considered for adoption by another agency for the purpose of increasing children's interpersonal social skills. It is also considered appropriate to evaluate directly the intended goals of any program, quite apart from their implementation or their relationship to the goals of other programs (Scriven, 1967; Stake, 1970a; and Worthen and Sanders, 1973).

Issue 11: Does Evaluation Unduly Influence Program Goals? This issue concerns the responsiveness of evaluation to unique, diverse programs. Critics of evaluation suggest that programs may unwisely concentrate upon program goals that are readily susceptible to evaluation rather than on goals of primary importance. Eisner expressed concern about the "tendency to reduce educational problems into forms that fit research paradigms instead of finding research and evaluation procedures that fit the problems" (1972, p. 577). To many, this deference to evaluation seems to be yet another case of the tail wagging the dog.

The link between this issue and Issue 7 is obvious and was noted in that prior discussion. A direct relationship also exists to Issue 3 in that measurable outcomes are principal components of many evaluations. Thus, Macdonald lamented "a wholesale miniaturizing of goals to satisfy the primitiveness of our measurement abilities. We have really gained very little and risked much if we allow our goals for schooling to be determined by our ability to measure" (1974, p. 3).

Appropriately, then, this eleventh issue can be broadened to ask whether suitable measuring instruments exist for effective program evaluation. White and his associates (1973a), in examining the measures most used in early childhood program evaluation, noted concentration on (1) achievement tests for assessing the effects of elementary education, with occasional use of affective measures, (2) IQ or language development measures for assessing preschool effects, with some use of affect measures (often unstandardized), and (3) infant tests of development, some of long standing, some newer and based on Piaget's work, and some adapted for measuring IQ in the older daycare children, for purposes of assessing daycare projects. Numerous educators have criticized the use of IQ tests and achievement tests as indexes of both individual performance and program effectiveness (see Anderson and Messick, 1974; Bentley, Washington, and Young, 1973; Hein, 1975; Lewis, 1973; and Sigel, 1973). Most of the authors just cited argue for the development of program-specific measures. This solution is not easily implemented, as the establishment of validity and reliability for any such newly developed measures would doubtless be a long process. While noting the widespread dissatisfaction with, and limitations of, both IQ and achievement tests, White and his colleagues (1973a) point out the general superiority of both types of measure over existing alternatives in terms of validity, reliability, and usability, including norming.

Issue 11 will probably never be fully resolved. Progress toward its resolution will be tied to the development of flexible and responsive evaluation models and to the associated creation of a wide range of appropriate measures. For example, the elements of social competence presented earlier in Table 1 could serve as a source from which a particular program could select competencies to emphasize; any evaluation of that program could then make excellent use of the measures developed for those competencies. Further, if evaluation is to serve and not dictate programs, measures are needed for other aspects of children's behavior, for the behavior of adults working with young children, and for assessment of the early childhood education program environments. Subsequent chapters present material related to this pervasive issue.

Issue 12: Is Evaluation Unethical When It Denies Services to Control Students? One evaluation design frequently recommended, but infrequently used, involves the (preferably random) assignment of students either to an experimental program or to a control group. Control students do not receive the special program, but are measured to provide comparative data for determining program effects. The merits and limitations of such an evaluation design are discussed in Chapter Twelve. It is sufficient for now to note the considerable agreement that "true experimental designs," in the Campbell-Stanley sense (1963) of randomly assigning subjects to groups, yield the most supportable cause-and-effect claims. The applicability of such designs to program evaluation has been widely demonstrated (Gilbert, Light, and Mosteller, 1975; Goodwin, 1971; Goodwin and Sanders, 1971; and Riecken and Boruch, 1974).

This issue arises frequently. Many evaluators or consultants on evaluation are prone to recommend the use of a control group because of their own academic training and because of its superiority in establishing cause and effect. Program directors seem at least equally prone to reject such an evaluation design. Apparently, the assumption is that the program (or treatment) being evaluated is beneficial; therefore, control children not receiving the program are being denied its benefits. As one example of this situation, note that local agencies conducting Head Start and Title I, ESEA, programs since the mid 1960s have been required to evaluate their efforts annually. The use of control groups in such evaluations has been rare. Several program directors and state education officials quizzed by the authors on the absence of such evaluation designs have remarked that establishing truly comparable control groups would be both unethical and illegal. They viewed the laws as requiring involvement of the most needy eligible children. Most program directors would probably respond in similar fashion. Unfortunately, the evaluation designs then employed are often perfunctory, lacking in rigor, notably flawed, and not helpful in either a formative or summative sense.

Riecken and Boruch have raised several relevant points about the use of control groups. First, the seriousness of the problem of failing to provide benefits to untreated groups is related to the certainty that the proposed program is beneficial. "If it were known for certain that the program was beneficial, there might be no need to experiment at all. . . . The more doubt there is about the efficacy of the program or about its superiority over existing alternatives, the less severe the moral dilemma, if any, created by the scientific need for random assignment" (1974, pp. 249–250). Second, the specter of control group formation as unethical conduct is less apparent if measures of eligibility and need are uncertain, such as when program officials cannot agree who is most deserving or needy. Third, if program resources are scarce and, clearly, all eligible persons cannot be served, then randomization into program and control groups may be as fair a way as any to select the small group that is to receive program benefits.

We view the assumption that an innovative educational program or intervention treatment is beneficial or effective (at least more effective than no program or than the traditionally maligned "traditional program") as just that: an assumption. However, the reality is that to receive the needed financial support to introduce such programs, proponents must create the expectation that the program will be effective. Be that as it may, the program introduced will most likely have both unintended and unanticipated effects, some of which may be deleterious. Despite this likelihood and the points raised by Riecken and Boruch, there is no glory in being assigned to the control group, apparently doomed to less learning or more cavities. Note, however, that the situational context of the evaluation and the exact nature of the treatment are critical. For instance, when Walter Reed initiated his studies of yellow fever, he had no trouble locating control subjects but found very few persons itching to receive the experimental treatment.

Two available procedures mitigate the concerns of Issue 12. First, it is sometimes possible to design a comparative evaluation in which all eligible students receive one of several new programs, each purported to be beneficial. Thus, one randomly assigned group of students might undergo a new procedure for developing prereading skills while the other randomly formed group receives a "cheapy competitor." Student outcomes under each procedure are then compared, and judgments are made. In essence, the programs compared are in competition with each other. The use of comparative evaluations is not without limitations. For example, the two programs being compared could lead to similar outcomes. In fact, finding "no significant differences" between programs in comparative evaluations is very common; however, an outcome of "no differences" should not be taken to imply "no knowledge," as important information will have been generated (Scriven, 1967). In such a case, it may be unclear whether the two programs are equally effective or equally ineffective. Adding suitable pretests to the study could help alleviate the problem, although the inclusion of a third, randomly formed, no-treatment control group would clarify the evaluation findings even more. Another limitation of many comparative evaluations is their failure to include also the traditional program, which may be very much "in the running" and which, as a known entity, can increase the meaning of the comparison and of subsequent generalizations. Alas, to many, being assigned to the traditional program is as onerous as assignment to the control group.

A second evaluative procedure that helps circumvent the twelfth issue is for program managers to adopt a policy of using "deferred-treatment" groups (a term used in psychotherapy outcome studies instead of "control group"). Such groups are especially appropriate when program resources are inadequate to include all eligible participants. Members of the deferred-treatment group do not receive the new program or treatment, but they are measured for comparison purposes. Subsequently, as a second wave of participants is started in the program or as more resources become available, many of those initially in the deferred-treatment group will have an opportunity to receive the treatment.

Therefore, Issue 12 often can be resolved satisfactorily by using some of the procedural variations and reasoning presented here. When such resolution is not possible, a large number of alternative evaluation models are available for use (Chapter Nine). Indeed, in many situations, other evaluation models would be preferred.

Issue 13: Is Evaluation Capricious Given the Varying Standards Employed by Different Evaluators? Many persons are concerned that measurement and evaluation undeservedly bask in an aura of objectivity and scientific rigor. They point out that much subjectivity enters every stage of the entire evaluative process, such as in the selection or development of measures, in the timing of data collection, or in the particular procedures or personnel used. They particularly question the judgments of program worth made by the evaluator, pointing out the heavy influence of social and political factors on such important evaluative decisions, as well as the widely varying background experiences, orientations, and standards of different evaluators. Given such variability, they argue, evaluation is more apt to be arbitrary than rigorously objective. This general position sounds much like the current criticism of the social sciences (which, incidentally, contain many evaluators) on the grounds that "expert" social scientists cannot agree on the interpretation of relevant data. (Criticism of social scientists is not a new phenomenon, however. Several persons have long since been credited with stating that if you laid all the economists in the world end-to-end, they still would not reach agreement.)

There is no denying that different evaluators will make somewhat different judgments when confronted with the same body of data or evidence. At the same time, steps can be taken to minimize or at least understand such differences and put them into a more meaningful perspective. One step is to require evaluators to explain which data or evidence they are according primary importance and why. The reasoning leading up to their judgments likewise should be fully disclosed. Each evaluator also should describe thoroughly the standards being utilized for each judgment. Bracht (1975) has suggested another means to reduce arbitrary judgments. In this procedure, audiences for the evaluation report make judgments about the data provided to them by the evaluator; the evaluator then processes, summarizes, and reports on the various judgments that result. Full and open disclosure of the principal components involved in making evaluation judgments or surveying the judgments of potential audiences will not eliminate all capriciousness. However, such procedures should lessen differences among evaluators' opinions and increase the level of understanding of judgments made. Scriven (1976) has labeled this general problem area *evaluation bias* and has presented available procedures to reduce, balance, or otherwise control bias (such as metaevaluation and the adversary model, described in Chapters Nine and Twelve, respectively).

Issue 14: Is Evaluation Inadequate Because It Does Not Explain Why a Program Is Effective? This issue questions the depth of evaluation. An evaluation typically might judge Program A to be moderately effective; or, if the evaluation is a comparative one, it might judge Program C to be more effective than Program B. However, it is not likely to be explained why A is moderately effective or why Program C did better than Program B on outcome measures. One might argue that program improvement generally is not possible when reasons for more effective performance are unknown.

In one sense, there is no counterposition on this issue, for it is true that evaluations usually do not answer the "why" question. In most cases, evaluations do not provide explanations. The purpose of evaluation is to determine worth, not to explain. Through evaluation, the information necessary for making rational judgments is collected. Since evaluation is not directed toward generating explanations, other procedures must be initiated to determine why a program is exemplary in a given regard or why certain outcomes were not achieved. In another sense, evaluation can provide clues to the "why" question, particularly if some elements of the evaluation focused on process—that is, on program activities as they occurred. The question of likely causes of program effects can more adequately be answered if key program features are systematically varied, and a series of corresponding evaluations take place (Bracht, 1975). Regardless of its applicability to explanations, however, evaluation itself is a significant undertaking.

Issue 15: Should Evaluation Be Abandoned Since Little Is Changed By It? This issue is a lively one. Those who contend that evaluation produces minimal effects cite four basic illustrations. First, evaluation results are too often tardy, and this severely limits their influence. Stake (1970b) expressed the opinion that evaluations typically take too long. He has proposed a Parkinson's Law for evaluators: "No matter how short the evaluation period, the critical decisions will be made before the evaluation results are available." Second, in many cases evaluation results have been used selectively: data that support a given (often preconceived) position are highlighted, while contrary data are suppressed, ignored, or denied. Third, programs and schools employing evaluators do not seem to have distinguished themselves as significantly more effective (owing to that fact) than those not using evaluation to any extent. Fourth, examples abound in which evaluation results have produced no more than a small and very temporary ripple of change.

Immediate responses to these four charges are possible, although they tend to seem somewhat weak. In answer to the first, clearly evaluation results should be timely. As to the second, failure to consider all available and sound evaluative data reflects a lack of good sense rather than any inherent lack in the worth of evaluation as a process. The third charge could be deflected by pointing out that programs and schools employing other types of specialists, such as counselors or curriculum planners, have also failed to demonstrate superior effectiveness. In all fairness, the contributions of such professionals in large agencies are quite diffuse and difficult to sort out in any highly analytical sense. The fourth charge can be countered more substantively in that it is also possible to note many examples of evaluations that could lead to important decisions and have significant impact. For instance, the appendix of the Riecken and Boruch book (1974) contains abstracts of many evaluative studies in delinquency and criminal reform, law, rehabilitative mental health, special education, fertility control, communication methods, research utilizations, and economics. A review of these evaluation abstracts makes it clear that many of them lay the groundwork and rationale for significant changes. Other examples can be obtained by reviewing the social program evaluations in Abert and Kamrass (1974) and the education, health, labor, welfare and social service, and crime and justice evaluations in the *Evaluation Studies Review Annual* (Cook and others, 1978; Glass, 1976; and Guttentag, 1977).

The responses to Issue 15 just summarized seem defensive and apologetic in tone. A more substantial rationale for evaluation might be established if it could first be determined whether or not evaluation has been adequately supported and systematically applied. Have resources allocated for evaluation been 10 to 20 percent of total program costs, particularly during program initiation? In most cases, the answer is no; expenditures for research and development in education have been a pittance compared with analogous outlays in the automotive, drug, electronic, medical, and aerospace industries. Have personnel assigned to evaluative responsibilities been competent, in general, and competent evaluators, in particular? If not, have arrangements been made for adequate training in evaluation? Have high-level administrators such as program directors and funding agency officials supported systematic, unfettered evaluations of organizational procedures, products, and outcomes? Conversely, have they, at the evaluation's start, strongly intimated to internal (or even external) evaluators the "results" that the evaluators should reach? Our point, relevant to Issue 15, is that in many cases evaluation has had no fair chance to influence or change anything or to demonstrate its potential benefits.

Influence of Measurement and Evaluation. This topic in effect is Issue 16. In essence, it questions whether measurement and evaluation are influential with early childhood educators. If not, one might proceed to question the legitimacy and utility of both measurement and evaluation in the field.

Let us look first at the stature of measurement and evaluation in education generally. In the past, educators usually have not looked to measurement and evaluation to supply the information required for rational decisions at the many choice points in their programs. The reasons for this are not clear; any number of forces, operating independently and in combination, may have been contributory. Regarding measurement, for example, it can be noted that in a majority (if not most) of teacher education programs, measurement is not a required course. Even at the graduate level, practicing teachers are likely to avoid a formal course in measurement. Possibly measurement is shunned because it involves numbers. Dyer deplored this avoidance of measurement and suggested that schools experience many difficulties because "too many educators have too little respect for the dignity of data" (1971, p. 2). Our impression is that testing itself is currently used less in elementary and secondary schools than at any time in the recent past; however, we have seen no hard data to support (or refute) such an impression.

Evaluation has met with no warmer reception. Most educators (and many others), act almost as if they were members of a secret club known as ONOE (pronounced "Oh, no!" and standing for the Organization for No Organized Evaluation). Membership in such a club is understandable as virtually all of us lean toward joining at times, such as when our employer's evaluation of us matches poorly our own estimate of self-worth or when a product of our making is judged harshly. For educators, the word *evaluation* is likely to evoke recollections of being rated during a brief visit by a principal or supervisor, or of preparing and performing for an external evaluation team, possibly for program continuation or accreditation. Considerable anxiety attends being evaluated or having one's program evaluated. Indeed, evaluation may be so threatening as to trigger anxiety and avoidance symptoms (Phi Delta Kappa Commission on Evaluation, 1970). Anxiety in some degree or form is probably a concomitant of most evaluative efforts of any substance. Some might contend that the large number of educational program evaluations conducted attest to educators' belief in and support for such undertakings. However, it could be argued that many evaluations are conducted only because they are required by the funding legislation, regulation, or agency. In fact, some question exists as to whether even the funding agencies requiring evaluation are committed to the process (House, 1972).

In early childhood education, the status of measurement and evaluation seems much the same as in education generally, but possibly for somewhat different reasons. To be more explicit, persons attracted to work in early childhood education settings appear to have characteristics notably different from those of teachers at the secondary school level. Thus, Jackson examined elementary school teachers' language and found it characterized by: "(1) an uncomplicated view of causality, (2) an intuitive, rather than rational, approach to classroom events, (3) an opinionated, as opposed to an open-minded, stance when confronted with alternative teaching practices, and (4) a narrowness in the working definitions assigned to abstract terms" (1968, p. 144). LaCrosse (1970) noted that such a description was equally appropriate for nursery school teachers. He viewed the intuitive, feeling orientation of the teacher of young children as in sharp contrast to the inquiring, rational outlook of the psychologist-researcher who "invaded" the field in the mid 1960s. The implication is that early childhood educators, with their uncomplicated view of causality and their allegiance to intuition, feel no need for the products of a solid evaluative effort. Most early childhood education programs do not use systematic evaluation strategies (Goodlad, Klein, and Novotney, 1973; and Goodwin, 1974).

We also observe that some early childhood educators are strongly antitesting, particularly in cognitive areas. In their view, such testing is counterproductive, at best. They place heaviest emphasis on affective orientation and status of the child as the primary desideratum in early childhood education efforts. For example, they have identified "positive image-building in kindergarten" as "what education is all about" (Jordan, 1971, p. 106) and indicated that early childhood teachers "must realize that no learning will take place until each child is at ease with himself" (Woolner, 1971, p. 60). Considering the affective outlook and self-concept of the young child as primary can cause adults in early childhood settings to see their major role as providing love and affection, and lead them to postpone more academic educational activities for a child until emotional foundations are laid. The psychologist-researcher, however, might argue as follows: "In the hands of a skillful teacher, favorable attitudes and emotional adjustment can be fostered just as readily through activities that serve specific learning purposes as through activities that otherwise serve only as amusements. This is a point that is well known to teachers at higher school levels but that many early childhood educators seem not to recognize" (Bereiter and Engelmann, 1966, p. 11). This difference of opinion has the earmarks of the renowned chicken-and-egg controversy. Must a healthy self-concept and a feeling of being loved precede any formal academic learning by a child, or will formal learning by a child lead to a state of affective well-being and self-satisfaction? If early childhood educators predominantly hold the view that affective well-being comes first, then they are likely to de-emphasize formal learning and consider testing unnecessary.

We consider this controversy somewhat illusory. Though we have high regard for Maslow's views (1970) that love, belonging, and security needs are prepotent over needs to know and understand, we believe that affective and cognitive development are mutually facilitating. In other words, formal learning and achieving competence over one's environment can lead to positive self-regard on the part of the young child, and, concurrently, emotional adjustment and a positive affect state can facilitate processes such as learning and establishing competence. Neither necessarily must follow the other; no simple cause-and-effect chain is implied. That is, learning might not lead to high self-regard and positive affect need not facilitate learning. We think, however, that the supporting-facilitating cycle is more likely to occur for most children. We also believe strongly that young children should be able to expect more than just love from adults.

We conclude that measurement and evaluation currently are not particularly influential with early childhood educators. We are optimistic, however, that there will be growing trends in support of both. Measurement will no doubt gain acceptance more quickly. As noted in the discussion of Issue 3, once a broad range of suitable measures are available—not just tests but also records, ratings, observation procedures, and performance indicators—early childhood educators should be more prone to use them. Personnel in the field seem less opposed to measurement itself than to the instruments now in wide use. It is clear to most that accurate child assessment can help an adult facilitate the learning of the child.

Bringing about a more positive attitude toward teacher and program evaluation may be more difficult. Measuring young children's behaviors and evaluating their performance is one thing—adopting a positive attitude toward the evaluation of one's own performance or of one's own program is quite another. Such a change may gradually come about as early childhood educators hear about instances in which evaluations have led to desirable personal and program improvement. Certainly, the external pressures exist to bring such a change about—pressures such as accountability and scarce resources for staff and program support. More important, though, is that any change be primarily due to the educators' own convictions that evaluation can improve early childhood education.

Current Trends

Certain broad trends in the use of measurement and evaluation in early childhood education can now be identified. For the most part, these trends should come as no surprise, as the bases for them were established in the previous discussion of issues.

The durability of the five trends cited here is questionable. Although the field of early childhood education has demonstrated considerable stability, the focus of its programs is mercurial, changing quickly in response to new developments both inside and outside the field. External funding contributes to this changeability. The injection of new funds can quickly stimulate a totally new area of interest within early childhood education; the withdrawal of funds has a slower, but still dramatic, reverse effect. As the focus within the field changes, so may the trends in measurement and evaluation.

Trend 1: A broader conception of the types of measure appropriate for the field. This trend implies that several types of measure—tests, rating scales, observation systems, questionnaires, unobtrusive measures, performance measures, work samples, records, and social indicators—are suitable for use in early childhood education. Concomitantly, it heralds less dependence on tests themselves or, as McReynolds (1968) put it, less equating of psychological assessment with test technology. Most writers consulted have predicted an increased emphasis on naturalistic observation as a measurement procedure in early childhood education.

We do not see a trend toward the use of automated assessment procedures in early childhood education. It is true that the general fields of measurement and evaluation have access to, and are increasingly using, new automated procedures and equipment available due to technological advances in other fields. Thus, for psychological assessment as a total field, such a trend has been noted (McReynolds, 1968, 1971a, and 1975b). Such innovations include steadily more sophisticated computers, improved audio and video recording and related capabilities, and advances in recording and telemetry apparatus in psychophysiology (yielding the current interest in biofeedback procedures). Numerous aspects of clinical psychological assessment have been built into a single automated equipment console (Klett and Pumroy, 1971). Further, young children in educational settings have been infrequently measured or evaluated via automated procedures or equipment. In the case of infants, however, automated assessment of physiological functions is very much in evidence; but such activity has a research rather than education orientation and the age level falls below our range of special interest.

Trend 2: An increase in the number of variables that can be measured well due to an expanding supply of usable measures. Related to the first trend, Trend 2 suggests that suitable instruments and procedures will increasingly become available to measure variables in early childhood education. Any number of variables would be welcome additions to the pool of measurable variables in the field. The social competence elements listed in Table 1 would be an appropriate start. It is to be hoped that all of these variables would be based on advances in child development research. In White's view (1973a), variables such as cognitive style, which deal with process rather than product, will gradually receive more emphasis. He also forecasted increasing emphasis on criterion-referenced measures rather than norm-referenced measures (see Chapter Two). Not all of the new variables will be directly child-related. For example, more and better situational assessment of social and physical environments would seem likely (McReynolds, 1975b). Substantial materialization of this trend would do much to resolve Issue 3 (concerning the need for appropriate measures for young children).

Trend 3: An increase in the emphasis on fair and rational interpretation of results from measures. Earlier, considerable attention was focused on the issue of the fairness of tests for young children (Issue 4). In Tyler's view (1974), that issue reflected the continued effort to extend the civil rights drive to all segments of American society. As previously discussed, a culture-fair test may be an impossibility, with a given test being to some degree unfair to anyone outside the dominant societal group. A tolerable alternative might be to use the performance on a test or measure as simply one piece of information to be interpreted within a much broader framework that includes experiential background, socioeconomic status, and ethnic group membership. Thus, test scores would not be viewed as absolute or even as approximations of true scores—rather they would be relative indexes requiring interpretation (McReynolds, 1971a). This trend denotes a shift away from a search for a culture-fair test and toward a culture-fair interpretation. Rights of children being measured and evaluated would increasingly be respected and protected.

Trend 4: More staff evaluation. Although the field apparently has had some immunity from staff evaluation in the past, we note a slight trend toward increased emphasis on the evaluation of early childhood education personnel. If the public attitude remains one of seeking accountability and if resources for social programs remain relatively scarce, then the trend toward more staff evaluation may accelerate.

Trend 5: More program evaluation. This trend would mean increased evaluation of most aspects of programs, such as methods, materials, processes, outcomes, and staff (as set out in the fourth trend). The reasons for this trend are the same as those just mentioned in connection with the previous issue—increased public demands for accountability and reduced resources for social programs.

Again, the five trends presented are only trends and therefore are far from certainties for the future. To the extent that the trends are accurate reflections of present emphases and likely directions, however, they forecast an extensive need for development activity in both measurement and evaluation as they relate to early childhood education.

Chapter 2

Basic Measurement Concepts and Types of Measures

Measurement was defined in Chapter One as "the process of determining, via observation or testing, an individual's behaviors or traits, a program's characteristics, or the characteristics of some other entity, and then assigning a number, score, or rating to that determination. Generally, the purpose of measurement is to quantify or categorize variables in a logical maner, so as to determine the presence or absence—and amount or type—of characteristic possessed by individuals, groups, or programs. "Mary is reading well below her grade level" and "the experimental mathematics program for five- to seven-year-olds was rated by math experts as substantially to highly relevant in subject matter content" are examples of statements that might follow the analysis and interpretation of measurement data.

To design or select and implement measurement procedures, certain terms and concepts must be understood. Basic statistical skills are necessary to aggregate and simplify data. Even if one does not actually perform statistical analyses "by hand," but rather uses electronic calculators and computers, an understanding of statistical terms and concepts is critical for the interpretation of calculator and computer output, test scores, ratings, and observation data.

A knowledge of basic statistics and measurement concepts helps users of measuring instruments understand the instruments' empirically derived characteristics—those properties that indicate how accurate, useful, and meaningful the scores are. Does the test really measure what it purports to measure? Would the same scores result from administration of the same test to the same group a second time? How difficult, time-consuming, and costly would it be to use this particular instrument? Such questions can be answered by investigating the properties of the instruments. To adequately assess prospective instruments and the credibility of any set of measurement data, the users must know what evidence to look for (primarily in the manuals of commercially available instruments), how to evaluate that evidence, and, in some cases, how to gather that information themselves. This chapter sets the stage for understanding these psychometric concepts, which are the subject of Chapter Three.

In the first part of this chapter, we define and explain basic statistical and measurement terms and concepts, excluding reliability, validity, and usability. We have limited our material to the essentials for comprehending the rest of this book. Basic statistical terms—those integral but not unique to the field of tests and measurement—are included in order to familiarize readers with their meanings. (For a more detailed explanation of the statistical concepts, interested readers may want to consult an introductory statistics text, such as Hopkins and Glass, 1978.) Also included in the first section are definitions of some common measurement terms, presented in glossary fashion.

The second part of this chapter is concerned with basic types of measure, such as standardized tests, teacher-made measures, questionnaires and interviews, and unobtrusive measures. Each type is briefly described, along with applications to measurement of young children. (One technique—observation—is so appropriate for use by early childhood educators that we devote Chapter Four to it.) Here we introduce the structure and use of other commonly used measurement approaches, which are further exemplified in Chapters Five through Eight.

Terms and Concepts

Almost everyone at some time has confronted a set of numbers and attempted to make sense out of them. Balancing a checkbook, determining and comparing unit prices for grocery items, calculating income tax, and proportionally increasing or reducing amounts called for in a recipe are all common situations involving numbers. Teachers are especially familiar with sets of numbers, as they score tests and assign grades to students. The kinds of questions teachers ask about a set of student scores—What is the "average" score? How much do the children differ in their scores? Is there any correspondence between these and earlier test scores?—are questions answered by using descriptive statistics. Measures of central tendency, measures of variability, and measures of relationship are all descriptive statistics.

The distinction between descriptive and inferential statistics should be made. *Descriptive statistics* are used to describe a set of data, such as a group's performance on a measure and any individual's effort relative to the group. *Inferential statistics* are used when one wants to take outcomes from a given set of data and generalize to a larger group. The data are drawn from a sample of persons or objects assumed to be representative of a much larger group, or population, of persons or objects. Descriptive statistics are calculated for the sample, and then, using inferential statistical techniques (based on probability theories), statements are made about the entire population.

Variables and Scales of Measurement. A *variable* is a characteristic of persons or things that differs in type for different persons or things. Height, weight, sex, age, reading speed, mathematical ability, and temperature are examples of variables. Almost any description of persons or things involves variables. The sentence, "Bobby is five feet tall, weighs ninety pounds, has blue eyes and blond hair, and wears a size four shoe," describes Bobby in terms of five variables—height, weight, eye color, hair color, and shoe size. In the context of person- or program-related evaluation, the variables most frequently encountered are test scores, results of ratings or observations, and questionnaire responses. To say, for example, that a student's raw score of 40 on a science achievement test places him at the 70th percentile is to describe him in terms of the variable "science achievement" in two ways—by raw score and percentile rank. As long as the characteristic of interest encompasses at least two different values within a group of persons, it is a variable. However, if all persons in a group are the same with respect to some characteristic, it is a constant for that group. For example, if all the children in a school are female, then sex is not a variable for that group.

Before tabulating or aggregating variables for a group of persons or objects, a uniform conversion of variable values to numbers must be defined. Four different scales of measurement convert values of variables to numbers. The type of scale used depends in part on the type of variable. Some variables (height, for example), are readily expressed in meaningful numerical units; but other variables (hair color, for example) do not have intrinsic numerical equivalents and numbers are assigned arbitrarily.

A *nominal measurement scale* is one in which assignment of numbers to values of a variable is arbitrary; the size of the number does not connote relative amounts of the characteristic. Sex, nationality, occupation, religion, favorite food, and predominant language are examples of nominal scale variables. To establish such a scale, persons or objects are grouped according to their different features of the characteristic. All the persons or items displaying the same features are assigned the same number. For example, if sex were the variable of interest, all males would be assigned one number and all females another number. It makes no difference what numbers are used, but the assignment procedures, once established, must remain uniform.

Nominal scale numbers have no meaning in terms of the amount of a given characteristic. If blue-eyed persons were assigned the number "3," brown-eyed persons the number "2," and green-eyed persons the number "1," we would not say that those given the value "3" had more eye color than those given a "2" or a "1." The numbers merely distinguish the three eye colors.

Other scales of measurement differ from the nominal scale in the correspondence of properties of numbers to properties of variables. An *ordinal measurement scale* involves rank-ordering of persons or objects with respect to amounts of a variable, and numbers are assigned in corresponding order. If ranks are assigned in descending order and one person's rank is greater or higher than that assigned to another person, the first person possesses more of the characteristic than the second person. Suppose that five children were rank-ordered according to height. The tallest child is assigned the number "5," the next tallest the number "4," and so on down to the shortest child, ranked "1." With this rank-ordering, we know that the larger the number, the taller the child. With ordinal measurement, however, we cannot say that child "4" is twice as tall as child "2," or that child "5" is five times as tall as child "1." Neither can we say that the difference in height between the child with the rank of "4" and the one with the rank of "2" is the same as the difference in height between child "5" and child "3."

As with nominal measurement, the numbers on an ordinal measurement scale cannot meaningfully be added, subtracted, multiplied, or divided. Unlike nominal measures, however, ordinal numbers reflect more or less of a characteristic when compared with each other. Other examples of the use of the ordinal measurement scale are military ranks (position in the chain of command), graduating-class rank, rank (placement by age) in one's family, and the ranked results of a foot race.

An *interval measurement scale* renders more sophistication to the assigned numbers by making the differences between numbers meaningful. Temperature, measured in Fahrenheit or Centigrade units, is a good example of interval measurement. The difference in temperature between 80°F and 60°F is the same—twenty degrees—as that between 50°F and 30°F. However, the zero point on this scale is arbitrary; 0°F does not indicate the absence of temperature. An arbitrary zero point is a constant feature of interval measurement scales. Thus, we cannot appropriately say that it is twice as hot today, if the temperature is 70°F, as yesterday, when the temperature was 35°F. We can only say that it is 35°F warmer today. It is appropriate to add and subtract values on an interval scale, but multiplying or dividing them is meaningless because of the arbitrary zero point.

Many measures used in education and psychology are interval scale measures. Interval measurement clarifies differences between test scores. For example, if a reading achievement test for children in kindergarten through third grade was constructed on an interval scale, we might note that the difference in reading achievement between kindergartners and first-graders was much greater than the differences in reading achievement between children in successive grades.

The *ratio measurement scale,* the fourth and final type, differs from interval in that the zero point is not arbitrary; rather, zero on this scale indicates absence of the property being considered. Weight, age, time required to travel a certain distance, length, width, and number of children are variables measured on a ratio scale. With ratio measurement, it is possible to add, subtract, multiply, and divide the numbers meaningfully. A boy who weighs ninety pounds is said to weigh twice as much as his sister who weighs forty-five pounds.

Most variables of interest to early childhood educators and psychologists are measured on the nominal, ordinal, or interval scale, with the exception of some ratio-level measures of physical performance, such as reaction time, running speed, and jumping height (see Chapter Eight on psychomotor measures). Most measures of cognitive abilities or aptitudes and of psychosocial characteristics, such as attitudes, are considered interval scales. The required assumption for an interval scale is that equal differences between numbers on the scale reflect equal differences in the property being measured. Although some psychologists have argued against assuming interval measurement for cognitive and attitudinal variables, the practice is prevalent and most standardized tests and measures assume the interval scale. (Glass and Stanley, 1970, discuss this controversy and give references.)

Measures of Central Tendency. Three descriptive statistics commonly used to describe the "average" or "typical" score for a set of data are the *mean, median,* and *mode.* These measures indicate how the scores "tend centrally"—that is, how they are concentrated. The three measures, based on three varying definitions of "average," are determined in different ways. Although the mean is the most commonly used measure of central tendency, it is often useful to determine all three measures for a given set of data.

In order to facilitate the discussion of measures of central tendency and variability (next section), a set of hypothetical data is presented in Table 2. Variables listed include age in months, number of siblings, IQ scores from the Wechsler Preschool and Primary Scale of Intelligence (WPPSI), and raw scores from the Boehm Test of Basic Concepts (BTBC); the measures are described in Chapter Five.

Mean: The *mean* is the arithmetic average. It is calculated by adding all the scores and dividing by the number of scores. The formula for calculating the mean is

$$\bar{X} = \frac{\Sigma X}{n}$$

with $\bar{X}$ representing the mean, ΣX the sum of all the scores, and n the number of scores. In Table 2, the means of the four variables are calculated. For age in months, the ages of all 10 children are first summed; that sum (650) is then divided by n, in this case 10, the number of children. The mean age of the 10 children, therefore, is 65 months (650 ÷ 10). The mean number of siblings, WPPSI IQ score mean, and BTBC raw score mean are calculated in the same manner.

Median: The *median* is the point below which half the scores lie. If the total number of scores is odd, the median is the middle score. Given the scores 3, 4, 5, 9, 10, 11, and 12, the median is 9 since three scores lie below it and three lie above

Table 2. Hypothetical Data on Ten Kindergarten Children

Name	Age in Months	Number of Siblings	WPPSI IQ	BTBC Raw Score
		Variable		
Maria	63	0	120	42
Bill	65	3	103	34
Robin	63	4	85	28
Melissa	66	0	104	34
Francis	64	0	100	32
Linda	67	6	100	33
Jason	67	1	106	35
Leroy	60	3	113	38
David	67	0	98	31
Kathy	68	3	101	33
ΣX	650	20	1030	340
n	10	10	10	10
$\bar{X}$ (Mean)	65	2	103	34
Median	65.5	2	102	33.5
Mode	67	0	100	33 & 34 (Bimodal)
Variance (s^2)	6.22	4.44	85.55	14.66
Standard Deviation (s)	2.49	2.11	9.25	3.83

it. For an even number of scores, the median is the midpoint between the two middle scores. Given the scores 4, 5, 6, and 7, the median is 5.5. To calculate the median for a small, ungrouped set of data (such as in Table 2), first order the scores from smallest to largest. Ordering the numbers in the "Age in Months" column results in a new listing: 60, 63, 63, 64, 65, 66, 67, 67, 67, and 68.

Since there is an even number of children, the median is the midpoint between the two middle-most ages, 65 and 66 months; the median, therefore, is 65.5 months. Half of the children's ages fall below 65.5. In like manner, the median for the other three variables in Table 2 can be determined. For example, setting the IQ scores in order from smallest to largest, the middle values are 101 and 103; the midpoint of these scores, the median, is 102. Calculating the median by hand is easily manageable for small, ungrouped sets of data. Once data exceed about twenty scores, this type of calculation becomes cumbersome. (For the interested reader, most basic statistics texts include formulas for calculating the median on grouped data.)

Mode: The *mode* is the most frequently occurring score in a set of data. In Table 2, the mode for age in months is 67 months, since that value occurs more often (three times) than any other age. The modal number of siblings is 0. The mode for the IQ scores is 100; it occurs twice, while no other score occurs more than once. If all scores occurred with the same frequency, there would be no mode. Thus, if one of the "100" IQ scores in Table 2 were to be changed to "99," there would be no mode. If more than one of the scores occurred with the highest frequency, there would be multiple modes for the data. Note that the BTBC scores in Table 2 have more than one mode. Since the scores 33 and 34 both occur twice, and no other score occurs more often, the distribution of scores is said to be *bimodal,* that is, having two modes.

    Comparison of mean, median, and mode: The three measures of central tendency yield different types of information about the concentration of scores. The mean takes into account every score in a set of scores, creating a "balancing point" for the scores. The median is the same as the 50th percentile (to be discussed later in this chapter) in that it indicates the point below which half the scores lie. The median does not consider the value of every score with the same emphasis, as does the mean. The extreme scores tend to be ignored by the median. For example, if the highest IQ score in Table 2 were 140 rather than 120, the median would still be 102. The mean, however, would be sensitive to the change, moving from 103 to 105. The mode is the least stable of all three measures of central tendency. A slight change in one score can result in a change in the mode—either changing the mode from one value to another (if, for example, the 101 and 106 IQ scores in Table 2 were changed to 103, that would be the new mode), changing a unimodal distribution to a multimodal one, or yielding a set of scores with no mode at all. Note, too (particularly in ungrouped data), that the mode could lie at one end of the set of scores or the other and not in the central region at all, as in the case of the number of siblings in Table 2.

    Which measure should be used? It is probably best to examine all three for any set of data, but choosing the best one to characterize a set of data will often depend on the occurrence of extreme scores. The mode, because of its instability, is rarely chosen as the single measure of central tendency. The mean gives the most precise information, since it considers every score, but can be misleading when there are extreme scores; the median is preferable as an indication of the "typical" score when there are very extreme scores. For example, consider the situation in which the seven members of a school team bowled games of 4, 5, 6, 7, 9, 12, and 300 (a perfect score). The mean score, 49, is hardly "typical" of the performance of the individual group members, although it is a good estimate of how the members, as a team, would place in a tournament. The median, 7, better indicates the standard performance of individual members. Optimally, one should look at all three measures. If they vary widely, a close examination of the distribution of actual scores should be made.

    Measures of Variability. To adequately describe a set of data, statistics other than just measures of central tendency are needed. Although the mean provides a useful reference point for determining whether a particular score is above, at, or below the "average," other statistics are needed to gain a clear picture of any score's distance from the mean. Measures of variability are descriptive statistics that convey information about the amount of spread or dispersion in a set of data. The measures of variability that will be described here are the range, the variance, and standard deviation.

    Range: A simple measure of variability is the *range,* the difference between the largest and the smallest values in a set of data. Two different ways of calculating the range result in slightly different values for the statistic. The *exclusive range* is the difference between the highest and lowest scores or values. Thus, for the IQ scores in Table 2 the exclusive range is 35 (120 – 85). The *inclusive range* is one unit more than the exclusive range, for the fractional half-units above the highest score and below the lowest score are included (that is, the inclusive range is 120.5 – 84.5, or 36). The range provides an easy, quick measure of the amount of spread but has the disadvantage of considering only the extreme scores. The range is unstable: any change in the extreme scores will alter the value of the range, even though all other scores remain constant.

Variance and standard deviation: The variance and standard deviation are more precise measures of dispersion or spread than the range because all scores are taken into account in the calculations of these statistics. They are the most widely used measures of variability. The *variance* is the average of the squared deviations of scores from the mean. The *standard deviation* is the square root of the variance and is somewhat more meaningful because it is expressed in the same units as the raw scores themselves. The usual symbols for the variance and standard deviation are s^2 and s, respectively.

The deviation of any score from the mean is simply the difference between that score and the mean, or $X - \bar{X}$. At first glance, it might seem that the sum of those deviations would provide a measure of the total amount of deviation, or difference from "average," in the distribution. However, the sum of all deviations will always be zero. For that reason, the deviations must be squared and then summed to yield a value for total amount of deviation. To obtain the variance—that is, the average amount of squared deviation—the sum of the squared deviations is divided by n (the number of scores), if the number of scores is large, or $n - 1$, if the number of scores is small, say thirty or less. (The reason for dividing by $n - 1$ rather than n is discussed in most basic statistics texts.) The square root of the variance yields the standard deviation.

Table 3 shows the steps involved in calculating the variance and standard deviation. The variable used in the illustration in Table 3 is "Age in Months," reproduced from Table 2. The formulas presented in Table 3 are known as the *definitional formulas* for the variance and standard deviation. The more expeditious *computational formulas,* found in standard statistics texts, should be used to calculate these statistics by hand for large sets of data.

The standard deviation of a set of scores provides a reference for assessing the extent of deviation from the mean—that is, for knowing within what limits proportions of the scores in a given distribution are contained. In most distributions, a majority of scores will fall between $-1s$ and $+1s$ from the mean. (In all normal distributions, 68 percent of all scores fall within these limits; this will be discussed in greater detail in the next section.) If we round the value of the standard deviation in our example to 2.5, the limits of $-1s$ and $+1s$ from the mean are approximately 62.5 (65 – 2.5) and 67.5 (65 + 2.5). Once we know this, we can be more precise in assessing the relative status of individual children. Whereas the children who are 63, 64, 65, 66, and 67 months old are all within one standard deviation of the mean, the other children (those who are 60 and 68 months old) are in the minority extremes. If we were told only that Leroy is 60

Table 3. Calculation of the Variance and the Standard Deviation

Age in Months	Deviation Scores or $X - \bar{X}$ (each score minus the mean of 65)	Squared Deviation Scores $(X - \bar{X})^2$
63	63–65 = −2	4
65	65–65 = 0	0
63	63–65 = −2	4
66	66–65 = 1	1
64	64–65 = −1	1
67	67–65 = 2	4
67	67–65 = 2	4
60	60–65 = −5	25
67	67–65 = 2	4
68	68–65 = 3	9
	Sum of the Deviation Scores or $\Sigma(X-\bar{X})$ = 0	Sum of the Squared Deviation Scores or $\Sigma(X-\bar{X})^2$ = 56

Step 1: Subtract each score from the mean to obtain deviation scores; determine that the sum of the deviation scores, or $\Sigma(X-\bar{X})$, equals zero.

Step 2: Square each deviation score.

Step 3: Sum the squared deviation scores; determine that $\Sigma(X-\bar{X})^2 = 56$.

Step 4: Find the number of scores minus one; determine that n–1 = 9.

Step 5: Substitute the results from step 3 and step 4 for the terms in the formula for the variance and perform the indicated operations:

$$\text{Variance} = s^2 = \frac{\Sigma(X-\bar{X})^2}{n-1} = \frac{56}{9} = 6.22.$$

Step 6: Take the square root of the variance to obtain the standard deviation:

$$\text{Standard Deviation} = s = \sqrt{s^2} = \sqrt{6.22} = 2.49.$$

months old and that the average age for his class (of ten students) is 65 months, we would not know how greatly he differs from his peers in age. Once we know the standard deviation, 2.5 months, we know that he is one of the youngest of the group. Francis, however, who is also younger than the average child (being 64 months old) is within one standard deviation; he does not, therefore, differ as much in age from most of the other children as does Leroy.

Normal Distribution and Interpretation of Scores. Raw scores can be transformed into a number of different, comparable units that aid interpretation. Grade-equivalent scores, age-equivalent scores, percentile ranks, and standard scores are common types of transformed score. As we will see, the meaningfulness of transformed scores is enhanced when the underlying distribution of raw scores is normal.

The "normal curve" and z-scores: Many physical characteristics are normally distributed; that is, their distribution forms a bell-shaped curve like the one in Figure 1. The *normal curve* is a theoretical distribution symmetrical about the mean; the mean, median, and mode coincide. The fact that many easily measured physical characteristics, such as height and weight, comprised a normal

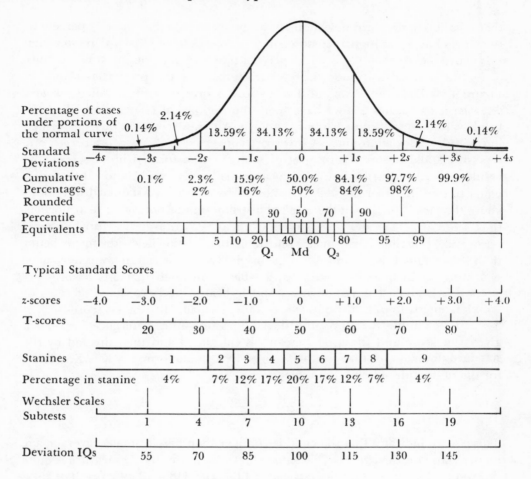

Source: Adapted from the Psychological Corporation, 1955, p. 8.

Figure 1. The Normal Curve, Selected Standard Scores, and Percentiles.

curve when values for a large number of persons were plotted led to the conjecture that psychological characteristics, such as intelligence, were similarly distributed. This assumption influenced many developers of intelligence and aptitude tests to use scoring and weighting procedures that resulted in normal or near-normal distributions of score for tryout samples.

Note in the sketch of the normal distribution (Figure 1) that by far the largest proportion of scores or cases falls under the central portion of the curve, with proportions getting smaller and smaller as one moves outward from the mean. Approximately two thirds of the cases (34.13 percent plus 34.13 percent) lie within the limits $\pm 1s$—that is, plus and minus one standard deviation from the mean. About 95 percent of the cases lie between $\pm 2s$, and 99 percent between $\pm 3s$. A person who scores at the mean surpasses 50 percent of the group (0.14 percent plus 2.14 percent plus 13.59 percent plus 34.13 percent). A score that falls at one standard deviation above the mean is higher than 84 percent of the scores but not as high as 16 percent of the scores (those that are greater than +1s above the mean—that is, 13.59 percent plus 2.14 percent plus 0.14 percent).

All normal distributions are characterized by the properties shown in Figure 1. It becomes meaningful to express scores in a form called *standard deviation units* because, as we have seen, the number of cases falling above or below various standard deviations is known. Any raw score can be transformed into standard deviation units. A raw score converted in this way is a *z-score,* one type of standard score. Once a set of scores is transformed into z-scores, the resulting z-score distribution has a mean equal to zero and standard deviation equal to one. A z-score of +2 indicates performance two standard deviations above the mean; further, if the original distribution was normal or near normal, the z-score of +2 lies above 98 percent of the other scores in the distribution. A z-score of −1 signifies performance one standard deviation below the mean, better than 16 percent of the other cases if the original score distribution was normal or near-normal. In most statistics texts, a table is provided that lists z-scores expressed in standard deviation units and indicates the percentage of cases or scores falling below each specific z-score for normally distributed scores.

To compute a z-score, the deviation score—the difference between a given raw score and the group mean—is calculated and then divided by the standard deviation for that group of scores. In formula form, $z = X - \bar{X}/s$. Thus, for the 60-month-old child in Table 2:

$$z = \frac{60 - 65}{2.5} = \frac{-5}{2.5} = -2$$

This z-score indicates that the child is younger than his classmates' average age by two standard deviations. That same child's status on the IQ measure is quite different. His z-score on that variable is 1.08 ($z = 113 - 103/9.25 = 10/9.25 = 1.08$). Converting scores on all the measures in Table 2 to the common unit of the z-score facilitates meaningful comparison across the measures.

Percentile and percentile rank: Any distribution of scores can be subdivided into units of equal size—that is, groups of scores with a certain proportion in each. The most common delimiters of this type are deciles, quartiles, and percentiles. *Deciles* divide the scores into ten equal groups, *quartiles* into four equal groups, and *percentiles* into one hundred equal groups. Whether the partition values are deciles, quartiles, or percentiles, they are represented by numerical points on the distribution. For example, Q_1 (the first quartile) is the point below which 25 percent of the cases, or scores, lie; P_{65} (the 65th percentile) is the point below which 65 percent of the scores fall. The median, which is equal to P_{50}, or the 50th percentile, divides the scores into two equal groups.

Since a percentile is a point on the distribution, it does not necessarily correspond to any actual, obtained score for a particular group of students. Percentiles provide references against which actual scores can be compared. For example, one might determine that a student performed above P_{80} on an aptitude test but below P_{50} on an achievement test.

Percentile rank is a type of transformed score that is closely related to percentile; whereas the latter is merely a point that may or may not equal a real score, the former corresponds exactly to a particular score. A student whose percentile rank on a reading test is 76, for example, scored better than or equal to 76 percent of the group with which he is being compared.* Expressing raw scores as percentile ranks is a popular practice. The computation involved in converting a raw score to a percentile rank is relatively easy, and the meaning of the transformed score is apparent to most people. Caution must be used, however, in interpreting the meaning of differences between percentile ranks. Note in Figure 1 that equivalent differences in percentile ranks do not reflect the same differences in z-scores or raw scores. The difference between the 50th and 60th percentile ranks is not the same as the difference between the 80th and 90th percentile ranks, in terms of standard deviation units. The latter difference is greater than the former, owing to the greater concentration of cases near the middle of the distribution. Interpretation of differences between percentile ranks for scores earned on different measures must take into account this characteristic of percentile ranks.

Standard scores: We have already introduced one type of standard score, the z-score. The z-score is the most basic type of standard score, expressing a raw score as a deviation from the group mean in standard deviation units. The transformation of raw scores into z-scores utilizes properties (mean, standard deviation) of a particular group—for example, a national norm group or a local group such as a particular class of students. The mean and standard deviations of a distribution of z-scores are always zero and one, respectively.

Other typical standard scores are merely further transformations of z-scores. *T-scores* are standard scores with a mean equal to 50 and a standard deviation of 10. Any raw score can be converted to a *T*-score by first calculating a z-score, multiplying it by 10, and adding 50. Presented in formula form:

$$T = 50 + 10 \ \frac{X - \bar{X}}{s} = 50 + 10z$$

T-scores are sometimes preferred over z-scores because they eliminate the necessity of expressing the scores below the mean as negative scores. (Standardized test scores are rarely presented as z-scores for this reason.)

Additional examples of standard scores are the College Entrance Examination Board scores, with mean equal to 500 and standard deviation equal to 100, and the Wechsler intelligence scales (WISC, WISC-R, WPPSI), with means of 100 and standard deviations of 15. Deviation IQs resulting from the Wechsler scales are represented in Figure 1.

Stanines: Another type of standard score scale is the stanine scale. *Stanines* are normalized standard scores, with a mean equal to 5 and a standard deviation

---

*Since the traditional use of the pronoun *he* has not yet been superseded by a convenient alternative meaning *he* or *she,* we will continue to use *he*—acknowledging here the inherent inequity of the traditional preference for the masculine pronoun.

of 2. The relationship of this nine-unit scale to the normal curve is shown in Figure 1. Stanines 2 through 8 are each approximately one half a standard deviation in width, whereas stanines 1 and 9 each occupy a larger proportion of space (in standard deviation units) under the curve. To convert raw scores to stanines, the scores are first arranged from highest to lowest, and then the appropriate percentage of scores is assigned to each stanine. For example, the top 4 percent of the scores fall into stanine 9 and the lowest 4 percent fall into stanine 1. In this way, the scores are "normalized," that is, forced into a normal distribution. Stanine scores are frequently reported for standardized tests. The Metropolitan Readiness Tests (see Chapter Five) present tables for the transformation of raw scores to stanines, for the subtests as well as total test scores. The transformation procedures are based on results from the norming samples. Although stanine scores lack the precision of percentile ranks or other standard scores, they are easy to calculate by hand and enable one to "normalize" a distribution whose raw scores are not normally distributed.

Grade- and age-equivalent scores: Achievement tests frequently yield *grade-equivalent scores,* which indicate the grade levels at which students are performing. A grade-equivalent score corresponds to the average raw score of students at a particular grade level. If a student in the first grade, for example, achieved a raw score of 60 on a standardized reading test, the grade-equivalent score, say 2.5, would indicate that a raw score of 60 is the average score earned by children who are halfway through the second grade. The reference group for the establishment of grade-equivalent conversions is usually the national norm group used in the standardization procedures, although it could be a local group, such as a school district. Since schooling traditionally takes place from September through June, each school month is considered one tenth of a year.

Grade-equivalent scores have a few distinct disadvantages. First, standardization testing usually occurs at only one or two times during the school year. Schools using the test at other times during the year must use conversion tables, which are not quite accurate. Another disadvantage of grade-equivalent scores is that they are subject to misinterpretation. The first-grader whose arithmetic grade-equivalent is 3.5 has probably not mastered the arithmetic processes and content representative of the middle of third grade; that child and the average third-grader have achieved their scores for different reasons (superior performance on first-grade arithmetic and average performance on third-grade arithmetic, respectively).

Age-equivalent scores are similar to grade-equivalent scores, except that they represent the typical performance of children at different chronological ages. A preschool developmental test might convert raw scores to age-equivalent scores; to know that a child's performance is better or poorer than the average for his own chronological age group might be very helpful in planning the instructional program for that child.

In the context of intelligence tests, age-equivalents are known as *mental age scores.* A person's "mental age" on an intelligence test is the chronological age at which his score is the average score. Previously, mental age was used extensively

in the computation of a *ratio IQ score,* namely: IQ = (MA/CA)100. A child's mental age (MA) was divided by his chronological age (CA), and the quotient multiplied by 100. This ratio IQ score has largely been replaced by a *deviation IQ score,* a type of standard score based on the extent of deviation (in standard deviation units) of a person's performance from the mean of his own age group.

The preferred modes of reporting developmental and achievement test scores include different types of unit: percentile rank, standard score, and age-equivalent or grade-equivalent scores. At least two different expressions for scores are desired since, as we have seen, different transformations of scores mean different things. Multiple scores make misinterpretation less likely. For example, a five-year-old child may receive an age-equivalent score of 6.5 on a developmental test. However, his percentile rank in his own age group may be only 55. The initial reaction to the age-equivalent—that this child is well advanced for his age—is tempered when the percentile rank is simultaneously considered.

If only one type of transformed score is to be reported, it should be one other than the age- or grade-equivalent score, if possible. Cronbach (1970) criticized equivalent scores and argued against their use: "In the writer's opinion, grade conversion should never be used in reporting on a pupil or a class, or in research. Standard scores or percentiles or raw scores serve better. Age conversions are also likely to be misinterpreted. A six-year-old with mental age nine cannot pass the tests a twelve-year-old with mental age nine passes; the two simply passed about the same fraction of the test tasks. On the whole, however, age equivalents cause less trouble than grade equivalents, if only because the former are not used for policy decisions in education" (p. 98).

Measures of Relationship. The relationship between scores on different measures is a common concern in instrument construction as well as in the synthesis and interpretation of measurement data. Typical questions include the following: To what extent do children who excel on a given readiness test in kindergarten also excel in first-grade achievement? Are low self-esteem ratings associated with low creativity scores? Is the child with psychomotor delays also likely to experience learning difficulties? These and an infinite number of similar questions are answerable through statistical measures of association, or correlations. An understanding of the concept of correlation and of related correlation coefficients is also required for the study of reliability and validity (Chapter Three).

The meaning of "correlation": Correlation refers to the relationship between two variables available for one group of persons or the relationship between pairs of persons on one variable. Height and weight are physical properties that are related; for any representative group, the taller people will tend to be the heavier people and the shorter people the lighter ones. Obviously, there are exceptions: the tall-slender and the short-plump. But, on the average, the person who is six feet tall will weigh more than the person who is five feet tall. The heights of fathers and sons are also related, in that the sons of tall fathers tend to be tall and the sons of short fathers, short. Many physical properties are related, as are some psychological characteristics. Intelligence and school achievement are moderately related. Although the relationship is far from perfect, children with above-average intelligence typically display above-average achievement.

The statistical expression for correlation is a *correlation coefficient (r),* which ranges from –1.0 to +1.0. A correlation coefficient of –1.0 or +1.0 signifies a perfect negative or perfect positive relationship, respectively. Assume two test scores are available for each of thirty children. A perfect positive relationship $(r = +1.0)$ exists if the child scoring highest on Test A also scored highest on Test B, the child scoring second highest on Test A also scored second highest on Test B, and so on, down to the thirtieth child, who scored lowest on both tests. A perfect negative correlation $(r = -1.0)$ exists when the rankings on two tests are exactly opposite, as when the child scoring highest on Test A scores lowest on Test B, and so on. (Perfect positive or negative relationships are extremely rare in education and psychology.) A correlation coefficient of zero $(r = 0)$ indicates no relationship between two variables. The relationship between age in months and number of siblings for a group of thirty preschoolers would most likely be zero or very close to zero. The number of siblings would vary independently of the ages of the children. No relationship $(r = 0)$ would also be likely to result if the thirty children mentioned above were assigned scores for the two tests by some chance or random method (such as a score pulled out of a hat for each child for each test). The child receiving the highest score on Test A could score at the top, middle, or bottom of the distribution for Test B. With such a random procedure, no systematic correspondence would be anticipated between the two test scores for each child.

The relationship between two sets of scores can be visualized by constructing a scattergram, which is comprised of points representing each student's standing on the two tests. For example, the relationship between the IQ (WPPSI) scores and BTBC scores (for the data originally presented in Table 2) is depicted in the scattergram in Figure 2. Each point in the scattergram represents one of the ten children. Note that the data points form a tight, nearly straight pattern running from the lower left corner to the upper right. Such a pattern is in evidence with high positive relationships; by calculation, $r = .98$, nearly perfect. Had the correlation been perfect (that is, $r = +1.0$), all the data points could have been connected by a single straight line. In analogous manner, a scattergram depicting a perfect negative relationship consists of data points lying on a straight line running from the upper left corner to the lower right.

The difference between a strong correlation and a negligible one can be seen by comparing the scattergram in Figure 2 with the one in Figure 3, which illustrates the relationship between age in months and number of siblings (from Table 2). The points in the scattergram do not form a discernible pattern; they appear almost as if distributed at random. In fact, calculation of the exact correlation between the two variables reveals that there is no association; that is, $r = 0$. With small samples of data like the two sets diagrammed in the last two figures, or even with samples of thirty to forty subjects, the construction of a scattergram by hand is relatively easy. With larger numbers of subjects, scattergrams can be

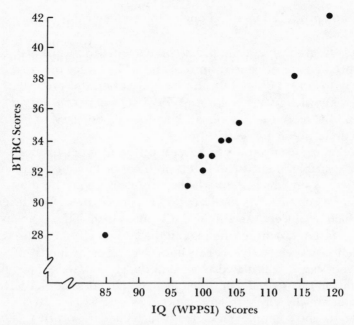

Figure 2. Scattergram Illustrating a Strong Positive Relationship
(*r* = .98) between IQ (WPPSI) Scores and
BTBC Scores for Ten Children.

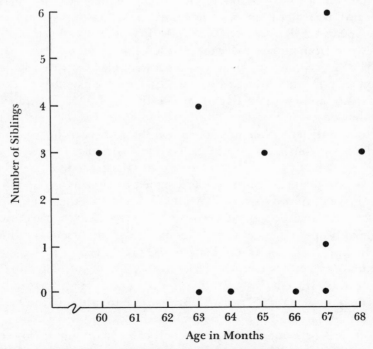

Figure 3. Scattergram Illustrating a Zero Relationship (*r* = 0) between
Age in Months and Number of Siblings for Ten Children.

more efficiently produced by using one of the commercially available computer programs.

If a scattergram shows a nonzero correlation, this means that it should be possible to predict one variable from the other. The larger the correlation (that is, the closer it is to +1.0 or –1.0), the more accurate the prediction. Figure 2 indicates that knowledge of a student's WPPSI IQ will permit very good prediction of his BTBC score (or vice versa). For the data depicted in Figure 3, however, no accurate prediction is possible.

Types of correlation coefficient: Several different types of measure of relationship are available; their use depends on the type of scale (nominal, ordinal, interval, or ratio) on which the variables are measured. The most commonly used correlation coefficient is the Pearson Product-Moment Coefficient of Correlation, which requires interval or ratio measures. The Pearson Product-Moment Coefficient quantifies the magnitude and specifies the direction of the correspondence between two sets of values, having as its limits –1.0 and +1.0. The coefficient can be calculated in several different ways. One common formula uses data in raw-score form. The calculation of correlation coefficients can be quite tedious, especially with large amounts of data. The advent of sophisticated calculators and computers has greatly facilitated the process. Table 4 shows the steps involved in calculating the correlation illustrated in Figure 2, between the IQ and BTBC scores for the children in Table 2.

The product-moment correlation coefficient is a measure of association for two interval or ratio variables. The correlation between two variables measured on ordinal scales (that is, variables expressed in ranks) can be calculated with the Spearman Rank-Correlation Coefficient (r_s). Educators often rank-order students from highest to lowest on test results or other characteristics, such as age. When a group is rank-ordered on two variables, or paired subjects (twins, for example) are rank-ordered on one variable, it is possible to calculate the degree of association with the Spearman coefficient. Table 5 illustrates the calculation of the Spearman coefficient, using the same data as was used in Table 4 for the Pearson coefficient. Note in Table 5 that the scores on the two variables (IQ and BTBC) are converted to ranks. For each variable, the ten children are ranked from highest to lowest, with the rank of "1" assigned to the highest scores. Tied ranks take the mean of the ranks assigned to them as a common rank. For example, in Table 5, two students have IQ scores of 100, the seventh and eighth highest scores; both are assigned a rank of 7.5. (With an excessive number of tied ranks, the appropriateness of using the Spearman coefficient is reduced.)

The Spearman coefficient between IQ (WPPSI) and BTBC scores is .99. This compares favorably with the Pearson coefficient, calculated in Table 4, of .98. The two coefficients are not identical because some information is lost in transforming the IQ (WPPSI) and BTBC scores into ranks. In most cases, unlike this one with its large number of tied ranks, the loss of precision associated with the rank-order correlation results in a coefficient value slightly lower than that obtained with nonranked data. However, the loss of precision is slight, and the Spearman coefficient is thus sometimes preferred if a calculator is not available.

Table 4. Calculation of the Pearson Product-Moment
Coefficient of Correlation between IQ (WPPSI)
and BTBC Scores for Ten Children

IQ (WPPSI) Score (X)	BTBC Score (Y)	X²	Y²	XY
120	42	14400	1764	5040
103	34	10609	1156	3502
85	28	7225	784	2380
104	34	10816	1156	3536
100	32	10000	1024	3200
100	33	10000	1089	3300
106	35	11236	1225	3710
113	38	12769	1444	4294
98	31	9604	961	3038
101	33	10201	1089	3333

$\Sigma X = 1030$ $\Sigma Y = 340$ $\Sigma X^2 = 106860$ $\Sigma Y^2 = 11692$ $\Sigma XY = 35333$
$(\Sigma X)^2 = 1060900$ $(\Sigma Y)^2 = 115600$

Step 1: Sum the raw scores for X; sum the raw scores for Y. Determine that $\Sigma X = 1030$; $\Sigma Y = 340$.

Step 2: Square the results of step 1. Determine that $(\Sigma X)^2 = 1060900$; $(\Sigma Y)^2 = 115600$.

Step 3: Square all X scores and sum the products; square all Y scores and sum the products. Determine that $\Sigma X^2 = 106860$; $\Sigma Y^2 = 11692$.

Step 4: Multiply X by Y for each student and sum the products. Determine that $\Sigma XY = 35333$.

Step 5: Substitute the results of steps 1 through 4 in the formula for the Pearson correlation coefficient and perform the indicated operations:

$$r = \frac{n\Sigma XY - \Sigma X \Sigma Y}{\sqrt{[n\Sigma X^2 - (\Sigma X)^2][n\Sigma Y^2 - (\Sigma Y)^2]}}$$

$$r = \frac{10\,(35333) - (1030)(340)}{\sqrt{[(10 \times 106860) - 1060900][(10 \times 11692) - 115600]}} = \frac{3130}{3188.1} = .98$$

Other statistical techniques must be used to measure association if one or both of the variables of interest are nominal. If one variable is ordinal and the other interval, no statistic is available and the interval measure must be converted to ranks. This chapter will not describe other types of measure of relationship or of multiple correlation. Glass and Stanley (1970) include a detailed description of these other statistics and their applicability.

Interpreting and using the correlation coefficient: The numerical value of a correlation coefficient indicates its magnitude; the sign indicates its direction. A correlation of −.70 is of the same magnitude as a correlation of +.70 but represents an inverse relationship rather than a direct one. The sign is sometimes a product of the scaling technique used. If teacher-assigned grades are correlated with number of days absent from school, the r is likely to be negative—those students with the higher scores being the ones with the fewer days absent and vice versa for the lower achievers. If, however, the correlation between those same teacher-assigned grades and number of days present in school is calculated

Table 5. Calculation of the Spearman Rank-Correlation Coefficient between IQ (WPPSI) and BTBC Scores for Ten Children

IQ (WPPSI) Score	BTCB Score	IQ (WPPSI) Rank	BTBC Rank	d	d²
120	42	1	1	0	0
103	34	5	4.5	.5	.25
85	28	10	10	0	0
104	34	4	4.5	−.5	.25
100	32	7.5	8	−.5	.25
100	33	7.5	6.5	1	1
106	35	3	3	0	0
113	38	2	2	0	0
98	31	9	9	0	0
101	33	6	6.5	−.5	.25
				$\Sigma d = 0$	$\Sigma d^2 = 2$

Step 1: Rank separately each set of scores, assigning 1 to the highest, and so on.

Step 2: Subtract to find the difference in rank (d) for each pair of ranked scores. Determine that the sum of all the difference scores (Σd) is equal to zero, which will always be the case if computations are correct.

Step 3: Square each difference in rank to obtain d^2.

Step 4: Sum the d^2 numbers. Determine that $\Sigma d^2 = 2$.

Step 5: Substitute the result of step 4 in the formula for the Spearman correlation coefficient and perform the indicated operations:

$$r_s = 1 - \frac{6\Sigma d^2}{n(n^2-1)}$$

$$r_s = 1 - \frac{6(2)}{10(100-1)} = 1 - \frac{12}{990} = .99$$

(for the same group of students), the resulting r will have the same value but be positive rather than negative.

The labeling of correlational values as "high," "medium," or "low" depends, in part, on the type of relationship being studied and is also somewhat arbitrary. The correlation between the scores earned by a group of children on a standardized test given twice within one week should be very large (.90 or above) to be considered "high." The correlation between two more diverse measures administered further apart (for example, scores on a first-grade readiness test given at the end of kindergarten and teachers' grades at the end of second grade) would be viewed as "high" if it fell in the .70 and .80 range. Although there are no set guidelines for translating the numerical value into a qualitative term, we have adopted the following general descriptors for values of r in the remainder of this book: r's in the .30 range and below are considered *low;* those in the .40's and .50's, *moderate;* those in the .60's and .70's, *substantial;* and those .80 or above, *high.* Our categorization is admittedly arbitrary, but we have decided upon it in order to facilitate later discussions.

A correlation coefficient cannot be directly interpreted as a percentage, as is commonly believed; that is, an r of .70 does not mean a 70 percent relationship. Nor is an r of .70 twice the relationship demonstrated by an r of .35. The *squared* value of a correlation coefficient does have meaning in terms of percentage, however, as r^2 is equal to the percentage of variance common to, or shared by, the two variables. (Advanced statistical texts present the rationale behind interpreting r^2 as percent of common or shared variance.) For an r equal to .70, it can be said that the two variables share 49 percent of the total variance.

More serious than the misinterpretation of r as a percentage is the common misconception that correlation signifies causation. For example, we would probably observe a high positive correlation between shoe size and running speed for a large group of four-, five-, and six-year-olds. Yet we could not conclude that a larger shoe size causes a child to run faster, nor that being able to run at a certain speed causes a child to require a certain-sized shoe. The real underlying cause is probably physical-developmental status, which influences both shoe size and running speed. Similarly, a substantial negative correlation between number of siblings and number of days present at school for one year does not signify a direct causal relationship. The notion that having many brothers and sisters directly causes a child to be absent from school is as fallacious as the reverse assumption—that being absent from school causes a child to have many siblings. A variety of environmental factors would actually explain the demonstrated correlation in causal terms, but it would be very difficult to determine the exact cause of either variable. Correlational analyses often provide clues to causal relationships, but evidence for causality requires carefully controlled experimentation. For exploratory studies, r is extremely useful; in no case, however, can a substantial or high correlation be correctly taken as evidence of a cause-effect relationship. When two variables correlate, it simply means that a change in the value of one corresponds systematically to a change in the value of the other.

Correlation is useful in measurement efforts as well as exploratory studies. Reliability and validity coefficients (to be discussed fully in Chapter Three) are correlation coefficients. Thus, one way to estimate the reliability or stability of a measure is to administer the same test twice to a group of students at close intervals; the correlation coefficient between scores earned on the two occasions is one type of reliability coefficient. As a second example, the validity of a test is sometimes measured by how closely the test corresponds, or correlates, to another measure of the same trait or ability. Scores on a reading achievement test might be correlated with reading grades assigned by teachers, for example. Investigation of the reliability and validity of an instrument often involves use of the correlation coefficient.

Prediction is closely associated with the concept of correlation. The higher the correlation between two variables, the greater is the predictive power of one for the other. If reading readiness scores from kindergarten correlate well with standardized reading achievement scores at the end of first grade, then we can predict the latter from the former. If r equals $+1.0$ or -1.0, our predictions should be perfectly accurate, whereas they will be right only by chance if r equals

0. The higher the correlation, the more accurate the predictions. The correlation between IQ (WPPSI) and BTBC scores, illustrated in Figure 2 and calculated in Table 4, is very high — .98. The predictive value of one variable for the other is therefore also high. Suppose we were to gather IQ (WPPSI) scores from another group of children very similar to those from whom the data in Table 4 were collected. Using the *r* we obtained from our sample, we could predict the new group's BTBC scores from their IQ scores. The accuracy of our predictions (as verified by later obtaining BTBC scores and comparing obtained with predicted scores) would be greater than that expected by chance alone, but not perfect.

We will delve no further into the statistical techniques associated with prediction; suffice it to say that the correlation coefficient is integral to the prediction formulas and that the larger the value of *r* (either in a positive or negative direction), the greater is the power to predict one variable accurately from another.

Other Measurement Terms. To conclude our review of basic measurement concepts, we will define, in alphabetical order, seven terms frequently used in discussions of measurement instruments, especially in reference to their relative strengths and weaknesses. Although far from exhaustive, this listing should alert the reader to common measurement problems, issues, and empirical procedures. Terms and concepts that relate directly to reliability, validity, and usability are covered in Chapter Three.

Ceiling: The upper limit of ability or performance that can be measured by an instrument is known as its *ceiling level.* If a student's abilities meet or exceed those at the highest level of the test, the student has reached the ceiling. Standardized tests designed to maximize the variability among a group (see the discussion of norm-referenced versus criterion-referenced measures later in this chapter) are inadequate for a group of children who are at the test's ceiling level; in such a case, the next level of the test or a different test should be used.

Correction for chance: Also called *correction for guessing,* this is a technique devised to prevent inaccurate rankings of examinees due to their guessing on test items. The underlying assumption is that, if a student guesses on an objective test, the number of right and wrong guesses will be proportional to the number of response options. For example, if a student guesses on each of sixty true-false items, he should, by chance, guess correctly on thirty of the items. If he were to guess on forty multiple-choice items, each with four response choices, the laws of probability suggest that he would guess correctly on ten of the questions, that is, one fourth. The correction for chance formula reduces the student's score to what it would have been if he had not guessed. Here is the formula:

$$S = R - \frac{W}{n - 1}$$

where: S = the student's corrected score,

R = the number of correct responses given by the student,

W = the number of wrong responses given by the student, and

n = the number of response alternatives per question.

The correction formula is applicable only in situations where some students omit some items and others do not; if there is no difference among examinees in tendency to omit items rather than guess, the ranking of students both before and after the formula is applied will obviously be identical. Further, the applicability, in general, of this procedure in the assessment of young children has been questioned by some test experts. Anderson, Messick, and Hartshorne (1972) pointed out that the correction formula "seems fairly sensible when applied to a population who have developed out of their experience some specific strategies for test taking. . . . It is highly unlikely, however, that children of five or six would have developed such strategies. Similarly, we can expect relatively sophisticated test takers to recognize that the correct answer is equally likely to appear in any of the response positions. When faced with difficult items, however, young children without this insight are more likely to respond in terms of position biases or other types of response sets" (p. 5).

We include the correction for chance technique here because it is still used and will be encountered in discussions of tests and other measures. At the same time, we believe that its use is currently less appropriate in early childhood education. With the increasing use of machine-scored answer sheets for young children, however, understanding the correction and the rationale for it could become more important. For additional information about problems associated with the correction for chance, see Stanley and Hopkins (1972).

Difficulty index: The *difficulty index,* or *difficulty value,* of an objective test item is the percentage of a specified group of examinees who answer the item correctly. A test that is very easy for a group of students will have many items with difficulty values above 80 percent. Norm-referenced tests aim for difficulty indexes around 50 percent so as to maximize the test's capability to differentiate between examinees' performances. With criterion-referenced tests, however, the difficulty index of individual items is not of major importance in test construction. If it can be defended on logical or empirical grounds that all students should be able to pass a certain item, an observed difficulty level as high as 100 percent would be acceptable.

Discriminating power: A test item is said to have good discriminating power if it differentiates between examinees who possess large amounts of the ability or skill being measured by the test and examinees who possess lesser amounts of that ability or skill. The discrimination index of an item indicates this capacity to differentiate. Like the difficulty index of an item, the discrimination index is primarily of concern in norm-referenced tests. Indeed, the two indexes are related—the discriminating index has the potential of reaching its maximum value when the difficulty index is 50 percent (Stanley and Hopkins, 1972).

The discrimination index can be determined in several ways. One common approach is to calculate the item-to-total test score correlation for a specified group of persons; a substantial positive correlation indicates that students passing the item are also scoring high on the total test, while those students missing the item are receiving relatively low total test scores. Conversely, if students doing poorly on the overall test tend to pass a particular item while students performing well on the total test are missing the same item, the item has poor or even negative discriminating power. For an explanation of other ways to calculate discrimination indexes, and the relation between discrimination and other test properties, see Stanley and Hopkins (1972). Note that determining the difficulty index and discriminating power of test items is the principal component of a process termed *item analysis.*

Factor analysis: One way of attempting to ferret out underlying components of a construct such as intelligence is to factor-analyze the test that purports to measure that construct. Through factor analysis, test items can be seen to cluster (or load) on one or more "factors," each of which is then named to reflect similarity among the items that belong to the factor. The intercorrelations among items or subsets of items are first determined; then factor analysis techniques further analyze those intercorrelations to produce the factors. Factor analysis is often used in content- and construct-validation procedures (see Chapter Three).

Power and speed tests: Tests can be differentiated on the "power versus speed" dimension. A *power test* is intended to measure the level of knowledge, aptitude or skill in some area without regard to the speed with which examinees complete the test. Time limits on power tests, therefore, should be very generous or not imposed at all. Unfortunately, this is not always the case. Further, items should be arranged from easiest to most difficult so that examinees have the chance to correctly answer all questions within their capability.

A *speed test* is one in which performance is equated with the number of tasks completed during a specified amount of time. Some psychomotor tests used with young children are speed tests. An example is the Fist/Edge/Palm subtest of the Frostig Movement Skills Test Battery (see Chapter Eight). In the Fist/Edge/Palm subtest, the child sequentially forms three positions with his hand: he makes a fist, then extends his fingers while resting the edge of his hand on a table, and finally places the hand palm down on the table. He repeats this cycle of three movements as fast as he can for twenty seconds, using his preferred hand, and then repeats the cycle for twenty seconds with his other hand. His score is the total number of correct cycles for the forty seconds. Speed is also an important part of tasks in other early childhood measures, such as measures of reading speed.

Practice effect: If the same test is administered to a group of students on two occasions, the scores from the second administration may be higher than the original scores because of the examinees' familiarity with the content or directions. This "practice effect" results in inflated scores on the second test. The threat of a practice effect accounting for observed changes in scores is greatest when the interval between testings is short; as time increases, the examinees are less likely to remember, and be influenced by, their first experience with the test.

Basic Types of Measure

A variety of ways to measure characteristics, abilities, or skills are available. The choice of a particular type of measure depends on the purpose of the measurement. The specific measurement instrument used will be selected on the basis of its relative validity, reliability, and usability. Thousands of measurement instruments and procedures have been developed for use in education. A great many have been published commercially, while others (sometimes called *fugitive instruments*) can be found in schools, project offices, and universities around the country. The source book section (following Chapter Twelve) includes a description of major sources of both published and unpublished instruments.

Systematic and objective measuring procedures have many advantages over intuition and subjective assessments.

> Strictly speaking, an objective measuring instrument is one on which the same score is assigned no matter who marks the test. When items can be scored right or wrong (as on multiple-choice or true-false tests), scoring is highly objective. When more complicated judgments have to be made, careful instructions are used to increase the likelihood of similar ratings by different teachers or graders.
>
> The logic of measurement, therefore, implies that most teachers and others are subject to biases and other unknown influences when attempting to intuitively measure the quality of behavior or performance. Measurement proponents urge the use of more objective means, such as "neutral" observers or the actual recording of events using videotape or the like, in order to increase the accuracy and generalizability of the measurements made. The logic of measurement does not seek to displace the human interpreter and judge but rather to provide the human judge with solid data relatively uncontaminated by various biases [Goodwin and Klausmeier, 1975, pp. 494–495].

Tests and measures can be categorized in a number of ways. Most common, perhaps, is to distinguish measures according to the types of human characteristic or ability they assess—cognitive, affective, or psychomotor ability, for example. This is the general approach we have taken in this book; Chapters Five and Six are primarily devoted to cognitive measures, while Chapters Seven and Eight deal with attitudinal and psychomotor instruments, respectively. Although the three domains often overlap when one tries to categorize behaviors of young children in this manner (Bradley and Caldwell, 1974), the scheme remains a useful one for general classification purposes.

Measurement instruments can also be differentiated along other lines, including purpose, scope, format, construction procedures used, administration and scoring procedures, nature of target audience, and so on. Here we will discuss differences and similarities among standardized tests, teacher-constructed measures, interviews and questionnaires, and unobtrusive measures. An additional category of measurement techniques—observational techniques—is so important in early childhood education that we have reserved the whole of Chapter Four for it. Comprehensive summaries of the strengths and weaknesses of various measurement techniques can be found in other sources (for example, Worthen and Sanders, 1973, pp. 280–289).

Before introducing the basic types of measure, we will discuss the differences between norm-referenced and criterion-referenced tests. Although the former tend to also be standardized and the latter nonstandardized and locally constructed, that distinction is not paramount; norm-referenced tests differ from criterion-referenced tests in other important ways. We include a description of the two types here because of the increasing concern and debate that these differences have evoked.

Norm-Referenced Versus Criterion-Referenced Measures. Performance is measured quite differently by norm-referenced and criterion-referenced tests. In a *norm-referenced test,* a student's performance is compared with that of other students. In a *criterion-referenced test,* the student's performance is compared against predetermined levels of mastery. Criterion-referenced tests show whether or not a student can do a certain thing, while norm-referenced tests show how the student performs in comparison with outside norm groups. Criterion-referenced achievement tests are becoming quite popular as replacements for norm-referenced achievement tests. Norm-referenced tests, however, continue to be used almost exclusively in the assessment of intelligence, aptitude, and many personality variables.

Before we extend our comparison of these two approaches, the meaning of *norm* and *norm-referenced* should be made clear. *Norms* are numerical descriptions of the test performance of reference groups of students. For many widely used tests, the reference group consists of the students in a national standardization sample; the reference group can, however, consist of a local group, such as students in one school district. In either case, tables of scores describing the norm group's performance are made available. Grade-equivalent scores, age-equivalent scores, standard scores, and percentile equivalents are common types of tabled norm. A student's score is referenced against the scores in the tables. With a norm-referenced measure, then, the meaning of a child's score is derived from its relation to the scores of other children on the same measure. The Cooperative Preschool Inventory and Wechsler intelligence scales (see Chapter Five) are examples of norm-referenced tests. Norms are useful to the extent that the normative group is truly representative of a definable group and that it makes sense to compare others' performance on the test with the results from that group. More will be said about the characteristics of norm groups when we describe standardized tests in the next section.

A norm is not a standard or goal to be reached. Rather, it is a description of the performance of a defined group. The intent during development of norm-referenced tests is to maximize the variance among students so as to allow very specific differentiations among students in terms of their knowledge or skills. In contrast, criterion-referenced tests de-emphasize specific individual differences; they usually categorize students into two groups—those who have mastered the material and those who have not. The predetermined criterion, not other individuals' scores, is the standard against which performance is measured on criterion-referenced tests. Passing the test means meeting or surpassing a minimum, absolute level of competence. The score or performance of other persons is irrelevant in interpreting the score achieved by any one person.

Criterion-referenced tests appropriate for young children include, among others, the Learning Aptitude Profile and the Basic Concept Inventory; the Denver Developmental Screening Test (DDST) also has several criterion-referenced features (see Chapters Five and Six). These measures are based on the premise that certain basic skills and abilities (conceptual or behavioral) are necessary for early academic progress. Assessment of the degree of individual students' mastery of various skills and abilities permits remedial instructional programs to be designed for those children with cognitive or developmental delays. Criterion-referenced tests are also used in some settings to measure the effectiveness of instructional programs aimed at fostering children's mastery of basic skills.

Perhaps the most difficult and controversial problem in criterion-referenced testing is the establishment of the standards or criteria. The determination of mastery levels on criterion-referenced achievement tests is often an arbitrary decision. Hence it may be difficult to justify a certain criterion (such as 80 percent correct) as the cutoff score for mastery of some universe of content (Stanley and Hopkins, 1972). The problem is complicated further by the difficulty levels of items. Two sets of items, both dealing with the same content, may differ greatly in their difficulty levels. Scores of 80 percent on these two tests will therefore mean very different types of "mastery." For a discussion of the problems associated with establishing standards for criterion-referenced tests, see Glass (1977, 1978).

The problem of determining cutoff scores is less acute in certain assessment areas, such as the psychomotor and developmental areas. Credible bases, both logical and empirical, can frequently be found for criterion scores on psychomotor and developmental tests. The DDST, for example, determines whether or not a child's developmental status is normal, questionable, or abnormal for his age by comparing his performance against empirically derived standards. After having administered the test to a large number of children, the test developers determined the types of performance frequently demonstrated by children judged to have developmental delays. In this case, procedures associated with norm-referenced measures were used to establish the mastery levels for a criterion-referenced test. In these and other ways, some tests combine norm- and criterion-referenced features.

The choice of a norm-referenced or criterion-referenced measure depends largely on the nature of the information required or the decision to be made. For example, if a test is to be used to select a certain number of "gifted" children for a special program, a norm-referenced test would be preferred. The children scoring in the top of the distribution would be selected. If, however, educators wish to know the extent to which children have mastered certain behavioral objectives in highly structured instructional programs, criterion-referenced tests will be preferred. Here the goal in testing is to determine the number of children who have achieved certain learning goals rather than to compare the children with each other.

Standardized Tests. Almost all types of measure used in education are designed to provide a systematic procedure for describing behaviors, whether in terms of numbers or categories. *Standardized tests* extend this effort to include fixed administration and scoring procedures, empirical testing of items, standard apparatus or format, and tables of norms (Cronbach, 1970; Stanley and Hopkins, 1972). Using the established materials and procedures sets a common task for students and permits interpretation of their performance relative to the norms established (if representative norm groups were used). Nearly all standardized tests are published commercially and are produced for widespread use. Because of this, most are based on common objectives of education that are shared widely by educational institutions in diverse settings. However, rarely will these common objectives coincide exactly with the specific objectives of the individual classroom teacher or project director.

The development of a standardized test can extend over a period of several years. During that time, the content is specified, items are written and edited, pilot testing is conducted, data are analyzed to eliminate items that are ambiguous, too difficult or too easy, or not sufficiently discriminating, and final versions produced. Included, too, in the preliminary phases of development is the establishment of norms.

Norms, as we noted earlier, permit comparative evaluation of scores. The tables of norms provided in the manual of a standardized test make it possible to convert an individual's raw score into a percentile rank, age-equivalent score, or grade-equivalent score. How does Johnny's performance compare with that of other children his age? Is he below average or above, and how much? Since norms are not standards or goals, but simply descriptions of the reference group, Johnny's percentile rank will not in itself tell whether his performance was satisfactory or not. Such decisions will depend on the type and level of the test, Johnny's aptitude, and so on.

Remember, too, that the usefulness of norms depends on the representativeness of the normative sample. If a test is intended for national use with children of different races, socioeconomic status, age, sex, and geographic location, then the normative sample should include children representing all levels of these demographic variables. In contrast, norming a standardized developmental inventory only on a group of white, middle-class children living in one suburb severely limits the representativeness of the norms and therefore restricts their utility for many other groups of children.

White and others (1973a) emphasized the importance of representative norms:

> The principal issues in norming arise out of the fact that this aspect of test development sets the stage for the judgment of children according to some public or near-public standard. Through the norming we establish the basis for saying that a child is "high" in intelligence, "retarded" in development, "nonanxious," and so on. Possibilities of libel occur (although not necessarily in the strict legal sense). A rural child will often learn a different vocabulary and a different subset of facts about the world than will an urban child. When the rural child is faced with an IQ test norm-referenced to urban children, this simple difference in his background will be translated into "less measured intelligence." A number

of subpopulations of children—rural children, bilingual children, children from distinctive subcultural backgrounds—run the risk of such unfair labeling when they confront imperfectly normed instruments [White and others, 1973a, p. 281].

Unfortunately, even well-developed norms have often been presented for the total sample only, with no breakdowns and separate tables for large definable subgroups. An admirable and increasingly common practice is to provide separate norms according to sex, income level, race, and the like. Such breakdowns are very helpful for proper score interpretation, especially on measures of aptitude and achievement. Also coming into vogue is the establishment of regional, state, or local norms to further facilitate interpretation. Some districts have supplemented national norms with locally developed norms, for it often is very useful to compare a class's performance with that of other classes in the same school district.

The representativeness of the norming sample is more important than its size. When this sample is classified on the relevant demographic variables, the percentages of students in various categories should approximate population percentages. Further, the sample should be randomly representative, meaning that all students in the population had an equal and independent chance to be sampled. Rarely is that actually the case, although some tests have approximated it quite closely. Test publishers are sometimes unable to obtain randomly representative samples because of school administrators' unwillingness to have their students participate. A close inspection of the norms provided with a standardized test is thus essential in determining the test's usefulness. Test content should also be scrutinized to determine if tasks and items are appropriate for the students to be tested, if they really appear to measure what the test title implies (see the discussion of content validity in Chapter Three), and if administration, scoring, and examiner instructions are clear. The very fact that a test is published does not ensure quality.

The differences between standardized and teacher-constructed tests are important to note. Although teacher-made tests could fulfill the requirements for standardized tests, it is very rare to find one that does. These two types of tests differ in both purpose and use. Thorndike and Hagen (1977) presented the differences between standardized and teacher-made (locally constructed) measures in terms of the types of decision to be made with test data:

1. Day-by-day instructional decisions must depend primarily on locally constructed tests, rather than standardized surveys, though some mini-tests are now being prepared for nationwide distribution.
2. Student appraisal decisions should be based primarily on locally constructed tests covering what has been taught specifically in a given unit or course.
3. Diagnostic and remedial decisions can with advantage use information both from published diagnostic tests and from focused tests developed locally.
4. Placement decisions call for a broad appraisal in an area and can often

use standardized tests to identify entry level of performance on a uniform score scale.

5. Counseling and guidance decisions usually call for the normative comparisons that standardized tests make possible.
6. Selection decisions tend to imply comparisons with others, and for these comparisons adequate norms are often important.
7. Curricular decisions between alternative programs imply a broadly based comparison in which standardized measures can play a role, often supplemented by measures developed locally for distinctive special objectives.
8. Public and policy decisions, as with curricular decisions, call for a comprehensive and comparative view of how well a school is doing, and for this the broad survey and comparison that a standardized test permits has significant value [Thorndike and Hagen, 1977, pp. 274–275].

Intelligence and aptitude tests: Intelligence tests are intended to provide an indication of an individual's general mental capacity. They usually include a wide variety of tasks, in order to sample several important cognitive functions. They also typically provide a single score (such as IQ) to represent the individual's general intelligence level. Most intelligence tests are patterned after the instruments developed by Binet and Simon in the early 1900s. The purpose of the original intelligence tests was to predict school performance, and that remains true of most intelligence tests in common use today. Although the notion of a generalized human intelligence has been questioned (off and on since the 1930s), the attempts to define separate, independent components of intelligence have been only partially successful (White and others, 1973a). Intelligence tests often include separate subtests, both verbal and performance, which are themselves subdivided into several specific parts. The intercorrelations among those subtests, however, tend to be at least moderate.

Some persons use the terms *intelligence* and *aptitude* interchangeably, although there are subtle differences between the two. *Intelligence tests* are general measures of ability or potential; *aptitude tests* measure one or more specific factors thought to be relevant to later learning, performance, or achievement in that specific area. Each Wechsler measure is considered a general intelligence test since it yields a global indicator of ability. The separate tests of each, however, do resemble some aptitude measures or subscales, and herein lies the overlap between the two types. Intelligence tests, either group or individual, are the preferred measure for making general predictions about future academic performance. Differential predictions of success in a specific area, however, require multiple aptitude tests or specific aptitude tests, respectively. For example, the Differential Aptitude Tests (Bennett, Seashore, and Wesman, 1974) measure high school students in eight areas (verbal reasoning, numerical ability, abstract reasoning, clerical speed and accuracy, mechanical reasoning, space relations, spelling, and language usage); such test results are used for occupational guidance. Other aptitude tests assess probable future performance in areas such as art, music, or even flying. In the case of young children, specific or differential aptitude tests are not frequently in evidence, whereas intelligence testing is quite common. The definitional distinction between intelligence and aptitude tests is not nearly as clear-cut as that between, for example, intelligence and achievement tests. Further, the term *aptitude* or *scholastic aptitude* is more acceptable to some persons than is the term *intelligence,* the latter tending to connote innate ability (Mehrens and Lehmann, 1969).

Intelligence testing has had a volatile history. The more recent controversies center around the nature-versus-nurture issue (that is, how much of one's intelligence is inherited and how much is a product of environmental factors) and the issue of culture bias in the tests. The relation of these issues to early childhood education was examined in Chapter One.

The intelligence tests used with infants and preschoolers are typically individual, rather than group, tests and usually require either performance or oral responses. At about the kindergarten level, group-administered and paper-and-pencil tests become much more prevalent. Anastasi (1976), reporting on the predictive validity of infant and preschool intelligence tests, concluded that infant tests generally have little validity in terms of predicting later intelligence test scores, but scores of preschoolers do correlate moderately well with later measures of intelligence. Infant intelligence tests are considered most useful for early detection of neurological and developmental abnormalities. Since Chapter Five describes in some detail the various intelligence tests developed for young children, we will not examine specific examples here.

What does an intelligence test really measure? White and others (1973a) offered five responses to this question:

1. It tests some set of cognitive achievements in the child, achievements which are a joint product of hereditary talent and cultural milieu.
2. It tests capacity to profit from schooling, to some extent. The correlation with school achievement is good, but by no means perfect.
3. It samples the cognitive achievements of the child in the same way, perhaps, that one might test for "athletic ability" by a sample of athletic skills and variegated game scores.
4. It has some biases, probably, with respect to what might be a full-range cognitive assessment of the child. Those biases are probably similar to the biases inherent in the demand of the school on the child, which is most likely what makes the test useful as a school-selection instrument. They are also probably weighted toward the ability of the child to deal with letters, words, and numbers, and with reasoning problems presented in those codes. They are, finally, probably biased against spatial reasoning, manipulative ability, and against competences in emotional self-management, social skill and leadership, and management ability.
5. There are most likely some noncognitive biases as well, relating to the test milieu as well as to the test substance. The tests are probably biased against children whose previous social experience has not included contests like the testing experience, and more generally, towards children who have a quickness of reaction, a quickness to "get things," and a flexibility in reaction to quickly changing demands [White and others, 1973a, p. 291].

Achievement tests: Achievement tests differ from *aptitude tests* in that the former assess a child's present level of knowledge, skills, or performance whereas the latter measure ability to learn new tasks. Thus, achievement tests are present- and past-oriented and pertain to specialized, formal instruction. Aptitude tests, by contrast, are future-oriented (that is, they are intended to predict future performances) and reflect the cumulative impact of learning experiences. Intelligence, aptitude, and achievement tests could be arrayed on a global-to-specific continuum, with intelligence tests at the global end, aptitude tests in the middle, and achievement tests at the specific end (since they are more dependent on certain school objectives and experiences). A similar alignment on an innate-environmental continuum could be made as well, in that performance on achievement tests is probably influenced more by environmental factors than is performance on intelligence tests. Although it is generally accepted that both genetic and environmental conditions affect performance on intelligence tests, the environment is relatively more influential on achievement test performance.

Standardized achievement tests, unlike some other school-related measures, are normed. The norming procedures used with standardized achievement tests are critical to the tests' usefulness. Norming samples should be representatively inclusive of the population of children for whom a test is designed. Otherwise, the norm-referenced scores will be meaningful for only certain types of children.

An additional concern in using achievement tests is whether or not their content accurately reflects local curriculum emphases. Since test development is focused on certain educational objectives and content, other areas may go unassessed. Generally, the achievement tests in use today tend to reflect the "structured" curriculums more than the "open" curriculums (White and others, 1973a).

Achievement tests are commonly used in the evaluation of preschool and Title I, ESEA, programs. Regardless of their drawbacks, "[they] remain today the single strongest and most trustworthy standard for the evaluation of programs for young children. . . . They assess a goal which is of recognized social utility—the attainment of literacy. Excepting IQ, they show correlations with indices of later life chances of a child that are about as good as any existing instrument. . . . Finally, [they] have a modicum of feedback utility for project development" (White and others, 1973a, p. 292). For a description of some specific standardized achievement tests available for use with young children, see Chapter Five.

Diagnostic tests: Diagnostic tests are actually closely related to standardized achievement tests. The difference between achievement and diagnostic tests is primarily a difference in purpose and in specificity of the information that is made available through testing. *Diagnostic tests* are intended to identify particular strengths and weaknesses of a student in a specific academic subject or field. They are primarily concerned with factors that subject matter experts believe underlie the learning process in a particular subject, such as reading, arithmetic, or spelling. Achievement tests survey a subject area in terms of content and process and might include one or two items on each of several aspects of the area. Diagnostic tests, however, concentrate on just a few types of operation and content and include many items under each. For example, an arithmetic achievement test intended to cover all that is included in arithmetic curriculums through the first grade might have two to four questions on the addition and subtraction of single-digit numerals. An arithmetic diagnostic test, by contrast, might examine only addition and subtraction of single-digit numerals, presenting a large number of each type of problem.

Diagnostic test results convey detailed information about a child's deficiencies in a subject. Unlike achievement tests, diagnostic tests usually do not generate any overall score. Rather, a detailed analysis of the student's level of knowledge and performance is provided, often as a series of scores. Instead of using diagnostic test results for program evaluation or grouping—uses frequently made of achievement test results—the teacher would use the results to design remedial instruction for the individual child.

Because of their specificity, diagnostic tests tend to be time-consuming to administer, score, and interpret. Some of the tests call for oral administration, with the examiner noting errors (such as omissions, substitutions, and reversals) as they occur. Identifying the nature of the errors as well as other behaviors of the child during the test can greatly aid the teacher in planning future instruction for the child. Often the child is asked to "think aloud" during the testing, so that the examiner may get some idea of the child's thought processes and attitudes. Diagnostic tests are usually given only to those children who are having learning problems, rather than to all students, because of the large amount of time required.

Diagnostic tests are standardized in their administration and scoring procedures. They also include norms, but the characteristics and uses of the normative data differ from those of standardized achievement tests. Diagnostic tests are normed, not on a representative sample of test takers (which is this case would mean students having learning problems), but on a cross-section of children including those possessing the entire range of abilities and skills. This procedure enhances the usefulness of the data, since one purpose of diagnostic tests is to confirm a suspicion that certain children are having difficulties. The norms that accompany diagnostic tests are also unique in that item-specific information (difficulty values) and classifications of types of error made are provided. It is critical that the norming sample be described in detail and be acceptable to the user before a particular diagnostic instrument is selected.

The major differences among intelligence tests, aptitude tests, norm-referenced standardized achievement tests, criterion-referenced tests, and diagnostic tests are summarized in Table 6.

Personality and attitude measures: Standardized tests may be used to measure noncognitive as well as cognitive characteristics. Both personality and attitude inventories are used occasionally to supplement subjective assessments of students' noncognitive behaviors. A third type of noncognitive measure is the interest inventory, designed for educational and vocational guidance of older children; since such measures are not designed for use with young children, however, we chose not to include them in our discussion.

Personality is as difficult to define as intelligence. Most persons acknowl-

Table 6. Summary Information on Five Types of Test

	Intelligence Tests	Aptitude Tests	Norm-Referenced Achievement Tests	Criterion-Referenced Tests	Diagnostic Tests
Purpose/ Use	Intended to provide an indication of an individual's general mental ability; used to predict overall school performance; sometimes used in preliminary screening or in clinical examinations.	Used to measure specific intellectual factors relevant to school achievement or performance in a defined area; used to predict success in specific academic areas or occupations; reflect cumulative impact of learning experiences.	Intended to rank students according to their levels of knowledge and skills in subject areas; used for program evaluation, grouping decisions, and prediction of later school achievement.	Used either to evaluate past mastery or to diagnose the state of a student's knowledge or skill in a particular area; applicable primarily in programs with explicit objectives; used often in evaluation of individualized instruction.	Intended to identify individuals' strengths and weaknesses (especially the latter) in a particular basic subject area; primarily used with children appearing to have learning problems; with results also useful in the design of remedial programs.
Scope of Content	Include content and problem solving items from diverse fields; sometimes include subtests, usually subsumed under two major headings (verbal and performance).	Contain items specific to the academic or performance area for which prediction is desired (such as arithmetic reasoning or clerical speed and accuracy).	Include a broad range of content within a subject area; comprehensive coverage of knowledge and skills dealt with by most curriculums; tests reflect general school objectives.	Include items specific to instructional goals and content, with relevance to objectives being the most important criterion for inclusion; difficulty levels are irrelevant.	Cover a narrow range of content thought to underlie learning in particular subjects (usually reading, spelling, or arithmetic); intensive coverage of content, processes, and responses.

Norms	Normed on a cross-section of persons, usually categorized by age; standard scores are frequently generated based on the performance of large, representative norming samples.	Normed on a representative cross-section of students (or other persons) categorized by age or grade level; published norms are used as referents for generated scores.	Normed on a cross-section of students representative of targeted audiences; published norms are used as the referents for generated scores.	Empirically derived norms not necessary (although such data may aid in determining criterion); usually, expert opinion used to establish criterion for mastery; the criterion, rather than norms, is the referent.	Normed on a cross-section of students, although primarily used with students having problems; detailed item-by-item information and classification of types of error are usually included with norms.
Administration Procedures	Administered to either groups or individuals (the Binet and Wechsler tests are individually administered); usually objective scoring.	Administered periodically (usually every several years) during schooling, especially at the secondary level; group administered and objectively scored.	Administered after formal instruction in the subject area has occurred; group administration and objective scoring.	Usually administered following instruction, but may also precede instruction to determine which students have not yet mastered certain objectives; group or individual administration and objective scoring.	Administered prior to formal instruction in the area of interest, to help in designing remedial programs; tests often entail individual administration and some subjectivity in interpretation.

edge that the term *personality* represents a wide variety of traits and characteristics and the interactions among them. Allport (1961) defined personality as a dynamic organization, within an individual, composed of psychophysical systems that determine his characteristic behavior and thought. Although personality obviously involves both cognitive and noncognitive characteristics, standardized personality measures typically make no attempt to assess cognitive factors that are measured in primarily cognitive standardized tests, such as achievement and diagnostic measures.

Not all measures of personality are standardized. Observational techniques (discussed in Chapter Four) and sociometric measures (Chapters Seven and Twelve), both of which tend to be nonstandardized, are sometimes used to assess personality variables. Projective tests fall somewhere between the standardized and nonstandardized categorizations. Those personality instruments that are clearly standardized are typically self-report inventories with relatively detailed structure. Examples are problem checklists, surveys of needs, and adjustment inventories. These measures present relatively clear stimuli that should be interpreted in much the same way by all respondents—for example, "Do you ever have nightmares?" These structured tests have objective formats and scoring procedures; they also have derived norms against which individual scores can be referenced. Although the administration and scoring of these inventories are fairly straightforward, proper interpretation of scores often requires professionals with special training.

Projective tests often have standardized stimuli, but administration, scoring, and interpretation tend to be relatively unstructured. Stimuli frequently are ambiguous (for example, inkblots or sketch drawings). The examinee interprets the stimuli, and his responses, in turn, are interpreted by the examiner. Each examiner uses a slightly different method of presenting the stimuli and probing for responses, and each has his own style of interpretation. Some projective measures claim to have norms, but they tend not to be specific, empirically derived norms as we have described them. Rather, they are subjective, general understandings (assumed to be held by the examiner) about appropriate scoring on interpretations. Obviously, extensive examiner training in administration, scoring, and interpretation is critical. Even then, projective tests remain very vulnerable to criticism.

At the same time, projective techniques have several advantages over self-report measures: they allow the examinee the opportunity to discuss or reveal many aspects of himself, not just answers to a specific set of questions; they are not as susceptible to faking as self-report inventories; they are relatively unaffected by *response sets* (the tendency to respond in a particular direction, independent of the question asked); and they are useful with young children, since some of them (such as doll play and finger painting) rely little on verbal abilities and can be treated almost as games. Disadvantages include the need for extensive training of administrators and the heavy reliance on subjective interpretation. Standardized self-report inventories, although likely to be influenced by faking and response sets to varying extents, do have the advantage of being more objective in administration and scoring procedures. Regardless of the type of personality measures used, early childhood educators should in most cases seek expert opinion on test interpretation before making decisions that affect children.

Turning now to *attitudes,* we note considerable agreement on definitions. Khan and Weiss indicated, "attitudes are selectively acquired and integrated through learning and experience; . . . positive or negative affect toward a social or psychological object represents the salient characteristic of an attitude" (1973, p. 761). Similarly, Thorndike and Hagen stated, "Attitudes relate to tendencies to favor or reject particular groups of individuals, sets of ideas, or social institutions" (1977, p. 365). Thus, in the words of Goodwin and Klausmeier, "attitudes are learned, emotionally cast predispositions to react in a consistent manner, favorable or unfavorable, toward certain objects, people, ideas, or situations. A person's attitudes are normally inferred from his behavior and generally cannot be measured as directly as skills or knowledge of facts or concepts" (1975, p. 303).

The measurement of attitudes most frequently occurs via inventories similar in structure to personality checklists and inventories. Most experts view attitudes as one aspect of the global construct of personality. Attitudes are generally much less stable than personality as a whole, and this instability is especially marked in young children, who daily are in the process of learning attitudes. Since affective factors such as attitudes are assumed to determine cognitive performance to some extent, educators frequently include affective objectives among their educational objectives. Appropriate influencing of attitudes requires, of course, that educators be aware of their students' attitudes. Standardized attitude measures are one means of assessing students' feelings and predispositions.

For the most part, standardized attitude measures are paper-and-pencil, self-report measures. Like other personality inventories of this type, they are subject to faking and response sets. However, they are easy to administer and score and generally require no special training. Commercially available are measures of attitudes toward school, work and study habits, and self. Unfortunately, many of the available instruments lack adequate validity, reliability, and norms. Normative information is often missing completely or based on nonrepresentative samples; local norms frequently must be developed. Still, attitude measures that have been carefully developed can contribute to a teacher's understanding of his students.

A detailed discussion of affective measures for use with young children is presented in Chapter Seven.

Teacher-Constructed Measures. Standardized measures are useful for many educational purposes, notably for student selection, guidance, and placement and for evaluation of programs. Equally important, however, are measures of students' daily progress in the attainment of skills and knowledge specific to the individual teacher's curriculum. For assessments of this second type, teachers must develop their own measures. Teacher-constructed tests serve diagnostic, instructional, and evaluative functions. They afford an objective check against subjective or "gut-level" assessments made by teachers all the time. Achievement tests, checklists or rating scales, and work samples are three assessment devices commonly used by teachers to monitor their students' individual progress. All three deal primarily with the cognitive domain. Teacher-initiated assessment in the affective domain, undertaken mainly through observation and unobtrusive techniques, will be covered in more depth in later sections of this chapter and in Chapter Four.

Achievement tests: Although teacher-made and standardized achievement tests both measure the student's level of current knowledge and sample course content, they differ on several dimensions. Teacher-made achievement tests are designed to measure specific classroom objectives and thus have much narrower content coverage than standardized tests. Because of their content specificity, the teacher's own tests often provide more precise assessment of the teacher's own objectives than do standardized tests. Teachers' test results are used in prescription of individualized programs, assignment of course grades, promotion, placement, and so on. For some educational decisions, such as student selection, placement, and individualized guidance, it is helpful to have results from both standardized and teacher-made tests. The teacher-made tests, because of their specificity, can supplement the information provided by the more carefully developed standardized tests. Further, by sampling a narrow content domain in great detail, teacher-made tests can contain a variety of types of question on the same instructional content, providing an opportunity to diagnose strengths and weaknesses in detail.

Teacher-made achievement tests are constructed with much less time, effort, and resources than are standardized tests. Because of the use of subject-area and test experts, as well as careful empirical tryout and revision, standardized tests are, generally, technically superior to the teacher-made ones. Nevertheless, teachers who are well schooled in the principles of test construction can achieve a sufficient degree of psychometric quality (that is, adequate reliability and validity) on their tests.

One of the major differences between teacher-made and standardized achievement tests is in the provision of norms. Whereas the latter typically include national norms (often stratified by geographic region, age, sex, ethnicity, and so on), it is rare that norms are developed for teacher-made tests. Teachers frequently construct criterion-referenced tests (whether they actually call them that or not), establishing certain levels of mastery as critical for the undertaking of subsequent work. The performance of previous classes of children on the same teacher-made test can be used to develop a sort of norm (although the classes will certainly differ from year to year in some ways), or the performance of previous classes can be used to help establish criterion levels. Generally, however, teachers are not quite so systematic in their testing procedures. Usually, tests are simply developed as the need arises and are tailored to the previous instruction.

In administration and scoring, teacher-made tests are not standardized. Nevertheless, careful teachers will administer their own tests under optimal conditions (quiet, lack of time pressure, and so on) and will have prepared scoring keys in advance. Detailed keys are especially important for tests with open-ended or essay questions, in which increased objectivity in scoring is desired. By preparing a set of scoring guidelines, scoring the questions "blindly" (that is, not knowing which student wrote the answers), reading and scoring all answers to one question before moving to the next, and, if possible, asking another teacher to also score the answers, teachers can do much to avoid subjective bias in test scores.

Because paper-and-pencil tests have less utility with very young children, preschool teachers may often opt for oral testing. Such an approach may necessitate individual testing. Whether group or individual testing is planned, the teacher should confine the testing period to a short time period and should conduct frequent short testings rather than infrequent long testings. The students' attention to task or mental alertness must be taken into account; otherwise, guessing, fatigue, or response sets could unduly affect test outcomes.

Many authors have written in considerable detail about test construction for the classroom teacher. The interested reader could consult Medley (1971), Stanley and Hopkins (1972), and Thorndike and Hagen (1977).

Checklists and rating scales: Checklists and rating scales can be constructed by the teacher to assess almost any student behavior. They do not require elaborate administration procedures. Also, they provide a convenient way of recording performance of children too young or unable to respond on paper-and-pencil tests. Teacher-made checklists and rating scales are most often criterion-referenced and can be tailored to closely match specific local objectives. Through them, the teacher receives direct and usable information.

Behaviors pertinent to the objectives are first listed. The typical *checklist* format simply provides spaces for the teacher or other observer to check "yes" or "no," indicating whether or not the student demonstrates the behavior. A *rating scale* format allows more varied descriptions of behavior since it includes grades of frequency (such as "usually," "about half the time," or "seldom") or degree of skill exhibited (such as "exceptional," "good," "satisfactory," and "poor").

Checklists and rating scales can be developed to assess behaviors in the cognitive, affective, and psychomotor domains. Thus, in the cognitive domain, behaviors appropriately assessed might include the abilities to count to ten, to recognize printed words by reading them aloud, to recall and follow verbal instructions, and the like. Checklists and rating scales in the affective area might assess coping with anger or frustration, expressing affection for peers or adults, and maintaining friendships with other children. Psychomotor examples might consist of checklists of the ability to perform certain movements or ratings of stamina, coordination, or accuracy. To be most valuable, checklists and rating scales should deal with important behaviors. Both the behaviors and, for rating scales, the response categories should be fairly explicit to reduce later subjectivity. For example, "sometimes" is not as explicit as "about half the time." For examples of checklists and step-by-step construction details, the reader is referred to Hendrick (1975).

Work samples: A popular assessment device of preschool and kindergarten teachers is the systematic collection of children's products as one source of information about their progress. Work or product samples are especially useful in individualizing instruction. Each student is basically compared against himself, rather than his peers, through the evaluation of his products over time. Evidence of a child's increasing motor skills, mastery of simple arithmetic and verbal concepts, and attention to detail can be seen over the course of a few weeks, months, or even years. The product collections can also inform parents, and possibly even the children themselves, of the nature of progress made or areas needing remedial attention.

In keeping samples, teachers should make sure that each product is correctly dated, that samples are collected at approximately equivalent time intervals, and that samples are carefully filed for easy access. Objections by the child or parents to storing products at school rather than sending them home are unlikely as only a representative sample need be collected, leaving many work products that can be sent home. Note, too, that not all work samples have to be drawings or written products. Use of tape recorders and cameras can help capture the progress made in speaking, playing, construction, or even physical growth. If such equipment is not available, the teacher can record the types of activity children choose to engage in.

The value of the information afforded through work sampling can be seen in the following examples of Fromberg: "In one group of three-year-olds, all easel paintings were collected and kept at the school until Christmas. The teacher sorted them by name and date, bound them in a roll with red ribbon, and planned to send them home. In addition to enjoying the sight of children's growing coordination and expressive abilities, she was able to see that Ross had not been to the easel even one time. Since he was always busy and productive with others in construction and sociodramatic play projects, she had not noticed the gap. When she suggested that he paint at the easel, he readily agreed. In his case, there appeared to be no problem" (Fromberg, 1977, pp. 222–223).

Interviews and Questionnaires. Common ways of gathering attitudinal, interest, and personality information are structured or unstructured interviews and questionnaires. Although such means can be used for some cognitive assessments, they are employed much more often in affective measurement. Our focus here is on locally developed interview schedules and questionnaires rather than standardized ones available commercially.

Interviews can be either structured or unstructured. Structured interviews have fixed questions and sequencing, with little opportunity provided for interviewer deviation to other topics or questions. Unstructured interview schedules are much less systematic in wording, directions to the interviewer, and phrasing of questions. In fact, some unstructured interviews require no pre-established schedules at all. Whereas questions in a structured interview tend to be specific and closed, and might even include multiple-choice questions, those in an unstructured interview are more open-ended and only generally stated. In the latter case, the interviewer usually is able to phrase the questions in a way natural for him. While this may have some advantages, such as making the respondent feel comfortable and eliciting additional comments of interest, it also creates the problem of tabulating responses gathered by several different interviewers in several different ways.

Interviews are of special value with little children. For example, by carefully preparing a set of interview questions on attitudes toward television, a researcher or teacher could obtain valuable information that might otherwise be unavailable—as in the cases where children are too young to answer written questions, or where they do not watch television at school, or where it is impractical for the teacher or researcher to observe them during home viewing. Kerlinger (1973) included a chapter on interview techniques, including examples of interview questions, ways to construct schedules, and related information. Rich (1968) presented some interesting observations on interviewing techniques to use with young children.

Questionnaires are widely used in assessing attitudes and in evaluating the affective components of many projects. With some background reading and technical assistance from persons schooled in test construction, teachers can develop creditable questionnaires. Attitude questionnaires or inventories are self-report measures that usually consist of numerous questions, each followed by a standard set of response options, such as "agree," "disagree," and "no opinion." A Likert scale—comprised of the five choices "strongly agree," "agree," "no opinion" or "undecided," "disagree," and "strongly disagree"—is often used for the responses. After reading each question, the respondent checks the one response that best describes his reaction to the statement.

The Likert scale itself is not appropriate for young children, but variations of it are frequently used. For children with basic reading ability, the words "yes" and "no" might be included, with directions for the respondents to circle the word that tells whether or not they agree with a statement. An alternate approach—one that is adaptable for even younger children—is to provide a series of faces as possible responses, such as a smiling face, a neutral face, and a frowning face. If the children responding are not able to read, the statements or questions are read by the teacher and the children individually mark the faces that tell how they feel. This approach has been taken with some of the commercially available affective inventories, as described in Chapter Seven.

As contrasted with the closed response questionnaires just described, open-ended questionnaires can elicit a variety of types of response—one- or two-word answers, longer statements, or even pictures or diagrams. With young children who can write, questions should be phrased simply and require relatively short answers. For even younger children, asking for pictures ("Draw a picture that tells me how you feel today") is more reasonable. In general, however, the more the questionnaire format departs from a standard, closed arrangement, the more difficult it is to objectively score and interpret the results.

As self-report attitude measures, questionnaires are prone to some of the problems mentioned earlier. For example, they are susceptible to "faking" and often yield the "socially desirable" responses rather than those actually held. If anonymity is assured, however, some of these problems become less acute. For assessing childrens' reactions to certain instructional methods or materials, carefully constructed questionnaires can yield more objective and reliable information than unsystematic collection means, such as asking questions to a few children during casual conversation or recording one's own impressions of what the children seemed to like or dislike about particular activities. Further, appropriately designed questionnaires and interviews can be used productively to assess parental attitudes toward their children and their children's early educational experiences.

Unobtrusive Measures. The use of unobtrusive measures was surveyed in 1966 by Webb and his colleagues in their delightful book *Unobtrusive Measures: Nonreactive Research in the Social Sciences. Unobtrusive measures* are ways of gathering data about persons or events without actually asking subjects to tell about themselves, to take an objective test, or to perform in a certain way. Rather, data are collected from records, physical traces of activities, or observation or recording (human or mechanical) of naturally occurring events. Thus, the process of measuring does not alter or intrude upon the event or person being measured. For example, shifts in sales of childrens' toys might indicate that educational toys are gaining in popularity as compared with war-oriented toys. Similarly, a count of the number of times that various books have been checked out of the school library might help a teacher gauge what types of book are most appealing to her students. (Of course, the fact that books are checked out does not necessarily mean that the books have been read. Children may check out books on orders from other teachers, without actually reading them. Nevertheless, library records constitute a prime source of information about reading interests.) The activity level of children could be measured, in part, by charting the rate at which they wear out their shoes—a study that actually was conducted, as reported by Webb and others (1966).

Use of unobtrusive measures avoids many of the problems associated with self-report measures. For instance, when asked to tell a teacher what type of book they like, some children might tell her what they think she wants to hear, rather than the truth. Another problem avoided by unobtrusive measures is the "practice effect" possible on performance measures, as described earlier in the chapter. Asking children to imitate the teacher in a construction activity, measuring them on their ability to do so, and then repeating the test task two weeks later might result in large performance differences due in part to learning on the first test. By observing children over time in a variety of similar activities, not just one, and not letting them know that they are being "tested," a teacher might gather data that more accurately represent changes in motor ability.

Other threats to the validity of self-report measures that are avoided by unobtrusive measures include reactivity and the problem of response sets. *Reactivity* means that respondents know they are being studied or tested and thus respond differently than they might under ordinary circumstances. The construction test just mentioned includes the possibility of reactivity; the fact that the two tests were just that—tests—could promote in the children increased attention to, or concern about, completing the task correctly. *Response sets,* as noted earlier, are tendencies to respond in particular directions, independent of the questions asked. One type is the tendency to acquiesce—that is, to agree more often with positively phrased statements than to disagree with the same statements when stated negatively (Webb and others, 1966). Such problems as these do not arise when the data collection effort neither requires direct answers from students nor makes them aware of being measured.

Settings for young children, such as preschools and elementary schools, offer many opportunities for unobtrusive measurement. The amount and type of food discarded after lunch yields information about childrens' eating preferences and habits. The comparative wear and tear on playground toys reveals something about play habits. Dirty edges to pages of childrens' books may show differential reading preference. Careful observation of childrens' interactions with peers, over a course of a few weeks, will help identify both the leaders and the loners.

Readers interested in unobtrusive measures should examine the previously cited book by Webb and his associates. It contains several types of unobtrusive measure and numerous, creative examples of each type. Helpful materials on the same general topic can be found in Bouchard (1976), Brandt (1972), Denzin (1970), and Sechrest (1969).

Chapter 3

Validity, Reliability, and Usability of Measures

In selecting or constructing a measurement instrument, it is important to ensure that it will actually measure what it is intended to measure, yield accurate
scores, and be relatively easy to administer and score. These characteristics refer
to the instrument's validity, reliability, and usability, respectively. It is unusual to
find a test that conforms uniformly well to all psychometric and use-related
specifications. Decisions as to which characteristics are more important will be
made according to the purpose of the assessment. For example, a very long
reading readiness test may yield more accurate scores than a shorter version of
the same test, but the longer test will require more class time for administration.
If an important selection or classification is to be made on the basis of the test
results, the loss of instructional time may be justifiable. If the assessment is just
one part of an ongoing program evaluation effort, however, the shorter test may
be the better choice.

Ability to judge the adequacy of published measures is critical. A test may
look appealing and useful but in reality measure something different from what
the potential user wants to measure. Seeking and evaluating evidence about the

test's validity and reliability can help prevent a user from selecting an inappropriate or worthless measure. Information on the established validity, reliability, and usability characteristics of a published measure is available from several sources. The manual accompanying the measure should contain all pertinent facts and findings. Unfortunately, published instruments vary greatly in the quality of their manuals. Whereas some manuals contain clear, complete descriptions of reliability and validation procedures and results, others provide only scanty information or none at all. In some instances, this insufficiency is due to poor manual construction; more frequently, however, the manual reflects the incomplete state of investigations on the measure. Test reviews, especially those that appear in Buros' *Mental Measurement Yearbooks* (described in the section on source books) are a valuable secondary source of information about a measure.

In this chapter, we will discuss validity and reliability as well as usability concerns such as administration, scoring, interpretability, and cost. The statistical concepts introduced in Chapter Two will be called into use in this chapter, especially in conjunction with validation and reliability procedures. The information presented here will enable the reader to make more informed judgments of tests and other measures designed for use with young children.

Validity

The *validity* of a measure is the extent to which it fulfills the purpose for which it is intended. A measure may be valid for one purpose but not for others; thus, the question of validity always pertains to specific uses. One does not ask, "Is this test valid?" but rather "Is this test valid for this particular purpose?" Validation is multifaceted, since different types of evidence are required to support various uses. Even if only one purpose is intended, validity information should come from several sources. Rarely will a single investigation provide sufficient validity data to satisfy all potential users. For example, suppose one wants to screen children to identify those with developmental delays. The instrument chosen for this purpose should contain tasks that experts agree are representative of a domain of developmental indicators. In addition, results from empirical investigations should provide evidence of the instrument's ability to accurately identify children with developmental delays. A strong correspondence between scores on this measure and psychologists' judgments for a group of children is an example of one such indicator.

Validity is a critical characteristic for any instrument. A test that measures something other than what the user wants to measure is virtually worthless for that user's purpose. Generally, validity refers to the appropriateness of inferences made from scores on the measure. As we shall see, different types of validity correspond to different types of inference from scores. A measure fulfills its intended purpose when its scores permit valid inferences to be made—such as inferences about examinees' knowledge in a field of study, their present or future performances on a related dimension, or other inferences dictated by the measure's purpose.

Validity has been categorized into three major types: *content, criterion-related,* and *construct.* This categorization scheme, which will be described shortly, was the work of a joint committee of the American Psychological Association, American Educational Research Association, and National Council on Measurement in Education. In its document *Standards for Educational and Psychological Tests* (American Psychological Association, 1974), the committee described the three types and made recommendations to improve the quality of validity data gathered by test authors and publishers. (The *Standards,* which contains a detailed list of recommendations pertaining to validity, reliability, and usability, is a useful resource guide for persons developing or judging instruments. In addition, Lerner (1978) cited the increasing reliance of the Supreme Court on the *Standards* as an authoritative source for objective answers to technical measurement questions.)

The three types of validity identified in the *Standards* correspond, generally, to three different types of inference to be made from test scores. *Content validity* makes it possible to infer how well a student would do on the larger population of items or tasks the test presumably represents. *Criterion-related validity* permits an inference to be made about the student's present or future performance on some other relevant test or task. *Construct validity* provides the basis for inference about the student's relative standing on some theoretical variable or construct that is assumed to be the major determinant of that performance (Martuza, 1977). Although the three types of validity are distinct and require different kinds of evidence, thorough validation of a measure often involves information of all three types. For example, a vocabulary comprehension test may be validated and used for all three types of inference: how well it samples a defined population of vocabulary words, how well it predicts future academic performance, and how well it measures the construct "vocabulary comprehension." Evidence for each type of validity is obtained via prescribed logical or empirical analyses of test content. In the sections to follow, the characteristics of each type are noted, as are the techniques used to obtain the appropriate evidence.

Content Validity. The extent to which test items or tasks represent the content and processes of a curricular universe or domain is known as *content validity.* Most often associated with achievement tests, content validity is determined primarily through logical analyses of a test by subject-matter experts and potential users. Content validity is relevant to both teacher-constructed measures and standardized achievement tests. With teacher-constructed tests, it is important to determine how well the test content mirrors the course content and instructional objectives. For published standardized tests, content validity is usually assessed by the test developers in relation to broad curricular goals. A reassessment in terms of locally established objectives is desirable prior to the use of the test in specific settings. Content validity is always determined in relation to a particular curriculum or set of objectives; to the extent that a test represents the objectives of a specific school or curriculum, it has content validity for use in that setting.

The procedure most commonly used in determining content validity consists of systematic logical analyses of the content of, and the mental processes required by, the measure, in the light of their appropriateness to the domain in question. For example, a reading readiness test intended for kindergartners can contain only a limited number of vocabulary items, comprehension items, grammar and spelling items, and so on. To assess content validity, the following questions should be asked:

1. Does this test cover a representative sample of the knowledge and behaviors that comprise the domain "reading readiness"?
2. Do the questions call on mental processes higher than memory (such as comprehension, application, analysis, synthesis, and evaluation)?
3. Are the major components of the domain covered in the right proportions?
4. Are the required modes of response (such as those required by multiple-choice items, true-false items, and matching items) relevant to the domain?
5. Have irrelevant difficulty factors (such as reading level of instructions) and speed factors been controlled in the test?

Developing a standardized achievement test with content validity is a complex process, requiring careful planning, detailed examination of curriculums and objectives, consultation with subject-matter experts, and revisions of items based on results from preliminary tryouts. First it is necessary to define the domain—that is, to enumerate tasks or list the instructional objectives, topics, and processes included in that domain. Then it must be determined how much weight to give to various topics and processes in the test; the importance and relevance of each topic and process must be estimated. Next begins the time-consuming activity of drawing up exact specifications for item writers. Explicitly defining the domain prior to test construction is greatly preferred to defining it after the fact. It is difficult to justify test content, emphasis, and structure without the aid of a previously prepared and well-detailed blueprint.

Content validity is a matter of judgment. Using the description of the domain, subject-matter experts determine whether the test items constitute a representative sample. One approach involves asking two or more judges to rate each item for correspondence to the objective it is designed to measure, and then computing an index of interjudge agreement (see the discussion of interrater reliability later in this chapter) as an indicator of content validity (Martuza, 1977). Another approach is to construct, based on the test blueprint, a matrix plotting topics against mental processes, and then to have experts place the written test items in the matrix. This procedure yields information about the fit between the blueprint for the test (the matrix) and the actual test items, and also gives an overall picture of the domain as measured—what aspects are included and to what extent. Items that do not seem to fit readily into the matrix are also identified. This procedure may make it obvious that a certain aspect, such as reading comprehension, is not covered adequately in the test while another aspect, say letter recognition, is overemphasized.

To evaluate a standardized achievement test for local use, the objectives of the local curriculum or program should first be specified. The test is then examined, item by item, for representativeness. A hypothetical example of the results of this process is shown in Figure 4. The objectives for a preschool program, based on the Primary Education Project (PEP) classification curriculum (Resnick, Wang, and Rosner, 1977), are listed as the columns of the matrix. The rows are the numbers of the twenty-five items in a standardized basic skills test being considered for use. The teacher and program director judged each item in terms of which PEP objective(s) it represented. Note that two items (21 and 25) were not judged as representative of any objective and that

Objectives

Item Number	Exhibits Basic Matching Skills	Discriminates Shape and Size	Names Colors	Names Shapes	Exhibits Advanced Matching Skills	Describes Size (Big and Little)	Describes Length (Long and Short)	Describes Height (Tall and Short)	Describes Width (Wide and Narrow)
1	X								
2					X				
3			X			X			
4									X
5								X	
6	X								
7		X							
8		X							
9				X					
10				X					
11					X				
12				X					
13								X	
14	X								
15							X		
16				X	X				
17				X					
18				X					
19	X								
20	X								
21									
22		X							
23				X					
24				X					
25									

Figure 4. A Matrix for Assessing a Standardized Preschool Test in Relation to Local Program Objectives.

some objectives were better represented than others. The objective "names colors" is not represented at all, whereas "names shapes" may well be overrepresented. Although it is time-consuming to scrutinize tests in this way, it is well worth the effort to assure that test results will be meaningful.

A teacher-constructed measure is ordinarily not based on an extensive item-development procedure. Nevertheless, the stating of objectives and guidelines for items prior to test construction will help guarantee adequate coverage of important instructional areas. As is true with a standardized achievement test, preplanning a teacher-made test makes it possible to build content validity into the test as it is written.

Determinations of content validity may involve empirical procedures as well as logical analyses. For example, on instruments that measure age-related developmental variables, it is important to determine that the percentage of children passing individual items does increase with age. Data collected from a representative sample of children are used to verify the age-related assumptions upon which the measure is based. For each item, the difficulty index (see Chapter Two)—the percentage of children passing it at each age level—is calculated. Those items that show little or no gain in percentages of children passing them from younger to older age groups are then eliminated. Although this procedure yields useful supplementary information, it alone does not constitute adequate validation. A test may contain items with good age discrimination without meeting content or other validity requirements for specific purposes. Another empirical approach to content validity is factor analysis (see Chapter Two). Essentially, factor analysis assesses the distinctiveness or independence of the factors allegedly making up the test content. For example, the revised, shortened edition of the Cooperative Preschool Inventory (1970), as described in Chapter Five, was factor analyzed to determine whether four original edition subtests (Personal-Social Responsiveness, Associative Vocabulary, Concept Activation-Numerical, and Concept Activation-Sensory) could also be identified in the revised instrument. In the analysis, the factors did not emerge as independent, so the new version of the test retained only the single total score of the Inventory and dropped the four former subtest scores. In other words, the factor analyses of the shortened test did not support the claim that the test measured four separate content areas.

Although content validity is most commonly associated with achievement tests, it is not restricted to that type of measure. Observation schedules should also possess content validity. The extent to which the behaviors covered on an observation schedule represent a domain of behaviors constitutes the content validity of the instrument. Specification of types of behavior belonging in the domain, and other factors such as stimuli or settings for the observation, should be made prior to constructing the schedule. In Chapter Four, validity requirements for observation techniques are discussed in greater detail.

Sometimes a measure is said to have *face validity*. This means that it appears to be appropriate and adequate. The format, content, administration and scoring procedures, and manner of reporting scores appeal to potential users.

Since face validity rests on loose subjective judgments, however, rather than on the systematic logical analyses required for content validity, it is an insufficient basis for instrument selection. Many otherwise valid measures may also have face validity, but the reverse is not necessarily true.

In concluding this section on content validity, we paraphrase several of the recommendations pertaining to content validity from the *Standards for Educational and Psychological Tests* (American Psychological Association, 1974). If the manual of a published test addresses content validation undertaken on the test, the following facts about the validation process should be stated:

1. A clear definition of the universe or domain of content and processes represented by the test.
2. A description of the procedures followed in sampling from the domain.
3. An indication of the number of items in each category of content and process covered by the test.
4. A description of the qualifications of any experts asked to judge the items.
5. A description of the procedures used by judges to rate items and an indication of the extent of interjudge agreement.
6. A list of relevant dates, such as the dates of any expert reviews, and the copyright or publication dates of any textbooks, syllabi, or objectives that were consulted during test construction.

The manual and test must first be examined and judged satisfactory on these and other points. If the measure fares well in this initial scrutiny, then its content validity is examined in terms of local objectives.

Criterion-Related Validity. This type of validity indicates the correspondence between test scores and present or future performance as measured in another way. When one wants to use a test score to infer an examinee's probable standing on some other variable (the criterion), then criterion-related validity is pertinent. If an aptitude test is designed to predict school performance, then the criterion might be school grades obtained later, or teachers' ratings, or scores earned on a subsequent achievement test. Students' scores on the aptitude test are compared with their performances on the criterion. The closer the correspondence between the test scores and the criterion, the more valid the test is as a predictor of the criterion.

There are two types of criterion-related validity: concurrent validity and predictive validity. *Concurrent validity* is relevant if the intent is to substitute the measure for another, already-available measure of the same trait, ability, or behavior (the latter measure serves as the criterion). *Predictive validity* is future-oriented; if the measure is designed to predict subsequent performance, evidence of predictive validity is needed.

Concurrent validity: Three categories of test development situations clearly call for concurrent validation:

1. When the purpose of a test is to provide a shorter or less expensive way of measuring a trait, ability, or behavior for which some adequate (but longer or more expensive) measure or procedure already exists.

2. When a new test purports to measure a psychological construct for which well-established, construct-valid measures are available.
3. When the purpose of a test is to identify present capabilities, strengths, and weaknesses in an instructional or behavioral area.

A measure representing the first category would be a shortened version of an existing reading readiness test. In the second category belong most new intelligence tests. Most intelligence tests developed now are validated against the Stanford-Binet or Wechsler, or against both of them. Strictly speaking, measures of intelligence require construct, rather than concurrent, validation; if developers of new intelligence measures are willing to accept the definitions and theoretical bases of the Stanford-Binet and Wechsler tests, however, then additional construct validation is possibly not as critical. In the third category are both diagnostic instruments and the developmental surveys popular in early childhood education. With diagnostic measures, the focus is on how well the measures identify present learning problems or weaknesses in need of remediation. The correspondence between the diagnostic test results and other indicators of academic deficiency represents one way to provide such concurrent validity data. With developmental surveys, concurrent validation might center on how well the survey's assessment of a child matches the assessment made by a team of professionals, possibly composed of a psychologist, or medical doctor, and others.

To obtain evidence for the concurrent validity of a test, the scores on the test and the criterion are obtained at approximately the same time from one group of examinees. The validity coefficient is the statistical measure of association between the test scores and the criterion. Usually, the Pearson correlation coefficient is calculated. The closer the correlation is to 1.0, the greater the concurrent validity is in terms of that criterion.

The Quick Test or QT (Ammons and Ammons, 1962) provides an example of concurrent validation procedures. Designed as a short version of the Full-Range Picture Vocabulary Test or FRPV (Ammons and Ammons, 1948), the QT is an individually administered intelligence test for persons aged two years and over. To obtain concurrent validity information for the QT, the correlations between it and the FRPV were determined for several samples of children and adults. For one sample of forty preschool-age children, the correlations for QT Forms 1, 2, and 3 with the FRPV were .76, .77, and .62, respectively—indicating a substantial relationship between the QT and the longer version, the FRPV. In other concurrent validation efforts, the correlations between QT scores and scores on the Iowa Test of Basic Skills and school grades were obtained for a group of forty-six seventh-graders. Those relationships were lower than the QT-FRPV relationships, with a median correlation of .45 (Ammons and Ammons, 1962). Numerous other validation studies have explored the correlations between the QT and the Stanford-Binet and Wechsler intelligence scales, and investigated relationships between the QT and other aptitude measures for specific groups, such as the mentally retarded or hospitalized persons. For more discussion of the QT, see Chapter Five.

Predictive validity: Whereas concurrent validity is necessary when one wants to infer an individual's present status on a criterion, predictive validity is necessary when the inference is to later performance on a criterion measure. Predictive validity is especially applicable to scholastic aptitude tests, since one major purpose of those tests is to predict future academic performance.

Predictive validity is specific to particular predictions. The nature of the prediction dictates the type of criterion measure used and the period of time that should elapse between the testing and the collection of the criterion data. For example, if the purpose of a readiness test for finishing kindergartners is to predict academic status at the end of first grade, then approximately one year should intervene between the time the readiness test is given and the measurement of the criterion, which might consist of teachers' grades or scores on an academic achievement test. If the purpose of an intelligence test for preschoolers is to make predictions about the child's academic performance in elementary and secondary school, then a much more extensive, longitudinal study is required. In some cases, concurrent validation is offered as a partial substitute for predictive validation when the length of time encompassed by the predictions is quite long. In such cases, however, test developers are obligated to provide supporting evidence of a predictive nature and should keep users informed of results of longitudinal studies as they become available.

Predictive validity coefficients are correlation coefficients. The correlation between the scores on the test and the subsequent criterion scores is calculated. The larger the correlation, the greater is the predictive power of the test. (Remember from Chapter Two that the magnitude of a correlation coefficient, rather than its direction, conveys its predictive value. Thus, correlations of $+.5$ and $-.5$ have the same predictive value. Be that as it may, the usual procedure is to score a test in such a way that its probable correlation with a criterion will be positive.)

To facilitate interpretation of predictive validity data, expectancy tables can also be constructed. An *expectancy table* shows the probabilities that a student will obtain various criterion scores, according to his score on the predictive test. For example, suppose that one hundred children take a reading readiness test at the end of kindergarten. At the end of first grade, teachers' ratings in reading (outstanding, highly satisfactory, satisfactory, and needs improvement) are obtained for the children. The correlation coefficient between readiness scores and teachers' ratings would be the predictive validity coefficient for the readiness test. To aid in interpretation, an expectancy table showing the number of children receiving different ratings according to their scores on the readiness test could easily be constructed. By converting the frequencies within each score interval to proportions, the probabilities of achieving various marks for each score interval are obtained. In Table 7, the expectancy table for this hypothetical situation is shown. The number in parentheses in each cell is the actual number of children who received the readiness score and the teachers' rating represented by that cell. The decimal represents the probability of achieving that mark, given the particular readiness score interval. For example, for the twenty-four children with readiness scores in the 40 to 45 range, the probability of

Table 7. Expectancy Table Giving Probabilities of Obtaining
First-Grade Teachers' Ratings According to Scores
on a Kindergarten Reading Readiness Test (*N* = 100)

		Scores on Kindergarten Reading Readiness Test						
		20	25	30	35	40	45	50
Teachers' Reading Ratings at End of Grade 1	Outstanding						.29 (*n*=7)	.92 (*n*=11)
	Highly Satisfactory				.28 (*n*=5)	.57 (*n*=17)	.67 (*n*=16)	.08 (*n*=1)
	Satisfactory	.25 (*n*=1)	.38 (*n*=5)	.50 (*n*=9)	.33 (*n*=10)	.04 (*n*=1)		
	Needs Improvement	.75 (*n*=3)	.62 (*n*=7)	.22 (*n*=4)	.10 (*n*=3)			

receiving a rating of outstanding, highly satisfactory, or satisfactory is .29(7 ÷ 24), .67(16 ÷ 24), and .04(1 ÷ 24), respectively.

Criterion-related validity coefficients, whether they be concurrent or predictive, are specific to the situations that produced them. The characteristics of the sample of examinees from whom validity data are gathered determine the generalizability of the coefficients. If the coefficients are obtained for a sample representative of only a certain type of student, the applicability of the coefficients to different populations is questionable. Along with the reporting of any validity coefficient should go a detailed description of the validation sample, including a breakdown by such characteristics as age, sex, ethnicity, socioeconomic level, and geographic location.

Characteristics desired in a criterion: Obtaining a suitable criterion measure for use in establishing criterion-related validity is not an easy task. For example, a readiness test is intended to predict subsequent "success" in school. How is such success to be measured? Teachers' marks and scores on later achievement tests are two frequently used criteria of success. However, teachers' marks are subject to unreliability, and many achievement tests contain irrelevant features or are of modest validity themselves. The criterion for a diagnostic test, designed to identify children with academic weaknesses, is equally difficult to develop or find. Teachers' ratings of students' academic deficiencies might be the most easily gathered data. Yet such ratings are likely to be confounded with the teachers' pre-established opinions on other dimensions (ones that are not the focus of the ratings). Further, the use of ratings raises the question: "If teachers' ratings are an acceptable and believable criterion, why bother with the diagnostic test at all?" Clearly, many people believe teachers' ratings are not entirely acceptable, and therefore a more precise measurement strategy is needed as a criterion.

Although it may be difficult to accomplish, suitable criterion measures can be identified. One desirable procedure is to use multiple criteria. In the case of the diagnostic test, for example, independent and external raters might be brought in, scores on other similar measures might be sought, and teachers'

ratings might also be obtained. A single criterion measure conveys limited information; with data from several measures, the criterion-related validity of the
test is strengthened.

Thorndike and Hagen (1977) cited four characteristics desired in a criterion measure: (1) relevance, (2) reliability, (3) availability, and (4) freedom from
bias. Relevance means that the criterion should correspond closely to the purpose of the measure being validated. Although grades are criticized for numerous reasons, they are a good indication of success in school and therefore are a
relevant criterion for measures purporting to predict later school success. Reliability, discussed in greater detail later in the chapter, is also critical. An unreliable
criterion cannot correlate well with another measure, even if the measure being
validated is itself quite reliable. Availability is a crucial characteristic for practical
reasons. Time, financial considerations, and other practical matters must enter
into decisions about which criterion measures to use. Finally, freedom from bias
is also an important characteristic in a criterion. Scores on the criterion are
biased to the extent that they reflect factors (such as differences in socioeconomic
status or reading level) other than what is supposed to be measured. This relates
closely to the discussion of test bias under Issue 4 in Chapter One.

One special type of bias that should be avoided in gathering criterion data
is *criterion contamination* (Anastasi, 1976). This contamination occurs when the
scores on the test being validated inappropriately influence the scores on the
criterion. Criterion measures that involve subjective ratings are especially susceptible to contamination. For example, in the process of validating a diagnostic test,
if teachers know of their students' diagnostic test performances and are then
asked to rate those students on the same dimensions, their ratings will probably
be influenced ("contaminated") by their prior knowledge of the test scores. The
resulting correlation between test scores and ratings would be spuriously high.
Preventing such contamination requires either withholding information about
the results of the test from the raters until after all ratings are made or obtaining
the ratings prior to administering the test.

Predictive validity for tests used for selection purposes is subject to
another type of problem. When a test is used as a basis for selecting students for
a special program, those students not chosen are usually unavailable for later
criterion measurement. Subsequently, only data on the specific students selected
are available to support predictive validity claims. The correlation between test
scores and criterion measures for the selected group will be attenuated, that is,
weakened, as a result of the lack of variance in the test scores. If all students—
both the selected and unselected—were available for measurement on the criterion, the correlation would probably be higher and the predictive value of the
test better estimated. This problem, stemming from the unavailability of the
unselected students for later criterion measurement, is known as *restriction of
range.* One way to avoid it is to make every attempt to track down the unselected
students for later measurement on the criterion. If that is impossible to achieve
(as it often is), statistical corrections can provide estimates of what the unat-
tenuated correlation would be. Most measurement texts include the statistical
correction for disattenuating a predictive validity coefficient.

Construct Validity. "A psychological construct is an idea developed or 'constructed' as a work of informed, scientific imagination; that is, it is a theoretical idea developed to explain and to organize some aspects of existing knowledge" (American Psychological Association, 1974, p. 29). Examples of psychological constructs are intelligence, reading comprehension, creativity, anxiety, and self-esteem. Construct validation is required for measures purported to assess the extent to which persons manifest abstract psychological abilities or traits. *Construct validity,* then, is an indicator of how well the test actually measures the theoretical construct of interest.

Construct validation requires a gradual accumulation of data from a variety of empirical studies. Investigations of a measure's construct validity are dictated by researchers' hypotheses about the nature of the construct and its behavioral indicators. After a measure of the construct has been developed through logical analysis, predictions of several kinds can be made about the relationships between scores on the construct and other variables. The predictions can be about correlations of the scores with other measures, about differences in scores among persons categorized into different groups on other dimensions, and about the effect on scores of experimental treatments or interventions (Thorndike and Hagen, 1977). As an illustration, the construct validity of intelligence tests (especially the early Stanford-Binet and Wechsler tests) has been investigated extensively via studies based on a variety of predictions. Those predictions included: that intelligence test scores would correlate positively and substantially with academic achievement measures; that children not promoted to the next grade would score lower than children who progressed as expected; that scores would correlate with age until maturity and then level off; and that persons with clinical mental problems would score lower than persons without such problems (Stanley and Hopkins, 1972).

Following the statement of hypothesis or prediction, actual empirical studies are conducted to test the hypothesis. The outcomes of the studies, primarily correlational or factor analytical, can lead to revisions of parts of the test that do not conform empirically to theoretical expectations, or can influence reformulations of the theories themselves. After a substantial amount of evidence has been collected from a variety of empirical studies, answers to the question "What is actually being measured?" become more convincing. These are the answers required for construct validity.

According to Campbell and Fiske (1959), construct validity is best demonstrated when a test correlates substantially with variables with which it theoretically should correlate, and also when it does not correlate with variables from which it should differ, or that the latter correlation is less than the former. In other words, a test should show evidence of both *convergent validity* and *discriminant validity.* (For more information on convergent and discriminant validity as well as on an experimental approach for the dual investigation of the two validities, see Campbell and Fiske, 1959.)

Operationally, construct validity often resembles criterion-related validity. Both emphasize obtaining substantial correlations with other measures of the same trait, ability, or behavior. The difference between construct and criterion-related validity involves purpose and, concomitantly, scope. Criterion-related validity, which is basically pragmatic, tells how well a measure correlates with other indexes of performance. Construct validity, however, addresses a broader question: how to psychologically interpret the scores from a measure. Because construct validity is highly theoretical, it requires much more extensive evidence than does criterion-related validity. (Amplification of the distinction between construct and criterion-related validity is contained in the *Standards for Educational and Psychological Tests* published by the American Psychological Association, 1974.) With the exception of some intelligence tests and an occasional personality test, it is difficult to find examples of elaborate construct validation efforts, especially for instruments designed for young children. Many test developers claim to have obtained evidence for construct validity, but a close examination of the procedures and scope of their investigations suggests attention to criterion-related validity rather than construct validation.

Reliability

A measure is reliable if the scores it yields are accurate and consistent. Assessing the reliability of a test or other measure requires determining the precision of the measurement technique. A reliability estimate gives the expected consistency of scores for the measure. As we shall see, consistency is defined in different ways, depending on the particular procedure used to determine reliability.

Reliability is necessary, but not sufficient, for validity. To be reliable, a measure must correlate reasonably well with itself. If it does not correlate with itself, it cannot correlate well with any external criterion, either. A measure can be reliable without being valid, however. For example, suppose a group of young children is given the same creativity test twice within the same week. Overall, the children's scores from the two testings are very similar, thus demonstrating substantial consistency, or reliability, of the test. However, does the test really measure creativity? The answer to this question requires evidence of construct validity. In reality, the test may measure reading ability, or artistic aptitude, or a combination of variables not directly related to the theoretical construct "creativity."

As compared with validity evidence, reliability evidence is relatively easy to obtain. For this reason, the reliability of many published instruments is documented in test manuals, while documentation on validity is scant or nonexistent. Reliability is secondary in importance to validity, however, and instruments accompanied only by reliability information have not been adequately prepared for widespread use.

The concept of reliability can be illustrated with any type of measurement technique. Suppose, as one part of a psychomotor test, the distance a ball is thrown by a group of preschoolers is to be measured. To measure throwing distance, we ask each child to stand in a specific place and throw a rubber ball as far as possible. Using a meterstick, we measure the child's "score" as the distance from the starting point to the landing point, reported to the nearest centimeter, such as 10.26 meters. What is the reliability of this measurement procedure? To find out, we can repeat the exercise one week later—using the same children and the same meterstick—and compare the results from the two occasions. A comparison of each child's two scores will show some disparity, but the differences for most of the children will be small. Further, the relative standing of a given child in each set of results will be about the same. The correlation between the paired scores will be positive and quite high. This correlation yields the reliability of the measurement procedure and is known as the *reliability coefficient*.

We could have used a different measure of distance, but it would be difficult to find one as reliable as the meterstick. For example, a teacher in the preschool could have estimated the distance thrown by each child, both on the initial day and one week later. This procedure would yield less reliable "scores" for each thrower. The correlation between the initial set of scores and the set obtained one week later, both being based on the teacher's distance estimates, would be lower than that which was found for the meterstick procedure. Subjective estimation lacks the precision of the standard meterstick. The teacher's perception of distances will vary somewhat from child to child and also from the initial day to one a week later.

To more fully understand the concept of reliability, the meaning of obtained score, true score, and measurement error must be understood. Theoretically, any obtained score is composed of two parts: a true score and an error component. Expressed as a formula:

$$X_o = X_t + X_e$$

where X_o represents the obtained score, X_t the true score, and X_e the error component associated with a particular obtained score. The *obtained score* is the actual score observed for a person. It is assumed that each person has a *true score*, that is, an indicator of his true ability, aptitude, or whatever the test is designed to measure. The *error component* is due to chance factors of several types: factors operating within the individual (such as fatigue or temporary inattention); factors associated with the test itself (such as a limited sampling of behaviors belonging to a universe or domain of content); and factors associated with administration or scoring procedures (such as limited time allotted for administration or subjectivity of scoring). Sometimes the error component raises the obtained score and other times it lowers it. That is, such errors are assumed to be random and independent, averaging (over repeated testings) to zero. No one obtained score is free of all measurement error. If it were, that obtained score would be the true score rather than just an estimate of it. Obviously, the intent in measurement is to minimize error so as to secure obtained scores as close to true scores as possible.

Just as any one obtained score is the sum of the person's true score plus the error component, the total variance for a set of obtained scores (s_o^2) is composed of two parts, true-score variance (s_t^2) and variance due to measurement errors (s_e^2):

$$s_o^2 = s_t^2 + s_e^2$$

The greater the influence of the true-score variance on the total obtained-score variance, the more precise the scores are as estimates of true scores. If most of the total obtained-score variance is variance due to measurement errors, however, then the obtained scores are heavily influenced by chance and lack reliability.

Theoretically, the reliability coefficient (r_{xx}) expresses how much of the total obtained-score variance is true-score variance:

$$r_{xx} = \frac{s_t^2}{s_o^2} \text{ or } r_{xx} = 1 - \frac{s_e^2}{s_o^2}$$

A reliability coefficient can range from 1.0, or perfect reliability, to 0.0, reflecting a complete lack of reliability. The closer r_{xx} is to 1.0, the less influential are the random measurement errors in the obtained-score variance. A measure with a high reliability coefficient, therefore, is accurate in the sense of producing stable or consistent scores. By contrast, the closer r_{xx} is to 0.0, the more the obtained scores represent only error and chance factors.

The basic meaning of any reliability coefficient is best expressed in terms of the above formulas—r_{xx} is the portion of total test variance that is not the result of errors of measurement. At the same time, note that the formulas for r_{xx} result from theoretical considerations; only rarely are they used in the calculation of reliability coefficients. Rather, as we will see in the next sections, product-moment correlation coefficients (see Chapter Two) are used in the operational (as distinct from theoretical) definitions of reliability. That is, correlation coefficients are calculated as estimates of reliability. (For more information on how this operational approach to determining reliability relates to the theoretical aspects of reliability, see Gulliksen, 1950, or Magnusson, 1967).

Generally, there are four types of operational reliability coefficients: the coefficients of stability, equivalence, stability and equivalence, and internal consistency. The four vary in the procedures used to collect relevant data and in the meaning or interpretation of the resulting coefficient. Differences in meaning basically derive from differences in how consistency is defined.

Coefficient of Stability. The coefficient of stability, also known as the *test-retest reliability coefficient,* was illustrated earlier by the ball throwing example. This coefficient is a measure of the consistency of scores over time—that is, across occasions. To obtain a stability coefficient, the same measure is administered twice to a single group of students. The correlation coefficient between the two sets of scores is the coefficient of stability. The closer the coefficient is to 1.0, the greater is the correspondence between the two sets of scores and the higher is the stability reliability.

The time interval between the two administrations influences the meaning of the stability coefficient. In general, the longer the time interval, the less the correspondence will be. The time interval used in determining test-retest reliability should relate to the purpose of the measure. If long-range stability is necessary for proper use and interpretation of the measure, then a reasonably long time period should be used when calculating the coefficient of stability. For example, if a school district gives an intellectual aptitude test in second grade and not again until fifth grade, the second-grade scores should be expected to exhibit stability over the full three-year period that they influence decisions about each student's instruction. In such a case, a one-year test-retest interval to establish stability reliability might be reasonable, although an even longer interval would be desirable. For most purposes, a short interval (a few days or a few months) is sufficient for this type of reliability estimate. In any event, the test manual should report the length of the test-retest interval.

Any random fluctuations in performance from the first testing to the second are categorized as errors of measurement and thus are included as error variance rather than true variance. Such fluctuations can occur because of changes within the respondents, due to such factors as fatigue, illness, or anxiety. Uncontrolled testing conditions, such as variations in administration procedures, weather changes, different noise levels, or other environmental distractions can also cause random fluctuations. The coefficient of stability indicates the extent to which test scores can be generalized over different occasions. A high coefficient implies that scores are influenced only slightly by random daily fluctuations in the conditions of the respondents or in the testing situation.

Test-retest reliability does not permit scores to be generalized over different test content since the test content remains identical from one administration to the next. The coefficient would convey the stability of scores on just the specific sample of items on the test; it would not infer the stability of scores on other forms of the test that are comprised of different items sampled from the same test-item universe.

An additional consideration in using the stability coefficient is that the scores from the second testing may be due, in part, to students' memory of the test given the first time—especially in cases where the time between testings is very short. The students may remember format, specific content, or even answers and respond as they did the first time, without going through the same processes as the first time. The coefficient of stability might be spuriously high—that is, higher than it would have been if the scores from the second testing had not been influenced by memory. In evaluating stability coefficients, the test user should be sensitive to this concern (also known as the practice or testing effect) if the test-retest interval is short.

Coefficient of Equivalence. The correlation between scores from two forms of a test given at essentially the same time is a *coefficient of equivalence* or an *equivalent-forms reliability coefficient.* Two or more forms of a test are said to be equivalent if they are alike in content, process, and difficulty levels of items, and if they yield similar means and standard deviations for a single group of respondents. Having equivalent forms of a test available is helpful in investigating the effects of intervention (using different test forms for pre- and post-testing) and in conducting follow-up studies.

Underlying equivalent-forms reliability is the concept of *item sampling*. Most educational and psychological measures are assumed to contain a sample of content, or items, that is representative of a much larger universe of content. For example, a vocabulary comprehension test for kindergartners, using a picture identification response format, is developed by randomly selecting 20 words from the 400 words originally identified as belonging to the relevant universe of items. Therefore, the test represents only a small portion of the universe of interest. Note that a large number of 20-item tests could be constructed by randomly selecting, with replacement, 20 words at a time for each test. (*Replacement sampling* means that a word, once randomly selected, would be replaced in the total pool of items and thus, by chance, could be reselected for a subsequent test.) Our interest is not so much in a student's score on one 20-item test as in his comprehension of the entire 400-word universe. An accurate estimate of his comprehension would be the average score he would receive by taking a large number of different 20-item tests.

A student's score on one of the 20-item tests would probably be different from his score on a second 20-item test because of a variety of factors, including the specific words that, by chance, are selected. He may be lucky on the first test, in that several of the words are ones he has just learned; but the second test may include an unusually large number of unfamiliar words. Another student may have the opposite experience. Thus, some of the variance in each set of scores is due to factors specific to the particular words selected as test items. In constructing a test of items by sampling from a universe, one goal is to eliminate as much error variance due to item sampling as possible.

In reality, a particular test is usually not constructed by randomly selecting items from a very large universe of developed items. Rather, the test is constructed to meet certain content specifications and to cover a certain range of difficulty. Nevertheless, it is assumed that the content represents a larger domain. If a second form of the test is then constructed using similar procedures—the same number of items and the same content, format, and difficulty specifications—then the two forms are considered to be equivalent. The extent to which they yield consistent results is determined by correlating the scores from the two forms for one group of students. The higher the coefficient, the less the scores on either one of the forms are influenced by error due to item sampling.

To establish a coefficient of equivalence, all students take both forms of the test at essentially the same time—that is, on the same day and with no time interval except possibly a rest period long enough to be consistent with good performance. Since the order in which the forms are taken may have an effect, it is a good practice to have some students take, say, Form 1 and then Form 2, while other students start with Form 2 and then take Form 1. Because there is no time interval between the two testings, the correlation between the two sets of scores gives the consistency across forms but not across occasions. Thus, a coefficient of equivalence should be established for measures purporting to be representative of a larger universe of items or behaviors (such as achievement tests); interest lies in inferring knowledge or mastery of the larger universe rather than in estimating the stability of that knowledge or mastery over time.

Coefficient of Stability and Equivalence. When two equivalent forms of a test are administered at different times, the correlation between scores is a *coefficient of stability and equivalence*. This coefficient conveys the consistency in scores across forms as well as across occasions. The factors considered as error variance include those for both the stability coefficient and the equivalent-forms—that is, factors within the individual that randomly fluctuate over testing occasions and factors due to item sampling. This coefficient will usually be lower than either the stability or equivalent-forms coefficients for the same measure would be, because of the accumulation of factors contributing to error variance.

This type of reliability should be established for measures that both need long-range stability and are to be used for making inferences to a domain of knowledge. When a coefficient of stability and equivalence is reported, the length of time between the two administrations should be indicated. In addition, the means and standard deviations for the two forms should be given, as they should be for any coefficient of equivalence.

On many occasions, the construction of equivalent (also called *parallel* or *alternate*) forms is impractical. Developing two good forms of a test approximately doubles both the time and cost necessary to develop just one. Thus, the coefficients of equivalence and of stability and equivalence are not used as often as are other coefficients that require only one form of a test. Several procedures exist to estimate the internal consistency of a single-form measure administered only once.

Coefficients of Internal Consistency. Determining reliability from a single administration of one form of a test yields reliability estimates known as *coefficients of internal consistency*. Such coefficients convey the degree of consistency of the content within the single test form.

The *split-half technique* involves dividing a test into two parts and measuring the degree of correspondence between the resulting two sets of test scores. Ordinarily, following the administration of the entire test to one group, the odd-numbered items are treated as one half and the even-numbered items as the other half. Two scores are determined for each person, one score for each half of the test. The correlation between the scores from the two halves is then calculated and yields the split-half coefficient indicating the consistency between the two halves. If most persons score about the same on the two halves, or if each half-test ranks the persons similarly, then the correlation is high and the test consistency is good. Note that the split-half technique results in the reliability of only a half-test. In a sense, then, it is analogous to an equivalent-forms coefficient for two forms, each form being one-half the length of the actual test administered.

The correlation obtained between the two halves can be used (or "stepped up") to estimate the reliability of the actual full-length test. The formula that produces this estimate is:

$$r_{xx} = \frac{2r_{\frac{1}{2}\frac{1}{2}}}{1 + r_{\frac{1}{2}\frac{1}{2}}}$$

where r_{xx} represents the reliability for the full-length test and $r_{\frac{1}{2}\frac{1}{2}}$ indicates the correlation observed between the two half-tests. The formula is one version of the Spearman-Brown Prophecy Formula. In its more general form, the prophecy formula can be used to estimate the effect that lengthening or shortening any test will have on its internal consistency coefficient. In the specific case of the split-half technique and the formula above, the effect on the coefficient of doubling the (half) test length is determined. To illustrate, suppose that the correlation between the odd- and even-numbered halves of a fifty-item test is found to be .70. The reliability for the full-length test is:

$$r_{xx} = \frac{2r_{\frac{1}{2}\frac{1}{2}}}{1 + r_{\frac{1}{2}\frac{1}{2}}} = \frac{2(.70)}{1 + .70} = \frac{1.40}{1.70} = .82$$

Note that the full-length test coefficient, .82, is larger than the reliability of the half-test. (Other things being equal, a longer test will be more reliable than a shorter version of the same test.)

Other approaches to internal consistency also yield indexes of the homogeneity of tests. Two formulas derived many years ago by Kuder and Richardson (1937), called KR_{20} and KR_{21}, are probably the most frequently used estimates of internal consistency. Either formula can be used to estimate a test's item-to-item internal consistency. That is, a determination is made of the degree to which all of the items on a test measure a common trait or ability of the persons tested. The KR formulas are not simple to calculate by hand. For example, KR_{20} entails obtaining the average intercorrelation of all the items, which is then assumed to be the reliability of a single item. The general Spearman-Brown Prophecy Formula is applied to that average intercorrelation to obtain the reliability of the entire test. KR_{21} is not quite as cumbersome, but also not quite as precise, as KR_{20}. Fortunately, with available computer programs, it is no longer necessary to calculate either coefficient by hand. The KR formulas are two of several similar approaches to inter-item, or internal, consistency. Coefficient Alpha (Cronbach, 1951) is a generalized formula, under which most other approaches can be subsumed. Coefficient Alpha is also typically calculated using available computer routines.

Internal consistency reliability is not appropriate for speeded tests. A speed test usually consists of relatively easy items, since the objective of the test is to measure not what one knows but how quickly one can complete a series of tasks. Internal consistency reliability coefficients, which indicate the degree of similarity among responses to the items (or halves, in the case of the split-half coefficient), will be spuriously high. The proper reliability estimate should indicate the consistency in speed of work, not consistency in number of right answers for a respondent.

An example will help clarify this problem with speeded tests. In a kindergarten class, the children have been learning to print the letters of the alphabet. After several months' practice, all children are capable of printing every letter, but some are much slower printers than others. After encouraging the children for a few days to work more quickly, the teacher decides to test them on speed. In a two-minute timed test, the children are asked to print in order the letters of the alphabet, starting over again if they complete all twenty-six letters before time is up. Scores are based on the number of letters printed in the two minutes.

Suppose that the teacher computes a split-half reliability coefficient for the test. She divides the test into two halves, one consisting of the even-numbered letters of the alphabet (that is, *b, d, f,* and so on) and the other consisting of the odd-numbered letters. A child who printed forty letters will have twenty correct even letters and twenty correct odd letters. Another child, who completed only ten letters, will have five correct even letters and five correct odd letters. Regardless of the number of letters completed, each child's two half-scores will be identical. Consequently, the correlation between odd and even scores for the total group of children will be perfect. When "stepped-up" with the Spearman-Brown Prophecy Formula, the correlation will remain perfect— that is, $r_{xx} = 1.0$. This coefficient, however, is entirely spurious and gives no useful information about the reliability of the test. By contrast, the reliability of the speed with which children work on the test would be helpful in evaluating the test.

Assessing the reliability of speeded tests requires two administrations of the test—either two administrations of the same form, to obtain a coefficient of stability, or two administrations of equivalent forms, to obtain a coefficient of stability and equivalence. Alternatively, the split-half procedure could be used, provided that the split is in terms of time rather than items. For example, the kindergarten teacher could have administered two separately timed tests, one for the printing of the even-numbered letters and the other for the printing of the odd-numbered letters. This technique is similar to using two equivalent forms of the test, except that each form is only half the length of the test itself. By applying the prophecy formula to the correlation between the scores (number of letters printed) from the two administrations, the teacher could obtain the reliability of the entire test.

The reliability procedures discussed to this point differ in several respects, especially in regard to data collection and analysis, and the meaning of resulting coefficients. A comparative summary of the four types of coefficient is presented in Table 8.

Interrater Reliability. The coefficients summarized in Table 8 all give estimates of consistency of subjects' responses to test content. Most tests and measures for which those coefficients are calculated consist of objectively scored items, so error variance due to scoring is small. For example, the scoring of a fifty-item multiple-choice test with a pre-established scoring key requires only

Table 8. Characteristics of Four Types of Reliability Coefficient

Type of Reliability Coefficient	Data-Collection Procedures	Correlation Between		Meaning of Coefficient
Coefficient of Stability (Test-retest)	Test A is given twice to the same group of subjects, with an arbitrary but meaningful time interval between testings.	Test A	Test A	Consistency of subjects' responses over time.
Coefficient of Equivalence (Equivalent, alternate, or parallel forms)	Forms 1 and 2 of Test A are given to the same group of subjects at essentially the same time.	Form 1 of Test A	Form 2 of Test A	Consistency of subjects' responses to equivalent samples of content.
Coefficient of Stability and Equivalence (Test-retest of equivalent, alternate, or parallel forms)	Forms 1 and 2 of Test A are given to the same group of subjects, with an arbitrary but meaningful time interval between testings.	Form 1 of Test A	Form 2 of Test A	Consistency of subjects' responses to equivalent samples of content over time.
Coefficient of Internal Consistency (Split-half, KR_{20}, KR_{21}, Cronbach's Alpha)	Test A is given once to one group of subjects.	For split-half: Half 1 of Test A For other coefficients: Intercorrelations among all items are used as basis for calculation.	Half 2 of Test A	Consistency of subjects' responses to content in two halves of one test or to all items in one test.

that the key be meticulously followed and the number of correct or incorrect responses carefully counted and recorded. Further, if objective tests are computer-scored, as is now the case with many widely used standardized tests, the possibility of scoring errors is reduced even further.

There are some types of measure, however, that entail subjective scoring. Projective personality tests, some tests of creativity, and cognitive essay tests are examples of measures that depend on the judgments of scorers or raters. For such measures, it is important to determine *interrater reliability*—that is, the extent to which two or more scorers are consistent in their judgments. Interrater reliability can be found by having two judges independently score one set of tests or rate the behavior for one group of students. The correlation coefficient between the scores assigned by the two judges is a measure of interrater reliability.

Related to interrater reliability is interobserver reliability, applicable to measurement via observation techniques. *Interobserver reliability* measures the extent to which different observers agree in their recordings of events or behaviors. The procedure for establishing interobserver reliability involves having two persons observe the same stimuli and independently record their impressions (using checklists, rating scales, or whatever form the observation schedule takes). Then the results from their observations are correlated. Interobserver reliability is discussed more fully in Chapter Four.

Standard Error of Measurement. As stated earlier, the variance of the obtained scores (s_o^2) for a group of students is theoretically composed of two parts: the variance of the students' true scores (s_t^2) and the variance due to errors of measurement (s_e^2). Reliability is a measure of the amount of total variance in a set of scores that is attributable to true differences among respondents' scores rather than differences attributable to errors of measurement (that is, $r_{xx} = s_t^2/s_o^2$ or $r_{xx} = 1 - s_e^2/s_o^2$). Reliability coefficients thus indicate the accuracy or precision of a measurement technique when used with a group of students.

For interpretation of individual scores, the standard deviation of the errors of measurement (s_e), also called the *standard error of measurement,* is more meaningful than the reliability coefficient. The standard error of measurement is a measure of the discrepancy between obtained and true scores. (Since $s_o^2 = s_t^2 + s_e^2$, then $s_e^2 = s_o^2 - s_t^2$.) In interpreting an individual's score, we wonder how much confidence to place in its accuracy or, stated differently, how much the observed score was influenced by irrelevant, temporary fluctuations within the individual or the testing situation. The standard error of measurement allows us to estimate the range within which the individual's true score lies.

By examining the formulas presented earlier for r_{xx}, it can be seen that the standard error of measurement, s_e, is closely related to the reliability coefficient. In fact, some simple algebraic operations of the formula $r_{xx} = 1 - s_e^2/s_o^2$ yields a computational formula for the variance of the errors of measurement:

$$s_e^2 = s_o^2(1 - r_{xx})$$

Thus, the standard error of measurement, s_e or the square root of s_e^2, is equal to:

$$s_e = s_0\sqrt{1 - r_{xx}}$$

As r_{xx} increases, the magnitude of s_e decreases; that is, the greater the reliability, the smaller the standard error of measurement. If $r_{xx} = 1.0$ (indicating perfect reliability), $s_e = 0$; therefore, the observed scores contain no error components and hence are the true scores. If, however, $r_{xx} = 0.0$ (indicating complete absence of reliability), $s_e = s_0$; that is, the standard error of measurement is just as large as the standard deviation of the test itself. All variability in the test is thus due to the errors of measurement, and there is only a chance relationship between the obtained and true scores.

The standard error of measurement is used to establish a range of scores within which an individual's true score probably lies. Remember, from our discussion of the standard deviation in Chapter Two, that a fairly uniform proportion of scores lies within any given number of standard deviation units from the mean. An analogous principle applies to interpreting the standard error of measurement. That is, there is a 68 percent probability that a person's true score lies in the band or range within one standard error of measurement (s_e) of his obtained score. If $\pm 2s_e$ are added to a person's obtained score, there is a 95 percent probability that the range established spans his true score; if $\pm 3s_e$ are added, instead, the probability rises to 99 percent.

An example should help clarify the meaning and use of the standard error of measurement. The Wechsler Preschool and Primary Scale of Intelligence (WPPSI) is given to a large group of young children. The standard deviation for the WPPSI is 15 points. The reliability for the Full Scale IQ, estimated via internal consistency, is .96 for this group of children. The standard error of measurement, then, is:

$$s_e = s_0\sqrt{1 - r_{xx}} = 15\sqrt{1 - .96} = 15\sqrt{.04} = 15(.2) = 3$$

For any individual child, we infer that there are two chances in three that his obtained IQ (WPPSI) score lies within ± 3 points of his true score. That is, if a child has an obtained Full Scale IQ of 110, the probability is 68 percent that his true score lies somewhere between 107 and 113. There is about one chance in six (16 percent probability) that his true IQ score is lower than 107 and one chance in six that it is higher than 113. Similarly, it can be calculated that there is a 95 percent probability that his true Full Scale IQ falls somewhere in the band from 104 to 116 (that is, 110 $\pm 2s_e$).

The standard error of measurement is thus extremely useful in interpreting the obtained score of an individual. The lower the reliability, the larger the standard error of measurement and the less likely we are to have confidence that the obtained scores closely correspond to the true scores.

Validity and Reliability:
Interpretation and Special Considerations

Validity and reliability are of concern to both test developers and users. Developers utilize the techniques presented in the previous sections for establishing the psychometric properties of their measures. Users examine the published validity and reliability evidence when selecting measures for use in specific circumstances. Through the published technical data, the user becomes familiar with the constructs being measured and is able to form opinions about the appropriateness of different measures for his intended uses. However, since much of the published information is inadequate or not relevant to a user's own needs, he will often need to conduct additional investigations prior to his own use of a measure. Thus, the actual techniques for determining reliability and validity are of importance to the user, too. In this section, we will discuss some of the factors to be considered when designing validity and reliability studies or when interpreting available data.

Conditions Affecting Validity and Reliability Coefficients. Both validity and reliability coefficients are calculated for particular groups of respondents, and the characteristics of those groups can affect the coefficients. One characteristic that affects both types of coefficient in similar ways is the heterogeneity of the group tested. Other things being equal, the larger the variance in a set of obtained scores, the greater the correlation possible between those scores and another set of scores. Thus, if a group of students are tested who vary greatly in ability level, the correlation between their scores on two equivalent forms of an achievement measure, or between their test scores and scores on a criterion measure, will be higher than for another group of students who are quite similar in ability level. The same phenomenon will occur for coefficients for a developmental inventory based, first, on a group of children covering a wide age range and, second, on a group of children of one age only. Reliability and criterion-related validity coefficients will tend to be lower for the second (more homogeneous) age group. This situation is similar to the restriction-of-range problem considered in the discussion of criterion-related validity.

Other sample characteristics affect the usefulness of the coefficients for particular types of student. A test may measure different functions when given to students who vary in sex, age, ethnicity, socioeconomic level, educational background, or other pertinent characteristics. The test may, therefore, demonstrate good stability and have high predictive validity when used with one type of student but be much less stable and valid with other types of student.

Reported reliability and validity coefficients should be accompanied by a full description of the samples used in obtaining them. If the samples are not representative of the persons with which the test is to be used, validity and reliability should be reassessed for more appropriate samples. Measures designed for use in early childhood education are especially susceptible to fluctuations in validity and reliability coefficients depending on the exact ages of the children tested. Since the coefficients typically are lower for very young children than they are for older children, manuals should report separate coefficients for the various age groups targeted.

In addition to sample characteristics, certain features of the test itself can affect the reliability estimates. As we have seen, internal consistency reliability of the Kuder-Richardson and Alpha types is a measure of the homogeneity of the test items. Therefore, the more similar the items are in content and format, the greater the reliability is likely to be. The item difficulty and discrimination levels of the items (see Chapter Two) also influence reliability. Items with difficulty values around .50 (that is, about 50 percent of the sample passing the item) contribute more variance to the total test variance than items that are either extremely easy or extremely difficult. Since reliability is increased when the variability of scores on the total test is increased (other things being equal), a large number of items around .50 difficulty are usually desired. Further, these items of moderate difficulty have the capacity of being good discriminators, meaning that they differentiate the students scoring well on the total test from those scoring poorly. On the other hand, very easy items cannot possibly differentiate well, since a large proportion of the students, including some of varying ability levels, will pass the items. With very difficult items, most of the students will fail, with a few passing only because of lucky guessing. Although items with difficulty values around .50 do not necessarily differentiate the stronger and the weaker students, they have the best chance of being good discriminators.

A final consideration with reliability is the length of the test. In discussing the split-half reliability procedure, we showed that doubling the length of a test increased its reliability. The Spearman-Brown Prophecy Formula was applied to obtain the reliability coefficient for a test twice as long as the half-length tests that were first correlated. Actually, the Spearman-Brown Prophecy Formula can be used to estimate the effect that lengthening or shortening a test to any extent will have on its reliability, or to determine the number of items needed to achieve a certain reliability. The general equation for the Spearman-Brown Prophecy Formula is as follows:

$$r_{xx} = \frac{nr}{1 + (n - 1)r}$$

where r_{xx} is the reliability of a test n times as long as the original test, n is the factor by which the length of the original test is increased, and r is the reliability of the original test. The formula presented earlier for the split-half technique is simply a specific example of this general equation, showing its use for estimating the reliability of a test twice as long as the original test; that is, for the split-half technique, $n = 2$.

In applying the formula to estimate the reliability of a lengthened test, it must be assumed that the items added would be of comparable quality and that the examinees do not undergo any changes (for example, in attention level) while taking the longer test. As the length of the test is increased, then, the random errors of measurement influencing an individual's score tend to cancel each other out; thus, his total obtained score is less determined by chance factors.

To illustrate the use of the general Spearman-Brown Prophecy Formula, let us suppose that a thirty-item aptitude measure has a reliability of .60. We want to know how reliable the test would be if the number of items were increased to ninety. Applying the prophecy formula, we obtain the reliability estimate for a test three times as long:

$$r_{xx} = \frac{nr}{1 + (n-1)r} = \frac{3(.60)}{1 + (3-1)(.60)} = \frac{1.80}{1 + 2(.60)} = \frac{1.80}{2.20} = .82$$

The increase in reliability is considerable, .60 to .82. As we said earlier, the estimate assumes that the examinees do not change, that is, become more fatigued, bored, inattentive, and so forth. Such an assumption bears closer scrutiny with young children than with adolescents or adults. If testing conditions can be kept practical and feasible, however, reliability can be increased by adding additional similar items to the test.

The above-mentioned test considerations also affect validity coefficients, but less directly. Reliability is necessary, but not sufficient, for validity. The more reliable a test is, therefore, the more valid it could be. In fact, the square root of the reliability coefficient of a test is the maximum criterion-related validity that that test can have; even then, however, the maximum can only be achieved if the criterion itself is perfectly reliable (Stanley and Hopkins, 1972). Obviously, taking steps to increase the reliability of a measure (for example, by lengthening the test and including a large proportion of items of moderate difficulty) potentially enhances validity, too.

Validity and Reliability of Criterion-Referenced Tests. Criterion-referenced tests present a special problem for determining validity and reliability. Most of the traditional validity and reliability coefficients are Pearson Product-Moment Correlation Coefficients; as we have seen, such coefficients are affected by the variability of the groups for which they are determined. With norm-referenced tests, which are designed to differentiate among students (see Chapter Two), the traditional approaches are appropriate. In criterion-referenced measurement, however, the intent is to assess whether or not an individual's performance meets a certain criterion or mastery level. Determining the individual's status in relation to the rest of the group is of minor importance, as is the corresponding concern with maximizing variability among students' scores. Because of this, the validity and reliability procedures based on product-moment correlation coefficients are inappropriate for criterion-referenced tests, and their use can actually produce misleading information. The problem is more acute with reliability than validity, since several of the traditional validation procedures do not depend on the product-moment correlation coefficient.

The content validity of criterion-referenced tests can be assessed in much the same way as for norm-referenced tests. Remember that content validity relies primarily on logical, rather than empirical, analysis of test content. Having experts categorize items according to objectives, and then examining the fit between the blueprint for the test and the experts' categorization, would yield information about the test's content validity. As was the case for norm-referenced tests, content validity of criterion-referenced tests should be addressed during test development.

Criterion-related and construct validity data are obtained by determining the correspondence between the criterion-referenced scores and scores on other measures. However, correlational techniques other than the Pearson must be used. Since most criterion-referenced tests sort examinees into two groups— passers and nonpassers—the scores do not constitute an interval-level variable (see Chapter Two), one of the prerequisites for use of the Pearson Product-Moment Correlation. Various other correlational procedures are available for assessing the extent of correspondence between criterion-referenced test scores and scores on the other measures employed for validation (see Millman, 1974).

Expectancy tables, illustrated earlier as an adjunct to criterion-related validity, can also be constructed for criterion-referenced test validation. The test itself results in categorizing students into two groups—passers and nonpassers. The other measure used for validation would be some pertinent external criterion or indicator of mastery, such as either promotion or nonpromotion to the next grade. The extent to which the classification of students based on the test and the external criterion coincide, as shown in the expectancy table, indicates how valid the test is as a classification device.

The ability of criterion-referenced test scores to differentiate criterion groups can also be assessed by a statistical technique called *analysis of variance* (discussed in most statistics texts). This approach is particularly applicable when the sensitivity of the criterion-referenced test, either to preinstruction-postinstruction changes in students or to the effects of different types of instructional treatment, is being judged as part of the validation effort (Millman, 1974).

As an example of this approach, consider a fifteen-item criterion-referenced test designed to measure basic concepts. The content of the test closely mirrors the content and activities of a special six-week summer program for preschoolers, which is offered twice during the summer. Children who have completed the program should perform better on the test than children who have not had the program. A group of forty preschool-age children are randomly divided into two groups of twenty each. One group is enrolled in the program during the first six weeks of the summer; the other group is enrolled for the second six weeks of the summer. At the end of the first six-week program, all forty children are given the criterion-referenced test. Analysis of variance techniques are then used to compare the two groups, either on the basis of their overall performance on the test or on the basis of how the children in each group performed on each separate item. The analysis of variance procedures take several factors into account. Generally, however, the larger the differences in performance in favor of the students who have already completed the program, the stronger the case can be made for the validity of the test. For more information on the special use of the analysis of variance, see Millman (1974).

The reliability of criterion-referenced tests is more problematic, due to the greater prominence of (and lack of substitutes for) Pearson correlation procedures in traditional reliability calculations. Efforts are currently being taken to develop relevant statistical procedures (Hambleton and others, 1978; Martuza, 1977; Millman, 1974; and Popham, 1975). A few of the recently proposed techniques will be briefly described here.

As with norm-referenced tests, test-retest and equivalent-forms procedures may be used to assess the stability and equivalence of forms, respectively. In the context of criterion-referenced measurement, however, stability refers to the extent to which students are consistently classified as passers or nonpassers of the criterion. Likewise, equivalence refers to the consistency of classification across two forms of the test. Thus, reliability is defined as the consistency of any classifying or decision making that is based on criterion-referenced test outcomes, rather than as the consistency of actual obtained scores.

To secure an indicator of stability, the criterion-referenced test would be administered twice to one group of students. To obtain an indicator of equivalence, two forms of the test would be administered at essentially the same time. An indicator of stability and equivalence would result if two equivalent forms were administered with a time interval between testings. The percentage of consistent classifications on the basis of these repeated testings would be used to estimate the test's stability or equivalence. The higher the percentage of consistent classifications, the more reliable is the test. Extensions and elaborations of this basic idea into more complex statistical procedures have been developed (see, for example, Martuza, 1977).

Usability

In addition to validity and reliability, a number of practical considerations must also be addressed in the selection of measuring instruments. These practical considerations are incorporated under the general heading of *usability*—the extent to which a test can be used. They include (1) provision of technical quality data, (2) administration, (3) scoring, (4) interpretation, (5) format, (6) sources of irrelevant difficulty, and (7) cost. Each of these considerations will be discussed in turn.

Detailed information on the evidence for the validity and reliability of a measure—*technical quality data*—should always be provided in the accompanying manual. The size and characteristics of the samples used for determining validity and reliability should be clearly specified. For content validity, information in the manual should include a description of the procedures used, qualifications of judges, and an estimate of interrater agreement (if appropriate). For criterion-related validity, a clear description of the criteria, including relevant reliability estimates for the criteria, should be given. Construct validation procedures should be fully explained, including the theoretical bases for the studies that were conducted. With regard to reliability, the manual should contain information on pertinent reliability coefficients and details of the procedures used for obtaining them. If subtests are to be interpreted separately, then reliability estimates for them should also be included. The standard error of measurement, important for interpreting individual scores, should be reported for all relevant age groups.

A pervasive concern with regard to test administration is the standardization of the stimulus situation. That is, the test manual should include sufficient detail to permit each child to receive an equivalent stimulus. Testing procedures and instructions must be fully specified. Other important aspects of test administration involve requirements such as time, administrator training, and testing group size.

The amount of time required for administration is an important usability feature, especially with measures for young children. Test tasks can fail to hold a child's attention for a sufficient time period. For example, as will be noted in Chapter Five, not all children sampled on the Circus battery of tests displayed appropriate attentiveness (*Circus Manual and Technical Report,* 1974–75, pp. 378–379). Consequently, measure reliability can be difficult to achieve with young children. Test reliability can theoretically be improved by adding comparable items, as we noted; however, an important assumption is that the increased test length will not cause the examinees to become bored or inattentive. If they do (and young children are likely to), the reliability will not necessarily be increased, as new sources of error, such as guessing and neighborpoking, may be introduced. A test that can be administered in several short testing sessions, with a few hours or a day intervening between sessions, is a reasonable compromise between technical and practical considerations when testing young children.

The usability of a measure is also influenced by the administrator training required. Measures that can be administered by classroom teachers are convenient and relatively undisruptive to students. The convenience of some measures, especially individually administered intelligence and personality tests, is limited because of the extensive examiner training required.

Testing group size is a final salient administration feature. Too large a test group can impair test performance. With young children, testing group size is an important consideration, especially if (as is often the case) the children have had little or no previous experience with formal school settings or tests. Unfortunately, many manuals of tests for young children fail to address the issue of proper group size. It might appear a simple problem to solve—just give the test to very small groups. The smaller the groups, however, the more groups there are to test and the more time it takes. Test manuals should contain information on proper group size and should report the testing group size used in establishing norms.

Scoring procedures affect a test's usability. Objectivity of scoring is particularly important. (Recall from Chapter Two that objective tests are those in which the same score is assigned no matter who marks the test.) For objective tests, detailed scoring instructions and scoring keys are often supplied by developers and permit relatively quick and accurate scoring. Many commercial test companies provide a scoring service (often computerized) for their objective, standardized tests. Such services, though costly, may be worthwhile since they save teacher time and normally result in the most accurate scoring. However, the time delay involved in getting scored results back from the test company can erode a test's usefulness.

Subjective tests present special scoring difficulties. As the objectivity of the scoring process decreases, the magnitude of measurement error due to unreliable scoring increases. Further, some subjectively scored measures, such as projective personality tests, require extensive training of scorers. From a usability standpoint, then, the subjectively scored instruments are less practical than the objectively scored ones.

Interpretation of test results also must be considered. The time required is important, and the additional personnel training needed to allow proper interpretation may represent a critical factor. That is, for many measures only minimal training of personnel is required to achieve satisfactory administration and scoring practices, but satisfactory interpretation of the results from the measure is far more complicated and demanding.

Ease of interpretation is also affected by the manner in which scores are transformed or reported. Age- or grade-equivalent scores can be misleading (see Chapter Two). Optimally, transformed scores of several types—standard scores, percentile ranks, and age- or grade-equivalents—should be available in the manual.

Interpretability is highly influenced by the norms reported in the manual. Norm tables should be accompanied by a detailed description of the characteristics of the samples on which they were based. A breakdown of norms by age, sex, geographic location, ethnicity, or other relevant demographic variables is an additional aid to interpretation of norm-referenced tests.

The test format should also be examined, from several angles. The appropriateness of the measure's format for the intended examinees is, of course, critical. The adequacy of the instructions to the examinee (that is, their brevity, clarity, appropriate vocabulary level, and so on), the number and quality of the practice items provided, the visual appeal and clarity, and the organization of the content should all be taken into account. With young children, instructions should be clear and complete, and read aloud to the children by the teacher or other examiner. A sufficient number of practice items should be provided, so as to eliminate irrelevant test difficulty due to misunderstanding of directions. Each page of a paper-and-pencil test should contain large, clear print and distinct pictures. Providing generous space between items and having each item complete on a single page helps eliminate examinee confusion. Further, items should be ordered by increasing difficulty levels to prevent children from becoming discouraged early in the test.

Several times in this and the previous chapter, we have alluded to sources of irrelevant difficulty in tests. *Irrelevant difficulty* refers to factors in a test that are irrelevant to the traits, abilities, or behaviors being measured, but contribute to the difficulty level of the test for some examinees. Irrelevant difficulty factors lead to less accurate test results, since examinees of equal ability can score differently solely because of the irrelevant difficulties. The extent to which irrelevant difficulties are minimized in a test is related to the usability of the measure.

Messick and Anderson (1970) cited four sources of irrelevant difficulty: test format, test content, testing conditions, and test-wiseness. Irrelevant difficulty in test format might be illustrated by a format that requires young children to read the directions for a test of listening skills, or one in which the answer-marking process is extraordinarily difficult. Test content can produce irrelevant difficulty when test items differentially favor children of one sex over the other, or one racial group over another, for reasons unrelated to what is being measured. Testing conditions that pose irrelevant difficulty problems are ones that make some examinees feel threatened, anxious, or alienated. Finally, differences among examinees in "test-wiseness," or familiarity and experience with test-taking procedures, can result in biases in scores favoring the more experienced children.

There are ways to reduce these sources of irrelevant difficulty in tests. For example, a test that directs the examiner to read instructions aloud, contains items with vocabulary words common to children of different racial groups, and is designed to be administered in the familiar classroom setting by the teacher has reduced the first three sources of bias. To reduce differential effects due to test-wiseness, a test should contain clear, detailed instructions and a sufficient number of practice items (or even an entire practice test) to make the children feel comfortable with the testing procedures. A further mitigating procedure would involve actually instructing the children in test-taking strategies prior to giving them an unfamiliar test.

A final practical feature germane to usability should not be overlooked—cost. In large-scale testing programs involving many children, small per-test costs quickly mushroom. Some savings are possible if the test booklets can be used over again, requiring only the purchase of new answer sheets for each subsequent year or testing session. However, use of separate answer sheets can be confusing to very young children (Cashen and Ramseyer, 1969), so such tests should be selected after a careful consideration of the trade-offs involved. In many cases, a suitable period of practice with separate answer sheets would permit young children to use them appropriately.

The several usability considerations presented above are important, but they should be kept in perspective. Undue weighting of cost, physical attractiveness, ease of scoring, or other usability features occurs all too often in test selection. The wise test user focuses first on the validity of measures under consideration, and next on their reliability. Only after the available measures have been narrowed down to those with high validity and reliability should the question of usability be addressed.

A System for Evaluating Measures

In judging the adequacy of measures proposed for specific purposes, it is helpful to use a systematic assessment procedure. The following form can aid prospective users of measures in weighing the pros and cons of different measures. Some aspects of the form were suggested by a related system presented by Cronbach (1970).

Measure Evaluation

I. Purpose of evaluating measure (Detail the principal reasons for evaluating the measure.)
II. Identification of measure (For each topic, record all available information.)
   A. Title and acronym
   B. Author(s) and address
   C. Publisher and address
   D. Date(s) of publication
   E. Materials available (forms, levels, parts, kits) and costs
III. Description of measure (For each topic, include (a) what is reported by the author(s) of the measure and (b) your judgments about the adequacy and worth of what is reported.)
   A. General type
      1. Purpose(s) of measure
      2. Traits assessed
   B. Intended test population
      1. Age
      2. Special groups
   C. Individual or group administration (and recommended group sizes)
   D. Time required
      1. Actual testing time
      2. Total administration time
   E. Stimulus items
      1. Content and appearance
      2. Examinee response mode
   F. Administration procedures
      1. Training needed for administration
      2. Administration assists provided
      3. Sequence of actions for administering measure
   G. Scoring procedures
      1. Training needed for scoring
      2. Scoring assists provided
      3. Types of score
      4. Sequence of actions for deriving scores
      5. Availability/cost of machine scoring
   H. Interpretation procedures
      1. Training needed for interpretation
      2. Interpretation assists provided
      3. Availability and description of norms (or if criterion-referenced, description of the nature, source, and importance of the criterion)
      4. Sequence of actions for interpreting scores

    I. Reporting procedures
       1. Training needed for reporting
       2. Reporting assists provided
       3. Sequence of actions for reporting scores
  IV. Support for measure (For each topic, include (a) what is recorded by the author(s) of the measure and (b) your judgments about the adequacy and worth of what is reported.)
    A. Item selection
       1. Process
       2. Rationale
       3. Measure progenitors
    B. Validity evidence
       1. Content
       2. Criterion-related
          a. Concurrent
          b. Predictive
       3. Construct
    C. Reliability evidence
       1. Stability
       2. Equivalence
       3. Stability and equivalence
       4. Internal consistency
       5. Interrator
    D. Cautions by the author(s) of the measure
    E. Comments by the author(s) of the measure
   V. Reviewer's overall judgments of the measure
  VI. Bibliographical references about the measure

                                      Reviewer's name: _____
                                      Date completed: _____

    To assist the reviewer in making the judgments of adequacy and worth for most of the categories presented under sections III and IV of this evaluation form, specific rating procedures could be developed. For guidance in defining and constructing such rating procedures, see the MEAN Evaluation System developed by the Center for the Study of Evaluation, described in the source book section (following Chapter Twelve).

Chapter *4*

Observational Measurement

Most readers of this book have no doubt reviewed research and evaluation reports that summarize and interpret measurement data. However, we would guess that few of the report summaries were anything like the one paraphrased below (which concerns an analysis of 200 quarrels of nursery school children):

> Among the 40 children, 3 to 4 quarrels per hour took place. They were short, averaging less than 24 seconds, with only 13 of the 200 exceeding one minute. Quarrels indoors were shorter, and were terminated more quickly by teachers, than quarrels outdoors. Girls were involved in quarrels less frequently, and at a less aggressive level, than boys. Quarreling was most common between older and younger (rather than same-age) children and, additionally, between members of the same sex. When boy-girl quarrels did erupt, however, they were only one third as likely to end in compromise as same-sex disputes. With age, quarreling behavior appeared to decrease, but extent of aggressiveness and tendency to retaliate increased. Most quarrels involved a struggle for possessions. Common physical activities accompanying nearly every quarrel included striking, pulling, and pushing. Silence during quarrels predominated, although vocal activities such as crying and forbidding were moderately common. Most quarrels were settled by the participants themselves, frequently with the younger child forced to yield to the older or the older voluntarily yielding the issue to the younger. In over three quarters of the cases, children apparently recovered rapidly from the quarrels, appearing cheerful rather than resentful quickly thereafter.

This passage, paraphrased from an early observational study by Dawe (1934), contains much interesting data on the frequency, nature, and process of quarrels. As a bonus, it suggests the antecedents of the quarrels and provocative relationships deserving further study. We are not first to cite Dawe's work for its richness of description and its heuristic value (see also Weick, 1968; and Wright, 1960). Curiously, direct observation was in steady use as a psychological research method in the early part of this century—and probably at its peak in the 1930s—but its popularity declined from 1940 to 1960 (Hutt and Hutt, 1970). Even in child development, observation gave way to other "more experimental" methodologies, an unhealthy trend in the eyes of some (for example, see Wright, 1960). However, this declining trend seems to have reversed itself in the mid and late 1960s, perhaps in part because of the accelerated interest in Piaget and his methodological variances (including a heavy reliance on detailed observation). As was noted in Chapter One, interest in and proponents of observational measurement procedures are currently on the increase—hence, this chapter.

For our purposes, *observational measurement* is the process of systematic recording of behavior as it occurs, or of a setting as it exists, in ways that yield descriptions and quantitative measures of individuals, groups, or settings. We make a distinction between formal and informal observational measurement. *Formal* observational measurement is most often developed for and used in research studies. It typically involves defining categories carefully, constructing elaborate data forms, training observers and establishing their interreliability, and recording, analyzing, and interpreting data using relatively sophisticated procedures. *Informal* observational measurement, by contrast, denotes a less structured and less elaborate attempt (usually by an individual) to use systematic observational procedures to learn about others or about a setting. Thus, a teacher might use informal observational measurement to assist in planning a student's instructional program or to assist in determining why one student appears to be shunned by his peers. Both formal and informal observational measurement are considered in this chapter, but the former receives greater emphasis because formal observational measurement relates somewhat more directly to the development of measures with clear validity, reliability, and generalizable use. Informal observational measurement seems more relevant to instructional planning and day-to-day program operation, important but lesser concerns of this book. Of course, much of the material presented during the discussion of formal observational measurement has relevance, at a less intense level, to informal observational measurement.

Importance of Observational Measurement

Much recent literature extols the virtues of using direct observational procedures in natural or somewhat staged settings for generating knowledge of human behavior. Some advocates of observational measures stress the alleged shortcomings of other research methodologies; others take a more balanced view (for example, see Bersoff, 1973; Brandt, 1972; Carini, 1975; Hutt and Hutt, 1970; Willems and Raush, 1969; and Wright, 1967). Our view is that observa-

tional measures are valuable in their own right, as are the several types of measures and procedures outlined in the previous chapter. Carefully conceptualized
and applied, observational procedures can complement other measures available
for use in various settings. Further, observation is especially well suited for
recording processes, such as classroom activities.

Observational measurement is of particular importance in early childhood education for three reasons. First, and possibly most important, it affords a
means of measuring many child behaviors that might otherwise be unmeasurable. Very young children, say five years and under, have a limited response
repertoire, and especially if verbal-related. Thus, they may be unable to make
the response or provide the information that a more conventional measure, such
as an interview or a paper-and-pencil test, may require. Observational measurement may offer particular advantages in the affective domain. Walker surveyed
socioemotional measures for youngsters (see the source book section) and de-
duced "the most reliable and valid measures available at the present time are the
observational, nonverbal techniques" (1973, p. 38). In reaching this position, she
noted young children's limited test-taking skills, their variability in understanding test directions even when no verbal response was required, their response
instability from day to day, their intense eagerness to please adults (by giving the
presumed adult-appropriate response), and their egocentrism, which tended to
muddle both their concepts of self and their attitudes.

A second reason for the appropriateness of observational measurement in
early childhood education is that young children frequently fail to take testing
procedures seriously. It is as if the child has not yet learned the import of words
like, "Now try hard . . . this is very important . . . do your very best." Hutt and
Hutt indicated, "In general, the younger the child, the less likely he is to cooperate in investigations involving traditional psychological paraphernalia" (1970, p.
9). In most observational measurement, there is no requirement that the child
stay on-task in, or exhibit proper respect for, the measurement endeavor—
rather emphasis is on recording the child's behavior as it occurs naturally.

The third reason relates to the generally held assumption that very young
children are open and relatively unchanged or unperturbed by being observed.
As Thorndike and Hagen put it, "the young child has not developed the covers
and camouflages to conceal himself from public view as completely as has his
older brother and sister, so there is more to be found out by watching him"
(1977, p. 508). Wright believed that the younger the child, the fewer the compli-
cations that accompany observation. Further, he noted that even if the observer's
"presence attenuates especially the bad extremes of behavior from cuss words on
down" one is still left with "much that experimenters are never going to see in
laboratories in their inestimable best" (1960, p. 118).

Observational measurement of young children has historically been either
informal or formal. Informal measurement has occurred in settings where
adults use observation to determine how children behave and then to plan educational or other experiences for them. These informal procedures are not well
documented in terms of either frequency or quality, although we presume they
could be more effectively implemented in early childhood education (as a later

section of this chapter makes clear). Formal observational measurement has appeared almost exclusively in child development research or (more recently) evaluation efforts. Interestingly, when this mode of research has occurred, it has been overwhelmingly centered on children under the age of six years. Wright's (1960) survey suggests that over 90 percent of observational studies since 1890 have involved preschoolers and over half of these have taken place in nursery school settings. This concentration bespeaks the importance and appropriateness of observational measurement for young children. Further, it portends well for our purpose of proposing observational measures for early childhood education, in that it suggests that the observational methods developed for child study have been shaped primarily by young children's behaviors in school-like settings. Nevertheless, given the expanding concept of desirable processes and outcomes for "schooling," Wright's point is well taken: "It seems a likely guess . . . that observational methods in child development would now be suited to more problems if they owed less to the American nursery school and more to stores, streets, parks, vacant lots, swimming pools, and other settings that child psychologists rarely visit for research purposes" (1960, p. 77).

One of our intentions in this chapter is to alert the field to the potential utility, for measurement in early childhood education, of some middle ground between the areas we have defined as formal and informal observational measurement. Our approach here is to discuss formal and informal observational measurement in turn and to provide examples of each. However, the observational measures with the greatest potential utility in the field might very well combine formal and informal characteristics. To be more specific, low utility would characterize any observational measure requiring the elaborate training of observers (formal) or any measure depending more on the interest and inclination of the early childhood educator than on any specific observation skill or training (informal). Conversely, greater utility would characterize an observational measurement procedure requiring only moderate training to use or one needing only a single observer (performing at a pre-established criterion level) for implementation. Similarly, both the observational measure requiring many hours of spaced observation time (formal) and the one produced from a very brief sample of behavior but with dubious reliability (informal) would have low utility. By contrast, the observational measure that could be obtained in relatively short time segments and that would exhibit durable reliability would have substantial utility. Our contention is that many of the observational procedures described in this chapter as either formal or informal could be adapted and developed to exhibit these middle-ground characteristics and therefore to serve as valid, reliable, and useful observational measures in early childhood education. We return to this topic in the brief concluding section of this chapter.

Formal Observational Measurement

Formal observational measurement systems in education have originated primarily in research studies. Since they have drawn on the various social sciences with which education is closely related, such as anthropology, psychology, and sociology, they exhibit some variation in methodology. For example, some systems reflect a behavior modification orientation (Bijou and others, 1969), others are oriented toward clinical assessment (Jones, Reid, and Patterson, 1975; Palmer, 1970) or comparative psychology (Miller, 1977), and so forth. Formal observational measurement systems also vary in terms of their particular focus, with many focusing on teacher, parent, or child behaviors themselves, while others focus on the characteristics of particular settings, such as their "climate," their generation of participation, or their manning level (for example, see Barker, 1968; Medley and Mitzel, 1963; and Moos, 1973).

More specific to the age group of special interest in this book is the collection of seventy-three observation systems contained in *Measures of Maturation: An Anthology of Early Childhood Observation Instruments* (Boyer, Simon, and Karafin, 1973). This three-volume source, also in the source book section, demonstrated the variety of formal observational measurement systems that have been developed. This variety is reflected in the extensive classificatory system used. Thus, the observation instrument titled the Florida Climate and Control System or FLACCS (Soar, Soar, and Ragosta, 1971), designed to record the expression of positive and negative affect by teachers and students in the classroom (climate) and the structure of the class and teacher control measures (control), is classified in the anthology as follows:

Summary Data Reported on FLACCS:
- Subject of observation: Children and teacher/aides.
- Age of child recorded: Kindergartener; primary schooler.
- Number of children recorded: Three or more (identities not maintained).
- Setting: Kindergarten; primary school.
- Collection methods reported: Live (no special equipment needed).
- Collecting/coding staff needed: One person only.
- Coding units: Time sample.
- Uses reported by author: Descriptive research.
- System developed: 1971.

Category Dimensions Recorded Via FLACCS:
Individual dimensions:
- Psychomotor: Facial expressions; body activity and movement; sensory perception.
- Activity: Playing.
- Other: Expressions of affect.

Materials and physical environment dimensions:
- Materials used: Kinds of contacts.
- Physical environment: Social environment (people present, group size).

Social contact dimensions:
- Type of contact: Leadership/followership; affective communication; reinforcement patterns; information processing.

Development level rating scales: Interpersonal.
Key descriptors: Classroom climate and control.

This listing indicates the complexity of many of the formal observation systems. The anthology also contains a narrative section for each system, which elaborates the categories and details the use of the instrument. Several topics relevant to the development and implementation of formal observational measurement systems such as FLACCS will be considered in this section. Such formal observational systems have not been used frequently as measurement devices in early childhood education (except in research studies as noted). Nevertheless, their importance here is undiminished because their development, if carefully done, lays an appropriate base for establishing high quality psychometric instruments.

Methods for Formal Observational Measurement Systems. Several basic methods exist for formal observational systems. They are discussed here as "pure" types although, in many cases, they have been combined in actual operating systems. Table 9 contains selected information about five such methods: (1) specimen records, (2) time sampling (signs), (3) time sampling (categories), (4) event sampling, and (5) trait rating. Our discussion of these methods represents a synthesis of ideas and materials drawn from a group of key references (Brandt, 1972; Gordon and Jester, 1973; Medley and Mitzel, 1963; Weick, 1968; and Wright, 1960). Before discussing each method in greater detail and providing relevant examples, we will make some general comments about Table 9.

One dimension of observational measurement to note is the tendency of a given method to preserve the raw data for later analysis or reanalysis. A method that does preserve the raw data is termed *open,* while one that does not is termed *closed.* A closed method is considered more efficient, as the data recorded are already in coded form; however, this efficiency is purchased at a cost, since the raw data and their sequence of occurrence are lost. In Table 9, specimen records are clearly the most open procedure, as a sequential, detailed record of everything occurring is produced. This record is then available for subsequent analysis or reanalysis. (Certain other open procedures are discussed in the section of this chapter on informal observational measurement.) All the other methods listed in the table are closed in that they institute a coding scheme at the point of initial data collection. The sign time sampling method, however, does have some partial open features, in that pre-established specific acts or incidents of behavior (signs) are recorded if and when they occur and, thus, their sequence can be recorded.

Three additional distinctions between the formal observational measurement methods, each indirectly related to the open-closed dimension already noted, can be made. First, the methods vary in the extent to which they are theoretically based. Thus, the specimen record is essentially atheoretical, as everything is recorded. Category time sampling methods, conversely, are fairly narrow in their focus on a single category system—a focus often determined by a specific theoretical formulation. Thus, open systems, in general, are less likely than closed systems to be theory-based. A second distinction concerns how selective the method is in specifying behaviors to be observed. Specimen records are unselective in that no specific elements are preset for recording. Sign time sampling methods are partially selective (in that observers may have to record as many as fifty to sixty specific signs), and the other formal methods are quite selective. The relationship of selectiveness to the open-closed continuum is quite pronounced, with open methods appearing most often as unselective and closed methods seeming notably selective. The third difference between the methods concerns the degree of observer inference required, which is also linked to the open-closed dimension. Of the methods listed in Table 9, trait rating probably calls for the greatest amount of observer inference, while specimen records require almost none, although some inferences are at times included (and marked as such) to enrich the record. In the three sampling methods (sign time, category time, and event) some observer inference is required, but great efforts are taken to control its character.

A final general comment relevant to Table 9 concerns typical applications of each method. Wright (1960) distinguished four possible application aims: (1) ecological, (2) idiographic, (3) normative, and (4) systematic. *Ecological* aims are evident when the observation method is used to link children's behavior with conditions existing in natural settings—a type of natural history objective. Use of observation for this purpose is uncommon, but ecological psychology (Barker, 1968) has been increasingly in evidence. As noted in the table, specimen records at times have ecological aims, while event sampling also has such a potentiality. *Idiographic* application aims are central when observational studies focus on individual children, for purposes such as description, testing, interviewing, or diagnosis. Of the methods described in the table, only trait rating frequently has idiographic applications, while specimen records might on occasion. *Normative* aims in observational studies involve establishing central behavior tendencies in children of a given age group or some other definable classification. Thus, they are analogous to such aims in psychological testing. The time sampling and trait rating methods often have normative aims, and specimen records of certain types can enrich such norms. *Systematic* aims are predominant in observation studies that examine relationships between behavioral variables in order to derive generalizations. This purpose is characteristic of all the methods described with the exception of trait rating. A short description of each formal observation method will now be provided, along with relevant examples.

Specimen records: The specimen record method involves the observer in continuous observation and recording of everything that occurs within a specified context. The permanent records that typically result (called *running behavior records* by some) preserve both the nature and sequence of what transpired and are thus available for analysis by any number of schemes. A common analysis procedure first divides the full record or behavior stream into segments called *behavioral episodes* for examination; other analysis procedures have also been developed (Wright, 1960). The permanent record itself might consist of just movies, videotapes, or audiotapes, if mechanical observation means have been used, or some combination of mechanical recording and observer's notes. In any event, the method serves well to describe existing behavioral patterns in a wide range of situations.

A classic example of a specimen record is *One Boy's Day* (Barker and

Table 9. Characteristics of Formal Observational Measurement Methods

Formal Observation Method	Purpose	Time Coverage	Material Coverage	Recording Procedure	Relevant Descriptors and Application Aims
Specimen Records	To provide a comprehensive, descriptive, objective, and permanent record of behavior as it occurs.	Continuous within limited time periods (such as one hour).	"Everything" related to behavior and setting.	Making, on the spot, detailed sequential notations to produce a continuous record of behavior and events; could involve audio or video recording.	Open (preserves data for later analysis or reanalysis); atheoretical; unselective; no to moderate inference; ecological and systematic application aims (possibly idiographic and normative).
Time Sampling (Signs)	To identify and record the occurrence of preselected, well-defined discrete behaviors.	Intermittent yet uniform time periods.	Selected behavioral or setting variables; often a long list of infrequently occurring behaviors.	Recording, on the spot, the occurrence of certain behaviors; entry and notation made only if and when one of the behaviors occurs.	Open in some regards, closed in others; less theoretical; partially selective; low inference; normative and systematic application aims.
Time Sampling (Categories)	To make elementary discrimination and to classify behavior or behavior unit observed into one category from an available set.	Intermittent yet uniform time segments, usually short (such as five minutes or less).	Selected behavioral or setting variables; only a single category system in use at one time.	Coding, on the spot, behavior or behavior units into one category of several available; entry or notation made for every time or behavioral unit sampled.	Closed (does not preserve "raw data" for later analysis or reanalysis); theoretical; selective; low inference; normative and systematic application aims.

Event Sampling	To record the occurrence of preselected events of a given class.	Continuous within limited time periods (such as one hour).	Selected behavioral events of a given class.	Coding, on the spot or subsequently, occurrence of certain events; entry and notation made only if and when one of the events occurs.	Closed; theoretical; selective; low inference; systematic application aims (possibly ecological).
Trait Rating	To observe and, subsequently, to rate a person's (or persons') behaviors in terms of underlying traits.	Continuous within substantial time period, usually over a number of occasions.	Selected behavioral variables.	Observing and, subsequently, rating the presumed traits of persons based on their behavior.	Closed; theoretical; selective; moderate inference; idiographic and normative application aims.

Wright, 1951), which gives a minute-by-minute account of seven-year-old Raymond Birch's activities at home and school during a single April day (from 7:00 A.M. to 8:33 P.M.). Eight different observers, known by Raymond, took half-hour shifts. During the thirty minutes, the observer on duty made brief notes on a writing board and noted the passage of each minute. Once relieved, the observer dictated an elaborated account into a tape recorder using the sketchy notes as a guide. A listener present during the dictation noted unclear passages and afterwards interrogated the observer in order to flesh out the record. After several editorial refinements, a final record of 420 pages resulted. This observational endeavor and the resulting book did much to stimulate the field of ecological psychology (see Chapter Twelve).

An illustration of the method's use in an educational setting is provided by Gump (1969). The activities of six third-grade classes were recorded to determine how certain settings affected teacher and student behavior. Observers dictated reports of classroom occurrences into steno-masks and hence onto audiotapes. Additionally, a wide-angle lens camera automatically snapped a picture of the classroom participants every twenty seconds. Two full-day chronicles were established for each classroom. Although the observers focused on teachers, Gump argued that the resultant record was not of teacher behavior itself but rather of environmental operations—which, at this grade level, are typically controlled to a great extent by teachers.

Resultant chronicles were divided into behavior segments (such as word usage drill for the Red Reader Group or gym preparations for the total class). Segments were then diagramed to present a visual structure of classroom events. The time-lapse photographs produced were matched to behavior segments and various measures were derived, such as involvement or noninvolvement of each student in specific portions of each segment. These analyses led to several findings. External pacing of students (that is, by the teacher) led to more student involvement than self-pacing. Similarly, student involvement was higher in small-group configurations. Involvement tended to be less during start-up phases of an activity than in the remaining phases. Defining a "teacher act" as the shortest meaningful bit of behavior directed toward students, Gump found teachers averaged 1,300 acts per class day. Further, those teacher acts described under the category of dealing with deviant behavior increased in frequency during transitions from one classroom activity to another. Using the specimen record method in general, and findings such as these in particular, Gump was able to weave an interesting account of classroom transactions and even to supply some provocative hypotheses as to likely cause-and-effect relationships.

A final example of specimen records, in this case generated completely by mechanical means, is the study of the daily language environments of two one-year-old infants reported by Friedlander and others (1972). The house of each infant was "bugged" using sensitive microphones that activated for five minutes three times per hour (from 7 A.M. until 9 P.M.) and that recorded all sound sources. Subsequent analysis revealed that in one home, family speech was the major source of sound, while in the other, electronic sound sources (television and radio) predominated. Excluding the electronic sound sources, the patterns of the amounts of utterances in the two homes were similar and in the ratio of 7:5:3 for infants, mothers, and fathers, respectively. The infants' utterances were, of course, often babbling sounds. Finally, it was determined that mothers directed the most speech specifically at the infants.

Time sampling: The two systems of time sampling—by category and by sign—are best described together. In the category system, the observer focuses on a single dimension of classroom behavior, such as verbal utterances of the teacher, students' classroom attentiveness, or children's style of interacting with peers on a playground. The categories in the system are independent, mutually exclusive, and usually limited in number (say, no more than ten). For each time segment, the observer must classify the behavior just observed into one of the categories; for this reason, a miscellaneous (or "junk") category is included. By contrast, in the sign system the observer has a fairly long list of infrequently occurring behaviors to watch for and record. During a given time segment, the observer may or may not make a recording entry. In general, then, important behaviors that occur often should be observed using a category system, while infrequently occurring behaviors can be observed via a sign system.

Medley and Mitzel (1963) reported that observers using a category system are likely to be more relaxed in their task since the number of aspects of behavior they must consider is small. Further, after each short time segment, they make a decision as to the appropriate category of behavior for whatever was just observed and routinely make a recording entry. The cycle repeats quickly, so that the observer feels reasonably busy, but not too busy. The observer using a sign system, however, must wait and watch for infrequently occurring behaviors. As the list of behaviors is usually long, the observer has much to keep in mind and may be uneasy about possibly missing a sign. Further, there is often ample time to fret about a decision made. Nevertheless, since a sign system does keep track of a large number of behaviors, it is often preferred in early stages of studying a phenomenon, when several types of behavior seem of equal importance. The more narrow focus of category systems is often more appropriate after preliminary studies have been conducted.

An interesting illustration of the sign time sampling method is the work of Friedrich and Stein (1973) on the effects of children's behavior of viewing different types of television shows. Nursery school children, varying in age from nearly four to five and a half years, were assigned to three different types of programming: (1) prosocial ("Mister Rogers' Neighborhood"), (2) aggressive ("Batman" and "Superman" cartoons), and (3) neutral (films with minimal prosocial or aggressive content, such as travelogues). The children were observed during free play time in the school for nine weeks in all: three weeks before the differential viewing began (baseline); four weeks during the daily twenty- to thirty-minute treatments (viewing); and a final two-week period (postviewing).

Each child was observed in one-minute blocks for five minutes at a time, on three occasions daily. Observers watched for any of eighteen types of behavior, recording up to two such behaviors per minute. Examples of the eighteen behaviors were physical aggression, verbal aggression, cooperation, nurturance, rule obedience, tolerance of delay, and task persistence. By comparing baseline, viewing, and postviewing observations and including other child descriptor variables in the analysis, the investigators reached several conclusions. In the group viewing aggressive programs, the children who had been above average in aggression during the baseline period showed more interpersonal aggression during and after the viewing period than either the prosocial or neutral viewing groups. Further, the entire group on the aggressive viewing diet declined in rule obedience and tolerance of delay. Prosocial program viewers, especially those of above-average IQ, showed higher levels of task persistence and, to a lesser extent, higher rule obedience and tolerance of delay than children in the neutral viewing group. Further, children from lower socioeconomic status families who watched the prosocial programming displayed increased prosocial interpersonal behavior. The time sampling system using signs served as an effective method for observing the behaviors of interest.

A noteworthy example of a category time sampling system is the Flanders (1968, 1969) Interaction Analysis procedure. Although some have expressed concern about the orientation of the system and its underlying assumptions (see Stubbs and Delamont, 1976), it has been widely used with fair success. The procedure is concerned with observing, recording, and interpreting student-teacher interactions. Only verbal behavior of the students and teachers is considered, the assumption being that it is an adequate reflection of their total behavior; additionally, it can be observed more reliably than nonverbal behavior. Every three seconds, an observer using the system must classify the behavior just viewed into one of the ten categories listed in Table 10. The two major divisions of teacher talk and student talk are composed of seven and two categories each, while Category 10, silence or confusion, serves as the miscellaneous category. Teacher talk contains four categories of indirect teacher influence, which maximizes student opportunity. The three categories of direct teacher influence, lecturing, giving directions, and criticizing or justifying authority, limit the students' opportunities to initiate talk and respond. Student talk is made up of two categories: response and initiation. Once the categories are recorded, they are entered into matrices that both preserve the sequence of the observations and allow broad pattern analysis and interpretation (for example, proportion of teacher talk or student talk; extent of emphasis on content or on constructive integration; degree of interested acceptance or indifferent acceptance; and the like). In all, the system illustrates well a category time system and has enjoyed many applications. Our feeling is that the system has great utility, in its present form, for elementary school classrooms, but is much less applicable to youngsters in preschool educational settings. With substantial modification, however, the system would probably prove useful. Such changes might involve reducing the emphasis on just verbal behavior, adding additional student behavior categories, and the like.

An example of a category time sampling system used with children at eighteen and twenty-four months of age is provided by Van Lieshout (1975).

Table 10. Categories in the Flanders Interaction Analysis System

Teacher Talk

Response

Indirect Teacher Influence	1. Accepts feelings: accepts and clarifies the feeling tone of the students in a nonthreatening manner; feelings may be positive or negative; predicting or recalling feelings is included.
	2. Praises or encourages: praises or encourages student action or behavior; jokes that release tension, but at the expense of another individual; nodding head, or saying "um hm?" or "go on" are included.
	3. Accepts or uses ideas of students: clarifying, building, or developing ideas suggested by a student; as teacher brings more of his own ideas into play, shift to Category 5.
	4. Asks questions: asking a question about content or procedure with the intent that a student answer.

Initiation

Direct Teacher Influence	5. Lecturing: giving facts or opinions about content or procedures; expressing his own ideas, asking rhetorical questions.
	6. Giving directions: directions, commands, or orders with which a student is expected to comply.
	7. Criticizing or justifying authority: statements intended to change student behavior from nonacceptable to acceptable pattern; bawling someone out; stating why the teacher is doing what he is doing; extreme self-reference.

Student Talk

Response

8. Talk by students in response to teacher; teacher initiates the contact or solicits student statement.

Initiation

9. Talk by students which they initiate: if "calling on" student is only to indicate who may talk next, observer must decide whether student wanted to talk; if he did, use this category.

Silence or Confusion

10. Silence or confusion: pauses, short periods of silence, and periods of confusion in which communication cannot be understood by the observer.

Note: No scale is implied by the numbers. Each number is classificatory; it merely designates a particular *kind* of communication event. Thus, to write these numbers down during observation is to enumerate, not to judge, a position on a scale.

Source: Flanders, 1968, p. 128.

This study is a relatively pure instance of the category time sampling procedure and provides an example of a longitudinal study in that the same youngsters were observed twice, the second time six months after the first. After eighteen-month-olds played five to ten minutes with an attractive toy, their mothers placed the toy in a Plexiglas box where the child could see the toy but could neither reach it nor lift the box. Observations were made of the children's responses to this situation. The same procedure was followed when the child reached two years of age. Observations were made through a one-way window. Every six seconds, observers selected one of four categories: positive overtures toward the toy or the box; crying, emotional upset, or angry behavior directed at the toy or box; positive overtures toward the mother; or crying, emotional upset, or angry behavior directed at the mother. Observers also made a distance judgment every time interval, scoring whether or not the child was within 1.1 meters of the mother. Analysis of the observations revealed that positive coping behaviors decreased with the introduction of the barrier, while crying and angry behaviors toward the box and the mother increased. Many children attempted to overcome the barrier alone and then later turned to the mother to get help. This help-seeking behavior consisted more often of positive overtures than crying and anger, particularly when the children were two years old. The findings were interpreted further in terms of instrumental dependency or "social tool using" (that is, using mother as a tool to help solve the problem).

Event sampling: Event sampling systems involve studying preselected events of a given type, such as anger episodes or humor episodes. The observer is positioned so as to be able to note if and when the event occurs during a given time period. Certain aspects of the event are normally also recorded, but emphasis is on description rather than interpretation.

We have already considered an example of event sampling in the early Dawe study described previously. The event focused on in that study was quarrels among nursery school children. The observer would move quickly to the vicinity of the quarrel, start a stopwatch, and attend to elements of the situation. Once the quarrel ended, several aspects of the event were recorded: duration; name, age, and sex of participants; what the children were doing that apparently led to the quarrel; behavior during the quarrel such as vocal and motor activity; the outcome of the quarrel; and the after-effects.

Another interesting use of event sampling is a study centering on kindergarten teachers' handling of classroom misbehavior during the first four days of school (Kounin, 1970). In this formal observational study, a teacher's effort to stop a misbehavior was termed a *desist,* and the influence of the desist on other class members (that is, the nonoffenders) was called a *ripple effect.* When a teacher directed a desist at a misbehaving child, the observer recorded what the deviant child had been doing as well as activities of the audience (watching) student, the nature of the desist and the deviant child's immediate reaction, and the behavior for the next two minutes of the nearest student witnessing the desist. As was done in the Dawe study, observers waited until after the event to record particulars but did so immediately afterward to help assure fidelity of memory.

Subsequent analysis and interpretation of the data on the events led to categorizing desists in three ways: (1) clarity: the amount of information the teacher provided; (2) firmness: the degree of immediacy or "I-mean-it" quality the teacher conveyed; and (3) roughness: the anger or exasperation expressed by the teacher. Similarly, several kinds of ripple effect were identified: (1) no reaction: the audience student appeared unaffected by the desist incident; (2) behavior disruption: the child was confused, anxious, and restless; (3) increased conformance: the student exhibited more conformity, that is, stood or sat even "straighter"; (4) increased nonconformance: the child engaged in misbehavior of his own following the desist; and (5) ambivalence: both conformance and nonconformance behaviors were displayed by the child following the desist. Audience students' behaviors just prior to the desist were also classified as deviancy-linked (also misbehaving or watching the deviancy) or deviancy-free (engaging in legitimate work).

With such classifications and further analyses, Kounin reached a number of conclusions. The ripple effect did, in fact, occur. Children witnessing a desist on the first day of kindergarten showed more overt reaction than on following days. On the first day, incidentally, they were more likely to behave themselves, to conform, or to show behavior disruption after viewing a desist. Deviancy-linked children showed more conformity, nonconformity, and a mixture of both after witnessing a desist than did deviancy-free children, and they were more likely to decrease deviancy and increase conformity if the desist was high in firmness. Clarity of desist influenced both categories of children in the direction of conformity and was, in general, more a determiner of the nature of the ripple effect than was firmness. Although rough desists upset many children, their overall effect on conformity and nonconformity was slight. These and other findings illustrate the utility of the event sampling procedure.

Trait rating: A final common formal observational measurement system is trait rating. In this method, the subject is observed over several spaced sessions, during which time the observer may or may not have in mind a set of scales describing various dimensions of behavior. At some subsequent point, the observer uses a battery of trait scales to sum up impressions of the subject. Thus, unlike the previous methods, trait rating does not involve describing behavior in progress. Rather, stable ways of behaving that have been observed are rated and recorded after the fact. The variety of behaviors that can be so rated is essentially limitless. Note, too, that the same procedure can be and is applied to adults working in early childhood settings.

As an illustration, consider the following attempt to rate the traits of six Head Start teachers (Beller, 1969). A Head Start supervisor was asked to select three "good and effective" teachers and also three who were less effective. The supervisor based her decisions on such teacher characteristics as being warm, prepared, and child-oriented. Beller had scales related to these characteristics that he wished to validate. Observers then conducted twelve fifteen-minute observations in each of the six classrooms. After the sixth and twelfth observations, they filled out teaching style scales on the six teachers. Ten traits were rated: (1)

controlling children, (2) exhibiting closeness to children, (3) being oriented to the individual child, (4) giving approval and positive reinforcement, (5) enjoying teaching, (6) making a distinction between work and play, (7) providing a flexible classroom arrangement, (8) allowing children to select and control materials, (9) encouraging exploration, and (10) adhering to an organized schedule or planned program. A nine-point rating scale was used, with points 1, 3, 5, 7, and 9 accompanied by word descriptions (for example, for the sixth trait, the points were: 1—distinguishes always; 3—distinguishes often; 5—permits some overlap; 7—permits much overlap; and 9—makes very little distinction). On the first eight scales, expected differences were found between the three effective and three less effective teachers. That is, the "good" Head Start teachers were rated as more likely (1) to allow children a range of choices, (2) to be sensitive and responsive to children's needs, (3) to emphasize individual needs over group needs, (4) to use positive reinforcement liberally, (5) to be enthusiastic about teaching, (6) to make little distinction between work and play, (7) to permit flexibility in classroom arrangements, and (8) to allow children control of their own materials. However, the three less effective teachers were rated somewhat more likely to encourage exploration rather than to provide facts, information, and demonstrations (trait 9) and also less likely to adhere closely to a preplanned program (trait 10). Examination of the word descriptions on the two scales where reversals occurred reveals some ambiguity and, thus, uncertainty as to how well the two traits (as defined on the scale) link to the general dimension of teacher effectiveness; further, the number of teachers involved in the validation study was quite small. In all, Beller found moderate support for his trait rating scales via this procedure.

Establishing a Formal Observational Measurement System. We now consider briefly several of the most important concerns in establishing a formal observation procedure.

Determining the setting: Concern over the setting for observation is quite justified. Too often it is assumed that settings are pretty much alike and that one need simply select a convenient one. Weick (1968) argued convincingly for great deliberateness in site selection and even for modifications in the setting when warranted. He cited several reasons for such planning or modification. The first is that when the behavior of interest occurs infrequently, extensive observation resources must be expended in the process of simply waiting. A planned setting could evoke this behavior much sooner. Secondly, planning can also increase the likelihood of selecting or creating a setting that is neutral or equivalent in important regards for the children of interest; that is, so the children's prior history would not unduly cloud the interpretation of behaviors observed therein. Other reasons might involve decreasing the obtrusiveness of the observer, increasing the range of behaviors observed, invoking novel responses, influencing the magnitude of certain outcomes, clarifying incipient responses, and establishing the generality of an outcome.

Extensive modification of a setting quickly runs afoul of a cardinal reason often advanced for using observation—namely, to observe behavior as it naturally occurs. At what point does modification render the setting unnatural? Weick (1968) maintained that well-reasoned "subtle modifications" can improve observational efficiency. He acknowledged that modifications are less appropriate and probably unwarranted if one's purpose is simply to describe or record everyday behavior as it occurs in natural settings. However, he contended that if the hypotheses to be tested involve only a selected range of problems, the setting can be modified somewhat without destroying its essential naturalness.

We believe that subtle modification of settings is appropriate for observation and measurement in early childhood education—in part because of the generally unsuspecting nature of the young child. Subtle changes in the setting are unlikely to be noticed, or even if noticed, are unlikely to destroy the young child's perception of the naturalness of a given situation. Thus, if one's purpose is to measure young children's tolerance for frustration in a preschool setting, and frustrating circumstances seem in short supply, we see nothing particularly unnatural about reducing the available supply of toys, or rigging the drinking fountain so that it does not work, or the like. Such modifications seem within the range of normal happenings and should increase an observer's opportunities to view young children's tolerance for, and reactions to, frustration.

Determining categories and the behavior to be observed: Most observational procedures involve categorization at some point. Often categorization occurs during the very act of observing. In other cases, categories are applied subsequently (and may even be derived from the observations themselves). Categories must be explicit and defined in appropriate terms so that an observer can make correct and consistent discriminations. Further, the categories should not rely too heavily on contextual information, such as preceding events; the observer should be able to base the selection of category on just the immediate situation encountered. Other relevant concerns are the number and exhaustiveness of the categories in the system. As already noted, on-the-spot categorizing necessitates a limited number of mutually exclusive categories, including a miscellaneous category. All categories (except miscellaneous) should occur with some frequency, say at least 5 percent of the time or more, for both reliability and usability purposes; the hoped for exception is the miscellaneous category, as minimal information accompanies such entries. Systems that categorize after the fact have more flexibility in number of categories; in fact, if raw data have been recorded (as in the specimen record procedure), any number of category systems could be sequentially applied later.

Other critical aspects of the category system utilized are its reliance on observer inference and its susceptibility to the halo effect. The inference issue was introduced in Table 9. Kerlinger (1973) suggested that systems requiring higher degrees of inference were likely more useful in research because hypotheses under test are often less concerned with the behavior itself than with its probable meaning in a given context; discerning such meanings requires some inference. We agree with Kerlinger, particularly if competent observers are skillfully implementing "informed inference." This capability of a human observer clearly is unmatched by mechanical observers, such as television or audio recorders. Such informed inference does not occur automatically. Both explicit category definition and substantial observer training are required.

The *halo effect* refers to the tendency for an assessment of the characteristic of a person to be influenced by another characteristic or by a general impression of the person. Thus, a positive general impression could lead to more favorable ratings, and a negative impression, to less favorable ones. This human tendency can create substantial, even invalidating, problems for observation systems. For example, instead of making independent assessments on several behaviors or traits of an individual, an observer strongly influenced by the halo effect might simply mark each in a highly positive (or negative) direction. Vague categories pose difficult discriminations for observers and can easily lead to uninformed and inaccurate inferences; in such situations, the halo effect can be pronounced.

Related to the problem of categorization is the selection of the exact behaviors to be observed. This question is a critical one in early childhood education. Many observation systems rely heavily on subjects' verbal behavior. Although this may be warranted in the case of older children and adults, it is often inadequate for observations of young children. We suggest that many less obvious behaviors might profitably be observed, such as those addressed by the unobtrusive measures discussed in Chapter Two. Indeed, several of the observation studies already cited concentrated on other than verbal behavior. Available reviews (Brannigan and Humphries, 1972; and Weick, 1968) suggest several varieties of behavior suitable for observation.

Weick, for example, described in detail the observational use of several classes of nonverbal behavior. One class, of vocal if not exactly verbal behavior, is termed *extralinguistic behavior.* It includes variations in vocal pitch, loudness, rate of speaking, rhythm, and the like, as well as tendencies to interrupt, dominate, and inhibit. A second class, spatial behavior, includes the frequency and range of a person's movements, how close one is to another (such as the "nearness-to-mother" index in the Van Lieshout study discussed earlier), clustering, density, and laying claim to space and maintaining discrete distances from others (or proxemics). A third class consists of the exchanging of glances—that is, looking directly into another's eyes—often considered an important index to comfort and discomfort. A fourth group of behaviors, recently much heralded, are labeled *body movements,* or, more commonly, *body language.* Attention focuses particularly on the feet, head, and hands. A final class discussed by Weick is facial expressions such as eyeblinks or micromomentary expressions—that is, momentary changes in facial expression that can only be caught by motion picture films or video recordings.

Observation of nonverbal behavior is highly appropriate for studying young children in educational and other settings. Important contributions have already been made. For example, Jones (1971) has detailed criteria for describing children's facial expressions. Using 500 still photographs of children aged two to five years, he identified eight segments of the face to attend to (brow position, mouth shape, lip position, eye openness, tongue position, eye direction, lip separation, and teeth) as well as a miscellaneous category (including such items as wrinkling the nose, tooth grinding, shaking the head, and indenting cheeks). Each of the eight segments was subdivided; for example, six brow positions, each fully described, were raised brows, general frown, oblique brows, weak frown, strong frown, and contraction around the eye. Photographs to illustrate the various positions were provided such as in Figure 5.

One should not get the impression that observing young children's non-verbal behavior is patently easy because of the behavior's naturalness, visibility, and discriminability. Jones' criteria, for example, represent long and painstaking

Source: Jones, 1971, p. 378.

Figure 5. Analysis of Facial Expressions, with Emphasis on Eyebrows. (A) Strong frown while tugging a toy held by another child. (B) Inner corner of eyebrow turned up; also eyes bit wide, mouth corners down. (C) Oblique brows. (D) Two girls screaming; left one shows brow-raising, while right one shows contraction around the eye.

work. Or consider studies of teachers' ability to predict student comprehension of an algebra lesson based on silent films of the students' faces (Jecker, Maccoby, and Breitrose, 1965; Jecker and others, 1964). Prediction was very poor until either verbal cues were added to the film or teachers were given training in detecting comprehension from nonverbal cues. Thus, observer training must be rigorous and systematic, whether verbal or nonverbal behaviors are featured.

Selecting human or mechanical observers: Which means of observation to use is a frequent concern. Advantages typically claimed for human observers include their ability to shift frames of reference promptly, to be sensitive (that is, to receive signals and input via all the senses), and to make inferences from subtle cues. Proponents of mechanical observers, such as audio, film, or video recorders, often criticize human observers for their tendency to make inferences, which, they suggest, are often misleading or wrong. They laud mechanical observers for their fidelity in reproducing actual events, behaviors, and speech. Of course, advocates of human observers criticize mechanical procedures for their lack of sensitivity, their inability to infer, their rigid focus or frame of reference, and their troublesomeness when they need repair and operate poorly.

We view this issue as somewhat academic. In observation related to early childhood education, there is clear need for both types of observers. Human observers are needed for their sensitivity, flexibility, ability to make inferences, and absence of significant "downtime." Mechanical observation means are needed to make permanent, sequential records. Such records are especially useful early in an investigation for they can help in establishing categories or in permitting successive tryout of preliminary category schemes, recording forms, and the like. They can also prove invaluable in the training of human observers. For example, if an episode that is difficult to categorize is on videotape, it can be replayed and analyzed until observers in training can agree on how it should be recorded. Thus, we see human and mechanical observers as complementing one another rather than being in competition. Used together, they can provide a depth and richness of recording not otherwise possible. Thus, in the previously discussed study of environmental operations in a third-grade classroom (Gump, 1969), both human observers and time-lapse photos were used. In another case, both types of observers were used to study three-, four-, and five-year-old children's exploration of a novel mechanical toy (Hutt and Hutt, 1970). A very "classy" toy was used—a red metal box, mounted on four legs, with a movable lever, that could be made to produce sounds, lights, and numerical counters which accompanied various manipulations of the lever by the child. A human observer used a category system to record the frequency and nature of exploratory acts by the child directed toward the novel toy. Simultaneously, a film record of the child's behavior was made. Subsequent analysis procedures involved synchronizing these diverse observations. It was ascertained that the holding power of the toy, in terms of children's attending to and investigating it, rapidly decreased over a six-day period. Other more complex and finer conclusions were also possible given the variety of observation data available. For example, the researchers discerned a qualitative shift over time in the children's responses to the toy—from investigation to play. That is, children's inspections of the toy during the first two days involved visual fixation, simultaneous manipulation, and serious facial expressions suggesting concentration; by the last two days, responses to the toy were almost nonchalant, with less concomitant vision and manipulation directed toward the toy, and relaxed, even smiling, facial expressions common.

Assuring the unobtrusiveness of the observer: Much has been written about observer interference or obtrusiveness. In general, concern centers on whether the presence of the observer might alter the very behavior or event being observed or measured. This concern is related to the earlier question about the naturalness of the setting—how natural is it to have someone intently watching your every action? The findings of the well-known study at the Western Electric Hawthorne plant (the Hawthorne Effect) demonstrated that workers' production improved when researchers began displaying interest in their work. Weick (1968) reported a study showing that psychotherapy clients made significantly more positive comments about themselves when being taped, and significantly more negative self-references when not being recorded. Closer to the field of early childhood education is a study in which mothers were observed through one-way glass as they interacted with their five-year-old children (Zegiob, Arnold, and Forehand, 1975). At different times, mothers were informed that the observation was occurring (informed condition) or led to believe that no observation was underway (uninformed condition). Under the informed condition, mothers played more with their children, structured their children's activities more, and used more positive verbal behavior. For other, related studies, see Kent and Foster (1977).

When adults are being observed, then, three key points deserve attention (Herbert, 1970; Medley and Mitzel, 1963; and Weick, 1968). First, the observed's anonymity must be assured, if so promised. Second, the purpose for the study and the use of the data collected must be set forth explicitly; this process should reduce suspicion of the motives behind the observation. Third, a sufficient number of observation periods must be scheduled to allow the novelty of the situation to wear off. This third point was well illustrated in a large study that shall remain unnamed (given pledges of anonymity made by us to the East Coast researcher). The study involved repeated visits to homes to observe mothers interact with their young children. On the first several early-morning visits, observers were frequently met at the door by immaculately dressed mothers and ushered into spotless homes. After a few visits, however, this "girdle-on phenomenon," as the researcher termed it, all but disappeared and the observers were made privy to more ordinary early morning appearances and routines.

Some persons might suggest circumventing the obtrusiveness problem by concealing the observation. However, this unleashes (particularly these days) a host of questions surrounding the ethics of concealed observation, unless the behavior or events being observed are already open to public inspection (such as behavior aboard a bus or on a playground). Other procedures to reduce observer obtrusiveness have been identified, such as recording behaviors not under the conscious control of the subject (for instance, nail-biting), ordering data collection so that the most descriptive measures are administered last, using persons naturally on the scene as observers, or using unobtrusive data such as archives or erosion and trace measures mentioned in Chapter Two (Weick, 1968).

When young children are being observed, we believe that assuring the unobtrusiveness of the observer is a much simpler task. Of course, even with young children, it is helpful for the observer to first "be around" for a while to seem more a part of the natural environment. In general, however, and as noted early in this chapter, young children seem only minimally concerned with concealing or camouflaging their behavior from observers. Connolly and Smith (1972) studied directly the reactions of preschool children to observers. In all, they concluded that most children quickly accommodate to a passive observer and, after a few sessions, respond minimally to the observer's presence. If, however, the observer openly responded to children by smiling and talking, children were likely to increase their approaches to the observer. Observer passivity and "commonness," achieved by being present for several sessions, should be sufficient in most cases to assure observer unobtrusiveness. To illustrate this point, consider this actual situation: A passive observer was seated and recording the behavior of two four-year-olds. A ball had rolled over by the observer and was resting against his shoe. One child asked the other where the ball was and was told, "It's over there by the leg."

Establishing reliability: Reliability speaks to the consistency, dependability, or generalizability of data recorded. Such consistency is important to ensure that a stable phenomenon is involved. Historically, users of observation systems have been most interested in interobserver agreement as the principal measure of reliability. Such a reliability coefficient estimates the extent to which two (or more) independent observers agree on the judgments they make. As noted, it is analogous to interrater reliability, discussed in Chapter Three. The usual procedure followed is to have two persons simultaneously but independently observe a given situation. The category codes assigned by the two observers are then compared to determine agreement. It has been well established that the extent of observer agreement is highly dependent on the degree of complexity of the coding system and of the discriminations required of the observers; the more complex the system and the discriminations, the lower the interobserver reliability (Jones, Reid, and Patterson, 1975; and Mash and McElwee, 1974).

Close observer agreement must usually be established before formal data collection can begin. This both assesses the adequacy and explicitness of category definition and justifies using individual observers on their own, a considerable saving in observer-time resources. Several procedures have been developed to increase interobserver agreement. They are listed below; the reader will recognize several of them from other contexts:

1. Establish explicit categories so that observers can be clear on coding distinctions.
2. Seek competent persons to serve as observers, especially those with previous observing experience.

3. Provide monitored training in use of the category system.
4. Compare observer judgments during training with some established standard or judgments by other observers of the same behavior events.
5. Utilize videotape when appropriate so that the stimuli for observer judgments can be repeated, discussed, and agreed upon.
6. Establish standard observational procedures for all observers, such as determining exactly how adults being observed will be informed of the purpose of the observation, setting "professional" and standard rules for observers regarding their general demeanor and approachability, their protecting of subject anonymity, and the like.

Even after interobserver agreement has been established, it is a common procedure to periodically pair observers to reassess their agreement and to ensure that slippage has not occurred. This procedure to assure maintenance of interobserver reliability at high levels has recently been questioned (Jones, Reid, and Patterson, 1975; and Reid, 1970). They suspect that such periodic rechecks overestimate interobserver reliability because during rechecks observers are more careful, or they tend to simplify their recordings and to avoid subtle and difficult discriminations, or they subtly influence subjects to act differently (possibly more simply) when being observed by both of them simultaneously.

The extensive attention given to interobserver agreement should not mask other legitimate reliability concerns. One of these is the stability of a single observer's judgments over time (analogous to the coefficient of stability addressed in Chapter Three). An obvious problem in establishing this type of reliability is having an event recur in essentially its original form, although a videotape recording might be used for such a purpose. Conceivably, too, internal consistency reliability (Chapter Three) might be established by examining an observer's single-session codings for consistency much as random halves of a test are compared. Another critical type of reliability, which actually takes precedence in importance over interobserver reliability, is the stability of the actual behavior or type of event being observed. Such stability can ordinarily be assumed if a sufficient number of observations of the same person or same setting are made. Thus, instead of conducting just a single observation and assuming that it is representative, an observer schedules a series of observations to increase the probability that they will average to a good estimate of typical behavior. Generalizability theory (Cronbach and others, 1972) provides a complex but appropriate means for addressing multiple types of reliability; actual examples applying generalizability theory to observational studies are available (for example, see Jones, Reid, and Patterson, 1975). Frick and Semmel (1978) have provided a comprehensive review of reliability and classroom observational measures.

The importance of establishing reliability in an observation system should not be underestimated. Under a general section titled "Calibrating the Observer," Weick (1968) presented additional, related concerns including training to neutralize known human biases such as reductionism, middle-message loss, bias toward central tendency, previous history as an observer, and the like. Mash and McElwee (1974) likewise suggested that observer accuracy is situation-dependent. Reliability must be thoroughly addressed as its adequacy sets an upper bound on the validity of an observational system or measure.

Establishing validity: It is critical to establish the validity of an observation system for its purported use(s). Validity is used here in the same sense as in Chapter Three. Thus, a formal observational measurement system can be assessed in terms of its content, criterion-related, and construct validity. However, developers of observation systems typically do not report on validity (for an exception, see Jones, Reid, and Patterson's Behavioral Coding System, 1975). Therefore, we present hypothetical validity applications rather than actual applications. Possibly observation system developers do not address validity concerns because they consider their procedure a direct assessment of a behavior or characteristic (as distinct from an indirect assessment, such as a paper-and-pencil test, for which validity must be established). Nevertheless, observations are only a measure of reality and not reality itself (especially when observer inference is high); thus, demonstrating the validity of observation systems is essential.

Content validity of the observation instrument refers to the representativeness of the behaviors recorded in terms of the universe of situations the instrument is supposed to assess. Suppose that an observation system purports to chart the variable "behaviors of five-year-olds that are noxious to teachers and parents." Immediate content validity issues are, first, the adequacy and exhaustiveness of the categories being used and, second, the coverage of the observations planned. With regard to the first issue, experts should be used to review the intended categories. Thus, an expert parent panel might review the existing list of noxious behaviors and add "whining" and "failing to come when called." Teacher-experts might review the list and suggest adding "bullying" and "refusing to wait to take one's turn." Use of the categories thus derived might result in further additions or deletions. The second issue involves examination of the scope and setting of the planned observations; thus, it partially overlaps with ensuring a stable view of the behavior assessed, as discussed previously under reliability. Given the behavior of interest, it would seem that both at-home and at-preschool observations are essential, as are several observation sessions in each setting to reduce the prominence of atypical events. Other settings might be included to provide even more complete coverage, such as routes between home and preschool or preschool-related evening or Saturday events. This expanded coverage might, in turn, lead to additional categories of noxious behavior such as "taking risks near traffic" or "disrupting others trying to watch a performance."

Criterion-related validity (predictive or concurrent) of formal observational measurement systems might often be an important consideration. Predictive validity might appropriately be required of many observation systems depending on their self-proclaimed utility. Thus, imagine that the system described earlier entailing children's reactions to the mechanical toy (Hutt and Hutt, 1970) was purported to predict preschoolers' subsequent tendencies to explore, to be inquisitive, and to persevere. A longitudinal investigation would provide criterion data, which could then be correlated with the initial observations of the children's exploratory behavior.

The other type of criterion-related validity, concurrent, might be pursued in the process of validating an observation system. As an illustration, recall the Van Lieshout study (1975) examining very young children's responses to having a Plexiglas box placed over an attractive toy. At the same time that those observations were made, other means of establishing the children's tolerance for frustration could also have been implemented. Thus, via a clinical assessment, psychologists could have judged each child's tolerance for frustration. These clinical outcomes and the results from the observations could then have been correlated to generate an estimate of concurrent validity.

Construct validity of an observation system involves determining the extent to which a theoretical construct or trait is measured. As such, construct validity concerns the gradual accumulation of data from a variety of sources (often including content and criterion-related validity). Assume that an observation system is designed to assess the anxiety of three-, four-, and five-year-olds. Derived from a theory of anxious behavior, the system and its categories are tried out in various empirical studies. If certain expected categories of anxious behavior never occur in the age group of interest, then the original theoretical construct of anxiety might well require modification (or even abandonment). Assuming, however, that the predicted categories do occur, this is only partial evidence of construct validity. Other procedures available to help establish construct validity include correlations with other measures, factor analysis, developmental changes, effect of other experimental variables on the construct as measured, and convergent and discriminant validation (Anastasi, 1976). For example, the anxiety levels observed in children could be correlated with clinicians' judgments of their anxiety; this determination of concurrent validity would also address construct validation. Or, assume that children's anxiety levels were first determined using the observation system, and then that a random half of the children were exposed to a situation thought to be anxiety-producing while the other half were not. The anxiety-producer might be news of an impending tornado alert, water crisis, or health crisis, or a fictitious horror story (ethics would demand that the children not be misled, however). Then, the observation system would again be used to assess amount and types of anxiety present. If the anxiety of the children exposed to the disquieting stimulus was found to be higher than that of the children not so exposed, this fact could be used in support of the construct validity of the categories and the observational method.

In general, many methodological issues surround the creation and operation of formal observational measurement systems. The most critical issues, in our opinion, center on reliability and validity. A similar orientation is reflected in the review of Kent and Foster (1977). They noted increased attention by researchers to directly studying methodological issues of observation in naturalistic settings. Further, they predicted a convergence of such investigations with considerations from more traditional test procedures.

Informal Observational Measurement

This section describes informal observational measurement techniques applicable in many early childhood educational settings. Whereas formal observational measurement techniques derive primarily from research investigations, informal procedures more often directly appeal (or even owe their origin) to adults in daily contact with young children in nursery schools and preschools. Further, informal observation of children is commonly practiced by early educators because its outcomes can be more immediately applied to instructional planning for, and daily operations with, children. The techniques would be equally applicable in school situations for older children, but possibly not as critically needed since several additional measurement methods are typically available for older persons. Focus here is exclusively on techniques that early childhood teachers might use in their work with young children, although persons other than teachers obviously could also utilize the procedures (such as aides, parents, student teachers, college or high school students, and the like).

In passing, it should be noted that teachers could and do use certain formal observational measurement procedures, although ordinarily with less rigor than was implied in that earlier discussion. The most obvious example is trait rating; many report cards or similar documents solicit teacher judgment of student traits, often performance- or personality-related. Also, a teacher highly motivated to initiate a time or event sampling procedure probably could. For example, an aide or other adults could work with the class while the teacher observes and records the behavior of one or more students. Or the teacher might, on days when not required to supervise outdoor activities, function as an observer of children as they interact on the playground. In quite another sense, a teacher might arrange for video or audio taping of the class in operation, and then apply category schemes to the recordings when class was not in session. In each case above, the teacher follows a formal observational measurement procedure, making modifications as necessary. The infrequency with which formal observational procedures are used by teachers should not suggest that the procedures are either impossible or inappropriate for their use.

The four informal observational measurement methods detailed here are frequency counts and charts, checklists, anecdotal records, and diary descriptions. Several sources (Brandt, 1972; Cartwright and Cartwright, 1974; Gordon, 1966; Rowen, 1973; and Wright, 1960) were consulted for our descriptions of the four methods. Interested readers reviewing the sources will find varying terminology used, but some general agreement on acceptable procedures. Other sources link observation to classroom activities and content areas (for example, see Lindberg and Swedlow, 1976).

Frequency counts, as the term implies, simply involve keeping a running tally of a certain type of behavior as it occurs. *Frequency charts* represent a graphic means to present the data collected. Frequency counting and charting have received much of their current impetus from behavior modification and precision teaching, but the methods have utility whether or not they originate from such sources. As in formal observation, precise definitions of the behaviors to be counted are necessary. Sometimes the behavior of interest is better represented by its duration than simply by a count of the times it occurs. In such situations, frequency counts and charts are, in effect, replaced by *duration records* and *charts.*

To illustrate frequency counts and charts, imagine that a preschool teacher is interested in children's cooperative behavior during free play. With the classroom aide, the teacher defines and writes out exactly what constitutes cooperative behavior, such as sharing a toy, helping on a group task, and the like. Then, a record form is made listing the children and leaving space to tally instances of cooperative behavior. The teacher and the aide agree to watch different children for five minutes each across several days, so that a total of twenty minutes—ten minutes by each observer—is accumulated for each child. The data generated on the cooperative behavior can then be charted, using any of several traditional means, such as bar graphs. Once these basic frequency data are available, several additional measures can be determined. For example, each child's rate of cooperative behavior per minute can be calculated by dividing frequency by twenty, and comparisons can be made between cooperative behavior rates for boys and girls or for older and younger children, and the like. Note, too, that the teacher and aide might select a few children who show little cooperative behavior, concentrate on helping them see the benefits of such behavior (the treatment period), and then recheck later, using frequency counts, to determine if any change has occurred in their frequency or rate of cooperative behavior. (If the frequency of cooperative behaviors were also monitored during the treatment period, the procedure would correspond to the traditional behavior modification paradigm, which consists of three steps: establish baseline, institute treatment, and determine effect once treatment is terminated; see Chapter Twelve.)

To demonstrate the use of duration records, suppose that a second-grade teacher wishes to record children's participation in fifteen-minute story-telling sessions in which the children are to provide the stories. The story-telling is done in groups of eight children, with the classroom aide facilitating the sessions. A form is designed with a place to list the children in the group and also to record, in seconds, the actual duration of each child's participation. Then, for several weeks, the aide uses a stopwatch and enters the number of seconds that each child participates. Before charting the results, the teacher must determine each student's rate of participation per fifteen-minute session since some students miss sessions because of absence from school. Then, the teacher charts the rates so that comparisons can be easily made.

Checklists involve recording whether or not specific behaviors are displayed in given situations. Usually, considerable effort is required to derive the list of behaviors that one could reasonably expect to be demonstrated in the situation. A list of the behaviors is provided for each child; the observer then simply marks those behaviors that are displayed by the child during the observation period. As was indicated in the discussion of checklists in Chapter Two, the checklist procedure is used by some teachers in criterion-referencing—that is, to indicate which behaviors a student can, in fact, display.

Suppose a Head Start teacher wants to chart changes in the ability of children in the class to perform certain physical movement tasks. Consulting books on psychomotor behavior, the teacher is able to construct a checklist of appropriate behaviors, such as "bouncing a large ball four or more successive times," "catching a tennis ball three times in a row," "skipping for a distance of twenty-five feet," and so forth. These behaviors are listed on a record form, with a box to check by each behavior if it is observed during the designated observation period.

Anecdotal records represent a well-known informal observational measurement method. Written by the teacher and filed for future reference, a complete anecdotal record would ordinarily have the following characteristics:

1. Results from direct observation of a child.
2. Describes promptly, accurately, and specifically a given event.
3. Includes sufficient detail and setting information to place the event in appropriate context and give it meaning (including direct quotes by the child or by principal respondents).
4. Separates, and identifies as such, any interpretation or inference made about the event by the recorder.
5. Represents either typical or unusual behavior for the child (if unusual, this is noted).

If an anecdotal record possesses all five characteristics, it should be a fairly dependable record of actual behavior.

An important question concerns what behaviors to record via this method. As implied in the fifth characteristic above, emphasis should be on events that demonstrate a child's typical behavior or strikingly unusual behavior. Some sources suggest recording events highlighting personality characteristics or adjustment rather than those bearing on achievement, creativity, intelligence, or problem solving. Their reasoning is that other types of measures are more appropriate than anecdotal records for documenting the latter behaviors. With very young children, however, we would encourage teachers to use anecdotal records more liberally, also covering these cognitive areas. Finally, note that anecdotal records take on greater utility if filed for ready access and if reviewed, summarized, and studied periodically.

As an example of an anecdotal record, consider the following written by a first-grade teacher.

> Date: 9/11/80   Student: Ben Miller
> Shortly after recess, Sharon screamed. A harmless garter snake was in her desk. After the class calmed down, Ben Miller produced a paper sack and offered to escort the snake outside. I agreed. After school I had Ben stay and asked him if he had put the snake in Sharon's desk. He said,

"Don't you like snakes, either?" I repeated my question. Ben started to cry, mumbling something about liking snakes and not knowing why others didn't. Once Ben stopped crying, I told him I would be glad to talk with him about snakes later on if he wanted to. Ben nodded "yes" and left.

(Interpretation: This was unusual behavior for Ben. My past impression has been that he tries to be friendly toward his fellow students. In fact, his relationship with Sharon has seemed especially positive. Could it be that he was actually sharing a valued prize with her even though that seems unlikely? I wonder where he got the snake? Whole situation bears close attention for a while.)

This brief introduction to anecdotal records should not imply that they are routinely easy to write and use. In fact, many problems can arise related to avoiding bias in determining what events to record, phrasing anecdotes appropriately, minimizing related clerical tasks, and using such records productively (Thorndike and Hagen, 1977).

A final informal observation method is the *diary description*. Diaries are similar in several ways to anecdotal records, but they differ in their planned longitudinal character and the ordinary requirement that there be a continuing, frequently occurring relationship between the recorder and the observed. Emphasis is on recording new behaviors demonstrated by a single child. These unique characteristics of diary description probably limit its utility for teachers in ordinary settings. Teachers seldom have a continuing, extensive relationship with a given student, and they are also unlikely to have the opportunity to attend closely to the behavior of a single child. Nevertheless, a descriptive diary or some modification thereof may make sense in certain special situations. Sources exist that detail the procedure of making diary descriptions (for example, see Wright, 1960).

Advantages and Limitations of Observational Measurement

The use of observational measurement in early childhood education has distinct advantages and limitations. Although several of these apply to both formal and informal observation, most apply more directly and intensely to the formal systems; this is especially true for the limitations.

Advantages of Observational Measurement. The first advantage apparent for observational measurement is that it gives a direct measure of actual behavior. One need not create an elaborate rationale to infer from indirect data sources what behavior might be displayed in an actual situation. In this regard, observation clearly provides more credible data, on the average, than attitudinal questionnaires or other self-report means. This advantage is well illustrated in a study reported by Sechrest (1969). Via a questionnaire, subjects reported they would be more likely to honk at, and show impatience with, a high-status, elegant car blocking traffic than a low-status, inexpensive car. In an actual empirical test, however, with latency before onset and frequency of honking as dependent measures, a stalled low-status car was honked at more quickly and more frequently. Although questionnaires might seldom be used with very young children, they are frequently used with adults working in early childhood education settings.

A second advantage, related to the first, is that observation avoids several limitations of other measurement methods. For example, it can avoid the distortion produced in after-the-fact reports by poor memory, reductionism, and other factors. It also avoids the problem of subjects' reluctance to respond frankly to interviews or questionnaires if they believe the information provided may reflect adversely on themselves or their friends. If appropriately unobtrusive, observation can, in general, avoid reactivity of the subjects to the situation, thereby increasing the probability that typical behavior is recorded. If truly unobtrusive, observation might even permit studying topics that would be "unsafe" or impossible to make "real" in laboratory studies (Weick, 1968). Examples might be observing the imposition of unfair hiring and employment practices against certain groups desiring to work in early childhood education settings, the rate and type of reinforcement provided by teachers to children representing different identifiable ethnic or socioeconomic groups, or the reactions of young children to learning of a classmate's serious injury or death.

A third advantage of observational measurement is its widescale applicability. Virtually every natural setting is open to observation of some sort. Thus, it is possible to imagine suitable observation procedures for essentially every aspect of early childhood education—from child to adult behaviors, from highly informal to heavily structured programs, and from elaborately furnished educational settings to those with the bare minimum. Of course, even given this advantage, some natural settings are easier and more appropriate to conduct observations in than others. Nevertheless, observational measurement's widespread applicability stands as an important advantage of the method.

A fourth strength of observation is its generation of extensive descriptive and detailed data. Certain formal observational measurement methods, like specimen records, preserve essentially the entire event or behavior with many embellishments; other formal methods record essential features and, sometimes, sequence of occurrence. This exhaustive approach to data collection has particular value in early stages of studying and measuring behavior, as has already been noted. The extensive data accumulated provide a fertile base for testing various hypotheses, applying different category systems, and the like. At the same time, the data serve a heuristic function, assisting in the generation of new, provocative hypotheses.

A fifth strength of observational measurement is its marked appropriateness for young children. This theme has threaded its way through the chapter. Observation opens for measurement many behaviors of young children that might otherwise be unmeasurable, particularly in the affective domain. To be observed, children need not be sophisticated in verbal communication—they need not be able to read or to understand directions. It has also been noted that young children are least likely to find observers obtrusive for any substantial time period and therefore are not prone to camouflage or alter their behavior.

Observation allows direct measurement of behaviors without requiring either introspection or retrospection, processes difficult and suspect even for adults. Available observational procedures assess numerous characteristics, such as accident-proneness, aggression, aspiration, attention, autonomy, creativity, curiosity, dependence, imitation, play behaviors, self-concept, sex-typing, and temperament.

A sixth advantage of observational measurement, periodically implicit in this chapter, should be made explicit. Whereas many measures in use in early childhood education focus on behaviors that are outcome-oriented (such as performance on a vocabulary or readiness test or on a series of psychomotor tasks), observation is uniquely suited to measure ongoing, interactive processes. One large and important class of such processes involves interactions of children with each other, with significant adults, and with their environment in general. For example, this chapter has detailed the use of observation to describe activities in a third-grade classroom (Gump, 1969), playground behavior after varied television viewing (Friedrich and Stein, 1973), teachers' approaches to classroom misbehavior (Kounin, 1970), and so forth. This capability of capturing ongoing processes is a distinctive feature of observational measurement—qualitatively different from the static tone of most measures attempting to assess outcomes.

A final advantage of observational measurement is its apparent appropriateness in the eyes of substantial numbers, probably a majority, of adults working in early childhood education. Observation matches well the philosophical leanings of these adults, in a way that paper-and-pencil tests and other more obtrusive measurement methods do not. Observational measurement, more than any other method, leaves intact the natural scheme of things, whether by this adults mean the spontaneous behavior and play of the child, the child's developmental unfolding from within, or the child's freedom from being subjected to tasks, problems, and situations contrived to generate various measurement outcomes. In some early childhood education settings, the popularity of adult observation is in dramatic contrast to the unpopularity of other measurement strategies.

Limitations of Observational Measurement. A major limitation cited for observational measurement is its cost. Each step of developing and implementing a formal observational measurement can involve large expenditures of time and other resources. Salient in this regard are developing a category system, training observers, conducting a full schedule of observations, and analyzing recorded data. Such time and resource expenditures may not be excessive for research studies (see Herbert, 1970), but for measurement purposes they may appear unacceptably high, compared with the costs for other measurement devices such as paper-and-pencil tests. As we noted in the section on informal observational measurement, inexpensive and relatively quick approaches to observation do exist, but such approaches have shortcomings. In general, cost limitations are real and must be addressed early in the development of an observational system.

A second limitation concerns the adequacy of any category system developed for use in recording or analyzing observational data. The importance of developing and using logical and explicit categories has been stressed throughout the chapter and need not be reviewed. At some point, every observation system becomes quite selective in terms of what behavior is attended to or what aspects of recorded behavior are analyzed—the category systems used are an embodiment of this selectivity. Thus, the significance of the eventual interpretation made of observations rests heavily on the adequacy of the categories themselves.

A third limitation stems from the shortcomings of the observers used. This limitation applies to both human and mechanical observers, even if used in combination. Since human observers are present in most cases, the principal concern is their subjectivity and bias. These tendencies can be controlled through extensive training and other procedures, but they are never fully eliminated. Human observers' ability to infer makes the data considerably richer than they would otherwise be, but the accuracy of inferences must be frequently examined.

A fourth limitation, previously noted, concerns the observer's obtrusiveness. This presents a problem especially when adults are being observed. It may be particularly disquieting to some adults if an observer refuses to supply information when requested, or observes a group while steadfastly refusing to participate in any way. Concealment of the observer might solve this problem, but leave in its place an even more significant ethical problem. It is apparent that some adults resist being observed, although such resistance may be overestimated (for example, see Herbert, 1970). A few adults might possibly persevere in presenting other than typical behavior for the observer to record, but there are obvious limits to extended efforts at "faking good." This limitation must be considered; open disclosure of the purpose of the observation and appeals to professionalism (say, to teachers of young children) might help alleviate it.

A final limitation concerns the nature of observation itself. In the process of developing discrete behavioral categories, a typical progression is to focus on smaller and smaller bits of behavior. Further, to help reduce observer subjectivity and bias, procedures are instituted to keep the observer detached from the situation. This focus on small bits of behavior and on "objectivity" can result in an artificiality in the data generated (that is, data that are narrow and antiseptic, possibly even trivial), even though observing in a natural setting and incorporating elaborate attempts at unobtrusiveness were components introduced primarily to preserve the "realness" of any behavior observed.

Practical Applications

The potential fertility of some middle ground between formal and informal observational measurement for early childhood education measures should be re-emphasized. Formal observation systems have primarily been developed for and used in research studies, while the informal systems have been emphasized in teacher-initiated undertakings. Nevertheless, any number of the observation studies and procedures described in this chapter could be adapted to produce practical measures for use in early childhood education. Adaptation might mean requiring a moderate amount of observer training—rather than either an extensive or a limited amount—and also a moderate period of observation to get a stable measure of some child or adult behavior. If it is intended that the early childhood educator be the observer, then some flexibility in the educator's schedule must be provided for, possibly by making an aide available to free the teacher for portions of the day.

To see how observation studies might be adapted for measurement use in early childhood education, let us consider three hypothetical, but realistic, applications of the methods developed by Chase (1905), Finlayson (1972), and Smith and Geoffrey (1968).

As a first illustration, assume that the kindergarten teachers in a given school were concerned about their physical education program. The district was unable to provide a specialist to assist them. The most noticeable problem was extensive disinterest and disagreement among the children about the outside games that they were directed to play. Arguments were frequent and different children seemed unmotivated to take part in particular games. The teachers attempted to survey the students but gave up because many children could not describe their favorite outdoor games and others, who could, often labeled the games differently or presented strange combinations of several games. As a result, outdoor physical education continued to be chaotic, and the teachers found themselves rejoicing when it rained.

Then one teacher, in connection with a college class, came across an early and simple procedure used by Chase (1905). Chase, the Head Worker at Maxwell House in Brooklyn, was somewhat distrustful of self-reports of street games liked by most New York City children. So he spent many days walking through tenement districts and tabulating the games played, the number of children involved, their apparent interest, and the date. He then tabulated the ten most popular games regardless of season. In order, they were: playing with fire (bonfires, fire in buckets), craps, marbles, potsie (an early form of hopscotch), leapfrog, jumping rope, baseball, cat (a short stick is made to bounce in the air and is then hit with a bat by one boy, while a second boy throws the short stick back as near the starting point as possible), buttons (buttons are thrown or rolled toward a curb or wall, with the object of ending up closest to it), and spinning tops. Inspired by Chase's work, the kindergarten teacher proposed to the other teachers that they establish categories and observe the outdoor games played by young children in the area served by the school. Agreement came quickly, and it was determined that the observations could be made at the same time that the teachers were conducting required home visitations. Within a month, the teachers had assembled considerable information on the types and frequency of outdoor games naturally played by area children about five years old. The teachers analyzed this information, made some adjustments to assure that all major parts of the body would receive exercise, and then developed an instructional plan for the next ten outdoor physical education periods. The improved motivation of the children and the heightened productivity of the outdoor sessions were dramatic. The teachers were then able to sequence outdoor physical education instruction appropriately and effectively for the entire year.

As a second instance, imagine that a Head Start center was located in a busy traffic zone and that most children had to walk to the center on their own. The staff at the center implemented an active instructional program on safety and checked on the children's learning by asking them to recite rules or simply asking them if they understood. Safety rule recitation improved noticeably, and the children invariably would respond "yes" when asked if they understood. Still, staff members on their way to and from the center noted numerous unsafe behaviors by these same children. (Note that the tendency of adults to ask "Do you understand?" is widespread, and it is matched by children's tendency to nod or respond "Yes," possibly to please the adult or to get a teacher to move on to the next student. At a time when Chris, the oldest daughter of Goodwin, was walking to her kindergarten class daily, several cases of child molesting were reported. The *modus operandi* of the culprit was to drive up and offer candy and a ride. Thus, Chris was given a long period of instruction by Goodwin detailing all the reasons for not accepting a ride with a stranger, regardless of any entice-ment. She was repeatedly asked, "Do you understand?" and always she re-sponded with a somber nod and a serious "Yes." At the end of all this instruction, she was asked, "Chris, do you have any questions?" She promptly answered, "Yes. What time is he going to pick me up?" The moral is that asking young children, or most persons for that matter, if they understand is a profoundly weak and suspect measure of comprehension.)

The center staff decided they needed a better measure of children's un-derstanding of traffic safety. Following Finlayson's (1972) strategy for studying the road-crossing behavior of children, they made arrangements for two volun-teer parents to use 8 mm cameras with zoom lenses to film the children's road-crossing behavior, unobtrusively, at two busy intersections. Then the staff studied the films and, like Finlayson, classified children's behaviors as safe, care-less, or unsafe. They observed, as Finlayson did, that boys were more likely to display unsafe behavior. Additionally, they noted a tendency for unsafe behavior to occur more often when the children were in groups rather than alone. Finally, certain children were singled out as needing extensive instruction. Armed with this information, the center staff resumed their instructional efforts, even add-ing direct experience at the most dangerous intersections for the children. Periodic reuse of the same measuring techniques allowed them to determine that the lessons were having the desired effect and also to plan appropriate additional instruction.

As a final example, consider the possible applications of the work of Smith and Geoffrey (1968). Smith, an educational psychologist, teamed with Geoffrey, a teacher of seventh-graders in a slum-area school. For a semester, both of them served as observers of Geoffrey's class—Smith as a nonparticipating observer and Geoffrey as a participating observer, as he was the teacher. They termed their anthropologically oriented method *classroom microethnography*, and they wrote a book about the insights reached in this shared observational experience.

Although their work was more along the lines of the specimen record method and not measurement-oriented, their teamwork and operating proce-dures imply how measurement of important behaviors might be facilitated. For example, one preschool teacher might join another for a week with both focusing on the observational measurement of child (or teacher) behaviors of principal importance. This arrangement, incidentally, might function as valuable in-service training for both teachers. A teacher of young children could make similar arrangements with a nearby professor or a competent university student. In many cases, the teacher might not be thought of as a participant-observer; rather the teacher would function as usual with the observer focusing on pre-established measures of student or teacher behavior. In some instances, such measures could be derived from informal observational measurement methods; that is, they could be patterned as frequency counts, duration records, or checklists.

The ways in which observation methods might be adapted for practical measurement uses in early childhood education are almost limitless. Further, a number of books are available to guide teachers of young children in the development and use of observational measurement (such as Almy, 1959; Boehm and Weinberg, 1977; Brandt, 1972; Carini, 1975; Cartwright and Cartwright, 1974; Medinnus, 1976; Stallings, 1977; and Wright, 1967).

Thus, observation allows an expansion of the measurement opportunities in early childhood education, both in terms of measures of outcomes and (especially) processes. As addressed in Table 9 and elsewhere in the chapter, measurement via observation often permits comprehensive description of what is observed. It can be used to identify the occurrence, frequency, and duration of certain behaviors, categories of behaviors, or events. If done carefully and systematically, it can result in accurate completion of checklists or of other records of behavior that subsequently can be reviewed to permit substantive trait rating, instructional guidance, or other reporting. Observational measurement can address behaviors of young children that might otherwise be unmeasurable. Possibly most important, the process of measuring via observation matches well the development of young children, for it tends to preserve the richness and elaborateness of children's behavior. Perhaps for this very reason, it also matches well the inclinations and preferences of most early childhood educators.

Chapter 5

Cognitive Measures: Intelligence and School-Related Tests

C*ognition* is defined as the intellectual process by which knowledge is gained. Thus, perceiving, knowing, thinking, learning, and intellectualizing all denote cognitive processes. In developing a taxonomy for the cognitive domain, Bloom (1956) started with two major categories: (1) knowledge and (2) intellectual abilities and skills. The latter category was subdivided into comprehension, application, analysis, synthesis, and evaluation. In Chapters Five and Six, we consider early childhood measures pertinent to this domain.

Determining the exact content of this chapter was difficult, for three reasons. First, human behavior does not divide itself neatly into the cognitive, affective, and psychomotor domains (the topics considered in Chapters Five and Six, Seven, and Eight, respectively); the interaction between these domains is substantial. Therefore, it is not clear which chapter is most appropriate for certain types of measure, such as language or motivation tests. After much discussion, and with a certain degree of arbitrariness, we decided to consider language as cognitive (Chapter Six), and motivation as affective (Chapter Seven). A second reason, related to the first, is the mixed nature of some measuring instruments. A single instrument might include some subscales that are primarily cognitive and others that are psychomotor or affective. This is true, especially, for certain measures of development, such as the Denver Developmental Screening Test. The typical procedure followed here in such cases is to consider the measure in its entirety once it is introduced. The third reason is that the very large number of cognitive measures available precludes a comprehensive treatment. We have narrowed our selection by concentrating on better-established instruments or somewhat different new ones and by excluding tests that fall outside our specified age range of interest or that are extensively considered in other sources.

Several categories of measure were excluded. Measures designed exclusively to assess behaviors of retarded children were considered to lie outside the scope of the book. Considerable attention has been given these measures elsewhere (for example, see Haywood and others, 1975). Measures associated with the cross-cultural study of young children's mental development were also excluded; interested readers should consult Glick (1975). No measure printed in a foreign language and not available in English is discussed here. However, a number of tests have been, or will be, translated into Spanish, and have even undergone content adaptations; Circo, for example, is being developed as the Spanish version of Circus. Recently, listings and descriptions of measures designed for students who speak a primary language other than English have appeared (see, for example, Jones and Spolsky, 1975; Locks, Pletcher, and Reynolds, 1978; Oakland, 1977; Rosen, 1977; and Silverman, Noa, and Russell, 1976); such measures receive some attention in the next chapter with regard to language testing.

Another large group of measures given only limited attention here are infant tests. They lie below the principal age focus of this book, and their educational implications often are not clear. However, realizing that many readers will be interested in infant testing, we have included a short section on recent developments in that area. Two other categories of test given limited attention are elementary-school level tests of intelligence and achievement. These measures apply mostly to the upper end of the age range of interest in this book, and they are well surveyed by many existing measurement books. Their occasional mention principally concerns their use for younger children in kindergarten and first grade.

A final category of instruments excluded deals with cognitive style, such as field independence or dependence, risk-taking or caution, attentiveness, and the like (see Banta, 1970; Kagan and Kogan, 1970; and Kogan, 1976). We initially intended to include substantial coverage of some of these instruments, such as the Kansas Reflection-Impulsivity Scale for Preschoolers, or KRISP (Wright, 1971), a downward extension of the Matching Familiar Figures Test (Kagan, 1965). Cognitive tempo, or reflection-impulsivity, may have substantial educational implications (for instance, see Kagan and Kogan, 1970; and Zelniker and Jeffrey, 1976). However, we finally decided to exclude measures of cognitive style, both because space was too limited and because most of the available instruments are used principally in research and have not been established as educationally relevant measures. We hope to add such measures in future editions as their direct relevance to education is established.

This chapter describes intelligence and instruction-related (readiness or achievement) tests. Chapter Six also deals with cognitive measures, specifically developmental and handicapped screening surveys, language measures (including attention to language dominance and bilingualism), and creativity tests. In both chapters, a concise overview of each major type of cognitive measure is followed by a section in which illustrative instruments are described. The reader should consider the test descriptions as surveys of available instruments rather than as in-depth critiques of their merits and limitations. The material presented here in no way relieves the test user from examining carefully any instrument that is contemplated for use or from consulting critical reviews relevant to the particular purpose envisioned (reviews such as those contained in the Buros' Mental Measurements Yearbooks; see the source book section). It should be noted that the authors do not intend any endorsement, explicit or implicit, of the instruments selected for discussion in Chapters Five through Eight. This caveat is especially pertinent to the discussion of affective measures in Chapter Seven. Systematic reviews of educational measures (for example, see Buros, 1978; Haney and Cohen, 1978; Hoepfner, Stern, and Nummedal, 1971; Hoepfner and others, 1972 and 1976; and Walker, 1973) have made it clear that considerable improvement is needed in most instruments. Therefore, as a general rule, the reader would be better served to think of the instruments "showcased" in these four chapters as representative, rather than exemplary, measures.

Intelligence Tests

In the United States, intelligence tests have constituted the most visible aspect of the complex testing movement. The history of such tests has been long and highly volatile. Reviews of the development and evolution of IQ tests in this century (such as Levine, 1966; and Sattler, 1974) have made it clear that avid proponents of such measures are counterbalanced by severe critics. Before reviewing various intelligence tests, we should make some general remarks concerning their nature and current status.

Nature and Status of Intelligence Tests. Historically, intelligence tests have been used in educational settings to predict success on school-related tasks. For example, in determining whether an underage child should be enrolled in school, an individually administered IQ test would yield highly relevant data. Since the validity of IQ tests for predicting school success is well established, we consider such a use appropriate. At the same time, for reasons examined in Chapter One, certain children do not have an equal chance to do well on such tests. Our concern grows with other uses of intelligence tests, such as grouping children for instruction or assigning them to special classes for the gifted or the retarded; in such cases, extensive qualifications seem necessary.

Since the mid 1960s, the IQ test has had an extensive impact on early childhood education itself. Legislation passed then, authorizing compensatory education, had as its aim better preparing children from poor families for school, so that they would neither start out behind nor fall further behind with each passing year. Many preschool program developers reasoned that if their programs increased measured IQ, then the children's school performance would correspondingly improve (given the substantial predictive validity of the IQ test for academic tasks). For them, IQ test scores became an important index of program effectiveness. This attitude is maintained to some extent even today. The widespread use of IQ tests with young children, for whatever the reason, justifies the considerable attention given them here.

Definitions of intelligence vary substantially (Bouchard, 1968), and so, too, do the IQ tests designed to measure it, as the illustrative tests in this chapter clearly show. Further, there is no guarantee that the items in a particular test will adequately reflect the definition of intelligence supposedly underlying the test. Some definitions emphasize innate or genetic determinants of intelligence, others stress environmental determinants, and yet others focus on interactions between the individual and the environment. From another perspective, definitions of intelligence can be classified in terms of their tendency toward a single pervasive ability factor or toward a multiple-factor (or differential aptitude) orientation. Reviewing the substantial material surrounding these definitional issues (such as did Scarr-Salapatek, 1975) is not central to the purpose of this chapter. Suffice it to say that we perceive trends toward an interactionist view (compatible with Piaget's view of intelligence as adaptation) and a multiple-factor approach (such as the extensive list of competencies presented in Chapter One, which was suggested by Anderson and Messick, 1974).

Several salient points should be made about intelligence and IQ tests for young children.

1. Intelligence is societally defined and its definition thus varies considerably over long periods of time. For example, imagine how the definition of intelligence might change as a society changed its principal orientation from hunting to agriculture to technical industrialization. It also can be noted that different nations have varying "tolerances" in their societal definitions of what constitutes low mental competence (Sarason and Gladwin, 1958).
2. The definition of what constitutes intelligent behavior varies with age. For example, McCall, Hogarty, and Hurlburt (1972) analyzed infant behavior and tentatively identified, using sophisticated statistical procedures, several components of infant intelligence that varied over six-month intervals and that resembled Piaget's developmental sequences from birth to age two. For school children and adults, quite different ideas of intelligent behavior emerge, and, depending on one's orientation, these may be quite different for children and adults.
3. The task of defining intelligent behavior for preschoolers is complicated by the lack of a substantial body of common experiences from which to draw test items (Anastasi, 1976).

4. IQ test scores generated after formal school entrance are relatively stable, in part because intellectual development is cumulative. Present scores predict subsequent IQ scores better over shorter time intervals between testings. Despite this general stability, especially for groups of individuals, recall from Chapter One that considerable variability can occur in an individual's IQ score over time (Honzik, 1973; McCall, Applebaum, and Hogarty, 1973; and Moriarty, 1966).

5. IQ tests have many limitations. A prime example is their supposed lack of fairness for certain children, as was discussed in Chapter One. Such limitations are treated extensively in the literature. For example, Sattler (1974) discusses several such limitations, giving special attention to the separate issues surrounding IQ tests and several different minority groups.

These points, along with the relevant issues from Chapter One, should be kept in mind as one considers the intelligence tests now described. An awareness of these questions can do much to prevent the abuses associated with IQ tests, such as making unwarranted interpretations and labeling children. Two additional points should be fixed firmly in mind. First, IQ test scores are merely descriptive and not explanatory. That is, such scores merely describe a person's test performance—they do not explain why the person performs as he does. Second, it is erroneous to equate an IQ test score with intelligence. An IQ is simply a score on a test and, as such, is far from synonymous with intelligence. This same caveat applies more generally to many of the measures subsequently described (Glick, 1968).

Before the illustrative intelligence tests are presented, three important topics related to intelligence tests will be briefly considered: infant "intelligence" scales; Piagetian scales of mental development; and attempts at developing culture-fair intelligence measures, highlighting the recent System of Multicultural Pluralistic Assessment.

Measures of infant intellectual development: Several excellent reviews have confirmed both that infant "intelligence" measures have a substantial history and that the assessment of infant intelligence, say from birth to age two, is a difficult task (Lewis and McGurk, 1972; Stott and Ball, 1965; Thomas, 1970; and Yang and Bell, 1975). The difficulty arises, for the most part, from dealing with so young a subject. Individual administration is nearly always the rule, with the subject lying, sitting, or being held by a caretaker. The psychometrician must find ways to keep the often uncooperative infant attending to, or focusing on, the situation at hand; often there is the dual requirement of establishing rapport with both the infant and a concerned caretaker. The chief causes of the difficulty, however, are the developmental characteristics of the infants themselves. Language is of dubious value for instructing the one-year-old during testing, and has only limited potential in testing the two-year-old. Rapid development of the infant complicates the assessment process, as does the fickle nature of some recently formed responses that are present only sporadically.

Cronbach (1970) pointed out that mental tests such as those for infants could be judged in any of three ways. First, the test tasks could be examined to see whether they really constituted a sample of behavior regulated by intellect. Second, an infant test could be judged in terms of its predictive validity—how well it forecasted a future criterion. Third, the test could be appraised in terms of whether the required behaviors represented steps or stages on a path toward mature intellectual performance. The first two procedures dominated infant test construction until recently and resulted in the development of measures such as those by Gesell, Cattell, and Bayley. The third orientation is more in tune with Piagetian approaches to assessment (discussed in the next section).

Three traditional infant assessment instruments are the Gesell Developmental Schedules, the Cattell Infant Intelligence Scale, and the Bayley (or California) Scales of Infant Development. The Gesell Developmental Schedules (Gesell and Amatruda, 1947) resulted from a series of longitudinal studies initiated in the early 1920s. The instrument contains a large number of age-graded items for children from one month through six years. Items consist of things that children normally do and are grouped into four major fields of functional organization: (1) motor (such as balance, reaching, and locomotion), (2) adaptive (alertness and tower building), (3) language (visual and vocal communication), and (4) personal-social (feeding and playing behaviors). The child's observed reactions to standard stimuli (toys and objects), supplemented by information supplied by the mother, resulted in an all-inclusive developmental quotient (DQ), although Gesell seemed to prefer more descriptive, qualitative performance reports. Gesell gave little attention to reliability and validity, but several other researchers did, especially as parts of longitudinal studies (see Thomas, 1970). In general, the Gesell did not predict well subsequent performance on the Binet.

The Cattell Infant Intelligence Scale (Cattell, 1960) was designed as a downward extension of the Stanford-Binet. Although starting with the Gesell as a base, Cattell was more interested in objectivity, standardization, and quantification than description. She also tried to reduce the Gesell scales' emphasis on motor items and on items susceptible to home training and influence. The scale was designed for infants from two to thirty months old, with five items and one or two alternates provided for each tested age level: every month, every two months, and every three months during the first, second, and third years of life, respectively. Representative items at the six-month level, scored pass or fail, were: follows ring in a circular motion with eyes; regards spoon; and regards cube. Split-half reliability of the scale at three months was only .56 but reached high levels (approaching .90) starting at six months. Nevertheless, correlations between Cattell scores of infants at one year and Binet scores at three years were generally low: .10, .34, .18, and .56 at three, six, nine, and twelve months, respectively. Cattell scores at eighteen and twenty-four months correlated better with Binet three-year performance, namely .67 and .71. Although noting the Cattell's outdated manual and inadequate, dated norms, Damarin (1978b) considered it possibly much better than these indicators would imply, especially if an efficient infant mental (as distinct from motor) scale was desired and if local norms were developed.

The Bayley Scales of Infant Development (Bayley, 1969), also known as the California Infant Scales, represent a third traditional infant assessment procedure. The scales originated in the 1930s and also owed much to the seminal work of Gesell. Unlike the Cattell, however, the Bayley has been revised and renormed. Intended for infants from two to thirty months of age, the scales have been used in several longitudinal research studies. They consist of a Mental Scale, a Motor Scale, and an Infant Behavior Record. The Mental Scale examines functions such as perception, vocalization, memory, learning, early verbal communication, and the like. The Motor Scale samples fine motor manipulations of hands and fingers and also more gross motor capabilities, such as walking, climbing, standing, and sitting. The Infant Behavior Record is a rating scale used by the tester to assess persistence, attention level, and personality characteristics. The Mental and Motor Scales yield separate developmental indexes, expressed as normalized standard scores (mean of 100, standard deviation of 16). Among the infant assessment instruments, the Bayley is clearly the leader in terms of representative norms and careful standardization (Anastasi, 1976; Collard, 1972; Damarin, 1978a; and Holden, 1972). The Bayley has substantial to high reliability. First-year scores on the Bayley, like those on other infant tests, do not predict well later measures of intellectual development; however, second- and third-year Bayley scores are somewhat better predictors.

Yang and Bell (1975), in an interesting overall comparison of the Gesell, Cattell, and Bayley, found them more alike than different. Although they made several important points, most important for our purposes here was their noting the limited predictive power of the measures. "In spite of the acceptable psychometric properties of all the scales, they have proved to be systematically poor predictors of later performance: the earlier in infancy the initial test, and the greater the time between initial and final testing, the poorer the predictive relationship. Thus, the loss of predictive power occurs precisely in the range for which there had been the most hope for strong relations: long-range prediction from a point early in life" (Yang and Bell, 1975, p. 175). These low correlations may be explained in part by the spurts of intellectual growth and periods of consolidation common in infants. Whatever their deficiencies as predictors, the infant measures (and especially the Bayley) do assess well an infant's current developmental status.

A relative newcomer to the infant assessment arena is the Brazelton Neonatal Behavioral Assessment Scale (Brazelton, 1973). The scale is qualitatively different from those just described in three key respects. First, the scale is designed for younger subjects, namely full-term newborns three days to four weeks of age (although some use with premature infants and other groups at risk is reported). Second, the manual makes it clear that every attempt should be made to secure the infant's best, rather than typical, performance. Third, and most significant, the scale assesses interactive behavior and neurological status.

Brazelton based his scale on extensive clinical pediatric practice. Forty-seven items are included. Twenty are elicited responses (such as the Babinski, Moro, and rooting responses), each scored on a three-point scale. The twenty-seven others are behavioral responses, each scored on a nine-point scale. (These responses include items gauging orientation toward, and response decrement to, external stimuli like a bell, a voice, and a pinprick; motor behavior in general and tremulousness, startle, and hand-mouth coordination; general arousal, including ratings of rapidity of buildup, peak of excitement, lability, irritability, and self-quieting activity; and social interaction, with indexes of cuddliness, consolability, and reflexive smiling.) On most of the twenty-seven behavioral items, the state of consciousness of the infant is important, with certain states being required before assessment on a particular item is undertaken. Six states are recognized, the first two being sleep states and the last four being alert states: (1) deep sleep, (2) light sleep with eyes closed, (3) drowsy or semi-dozing, (4) alert with bright look, (5) active with eyes open, and (6) crying. Thus, for assessment of cuddliness, the infant must first be in state 4 or 5, and then his response to being held in a cuddled position against the examiner's chest is scored on the following nine-point scale:

1. Actually resists being held, continuously pushing away, thrashing or stiffening.
2. Resists being held most but not all of the time.
3. Doesn't resist but doesn't participate either, lies passively in arms and against shoulder (like a sack of meal).
4. Eventually molds into arms, but after a lot of nestling and cuddling by examiner.
5. Usually molds and relaxes when first held, that is, nestles head in crook of neck and of elbow of examiner. Turns toward body when held horizontally, on shoulder he seems to lean forward.
6. Always molds initially with above activity.
7. Always molds initially with nestling, and turning toward body, and leaning forward.
8. In addition to molding and relaxing, he nestles and turns head, leans forward on shoulder, fits feet into cavity of other arm, all of body participates.
9. All of the above, and baby grasps hold of the examiner to cling to him [Brazelton, 1973, pp. 29–30].

Administration of the Brazelton appears quite difficult (Sostek, 1978). Nevertheless, the manual reported a study using an earlier version of the scale in which substantial interrater reliability was observed, as well as substantial stability reliability of rated infant behavior, with testing occurring at three and twenty-eight days of age. The reported reliabilities varied considerably, depending on the particular item examined. Training in the proper use of the scale appears very important. To help assure proper administration of the scale, three training sites for examiners have been officially established in Boston (Dr. T. Berry Brazelton at Children's Hospital), Lawrence (Dr. Frances Degen Horowitz at the University of Kansas), and Seattle (Dr. Kathryn Barnard at the University of Washington). Some attempts to research relationships between Brazelton performance and mother-infant interaction have been made (see Yang and Bell, 1975). At the present time, however, the Brazelton, like the other infant scales presented here, should be considered descriptive rather than predictive.

It is unclear what the future trends in infant assessment will be. Three elements likely to be influential are the recent assault on IQ tests for older children, the increasing research efforts directed at unveiling heretofore unestablished competencies of infants (for example, see Appleton, Clifton, and Goldberg, 1975; Connolly and Bruner, 1974; Stone, Smith and Murphy, 1973; and White, 1975), and the continuing attention to the work of Piaget.

Piagetian scales of intellectual development: No measure based on Piaget's theory of intellectual development is included in the section Illustrative Intelligence Tests because Piagetian intelligence tests are not in widespread use. Many such measures are still under development; however, given the likelihood of their eventual general use, we briefly examine their typical nature and potential application.

Infant scales extrapolated from Piaget's writings have been developed, such as the Einstein Scales of Sensorimotor Development (Corman and Escalona, 1969; and Escalona and Corman, 1969), the Piagetian Infant Scales (Honig and Lally, 1970), and the Ordinal Scales of Psychological Development (Uzgiris and Hunt, 1975). The Uzgiris-Hunt scales serve nicely to illustrate their general tone. Considered provisional and available primarily for research purposes, the scales cover an age range from two weeks to two years, comparable to Piaget's sensorimotor stage. Scale administration, obviously individual, is considered valid and feasible only when the infant is fully cooperative. Some thirty-four material objects are suggested to serve as eliciting stimuli (such as a bell, a pull-toy, a slinky, and a stuffed animal). The six scales included are as follows:

1. The development of visual pursuit and the permanence of objects. (A four-month-old infant playing with a toy, such as a ball, will not search for it if it rolls out of sight. The interpretation is that the object has ceased to exist once it leaves his field of vision. During the second year of life, most children will seek toys that disappear from view.)
2. The development of means for obtaining desired environmental events (such as using hands to reach objects).
3. The development of vocal and gestural imitation.
4. The development of operational causality (such as picking up an object and giving it to the examiner to activate).
5. The construction of object relations in space (such as coordinating looking and listening to locate objects in space or exploring the fall of dropped objects).
6. The development of schemes for relating to objects (such as constructing with blocks or naming objects).

Each of the six scales is further subdivided and differentiated. Record forms list the critical infant action for each step of each scale (that is, critical for inferring achievement of that step). When completed, the forms permit determination of the highest step obtained by the infant in each scale.

More relevant to older children, say of preschool and school age, are the instruments developed by Laurendeau and Pinard (1962, 1970), Goldschmid and

Bentler (1968a, b), and Struthers and De Avila (1967). Still being used principally for research and not available for general use, the Laurendeau and Pinard scales are derived directly from Piagetian tasks and intended for children between four and twelve years old. Many scales are under development. Ten such scales have been tried with a substantial number of Canadian children and the results reported. Five scales involve examining children's causal explanations of the character and origins of dreams; the concept of life in terms of animate and inanimate objects; why it is dark at night; why clouds move; and why some objects float and others sink. The other five scales center on the children's concept of space, particularly as influenced by the children's egocentrism (that is, their tendency not to recognize objects from any point of view other than their own). The scales are given individually and orally. Each scale is composed of a series of standard questions, somewhat vague in their wording. The examiner must use these questions to determine, for example, the child's current explanation of why it is dark at night. To accomplish this, however, the examiner can vary the number and sequence of questions used, depending on the answers obtained. (This procedure represents an interesting compromise between Piaget's free-wheeling *méthode clinique* and the objective tradition of psychological testing.) Using their sample, the developers of the scales generated age norms for specific responses indicating different levels of intellectual development, checked for ordinality (the extent to which different children went through a uniform sequence as they exhibited more and more sophisticated responses), and examined the relationships between the levels of development reached on the various scales by an individual child.

The Concept Assessment Kit-Conservation (Goldschmid and Bentler, 1968a, b) is a Piaget-based, commercially available instrument intended for children from four to seven years old. Central to the test is the most famous of Piaget's concepts—conservation. (Conservation is being able to understand that an amount of something, such as a liquid, has permanence, and that this amount does not change, even if its form is altered.) Test procedures for nearly each conservation task call for the examiner to show two identical objects to the child and then to transform one of them. The child is then asked if the objects are the same or different (one point) and to explain why (one point). Preliminary norms, reliability and validity data, and cross-cultural studies suggest that the instrument is functioning as one would expect given its theoretical foundation; that is, with increasing age, more children conserve. Several reviews qualifying the use of the Concept Assessment Kit have appeared (Ayers, 1972; De Vries and Kohlberg, 1969; Hall and Mery, 1969; and Smock, 1970). Another commercially available cognitive measure based on Piaget's work—Let's Look at First-Graders—is considered later in this chapter.

The Cartoon Conservation Scales (CCS), originally developed by Struthers and De Avila (1967), were used to examine elementary school children's acquisition of key Piagetian concepts (De Avila, Struthers, and Randall, 1969; and De Avila and Havassy, 1975). These scales, still used primarily in research contexts, have an unusual format for Piaget-based measures in that no individual interviewing occurs. Rather, group administration is used, with each child responding to questions in cartoon form:

> Three cartoon frames are presented in which two children discuss a Piagetian task. In the first frame an equality is established between two objects according to the dimension being studied (number, length, substance, and so on). In the second frame an identity transformation takes place and a question of equivalence is asked. On the right side of the panel three possible answers are presented. The three alternatives, which show the characters responding to the question, are randomly ordered to avoid the possible effects of position set or acquiescence. The CCS consists of thirty cartoon panels, six examples for each of five conservation tasks. The panels are presented to the subjects, and the story line is read and elaborated upon in order to facilitate understanding of the question. The subject's task is simply to mark the one alternative "that makes the story true." Incorrect alternatives were based on those most popularly given by children of similar ages and backgrounds [De Avila and Havassy, 1975, p. 252].

Many studies have examined the relationship between performance on Piagetian-oriented scales and on more traditional assessment instruments (for example, see De Avila and Havassy, 1975; De Vries, 1974; Dudek, Lester, and Goldberg, 1969; Stephens and others, 1972; and Wachs, 1975). In general, significant positive correlations were found, although the tests appeared to be measuring different aspects of cognitive functioning. (Note, too, that De Avila and Havassy (1975) found Chicano school children faring better in comparison with other ethnic groups on the CCS than on more traditional intelligence tests.) Kohlberg (1968) suggested that Piagetian measures, as contrasted with traditional measures, apparently eliminated or reduced effects due to distractibility, shyness, or verbal experience and therefore were more reliable. Keep in mind, however, that Piagetian measures focus on determining the child's current developmental stage—a notably different function from that served by traditional child measures. Additionally, the practical utility of Piagetian scales remains to be established. Elkind provocatively stated, "I cannot see, at the present time at least, much point in substituting a scale of Piagetian tasks for intelligence, achievement, or clinical tests that are already in use. A great deal of theoretical and empirical work needs to be done before the information provided by Piagetian tasks will be relevant to laymen, educators, and clinicians. That is to say, until educators and clinicians come to see their problems in cognitive developmental terms, a subject's performance on a scale of Piagetian tasks will have little practical value for them" (1971, pp. 27–28). In many ways, Elkind has been proved right, although Piaget's influence continues to spread and an increasing number of attempts have been made to develop and employ Piagetian measures. By and large, the principal uses of the Piagetian measures are still research-related. More in-depth information on the implications of Piaget's theory for measurement is found in Green, Ford, and Flamer (1971).

Culture-fair tests and the System of Multicultural Pluralistic Assessment: In our discussion of Issue 4 in Chapter One, we noted the continuing interest in designing culture-fair measures (that is, measures equally fair for children from all cultures). We also observed that it is extremely difficult, if not impossible, to design such measures. Nevertheless, many such attempts have been made, and some resultant measures are in relatively frequent use with young children, among them the Goodenough-Harris Drawing Test, the Culture Fair Intelligence Test, the Leiter International Performance Scale, and the Coloured Progressive Matrices. The Drawing Test is discussed later in this chapter. The other three measures are described briefly now.

Scale 1 of the Culture Fair Intelligence Test (Cattell, 1962) is intended for children four to eight years old and for "mentally defective" adults and purportedly measures general mental capacity (g). A paper-and-pencil test, it consists of eight subtests, some of which must be individually administered. Cattell believed that four subtests were culture-fair (Substitution, Classification, Mazes, and Similarities), while the other four were not sufficiently so (Selecting Named Objects, Following Directions, Wrong Pictures, and Riddles). Ratio IQs result, and the normative procedures fail to meet desirable test-construction standards. Anastasi (1976) reported her concern that the test involved extensive verbal instructions and that the test's reliability and validity were usually estimated as only moderate. Possibly more significant, given the test's purpose, she considered the measure of questionable fairness for certain cultural groups. Other reviewers (Milholland, 1965; and Tannenbaum, 1965) likewise believed that insufficient evidence had been presented to judge the test as culture-fair.

The Leiter International Performance Scale (Leiter, 1948, 1950), individually administered to children two to eighteen years old, has the distinctive feature of using very few instructions of any type. In each test, the initial task—a very easy version of the exercises about to be encountered—serves as the "instructions," and comprehending it is part of the test. Many tasks are included: matching colors, shapes and forms; completing series and pictures; recognizing analogies, age differences, similarities, and footprints; copying designs; and the like. Tasks are presented on a response frame with a stimulus picture card attached; the child must select blocks containing the response pictures and insert them appropriately into the frame. Ratio IQs result from the scale. Reliability and validity data for the Leiter are considerable, but often were derived from groups with limited representativeness. More suitable for testing young children (ages three to eight) is the Arthur Adaptation of the scale (Arthur, 1952), but its norms, based on midwestern middle-class children, are also limited (Werner, 1965).

The Coloured Progressive Matrices (Raven, 1947) is a test designed for children five to eleven years old and mentally impaired adults. Used widely in England and increasingly in the United States, it requires the subject to perceive relationships and is thought by many to be a relatively good measure of general intellectual ability, or g. It is primarily nonverbal, although simple oral instructions are used. On each test item, the child is presented with a pattern from which a piece is missing and must select an appropriate piece to complete the pattern from several response alternatives. Anastasi (1976) noted good reliability for the matrices, especially for older children, and modest correlations with more usual intelligence tests (somewhat higher with performance tests).

Quite a different orientation to the cultural fairness issue is exhibited by the System of Multicultural Pluralistic Assessment, or SOMPA (Mercer and Lewis, 1977, 1978). Although the system was just recently published, workshops on the proper use of SOMPA are already taking place around the United States under the auspices of Jane Mercer and the Institute for Pluralistic Assessment, Research, and Training, University of California, Riverside. SOMPA is included here because it claims to be a comprehensive approach and because its chief architect has been a severe critic of many existing assessment procedures. Recall from Chapter One that Mercer proposed a set of rights for children undergoing assessment, including the right to be evaluated within a culturally appropriate framework and the right to be treated as a multidimensional human being; presumably her involvement in SOMPA signals an attempt to assess while respecting such rights. Readers with measurement responsibilities who work extensively with culturally different children will want to examine and evaluate SOMPA.

SOMPA, intended to be used with children between five and eleven years of age, integrates information from three separate models or perspectives on what constitutes normality—a medical model, a social system model, and a pluralistic model. The models, in turn, synthesize data from two primary sources, tapped by three and four measures, respectively. The first primary source is a one-hour interview with the mother (conducted in English or Spanish). Three measures are used:

1. Sociocultural Scales, which identify the social, cultural, and economic characteristics of the child's family and compare these with the predominant school culture.
2. The Adaptive Behavior Inventory for Children (ABIC), which examines the child's performance of six social roles.
3. The Health History Inventory, which records the child's health history.

The second primary source is a test session that yields data from four additional measures:

4. The WISC-R (or WPPSI if the child is not yet six years old), which is an individually administered intelligence test (described later in the chapter).
5. The Bender Visual Motor Gestalt Test, in which the child reproduces a series of designs and his departures from the originals are interpreted according to Gestalt principles of perception and organization.
6. Physical dexterity tasks.
7. Weight by height, visual acuity, and auditory acuity.

These seven data sources are profiled and variously interpreted under the three models. The *medical model,* which is independent of culture and deficit-oriented, looks for possible biological causes of poor functioning (by incorporating measures 3, 5, 6, and 7). The *social system model* views normality and abnormality in terms of roles and social systems. Pertinent to this model are measures 2 (the ABIC providing information on community, family, peer, and other roles) and 4 (the WISC-R, termed "School Functioning Level," reflecting likely success in the student role in the school social system). The *pluralistic model* considers tests as a measure of learning and views as abnormal poor test performance relative to others from similar sociocultural backgrounds. Relying principally on measures 1 and 4, this model identifies assets and potential possibly masked by cultural differences, compares the child with his own ethnic group on the sociocultural scales, and yields an Estimated Learning Potential, which essentially is an adjustment of the earned WISC-R scores. (This adjustment is upward given certain sociocultural scale values.)

In other words, the measures are considered variously under the three models. SOMPA requires examining the outcomes from all three models. If the models generate similar or highly compatible findings, then interpretations are made with more assurance and appropriate interventions prescribed. If the three models generate disparate findings, then interpretations and subsequent proposed interventions must be made cautiously. SOMPA is an involved process, and costly in terms of time and resources. Although it represents a significant departure from most assessment procedures, judgments of its worth in light of its resource costs are several years in the future.

Illustrative Intelligence Tests. Seven intelligence tests are described in this section (see Table 11). Topics covered for most tests include the test's nature and construction, validity, reliability, and usability (including matters such as norms, interpretation, and criticisms). These discussions, which are necessarily brief, are primarily descriptive rather than evaluative; accordingly, potential users of a particular test should consult critical reviews in Buros and other sources (see the source book section). The Stanford-Binet and the two Wechsler instruments are considered first because of their preeminent positions in the field; after them, the order is alphabetical.

Stanford-Binet Intelligence Scale (Binet): The Binet (Terman and Merrill, 1960, 1973) is administered individually by a highly trained examiner in about one hour. The test session resembles a clinical interview in that several characteristics of the examinee may be observed and rated, such as attention, reactions during test performance, problem-solving behavior, and independence of examiner support.

The Binet features a special materials kit and 142 tests or items; Binet items are often called "tests" since each is administered separately and many contain several parts. Since the Binet is used in testing two-year-olds up through adults, the tests range dramatically in type and difficulty. For young children, typical items involve picture vocabulary, vocabulary, identifying parts of the

Table 11. Illustrative Intelligence Measures in Early Childhood Education

Title and Date	Age Range	Administration	Scales or Scores	Source
Stanford-Binet Intelligence Scale (1960: Items; 1972: Norms)	2 to 18 years	Individual; 1 hour	IQ	Houghton-Mifflin 110 Tremont St. Boston, Mass. 02107
Wechsler Intelligence Scale for Children—Revised (1974)	6 years to 16 years, 11 months	Individual; 1 hour	Verbal IQ Performance IQ Full Scale IQ	Psychological Corp. 304 E. 45th St. New York, N.Y. 10017
Wechsler Preschool and Primary Scale of Intelligence (1967)	4 to 6½ years	Individual; 50 to 75 minutes	Verbal IQ Performance IQ Full Scale IQ	Psychological Corp.
Goodenough-Harris Drawing Test (1963)	3 to 15 years	Individual or Group; 10 to 15 minutes	Unnamed Standard Score (presumably intellectual maturity)	Harcourt Brace Jovanovich 757 Third Ave. New York, N.Y. 10017
McCarthy Scales of Children's Abilities (1972)	2½ to 8½ years	Individual; 45 to 60 minutes	Verbal Perceptual Performance Quantitative General Cognitive Memory Motor	Psychological Corp.
Peabody Picture Vocabulary Test (1965)	2½ to 18 years	Individual; 10 to 15 minutes	IQ	American Guidance Service Publishers Bldg. Circle Pines, Minn. 55014
Quick Test (1962)	2 years to Adult	Individual; 3 to 10 minutes	Mental Age (children) IQ (adults)	Psychological Test Specialists Box 1441 Missoula, Mont. 59801

body, copying geometric shapes, and noting pictorial similarities, differences, and absurdities. Tests are grouped by age level, with each year represented by six tests plus one alternate test—except for ages two to five, which have six tests for each half year. No person takes all the tests. Rather, the examiner first establishes a basal age (where all six tests are passed); continues upward, giving the examinee additional credit for each item passed; and stops when a ceiling level is determined (the first age level where all six tests are failed). Total credit is then calculated for the examinee in order to determine a single deviation IQ score. This is essentially a standard score with mean of 100 and standard deviation of 16; the tested person's IQ is found by comparing his or her performance with that of the norm group of the same age.

Validity information on the Binet is substantial; quantities of data have been collected since its origin early in the century. Content validity is assessed by examining the items to see if they reflect what is commonly called *intelligence;* for many judges, the Binet appears appropriate in this regard (see Anastasi, 1976, for an elaboration of the Binet's content validity). At the older age levels, the preponderance of verbal items is obvious; to a lesser extent, verbal ability also is important for younger examinees. More apparent at the earlier age levels are tests calling for following directions, coordinating eye and hand, and making perceptual discriminations. Scattered throughout are items requiring conceptual thinking or judgment; for example, a test at the age four level asks the child to explain why we have houses. In all, analyses of the makeup of the Binet reveal content categories thought by many to relate substantially to intelligence. For example, the sixty regular Binet tests for ages two through eight were classified by Sattler (1974) as follows: Language, 22 percent; Reasoning, Visual-Motor, and Social Intelligence, 18 percent each; Conceptual Thinking, 12 percent; Memory, 10 percent; and Numerical Reasoning, 2 percent.

Criterion-related validity has been assessed by noting how well the Binet IQ both forecasts later scholastic performance (predictive) and corresponds to current performance in classes, grades, achievement test scores, and teacher ratings (concurrent). The Binet fares well in such examinations, with correlations between .40 and .75 common (McNemar, 1942). Construct validity has been addressed by selecting tests that do differentiate between groups of persons at successive age levels. Revisions of the Binet have retained tests that differentiate appropriately and correlate well with overall performance on the scale. Factor analyses of the Binet normally result in the identification of a common factor (increasingly a verbal factor at higher age levels), with some special ability factors making small contributions at different age levels.

Reliability of the Binet is likewise highly creditable. Cronbach (1970) estimated that an appropriate internal consistency reliability coefficient for the Binet is around .90. Anastasi (1976) agreed and noted somewhat higher reliabilities for older and less able examinees and somewhat lower ones for younger and "brighter" subjects. Prior to the 1960 revision, two forms of the Binet were available. Coefficients of equivalence established for them were impressively high (Terman and Merrill, 1960). The standard error of measurement for the revised version is five IQ points.

The Binet was re-normed in 1972 by anchoring it to the Cognitive Abilities Test, a group test standardized on a stratified sample (community size, geographic region, and economic status) of approximately 200,000 students in grades three through twelve. The much smaller Binet sample was selected by ensuring that the sample students' verbal scores on the Cognitive Abilities Test corresponded to the distribution of the larger sample. For ages two to eight years, younger siblings of the group-tested children were identified and tested. Children were excluded if the primary language spoken in the home was not English. The resulting 2,100 person sample was clearly more representative than the previously available 1937 norm group.

Because of its well-established reputation, the Binet is heavily used. Thus, in Buros' *Eighth Mental Measurements Yearbook* (1978), 1,590 research references were cited for it. Further, the Binet, along with the Wechsler, continues to be a very common standard or criterion used by others in establishing concurrent validity for recently developed instruments. For example, the Slosson Intelligence Test (Slosson, 1963) was designed to be a short version of the Binet that relatively untrained examiners could give. It borrowed many items from the Binet and also from the Gesell Developmental Schedules in order to permit testing down to the age of two weeks. Critical to its purpose was establishing concurrent validity with the Binet and Wechsler. It achieved this sufficiently well for most reviewers to endorse it, with qualifications, as an intelligence screening instrument for all except very young children (say, under four years) and those with language problems (Datta, 1975b; Eichorn, 1975; Himelstein, 1972; and Hunt, 1972).

Common criticisms of the Binet include its heavy emphasis on verbal and rote memory tests, its yielding of only a single IQ score to represent the complex concept of intelligence, its omission of creative abilities (most IQ tests can be similarly faulted), and its unsuitability for testing adults (Sattler, 1974). In most regards, however, the Binet has stood the test of time very well. Its general orientation and verbal emphasis do predict school performance well. The Binet has substantial validity, excellent reliability, and pronounced utility if interpreted judiciously and in full cognizance of the several relevant issues addressed in Chapter One.

Wechsler Intelligence Scale for Children—Revised (WISC-R): The original version of this scale, WISC, was published in 1949 as a downward age extension of the popular Wechsler Adult Intelligence Scale (WAIS); WISC-R represents the revised version (Wechsler, 1974). Like the Binet, WISC-R is administered individually by a thoroughly trained examiner, has a special kit of materials, and requires an hour or slightly more to complete. Together, the Wechsler scales and the Binet dominate the individually administered intelligence test scene. WISC and WISC-R have been extensively utilized; their accumulated research references in Buros' *Eighth Mental Measurements Yearbook* totaled 1,585, finishing just a hairbreadth behind the much older Binet.

The WISC-R is composed of ten separate tests, verbal and performance, plus two supplementary measures:

Verbal Tests	*Performance Tests*
Information	Picture Completion
Similarities	Picture Arrangement
Arithmetic	Block Design
Vocabulary	Object Assembly
Comprehension	Coding
Digit Span (Supplementary)	Mazes (Supplementary)

The supplementary measures are used in full clinical workups or as a substitute if another test cannot be properly given (say, because of a child's handicap) or is invalidated. (Similarly named tests, except for Coding and Mazes, make up the WAIS.) Much of the content of the Verbal Scale tests is similar to the Binet and to other group tests of intelligence. The content of the Performance Scale tests is more distinctive. For example, on the Picture Arrangement test, the child must correctly order a series of pictures to depict a logical sequence for a fire or to tell a story that makes sense about a burglar; on the Object Assembly test, cardboard pieces must be fitted together to make an animal or, on another item, a vehicle. The Verbal Scale and Performance Scale tests are given alternately; most tests are discontinued after a specified number of consecutive failures. An examinee is scored on each test, and these scores are converted to scaled scores appropriate to the child's age. The scaled scores can be plotted to form a profile, but one is warned to be cautious in interpreting small differences between scaled scores on any two tests. Appropriate scaled scores are also summed to yield a Verbal Score and a Performance Score, each based on five tests. The Verbal and Performance Scores are added to form the Full Scale Score; these three scores are then converted to Verbal, Performance, and Full Scale deviation IQs (mean of 100, standard deviation of 15).

Surprisingly, the WISC-R manual contains no separate section on validity (nor did the earlier WISC manual). Content validity might be addressed by analyzing the separate tests and showing that they represent legitimate components of intelligence; this is not done in any systematic fashion in the manual. However, concurrent criterion-related validity information is presented. A sample of fifty six-year-olds was given both WISC-R and WPPSI (see the following section); a correlation of .80 was found for both the Verbal IQs and the Performance IQs, while a .82 correlation was observed between the Full Scale IQs. Actual IQ differences were slight, with WPPSI IQs averaging two points higher than WISC-R IQs. At the other end of WISC-R's age range, a similar close correspondence with the WAIS was reported. Small samples of children aged six, nine and a half, twelve and a half, and sixteen and a half (about thirty children at each age level) were given WISC-R and the Binet. Average correlations of .71, .60, and .73 were observed between the Binet IQs and the WISC-R

Verbal, Performance, and Full Scale IQs, respectively. Binet IQs averaged about two points higher at the three younger ages, while WISC-R Full Scale IQs were about two points higher at age sixteen and a half. Although no correlations between WISC-R scores and academic performance are provided, earlier studies involving the WISC demonstrated substantial correlations, especially for the Verbal IQ, although not as high as for the Binet. Some factor-analytic information presented in the WISC-R manual shows considerable independence of the separate tests and might be interpreted as bearing on construct validity. Although Verbal and Performance IQs correlated .67, reporting them separately is probably warranted. Other interpretations of the validity of the earlier WISC are well summarized by Sattler (1974).

Reliability of the WISC-R, in terms of both internal consistency and stability of the separate test scaled scores and all three IQs, is extensively reported. Both types of reliability for the separate tests are substantial and an improvement over WISC. (WISC-R tests were, in general, lengthened.) Average internal consistency reliability across the several age groups involved was .94, .90, and .96 for the Verbal, Performance, and Full Scale IQs, respectively. Corresponding coefficients of stability, over a testing interval averaging one month, were .93, .90, and .95. A practice effect was noted during this retesting, amounting to three and a half, nine and a half, and seven IQ points on the Verbal, Performance, and Full Scale IQs, respectively. In all, these reliabilities are very high and commendably well reported; the associated standard errors of measurement for the Verbal, Performance, and Full Scale IQs are, in order, about three and a half, four and a half, and three points.

The norms for WISC-R are likewise exemplary. In all, 2,200 children were sampled, 200 in each of eleven age groups from six and a half to sixteen and a half years. Equal numbers of boys and girls were included. The sample was stratified proportional to the 1970 Census in terms of geographic region, race (white-nonwhite), head of household's occupation, and urban-rural residence. Bilingual children were included if they could speak and understand English. The sample was limited to "normal" children; institutionalized mental retardates and children with extreme emotional problems were excluded.

WISC-R represents highly technical and advanced approaches to instrument construction, especially in terms of reliability and norming. Improvements in the former WISC have clearly been achieved (Freides, 1978; and Whitworth, 1978). Failing to address validity systematically and completely in the manual is a weakness. Results from factor analyses and correlations within the scales and with other instruments are certainly relevant to validity, but even more convincing would be the inclusion of other types of datum generated from observed or measured behavior separate from the instrument itself.

Wechsler Preschool and Primary Scale of Intelligence (WPPSI): The administrative features of the WPPSI (Wechsler, 1967) are similar to those of WISC-R. It, too, is individually administered, requires a well-trained examiner, and features a special kit of materials. Administration reportedly takes fifty to seventy-five minutes; the manual acknowledges that testing may have to be spread over two different days in special cases but does not encourage this. (For a critical look at the WPPSI's long administration time, as well as at other limitations and strengths, see Eichorn, 1972.) As was true for the WISC-R, the WPPSI manual emphasizes that the examiner must establish rapport with the child before testing can begin.

The similarity between WPPSI and WISC-R also extends to their construction. WPPSI is composed of ten separate tests, plus a supplementary measure:

Verbal Tests	*Performance Tests*
Information	Animal House
Vocabulary	Picture Completion
Arithmetic	Mazes
Similarities	Geometric Design
Comprehension	Block Design

Sentences (Supplementary)

All five of the regular verbal tests are similar in design to the WISC-R tests of the same name, and they contain a mixture of different and identical items, the latter estimated to be one third of the total by Buros (1972). Sentences, the supplementary verbal test, is a memory test in which the child repeats each sentence after the examiner says it orally. Essentially, then, it substitutes for the WISC-R Digit Span test, in which the examinee must remember and repeat numbers in sequence.

Three of the performance tests have counterparts in WISC-R, while Animal House and Geometric Design are different. In Animal House, a form board is used: at its top are pictures of four animals, each with a different color cylinder (house) under it, and lower on the board are twenty pictures of the same animals, randomly ordered, each with an empty hole under it. The child must associate a color with each animal and place a cylinder of the proper color into the empty hole under each animal. The examiner records the time taken, errors, and omissions. (Wechsler viewed Animal House as similar to the Coding test on WISC-R.) In the Geometric Design test, the child is shown a series of designs to draw as similar to the stimulus as possible. The child's figure is then scored for accuracy of reproduction.

Procedures used with WPPSI parallel those used with WISC-R. Verbal and performance tests are alternated, discontinuance occurs after a specified number of consecutive failures or after a time limit is reached, and points earned are converted to scaled scores for each test. Appropriate scaled scores are summed to yield a Verbal Score and a Performance Score; in turn, these two scores are added to determine the Full Scale Score. Finally, with these collective scores, age-appropriate tables are entered to read out Verbal, Performance, and Full Scale deviation IQs (mean of 100, standard deviation of 15).

No validity section appears in the WPPSI manual. The comment made above pertaining to the absence of content validity information in the WISC-R manual is equally appropriate here. We previously noted that fifty children taking both WISC-R and WPPSI earned Full Scale IQs that correlated .82 and that, on average, were only two IQ points different. Other studies reviewed by Sattler (1974) reaffirm this significantly close relationship. Still other concurrent validity information presented in the manual concerns the relationships between WPPSI and three other individually administered intelligence tests—the Binet, the Peabody Picture Vocabulary Test (PPVT), and the Pictorial Test of Intelligence (PTI). Somewhat under one hundred students between five and six years of age enrolled in the same school took all three tests. The WPPSI Full Scale IQ correlated .75, .58, and .64 with the IQs derived from the Binet, the PPVT, and the PTI, respectively. In terms of the actual IQs scored, all four measures averaged about the same, with the average WPPSI Full Scale IQ within two IQ points of each of the other three tests. However, Sattler (1974) reviewed thirteen studies that compared performance on the WPPSI and the Binet. Median correlations (and ranges) were .81 (.33 to .92), .67 (.33 to .88), and .82 (.44 to .92) for the Binet with the Verbal, Performance, and Full Scale IQs, respectively. These correlations indicate substantial concurrent validity for the WPPSI using the Binet as the criterion. However, the studies consistently reported higher IQs with the Binet than with the WPPSI, ranging from one to seventeen points. Since the studies all preceded the 1972 Binet restandardization, excessive alarm over this discrepancy is not warranted.

Factor analysis of WPPSI, relevant to construct validity, demonstrated adequate independence of the separate tests, with a correlation of .66 between the Verbal and Performance Scores (in all, quite close to analogous analyses done with WISC-R). Another series of factor analyses (Hollenbeck and Kaufman, 1973) yielded a general factor for the WPPSI as well as two group factors—verbal and performance—with each separate test loading appropriately.

The WPPSI manual is considerably more explicit about reliability. Wechsler estimated a coefficient of internal consistency (split-half) for each separate test except Animal House at six half-year age levels from four to six and a half years; these coefficients all averaged in the .80s. Since Animal House is a speed test, split-half was inappropriate; therefore, Animal House was readministered after the completion of the entire scale, resulting in a correlation of .77. Average reliabilities for the Verbal, Performance, and Full Scale IQs across the six age levels were .94, .93, and .96, respectively; corresponding standard errors of measurement were approximately three and a half, four, and three IQ points. In a separate study, fifty kindergarten children were retested on the WPPSI after an average interval of eleven weeks. Coefficients of stability observed were .86, .89, and .92 for the Verbal, Performance, and Full Scale scores, while average second-testing IQs were three, six and a half, and three and a half points higher than those earned on first testing. In all, these reliability data are commendably high and impressive for subjects so young.

The standardization of WPPSI in terms of normative groups was systematic and thorough. In all, 1,200 children were used, 100 girls and 100 boys in six groups, ranging by half years from four through six and a half years. Based on the 1960 Census, the national sample obtained was stratified according to geographic region, urban-rural residence, color (white or nonwhite), and father's occupation. As was true for WISC-R, the approaches taken by WPPSI toward standardization and reliability are highly sophisticated.

Goodenough-Harris Drawing Test (Draw-a-Man): The Goodenough-Harris Drawing Test (Harris, 1963) was published as an extension, revision, and restandardization of the earlier Goodenough Draw-a-Man Test (1926). In both administration and content, the measure departs significantly from the usual type of intelligence test. Unlike the three previous measures discussed, it can be given to groups as well as individuals and does not require a highly trained examiner. The examiner need only have experience with children and be competent at following directions. Precise scoring and meaningful interpretation, however, are much more complicated matters (Ernhart, 1975a). The original 1926 measure required children to draw a man; the revision calls for the drawing of a man, a woman, and oneself. The rationale for using such drawings as a measure of intellectual maturity is provided by Harris: "The child's drawing of any object will reveal the discriminations he has made about that object as belonging to a class, that is, as a *concept*. In particular, it is hypothesized that his concept of a frequently experienced object, such as a human being, becomes a useful index to the growing complexity of his concepts generally" (1963, p. 7).

The instructions are very simple. The child is instructed "to make a picture of a man. Make the very best picture you can; take your time and work carefully. . . . Try very hard, and see what good pictures you can make. Be sure to make the whole man, not just his head and shoulders" (Harris, 1963, p. 240). Similar short, simple instructions precede the drawing of a woman and oneself. There is no time limit, and it is reported that ten to fifteen minutes are usually sufficient for young children. Elaborate materials or props are not needed to give the test. It is primarily intended for persons five to fifteen years old, although some "cautious" norms are provided for children as young as three. The test manual is just a section of the complete book by Harris (1963); the user is well-advised to obtain and to study the entire book.

Two scoring procedures are available. A rapid evaluation of the children's drawings of men and women can be made by comparing them against the Quality Scales—twelve sketches of men and twelve of women rated 1 (least mature) to 12 (most mature). These sketches were derived through a long process of having judges rate actual drawings. Important in the scoring of a child's drawing are the basic structure of the drawing and attention to detail and clothing. Once the Quality Scale score is determined, it and the child's age and sex are used to enter a table to obtain a standard score.

The second scoring method, which is more precise but also more time-consuming, uses Point Scales. The child's drawing of a man is examined for the inclusion of seventy-three separate items—body parts, items of clothing, and proportion. For example, one item is "eyes present," and four additional items concern eye detail (brow or lashes, pupil, proportion, and glance). The drawing of a woman is scored for seventy-one separate items. More detail and appropriate proportions in a drawing are taken as signs of a more advanced concept of a man or woman. Point Scale scores (the total points earned) are converted to standard scores in the same way that Quality Scale scores are. Scores generated by the two scoring methods typically correlate about .80.

The standard scores generated, whether by the Quality or Point Scale scoring procedure, have a mean of 100 and a standard deviation of 15, identical to both WISC and WPPSI. The manual indicates that the standard score earned is not identical to an IQ derived from an individually administered test such as the Binet, WISC, or WPPSI. However, the choice of the standard score scale based on Wechsler's precedent-setting deviation IQ and the use of phrases like "intellectual maturity" and "general ability level" to indicate what the Drawing Test assesses both imply a conscious effort to develop a measure and a score with substantial equivalence to the more usual IQ test and score.

Validity information for the Goodenough-Harris Drawing Test is of several types. Item analysis data were examined during the revision of the scales. Items retained had to show a regular and rapid increase with age in the percentage of children passing, be related to some general intelligence measure, and differentiate between children doing well and poorly on the test as a whole. Other relevant validity information noted the relationships between performance on the Drawing Test and on other measures. With the Binet, widely varying correlations are reported by different investigators but most exceed .50; with the WISC and the Primary Mental Abilities subscale, somewhat lower correlations are noted (Harris, 1963). Tangential evidence related to validity is also provided—namely, that an external examiner and a classroom teacher secured equivalent performances from students and that artistic ability had little influence on the standard score earned.

The principal use suggested for the Drawing Test is as a measure of intellectual maturity, either by a psychologist, in conjunction with other tests and clinical assessments, or by a classroom teacher "to arrange her children in order of intellectual maturity" (Harris, 1963, p. 247). Our impression is that validity is better established for use by psychologists than for use by teachers, primarily because skilled interpretation of scores requires training that teachers are not likely to have. The manual does not speak directly to this point. Commendably, the manual does not make claims to be culture-free (an early hope for the test). In a similarly cautious tone, the manual states, "There has been a tendency in recent years to interpret a child's drawings in terms of his 'creativity,' special interests, or deep psychological problems or conflicts. The literature review . . . shows that there is little confirmed basis for such use of children's drawings" (Harris, 1963, p. 247). Likewise, expectations for establishing the Drawing of the Self as a projective measure of personality have been, for the most part, unmet.

Reliability of the Drawing Test has been examined in several ways. Interscorer reliability of identical drawings is typically reported to be over .90 (Anastasi, 1972; and Harris, 1963). The coefficient of equivalence reported for scores on the male and female drawings (as if they were alternate forms) was .75. Considering this somewhat low, Harris suggested combining the two scores "to give a more reliable estimate of test achievement" (1963, p. 107). Turning to stability estimates, Harris administered the test on ten consecutive days to four kindergarten classes and found consistent performances by individual children. In a large study of the original scale, McCarthy (1944) noted a coefficient of stability of .68 for nearly 400 third- and fourth-graders over a one-week test interval; McCurdy (1947) reported a stability coefficient of .69 over a three-month interval for fifty-six first-graders.

For standardization of the 1963 revision, 2,975 children were sampled from four geographic regions of the country, approximately 75 from each region at each age level from five to fifteen years. Equal numbers of boys and girls were selected when possible, and attempts were made to select children from families representative of the occupational distribution in the country.

In all, the Goodenough-Harris Drawing Test represents a unique approach to the measurement of intellectual development. Its greater contribution could be to the general study of children's drawings (Kaplan, 1965). Administration is simple, but scoring and (especially) interpretation remain complex. The test has fair reliability and appropriate norms, although racial composition of the latter is not indicated. It has substantial validity as a supplemental measure for use by clinicians, but its validity in educational settings is neither thoroughly addressed nor established.

McCarthy Scales of Children's Abilities (MSCA): The McCarthy Scales of Children's Abilities (McCarthy, D., 1972) represent a new entry into the field of children's intelligence tests. This measure, which is individually administered by a trained examiner and requires a substantial kit of materials, is designed for children from two and a half to eight and a half years old. Administration reportedly takes forty-five minutes for children under five, and one hour for older children.

In construction, MSCA is similar in content to several measures already discussed. Eighteen tests are included: (1) block building, (2) puzzle solving, (3) pictorial memory, (4) word knowledge, (5) number questions, (6) tapping sequence, (7) verbal memory, (8) right-left orientation, (9) leg coordination, (10) arm coordination, (11) imitative action, (12) draw-a-design, (13) draw-a-child, (14) numerical memory, (15) verbal fluency, (16) counting and sorting, (17) opposite analogies, and (18) conceptual grouping. However, MSCA's combination of these eighteen tests to form six overlapping composite scales is unusual. The six scales and the numbers of the tests that compose them are:

- Verbal (V): 3, 4, 7, 15, and 17.
- Perceptual Performance (P): 1, 2, 6, 8, 12, 13, and 18.
- Quantitative (Q): 5, 14, and 16.
- General Cognitive Index (GCI): V plus P plus Q.
- Memory (Mem): 3, 6, 7, and 14.
- Motor (Mot): 9, 10, 11, 12, and 13.

The General Cognitive Index (GCI), made up of all the tests except 9, 10, and 11, probably comes closest to IQ as previously discussed. McCarthy purposely opted for the GCI to avoid some of the troublesome connotations that swirl about the term *IQ.* The GCI purportedly represents an index of a child's functioning at the time of testing, rather than any fixed or unchangeable quantity. However, like the developers of the Goodenough-Harris Drawing Test, McCarthy decided to express GCI as a standard score with IQ-like dimensions—namely, a mean of 100 and a standard deviation of 16. Sattler (1978) considered the GCI and the IQ "barely distinguishable." The other five scales are expressed as standard scores with mean of 50 and standard deviation of 10.

Validity for the MSCA is not extensively addressed, possibly because of the newness of the test. Predictive validity is addressed, but somewhat skimpingly, the sole criterion used being an achievement test given at the end of first grade to a small group of students. Somewhat more substantial, relating to construct validity, is information on the initial selection and grouping of tests. Such decisions were made on the basis of reviews of developmental psychology, experience gained in clinical settings, and factor-analytic studies. Subsequently, more exhaustive factor analyses of the standardization data substantially supported the structure of MSCA (Kaufman, 1975; and Kaufman and Hollenbeck, 1973).

Reliability data are substantial. For GCI, an average split-half reliability of .93 is reported, as is a coefficient of stability averaging .90 over three age groups retested after a one-month interval. For the five other scales, split-half reliabilities were principally in the .80s, while one-month stability coefficients ranged from approximately .70 to .90. The reliability of the Motor scale is relatively low compared to the other scales.

Norms and standardization involved over 1,000 children, about 100 at each of ten age levels—every half year from two and a half to five and a half years and then every year until age eight and a half. At each age level, equal numbers of boys and girls were tested, and the sample was stratified proportionate to the 1970 Census in regard to color, geographic region, urban-rural residence, and father's occupation. Bilingual children were included if they could speak and understand English. Children who were institutionalized for retardation or who had pronounced emotional or behavioral problems were excluded.

The McCarthy Scales represent an interesting addition to the field of early intelligence testing. MSCA's validity remains to be established, but its reliability and standardization are creditable. Its uniqueness lies in its separate scales for different functions, and the profile of abilities that they yield—characteristics that should make this measure quite valuable in clinical and other settings (in this regard, see Kaufman and Kaufman, 1977). However, it is precisely in this realm—the diagnostic potential of the profile of abilities—that additional work on validity is required (Hunt, 1978b; Sattler, 1978; and Silverstein, 1978). Further, whether the McCarthy will gain the widespread use and popularity of the Binet and the Wechsler remains to be seen.

Peabody Picture Vocabulary Test (PPVT): The Peabody (Dunn, 1965) requires no special qualifications for administration except that the examiner must know the test thoroughly, establish good rapport with the child, and be able to pronounce all the words correctly. Only ten to fifteen minutes are ordinarily required. The PPVT's unique construction feature is a multiple-choice picture format. The examiner reads a word, and the child chooses the picture to which the word corresponds, either pointing to or otherwise indicating a preferred picture of the four provided for each item. Since no verbal response is required, the PPVT can be used with subjects who cannot take tests such as the Binet, WISC-R, or WPPSI. Two forms are available; word lists are different, but the same plates of pictures are used for the two forms.

Like the Binet, the Peabody covers a wide age range and is administered only over a critical range of items, ordered by increasing difficulty, to determine a basal score (eight consecutive correct answers) and a ceiling (six misses out of eight consecutive responses). In content, the PPVT is even more verbal than the Binet in the sense that it involves just vocabulary. However, the Peabody, in Guilford's (1967) Structure of the Intellect terms, measures primarily cognition of figural units, that is, recognition of pictures—word correspondences, rather than language more generally conceived (the latter being more similar to that measured by the Binet). Although designed to be administered individually, the PPVT was standardized on groups of children, nine years of age or older, by using photographic slides of the response pictures. A pilot test of this procedure has yielded performances similar to those observed in individual testing. The raw score earned is the total number of correct responses; all items below the basal score are assumed correct, and items missed enroute to the ceiling are subtracted from the total number of items represented by the last item presented. Tables relating raw score earned and chronological age of the subject yield deviation IQs (mean of 100, standard deviation of 15).

Content validity was purportedly addressed by having 2,055 line drawings made of illustratable words, selected from a population of 3,885 such words identified through a dictionary search. Although starting with over fifty percent of all available words is commendable, selection criteria for this initial decision were not indicated in the manual. The items were then piloted with several groups and sequentially retained, revised, or eliminated, based on difficulty at varying age levels and suitability of distractors (incorrect choices in multiple-choice items, also called decoys or foils), until two forms of 150 words each were produced. Since the Peabody is often proposed as equivalent to longer IQ measures, concurrent validity is important. Sattler (1974) listed thirty-seven studies relating the PPVT and the Binet with a median correlation of .66, but noted significantly lower IQs for minority children on the PPVT (this disparity may have been reduced by the 1972 Binet norms). Reviewing the studies relating the PPVT and the WISC, Sattler reported median correlations of .66, .54, and .63 with the Verbal, Performance, and Full Scale IQs. Generally, for other intelligence measures, a median correlation of .53 with the Peabody was noted; with measures such as achievement tests and teacher ratings, a median correlation of .40 was observed (Sattler, 1974). Other validity information of quite varied nature is presented in the PPVT manual (Dunn, 1965).

Using the standardization sample, alternate form reliabilities from .67 at age six to .84 at ages seventeen and eighteen were observed; these correspond to standard errors of measurement of eight and a half to six IQ points, respectively. Under age six, equivalence reliabilities were primarily in the .70s, with standard errors of measurement averaging almost seven and a half IQ points. Sattler (1974) reviewed several studies of the PPVT and reported median coefficients of .77 for equivalence and .73 for stability over retest intervals from four weeks to two years.

The PPVT normative group consisted of over 4,000 subjects, aged two and a half to eighteen years, from the Nashville, Tennessee, area. Schools were selected where previous IQ performance approximated a normal distribution, or, in some cases, random samples of children in the lower grades were drawn until a normal distribution of their previous readiness or IQ test scores was approximated. For the preschool sample, a geographic area was canvassed after determination that it was served by four elementary schools whose students had previously earned IQ scores approximately normally distributed. Despite these efforts, the sampling was inadequate due to its regionality and its inclusion of only white subjects.

Overall, the Peabody is substantially reliable and moderately valid. However, it lacks culture-fairness (Datta, 1975a), and its norms could be markedly improved. The Peabody's uniqueness lies in its format and its simple administration and scoring. Further, it permits testing of retarded or certain handicapped children in terms of their developed vocabulary—or at least their "recognition" vocabulary (Hunt, 1975b)—independent of their ability for expression of ideas. At the same time, it does not serve as a substitute for IQ measures such as the Binet or the Wechsler tests, especially for minority children.

Quick Test (QT): The Quick Test (Ammons and Ammons, 1962) lives up to its name by requiring very little time (between three and ten minutes per person). Described as the "little brother" of the Full-Range Picture Vocabulary Test or FRPV (Ammons and Ammons, 1948), the QT was developed to be a very brief, individually administered intelligence test with strengths similar to the FRPV.

In construction, the QT resembles the Peabody. In fact, its development preceded the PPVT by several years. Like the PPVT, the QT uses a four-choice pictorial response format from which the testee simply has to point to the picture that "best fits" the given word. Further, only moderate training is needed to give and score the QT. Items are also arranged by difficulty but, unlike the PPVT, the QT uses a single plate of four pictures or scenes (such as a couple dancing or a policeman directing traffic) for all fifty items; that is, each of the four pictures serves as the correct response for ten or so of the items. Three forms of fifty items each, each with an accompanying plate of four pictures, are available. While a single form is reported as adequate for a general indication of intellectual ability, giving more than one form is encouraged if the QT is the only intelligence test being used. The range of the QT, extending to adult, is somewhat greater than that of the Peabody. Six consecutive passes set the base for the test, with the ceiling established at six consecutive failures. Raw scores earned on a single form or any combination of forms can be converted to mental ages for children or to deviation IQs (mean of 100, standard deviation of 15) for adults. Not providing deviation IQs for children seems a curious omission.

Criterion-related validity of a concurrent nature is provided in the QT manual. With the FRPV, high correlations are reported, with a median at .85. With tests such as the Ohio Psychological Exam and the Iowa Test of Basic Skills and with criteria such as school grades, the manual reports a median correlation of .45. Also noted are the age differentiation of items and matters that the test authors consider "indirect indications" of validity. Sattler (1974) reviewed many studies and reported correlations between the QT and several measures—the FRPV with a median at .76, the Binet at .17, .61, and .62, the WISC Full Scale with a median at .41 (somewhat higher for the Verbal Scale), and the Peabody with a median at .76. He also noted that, frequently, mean QT IQs are substantially different from mean IQs scored on other tests.

Reliability data concerning the equivalence of forms appears in the manual and ranges from .60 to .96, with a median of .70. Sattler (1974), reporting on subsequent studies, noted a median equivalence coefficient of .77 and stability coefficients principally in the .80s.

Norms are based on 458 white children and adults and some supplementary small samples. Equal numbers of males and females were used. Controls were instituted for age, grade placement, and father's (or husband's or own) occupation, the latter to be proportional to the 1950 Census. Geographic region was not included as the sample was drawn from Louisville, Kentucky.

Many have criticized the Quick Test for the poor and ambiguous quality of its response drawings (for example, see Piers, 1965; and Semeonoff, 1964). Semeonoff also lamented the QT's encouragement of the "loose use of language" (it seems somewhat appropriate that this criticism appears in a British journal). Its norms could be improved—for example, as by adding nonwhites. The Quick Test serves most appropriately as an initial rapid screening device, or possibly as a rough measure of intellectual ability needed in a large research venture. Its validity is moderate and its reliability even better in view of the short testing time. However, for assessment bearing on important decisions concerning an individual, it would seem that the increased testing time and expense involved with the use of longer, better-validated measures would be warranted. Use of the QT for decisions involving two- to four-year-olds would appear particularly ill-advised (Ernhart, 1975b).

In surveying early childhood intelligence measures, one cannot help but be impressed by the stature and well-researched nature of the Wechsler and Binet measures. Granted, these measures have been heavily criticized for their apparent unfairness to certain children (recall Chapter One). But the other available tests, such as the Drawing Test, the PPVT, or the QT, have addressed the fairness issue no better. Further, with the latter measures, savings in administration time and resources (in that highly trained examiners are not needed) are offset by reductions in reliability and, particularly, validity. It is unclear what long-range impact new measures of intelligence will have, such as the McCarthy,

SOMPA, and Piagetian scales. Their orientations, however, especially in the latter two cases, are sufficiently different that they deserve extended use and examination for possible new benefits.

Instruction-Related, Readiness, and Achievement Tests

The instruments examined in this section are all specifically related to school or instruction. They represent only a small sampling of the many readiness, achievement, and other instruction-related tests that have been developed for young children. Our selection criteria were not hard and fast but tended toward such things as recency of development, likelihood (or history) of substantial use, and relevance to children in preschools or in the initial school years (usually interpreted by us as kindergarten or first grade). Because the domain of available measures is so vast, we normally excluded tests that measure achievement in just a single area, such as reading or mathematics. The measures included, however, do give the reader a fairly representative sample of school- and instruction-related tests for young children.

Nature and Status of Instruction-Related, Readiness, and Achievement Tests. It was difficult to decide what types of measure to include in this section—not only because of the great number of measures available but also because of the misleading titles and vague purposes of some tests. For example, an achievement test is usually assumed to be designed to measure the effects of a specific program of instruction. Yet for a substantial part of early childhood education there is no set or established curriculum—in such cases, do achievement tests make sense at all? One could argue that there are certain general achievements that a child must master, either at home or in preschool, to be "ready" for kindergarten or first grade; should such achievements be measured by an achievement test or a readiness test? Further, the concept of readiness is far from well defined—a child ready for one type of kindergarten could be poorly prepared for another type or could be ready for instruction in some subjects but not in others. The notion that readiness is primarily maturational seems outdated, a more functional view of readiness is one that recognizes that both certain physical developments and considerable learning are required for a young learner to benefit substantially from formal school instruction. Note too that "readiness for school" might be extended downward to ask about "readiness for preschool." Some achievement tests explicitly claim not to be readiness tests, yet in content and construction they closely resemble readiness tests.

Rather than get bogged down in a series of unproductive verbal tangles, we (like others) have simply lumped together many of these measures of early learning regardless of their titles or claims, noting that they do have in common some relationship to learning or instruction. Helpful in reaching this decision was the typical distinction made between achievement and aptitude tests. Whereas an achievement test is designed to measure outcomes of specific instruction, an aptitude test is supposed to predict subsequent performance. This distinction of purpose does not necessarily imply highly disparate material in the two test types. In general, though, one would expect achievement tests to be more content-specific and more likely designed to tap the outcomes of presumably common experiences (Anastasi, 1976). Thus, if a test claims to be assessing a specific body of knowledge, it should be treated as an achievement test and evidence of content validity should be sought. Analogously, if a test is purporting to predict later performance (like succeeding in school or learning to read), it should be considered an aptitude test and expected to provide predictive validity information.

Note that tests of this general type can have functions beyond assessing knowledge of content or predicting future performance. That is, they can give clues to the types of experience or instruction needed by an individual (although specific diagnostic tests typically serve this function better) or to the strengths and limitations of set instructional programs. They can also provide valuable knowledge of results to the young learner and may possibly be motivational.

Before considering a series of illustrative tests, we would like to point out a promising instrument used primarily for instructional purposes and only secondarily for assessment. Based largely on Piaget's theory, Let's Look at First-Graders represents a joint venture of New York City's Board of Education and Educational Testing Service that commenced in 1965. Some of the materials explain Piaget's theory to teachers in terms of likely instructional applications, while others are related games and tasks for instructional use with first-graders. A series of written exercises, quite testlike in appearance, are also provided for children covering six areas: shapes and forms, spatial relations, time concepts, understanding mathematics, communication skills, and logical reasoning. Although the exercises are given and scored like tests, they are used by the teacher primarily for observing and understanding children's learning and development, for planning instruction, and for fostering intellectual development. Addison-Wesley has announced plans to completely revise these materials and to issue them in 1979 under the title Let's Look at Children.

Illustrative Instruction-Related, Readiness, and Achievement Tests. The eight tests presented now will convey well the general status of instruction-related, readiness, and achievement tests in early childhood education; they are listed in Table 12. A very large number of similar instruments exist, but space limitations preclude their inclusion here. The administration times given in the table are approximate in some cases, but give an indication of likely time requirements.

Basic Concept Inventory (BCI): This test was published as a "field research edition" (Engelmann, 1967). Purposes identified for the BCI are to evaluate instruction in beginning, academically related concepts received by a group or by an individual and to place children in small, homogeneous groups for instruction. The BCI is criterion-referenced only, with no norms provided. The measure is given individually, in about twenty minutes, by either a teacher or a trained examiner—depending on whether results are to be used for remedial instruction or diagnostically for special treatment or placement.

The BCI is divided into three parts, each featuring a different type of item. In Basic Concepts, the first part, the child must find in pictures things that

Table 12. Illustrative Instruction-Related, Readiness, and Achievement Tests in Early Childhood Education

Title and Date	Age Range	Administration	Scales or Scores	Source
Basic Concept Inventory (1967)	Preschool and Kindergarten	Individual; 20 minutes	Basic Concept Score (criterion-referenced)	Follett Publishing Co. 201 N. Wells St. Chicago, Ill. 60606
Boehm Test of Basic Concepts (1969, 1971: Items; 1971: Manual)	Kindergarten to Grade 2	Group; 30 to 40 minutes	Total Concepts Correct (norm- and criterion-referenced)	Psychological Corp. 304 E. 45th St. New York, N.Y. 10017
Circus, Levels A and B (1972–1976: Items; 1974–1976: Manuals)	Preschool to Grade 1	Group; variable time required	Multiple Measures such as Language, Reading, Perception, Mathematics, Information Processing, Creativity, Attitudes, and Interests	Addison-Wesley Testing Service South St. Reading, Mass. 01867
Comprehensive Tests of Basic Skills, Levels A and B (1973: Items; 1973–1974: Manuals)	Kindergarten to Grade 1	Group; 2½ to 3 hours	Multiple Measures Related to Prereading, Reading, Language, and Mathematics	CTB/McGraw-Hill Del Monte Research Park Monterey, Calif. 93940
Cooperative Preschool Inventory (1970)	3 to 6 years	Individual; 15 minutes	Total Items Correct	Addison-Wesley Testing Service
Metropolitan Readiness Tests, Levels I and II (1976)	Kindergarten to Grade 1	Group; 2 hours	Skill Areas such as Auditory, Visual, Language, and Quantitative	Harcourt Brace Jovanovich 757 Third Ave. New York, N.Y. 10017

Test	Grade Range	Administration	Subtests	Publisher
Stanford Early School Achievement Test, Levels I and II (1969–1970: Items; 1969–1971: Manuals)	Kindergarten to Grade 1	Group; 1½ to 2½ hours	Environment Mathematics Letters and Sounds Aural Comprehension Word Reading Sentence Reading	Harcourt Brace Jovanovich
Tests of Basic Experiences, Levels K and L (1970; Items; 1970–1972, 1975: Manuals)	Preschool to Grade 1	Group; 2 hours	Mathematics Language Science Social Studies General Concepts	CTB/McGraw-Hill

are described by the examiner, or answer questions about the pictures, or identify body parts. The plates of pictures are well sketched and are the only special materials needed to administer the BCI. In part two, Statement Repetition and Comprehension, the child must repeat sentences read by the examiner and answer questions based on the statements. The final part, Pattern Awareness, requires the child to imitate movement patterns and number sequences and to recognize words from sounds blended very slowly by the examiner. In all, one can recognize many direct correspondences between the test items and the program model for instructing young children that Engelmann helped develop (Bereiter and Engelmann, 1966). Errors made by the child are summed for each part and then totaled; the smaller a child's score, the better the performance. The manual contains extensive discussion on interpreting inventory performance, including item-by-item examples for hypothetical children and a series of case histories. Some limited attention is also given to possible remedial instruction based on inventory performance.

Technical information contained in the manual is disappointing. The "intuitive and informal" approach to item construction and selection lacks the substance to support content validity (McCandless, 1972; and McCarthy, J. J., 1972). However, the items selected as representative by the developer should not be lightly dismissed, in view of his extensive experience with young children. The manual states clearly that predictive validity, construct validity, reliability, and age norms are not provided. (It predicted that adequate reliability data would be available by 1968, but to date these have not appeared.) After the solid promise of an effective link between assessment and instruction and a decade of existence, it is unfortunate that additional substantiating material for the BCI has not been provided to increase its utility.

Boehm Test of Basic Concepts (BTBC): The stated purpose of the BTBC is to measure children's mastery of concepts felt necessary for achievement in the first years of school, thereby identifying individual children needing special help or particular concepts unfamiliar to a sizable proportion of a class (Boehm, 1971). Intended for kindergarten to second grade, the Boehm is designed to be administered by a teacher to an entire class or to small groups of eight to twelve if the children are unfamiliar with marking workbooks. Each item consists of a drawing; the teacher reads a question and the child must mark the appropriate part of the drawing with a crayon or pencil. Use with preschoolers is possible if the BTBC is given individually with children pointing to, rather than marking, the answer.

Items were selected by reviewing preschool and primary-grade curriculum materials in reading, arithmetic, and science for concepts that occurred frequently, were seldom explicitly defined, and were relatively complex. The concepts were translated to pictorial, multiple-choice form and tried out to eliminate items that were ambiguous or too easy. Ultimately, fifty items were selected and arranged in order of increasing difficulty. The items were classified in terms of the content category represented—either space, quantity, time, or miscellaneous (a few items were classified in more than one category). Proportionately, space concepts are most frequent, then quantity, and time; very few are classified as miscellaneous. To create two parallel forms, a second set of multiple-choice pictorial responses was designed. That is, the fifty concepts (such as farthest or few) remained the same, but the illustrated choices and verbal instructions (compatible with the new pictures) changed. Both forms were divided into two parts of twenty-five items each so that two test sessions could be used with young or inattentive students. Raw scores are converted to percentile ranks; separate conversions are provided for socioeconomic class (low, middle, or high), grade (kindergarten, one, or two), and time of year (beginning or middle). The manual contains considerable information on using the results for planning remedial instruction for individuals and groups—the content of the instruction being the missed concepts themselves.

Unfortunately, validity is minimally addressed in the Boehm manual. There, only content validity is considered applicable; the position taken is that using relevant curriculum materials to select concepts assured such validity. However, both we and Noll (1970) believe that the actual curriculum materials and criteria used are inadequately described to support such a contention. On their surface, the concepts seem to be highly relevant to early instruction, but solid convincing evidence is lacking. Further, predictive criterion-related validity should have been examined to establish that mastery of the concepts does indeed forecast successful performance on related curriculum tasks and high achievement in the first years of school (Dahl, 1973; and Noll, 1970). Neither criterion-related nor construct validity is mentioned in the BTBC manual.

Split-half reliability coefficients were substantial, being .90, .85, and .81 on Form A and .84, .83, and .87 on Form B, for kindergarten, grade one, and grade two, respectively. These generally corresponded to standard errors of measurement of two to three raw score points (or items), with larger standard errors for the younger students. Split-half reliabilities were also reported by socioeconomic level within each grade. These estimates were satisfactory except for second-graders from the high socioeconomic level, whose scores varied so little from child to child (all being near the maximum score possible) that the correlation was depressed. Also of interest was the correlation between Forms A and B since a deliberate attempt to make the forms parallel had been made. Alternate forms were given with testing intervals from one day to less than one week. The coefficients of stability and equivalence observed were .72, .87, and .88 for kindergarten, grade one, and grade two, respectively. While adequate, these correlations may appear somewhat lower than expected. Alternate form reliability was also reported by socioeconomic level within each grade and ranged from .55 to .92.

Norms are provided and commendably are broken down by socioeconomic level. School children from over twenty cities were included in the standardization sample, but no attempt was made to make it representative of the entire nation. The test developer contends a representative sample was unnecessary since the BTBC was intended primarily for screening and planning instruction rather than for prediction. Norms became, therefore, a bonus provided and not essential to interpretation of the Boehm performance. We believe the test author relies too heavily here on the criterion-referenced nature of the test; clearly many users will rely on the norm-referencing, and norms established as nationally representative and fully differentiated would be of greater value to them. Note further that the near-perfect performance on the Boehm by nearly all second-graders and the excellent performance by first-graders from middle to high socioeconomic levels make the test only minimally pertinent to them.

In summary, the Boehm is a promising test including such features as alternate forms, links to instruction, short administration time, teacher administration and interpretation, and both criterion- and norm-referencing (although we agree with Dahl, 1973, that the BTBC lacks consistency with regard to referencing intentions, thus causing confusion). Its value could be increased substantially, however, by the addition of convincing content and predictive validity information and fully differentiated and nationally representative norms. The BTBC should be considered a test for just kindergartners and lower socioeconomic level first-graders unless substantial numbers of more difficult concepts are added. The reader interested in the Boehm also will want to examine a related but more comprehensive instrument, namely, the Cognitive Skills Assessment Battery (Boehm and Slater, 1974); issued only as a preliminary edition at this time, it also could be improved by the addition of substantive technical data, especially on validity (Keogh, 1978).

Circus: This test, developed by Educational Testing Service (ETS), represents a recent entrant into the field. The two major purposes established for Circus are to diagnose the instructional needs of children and to monitor and evaluate early childhood education programs (*Circus Manual and Technical Report,* 1976). Considerable user choice exists in deciding which measures to give; Level A (preschool and early kindergarten) has seventeen separate measures, and Level B (late kindergarten and first grade) has fifteen. Of the fifteen Level B tests, three are identical to Level A tests and two are completely different, while the remaining ten have analogous counterparts. Most measures are responded to by children, but three at each level are completed by teachers. The tests in Levels A and B are indicated in Table 13. In 1979, ETS and Addison-Wesley Testing Service plan to introduce Circus Levels C (mid-first to mid-second grades) and D (mid-second to mid-third grades); however, this discussion focuses on Levels A and B.

Circus claims several unusual features, such as having preliminary practice materials, focusing on a child's multiple capacities and avoiding any global score (such as IQ), being an enjoyable experience for young children, and providing sentence reports of performance as well as percentile rank norms. Construction features include having very few items per page, using untimed tests for the most part, and giving the tests to small groups of children (except on Say and Tell, which is individually administered). The teacher reads each item aloud, and the children mark directly the picture they choose as the answer. Circus appears to have "covered the bases" quite well in terms of construction, although the following features must be noted: (1) many of the picture drawings lack clarity; (2) a small but significant proportion of children did not find the experience pleasant or displayed inappropriate test-taking behavior (*Circus Manual and*

Technical Report, 1974–75, pp. 378–379); and, (3) group testing might not run as smoothly as suggested (Raths and Katz, 1975), often because the very young children may not have developed test-taking etiquette (Ambron, 1978).

Curiously, the manual does not address content validity, although child development experts might have been polled on the representativeness of the items and the comprehensiveness of the total Circus package. Predictive validity was examined by noting the relationship between over 1,000 kindergartners' fall scores on Level A and, six months later, their spring scores on Level B. Although an average of .57 (obtained via Fisher's Z-transformation of r) was noted for the nine correlations generated, this looks to us less like a true measure of predictive validity than like a reliability coefficient of stability and equivalence (given the construction similarities between Levels A and B and the unknown quality of Level B as a criterion). Concurrent validity was addressed by comparing teachers' ratings of children's abilities with their performance on associated Circus measures. Calculated separately for Levels A and B, average correlations of .41 were observed. Finally, in an attempt related to construct validity, performance on Circus measures was factor-analyzed for each level. A substantial general ability factor was identified at each level, suggesting that the measures making up Circus were not as independent as developers might have wished. Although these reported procedures contribute to understanding Circus, they unfortunately do not address directly the stated purposes of Circus—that is, diagnosing instructional needs and monitoring or evaluating early education programs (Goodwin, 1978a).

Reliability is reported in the manual chiefly in terms of the internal consistency of each measure and subscales within measures. Alpha reliabilities are, generally, substantial to high, ranging from .60 to .90; associated standard errors of measurement are also reported and are satisfactorily small. Reliability estimates are especially impressive given the young age of the respondents. Further, data on each individual item are presented in the user's guide accompanying each measure. The percentage of children selecting each response appears, and also biserial correlations (relating subjects' performance on each item to their overall performance on the measure). No reliability information is presented for the "creativity" measure (Make a Tree); this is also the only test for which scoring service is not available from ETS. Unfortunately, no stability reliabilities are reported.

The norming of Circus has been systematic and impressive. For Level A, a sample of nearly 2,000 kindergarten and 1,000 nursery school children was selected from the population of preprimary education centers in the country that met certain criteria (had been in operation for at least one year, had a "professional" director, met at least twelve hours weekly and thirty weeks annually, and enrolled at least ten children). For Level B, a national sample of first grade classrooms was randomly selected, involving over 6,000 children in nearly 300 classrooms. Actual test sites are listed, and sampling procedures are well described. Tables contain means and standard deviations on each measure for the norm group characterized by sex, ethnicity, previous school experience, age, socioeconomic status, and region of the country. (Even with these exemplary

Table 13. Circus Instruments for Level A (Preschool and Early Kindergarten) and Level B (Late Kindergarten and First Grade)

General Area	Instrument Title (and Content Area)	Designed for Level(s)
Language and Reading	How Words Sound (auditory discrimination)	A only
	What Words Mean (receptive vocabulary)	A only
	How Words Work (functions of language)	A only
	Listen to the Story (comprehending, interpreting, and recalling oral language)	A and B (similar)
	Say and Tell (productive language)	A and B (similar)
	Word Puzzles (identifying, recognizing, and blending sounds)	B only
Perception	Look-Alikes (visual discrimination)	A and B (similar)
	Copy What You See (perceptual-motor coordination)	A and B (similar)
	Finding Letters and Numbers (recognizing and discriminating letters and numbers)	A and B (identical)
	Noises (discriminating real-world sounds)	A only
Mathematics	How Much and How Many (quantitative concepts)	A and B (similar)
Information Processing and Experience	Do You Know . . . ? (general information)	A and B (similar)
	See and Remember (visual and associative memory)	A and B (similar)
	Think It Through (problem solving)	A and B (similar)

Divergent Production	Make a Tree (divergent pictorial production)	A and B (identical)
Attitudes and Interests	Things I Like (activity preference)	B only
	Activities Inventory (teacher ratings of child's typical activities)	A and B (similar)
Test-Taking Behavior	Circus Behavior Inventory (teacher ratings of child's test-taking behavior)	A and B (identical)
Teacher/Program Measure	Educational Environment Questionnaire (teacher ratings of self and environment)	A and B (similar)

norming procedures, some concern is warranted about the representativeness of the resultant Level A sample for several measures. For example, the nursery school sample for Look-Alikes consists of 88 percent white children and essentially no Chicano children, while 80 percent of the sample is either middle or high socioeconomic status—nearly 50 percent are high. These seeming imbalances are ameliorated considerably in the case of the kindergarten sample.) Tables are available to transform raw scores to percentile ranks, to six-month growth expectancies (when analogous Level A and B measures exist), and to sentence reports. We believe that the sentence reports need reconceptualization if they are to have utility for Circus' primary purpose of diagnosing instructional need. Considerable information is lost when raw scores are transformed to a limited number of sentence reports, as each encompasses a substantial range of raw scores. Further, the sentences themselves were based on a very broad definition of "average competence," thus reducing the preciseness of the sentence reports.

In all, Circus is quite promising. It provides multiple measures that can be used flexibly—meeting well the recommendations of the Anderson and Messick (1974) article presented in Chapter One (both Anderson and Messick work for ETS). The internal consistency reliability estimates are excellent and the sampling procedures noteworthy (although some subgroups should be more adequately represented in the norms for certain measures). With more attention focused on validity and test-retest reliability, Circus could become a very valuable measure for early childhood education. (In the following chapter, Circus language and divergent production tests are considered in greater depth.)

Comprehensive Tests of Basic Skills (CTBS): This measure, like the Stanford Early School Achievement Test described later, represents a downward age extension of a series of achievement test batteries originally developed for students at higher grade levels. Here we consider only the single forms available for Levels A (early kindergarten through early first grade) and B (mid-kindergarten through late first grade); five other CTBS batteries extend upward through grade twelve. Designed for group administration by the classroom teacher along with several proctors, both Levels A and B are quite long (four separate testing days are suggested) and contain a practice test and eight other tests:

Level A	*Level B*
1. Letter Forms	1. Letter Sounds
2. Letter Names	2. Word Recognition I
3. Listening for Information	3. Reading Comprehension
4. Letter Sounds	4. Word Recognition II
5. Visual Discrimination	5. Language I
6. Sound Matching	6. Language II
7. Language	7. Mathematics Concepts and Applications
8. Mathematics	8. Mathematics Computation

The predominance of test activities related to language and reading is obvious at both levels, though Level B is more "school-like" in content. In addition to separate scores for each test, Level A yields three composite scores: Total Alphabet Skills (tests 1 and 2), Total Visual and Auditory Discrimination (3 through 6), and Total Prereading (1 through 7). Level B yields four composite scores: Total Reading (1 through 4), Total Language (5 and 6), Total Mathematics (7 and 8), and Total Battery (1 through 8).

Special construction features include having classroom teachers work with curriculum and testing specialists in item writing; attempting to reduce racial and ethnic bias by eliminating suspect items after preliminary tryout and by having knowledgeable minority group members review the tests for content bias; and providing a machine-scorable option. Raw scores earned can be transformed into percentile ranks, stanines, and "expanded standard scores" (provided by a single standard score scale, with equal intervals from 0 to 999, that ties together all the levels of the CTBS). Additionally, grade-equivalent conversions are provided for the four composite scores on Level B.

Validity claims for the CTBS are presented (Comprehensive Tests of Basic Skills, Technical Bulletin No. 1, 1974). Most emphasis is placed on content validity; criterion-related validity, such as predictive and concurrent, was not deemed useful for the evaluation of an achievement test. (One might question this logic in the sense that Level A performance should predict later school success.) The test developers indicated that highly experienced primary and nursery school teachers were employed to evaluate existing test materials, to make recommendations for improvement, and to indicate needed test materials. Recommendations from these teachers plus a thorough literature review formed the basis for test specifications; actual items were written by teachers and content area specialists. This process sounds appropriate for laying a base for content validity, but there is a disappointing lack of information about the training and expertise of both the teachers and the content specialists used. Tryout of the new tests led to retention of items that showed greater passing percentages for each higher grade level, that differentiated between students doing well and poorly on the test as a whole, and that correlated well with entire test performance. The last procedure was done separately for white and black samples to reduce bias. In general, these practices seem creditable. However, validity would be further enhanced by an even fuller description of the process and the participants. (Why, for example, was only one minority group consulted in determining items retained?) Intercorrelation coefficients are provided separately for the Level A and Level B tests, but are not interpreted in terms of validity. The intercorrelations between the tests (not including composite scores) are moderate, with median correlations at .50 and .56 for Levels A and B, respectively.

The reliability information for the CTBS is primarily phrased in terms of internal consistency (KR_{20}) and standard errors of measurement. For Level A, coefficients for separate tests and two age groups range from .72 to .92 (median .89); for Level B, with three age groups, the range is .62 to .91 (median .79). For composite scores, even larger coefficients are reported (such as .96 for Level A's

Total Prereading and .94 for Level B's Total Battery). Additional information concerned the articulation between Levels A and B. Over 2,000 students took Level A early in first grade and then, six months later, Level B. The similarity between this procedure and determining a coefficient of stability and equivalence probably explains the appearance of this procedure in the reliability section; note that it also bears some indirect relation to predictive validity. Most interlevel correlation coefficients fell in the range of .40 to .70; Total Prereading from Level A correlated .78 with Level B's Total Battery.

Norms were determined by an elaborate and extensive sampling procedure. All school districts were characterized by average enrollment per grade, geographic region, community type, and school type (greater cities public, other public, and Catholic); a sample of districts was then drawn. Within selected districts, a random sample of schools was chosen. Considerable information was then secured from participating schools, such as size, neighborhood self-description, student characteristics (such as percentage with employed mothers and ethnic composition), and staff and materials characteristics (such as text dates and staff specialists). In all, over 16,000 students were involved in the standardization of Level A, over 13,000 in that of Level B. The test developers' claim that the sample was representative of the nation's schools seems reasonable. With this elaborate standardization, it is curious that norm tables provided are not differentiated according to the sampling characteristics.

In all, the CTBS exhibits characteristics similar to many other measures of the same type—substantial content coverage, good reliability, and extensive standardization samples. Content validity is partially addressed; validity in general should be more fully elaborated (see also Nitko, 1978).

Cooperative Preschool Inventory (CPI): Developed for use with three- to six-year-olds, the CPI is designed as a brief (fifteen-minute) assessment and screening procedure to measure achievement in areas considered necessary for success in school (Cooperative Preschool Inventory Handbook, 1970). It was originally constructed to identify the extent of early academic disadvantagement of children from impoverished homes. Only simple, easily obtained materials are needed for administration. The CPI is individually administered by the teacher, who at times must use a probing technique (that is, asking additional, clarifying questions when a child's answer is vague, ambiguous, or marginally correct) to determine if credit should be given for the item.

An initial pool of 161 items was developed. After tryout and factor analyses, sixty-four items constituted the final inventory. Many items are of the information type, while others involve labeling quantities, perceiving shapes, identifying serial positions, and exhibiting basic visual-motor drawing skills (French, 1972). Thus, several blocks of items call for the child to identify body parts, to follow simple instructions, to answer questions to demonstrate knowledge of a concept, to indicate awareness of more or less or bigger or slower, to identify colors and shapes, and to copy geometric figures. Although earlier, longer versions of the CPI included subtest scores, factor analyses of the eventual sixty-four item test did not support retention of distinct subtests. Thus, a single score is derived—simply the total number of correct items—which can be converted to a percentile rank.

Unfortunately, the CPI Handbook contains no section on validity. Some information relevant to validity does appear here and there, but in other contexts. Apropos of content validity, Bettye M. Caldwell, the inventory's principal architect, is clearly an expert in the field of early childhood education and development (but one would still want additional expert opinion). Further, most items do show moderate correlations with total test score and a sizable increase in percentage of passing scores from four- to five- to six-year-olds. Concurrent validity is examined, in a sense, in that Binet IQs were available for over 1,400 children in the CPI standardization sample. An overall correlation of .44 was noted, lower for younger and higher for older children (that is, .39 for three-year-olds, and .65 for those just over five). The Handbook reports that this is evidence that the CPI is measuring something in addition to intelligence, rather than simply noting (more defensibly, we believe) a modest correlation with a well-established predictor of school success—that is, the Binet. In general, one finds little in the way of predictive validity information, even though measuring achievement necessary for success in school is the principal purpose set for the Cooperative Preschool Inventory.

Reliability in the Handbook involves two measures of internal consistency—KR_{20} and split-half—which were calculated for several age groups. These coefficients are quite satisfactory, hovering around .90. The associated standard errors of measurement for different age groups range from three to four raw score points, again quite satisfactory. Unfortunately, no data on stability reliability are reported.

Norming of the CPI involved over 1,500 children in more than 150 Head Start classes in the United States. The selection of the actual classes is not detailed, but the sample is described in terms of age, sex, and ethnic group. Regional norms are provided when over 100 children were tested from a region. This concentration on Head Start Centers may make the norms valuable for other such centers, but it limits their utility for young children in general. For example, over two thirds of the sample was black. The developers of the CPI are evidently aware of the limitations of the norms and attempt to compensate by reporting performance of three additional groups of young children from Kentucky, Arizona, and North Carolina; only the latter included children from middle and high socioeconomic families.

Overall, administration by teachers is an attractive feature, as is the brief time required. Although internal consistency reliability is impressive, the Cooperative Preschool Inventory requires additional work on norms, on stability reliability, and, particularly, on validity if it is to attain its full utility.

Metropolitan Readiness Tests (MRT): First appearing in 1933, the Metropolitan Readiness Tests represent a widely used and fairly typical readiness instrument. Its primary purpose is to predict readiness for grade one instruction. In its 1976 revision, MRT is available in two forms for each of two levels; Level I is for early or mid-kindergarten, and Level II is for the end of kindergarten or start of grade one (Metropolitan Readiness Tests, Teacher's Manual, 1976). A practice booklet prepares the child; the actual test is given orally, with the child marking directly on pictures, numbers, or letters. Like the CTBS, MRT can be hand- or machine-scored and includes a practice test.

Tests in the MRT at each level are indicated below:

Level I	*Level II*
Auditory Skill Area	*Auditory Skill Area*
1. Auditory Memory	1. Beginning Consonants
2. Rhyming	2. Sound-Letter Correspondence
Visual Skill Area	*Visual Skill Area*
3. Letter Recognition	3. Visual Matching
4. Visual Matching	4. Finding Patterns
Language Skill Area	*Language Skill Area*
5. School Language and Listening	5. School Language
6. Quantitative Language	6. Listening
	Quantitative Skill Area
	7. Quantitative Concepts
	8. Quantitative Operations

In addition to composite scores for each skill area, tests 1 through 6 at both levels yield a prereading skills composite. The Metropolitan is similar to the CTBS in content and length; no two tests are to be given at a single sitting, so several days are required. For both levels, raw scores for skill areas and the prereading skills composite can be converted to either stanines or performance ratings of low (stanines 1 to 3), average (stanines 4 to 6), or high (stanines 7 to 9); percentile ranks are available just for the prereading skills composite. Additionally, on Level I only, raw scores on individual tests can be transformed to performance ratings.

Validation efforts centered on content and predictive validity. For content validation, the beginning reading process was analyzed and reading research literature reviewed to identify the skills necessary for beginning reading; tests to measure these skills were then designed, tried out, and item-analyzed. The over-all process sounds appropriate but is not explicated sufficiently; expert review is not mentioned. Further, the individual tests for each level are moderately related (median correlations of .55 and .51 for Levels I and II, respectively), so the content for each test might not be as separate as MRT developers hoped. Predictive validity involved relating MRT scores to later achievement test performance. Level I was given to over 700 kindergartners in November who then took the Metropolitan Achievement Test, Primer Level, the following April. Correlations of MRT's individual tests with the primer's listening for sounds, reading, and math tests were moderate, averaging about .55. Correlations of MRT's skill areas and composite with the primer's three tests were somewhat higher, averaging .63 and .70, respectively. Level II was administered in the fall to over 4,000 students who, the following spring, took either the Metropolitan or Stanford Achievement Test, Primary I Levels. Correlations of MRT's skill area scores with the achievement test scores were moderate to substantial, falling primarily in the .50s and .60s; correlations of MRT's composite score with the achievement tests' scores and battery composite scores fell in the .70s.

The MRT's reliability involved coefficients of internal consistency (split-half and KR_{20}) and equivalence between forms. For both levels, internal consistencies for the prereading skills composite were in the .90s, while skill area scores ranged from .68 to .93 (median of .85). On Level I, individual tests had internal consistencies ranging from .66 to .88 (median of .76). Considering the age of the children involved, these reliabilities are impressive. Alternate-form reliability was substantial for the composite prereading score (in the mid .80s), but lower than might be hoped for skill area scores (median of .75) and Level I individual test scores (median of .68).

The norming of the MRT was extensive, with over 100,000 kindergarten and first-grade children involved. School districts first were stratified using enrollment and socioeconomic criteria, then a random sample of districts was selected to participate; additional provisions were made to include parochial, very small, and large city school districts. The sample, described in terms of sex, ethnicity, geographic region, and previous school experience, was nationally representative. The manuals also contain extensive discussions on how to interpret scores.

In summary, the MRT continues to be a solid instrument with much to recommend its use. Its reliability and norming are exceptional, and validity has been conscientiously addressed. Improvements might be effected by providing appropriately differentiated norms for distinct subgroups and by examining predictive validity on additional criteria—that is, other than just achievement test scores.

Stanford Early School Achievement Test (SESAT): The stated purpose of the SESAT is to measure children's cognitive abilities during kindergarten and grade one, apparently so that the teacher will know where to begin instruction. Although the SESAT claims not to be a readiness test (Madden and Gardner, 1969 and 1971), it is similar in content to the CTBS and the MRT, previously discussed. Further, the SESAT resembles the other two tests in being long (requiring multiple sittings), teacher-administered, hand or machine scorable, available at two levels (Level I for kindergarten and early grade one and Level II for grade one), and prefaced by a practice test. SESAT's item format, however, may cause unnecessary difficulties for some children in that many items containing tiny pictures are crowded onto each page (Cazden, 1978).

The tests of SESAT at each level are indicated below:

Level I	*Level II*
1. The Environment	1. The Environment
2. Mathematics	2. Mathematics
3. Letters and Sounds	3. Letters and Sounds
4. Aural Comprehension	4. Aural Comprehension
	5. Word Reading
	6. Sentence Reading

The Environment is a general information test about science and social studies. Aural Comprehension is a test in which the child listens to a paragraph read aloud and then marks a picture to answer a question, to follow a sequence, or to make an inference. Although the first four tests have identical names, the Level II tests contain additional and different items. For both levels, total scores are obtained by summing across all tests. Raw scores can be converted to percentile ranks and stanines.

The manuals do not include specific sections on validity, nor do they indicate the source of the test items or whether content experts were consulted. Item difficulty tables are included, but for only one age on Level II; items on Level I show a satisfactory increase in percentage of children passing from beginning kindergartners to beginning first–graders. Of some concern are the high intercorrelations between tests at each level. For Level I, the median inter-correlations are .65 for the kindergarten sample and .70 for the first-graders; on Level II, the median correlations are .52, .62, and .58 for starting, midyear, and completing first-graders, respectively. These are higher than those for the MRT and cause one to question how separate the cognitive abilities measured by SESAT are. The only other manual information pertinent to validity is a report of correlations between SESAT measures and the Otis-Lennon Mental Ability Test. For Level I and the first-grade sample, a median correlation of .65 was reported between the four SESAT tests and the Otis, and a correlation of .74 between the total SESAT score and the Otis; for the three first-grade samples and Level II, the analogous median correlations were .59 and .67. Again, the distinctness of the separate SESAT tests failed to clearly emerge as most of them correlated moderately to substantially with the Otis.

Split-half reliability coefficients are reported for Level I; the median cor-relations are .79 for the kindergartners and .82 for the first-graders. On Level II, median KR_{20} reliability coefficients for the individual tests are .80, .90, and .90 for the early, middle, and late first-grade samples, while the reliabilities for the total score are .94, .97, and .97, respectively.

Normative procedures appear appropriate. Large national samples were used (over 20,000 kindergartners and first-graders for Level I, and over 7,000 first–graders for Level II). Appropriate representativeness in terms of geo-graphic region, size of city, and socioeconomic status was sought and essentially attained. The discussion of score interpretation in the manuals is generally good—except for very misleading sample individual profile charts for four hypothetical students in the Level I manual (Hagen, 1972; and Mehrens, 1972).

Overall, SESAT has moderate reliability and acceptable norms. However, it is questionable how well it fulfills its purpose of measuring cognitive abilities. The content validity of the Level I Environment test has, in particular, been challenged (Cazden, 1978). Different SESAT measures have much in common with each other and with IQ tests. If the SESAT does intend to establish itself as different from readiness tests and from IQ tests, and does intend to provide separate measures of several cognitive abilities with instructional implications, extensive additional work on validity appears necessary.

Tests of Basic Experiences (TOBE): These tests are designed to measure how well prepared individual children or entire classes are for scholastic activities (Moss, 1970–1972, 1975). The manual implies that (1) the TOBE measures a child's past experiences and concept formation rather than information and facts, and (2) that data from it can be used as a concrete base for instruction by analyzing either individual or class performance on an item-by-item basis, and then planning instruction on those concepts not yet acquired. Two levels of the TOBE are available: Level K for preschoolers and kindergartners and Level L for kindergartners and first-graders. TOBE is designed for group administration on separate days (no more than one test per day). The teacher, assisted by one proctor for every four to six children, reads each item while children mark one of four pictures in the test booklet; only one item per page characterizes Level K, while Level L has two items per page. No practice test is provided. Since 1975, a computer-scored version of the TOBE has been available.

Each level contains distinct items, but the content areas are the same, namely mathematics, language, science, and social studies. Additionally, a general concepts test is available, composed primarily of items selected from the other four tests; it need not be given if the other four tests are all used. Each test contains twenty-eight items and is untimed (each is estimated to take about twenty-five minutes). Raw scores on any test can be converted to percentile ranks, stanines, or standard scores (mean of 50, standard deviation of 10). Diamond (1978) has expressed her concern that the items show evidence of sex bias.

The manual emphasizes content validity, although information relevant to other types of validity is presented in a supplementary validity section. The content validation study involved printing each TOBE item separately without indicating which test it was from and having thirty-four teachers from six states independently classify the items as relevant to mathematics, language, science, or social studies. Teachers also indicated any items they would not use. Seventeen kindergarten teachers examined Level K, while seventeen first-grade teachers examined Level L. For about two thirds of the items, the teacher classification of content area and the test designation were in agreement. Less than 10 percent of the items were designated by the teachers as ones they would not use. The results from this fairly innovative procedure speak well for the TOBE's content validity from the perspective of the experienced user, although thirty-four teachers is still a small group. Missing are judgments from child development experts as to the representativeness and importance of the content. A potpourri of information appears in the supplemental validity section. Noted are low to moderate correlations between TOBE scores and criteria obtained several months later, such as teacher ratings of achievement and Metropolitan Readiness Test scores. Moderate correlations are reported between TOBE and measures given at the same time, such as MRT, Draw-a-Man, and the Cooperative Preschool Inventory. Other information shows scores on the TOBE to be influenced by school instruction. Elsewhere, the articulation between the analogous tests for K and L Levels is shown to be substantial, with correlations centering in the .70s.

Principal reliability information includes coefficients of internal consistency (KR_{20}) and associated standard errors of measurement. Coefficients are substantial, with median values on Level K of .80 and .84 for prekindergarten and kindergarten children, respectively, and on Level L of .77 and .79 for kindergartners and first-graders, respectively. Standard errors of measurement hover just over two raw score points (or items). Coefficients of stability over a six-week interval are also reported, with a median coefficient of .78 for kindergartners repeating Level K and median coefficients of .70 and .74 for kindergartners and first-graders, respectively, retaking Level L. These seem lower than might be expected, although the young age of respondents and short test length (only twenty-eight items) must be kept in mind.

Standardization of the TOBE involved over 10,000 children, but systematic sampling procedures were not used. Performance on each separate test is reported by grade, community type, and region. Conversion tables are available for both levels; however, it is recommended that these tables be used only for early-year performance and that local norms be used for end-of-year performance. It is clearly stated that the tables do not represent national norms. The manual does indicate, but relatively briefly, how test results can be used for instruction or program evaluation. The Class Evaluation Record is well designed and can be helpful to the teacher in interpretation.

In total, the TOBE demonstrates good reliability and considerable information related to validity. It is not clear, however, just what purpose the TOBE seeks to meet that would mark it as distinct from IQ, readiness, or achievement measures; its manual lacks integration in terms of an overall purpose. If its principal purpose is to prescribe needed instructional activities, this should be clearly stated and relevant validity established. Additionally, its large-scale but unsophisticated norming leaves much room for improvement.

Recently, CTB/McGraw-Hill released TOBE 2 (Moss, 1978); provided were items and examiner's manuals for both levels K and L. The principal changes involved the elimination of the general concepts test (with the suggestion that a combined mathematics and language score be substituted), the provision for spring norms, and the reduction of each test to twenty-six items. However, at the time of this writing (early 1979), the Norms and Technical Data Book has not yet become available, precluding judgments about TOBE 2's adequacy in several important regards.

In surveying the eight measures described in this section, we are impressed by their apparent appropriateness for assessing instruction-related cognitive abilities in young children, but we are also concerned about the general lack of definitive validation. Three possible reasons for this situation come to mind. First, instrument developers often seem uncertain as to the exact purposes of their tests. This uncertainty, in turn, makes it unclear how to approach validity and what evidence to seek and report. Second, the relative recency of these measures may indicate insufficient time, in many cases, to build up a substantial base of validity-related data. Maybe researchers must take the lead by conducting relevant validation studies. Both these reasons seem related to a third—the general uncertainty about the early educational experiences that are desirable for children. (This issue was addressed in Chapter One.) Particularly vulnerable on all three grounds are the newer types of test related to preschool experiences, early school achievement, or preschool and kindergarten instruction. Less vulnerable are readiness tests; they are of relatively long standing and can usually claim later school achievement as a validation criterion. With time for "maturation" and more certainty about their purposes, measures such as those discussed in this section should acquire greater validity.

Chapter 6

Cognitive Measures: Developmental and Handicapped Screening Surveys, Language and Bilingual Tests, and Creativity Tests

T his chapter continues our discussion of cognitive measures. The measures described here, although education-related, are not as directly and traditionally linked to schools as the measures in the previous chapter. Further, they demonstrate a greater concern with the affective and psychomotor domains. For example, the developmental surveys, in addition to assessing cognition, also examine social and motor functioning, while certain of the language measures assess aspects of speech that are heavily psychomotor. Generally speaking, the types of measure described in this chapter represent more recent emphases in test development than the intelligence tests and directly school-related measures. Recent interest has focused particularly on screening surveys to assess development and to identify handicaps, measures concerned with bilingualism, and tests related to creativity.

Developmental and Handicapped Screening Surveys

Developmental surveys connote comprehensive instruments that examine many aspects of development, not just intellectual maturity. Their typical content spans not only both of these chapters on cognition but the subsequent two chapters as well. We consider developmental surveys here because significant cognitive sections are integral to them and also because the surveys in some ways represent an outgrowth of the early developmental schedules for infants that were principally oriented toward predicting later intellectual functioning. We also attend to the use of surveys for screening populations of young children to identify those with handicaps or those who are, in some sense, at risk. Considerable activity in this regard has recently been evident in early childhood education. Since developmental surveys have frequently been used as screening instruments, we considered it appropriate to treat these related topics together.

Nature and Status of Developmental and Handicapped Screening Surveys. The recent expansion in the use of developmental surveys in early childhood education is a curious phenomenon. Several explanations—largely untested—have been advanced. One is that developmental surveys, with their claims of multifaceted assessment of children's development, have appeared to accord well with the commonly expressed aim of nurturing the development of "the whole child." A second plausible explanation is that early childhood educators have become increasingly aware that children's learning is intimately linked with other aspects of development, such as health, stamina, strength, perceptual abilities, and social relations with peers and adults. This awareness may have been generated by the new programs (that is, since the mid 1960s) for children of poor families, as many such children have exhibited a combination of cognitive, social, and physical limitations. To promote learning and more appropriate development, early educators have increasingly turned to physicians, clinicians, and other professionals for whom developmental surveys were standard assessment instruments. A third explanation for the growing use of developmental surveys in early childhood education, already alluded to, is that the tradition of assessing infants with developmental instruments carried over to education when younger and still younger children entered educational settings.

Recent legislation will probably stimulate an even greater use of screening surveys. The Education for All Handicapped Children Act, Public Law 94-142, was enacted by the federal government in 1975. It requires the following: (1) the identification of all handicapped children via screening instruments (now typically termed "Child Find"), (2) further evaluation by a team of specialists to ascertain each identified child's specific problems and educational needs, and (3) development and implementation of an individualized educational program for each handicapped child. These three procedural phases are commonly referred to as (1) screening, (2) diagnosis, and (3) treatment or intervention. The reliance on a medical model is obvious, although many conditions screened for are more the province of developmental psychologists than physicians. The usual rationale given for screening young children is that early identification of developmental disabilities or of children otherwise at risk will allow early preventative treatments or programs to ameliorate or reverse such conditions. Meier's thinking is representative:

> A massive screening program promises to reveal those factors which contribute to developmental risks in varying degrees and thereby to allow them to be weighted in terms of their relative contribution to handicapping conditions. Early detection and appropriate intervention will, in turn, help to prevent more serious disabilities. Moreover, the appropriateness and efficacy of various intervention/prevention methods and materials can be determined.
>
> Also, the results from such massive screening and assessment procedures, systematically applied to a representative sample of the population, will help to document the prevalence of various incipient and full-fledged developmental disabilities [Meier, 1975, p. 502].

Despite such compelling rationales, however, the execution of the seemingly simple legislative mandate (Public Law 94-142) has become a complex, troublesome process. At least six reasons might be given for this state of affairs.

1. The legislation did not detail how the screening (or the entire process) was to be conducted. Predictably, state and local education officials have settled on widely varying procedures and measures.

2. The screening and diagnostic phases have not been kept distinct. Since large groups are to be screened (relative to diagnosis), the need is for screening instruments and procedures that are valid, administered quickly, and at reasonable cost. By contrast, diagnosis of those identified via the screening should involve in-depth measurement and reflective examination by a team of professionals. Too often the screening and diagnostic phases are collapsed into one, use instruments more appropriate for the other phase, or are otherwise confused. In this connection, we find Eaves and McLaughlin's (1977) *mush—melon—rock* distinction appropriate. Adapting Yarger's (1975) scheme, they colorfully characterized three levels of child assessment: (1) *mush:* screening assessment dependent for data on informal consultation, structured interviews, archival data, and screening devices; (2) *melon:* clinical or diagnostic assessment using data from standardized and nonstandardized tests, and observation systems; and (3) *rock:* follow-up assessment to determine the effectiveness of intervention using nonstandardized tests and observation systems. Note that while such distinctions aid in conceptualizing the qualities of the three distinct assessment phases—screening, diagnosis, and treatment—they also hint at the heavy costs of a comprehensive three-phase system.

3. The purpose of the screening is not always definitive. Many have pointed out the folly, or even unethical practice, of identifying persons with

handicapping conditions or those at risk when there are insufficient resources available to treat many of those so identified. Further, if its purpose is ambiguous, the screening phase seems more prone to result in a dysfunctional labeling of children (as discussed in Chapter One), obscuring the essential normality, individuality, and variability of those classified and labeled.

4. The need during both screening and (especially) diagnosis for well-trained personnel has too frequently not been met.

5. The screening and diagnostic phases have been beset by definitional problems. The confusion over definitions may be greatest with regard to "learning disabilities," as dissatisfaction with existing definitions is extensive (for example, see Farnham-Diggory, 1978; Goldstein and others, 1975; Hobbs, 1975; and Torgesen, 1975). Cruickshank (1967) noted how the same "learning disabled" child would be classified differently as he moved from state to state, and Fry (as reported in Farnham-Diggory, 1978) sarcastically provided a do-it-yourself terminology generator to crank out hundreds of new terms that could be used as interchangeable labels for such persons.

6. The array of tests available and used in screening and diagnosis is extensive, but this quantity (for the most part) is not buttressed by evidence of quality, especially in regard to validity. Publishers, not surprisingly, have earmarked numerous instruments in their catalogs that they believe meet the requirements of Public Law 94-142. However, many such instruments lack strong validation data to support their purported uses. For example, Coles (1978) reviewed ten instruments and procedures commonly used to diagnose learning disabilities, and found them by and large wanting. The validity issues involved in the use of such measures are not simple ones. For example, Gallagher and Bradley (1972) examined the central decision of establishing a screening or diagnostic instrument's cutoff point—that is, the point separating those thought to have the condition from those thought not to have it. They noted the desirability of setting the score to achieve high correct identification and the desired balance between the two types of possible error: false positives, classified to have the condition but in reality not having it; and false negatives, classified as not having the condition although in reality having it. Moving the cutting point could lower the incidence of one type of error but at the cost of increasing the other. They lamented that the designers of most instruments failed to investigate and report the usefulness of their measures in this regard. (Note, too, that a screening instrument should do more than simply identify those children already known to have a given condition.) In the detection of learning disabilities in preschool children, this prime validity issue is clouded even further because the clinician is trying to predict which children may experience learning failures. That is, the debilitating condition has not yet manifested itself, and therefore the process involves hypothesizing rather than confirming (Keogh and Becker, 1973).

Hobbs (1975) directed the Project on Classification of Exceptional Children as requested initially by U.S. Secretary of Health, Education, and Welfare Elliot Richardson. Concluding that it was essential to classify exceptional children to secure funding and to implement and evaluate services for them,

Hobbs and his colleagues proceeded to raise a series of critical research questions. These questions serve as an effective summary of the issues surrounding screening:

1. What qualifications are necessary for personnel who staff screening programs?
2. How reliable and valid are the tests used in screening programs and how may they be improved?
3. Do currently available screening procedures reliably identify a significant number of children whose difficulties were not already known?
4. How frequent and important are "false positives" and "false negatives" in screening studies?
5. How many children who are identified in screening programs as in need of further diagnostic studies and possible treatment actually get the further help they need?
6. Which is the more cost-effective, mass screening programs or periodic, comprehensive examinations of children in facilities capable of providing comprehensive care? [Hobbs, 1975, pp. 92–96]

Large-scale screening of young children is likely to become more prevalent during the 1980s. Such screening will extend far beyond the sight and hearing checks that have been commonplace in schools in decades. Quite possibly the emphasis will be on identifying more subtle handicaps or partial handicapping conditions, previously undetected, that adversely affect learning and daily functioning. Important for such comprehensive screening efforts will be careful validation studies of the types implied above.

Screening programs have made use of an extensive array of instruments. Key factors in the selection of instruments are the particular purposes of the screening and the professional orientation of the persons in charge. The several collections or charts of screening measures that we examined (Coley, 1978; Davidson and others, 1977; Frankenburg and Camp, 1975; Gallagher and Bradley, 1972; and Meier, 1975) highlighted the diversity of instruments used in screening. Many of the designated instruments are treated under other headings in Chapters Five through Eight. Here we have selected illustrative measures that are fairly comprehensive, that relate to both development and education, that are appropriate for the age group of interest, and that could be (and frequently are) used in screening contexts.

Illustrative Developmental and Handicapped Screening Surveys. Four representative developmental surveys often used for screening are listed in Table 14. The Denver Developmental Screening Test (DDST) and the Learning Accomplishment Profile (LAP) are currently in wide use, particularly in Head Start, while the Comprehensive Identification Process (CIP) and the Developmental Indicators for the Assessment of Learning (DIAL) are of somewhat more recent origin. A brief examination of the table reveals the numerous scales in the tests, as well as considerable overlap between the measures. Note that the CIP lives up to the comprehensive label in its name in that it assesses a large number of areas. Not obvious in the table are the relationships between each survey and educa-

Table 14. Illustrative Developmental and Handicapped Screening Surveys in Early Childhood Education

Title and Date	Age Range	Administration	Scales or Scores	Source
Comprehensive Identification Process	2½ years to 5½ years	Individual by testing team; 25 to 35 minutes	Hearing Vision Cognitive-Verbal Fine Motor Gross Motor Speech and Expressive Language Socio-Affective Medical History	Scholastic Testing Service, Inc. 480 Meyer Rd. Bensenville, Ill. 60106
Denver Developmental Screening Test (1969: Items; 1975: Manual)	2 weeks to 6 years	Individual; 15 to 20 minutes	Personal-Social Fine Motor-Adaptive Language Gross Motor	LADOCA Foundation E. 51st Ave. and Lincoln St. Denver, Colo. 80216
Developmental Indicators for the Assessment of Learning (1975)	2½ years to 5 years, 5 months	Individual by testing team; 25 to 30 minutes	Gross Motor Fine Motor Concepts Communication	Dial, Inc. 1233 Lincoln Ave. South Highland Park, Ill. 60035
Learning Accomplishment Profile (1974)	1 month to 6 years	Individual; time required not stated	Gross Motor Fine Motor Social Self-Help Cognitive Language	Kaplan School Supply Corp. 600 Jonestown Rd. Winston-Salem, N.C. 27103

tion; of the four, the LAP has made the most direct claim to link to instructional planning and curriculum units. These instruments might well have been included in other sections of this book (indeed, the *Mental Measurements Yearbook* classified the DDST as an intelligence test and the CIP and DIAL as learning disabilities measures). We consider them separately to highlight their distinctiveness and their increasing use in screening processes.

Comprehensive Identification Process (CIP): This recently marketed system is broad in scope and directly related to developmental screening. The purpose of the Comprehensive Identification Process is "to identify every child in a community who is eligible for a special preschool program or needs some kind of medical attention or therapy to function at full potential when he or she enters school" (Zehrbach, 1975a, p. 1). Constructed for children two and a half to five and a half years old, CIP thus is intended as a screening process for identifying the mildly or moderately handicapped. The CIP stops short of actual diagnosis, although for certain children further diagnostic and evaluative activities are advised, as are programs designed to prevent or ameliorate handicapping conditions.

In the Screening Administrator's Manual (Zehrbach, 1975b), considerable information is given on locating children within the community, arranging the site, conducting the actual screening, and the like. The estimate of thirty minutes to screen each child does not convey well the total personnel resources required, for a full screening team consists of a team leader/greeter, one parent interviewer, three to five child interviewers, a speech clinician or language interviewer, and two hearing and vision screeners. Such a team purportedly can screen twenty children per hour. Although some members of the screening team obviously need extensive training for their roles (such as the speech clinician), the CIP manual claims that paraprofessionals trained for three to four hours can perform adequately as interviewers. Anderson (1978) questioned the sufficiency of such brief training and was concerned that many interviewers so trained would lack the objective attitude necessary to transcend their desire to help the child tested do well (that is, artificially well on the developmental tasks).

Although only eight scales or scores are listed for the CIP in Table 14, a detailed analysis reveals one overall recommendation based on twenty-four "scores" recorded on four forms:

1. Child Interviewer's Record Form, five scores: hearing screening, vision screening, and developmental—cognitive-verbal, fine motor, and gross motor. These latter three areas are most test-like; for each half year of age, fifteen age-graded tasks are available, five in each area. Anderson (1978) noted that many tasks were adapted from the Binet and wondered why some were misplaced age-wise (compared to Binet placement) and scored somewhat arbitrarily.
2. Speech and Expressive Language Record Form, five scores: articulation, voice, fluency, expressive language, and total. Newcomer (1978) expressed concern that the evaluative criteria were unclear in each area except articulation.

3. Observation of Behavior Form, seven ratings: hearing and receptive language, vision, physical/motor, speech and expressive language, affective behavior, and social behavior—response and interaction.
4. Parent Interview Form, seven ratings: pregnancy/hospitalization/accidents, walking and toilet training, hearing, vision, speech and expressive language, medical, and social effect.

In each of these twenty-four areas, some of them obviously overlapping, scores as such are not calculated. Rather, in each area the child is rated pass (P), refer or rescreen (R), or evaluate (E). Zehrbach (1975b) considered such ratings in developmental areas as consonant with a Minimal Acceptable Behavior (MAB) approach to screening. In other words, children were asked to perform behaviors indicative of at least a minimum level of functioning for a given chronological age, with those unable to perform such behaviors referred for additional assessment. Thus, after the four forms are completed, the screening team staff identifies the children who can clearly be rated pass (have no significant problems) or evaluate (need detailed diagnosis or evaluation in one or more areas). Additional time is spent by the team in reviewing the data on children who fall between these two categories, so that a judicious decision can be made—either to pass the child because the R-checked areas seem to represent minimal problems, to schedule the child for rescreening in a few weeks, or to refer the child to a specialist (such as in hearing or vision).

Validity data for the CIP are, for the most part, skimpy. Zehrbach claimed content and construct validity because two school psychologists and a motor development specialist knowledgeable about young children selected the initial items to be tried out and because the selections were made from a comparative listing of items from "nine tests and procedures," apparently established instruments. However, judging the CIP's degree of validity in these regards is difficult, given that such a small group of experts can hardly be representative of child development specialists and that the nine tests are unnamed. Further, no item analysis data are reported on the performance of the items in their new (that is, CIP) configuration. Since items were sometimes adapted and sometimes placed at new developmental levels, the absence of data on item characteristics and functioning is particularly disturbing. Further, the CIP manuals contain essentially no information on criterion-related validity. In one interesting but not totally unconfounded presentation, tangentially related to validity (Zehrbach, 1975b, c), children referred via CIP were compared with those referred by more traditional means. "The children referred through CIP tend to be intellectually more capable, immature in speech, short of attention, shy, fearful, withdrawn, and/or to have problems relating to their parents. Children referred through an agency or professional tend to have receptive language problems, articulation problems, more severe intellectual retardation, cerebral palsy, and/or orthopedic problems" (Zehrbach, 1975b, p. 31).

Reliability data for the CIP are nonexistent. This is a serious omission given the young age of the children involved, the probable strangeness to the children of the screening site, and the short duration of training for the paraprofessionals serving as interviewers. Related to the latter, the absence of inter-rater reliability estimates is also of considerable concern.

Norms in the usual sense are not provided. Of course, norms were used to establish the cutoff points between pass, rescreen (refer), and evaluate, and apparently were based on the performance of essentially all Caucasian children from rural areas and small communities in the Midwest. This raises serious questions about the appropriateness of these cutoff points for children from other ethnic groups and other regions of the country. Although Zehrbach suggested the development of local norms in using the CIP, such a practice is rarely undertaken because of costs and limited test development expertise (Anderson, 1978).

Overall, CIP stands as a comprehensive procedure for locating and screening handicapped children. This broad-based and systematic approach to identification and screening is appropriate. At the same time, inadequate attention has been given to the psychometric properties—particularly the reliability and validity—of many measures within the CIP framework. Careful development of CIP in these regards is essential if it is to reach its full potential as a screening process.

Denver Developmental Screening Test (DDST): This developmental assessment instrument has experienced considerable popularity since its appearance in the late 1960s. Its purpose is to detect developmental delays or problems early in life. Although individually administered, the DDST reportedly takes only fifteen to twenty minutes to give. Further, the amount of training necessary to give the DDST is claimed to be modest. The reference manual (Frankenburg and others, 1975) contains a self-test to assist one to learn proper administration procedures, and a proficiency exam consisting of a written test and a film is available to check testing accuracy.

The DDST's construction features 105 items selected from a dozen existing developmental tests appropriate between birth and six years of age. This eclectic nature of the test plus its unusually compact form prompted us to reproduce it here as Figure 6. Each item, drawn as a bar, is positioned appropriately by age (the long axis of the figure is an age scale from birth to six years). Based on the standardization sample, computer analyses yielded the exact ages when 25, 50, 75, and 90 percent of the norm group passed the item; these percent-passing points are noted on each item's bar, that is (in Figure 6) by the left edge, the small tick mark, the beginning of the shaded portion, and the right edge, respectively. In the figure, the items are grouped in one of four sectors:

1. Personal-social: ability to get along with people and to care for oneself.
2. Fine motor-adaptive: ability to see, to pick up objects, and to draw.
3. Language: ability to hear, to understand, and to use language.
4. Gross motor: ability to sit, walk, and jump.

This visual display of the items both facilitates administration and demonstrates the pronounced age variability in performing some of these behaviors. For example, in the gross motor sector, some children can balance on one foot for ten seconds at age three, while others are almost six before achieving this. Note too that the personal-social sector is underrepresented at the older ages.

Administration occurs in the presence of a parent. The child's precise age is determined and, accordingly, an age line is drawn across the sheet of items. Testing is begun to the left of the age line—that is, on items normally passed by younger children. Testing continues on progressively more difficult items by moving right on the page until the child fails three consecutive items within a sector. This procedure is repeated for each of the four sectors. Over 45 percent of the items can be passed by parent report, although the examiner is encouraged to observe what the child can do, rather than simply asking the parent. Such parent-report items, denoted by an *R* at the left side of the item bar (see Figure 6), are most apparent in the personal-social sector and least frequent in the fine motor-adaptive area. Each item is marked as a pass (P), failure (F), refusal (R), or no opportunity (N.O.). For example, if a child has had no chance to ride a tricycle, "N.O." is entered on the "pedals tricycle" item.

Performance on the DDST does not result in a score but rather, similar to the CIP, in a rating of abnormal, questionable, untestable, or normal, depending on the number and distribution of "delays." A delay is any item failed that is completely left on the age line; that is, the child fails an item that is normally passed by 90 percent of children at a younger age. It is advised that any child classified abnormal, questionable, or untestable be retested two or three weeks later; if not found normal on retesting, referral to specialists is advised.

Validity information in the manual is quite limited, consisting of a brief paragraph and one table, presumably based on Frankenburg, Goldstein, and Camp (1971). Some confusion is caused by numerical inconsistencies between the information in the manual and that in the article and between the paragraph and the table in the manual itself. Nevertheless, the following validity information appears pertinent. Evidently three sequential studies took place, and some re-scoring of DDSTs occurred based on the first two (Frankenburg, Goldstein, and Camp, 1971). The third study, probably the basis for the table in the manual, involved cross-validation. A type of concurrent criterion-related validity was addressed in that 246 children were given the DDST—considered a screening test—and either the Binet or the Bayley—considered, in this case, diagnostic tests. The process involved giving the tests at the same time and comparing the results of the screening test with those of the diagnostic test, while recognizing that the latter might also be in error. Agreement between the screening and diagnostic tests in the classification of positive (suspected of or having the condition) is termed *copositivity*, while negative classification made jointly by both tests is termed *conegativity*.

Based on the data in the table (identical in both the DDST Manual and the article), Frankenburg, Goldstein, and Camp reported a copositivity of .92, a conegativity of .97, an overreferral rate of 3.2 percent, and an underreferral rate of 0.4 percent (1971, p. 993). Our calculations, using the system reported by Frankenburg and Camp (1975, pp. 29–35) agreed except for a discrepancy in

Figure 6. Denver Developmental Screening Test

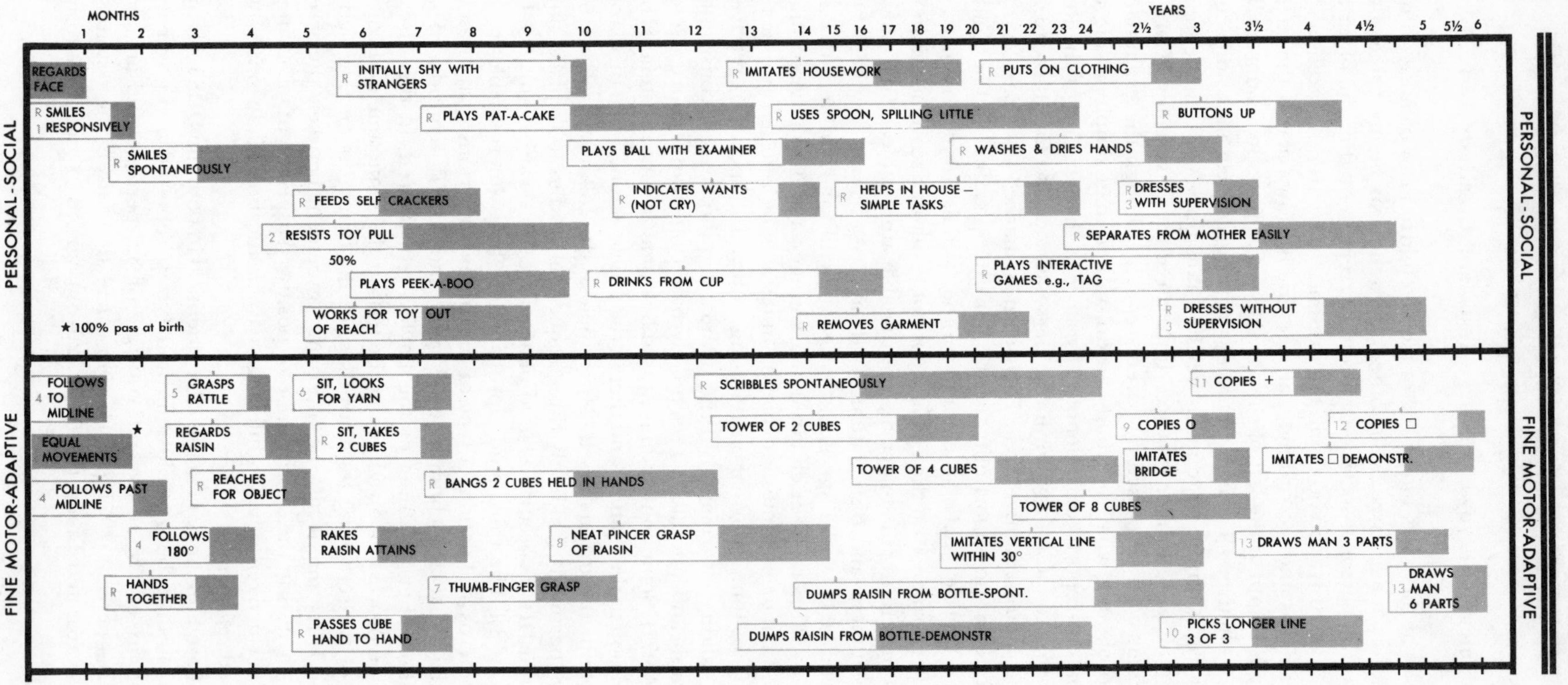

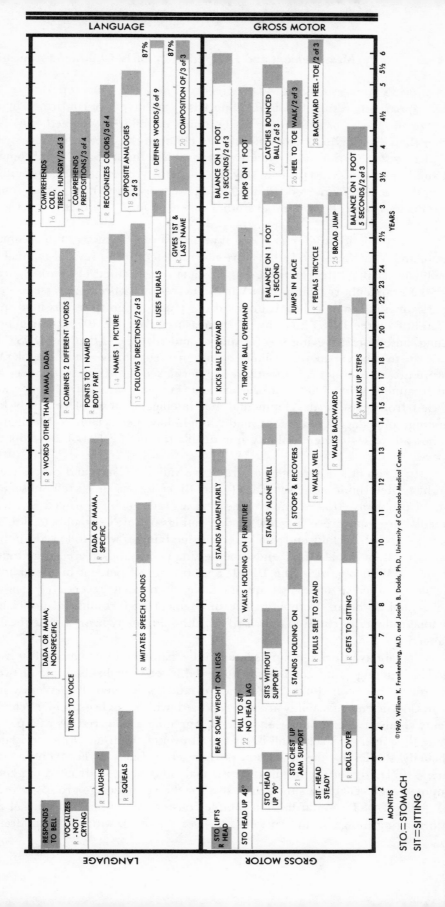

LANGUAGE

GROSS MOTOR

©1969, William K. Frankenburg, M.D. and Josiah B. Dodds, Ph.D., University of Colorado Medical Center.

STO. = STOMACH
SIT = SITTING

overreferrals (our rate being 40.0 percent). The lower rate reported in the article apparently resulted from dividing DDST positives not confirmed by the Binet or the Bayley ($n = 8$) by the total number of children screened ($n = 246$), rather than dividing by the total number of children classified as positive by the DDST ($n = 20$). Curiously, the validity paragraph in the DDST Manual contains yet another set of figures for copositivity, conegativity, overreferrals, and under-referrals (.73, .92, 7.2 percent, and 2.95 percent, respectively); these data resemble outcomes from the two initial studies (Frankenburg, Goldstein, and Camp, 1971).

Other validity studies had been conducted by 1975 (such as Frankenburg, Camp, and Van Natta, 1971), but were not reported in the revised manual (or possibly overlapped the reported data in some nonspecified fashion). Concern over the Frankenburg, Camp, and Van Natta study had been expressed since a significant number of children under three years of age were classified quite differently by the DDST than by other measures (Werner, 1972). Our general feeling, based on surveying several studies and reviews, is that the DDST has moderate to good concurrent validity, although it tends to overrefer—a tolerable feature in a screening instrument. We are perplexed, however, by the very limited treatment given validity in the manual. Further, since DDST items were selected from existing developmental and intelligence tests of relatively long standing, some degree of content validity might have been claimed. The manual neither addresses content validity nor details the item selection-development process.

In a recent study related to predictive validity, Camp and others (1977) sought to determine how well DDST and Binet results predicted subsequent "school problems" (for example, repeating a grade, being enrolled in special remedial programs, receiving low teacher ratings on one's school behavior, and the like). Sixty-five children from lower-income families were followed up three years after their initial DDST and Binet testing (which took place at age four to six years). With regard to the DDST, 88, 66, and 32 percent of the children initially classified as abnormal, questionable, or normal, respectively, showed later school problems. Combining the Binet and DDST results did not change the total number of children misclassified, although the type of misclassification changed.

Reliability information presented in the manual is of two types. Interrater reliability among four examiners, who tested a very small subsample of twelve children in common during the standardization, averaged 90 percent agreement. Coefficients of stability are also reported, with a single examiner retesting twenty children after a one-week interval. Agreement occurred over 95 percent of the time averaged across all items for all twenty children. Other and larger reliability studies by the test authors themselves (such as Frankenburg and others, 1971) are not reported in the manual. The latter study cited in general connoted high reliability although less so for the younger age groups tested.

The DDST standardization sample consisted of over 1,000 normal children ranging in age from two weeks to over six years, with more children at younger age levels. Somewhat more boys than girls were sampled. The sample was drawn from Denver, and data presented in the manual show the sample to be comparable to the racial and occupational breakdown of Denver in the 1960 Census. The circumscribed nature of the sample has been criticized (Moriarty, 1972; and Werner, 1972), although the revised manual hints of forthcoming results that make the DDST "useful throughout the country." Sandler and others (1970), using the DDST with urban preschool minority children, questioned the appropriateness of the norms and also reported reduced interrater reliability, ranging from .62 to .79 for the four sectors.

In summary, the DDST appears to have a high degree of usability as an easily and quickly administered initial screening instrument (Hunt, 1975a; Moriarty, 1972; and Stedman, 1975). For this screening purpose, some preliminary validity information exists. It is difficult to understand, however, why the revised manual does not incorporate fully and systematically validity and reliability data available and known to the test authors. Continuing and careful attention to such studies could well be the key to future improvements in the instrument.

Developmental Indicators for the Assessment of Learning (DIAL): The stated purpose for DIAL (Mardell and Goldenberg, 1975) is to efficiently screen preschool children (ages two and a half to almost five and a half years) for gross motor, fine motor, concepts, and communications skills. Emphasizing that DIAL is not a diagnostic measure, the test authors indicated that it is designed to identify children in need of follow-up services, as are the CIP and the DDST.

DIAL is administered by a team, composed of a coordinator (professional) and four operators (professionals and/or paraprofessionals), with the use of three volunteers optional. No specific training for administration is specified in the manual; however, the criteria and responsibilities listed for each position, and the test items themselves, imply that training requirements would be modest. The operators are placed at four stations in a large room, one station for each skill area screened. In addition to determining performance related to the skill area, each of the four operators also circles on the recording form the number of any of twelve behaviors exhibited by the child while at the station (such as crying, clumsiness, squinting, and impulsiveness). The room also has areas for registration, warm-up and orientation, photos, and parent observation. Children proceed through the stations individually, completing DIAL in twenty-five to thirty minutes. Although screening each child takes relatively little time, the requirement of several adults for administration represents a considerable expenditure of human resources.

The four skill areas assessed are Gross Motor, Fine Motor, Concepts, and Communications. Each is represented by seven items. The gross motor skills observed are throwing, catching, jumping in place, hopping in place, skipping, standing still, and balancing on a beam. The seven fine motor items are matching geometric designs, building block structures, cutting with scissors, copying shapes, copying letters, touching fingers, and clapping hands. The concepts skill area involves sorting blocks and classifying, naming colors, counting, positioning (on, under, and the like), following directions, identifying concepts, and identifying body parts. The communications items require articulating designated consonants, remembering and repeating back, naming nouns and verbs, answering questions to indicate coping style, naming self as well as age and sex, naming foods, and telling a story to fit stimulus cards.

The scoring criteria for most items appear clear and usable. Point credit on each item is converted (directly on a convenient and compact one-page recording form) to a scaled score from 0 to 3. For example, on the communication item requiring the naming of different foods, a scaled score of 0, 1, 2, or 3 is assigned to the naming of no, one-to-three, four-to-five, or six foods, respectively. Thus, in each skill area of seven items the maximum total scaled score is 21.

Separate cutoff points are provided for boys and girls in quarter-year age groups (such as 6 for a boy between three years and three years, two months, and 16 for a girl between four years, nine months and four years, eleven months). A child's performance in each of the four skill areas is compared with the relevant cutoff point to make one of three decisions. An "OK" decision results if the child is above the cutoff in every area or in three of the four (unless the below-norm performance occurs in the communications area). A "Redial" decision results if a child's scores are below the cutoff in two areas, again excepting communications. The child is then retested in the areas of low performance. The manual does not specify what procedures should accompany redial results. Presumably, if the child no longer is below cutoff in one or both areas, he can be judged "OK." However, if he continues to perform below cutoff in both skill areas, is he redialed repeatedly? Or is he assigned to the last category? A "Follow-up" decision is made if a child falls below the cutoff in three of the four areas or if a below-cutoff performance occurs in the communications area. (In other words, below-cutoff performance in communications must result in follow-up.) Follow-up signals the need for a diagnostic evaluation to determine if remedial or ameliorative placement is warranted.

Several types of validity are addressed in the DIAL manual. Content validation involved having eight child development experts review the test and make recommendations. Although specifics of this process are not included in the manual, it is reported that "All consultants were in total agreement with the course of development of the DIAL battery" (Mardell and Goldenberg, 1975, p. 55). (Curiously, this may be one of the few instances recorded of "total agreement" among a group of behavioral scientists.) The consultants were concerned about the shortage of social-emotional development items, but apparently no action was taken to address this concern. Content validity of DIAL, like that of the DDST, relies to some extent on the fact that items were selected largely from existing developmental instruments.

Several criterion-related validity studies are reported; three deal with concurrent validity (another two are mentioned but not in sufficient detail to permit assessment). In the first, twelve Head Start children were screened by DIAL and five identified as high risk and in need of follow-up. The same twelve children were given a complete diagnostic evaluation by a team of specialists using an extensive battery of instruments. The diagnostic reports concurred with the DIAL screening results for ten of the children. One child was not available for the full diagnostic evaluation, while the twelfth was identified as high risk by DIAL but not by the team of specialists. Unfortunately, this study involved very few children and their mobility and other factors prevented longitudinal follow-up. In the second concurrent validation effort, 181 children were given both DIAL and the Peabody Picture Vocabulary Test (PPVT), one of the intelligence tests described in Chapter Five. Statistically significant positive correlations were found between combined DIAL scores and chronological age, mental age, and intelligence quotients for all the DIAL decision-sex groups and age-sex groups formed (such as redial males and five-year-old females). The relationships existed in many cases, but less strongly, for each of the four DIAL skill area scores. The manual reported, "performances on the DIAL tasks were found to be statistically related to mental ages for all groups tested and suggest that the DIAL evaluates factors which are sex, age, and intellectually related" (Mardell and Goldenberg, 1975, p. 45). In the third concurrent validity study, Milwaukee school officials compared DIAL decisions and those from two other preschool screening instruments with decisions made by a multidisciplinary diagnostic team. The DIAL results corresponded best to the team decisions. In the only predictive validity study reported, about 250 kindergartners and first-graders were followed up after being tested with DIAL two years before. It appeared that the DIAL skill area scores, used as predictors in a multiple correlation analysis, could be weighted in a way to provide moderate to substantial multiple correlations with readiness and achievement test scores earned two years later. The information in the manual, however, is not presented clearly enough for the reader to be certain just what procedures were followed. Further, the study involved only older children and could not be viewed as relevant to predictive validity for the lower age range that DIAL attempts to address.

The reliability of DIAL has not been extensively addressed. No interrater reliability data are presented, and only one test-retest study is reported. In it, 520 children were retested after a one-year interval. "Half of these children were randomly selected from the upper 90 percent according to DIAL scores while half of these children were in the lower 10 percent. The two groups remained very distinct, indicating high test-retest reliability, even after a full year" (Mardell and Goldenberg, 1975, p. 56). This limited report is inadequate to judge DIAL's stability. Elsewhere in the manual, the test authors indicated that young children are easily affected by extraneous circumstances and used this reason for redialing. The absence of full reports on reliability in the manual is unfortunate. The reliability of DIAL scoring was addressed by having operators, trained by the test authors themselves, observe a small sample of children on videotape and rate their skills. High agreement occurred in this situation. The test authors indicated that further study was needed to determine scoring reliabilities for more typical use of DIAL in field settings by operators trained in various ways.

The standardization and normative information presented in the manual is not entirely clear. Reported first is an extensive test standardization on over

4,000 children from eight Illinois cities in 1972. Although the sample is described at length, several concerns can be raised. First, as mentioned by the test authors themselves, the sample was skewed toward the upper age ranges. Second, participation in the testing was voluntary, possibly creating a self-selection bias. Third, although an attempt was made to stratify the sample by sex, demographic setting, race, and socioeconomic status (SES), no procedure was used to provide separate norms for these subgroups (except by sex) or to weight them to reflect national census proportions. Given that 45 percent of the sample was classified rural, 30 percent black, and 63 percent low SES, considerable disparity from national proportions is obvious.

Because of the overrepresentation of older children, the norms were "reconstituted" a year later using 3,100 children, 100 randomly selected for each month of age (thirty-six to sixty-six months) and controlled for sex. Apparently, these reconstituted norms were used to derive the cutoff scores for boys and girls at quarter-year intervals, as previously mentioned. These scores were set to mark off the lowest 10 percent of the performers. However, information on the "reconstitution" procedures is scanty. It is unclear what the characteristics of the second sample were and what its relationship was to the original sample.

In general, DIAL appears to have a highly workable format for the developmental screening of preschool children. Some moderate attempts have been made to establish the validity and reliability of the instrument. Despite the claims in the DIAL promotional literature, however, considerably more needs to be done, particularly with regard to criterion-related validity (both concurrent and predictive) and reliability. In addition, although DIAL appears highly usable from an administration and scoring perspective, the actual nature of the normative group used to establish the cutoff points is inadequately specified in the manual. The user cannot, therefore, make judgments about the representativeness of the norm group. Possibly several of the vague areas could be cleared up by rewriting various portions of the existing manual. (For other reviews of DIAL, see Grill, 1978, and McCarthy, 1978.)

Learning Accomplishment Profile (LAP): This instrument departs from most others that we have discussed in that its manual (Sanford, 1974) contains no information on validity, reliability, or norms. Nevertheless, we have included the LAP here because of its unusual nature and its widespread use in Head Start centers. The general nature of the LAP can be conveyed by comparing and contrasting it with the DDST. Like the DDST, the LAP contains items from a large number of development instruments and organizes them into separate areas, namely Gross Motor, Fine Motor, Social, Self-Help, Cognitive, and Language. Both the DDST and the LAP are designed for simple administration, usually by the teacher in the case of the LAP. Also, items are recorded as either passed or failed until four out of five consecutive items are failed in each of the six areas. At this point, however, most of the similarity between the LAP and the DDST ends.

Whereas the purpose of the DDST is to screen children quickly for possible developmental delays, the LAP's purpose is to profile a child's developmental status, to set objectives based on the profile, to indicate relevant curriculum activities, and to evaluate subsequent progress. To this end, the LAP presents an average of about eighty items for each area. One of the over ninety items in the cognitive area requires the child to follow three separate commands in proper order, such as, "Put the pencil on the chair, then close the door, and then bring me the box from the table." If a child can do this, he passes the item and receives credit according to its set developmental age level of fifty-four months. If the item is failed, it signals the teacher to set an objective for the child highly similar to the item. Other curriculum materials related to the assessment process are included in the total LAP package.

The primary score resulting from the LAP is a developmental age in each of the six areas. For measuring student change, the manual suggests dividing a child's developmental age by chronological age to secure a rate of development, expressed as a percentage. Subsequently, say six to twelve months later, a new rate is determined for the child and compared with the previous rate. No evidence is presented for the appropriateness of this procedure; at first blush, it appears to hazard some of the same criticisms leveled at the now defunct ratio IQ (which preceded the now common deviation IQ).

No supporting evidence is presented for LAP's validity or reliability, although the sources used for the items suggest considerable content validity and age-differentiating items. What is clear is that the LAP is highly usable and, apparently, popular with users. A shortened version (the Smithfield Revision) has been developed, as well as a further refinement known as the Diagnostic Edition (LeMay, 1977). It is to be hoped that the developers of the Learning Accomplishment Profile will give immediate and sustained attention to its validity and reliability so that a better estimate can be made of its true value.

Language and Bilingual Tests

In this section, we consider the testing of language in young children. Why focus on language? Because we, like most others, believe effective language and communication to be critical for success in this country's schools. This belief in the centrality of language has been a major factor in the recent social concern over the need for bilingual instruction and programs, an issue receiving some attention in this section.

Researchers have demonstrated a continuing interest in unraveling the mysteries of language acquisition. Recent reviews have shown the broad front on which language research is being conducted (for example, see Appleton, Clifton, and Goldberg, 1975; Bloom, 1975; Cazden, 1971; and Glucksberg, Krauss, and Higgins, 1975). Much work has concentrated on two rival interpretations of how language is acquired—the environmental interpretation, which stresses the role of experience and imitation (Mowrer, 1960; and Skinner, 1957), and the nativistic position, which emphasizes innate structures. The latter is the basis for the Language Acquisition Device, a hypothetical device designed to activate at a given developmental age; it processes raw linguistic data heard by the child and then generates a basically consistent set of grammatical rules for the child (Chomsky, 1972; and Lenneberg, 1967). For the most part, these lines of research have not yet led to the development of measures with immediate, operational implications for early childhood education. This does not mean, however, that there are no language measures available. Several will be discussed in this chapter.

Nature and Status of Language and Bilingual Tests. Most early childhood education programs reflect a keen awareness of the importance of language, both as a logical precursor for reading and concept attainment and as a vehicle for establishing and maintaining rewarding interpersonal relationships and communication. Some programs approach the acquisition of language skills with rote procedures and intense systematization (such as DISTAR, the Direct Instruction approach, or the Kansas Behavioral Analysis Classroom), while other programs encourage many informal activities between adults and children, or among children themselves, through which language capabilities are expected to flourish (as in the British Infant School or Bank Street models).

Cazden (1971) nicely laid out the range of objectives appropriate for early language development and demonstrated that many were found in various forms in childhood education programs. Her presentation conveyed well both the breadth and complexity of language concerns incorporated in most preschools. She expressed considerable hope and optimism that teacher observational skills and methods might be developed to yield, in time, effective measures of children's language. She also urged that achievement in language skills be tested "as specifically as possible"—that is, that separate attention be paid to pronunciation, vocabulary, and so forth. She then reviewed many standardized tests of oral language skills. Her review prompted us to remind the reader that many measures already discussed in other contexts have significant linguistic features or even language subtests. Let us note quickly the language-related elements in measures previously described.

Forms of language testing: Among the intelligence tests, both the Binet and the Wechsler Verbal Scales have heavy verbal loadings. Children must respond to questions posed by the examiner, and those with effective language skills make a much better go of this. Children unable to speak and understand English were excluded from the WISC-R normative samples, and the Binet norming excluded children from homes where the primary language spoken was not English. The McCarthy Scales of Children's Abilities include a verbal scale comprised of five tests: pictorial memory, word knowledge, verbal memory, verbal fluency, and opposite analogies. The Peabody Picture Vocabulary Test and the Quick Test are both vocabulary tests.

In the instruction-related, readiness, and achievement tests described, language tests are common. Understanding language and following directions are important abilities on the Basic Concept Inventory, Boehm Test of Basic Concepts, and Cooperative Preschool Inventory (as indeed they are on all the measures). All the Circus measures under the language and reading areas are pertinent, requiring auditory discrimination, receptive vocabulary, language functions, comprehending and acting on oral language, identifying and blending sounds, and speaking (these measures are soon reviewed in depth). Separate, relevant subtests are available on all the other school-related measures that were considered in Chapter Five. Most of the subtests on the Comprehensive Tests of Basic Skills and the Metropolitan Readiness Tests apply to language. On the Stanford Early School Achievement Test, the tests of letters and sounds, aural comprehension, and word and sentence reading are applicable. The Tests of Basic Experience have a separate language test.

All four developmental and handicapped screening surveys examined in the first part of this chapter contain language-related components. The Comprehensive Identification Process (CIP) estimates the child's capabilities in the cognitive-verbal area, as well as in speech and expressive language. The Denver Developmental Screening Test (DDST) includes a language section with items that require using, combining, defining, and comprehending words (Figure 6). In the Developmental Indicators for the Assessment of Learning (DIAL), both the communications skills area (including articulating, naming nouns and verbs, telling a story, and the like) and, to a lesser extent, the concepts skill area (involving following directions, identifying concepts, and so forth) have clear links to language development. The Learning Accomplishment Profile (LAP) also has a language area consisting of almost one hundred items. Like the DDST items, LAP items range from early responding and vocalizing to defining words and using language in a number of ways. Additionally, some of the items in the LAP cognitive area are language-related.

Thus, there is no shortage of language and language-related tests in the various measures already described. There are also a number of somewhat more clinical instruments available. For example, the Illinois Test of Psycholinguistic Abilities or ITPA (Kirk, McCarthy, and Kirk, 1968) is designed for children two to ten years old with learning disabilities. Essentially a test of language, perception, and short-term memory, the ITPA is based on Osgood's theory of communication process (Kirk and Kirk, 1971). Assessment is made individually, on the basis of input in the visual and auditory channels and output in the vocal and motor channels. The developers believed their test could detect causes for learning or school difficulties that more standard educational measures could not. Cazden observed in 1971 that the three most frequently used standardized tests for measuring preschools' attainment of language objectives were the Stanford-Binet, the Peabody Picture Vocabulary Test, and the Illinois Test of Psycholinguistic Abilities. However, the decade of the 1970s has not been particularly favorable for these three measures, particularly the ITPA. In the case of the Binet and the PPVT, serious objections have been raised, principally by minority groups, about the norms, the language, and the likely cultural bias of such tests (see Laosa, 1977); a thoughtful article concerning language testing and young black children is also available (Dickie and Bagur, 1972). In the case of the ITPA, reviews have tended to be more incisively critical than generously supportive, with criticisms ranging from mild (such as, "much of the ITPA does not really test language") to severe (such as, "an expensive and inferior substitute for the matchbox test"): see reviews by Carroll (1972), Chase (1972), Coles (1978), Lumsden (1978), Waugh (1975), and Wiederholdt (1978).

We foresee a wave of new language instruments with direct educational applications. Basically, language can be thought of as either receptive (primarily listening and reading) or productive (primarily speaking and writing), with vocabulary playing a key role throughout. New, educationally relevant instruments will no doubt address all these functions, even in early childhood settings (although reading and writing might better be thought of as prereading and prewriting for very young children). The beginning of such a wave may already be in evidence with instruments such as some of the separate tests in Circus; the Preschool Language Assessment Instrument (Blank, Rose, and Berlin, 1978a, b); the Sequenced Inventory of Communication Development (Hedrick, Prather, and Tobin, undated); the Productive Language Assessment Tasks (High/Scope Educational Research Foundation, 1976); and Developmental Sentence Analysis (Lee, 1974). Circus and the Preschool Language Assessment Instrument are discussed in depth in the coming section on illustrative language tests; the other three measures require brief mention.

The Sequenced Inventory of Communication Development (SICD) is a diagnostic test appropriate for children functioning between four months and four years of age (Hedrick, Prather, and Tobin, undated). An attempt has been made to detail the communicative behaviors expected of the young child, in a sequence of small steps. The examiner, with the assistance of a data recorder, uses a fairly elaborate kit of materials to determine both the receptive and expressive language of the child. Receptive language includes items dealing with the child's awareness, discrimination, and understanding, while expressive items involve imitating, initiating, and responding. The expressive output, similar to Circus' Say and Tell's narrative, is measured in terms of length, grammar, syntax, and articulation.

The Productive Language Assessment Tasks (PLAT) have been developed by the High/Scope Educational Research Foundation (1976), also known for its Piagetian-based Head Start and Follow Through program model. This model, designed by Weikart and called the Cognitively Oriented Curriculum, has productive language objectives (oral and written) and minimizes language mechanics. Believing that existing standardized tests of language and reading achievement did not measure such objectives and possibly even violated their assumptions about child development, the model sponsors decided to pioneer the construction of PLAT. Intended for second- and third-graders, an older age group than Circus' Say and Tell targets, the PLAT elicits children's written responses to two tasks. In the reporting task, children are given unstructured materials to use in constructing whatever they want. After about twenty minutes, they are asked to write about how they made whatever they made. In the narrative task, children again receive a set of unstructured materials, but this time they are asked to make up a story involving the materials. After fifteen minutes, the children are asked to write for thirty minutes a story that might begin, "Once upon a time." Apart from the written aspect of the tasks, another unusual feature is that children are free to interact with one another throughout the entire activity. The children's written responses are then scored for a large number of variables, such as fluency, syntactic maturity, diversity of vocabulary, descriptive quantity and diversity, narrative organization, explanatory statements, and decodability. Scoring appears complex and time-consuming.

Developmental Sentence Analysis or DSA (Lee, 1974) is more a classification procedure than a test, but it does represent a thorough assessment of children's speech. Designed for use by speech clinicians (and often with handicapped, retarded or language-delayed children in the two- to seven-year-old range), the procedure is appropriate only for children learning standard American-English grammar. Essentially, "Developmental Sentence Analysis is a method for making a detailed, readily quantified and scored evaluation of a child's use of standard English grammatical rules from a tape-recorded sample of his spontaneous speech in conversation with an adult" (Lee, 1974, p. xix). Required for scoring and analysis is a fifty-sentence block of consecutive, different utterances. The utterances are then scored in terms of the developmental progression or sophistication they reveal in eight grammatical form categories, such as personal pronouns, main verbs, negatives, conjunctions, and the like. On the basis of this analysis, remedial teaching techniques are proposed to support the child's developmental progression where needed.

This brief sampling of recently developed language instruments, together with the instruments described later in this section, could suggest a potential trend in early childhood education measures over the next decade. Since they are either individually administered or elaborately scored, or both, they are time-consuming, compared with many educational measures. Yet they appear to tap abilities critical to the long-range success of children in educational and life settings.

Bilingual measures: Although some bilingual instruction was available in this country as early as the 1890s, primarily in parochial schools, the main push for such programs has come since 1965 (Law, 1977). As part of the educational reforms in the federal Elementary and Secondary Education Act of 1965, some initial efforts were made to help students with an inadequate command of English. These early efforts were called *English as a Second Language,* or simply *ESL,* and their principal purpose was to develop competence in written and spoken English. More comprehensive approaches were endorsed in the 1967 amendments to Public Law 89-10, specifically the Bilingual Program (Title VII) with its vision of a multicomponent program incorporating community involvement, instructional material development, and staff training. From this impetus, bilingual/bicultural programs were formed around the country.

In the 1974 *Lau* v. *Nichols* case, the U.S. Supreme Court held that a conventional ESL program was insufficient compliance with the intent of the law and that, where necessary, instruction must be conducted in the student's own language. "The Lau remedies require, as a minimum that: (1) schools systematically and validly ascertain which of their students are linguistically different;

(2) schools systematically and validly ascertain the language characteristics of their students; (3) schools systematically ascertain the achievement characteristics of their students; and (4) schools match an instructional program to the characteristics as ascertained" (Law, 1977, p. 3). Given such an explicit directive and other related legislation, the need to establish measures of language development in languages other than English is obvious, as is the need to develop measures of language dominance.

The response, in terms of the quantity of measures developed, has been substantial, but questions can be raised about the quality of the measures. Four recent sources have provided reviews of available instruments for bilingual students. One, from the Head Start Test Collection at Educational Testing Service (see the source book section), is an annotated bibliography titled "Tests for Spanish-Speaking Students" (Rosen, 1977). This document provides generally nonjudgmental paragraph descriptions of fifty-nine tests, and a supplement to it describes another nine. Another source, like the first primarily descriptive rather than judgmental, is the "Annotated Bibliography of Language Dominance Measures" (Oakland, De Luna, and Morgan, 1977). This source provides more information on each of the twenty-seven tests reviewed than does the ETS document, and it categorizes the information provided under the following headings: title, author, publisher, copyright date, purpose of test, examiner qualifications, type of test, description, cost, time limits, ages, validity, reliability, and other. Although no formal judgments have been made of the instruments, some evaluative comments appear occasionally. Further, the most common validity entry, made for over 60 percent of the measures, is that no information or data were available; another 15 percent of the measures only partially addressed validity concerns. Similarly, reliability information provided by the measure developers was often insufficient.

The other two sources are more directly evaluative. The *Oral Language Tests for Bilingual Students* (Silverman, Noa, and Russell, 1976) provides a brief review of issues involved in language testing. It also conceptualizes the school language domain as a two-by-four matrix, with the communication skills of speaking and listening intersecting with four linguistic structures—vocabulary, grammar, semantics, and phonology. Twenty-five instruments are reviewed in the book: seventeen measures commercially available (fourteen considered language skill tests and three sociolinguistic); six tests undergoing field tests; and two experimental measures. Each of the instruments is first systematically described using the following categories: publisher, oral language domain coverage (in terms of the two-by-four matrix), description, age/grade level, availability of alternate forms, administration time, administration procedures, materials used, scoring procedures, interpretation procedures, validity, reliability, field tryouts, and cost. Then each measure is rated using a set of criteria similar to the MEAN system developed by the Center for the Study of Evaluation (see the source book section). Based on a point system, ratings of good, fair, or poor are made of each measure's measurement validity, examinee appropriateness, technical excellence, and administrative usability. From the ratings, it is clear that the collection of instruments fared best on examinee appropriateness (most having "good" ratings and only one rated "poor") and least well, unfortunately, on measurement validity and technical excellence (80 percent of such ratings being "poor," 20 percent "fair," and none "good").

The last source, *Assessment Instruments for Limited-English-Speaking Students* (Locks, Pletcher, and Reynolds, 1978), is also evaluative. Its purpose is to provide information on the adequacy of available instruments for assessing the performance of limited-English-speaking students and to indicate areas of need. The report, prepared by the American Institutes for Research under contract with the National Institute of Education (NIE), is a companion document to the 1977 NIE document, the *Catalogue of Assessment Instruments for Limited-English-Speaking Students* (apparently soon to be available through Santillana Publishing Company). In the 1978 document, instruments available by mid April 1977 and intended for children in kindergarten through grade six are evaluated in terms of technical information (acceptable, unacceptable, or unavailable) and cultural information (acceptable or unacceptable). Instruments are reviewed and evaluated separately for students whose first language is Chinese, French, Italian, Navajo, Portuguese, Spanish, and Tagalog. (The three source books already considered focus primarily on Spanish-English measures.) For each language area, categories of measures considered include the following: language dominance, language proficiency (in both the language being examined and English), mathematics achievement, science achievement, social studies and ethnic studies, multisubject areas, attitude and self-concept, learning style assessment, and general ability and scholastic aptitude. In each language area, the report provides a brief review of the crucial assessment needs (and, in most areas, these are substantial needs).

It is unclear at this time whether the recent upsurge of activity in bilingual test development will persist. It is clear from the source books just cited that many instruments have been, or are being, developed, including efforts by major test publishers (such as the Language Assessment Battery, a Spanish-English measure, developed by the New York City Board of Education and now published by Houghton Mifflin). However, the children who will be needing such instruments represent a relatively small proportion of all the preschool- and school-age children in this country. More specifically, the NIE report discussed above (Locks, Pletcher, and Reynolds, 1978) gives the following K–12 enrollment figures for fiscal year 1976, ESEA Title VII bilingual education projects:

Chinese:	8,466 students
French:	7,871 students
Italian:	5,155 students
Navajo:	4,820 students
Portuguese:	4,317 students
Spanish:	199,360 students
Tagalog:	4,417 students

These figures undoubtedly would increase if all students with such needs were being served, but still the absolute numbers are small except for students with Spanish as a first language. It will be of great interest to note the status of bilingual instruments a decade from now. Our prediction is that development activity in the area will have abated considerably, but that some instruments of reasonable quality will be available in most of the languages.

Illustrative Language and Bilingual Tests. The extensive array of available language and bilingual measures made the selection of representative tests difficult. The three instruments finally chosen are listed in Table 15 along with several of their major characteristics. The six language and reading tests from Circus were selected because of their fairly comprehensive coverage and the recency of their development. The Preschool Language Assessment Instrument was reviewed because it links an interesting theoretical perspective on language directly to the teacher-learner dyad in early education. The bilingual measure included, the Pictorial Test of Bilingualism and Language Dominance, is of recent origin and was developed with considerable attention to technical concerns such as validity and reliability. Had space not been so limited, we would also have liked to discuss other bilingual measures.

Circus language and reading tests: In the previous chapter, Circus was discussed as a collection of many measures. Here, we concentrate on six tests in Circus that deal with language and reading (or, more appropriately, prereading) skills. Discussion concerns only two levels of Circus: Level A (preschool and early kindergarten) and Level B (late kindergarten and first grade). All the tests are given to small groups of children except Say and Tell, which is given individually. Each of the six measures is described in terms of types of item and construction; then matters pertaining to validity, reliability, and norms are considered for all the measures simultaneously, with the appropriate cross-references to the Chapter Five presentation of Circus.

How Words Sound is a test of auditory discrimination, available only for Level A. Designed to assess a child's ability to discriminate among phonemes heard in meaningful words, the measure results in scores for initial consonants, medial vowels, final consonants, and total. On each item, the teacher reads three words corresponding to three pictures in the child's test booklet—then, the teacher repeats one word and the child must mark it. For example, on an Initial Consonants item, the teacher reads: "Here is a picture of toes . . . rose . . . nose. Mark the picture of rose." Circus' authors acknowledged that the test ran the risk of measuring a vocabulary factor as well as auditory discrimination (a concern amplified by moderate to substantial correlations with other Circus vocabulary-related measures). They also noted that How Words Sound was not a formidable task for most children—average scores being above 37 and 39 (out of 44) for the nursery and kindergarten samples, respectively. Still, they believed the measure would function to identify children with severe handicaps in auditory perception.

What Words Mean, also available for Level A only, is designed to test receptive vocabulary. Based on content words (as distinct from functor, or operator, words such as prepositions, articles, and pronouns), the test includes items on nouns, verbs, and modifiers. For the nouns and all but one verb, the teacher reads the stimulus word and the child marks one of three response pictures. For the modifiers and remaining verb, the teacher reads the stimulus word and directs the child to the pictures. For example, "Shiny. Mark the picture of the one that is shiny" (a coin, not a dollar bill or a tree). The basic source for the words used was the Wepman and Hass (1969) spoken word count of five-, six-, and seven-year-olds. Raizen and Bobrow (1974) recommended the use of What Words Mean for Head Start children, considering it preferable to vocabulary tests with likely cultural bias, such as the Peabody Picture Vocabulary Test.

How Words Work, another Level A only measure, purports to assess aspects of functional language. The ability tapped is comprehension of sentences, with emphasis on syntax and on functor words. Three types of item are included: verb forms, prepositions/negations/conjunctions, and syntax (incorporating word order and subject-verb agreement). Several forms of teacher stimulus instruction are used, with the child marking pictorial responses. For example, "Here are two acrobats. Mark the one who is falling," as distinct from one who has fallen (verb form); or "Here are some lions. Mark the lion who is neither on the cage nor beside it," as distinct from those on and beside the cage (negation). The items involving prepositions, negations, and conjunctions were, as a group, the most difficult. The nursery school children did almost as well on this measure as did the kindergartners, and there was only a small improvement of performance with increasing age—surprising findings given the typical pattern on the other Circus tests.

Listen to the Story, available for both Levels A and B, tests the child's ability to comprehend, interpret, and recall oral language. Obviously of great significance in education, listening is a critical receptive language skill (reading being the other). The Level A version contains items dealing with comprehension and interpretation, making the measure seem like How Words Work, inasmuch as both assess comprehension. However, Listen to the Story emphasizes the content of messages, while How Words Work focuses on their syntax or word order and their functor words. Level B of Listen to the Story also concerns comprehension and interpretation; further, it includes a set of vocabulary items covering both content and functor words. Its authors deemed Level B of Listen to the Story as roughly equivalent to three Level A measures: What Words Mean, How Words Work, and Listen to the Story. For both levels, items are read aloud by a teacher and form a loose story line about young people planning to attend a circus and then actually doing it. Children are asked comprehension or interpretation questions throughout and mark a pictorial response for each (typically from arrays of three or four pictures for Level A and Level B, respectively). On both levels, comprehension items turned out to be somewhat easier than interpretation items for the norming samples, with vocabulary items on Level B easiest of all.

Say and Tell, also available for both levels, involves productive rather than receptive language. The measure is given individually (unlike any other Circus test). Each level contains three parts: description, functional language, and narration. In description, the child first must answer direct, structured questions about a pencil and then must describe (not in response to specific questions)

Table 15. Illustrative Language and Bilingual Measures in Early Childhood Education

Title and Dates	Age Range	Admin-istration	Scales or Scores	Sources
Circus:				
a. How Words Sound: Auditory Discrimination	a. Preschool to Kindergarten	a. Group; Untimed, but 15 to 20 minutes likely	a. Initial Consonants Medial Vowels Final Consonants Total	Addison-Wesley Testing Service South St. Reading, Mass. 01867
b. What Words Mean: Receptive Vocabulary	b. Preschool to Kindergarten	b. Group; Untimed, but 15 to 20 minutes likely	b. Nouns Verbs Modifiers Total	
c. How Words Work: Aspects of Functional Language	c. Preschool to Kindergarten	c. Group; Untimed, but 15 to 20 minutes likely	c. Verb Forms Prepositions/ Negations/ Conjunctions Syntax Total	
d. Listen to the Story: Comprehension, Interpretation, and Recall of Oral Language	d. Preschool to Grade 1	d. Group; Untimed, but 20 to 30 minutes likely	d. Comprehension Interpretation Vocabulary (B only) Total	

Test	Age	Administration	Description	Publisher
e. Say and Tell: Productive Language	e. Preschool to Grade 1	e. Individual; Untimed, but 20 to 30 minutes likely	e. Description Functional Language Narration	
f. Word Puzzles: Phonetic Analysis (1972–1976: Items; 1974–1976: Manuals)	f. Kindergarten to Grade 1	f. Group; Untimed, but 20 to 30 minutes likely	f. Sounds Ending Consonants Beginning Consonants Whole Words Total	Grune & Stratton, Inc. 111 Fifth Ave. New York, N.Y. 10003
Preschool Language Assessment Instrument (1978)	3 to 6 years	Individual; 20 minutes	Matching Perception Selective Analysis of Perception Reordering Perception Reasoning about Perception Qualitative Analysis	
Pictorial Test of Bilingualism and Language Dominance (1975)	4 to 8 years	Individual; 15 minutes	English Oral Vocabulary Spanish Oral Vocabulary Bilingual Oral Vocabulary Total Oral Vocabulary Language Profile Classification Level of English Oral Language Production Level of Spanish Oral Language Production	Stoelting Co. 1350 So. Kostner Chicago, Ill. 60623

either two pennies (Level A) or a dollar bill (Level B); more complete answers receive greater credit. In part two, Functional Language, measurements are made of the child's ability to use plurals, verb tenses, and comparatives (Levels A and B); to use prepositions, subject-verb agreement, and possessives (A only); and to use conjunctions (B only). Typically, a pair of drawings is presented to the child, a statement is made about one, and the child must complete a statement about the second. For example, "Here is a tree. Here are two _____ (trees)," or "This clown likes to swing. Here he is _____ (swinging)." In part three, Narration, the child is required to tell a story about a large colored drawing (for Level A, of a circus ring, and for Level B, of a fire station with a road leading to a circus and many children engaged in different activities enroute). The child's story is recorded verbatim and then analyzed in terms of the number of words and the number of different words (Levels A and B), the quality of the syntax, verbs, modifiers, sequence, and descriptions (A only), and the number of different situations and external events described (B only).

Word Puzzles, the final Circus test dealing directly with language, is available only for Level B. It measures some aspects of a child's understanding of the phonetic and structural properties of words. Set in the context of whole words, four tasks are required of the child. In Sounds, the child must select one of four pictured words that has the same sound as an initial pictured word (all the actual words are read by the teacher). For example, "Which word begins with the same sound as pig—knot, pot, cot, dot?" The second and third tasks, Ending Consonants and Beginning Consonants, involve recognizing a letter's sound and blending it with a word to form a new word. For instance, "Put 'car' and the sound of the letter 'd' together to make a new word." The child must select a picture of a card (not those of a cart, corn, or a car) as the teacher reads the four response options. In the Whole Word task, the child must look at a printed word (such as "fox") and select that pictured response (of four) that goes with the word; the teacher does not pronounce the word, although she does label each picture.

Validity considerations related to Circus as a total battery were presented in Chapter Five, and the reader may want to review that material. With regard to the specific measures reviewed here, it should be noted that content validity was not addressed, although experts in child development could easily have been queried as to the adequacy of Circus. Predictive validity of certain Level A measures was examined by ascertaining how well the Level A scores of over 1,000 kindergartners predicted their Level B scores (after a six-month interval). Correlations between the total score on Level B's Listen to the Story (the criterion) and its three associated Level A measures—What Words Mean, How Words Work, and Listen to the Story—were .64, .74, and .68, respectively. In addition, concurrent validity estimates were obtained by comparing teachers' ratings of children's capabilities with their performances on Circus. Relevant correlations appear in Table 16. Low to moderate agreement was generally found, with higher correspondence for the Level B measures. The exception to this pattern was very low correlations for Say and Tell, the measure of productive language. The .19 reported for its Level A narration score was composed of correlations of .31, .34, and –.11 for the total number of words, the number of different words, and the quality of words, respectively. This outcome prompted Circus' authors to hypothesize "that teachers are more influenced by how much children talk rather than by the quality of their productive language" (Circus Manual and Technical Report, 1976, p. 50). The .16 reported for narration on Level B involved just the total number of words. Finally, with regard to factor analyses to examine construct validity, a substantial general ability factor was noted, with high loadings on the factor for What Words Mean, How Words Work, and Listen to the Story (both Levels A and B). Somewhat more separate skills among the Level A measures were How Words Sound and Say and Tell, while for Level B, Word Puzzles and Say and Tell formed a moderately distinct cluster. In all, the language measures display promise with regard to validity although additional work is clearly warranted. Criterion-related validity would be of particular importance, especially for Say and Tell.

The Alpha or internal consistency reliability of the measures also appears in Table 16. The correlations reported for the narration subscale of Say and Tell were based on the quality score for the nursery school and kindergarten samples (Level A) and on the number of external events described for the first grade sample (Level B). In general, these estimates of internal consistency tended to be substantial to high, to be higher as the number of items increases (as one would expect), and to be especially impressive given the young ages of the children. However, no stability reliability is reported, a serious omission given the subjects involved.

As indicated in Chapter Five, the norming process for Circus was systematic and generally impressive. In all, Circus provides a valuable collection of measures of young children's language, especially as it relates to schools. Additional attention to its technical characteristics would enhance the utility of Circus.

Preschool Language Assessment Instrument (PLAI): Quite recently, an effort has been made to assess a child's competence in meeting the language demands of the teaching-learning situation. Based on an extensive research investigation (Blank, Rose, and Berlin, 1978b), the Preschool Language Assessment Instrument, or PLAI, has been released as an experimental edition (Blank, Rose, and Berlin, 1978a). Two principal purposes are set for the measure: (1) to describe a child's language skills so that teaching encounters can be structured to match the child's level of functioning, and (2) to identify early those children who might experience severe difficulties in school, so that they can be referred for extensive diagnostic testing. PLAI is intended for children three to six years old, although it reportedly can be useful with even ten-year-olds who have questionable language skills and are performing poorly in school. The sixty-item test (an abbreviated version of the instrument used in the research investigation) is administered individually by a professional who is familiar with young children (such as a school psychologist, a speech and hearing clinician, or a resource-room or classroom teacher); some experience in individual testing of children is desirable. A single twenty-minute test session in a quiet location is normal and preferred, with split sessions allowed if the second period occurs within a few days of the first.

The theory upon which PLAI is based is derived from Moffett (1968) and

Table 16. Validity and Reliability Estimates for Circus Language Measures

Circus Test	Number of Items	Validity (Concurrent with Teacher Ratings)		Reliability (Internal Consistency or Alpha)		
		K(A)[a]	FG(B)[b]	NS(A)[c]	K(A)	FG(B)
How Words Sound						
Initial Consonants	10			.68	.70	—
Medial Vowels	14			.77	.63	—
Final Consonants	20			.87	.77	—
Total	44	.25	—	.92	.87	—
What Words Mean						
Nouns	20			.73	.70	—
Verbs	12			.71	.66	—
Modifiers	8			.66	.55	—
Total	40	.39	—	.86	.83	—
How Words Work						
Verb Forms	8			.63	.57	—
Prep./Negation/Conj.	10			.54	.43	—
Syntax	8			.67	.51	—
Total	26	.36	—	.78	.71	—
Listen to the Story						
Comprehension	15/16[d]			.67	.68	.74
Interpretation	10/9			.60	.61	.61
Vocabulary	—/13			—	—	.71
Total	25/38	.47	.56	.77	.79	.87

Say and Tell						
Description	16/15	−.14	—	.72	.49	.71
Functional Language	38/31	.14	.23	.89	.90	.78
Narration	12/Open	.19	.16	.78	.78	.61
Word Puzzles						
Sounds	9			—	—	.70
Ending Consonants	9			—	—	.79
Beginning Consonants	8			—	—	.81
Whole Words	13			—	—	.84
Total	39	—	.52	—	—	.93

[a]Kindergarten Sample; Circus Level A.
[b]First-Grade Sample; Circus Level B.
[c]Nursery School Sample; Circus Level A.
[d]Numbers of items in Level A/Level B.

is presented in *The Language of Learning* (Blank, Rose, and Berlin, 1978b), a book that serves as a back-up document for the test. Moffett's model of communication is tripartite, consisting of the speaker-listener dyad, the topic or subject being discussed, and the level or complexity of discussion. In developing PLAI, Blank and her colleagues subtly adapted Moffett's model to young children in educational settings. First, they restricted the speaker-listener dyad to the teacher-child pair (while recognizing that meaningful discourse also took place between young children). Second, they limited the topics of discussion to perceptually based experiences within young children's comprehension level, focusing on activities that go on in most preschool programs. Finally, they conceptualized the level of discussion in terms of *perceptual-language distance.*

> This term has been chosen to reflect the two types of information that any discussion involves. First, there is the material being discussed (for ease of communication, the material is represented by the term *perceptual* in the perceptual-language distance rubric). Second, there is the language that the teacher uses to direct the child's analysis of the material (again, for ease of communication, the teacher's language is represented by the term *language* in the preceding rubric). According to the way it is formulated, the teacher's language can be quite close to or quite removed from the material. During a trip to the zoo, for example, a teacher could point to some animals (a tiger and a giraffe) and ask, "What are the names of those animals?" Alternatively, he or she could point to the same animals and say, "What is the same about both of them?" Although both questions deal with material that is before the child, the demands involve different relationships between the perceptual and verbal components. In the former, an almost one-to-one correspondence holds between what the child sees and says; in the latter, the language no longer has this tight relationship to the perception. Instead, the child must think of a verbal response that is appropriate to the two different objects but not immediately evident in either. As such, in the request for a judgment of similarity there is a considerably greater distance between the perception and the language than there is in the first question.
>
> These different types of relationships are what we are attempting to capture in the term *perceptual-language distance.* As the distance between the material and the language widens, increasingly greater demands are placed on the children to abstract the information from the material that is available to them [Blank, Rose, and Berlin, 1978b, p. 13].

The perceptual-language distance construct was operationalized as a continuum of four levels of discourse skills, each level more complex and abstract than the previous one and each composed of fifteen interspersed items:

1. Matching perception: Minimal distance between the perception and the language used, requiring the child to answer simple questions or to follow directives. For example, "What is this called?" (cup) or "Touch your nose."
2. Selective analysis of perception: Increased distance between the perception and the language used, necessitating that the child resist his attraction to global perceptions and, instead, respond more selectively. For instance,

"What do we do with it?" (scissors) or "What were the names of the children in the story we just read?"

3. Reordering perception: Considerable distance between the perception and the language used, requiring the child to reject appealing action characteristics and internally rework his experiences to fit the verbal demands of the task. For example, "Now say: what does a dog say?" (with full credit given for perfect imitation of the sentence) or "If I wanted to dress this doll, show me all the things I *don't* need. Point to them."

4. Reasoning about perception: Extensive distance between the perception and the language used, requiring the child to think about what might, could, or would happen to the materials. For instance, "If this bowl were filled all the way up with playdough, could we pour these marbles inside?" and, after the child's response, "Why?" (or "Why not?"). Or, in another item, "What will happen to the man if he closes his umbrella?"

Seated facing the child across a table, the examiner uses a large booklet to administer the test. On many items, the booklet is placed so the child can view large pictures filling a complete page (such as a man standing in the rain under an umbrella); on other items, the examiner lifts the test pages so that the child sees only a blank page. After two unscored demonstration items, testing begins. When a verbal response occurs, the child's precise words are recorded as well as any important gestures accompanying the verbalization.

Scoring is of two types: numerical and qualitative. In the numerical procedure, each item is scored 3 to 0 on fairly well-defined criteria, with 3 being fully adequate, 2 acceptable, 1 ambiguous, and 0 inadequate. An average score is obtained for the fifteen items making up each of the four levels of discourse skills. The test authors suggested that average scores below 1 indicated weakness, between 1.0 and 1.5 moderate weakness, between 1.5 and 2.0 moderate strength, and above 2 strength. Further, they believed that a profile of the child's four average scores would assist in effectively matching teaching to the child's performance level. This criterion-referenced function (that is, indicating the child's mastery of discourse) was seen as primary. Comparing the child with others in traditional norm-referenced fashion was viewed as secondary but particularly helpful in deciding about special educational placements, in referring for further diagnostic testing, and in identifying (and then stimulating) children with considerable discourse skills who have chosen not to display this capability in the give-and-take of classroom discussion.

Qualitative analysis or scoring is an optional procedure used to obtain a detailed analysis of a child's characteristic response modes. During the administration of PLAI, the responses to forty-five items are coded in seven quality categories:

1. FA: Fully adequate.
2. Acc: Acceptable.
3. Amb: Ambiguous.

4. Inv: Inadequate-invalid.
5. Irr: Inadequate-irrelevant.
6. DK: Inadequate-don't know.
7. NR: Inadequate-no response.

This listing bears an obvious relation to the numerical scoring procedure, as responses in the first three categories count 3, 2, and 1 point(s), respectively, while the four inadequate categories count 0. In qualitative analysis, the forty-five responses are considered as a group, independent of the level of discourse skill involved. A child's responses in the first three categories—FA, Acc, and Amb—are summed to yield the total number of adequate responses (with ambiguous responses being considered adequate in this analysis to give a child optimum credit for his answers). Then the percentage of this total represented by the FA, Acc, and Amb response categories is calculated. In similar fashion, the four inadequate categories are summed; then the Inv, Irr, DK, and NR responses are calculated as a percentage of the total inadequate responses. The test authors indicated that qualitative analysis of inadequate responses required a minimum of ten such responses. Considerable information is presented in the test and, especially, in the accompanying book on interpretation of resultant scores.

The PLAI manual addresses three aspects of validity: content, concurrent criterion-related, and construct. Content validity was examined by having five school psychologists and special education teachers, with no previous knowledge of the test, read about the adapted Moffett model (in Blank, Rose, and Berlin, 1978b) used in developing the test and then sort the sixty items into the four discourse skill levels. Total agreement was reached on 75 percent of the items, and four out of the five raters agreed on 95 percent of the items. While this procedure provides information on the adequacy of the content grouping of the items, it does not evaluate the adequacy or representativeness of the items as a sampling of the universe of language discourse items.

A type of concurrent criterion-related validity was also presented in support of PLAI. Fourteen middle-class children, half four years old and half five and all with normal intelligence, had been extensively tested and diagnosed as having language disabilities; they had been placed in a special program to improve their language functioning. When they were tested on the PLAI, their average performance was found to be markedly poorer than that of other same-age, middle-class children (this was particularly true for the seven five-year-olds). All fourteen children scored below the 25th percentile on two or more of the four discourse skills, while eight of the fourteen were below that level on all four skills. This outcome does lend support to the PLAI, although one would hope for larger samples (and, with time, examination of the PLAI's predictive validity).

Construct validity was assessed by noting how well the test results matched the postulated theoretical model. The developers of PLAI expressed encouragement in three regards. First, a steady improvement in performance was noted with increasing age, matching what is known about children's language development. Second, all groups of children experienced increasing difficulty as the perceptual-language distance increased (that is, items were easiest on the matching perception end of the continuum and got progressively more difficult with movement toward the reasoning about perception end of the continuum. Third, middle-class children performed better on PLAI than lower-class children. Curiously, although considerable attention is given in *The Language of Learning* to the significant positive relationship between IQ and discourse skill scores, the manual is silent on this. Apparently more important in the developers' judgment was the fact that PLAI yielded specific information on where a teacher could modify interactions with a child to facilitate learning, whereas an IQ test did not. Further, after controlling for IQ differences, they continued to note relatively better performance by lower-class children on the simple skills (matching perception) and by the middle-class children on the more complex skills (reordering perception and reasoning about perception).

Reliability assessments of PLAI took three forms: Interrater reliability was estimated by having four raters independently score the sixty items for each of ten children. All four raters gave identical scores 81 to 93 percent of the time across the protocols of the ten children, while three of four raters agreed at the level of 92 to 98 percent. Further, on examination of the four average discourse skill scores assigned by each rater to each of the ten children, an average discrepancy of only .1 was observed across all occasions. The discrepancies never exceeded .3, and identical mean discourse skill scores occurred 83 percent of the time. Internal consistency reliability was assessed by the split-half method, apparently using 120 children; observed correlations (corrected for attenuation using the Spearman-Brown formula) of .64, .80, .83, and .86 were found for the four levels of discourse skills, respectively. Stability reliability was determined by readministering PLAI to thirty-four children after an interval of one to two weeks. Test-retest correlations of .73, .83, .86, and .88 were calculated for the four discourse skill levels, respectively.

The PLAI, being an experimental edition, does not purport to have comprehensive normative data available (in fact, the manual includes a request that users send data to the test authors on PLAI results and children's demographic characteristics). However, the performance of 120 New York children is reported, 10 lower-class and 10 middle-class children in six six-month age groupings from three to six years old. Means and standard deviations on each of the four discourse skill scores are reported for each of these twelve groups; selected percentile ranks for PLAI are also presented by age and socioeconomic background. Scores were not reported by sex as no significant differences were found.

In summary, PLAI appears to be an important measure of language; with its age range and its discourse skills tied closely to the educational arena, it has high potential utility for early childhood education. Validity data generated to date are generally favorable; more attention to concurrent and predictive validity is needed. Reliability information is likewise substantial. Interrater reliability is quite encouraging, while internal consistency and stability reliability are substantial—with the exception of the estimates for the matching perception discourse skill. Extensive work is required on norms if PLAI is to become exemplary in this regard.

Pictorial Test of Bilingualism and Language Dominance (PTBLD): The recent surge of interest in bilingualism and language dominance has led to the development of many instruments. Representative of such measures and noteworthy in its efforts to address technical concerns is the Pictorial Test of Bilingualism and Language Development (Nelson, Fellner, and Norrell, 1975). Developed in Texas in the early 1970s and normed using Mexican-American children only, the PTBLD's primary purpose "is to provide procedures for the objective measurement of language facility in English and Spanish. The instrument provides an objective approach to establish a child's language development in English and Spanish (bilingualism) and additional procedures to determine the favored or predominant language (language dominance)" (Nelson, Fellner, and Norrell, 1975, p. 1). With such information, the test authors believed that accurate and appropriate placement in a bilingual class, rather than in a predominantly English-speaking one, could be accomplished. The PTBLD is designed for Mexican-American (Chicano) children between the ages of four and eight years, is given individually, and emphasizes speaking aspects of language (as distinct from writing, listening, and reading). Purportedly, a bilingual paraprofessional familiar with the test can administer it adequately; testing requires about fifteen minutes. Substantial attention is given in the manual to administration conditions, such as securing a quiet testing location, establishing rapport, and respecting the child's unique personality during testing.

The PTBLD consists of two parts: (1) oral vocabulary and (2) oral language production. Development of the oral vocabulary part extended over several phases. To generate potentially suitable words, early education materials were scanned, educational personnel working with target children were consulted, and other measures with similar purposes were reviewed. One hundred words were selected to constitute the initial content of the PTBLD. Original line drawings were made, each intended to depict a single word. On the basis of field tryout data, forty items were retained that met the following criteria: "(1) The word was correctly known in both English and Spanish at a given grade level by at least 50 percent of the sample at that grade level; (2) When a word was English-favored (known by a larger percentage of the sample in English than in Spanish), it was offset by choosing a Spanish-favored word. This procedure assured language balance (equal degree of difficulty in both languages) by grade level and throughout the entire range of the instrument; . . . (3) Point biserial coefficients of correlation were computed to objectively establish the relationship of grade level and knowing the word correctly in both languages. All words included in Part I of the instrument were positively correlated with grade level" (Nelson, Fellner, and Norrell, 1975, p. 7).

Each item consists of a sketch on a separate page in a small booklet and is shown to the child being tested. The examiner instructs the child, in both English and Spanish, to tell him what the picture is. The child can respond in Spanish or

English; after his first response, the child is asked to name the object in the other language. Each item is scored 1 point if correct, and 0 if incorrect. Four scores, each with a maximum of 40 points, derive from Part I:

1. English oral vocabulary: Total number of words known correctly in English.
2. Spanish oral vocabulary: Total number of words known correctly in Spanish.
3. Bilingual oral vocabulary: Total number of words known correctly in both languages.
4. Total oral vocabulary: Total number of words known correctly in either English or Spanish.

Tables are used to convert these four raw scores to corresponding "language quotients" (mean = 100, standard deviation = 15). The language quotients —English, Spanish, bilingual, and total—are plotted on a 16 × 16 language-profile matrix. Depending on the area of intersection of his English and Spanish language quotients, the child is classified in one of six ways: (1) English dominant, (2) Spanish dominant, (3) bilingual, (4) language deficient, (5) possible learning problem (mental retardation or language/learning disabilities), or (6) pseudobilingual (knowing some words in English and some in Spanish, but not the same words in both). The bilingual language quotient helps in determining between classifications 3 and 6, while the total language quotient reportedly can be interpreted cautiously as an indicator of general ability.

   Whereas the oral vocabulary part (Part I) of the PTBLD is used to establish language dominance, the oral language production part (Part II) is administered only when additional information is needed regarding the child's bilingual language facility (that is, his differential ability to communicate orally in Spanish and English). Part II is roughly comparable to aspects of Circus' Say and Tell, although the second language feature marks it as distinct. The child is shown a full-page drawing titled "Pinata Hanging" and is asked to tell a story about what he sees. The child's response is recorded verbatim. He is then asked to tell the story for the same picture in the "opposite" language, and this is also recorded verbatim. (A tape recorder might be necessary for the verbatim recordings.) Then a series of four structured questions is asked, in both English and Spanish—two about the pinata picture and two about a picture called "House Builders" (depicting a man and a child in a cooperative house-building effort). Again responses are recorded verbatim. All the child's English responses are then given a global rating at one of four levels:

Level 3: Uses grammatically correct sentences that express subject-verb-object relationships and that communicate complete thoughts.
Level 2: Uses sentences that communicate complete thoughts but that are grammatically incorrect or incomplete.
Level 1: Uses single or linking words to identify objects or describe actions but does not use complete sentences or express complete thoughts.
Level 0: Is unable to respond in the language, possibly lacking expressive vocabulary and/or the capability to understand the directions in the language.

Then the process is repeated in order to assign a global rating to the child's Spanish responses. A table of representative responses facilitates this rating process. The test authors suggested that responses by children who blend English and Spanish—that is, who relate a mixed-language response—could also be rated on the four-point scale. The authors envisioned results from Part II as providing additional information on the child's extent of bilingualism and dominant oral language as well as information useful for devising individualized instructional strategies and curriculum.

Considerable attention is given in the manual to validity. At the outset, the authors of the measure reviewed the development process, describing it as unique, particularly in its attempt to achieve language balance between the English and Spanish words utilized. (Had certain other elements in the development effort been examined more fully—as by detailing the educational materials and psychometric instruments reviewed to obtain words initially, or describing better the educational personnel involved, or having experts review and critique the words selected—the PTBLD developers could have made a stronger claim for content validity.) The test authors also predicted that PTBLD results would differ from outcomes on other measures, and reminded the reader that PTBLD was normed and developed using only Mexican-American children.

Concurrent criterion-related validity formed the heart of the validation claims, with six pertinent studies reported. In the first, twenty-five Chicano children who had been diagnosed as mentally retarded (scoring two or more standard deviations below the mean on the Wechsler or the Binet) and who were enrolled in a special education class were given the PTBLD. Their average English oral vocabulary and total oral vocabulary scores were significantly lower ($p < .05$) than those of a similar-age normal group of 182 Mexican-American kindergarten and first-grade children.

The second, third, and fourth studies involved teacher ratings. In one, 176 Mexican-American children attending migrant and bilingual education classes were divided into an English-dominant group and a Spanish-dominant group on the basis of teacher ratings of dominant home language. The children were then given the PTBLD. For both kindergartners and first-graders, the English-dominant home language group did significantly better on English oral vocabulary, while the Spanish-dominant home language group did significantly better on Spanish oral vocabulary ($p < .01$). In another study, bilingual teachers were instructed to rate each of their students on a five-point continuum: (1) English monolingual, (2) English dominant, (3) Bilingual, (4) Spanish dominant, (5) Spanish monolingual. The PTBLD was then administered. Fifty kindergarten and first-grade children were randomly selected; their English and Spanish oral vocabulary scores correlated .85 and .52, respectively, with the teacher ratings of language dominance. In the third study using ratings, teachers used a five-point scale to rate the overall school achievement of their Mexican-American students. Then, the PTBLD was given and fifty K-1 students were randomly selected. Correlations calculated between the achievement ratings and the PTBLD English, Spanish, bilingual, and total oral vocabulary scores were .81, .49, .75, and .79, respectively.

The two remaining concurrent validity investigations involved relationships between the PTBLD and other tests. Fifty Mexican-American children in kindergarten and grade one were given both the PTBLD and two tests in the Inter-American Series, one English (Tests of General Ability) and one Spanish (Habilidad General). The English, Spanish, and total vocabulary PTBLD scores were correlated with comparable scores from the Inter-American tests. Considerable correspondence was noted on the English oral vocabulary scores of the two instruments (r's of .81 and .50 at kindergarten and first grade, respectively). The PTBLD English oral vocabulary correlated .77 with the total English score on the Inter-American Series English test for kindergartners, but only .28 for the first-grade sample. Correlations involving the two tests' Spanish oral vocabulary scores were very low (.28 for kindergarten and .16 for first grade), and those between PTBLD's Spanish oral vocabulary score and Inter-American's total Spanish score were both negative and near zero. The PTBLD developers believed that these last low correlations may have been due to the different response formats (oral and in Spanish on the PTBLD and pointing after Spanish instructions on the Inter-American) or to the failure of Inter-American to control difficulty through some technique like PTBLD's language balance procedure.

The second measure examined in relation to PTBLD was the Peabody Picture Vocabulary Test (PPVT), reviewed in Chapter Five. A group of Mexican-American children were given both instruments in a three-week period. From among the students scoring at or below the normal range on the PPVT, twenty-five were randomly selected. Correlations between these students' PPVT scores and their PTBLD English and total oral vocabulary scores were .51 and .60, respectively. The test authors also noted that Spanish-dominant Mexican-American children tended to receive extremely low IQ scores on the PPVT.

Reliability of the PTBLD was examined in terms of internal consistency and stability. Split-half procedures were used with a random sample of twenty-five kindergarten and first-grade students. Obtained coefficients were stepped up using the Spearman-Brown technique, resulting in correlations of .85 and .89 for English and Spanish oral vocabulary scores, respectively. Stability reliability was assessed using two separate samples of fifty students. Retesting on the PTBLD occurred after two months for one group and after six months for the second. Resultant correlations on the four vocabulary scores were:

Oral Vocabulary Score	*Two-month Stability*		*Six-month Stability*	
	K	1	K	1
English	.89	.92	.79	.93
Spanish	.90	.70	.35	.82
Bilingual	.87	.96	.65	.69
Total	.69	.82	.67	.80

The stability coefficients were generally substantial to high and, as expected, lower over the longer retest interval (the .70 entry may be .77, as this correlation was reported differently at different places in the manual). Although these are encouraging estimates for young children, the six-month kindergarten scores were not as stable as one might hope, especially the .35 for Spanish oral vocabulary. Standard errors of measurement were reported for the four language quotients corresponding to the four PTBLD vocabulary scores; based on the two-month stability reliabilities, they averaged between 5 and 6 points.

Norms as such are provided only in the language quotient conversion tables. Raw scores for any of the four vocabulary tests can be entered into one of four age-appropriate conversion tables—preschool, kindergarten, first grade, or second grade, based on 48, 158, 167, and 95 children, respectively. These tables make it clear that the PTBLD was more appropriate for the younger students sampled, being on the easy side for second-graders. The norm group consisted of Mexican-American children from South Texas, but otherwise was undescribed. The test authors appropriately urged users to develop local norms and noted, "Numerous studies indicate that linguistic and cultural patterns among Mexican-American children populations differ significantly by region and to a lesser extent even among towns within the same region" (Nelson, Fellner, and Norrell, 1975, p. 37).

In all, the PTBLD appears to have undergone substantial early development. Reliability and validity studies are creditable, especially compared with the studies done for other measures attempting to assess the same constructs. Additional work is probably needed on the Spanish oral vocabulary portion of the test and definitely needed on Part II. The utility of the measure would be improved if it were made more difficult for the older children in the target age group, if more elaborate information on using the test scores were provided, and, particularly, if more broadly representative norms could be developed for it. One must wonder how the language balance of the words would hold up in various regions of the country and whether extensive reworking of the instrument would be required to match regional differences.

Creativity Tests

Research on creativity has flourished since midcentury—in part, according to writers such as Razik (1967), because world forces, such as the creation of the atomic bomb and the international Communist threat, persuaded many Americans that creativity must be nurtured directly in the schools rather than left to chance. Influential papers by Guilford (1950), who, in his "structure of intellect," redefined intelligence in terms of five mental operations, including divergent thinking, and Thurstone (1951), who highlighted the roles of inductive reasoning and ideational fluency as well as temperamental factors in creative production, served as early stimulants. By the 1960s, great interest in creativity was apparent. Getzels and Jackson's provocative study (1962) sought to demonstrate that highly intelligent secondary students were not necessarily the highly creative ones, and that many of the latter would go unidentified if only traditional intelligence tests were used. The authors also contended that highly creative students were discriminated against by too many teachers; that is, teachers tended to neither accept nor reinforce students who exhibited questioning, non-conforming, unconventional, or independent behaviors. Torrance (1962) reported similar findings. Both lines of work were criticized heavily for methodological reasons, especially that of Getzels and Jackson, and at times with substantial justification. Nevertheless, because of such pronouncements, the general topics of creativity, the schools' relation to it, and its measurement were thrust onto center stage.

Considerable controversy has surrounded the definition of creativity. A number of widely varying definitions have been proposed (for example, see Carroll and Laming, 1974; Dellas and Gaier, 1970; Getzels and Dillon, 1973; and Wallach, 1970). Exactly what constitutes creative behavior for an adult? Must the product or idea have utility? What constitutes creative behavior for a child? Or, in considering children, are we simply trying to identify the antecedents of later creative behavior? Should creativity be judged relative to some general societal or international norm or relative to an individual's own previous efforts? Questions about creativity are easily formulated but not easily answered. Nevertheless, certain distinctions have helped to organize thinking about creativity. For example, it has been useful to conceptualize two levels of creativity—one that is societal, quite restrictive (in that only a very few display it), and very high in quality, and a second that is personal, less restrictive, and less high in quality (Barron, 1969). Another aid has been provided by Tryk (1968), who distinguished four theoretical orientations and the implication of each for measurement—namely, creativity as a product, a capacity or aptitude, a process, or an aspect of the total person.

Nature and Status of Creativity Tests. Some have felt the need to defend the legitimacy and current state of the art of creativity testing in education (such as Torrance, 1975). Our own view, and that of many, is that the present creativity tests leave much to be desired in terms of validity and reliability. But a similar statement might be made about many types of tests in all three domains of behavior—cognitive, affective, and psychomotor. Given the relative recency of creativity tests, we believe that many additional years for development and study are warranted before definitive judgments are reached. Further, we agree with Anastasi that "creative talent is not synonymous with academic intelligence and is rarely covered by tests yielding an 'IQ'. . . . Studies of scientific talent have become increasingly concerned with creative abilities. Interest has shifted from the individual who is merely a cautious, accurate, and critical thinker to the one who also displays ingenuity, originality, and inventiveness. Thus creativity, long regarded as the prime quality in artistic production, is coming more and more to be recognized as a basis for scientific achievement as well" (1976, p. 389). Further, there currently appears to be a rekindling of interest in programs for both gifted and creative students (variously defined) in American schools—possibly a reaction to the 1965–1975 decade of special programs for children with pronounced learning difficulties.

Unlike the "basics" (reading, writing, and arithmetic), creative thinking and acting have not generally been established as principal objectives of educational programs. Without such objectives, creativity assessment was not needed. Thus, compared with available intelligence and achievement tests, the supply of creativity measures is small. Those measures that do exist are subject to a whole host of psychometric problems attributable to complexity of the construct *creativity* (Treffinger and Poggio, 1972). For example, a rather common difficulty has been establishing appropriate concurrent and predictive validity criteria (Forteza, 1974).

Paradoxically, although many early childhood educators are very much in favor of creative behavior in children such as original thinking, independence, inventiveness, and artistic individuality, they are often opposed to any attempts to measure or quantify such behavior. Apparently, they fear that overly prescriptive instructional guidance and restriction of children's natural and varied performances would invariably result. The short- to long-range prognoses for early childhood education objectives that stress unusual thinking and varied artistic production are uncertain. Probably emphasis on such objectives will fluctuate dramatically from program to program. Our position is that encouragement of creativity and individuality, even in preschoolers, is to be applauded— particularly in view of the strong societal pressures for conformity. We do not view attempts at measuring creativity or potential for creativity as being in any way restrictive; hence, the examples that follow.

Illustrative Creativity Tests. There was no problem of sampling representative tests to include in this section; we have included most of those that are readily available. There are several other sources of information relevant to creativity testing, however. Two are journals: the *Gifted Child Quarterly* and *Journal of Creative Behavior.* As an example from the former, one article described a checklist that reportedly can be used to identify creative talent among disadvantaged children (Torrance, 1973). As an example from the latter journal, a recent article described the Group Inventory for Finding Creative Talent (GIFT), a quick screening instrument designed to identify students from grades one to six for programs for the "creatively gifted" (Rimm and Davis, 1976). A third source is an appendix to a book (Davis, 1973), which lists tests and measures of creativity; especially valuable is its extensive list of noncommercial tests and attitude surveys, although the measures generally are for older children and adults. Johnson (1976) also includes a few creativity measures for very young children, among them a rating scale and an observation schedule. The salience of Wallach and Kogan's research (1965) should also be noted. Their approach to the measurement of creativity was quite different from that of Torrance, whose work is detailed here (for analysis and criticism of their approach, see Crockenberg, 1972 and Cronbach, 1968). However, the Wallach and Kogan measures generally were prepared for children aged eight years and older and thus are not included here. A final source of note is Guilford's work, especially an important chapter with Hoepfner on abilities in creative thinking and planning (1971) and his article describing his Creativity Tests for Children, which emphasize divergent production abilities (1975). The Creativity Tests for Children are not described here as they were designed for children in grades four through six.

The creativity tests considered in detail are listed in Table 17. The broad Torrance series is considered first because of its more comprehensive nature.

Torrance Tests of Creative Thinking (TTCT): The Torrance tests represent the most comprehensive battery of creativity measures for children in kindergarten and the early primary grades. The purpose of the tests is to detect and measure creative thinking potential in children. It is implied that such knowledge will help in individualizing instruction and evaluating effects of innovative programs and procedures (Torrance, 1966). Two separate tests are now available, each in two forms. A verbal test, Thinking Creatively with Words, takes about an hour and is given individually to children in kindergarten to grade three. The figural test, Thinking Creatively with Pictures, is group-administered (although smaller-than-classroom groups are recommended from kindergarten to grade four) in about forty-five minutes. If both tests are given, an hour and forty-five minutes are required, with separate sittings advised. Interestingly, the same tests used with young children are also used with adults.

Each test is made up of a number of measures or tasks. Since the tasks' titles are unusual and do not always convey their content, some elaboration is provided below.

Thinking Creatively with Words (verbal):
1. Ask-and-Guess: Provided with a provocative sketch, the respondent is directed (a) to ask all the questions necessary to know what is happening in the drawing, (b) to guess as many causes as possible for the action shown in the picture, and (c) to guess possible consequences of what is occurring in the picture. Five minutes are allowed for each of the three parts. The examiner writes all responses if the child is in kindergarten to grade three (this procedure is followed in all five of the verbal tasks).
2. Product Improvement: Given a picture of a stuffed animal, the child suggests ways it could be changed, regardless of cost, to make it more fun to play with; ten minutes are allowed.
3. Unusual Uses: The student is allowed ten minutes to indicate interesting and unusual uses, as many as possible, for a common object, like a cardboard box or tin cans.
4. Unusual Questions: Using the same object as in task three, the child asks as many unusual questions as possible about the object within five minutes.
5. Just Suppose: An unusual situation appears in a sketch and is described (such as clouds having strings that hang down to earth). In five minutes' time, the child must guess and give ideas about what would happen.

Thinking Creatively with Pictures (figural):
6. Picture Construction: The child is given a shaped piece of colored paper to use as the nucleus of a drawing that no one else would think of; it is to be completed and given a title within ten minutes.

Table 17. Illustrative Creativity Measures in Early Childhood Education

Title and Date	Age Range	Administration	Scales or Scores	Source
Torrance Tests of Creative Thinking: (1966: Items; 1966, 1968, 1972: Manual)	Kindergarten to Adult	Group (except individual on Verbal Battery, kindergarten to grade 3); 1¼ hours	Fluency Flexibility Originality Elaboration	Personnel Press, Inc. 20 Nassau St. Princeton, N.J. 08540
Circus: Make a Tree: Divergent Pictorial Production (1972–1976: Items; 1974–1976: Manuals)	Preschool to Grade 1	Group; 2 sessions of about 15 minutes each	Appropriateness Unusualness Difference	Addison-Wesley Testing Service South St. Reading, Mass. 01867
Starkweather Originality Test (1974)	3½ to 6½ years	Individual; Time required not stated (our estimate is 20 minutes)	Total Number of Different Responses	Dr. E. K. Starkweather FRCD Department Oklahoma State Univ. Stillwater, Okla. 74074

7. Picture Completion: Ten incomplete figures, resembling the start of doodles, must be completed and titled in ten minutes.
8. Repeated Figures: The student is given thirty sets of parallel lines (or forty circles, on the alternate form) and is instructed to make objects or pictures using the given figures as main elements. Names or titles are also to be added, all in ten minutes.

Administration does not require special training, and scoring reportedly can be done by teachers or any adult willing to carefully study and adhere to the detailed scoring guide. Four scores are derived, but not from all tasks; they are:

1. Fluency: the number of responses relevant to the test task.
2. Flexibility: the number of different categories of responses relevant to the test task (lists of categories are provided).
3. Originality: the unusualness of a response relevant to the test task, based on its frequency of occurrence among norm groups.
4. Elaboration: the adding of detail to a response relevant to the test task.

Additionally, the four scores above are considered separately for the verbal and figural tests.

Thus, on the figural test, Thinking Creatively with Pictures, the Picture Completion and Repeated Figures measures yield all four scores, while Picture Construction yields only Figural Originality and Figural Elaboration scores. To be even more specific, consider the four scores on the Picture Completion task: Figural Fluency (the number of figures completed with a relevant response, out of ten), Figural Flexibility (the number of categories into which relevant responses fall), Figural Originality (the unusualness of relevant responses, with more points awarded for a response only rarely observed in norm groups), and Figural Elaboration (points awarded for detail added to or around the original stimulus figure). The raw score points from the several tasks contributing to a given score category (such as Figural Fluency) are summed and then converted, by using tables, to standard scores (mean of 50, standard deviation of 10). In similar fashion, Thinking Creatively with Words results in Verbal Fluency and Verbal Originality scores (with all five tasks contributing) and a Verbal Flexibility score (with all tasks except Unusual Questions contributing). Although Elaboration scoring guides are provided for three verbal tasks (Product Improvement, Unusual Uses, and Just Suppose), Torrance did not encourage the use of a Verbal Elaboration score.

Examination of the test manual (Torrance, 1966) reveals extensive information on validity, but it is presented in an often indirect and sometimes confusing fashion. Little emphasis is placed on content validity. Also, only one predictive validity study is noted—a study suggesting that adult creative activities (such as learning a foreign language, writing poetry, or giving public performances) could be predicted partially on the basis of Torrance Test performance seven years earlier during the last year of high school. Rather, emphasis is on construct and concurrent validity, with some fifty studies cited. The typical approach in the construct validation studies involving children was to analyze personalities and behaviors of high and low scorers on the creativity tests. For example, in one study of elementary school children, high scorers as compared with low scorers were found to generate more original and elaborate drawings and other productions, to have "wild and silly" ideas, and to use more humor and playfulness in their daily responses. Although many of the studies could be faulted for design and methodological shortcomings, and correlations reported were often quite low, in total their results tend to suggest that the TTCT measures behaviors consistent with those identified in the creativity literature (Baird, 1972). The concurrent validity studies examined the relationship between TTCT performance and criteria such as peer nominations, teacher nominations, and educational achievement. In Torrance's view, these studies supported his tests' validity; Crockenberg (1972), however, noted several qualifications to such an interpretation. Several reviewers (Baird, 1972; and Wallach, 1970) have expressed concern over the substantial correlations between performance on intelligence tests and on the TTCT, wondering to what extent the measures are indeed distinct. Baird (1972), Hoepfner (1967), and Thorndike (1972) have noted high correlations between the four scores on either battery of the TTCT and have suggested that a composite verbal score and a composite figural score might be more appropriate.

The heart of the validation question for the Torrance tests is their ability to predict long-range creative behavior in the real world. Because of the short shrift given predictive validity in the manual, Holland (1968) remarked that until the TTCT is linked to reality by external validity studies, it could not be known if "high scores identify original people or crazy bricklayers and packers." Torrance (1972) subsequently addressed the predictive validity of his tests in a separate publication. Most of the short-range predictive studies that he discussed were ones that had been included in the earlier manual's construct validity section. The major long-range predictive study presented was an elaboration and extension of the single predictive validity study previously cited in the manual. In general, Torrance built a moderately substantial case for the TTCT's predictive validity. However, others have challenged it (for example, see Crockenberg, 1972, and Kogan and Pankove, 1974). In terms of young children, questions about the tests' predicted validity are particularly unexplained.

Reliability estimates reported in the manual for the Torrance tests are of several types. Since considerable judgment is involved in scoring, interscorer reliability was determined. Between inexperienced and experienced scorers, such correlations were high, typically above .90. If both scorers were inexperienced, somewhat lower reliabilities would be likely. Numerous coefficients of stability and of stability and equivalence resulting from a host of diverse studies are reported in the manual; correlations were typically in the moderate to substantial range (say, .50 to .80). In scattered studies not reported in the manual, however, lower correlations were observed (see Crockenberg, 1972).

No large-scale sampling of representative groups has been done. The norms appear a curious collection, which the user must sort through to find an appropriate comparison group. Of course, the TTCT manuals are labeled as research editions (except for the 1972 revised manual of directions for one booklet of the figural test), and shortages in norms, validity data, and the like are more readily allowed in research editions. Strangely, though, the tests themselves are not identified as research editions; some have chastised Torrance for releasing research editions but marketing them as fully developed products (for example, see Wallach, 1968).

In summary, the Torrance tests represent a provocative addition to the growing arsenal of cognitive tests. Their unusual nature bears full investigation. At present, however, their reliability status far exceeds that of their norming and, much more critically, their validity (and, hence, their utility). Since the tests are being widely used, at least in research (the *Eighth Mental Measurements Yearbook* listed 560 references for them), we are hopeful that clarifications of their validity will soon be forthcoming.

A brief note is warranted about the most recent addition to the Torrance tests. A research edition of a new type of creativity measure has been made available, Thinking Creatively with Sounds and Words (Khatena and Torrance, 1973; and Torrance, Khatena, and Cunnington, 1973). Children or adults listen to phonograph recordings of strange sounds and write down descriptions of the mental images stimulated by the sounds. In another portion of the test, onomatopoeic words are pronounced, like *growl* or *crackle,* and respondents describe the pictures that come to their minds. We note the test here because of its unusual nature, but do not supply details as the age range is above our principal focus—one level is for grades three through twelve, while the other level is for adults.

Circus: Make a Tree: This test of divergent pictorial production is in the Circus battery presented earlier. We consider it in detail here given its relevance to creativity. The child's task is to construct a tree in about ten minutes using a blank sheet of paper and brightly colored gummed stickers of various shapes and sizes. The child is told to make "any kind of a tree you like." As each child finishes, the teacher or aide takes him aside and asks three questions: "What kind of tree is it? Have you put anything special in your picture? Is there anything else you'd like to tell me about it?" The child's answers are recorded and filed with the picture. Then, on another day but within one week, each child is shown his original picture, told it was a good tree, and instructed to make "a tree just as different from your first one as you can." After ten minutes, the three questions are asked again and the answers recorded.

Three scores result from Make a Tree: Appropriateness, Unusualness, and Difference. Each is expressed as a 1 (low), 2, 3, 4, or 5 (high). Appropriateness refers to the extent to which the child's picture looks like a tree; the score is the average of the ratings for the two trees made. Unusualness rates how novel or imaginative the tree is compared with trees made by other children; again an average rating for the two trees is computed. Difference is a rating of how different the child's two trees are from one another. The three scores are interpreted together, with the help of sentence reports. The most creative performance is assumed to be represented by a high Difference score and average or high Appropriateness and Unusualness scores.

Unfortunately, very little validity information and reliability data are provided for Make a Tree. Recall from the earlier discussion that as an index of predictive validity the Circus developers used Level A performance to predict Level B performance six months later; this procedure evidently did not include Make a Tree, as no correlations for it are reported. Likewise, no measures of internal consistency (Alpha reliabilities) are included for Make a Tree. Some relevant data for Level A appear in the *Circus Manual and Technical Report* (1974–1975). First, interjudge reliability for Appropriateness, Unusualness, and Difference scores was high, usually in the .80s. Second, test-retest coefficients of stability for the Appropriateness and Unusualness scores of children's first and second trees were moderate to substantial, with a median at .60. Third, the intercorrelations between the three scores themselves were low to moderate (except between Appropriateness and Unusualness in the nursery school sample, where $r = .77$). Finally, the Appropriateness and Unusualness scores have low to moderate (and positive) correlations with other Circus measures, while the Difference score appears quite independent.

The standardization and norming of Make a Tree seem generally appropriate, as they did for the Circus battery described earlier, although the shortage of Chicano and lower socioeconomic status children in the nursery school sample is of concern. It can be noted that somewhat higher ratings on all three scores occurred as the child's age increased, while higher scores were displayed in the nursery school sample by children who had previously attended preschool and by those from higher socioeconomic levels. Differences between scores of boys and girls were negligible.

In all, Make a Tree stands as an interesting measure, but one about which little is known. This lack of knowledge prompted the appropriate cautions that appear in the user's guide and that limit interpretations of scores. Careful validity studies are needed, particularly of a predictive and concurrent nature.

Starkweather Originality Test: This test (Starkweather, 1974) is given individually and includes a practice or warm-up session. For the test proper, available in two forms, forty plastic foam pieces are used, four each of ten different shapes. In all ten cases, the four identically shaped pieces are painted red, blue, yellow, and green. During the test, the examiner follows specific procedures and the child takes each piece, one at a time, and tells what the piece might be. These responses are recorded in the order in which they occur for each of the ten different shapes. Credit is given for each response that is different from all previous responses, but not for names repeated a second time, those altered only by a minor adjective (such as ball and little ball), or those representing a play on words (such as pigless, kigless, sigless). Thus, a maximum possible score is 40.

Validity information is primarily of a concurrent type. In one study, teachers made judgments of which of two children was more original; pairs of children were made up of one child scoring high on the test and one scoring low.

Teachers and test results agreed for 106 of the 153 pairs. In a second study, children's freedom of expression when playing with toys was found to be significantly related to their originality test scores (.69), although only thirteen children were involved. Two other studies correlated originality test scores with scores on the Peabody Picture Vocabulary Test. Since the sets of scores were not significantly related, Starkweather concluded that originality scores are independent of verbal ability; sample sizes were small, however.

Reliability information of three types is provided. Interjudge reliability in scoring children's responses is reported as very high. Internal consistency, determined by split-half, is given as .86 and .81 for the two forms of the test. Finally, data are presented that suggest that there is substantial equivalence between forms.

Unfortunately, no norms are provided for the Starkweather Originality Test. With the moderately successful initial attempts at validity and reliability, one would hope that additional work on validity, reliability, and norming will occur. The test's unique feature of having each child serve as his own control (in the sense that each child's initial responses determine the unusualness of his later responses) deserves further investigation.

It is also worth noting that Starkweather (1971) has other creativity instruments for young children under development. The Starkweather Form Board Test purportedly provides a measure of impersonal conformity-nonconformity based on a child's choice of objects to complete a picture. The Starkweather Social Conformity Test is a color preference situational measure. The Starkweather Target Game reportedly measures a child's willingness to accept the challenge of trying a very difficult task—a characteristic of creative persons. For more information on these tests the reader should consult Starkweather.

In reviewing this section on creativity tests in early childhood education, we are impressed by the cleverness and unusualness of the test tasks. At the same time, validity information remains meager. If substantiating validity data become available, creativity tests can be put into service as another means of understanding children and nurturing their development.

Chapter 7

Affective Measures

There is a widespread belief among early childhood educators that cultivation of young children's affect—their self-concepts, attitudes toward school, social skills, and so on—is of equal or perhaps greater importance than cultivation of their intellects (Deutsch, 1966; Frank, 1969; Hartup, 1968; and Zigler, 1970). An increasing number of early childhood programs include goals pertaining to affective development (Evans, 1974). Although many programs place affective development second in importance to cognitive development, there are some, such as the Bank Street model (Maccoby and Zellner, 1970), in which primary emphasis is on the affective domain. Obviously, there is a need in program evaluation efforts for affective measures appropriate for use with young children. It should be noted, however, that many of the assumptions that educators and psychologists hold regarding the critical importance of nurturing early social and emotional development are unproven and in need of validation (Walker, 1973).

Much has been written about the affective characteristics of children and adults. Organization schemes and definitions of affective components vary. Personality, attitudes, values, self-concept, and interests are commonly discussed, yet are given various definitions and emphases by different writers. For example, attitudes and values are often used interchangeably, although we and others see them as quite different. This lack of agreed-upon definitions and classifications is reflected in the diversity of affective measures available. Measures of self-concept, for example, vary greatly in theoretical foundations, definitions of

242

terms, types of subscale included, and subsequent style of interpreting the scores.

The affective domain deals with the social and emotional aspects of behavior. Included are emotions, preferences, interests, attitudes, values, morals, and philosophies of life. According to Ringness (1975), any behavior with an emotional tone can be considered part of the affective domain. As noted in the previous chapter, many behaviors with emotional tones also contain cognitive components. Johnson (1974) stated it well: "Yet it should be emphasized that a person's affect and cognitions cannot be separated. Each affective behavior has a cognitive counterpart, and for every cognitive outcome there are changes in affect. To teach any concept, principle, or theory is to teach not only for its comprehension but also for an attitude toward it. For example, a school not only wants to teach the student to read, but to enjoy, appreciate, and value reading. Correspondingly, in order for a person to be aware of his feelings, he has to conceptualize them and place them in the context of the situation he is experiencing. At the very least this calls for cognitions about his feelings; generally, it means that there is a cognitive component in experiencing a feeling" (p. 100). This intermingling of the two domains exacerbates the problems of isolating affective dimensions for measurement purposes.

Krathwohl, Bloom, and Masia (1964) attempted to help educators formulate affective instructional objectives by providing a Taxonomy of Educational Objectives in the Affective Domain. The taxonomy portrays several behavioral dimensions, ordered on a continuum of increasing internalization: receiving, responding, valuing, organizing, and characterizing. Also discussed as part of the taxonomy are interests, appreciations, attitudes, values, and personal adjustments, each of which encompasses several dimensions of the continuum—interests, for example, encompass receiving, responding, and part of the valuing dimensions. It becomes clear that the divisions on the continuum and among the aspects of affective behavior are far from clear-cut. Nevertheless, the taxonomy provides a useful guide for developing affective objectives, as well as a sense of the scope of the affective domain.

In this chapter, we present illustrative affective measures designed for young children. Following a brief section on the status and nature of affective measures in early childhood education, fourteen measures, categorized into four general areas, are described. The reader is reminded of the caveat given in Chapter Five—that inclusion of particular measures in these chapters does not indicate endorsement. Rather, the chosen measures are meant to be representative of the pool of measures currently available for use with young children. Potential users of any of the measures should carefully examine the measures and all supporting materials.

Nature and Status of Affective Measures

The increased interest in promoting the affective, or socioemotional, development of young children has led to an increased demand for measurement and evaluation in this area. The need for affective measuring instruments became especially apparent with the funding of early childhood programs for disadvantaged children in the 1960s. Five of the seven stated goals of Head Start were in the affective domain and concerned the social and emotional development of children; specifically, they included the encouragement of self-concept, self-confidence, self-discipline, self-worth, and positive attitudes toward society and family (Walker, 1973). Given this concentration on the affective domain, the criticisms of the early Head Start evaluation efforts—which focused primarily on cognitive assessment—seem justified. Such criticism and concern prompted the development of several of the affective measures now available for use with young children. A number of measures have been developed by the Educational Testing Service for the Head Start Longitudinal Study (Education Testing Service, 1968; and Shipman, 1970). (See the section on source books following Chapter Twelve for a description of the Head Start Test collection. The current program goals for Head Start similarly reflect extensive attention to affective outcomes (Administration for Children, Youth, and Families, 1975).

     The assessment of affects in young children presents a multitude of problems. For instance, White and his colleagues pointed out, "Noncognitive instruments do not seem to be a problem to be solved by test development alone. There is a substrate problem. We do not understand the basic issues of noncognitive processes in human development sufficiently to make convincing moves toward index or test development" (White and others, 1973a, p. 322). Similarly, Ball (1971) cited several problems inherent in measuring young children's attitudes:

1. Young children tend to have mercurial attitudes. A child in a Head Start center, having just fallen and skinned his knee, may confidently tell an examiner that he hates school; ten minutes earlier or the next day, however, he may just as confidently express positive feelings toward school.
2. Young children frequently lack the skills necessary for many test-taking situations. A number of techniques used for assessing attitudes in older children and adults do not work satisfactorily with children who cannot read and write and who have difficulty following instructions.
3. Young children are exceedingly eager to please adults, including adults administering attitude tests. They may respond with what they think the adult wants to hear (the "socially desirable" response) rather than telling how they really feel.
4. Young children may exhibit a response set, such as consistently answering "yes" regardless of the questions asked. This problem can be especially acute when children are confronted with situations that puzzle them.

To Ball's list, Walker (1973) added the short attention span of young children. For more meaningful results, children should probably be tested in several sessions scattered over time with a limited number of items presented at each session—certainly a costly and inconvenient procedure.

Well-constructed and carefully administered tests can alleviate several of the problems noted by Ball and Walker, although the first—instability of children's answers—is extremely difficult to overcome. (Indeed, even affective measurements of adults are afflicted by this problem to some extent.) This lack of stability lessens the reliability of attitude assessment in young children and reduces the interpretability of the reponses given by any particular child. Use of such measures is more credible for research or program evaluation efforts that emphasize differences in responses between groups or changes over time in group averages; it is less credible for diagnostic or guidance purposes involving an individual child.

Another frequently mentioned problem with attitude assessment, and one that is not unique to young children, is the gap between attitudes and behavior. "There is little consistent evidence to support the hypothesis that knowledge of an individual's attitudes will allow one to predict how he will behave. A learning theorist would argue that the learning of behavior occurs independently, so that there may be little relation between a person's attitudes and his behavior. For example, a student may learn to have positive attitudes toward teachers, but whether he engages in friendly behavior toward a particular teacher depends on the reinforcement he receives for doing so. Another problem in trying to predict a person's behavior from a knowledge of his attitudes is that most situations are so complex that several attitudes may be relevant to any action taken" (Johnson, 1974, p. 102).

Generally, measures in the affective domain can be divided into projective and nonprojective techniques. *Projective* techniques, used primarily in personality assessment (see Chapter Two), tend to consist of unstructured situations that are supposed to evoke the respondent's unconscious feelings, attitudes, emotions, and thoughts. The stimuli include inkblots, incomplete sentences, dolls, or drawings. These techniques require considerable time and special training for administration, scoring, and interpretation. Their use in the average classroom by regular teachers, therefore, is impractical. *Nonprojective* techniques, including self-report inventories, rating scales and checklists, and observational measures are much more feasible for most classroom settings. Much recent work on attitude measures for young children has been in the development of self-report and rating scales (White and others, 1973a).

Self-report inventories for young children are often designed so that the child (1) chooses the picture or words with which he identifies himself, (2) reveals his perceptions of how others see him, or (3) indicates his preferred interests or activities. Rating scales are used to gather information about the child from someone familiar with the child, usually the teacher or parent. These two types of technique, plus observational measures, are most common in affective measurement with young children. Most of the illustrative measures we present in the remainder of this chapter are either self-report or rating scales. Observational measures, because of their extensive coverage in Chapter Four, are not included here.

Recent compendiums dealing with affective measures for young children include Coller (1971a), Guthrie (1971), Hoepfner and others (1972, 1976), Hoepfner, Stern, and Nummedal (1971), Johnson (1976), Johnson and Bommarito (1971), Walker (1973), and White and others (1973a). A review of their works (many of which are discussed in the source book section) yields a large number of titles of measure designed for preschool, kindergarten, and early elementary school children. For example, Walker (1973), probably the most comprehensive listing of young children's affective measures to date, describes 143 measures grouped into six areas: (1) attitudes, (2) general personality and emotional adjustment, (3) interests or preferences, (4) personality or behavior traits, (5) self-concept, and (6) social skills or competency. In the handbooks prepared by Johnson (1976) and Johnson and Bommarito (1971), many more instruments—all "fugitive," or unpublished—are described. A striking feature of the compendiums is the relative recency of a majority of the measures; most have been developed within the last ten or fifteen years.

An inspection of the technical data available for these measures reveals several shortcomings. The most glaring of these is the dearth of meaningful information on validity. Although some developers make claims for content validity based on their test construction procedures, very few show any data on criterion-related or construct validity. An oft-expressed reason for not correlating scores on an affective measure with scores from another measure of the same trait or characteristic is that no such alternate measure exists. This is true in some instances, but, generally, the weakness goes deeper than simply a lack of other available measures; it reflects a lack of meaningful construct-level definitions of the variables purportedly measured by the affective instruments. As Walker (1973) pointed out, "Without an adequate theory against which a variable such as self-concept can be validated, it is likely to be defined as 'that which a self-concept test measures'" (p. 36). Given developer-specific definitions of terms and the frequent lack of theoretical foundations, it is no wonder that the affective measures are characterized as idiosyncratic. This problem, highlighted by the widespread neglect of empirical validation, seriously weakens the interpretability and usefulness of many affective measures.

A second technical shortcoming relates to the reliability of the measures. Although many of the available measures do have reliability estimates—and in this respect they fare much better than in terms of validity—the estimates are often based on small, select samples of children. Further, the coefficients tend to be low to moderate, especially for single items or subscales, and all too often only internal consistency coefficients are presented when stability or interrater coefficients would be more suitable. Finally, even those measures with acceptable reliability data usually lack the critical validation evidence needed to support their use.

Inadequate standardization norms constitute a third shortcoming of most of the measures in this area. With a few notable exceptions, the norms either do not exist or are unrepresentative for children of varying socioeconomic levels, ages, racial groups, geographic locations, or intelligence levels. That is, most norms are based on a small group from one geographic locale and comprised primarily of white children enrolled in a limited number of schools. Using the norms in interpretation is thus unwarranted in many cases.

The fourteen measures described in this chapter are illustrative of the affective measures used in early childhood education, and, inevitably, many of them manifest the problems noted above. Decisions as to which measures to include were arbitrary at times, as several measures similar in purpose, content, and format were often available. Nevertheless, we included those that were relatively widely used and that represented a variety of measurement approaches (excluding observational methods). The measures are grouped into four categories: (1) personality, (2) self-concept, (3) social skills and competencies, and (4) attitudes and preferences. The categories represent broad divisions only; as is true with categorization of the affective domain in general, there is much overlap among categories in content coverage and types of stimuli presented.

The reader might be expecting to find measures described here that are based on the increasingly influential moral development theory of Kohlberg (1973, 1976), a stage theory that extends and dramatically elaborates earlier work by Piaget (1965, originally published in 1932). (Kohlberg started his basic longitudinal research study over twenty years ago, using as his youngest group ten-year-old boys. The essential measure he used involved presenting subjects with a series of moral dilemmas in the form of hypothetical stories and related questions to probe their moral reasoning; their free responses were then scored as being in one of several stages of moral development.) However, no such measures are included here as, to our knowledge, none are available for very young children. Some scholars are considering Kohlbergian implications for younger children (see Damon's formal research, 1977, and King's informal study, 1973, pp. 30–34), and this activity might lead to instrument construction at some point. Further, to avoid the inherent difficulty in categorizing and scoring subjects' free responses to Kohlberg's stories, Rest (1976) has proposed some new scoring approaches for assessing moral judgment; such simplified procedures probably would increase the likelihood that related measures would be developed for children eight years old and under.

Illustrative Personality Measures

We briefly discussed personality assessment in Chapter Two, adopting Allport's (1961) definition of *personality* as dynamic organization, within an individual, of psychosocial systems that determine his characteristic behavior and thought. Personality is a global concept, representing an aggregate of such elements as attitudes, self-concept, preferences and interests, values, and so forth. Whereas some elements are viewed as quite malleable (attitudes, especially), personality itself is usually considered a relatively stable representation of a person. Even so, however, little is known about the stability of human personality characteristics over time. "It is difficult to be certain that the same trait is being assessed at different ages. Currently, two characteristics have shown some correlation from the preschool years to maturity—aggressiveness in males and dependence/passivity in females" (White and others, 1973a, p. 11).

Much has been written about personality assessment in general (for example, see Goldberg, 1971; McReynolds, 1975a; and Mischel, 1968). In regard to personality measures specifically for young children, Walker (1973) suggested two categories: (1) general personality and emotional development, and (2) personality or behavior traits. Although the former measures generally have employed projective techniques, the two global measures we include in this section, the California Test of Personality: Primary Form (Thorpe, Clark, and Tiegs, 1953) and the Child Behavior Rating Scale (Cassel, 1962), are not projective. (Indeed, we chose not to include any projective measures, since the extensive training ordinarily required for administration, scoring, and interpretation precludes their use in most classrooms; for a review of projective techniques used with children, see Palmer, 1970.) Walker's second category of measures—personality or behavior traits—are those that focus on more specific aspects of personality. Two such measures are discussed in this section: Animal Crackers (Adkins and Ballif, 1973) and the Primary Academic Sentiment Scale, or PASS (Thompson, 1968). Both focus on academic motivation, and PASS also includes a dependency scale. Motivation, like personality in general, has been the subject of extensive work; for a thorough review of assessment attempts in this area, see McReynolds (1971b).

Another personality characteristic that has been given increasing attention recently is locus of control (see Lefcourt, 1976). Generally, *locus of control* refers to a person's feelings about the extent to which he has power over what happens to him. The concern with locus of control in early childhood assessment is relatively recent, and the available measures are few in number and somewhat difficult to locate. Educational Testing Service used a locus of control scale in its Head Start Longitudinal Study (1968). Closely related to that scale and more readily available is an instrument for older children, the Intellectual Achievement Responsibility Questionnaire, or IAR (Crandall, Katkovsky, and Crandall, 1965). Developed for children in grades three through twelve, the IAR is a self-report measure that assesses children's beliefs that they, rather than other people, are responsible for their intellectual-academic successes and failures. Although some validation data have been reported for the IAR, House and others (1978) were critical of the use of this questionnaire in the Follow Through evaluations (see Chapter Eleven) because the validation evidence appeared insufficient and inadequate.

Two rather new measures appropriate for younger children include the Preschool and Primary Nowicki-Strickland Internal-External Control Scale (Nowicki and Duke, 1974), discussed fully later in this section, and the Stanford Preschool Internal-External Scale, or SPIES (Mischel, Zeiss, and Zeiss, 1974). Developed primarily for use in research with young children, the SPIES was patterned after the IAR and requires individual administration. Preliminary reliability and validity studies have been conducted in experimental settings.

The five measures discussed in this section represent both established and relatively new attempts at personality assessment of young children. An overview of the section is presented in Table 18.

Animal Crackers: A Test of Motivation to Achieve. Designed for children from preschool through first grade, Animal Crackers (Adkins and Ballif, 1973) measures achievement motivation. The measure focuses on five aspects of achievement-oriented behavior that purportedly are not primarily attributable to intellectual capabilities: (1) school enjoyment, (2) self-confidence, (3) purposiveness, (4) instrumental activity, and (5) self-evaluation. "Achievement-oriented behavior is regarded as a result of the dynamic interaction of all these variables. A child will be motivated to achieve in school only when he expects that achieving in school will bring him pleasure; he thinks that he can achieve in school; he can set up his own purposes to achieve; he knows the instrumental steps that will lead to achievement; and, finally, he can evaluate his own performance" (Adkins and Ballif, 1973, p. 2).

Animal Crackers is administered either individually or in group sessions. Using proctors is strongly advised in the latter case. No special training is required for administration. The total time for testing, including directions and practice exercises, is estimated at thirty to forty-five minutes, depending on the age and maturity of the children. No time limits are observed. Although a single session is preferred, the test may be given on two successive days.

Animal Crackers is an outgrowth of an earlier achievement motivation test, Gumpgookies (Adkins and Ballif, 1970). The original measure contained one hundred items, each an orally presented description of two amorphous figures called gumpgookies that were depicted in different stances in the test booklet. After hearing the description, the child marked the gumpgookie with which he identified. (For example, one item instructed the child to mark either the "working" or "watching" gumpgookie.) Subsequent studies (Adkins and Ballif, 1972, 1973) suggested that children were inappropriately influenced by their non-test-related preferences for particular illustrations and by the left-right position of keyed responses in relation to which was read first by the examiner. (Note that these problems are types of response set, as described in Chapter Two.)

Accordingly, Gumpgookies was revised to form the sixty-item Animal Crackers. The illustrations for each item were changed from the two imaginary figures (Gumpgookies) to a pair of identical animals depicted in different stances. The keyed responses were counterbalanced with respect to order of presentation and position. These changes reportedly alleviated many of the problems originally encountered.

Of the sixty items in Animal Crackers, every fifth one is categorized as belonging to one of the five subtests, resulting in twelve items per subtest. In the introductory directions, the child is told that he has his "own" animals, which like the same things and behave the same way he does. The examiner points to each of the two alternative animals in turn and describes the attitude or behavior of each. Following the verbal description, the child identifies "his" animal in each

Table 18. Illustrative Personality Measures in Early Childhood Education

Title and Date	Age Range	Administration	Scales or Scores	Source
Animal Crackers: A Test of Motivation to Achieve (1973)	3 to 8 years	Group or Individual; 30 to 45 minutes	School Enjoyment Self-Confidence Purposiveness Instrumental Activity Self-Evaluation Total Score	CTB/McGraw-Hill Del Monte Research Park Monterey, Calif. 93940
California Test of Personality: Primary Form (1953)	Kindergarten to grade 3	Group or Individual; 45 to 60 minutes	Self-Reliance Sense of Personal Worth Sense of Personal Freedom Feeling of Belonging Withdrawing Tendencies Nervous Symptoms Total Personal Adjustment Social Standards Social Skills Anti-Social Tendencies Family Relations School Relations Community Relations Total Social Adjustment Total Adjustment	CTB/McGraw-Hill
Child Behavior Rating Scale (1962)	Kindergarten to grade 3	Individual; time required not stated (our estimate is 20 minutes)	Self-Adjustment Home Adjustment Social Adjustment School Adjustment Physical Adjustment Personality Total Adjustment	Western Psychological Services 12031 Wilshire Blvd. Los Angeles, Calif. 90025

| Preschool and Primary Nowicki-Strickland Internal-External Control Scale (1974) | 4 to 8 years | Group; 15 minutes | Externality | Stephen Nowicki and Marshall Duke Dept. of Psychology Emory University Atlanta, Ga. 30322 |
| Primary Academic Sentiment Scale (1968) | 4 to 7 years | Group; 20 minutes | Sentiment Dependency | Priority Innovations, Inc. P.O. Box 792 Skokie, Ill. 60076 |

pair by blackening the circle below it. Twelve different animals are used as stimuli, each appearing once in each of the five subtests. Illustrative tasks for each subtest include:

1. School Enjoyment: the child chooses between a lion that likes school very much and a lion that likes school a little bit.
2. Self-Confidence: the child chooses between a giraffe whose schoolwork is good and a giraffe that is not sure if its schoolwork is good or bad.
3. Purposiveness: the child chooses between a kitten that feeds its pet every day and a kitten that sometimes forgets to feed its pet.
4. Instrumental Activity: the child chooses between a duck that tries to write and a duck that watches others write.
5. Self-Evaluation: the child chooses between a rabbit that tries only easy things and a rabbit that tries some hard things.

Scoring can be done by a hand-scoring key or via a machine-scoring service available through the test publisher. The response of each pair demonstrating the greater degree of motivation is scored 1, while the other response is scored 0. A raw score for each subtest is found by summing the twelve item scores, and a total raw score results from summing all sixty item scores. Such scores for kindergartners and first-graders can be converted to percentile ranks by using tables in the manual.

Validity evidence in the manual is scanty. Content validity "is claimed through the construction of items in accord with the general theory" (Adkins and Ballif, 1973, p. 59). For criterion-related validity, the authors cited findings from empirical work with Gumpgookies: correlations with the Stanford-Binet, ranging from .20 to .35, and similarly low correlation with age; and statistically significant correlations with teacher ratings of motivation (although closer examination of this finding reveals uneven practical significance in that not all teachers made ratings comparable to the test scores; see Johnson, 1976, p. 424). Walker (1973) reported generally low correlations between Gumpgookies and three other self-esteem and locus of control measures for nearly 200 second- and third-graders in Follow Through classrooms. Bridgeman and Shipman (1978) reported some moderate but significant correlations between kindergarten Gumpgookies scores in a rural site and third-grade reading and mathematics achievement scores (as part of Head Start Planned Variations longitudinal study). Construct validity evidence for Animal Crackers itself was based on factor analyses. Data from kindergarten and first-grade tryout samples, involving over 1,000 children, were item- and factor-analyzed to aid in the identification of the five subtests and in final item selection.

Internal consistency reliability coefficients (Kuder-Richardson) were calculated for the tryout samples. The total test coefficient was .90 for both samples. Subscale coefficients ranged from .65 to .82, with the median at .73 and .72 for the kindergarten and first-grade samples, respectively.

The tryout sample of 1,212 children, 624 kindergartners and 588 first-graders, also provided the percentile rank norms. The children resided in seventeen cities and rural towns, and attended seventy-one public schools in Northern California. Data reported include total score means and standard deviations for various ethnic groups and for males and females. Differences among ethnic and sex groups are apparent; black and Spanish-speaking children scored lower than white ("Other") children, while females scored slightly higher than males. The conversion tables for subscale and total scores are presented separately for kindergartners and first-graders, but no further breakdowns are available. The authors commendably cautioned against strict adherence to these normative data, given the limited size and representativeness of the sample. Additional standardization data are mentioned as forthcoming in the 1973 manual, but, to our knowledge, they have not yet appeared.

Animal Crackers is an attractive measure. During development, many irrelevant response set features were eliminated and discriminating items were selected. Group administration is an advantageous feature and helps offset the considerable time required as well as the need for proctors. Internal consistency reliability is promising, but stability information is needed. Unfortunately, validation is far from complete (also see Weintraub, 1978). At the very least, the types of study conducted with Gumpgookies should be replicated with Animal Crackers. Larger, more representative samples are also needed, and norm tables should be more highly detailed.

California Test of Personality (CTP). The primary form of the California Test of Personality (Thorpe, Clark, and Tiegs, 1953) is intended for children in kindergarten through third grade; other forms are available for older children and adults. The purpose of the test is "to identify and reveal the status of certain highly important factors in personality and social adjustment usually designated as intangibles. These are the factors that defy appraisal or diagnosis by means of ordinary ability and achievement tests. . . . Personality . . . refers . . . to the manner and effectiveness with which the whole individual meets his personal and social problems, and indirectly the manner in which he impresses his fellows" (Thorpe, Clark, and Tiegs, 1953, p. 2). Teachers and counselors are advised, in the manual, on ways to use individual reactions to items to identify, classify, and treat personal and social adjustment difficulties. The test thus was purported to have diagnostic uses.

The CTP, available in two parallel forms, is untimed and can be administered either individually or to groups. Three sets of directions are provided: one for individual administration to children too young or immature to read the questions or to mark their own answers; a second for older children who need the questions read aloud to them, but are able to mark their own answers; and a third for children who can both read the questions and mark their responses. The entire test takes forty-five to sixty minutes; if needed, rest periods after each fifteen minutes of work are recommended. A teacher or counselor can administer the test; no special training is needed.

The CTP is based on the notion that a good adjustment to life requires a balance between personal and social adjustment. Accordingly, the two major parts of the test are Personal Adjustment and Social Adjustment, with six components subsumed under each. The six components of Personal Adjustment are:

1. Self-Reliance: being independent of others, depending upon yourself in various situations, and directing your own activities.
2. Sense of Personal Worth: feeling that you are well regarded by others, that others have faith in your future success, and that you have average or better ability.
3. Sense of Personal Freedom: feeling that you have a reasonable share in the determination of your own conduct and in the setting of general governing policies for your own life.
4. Feeling of Belonging: feeling the love of your family, the well-wishing of good friends, and the cordiality of other people.
5. Withdrawing Tendencies: inclining to substitute the joys of a fantasy world for real-life successes.
6. Nervous Symptoms: showing physical signs of emotional conflicts, such as loss of appetite, frequent eyestrain, sleeplessness, or chronic fatigue.

The six components of Social Adjustment are:

1. Social Standards: recognizing commonly held standards of what is right and wrong, understanding the rights of others, and subordinating certain desires to the needs of the group.
2. Social Skills: showing regard for people, assisting others, and being diplomatic in dealings with friends and strangers.
3. Anti-Social Tendencies: tending to bully, quarrel, disobey, and destroy property.
4. Family Relations: feeling well loved and well treated at home, and enjoying security and self-respect among family members.
5. School Relations: feeling liked by teachers, enjoying other students, and perceiving school work as personally appropriate.
6. Community Relations: mingling happily with neighbors, taking pride in community improvements, and being tolerant when dealing with strangers or foreigners.

These twelve components were arrived at during test construction. A large number of items had been written, judged for significance and appropriateness by teachers, counselors and others, and empirically tried out. Surviving items were grouped into sixteen categories (derived from the psychological literature) and administered to more students. Analyses of these data resulted in the elimination of four categories. Eight items were then selected for each of the remaining twelve categories. The ninety-six items are phrased as questions, to which the child answers either "yes" or "no." The questions deal with a variety of feelings, perceptions, and activities. For example, the child is asked whether or not he needs help in dressing, thinks most other children are brighter than he is, likes to push or scare other children, is punished for many things he does, finds it difficult to talk with his parents, and so forth.

Each of the twelve CTP sections is scored separately, with possible scores ranging from 0 to 8. An item is "correct," and given one point, if the response indicates personal or social adjustment. By scanning the six subscale scores for each of the two major sections, total Personal Adjustment and Social Adjustment scores are obtained; the latter two scores are summed to yield a Total Adjustment score for the entire test. The manual contains tables for converting raw scores to percentile ranks, as well as instructions for constructing individual student profiles. The profile is divided into two parts (personal and social adjustment), and shows the differences among scores on the component parts of each.

The CTP fares well in regard to content validity, owing to steps taken during development to obtain logical and empirical analyses of the content. Some studies suggestive of other types of validity are reported in the manual. However, direct evidence of criterion-related validity is not presented.

Kuder-Richardson internal consistency reliability coefficients are presented for 255 children in grades one through three. The coefficients for the twelve separate components ranged from .51 to .87, with a median of .73. The reliability coefficients for Personal, Social, and Total Adjustment scores were .83, .80, and .88, respectively. Regrettably, the manual contains no information on equivalent form or stability reliabilities, the latter being of special concern given the short length (eight items) of each of the twelve scales.

Norms for the primary form were based on responses of 4,500 children in kindergarten to grade three. The children resided in California, Colorado, Ohio, and South Carolina; about 85 percent were white children, the remainder being black, Mexican-American, and "other." In terms of school progress, 70 percent were considered normal; 20 percent retarded; and 10 percent accelerated. In all, the norm group was fairly representative; further, norms for special groups were reported and available through the California Test Bureau.

The manual contains extensive suggestions for interpretation and use of the test results by teachers, counselors, and supervisors. Other strengths of the measure include the evidence for content validity and the presentation of the norms (although the norms are now outdated). The lack of stability and equivalence reliability data represents a substantial shortcoming. More important, the CTP's major weakness is the lack of data pertaining to criterion-referenced validity, a serious omission given the intended diagnostic use of the measure. Accordingly, use of the CTP should be limited to group assessment or research studies, since supporting evidence for its use as a diagnostic instrument is not provided.

Child Behavior Rating Scale (CBRS). Designed to assess the personality adjustment of preschool and primary grade pupils, the Child Behavior Rating Scale (Cassel, 1962) provides a means for parents or teachers to rate children in five areas of adjustment, namely, self, home, social, school, and physical. According to the manual, teachers and counselors can use the data obtained to better understand the personality adjustment of individual children and to note changes in personality and emotional growth over time. Other intended uses are to provide information on children referred to psychologists and social workers; and to compare a child's ratings made by different persons, such as mother and father, to gain an understanding of the interpersonal relationships between raters and the child, and of the dynamics of the home.

No special training is required prior to using the CBRS. No time limits are imposed. To complete the scale on one child, about twenty minutes are needed. For each of the seventy-eight items, the rater checks the place on a six-point scale that best describes the behavior of the particular child. Only the end points of the six-point scale are defined, with "yes" at one end and "no" at the other end.

Construction of the CBRS began with the screening of over 1,000 case studies of elementary school students referred for psychological or psychiatric services. Statements appearing most often in the records, and considered critical for understanding children and their problems, were converted to items for the CBRS. Six psychologists then classified the items into the five adjustment areas. The items are short descriptive statements, some referring to behaviors but others referring to preferences, attitudes, childrearing practices of parents, living accommodations, and so forth. Most statements begin with the word "often." Examples of behaviors described under one of the areas—social adjustment— include playing mean tricks, being a "show-off," and not attending Sunday school or church. The phrasing of all statements is such that "yes" indicates adjustment problems. If the rater has not observed or does not know the behavior of the child for any item, he is instructed to check "no" for that item.

Each item receives a score from 1 to 6, with 1 for "yes" and 6 for "no," and intermediate values for the middle points. A score for each of the five adjustment areas is the sum of the item scores. The higher the score, the better the adjustment. A total score, the Personality Total Adjustment Score (PTAS), is obtained by weighting and summing three scores: the scores on the Self-Adjustment and Home Adjustment scales are each multiplied by 2, and these values are added to the School Adjustment score. A table in the manual can be used to convert each adjustment area score and the PTAS to two sets of T-scores: one based on normative data for "typical" children and the other based on normative data for "maladjusted" children. The two sets of T-scores can then be entered on a profile form.

Information on the construct validity of the CBRS is available in the manual. Presented are correlations between the PTAS for 600 children (as determined by ratings made by teachers, mothers, and fathers) and several criterion measures—specifically, the reading, arithmetic, and language subtests of the Metropolitan Achievement Tests, an IQ test (not specified), and the Vineland Social Maturity Scale (discussed later in this chapter). In addition, the correlations of the CBRS ratings with the chronological age of the child were determined. Most of the coefficients were low, with the teachers' ratings correlating slightly higher with the criterion measures than did the parents' ratings. The highest coefficients were .49 and .48 between teachers' ratings and the language subtest of the Metropolitan and the Vineland Social Quotient, respectively. (In contrast, the correlations between the children's grade point averages and the criterion measures were substantial, ranging from .53 to .73.) Accentuating the concern over the low correlations of the PTAS ratings and the external criteria is the absence of information in the manual about the demographic characteristics of the student sample and about analogous coefficients for the five adjustment area subscales.

A second set of validity data compared CBRS subscale scores of 200 well-adjusted or typical children with those of 200 children diagnosed as maladjusted. The children ranged in age from five to nine years. Statistically significant differences were found between the two groups. Again troublesome is the manual's absence of information on the characteristics of the student sample and even on the type of rater used.

Split-half reliability coefficients were calculated for a sample of 800 typical children and another sample of 200 maladjusted children; the coefficients (for the entire CBRS) were .87 and .59, respectively. Coefficients of stability are also reported in the manual: .91, based on ratings made by fifty parents on two occasions, and .74, based on ratings made by fifty teachers on two occasions. Unfortunately, the time intervals between ratings and information on the stability of subscale scores were not reported. The interrater reliability coefficients, for a group of 800 children, were .28 between teachers' and mothers' ratings; .33 between teachers' and fathers' ratings; and .66 between mothers' and fathers' ratings. The high mother-father coefficient led the scale's author to conclude that ratings by both mothers and fathers are not necessary; that is, either parent's ratings would suffice.

The norms, expressed as T-scores in the manual, were based on a group of 2,000 typical children and a group of 200 maladjusted children. Again, no descriptive information about the groups is provided, and there are no breakdowns according to variables like age and sex. Similarly, the manual contains only very general information pertaining to interpretation of CBRS scores.

Dunn (1972) raised several serious questions about the CBRS. For example, he noted the lack of instructions on the use of the scores for several of the intended purposes, such as understanding the dynamics of the home. In regard to content, he questioned the appropriateness of the six-point scale for certain items worded so that only a binary "yes" or "no" response is appropriate. He also noted that many items did not involve actual child behaviors *per se*. Further, he criticized the manual's treatment of validity, reliability, and normative data, especially in terms of the lack of details about the samples. He considered profile analysis with subscale scores inappropriate since no separate subscale reliability or validity data were provided.

We agree with Dunn's critique. It is unfortunate that the scale, which appears to have been developed relatively carefully, falls so short on technical and usability considerations. The problem may stem in part from an overly casual approach to manual preparation. Regardless, the potential user is left with too many unknowns in regard to the measure's worth.

   Preschool and Primary Nowicki-Strickland Internal-External Control Scale (PPNS-IE). This locus of control measure (Nowicki and Duke, 1974) is intended for children from four to eight years of age, and was developed primarily for use in research studies. It is one of a series of comparable forms developed for various age groups, all of which are based on the original Nowicki-Strickland scale—the Children's Nowicki-Strickland Internal-External Control Scale, or CNS-IE (Nowicki and Strickland, 1973). Construction of the entire series was based on the work of Rotter (1966), who distinguished between internal and external locus of control of reinforcement. According to Rotter, a belief in internal control is held by those persons who perceive that reinforcements or events are contingent upon their own actions or their own relatively permanent characteristics. In contrast, belief in external control is held by those persons who perceive events in their lives as being under the control of others, or due to luck, fate, or chance.

   The PPNS-IE consists of twenty-six questions, to which the child responds either "yes" or "no." Each question is presented as a cartoon drawing of two small children. The question is written in a bubble above the head of one of the children in the drawing, while the words "yes" and "no" are in the bubble above the other child's head. The child must answer such questions as, "When a kid your age decides to hit you, is there anything you can do to stop him or her?", "Most of the time do you find it easy to get your own way at home?", and "Do you have a lucky number?" In answering the question, the respondent is instructed to draw a line through or circle either the "yes" or "no." Both a male and a female form are available. In the male form, a little boy is asked the questions, half of them by another little boy and half of them by a little girl. The female form uses a little girl as respondent, again with half the questions presented by a girl and half by a boy. Each form begins with one sample question.

   The measure is group-administered. After a practice session, the questions are read aloud to the children. Approximately fifteen minutes are needed to administer the PPNS-IE, except in the case of very young children who may require more time. Administration purportedly does not require any special training. The items are keyed and scored in the external direction (with thirteen keyed "yes" and thirteen keyed "no" to reflect the external direction). The total score is thus the number of questions to which the respondent gave an answer indicating belief in external control (or, stated differently, the higher the score, the more the respondent was oriented toward external control).

   Construction of the PPNS-IE began with several psychologists and preschool teachers generating a list of seventy-eight possible questions. Items from the CNS-IE were included. After a review of these items by other psychologists and psychology students for content validation, the remaining forty-four items were piloted with eighty white, predominantly middle-class preschool children. Eight items were subsequently eliminated on the basis of an item analysis of these data. (See Chapter Two for a description of difficulty index and discriminatory

power, the major components of item analysis.) Results from a second preliminary study (with twenty-one preschoolers) led to the elimination of an additional
ten items. The criteria for inclusion consisted of difficulty levels between .30 and
.70 (Chapter Two) and moderate correlations between individual items and the
total test score, that is, good discriminating power.

To obtain reliability and validity data, the PPNS-IE was administered to
240 white children (120 boys and 120 girls), ages five through eight. The children
were randomly selected from two schools just outside Atlanta, Georgia. Black
children were excluded from the sample, as was any child with an IQ below 80.
Children were tested in same-sex groups of ten in their regular classrooms. The
sixty seven-year-olds in the sample were administered the PPNS-IE twice, with a
six-week internal, to assess the stability of the measure. The resultant reliability
coefficient was .79.

The construct validity of the PPNS-IE was assessed by testing several
hypotheses that had been formulated prior to conducting the tryout:

1. That PPNS-IE scores would become more internal with age.
2. That the scores would not be related to social desirability scores.
3. That scores would be significantly related to CNS-IE scores (for eight-year-
   olds).
4. That factor analysis would reveal a similar factor structure to that of the
   CNS-IE.
5. That PPNS-IE scores would be negatively related to achievement and negatively related to desired interpersonal distance from others (that is, the higher
   or more external a child's PPNS-IE score, the less likely he was to indicate that
   he was comfortable having others close to him).

To test the second hypothesis, eight social desirability items (for example, "Do
you sometimes tell a little lie?") were included with the twenty-six PPNS-IE items
in the tryout. To obtain data for the third hypothesis, the CNS-IE was administered to the eight-year-olds following the administration of the PPNS-IE. School
records yielded achievement test data pertinent to the fifth hypothesis; in addition, an interpersonal distance scale, measuring the extent to which children feel
comfortable in the presence of others, was administered to the seven-year-olds.

Results showed mean scores to be slightly more internal for seven- and
eight-year-olds than for five- and six-year-olds; the difference for boys in the two
age groups compared was just under one raw score point, while for girls the
difference was almost three points. Correlations between PPNS-IE scores and
social desirability scores were low and nonsignificant. The correlation between
the PPNS-IE and CNS-IE scores for the eight-year-olds was .78. Factor analysis
revealed three factors: power versus helplessness, persistence-in-dealing-with-
parents, and luck. This structure was similar to that found in earlier studies of
the CNS-IE. Finally, correlations between PPNS-IE scores and standardized
achievement test scores showed moderate negative relationships. With verbal
achievement, PPNS-IE correlated −.17 and −.34 for boys and girls, respectively.

With math achievement, correlations were −.20 and −.45. As expected, more internality (low scores) was related to comfort with less interpersonal distancing; the correlations for these data were moderate. Generally, these results supported the hypotheses; the disappointing features were the low to moderate sizes of the correlations with achievement test data and the small differences between scores for the different age groups.

Additional work remains to be done on the PPNS-IE. Its reliability when used with children younger than seven has not been reported. In addition, its relationship with other measures of self-responsibility should be explored. Neither it nor the CNS-IE seems to make very fine discriminations among children of various age groups—thus failing to corroborate the theoretical assumption regarding increased internality with age (see Nowicki and Strickland, 1973, for a report on the validation of the CNS-IE). Nevertheless, the PPNS-IE—as well as the other forms in the NS-IE series—shows promise. The PPNS-IE is quick and easy to administer and score, and its format is an attractive one that should appeal to young children. It is to be hoped that additional validity and reliability data will be obtained to strengthen its support. Further, it is critical that representative norms be developed for the PPNS-IE.

Primary Academic Sentiment Scale (PASS). This measure was developed "to obtain objective information about a child's motivation for learning and his relative level of maturity and independence" (Thompson, 1968, p. 1). It yields two scores—a Sentiment, or academic motivation, score and a Dependency score.

PASS is an untimed self-report measure for children four to seven years old. It contains two parts of nineteen items each, the second given after a recess break or on the following day. No special training is required for administrators. A teacher or paraprofessional reads PASS to children assembled in groups. For groups larger than ten children, an assistant should be available to help children turn pages, hold pencils, and so on; for groups larger than twenty-four, a second assistant is recommended; and groups larger than forty are not advised. Special instructions are included to help children inexperienced with this type of measure to attain basic prerequisite skills, such as turning pages and attending to visual and auditory stimuli.

The manual contains little information on the procedures used to construct PASS. In general, construction of the Sentiment scale was based on "the notion that a child's attitudes toward various components of successful academic performance will be displayed in three-choice items. The desired component is presented pictorially, competing with academically nonessential activities [and with activities suggesting dependency], also pictorially presented. The competing activities in the test are frequently those which would likely play the role of competing activities in the real world. Children who score high . . . are therefore seen, on a theoretical basis, as those who have been instilled with strong positive attitudes toward learning" (Thompson, 1968, pp. 12–13).

The child is given a test booklet. He is asked to indicate his preference or attitude, in response to a situation presented orally by the administrator, by marking one of the three drawings on the page (each item is on a separate page of the booklet). The response choices on most items are such that one choice is closely associated with traditional academic tasks, another with an interesting but academically nonessential activity, and a third with an activity that should appeal to a dependent or immature child. Examples of such choices are learning all about what makes fire, playing with balls, and sitting on mother's lap, respectively. Fourteen of the thirty-eight items present one happy and one sad face (some items have only two response choices) or a happy, neutral, and sad face as response alternatives instead of actual drawings.

A PASS scoring form is used to score each child's booklet for sentiment and dependency. All thirty-eight items are scored first for the Sentiment scale, with one point given for each response choice indicating academic interest or motivation. Twenty-eight of the items are scored again, this time with responses indicative of dependency receiving one point each on the Dependency scale. For most items, then, the child receives either a point for sentiment, a point for dependency, or no point on either scale. (The response choices that represent the competing, academically nonessential activities receive no credit on either of the two scales.)

With the aid of two tables in the manual, raw scores can be converted to Sentiment Quotients, standard scores with a mean of 100 and a standard deviation of 15, and Dependency Stanines (see Chapter Two for a review of stanines). Each table contains conversions according to four-month chronological age groupings beginning with age four years, four months and ending with age seven years, three months.

Information on the validity and reliability of PASS is available in the manual. Although a variety of studies apparently have been conducted, unfortunately only brief accounts of the results and no back-up references are provided. Missing are specifications of the procedures used in the studies as well as detailed descriptions of the subjects.

With regard to concurrent and possibly construct validity, correlations between PASS scores and certain other measures are reported for small groups (ranging from about thirty to sixty children). For example, correlations between the Sentiment Quotients and Otis-Lennon IQ scores, Metropolitan Readiness scores, and scores on the Screening Test of Academic Readiness (or STAR, a measure presumably developed by the author of PASS) were .34, .44, and .32, respectively. Correlations between the Dependency Stanines and Otis-Lennon IQ scores and Metropolitan Readiness scores were .34 and .22, respectively. Other validity reports revealed statistically significant differences between "high" and "low" groups of kindergarten and first-grade children, as ranked by their teachers on academic interest, on both their Sentiment Quotients and Dependency Stanine scores. In another table, a statistically significant difference on Sentiment scores among three first-grade classrooms grouped by performance is reported, with the class of high performers having the highest average academic sentiment score and the low-performing class the lowest average score.

Internal consistency (split-half) reliability coefficients and standard errors of measurement are given for groups of over sixty kindergartners and over sixty first-graders. For the Sentiment scale, the coefficients were .76 and .77, respectively, with standard errors of measurement of 7.3 and 7.2. Coefficients of .55 and .78 and standard errors of 1.3 and .9 were reported for the two age groups for the Dependency scale.

The norming sample consisted of 480 preschool, kindergarten, and first-grade children located in the suburbs outside Chicago. No additional information on the characteristics of the sample is provided. In regard to interpreting PASS scores, the test author noted a similarity between the meaning of high and low Sentiment Quotients and high and low IQs as many IQ tests employ the same type of standard score (mean of 100 and standard deviation of 15). Thus, a Sentiment Quotient between 86 and 114 is considered "average," as is the middle range of Dependency Stanines (four through six).

Rosner (1972) reviewed PASS and raised several concerns, which we share:

> The premise that a child cannot display high dependency and high motivation on the same item should be questioned seriously. Highly dependent children frequently are motivated toward academic success if only for the resultant social approval. Eight items are included that do not provide for a choice of activity but, instead, question the child on whether his parents take him to the zoo, museum, or on trips, and about mother's and father's favorite activity (read, talk on the phone, watch television?). The validity of these items is tentative at best.
>
> The manual is clearly written. Instructions are specifically stated. Each item is presented in a standardized manner; a script has been written for each. Following the script may cause trouble, however, because the examiner is told to offer such reinforcing comments as "good" and "you are doing it right" after the children respond to many of the items. It is conceivable that these comments might well reinforce responses in a way that would distort the test's validity [Rosner, 1972, p. 1183].

PASS was intended to fulfill several purposes: assess the effectiveness of instructional programs, especially those that attempt to increase achievement motivation; aid teachers in identifying highly or poorly motivated children; measure motivation and dependency in cross-cultural studies; and contribute, as part of a battery of tests, to decisions about placement of children in specific educational programs (Thompson, 1968). We are hesitant to accept PASS as a valid measure for these purposes because of the paucity of validity and reliability data. The few correlations that are reported are low to moderate. Additional and better-described validity data are needed, especially to substantiate the use of PASS as a diagnostic instrument. Given the young age of children for whom the measure is intended, stability reliability coefficients are also needed. PASS is an attractive and relatively quick and efficient measure. It is to be hoped that the necessary technical information will become available to better support its use.

Illustrative Self-Concept Measures

Measures of self-concept have become increasingly popular among early childhood educators, especially those guided by the humanistic psychologies

(Evans, 1974). As previously noted, the measures tend to vary widely as a result of the differing interpretations of the concept and its component parts. Generally, the term *self-concept* has referred to how one views, knows, or feels about himself. Ringness, for example, viewed self-concept as a very global construct:

> It is clear that the ways one regards himself are influential in determining how he views his life experiences and, in turn, how he behaves. The total of one's attitudes about himself is called the self-concept, the function of which is to act as a mediator between one's motives, the stimuli impinging upon him, and his responses to the situation.
>
> For example, if a child is certain that he is stupid, he may not try to learn. If he feels unaccepted by others, he may withdraw. If he feels self-accepting, he may try hard to excel. How he feels about himself affects not only the ways he interacts with others but the ways he deals with any situation. Children's self-attitudes directly affect their learning in the classroom, their interactions with teachers and peers, and indeed every aspect of their school lives.
>
> The self-concept is formed cognitively, largely from the feedback one gets from others. It is affective, however, in that one is happy or unhappy with this feedback. One tends to internalize it and, in turn, evaluates oneself as adequate or inadequate, acceptable or unacceptable, and so on in other dimensions, each of which has emotional tone [Ringness, 1975, pp. 32–33].

In the literature, marked discrepancies can be found in the opinions of writers and test developers regarding both the ways in which the self-concept is manifested and the constructs that underlie it. According to Wylie, "The basic constructs as defined in the writings of self-concept theorists frequently seem to point to no clear empirical referents. Thus, it is no wonder that a wide array of 'operational definitions' of some of these constructs have been devised by various experimenters. And by the same token it is understandable that some constructs have received no empirical exploration" (1974, p. 8). Shavelson, Hubner, and Stanton (1976) reviewed the literature on self-concept and revealed seventeen different conceptual dimensions on which self-concept definitions could be classified. Included among them were: an emphasis on a stable or changing self-concept; methods for changing self-concept; determinants (situational, phenomenal, or internal) of self-concept; types of evaluation (normative standard, absolute personal standard, or nonevaluative); and unidimensionality versus multidimensionality of self-structure.

A number of self-concept measures appropriate for preschool, kindergarten and early elementary children have become available in the last fifteen years (Coller, 1971a; Walker, 1973). The majority are self-report inventories in which the child responds to pictures or other stimuli by choosing one that best represents himself or how he perceives being viewed by others. The types of stimulus include expressive faces, pictures or drawings of other children, and a Polaroid picture of the child himself. The latter stimulus is used in the Thomas Self-Concept Values Test (Thomas, 1972) and in the Brown-IDS Self-Concept Referents Test (Brown, undated). In very few cases are children required to actually read or write to complete the tests; rather, the descriptions and directions are read to them and the child points to or marks his response choice.

We decided not to treat fully several well-known self-concept measures in this section because of their intended age range (most start at about third grade). However, since we know of situations in which they have been used—or adapted and then used—with younger children, we briefly describe them here.

The Piers-Harris Children's Self-Concept Scale, also called The Way I Feel About Myself (Piers and Harris, 1969), is an eighty-item self-report scale for children in the third through the twelfth grades. The student reads each of the eighty declarative statements (half of which are phrased positively and half negatively) and circles either "yes" or "no" to indicate whether the statement is generally like him or not. Subscales include self-concept with regard to behavior, intellectual and social status, physical appearance and attributes, anxiety, popularity, and happiness and satisfaction. Moderate to substantial validity coefficients are reported between the test and other self-concept measures (Coller, 1971a; Wylie, 1974). Internal consistency and stability reliability coefficients are substantial to high. Norms for the test are available for children in grades four through twelve. The test is purported to be appropriate for children below the third grade level, if the statements are read aloud by the examiner (Bentler, 1972).

The Self-Esteem Inventory (Coopersmith, 1967) consists of fifty-eight statements concerning a student's feelings about himself, the way he thinks other people feel about him, and his feelings about school. The child indicates whether each statement is "like me" or "unlike me." This measure is intended for children from the third grade on up. However, the limited data bearing on the validity and reliability of the measure are not supportive (Dyer, 1963; Wylie, 1974). Further, the inventory's use with third-graders in Stanford Research Institute's Follow Through Classroom Observation Evaluation (Stallings and Kaskowitz, 1974; also see Chapter Eleven on this evaluation) has been criticized because of lack of strong validity or reliability data (House and others, 1978).

The Self-Perception Inventory (Soares and Soares, 1975) consists of forms for students (grades one through twelve), teachers, and other adults (high school age and older). The student form measures six components of self-perception: how the student sees himself; how he perceives that his classmates, teachers, and parents see him (three components); how he sees himself in the role of student; and how he would like to be. In addition, there are measures designed to obtain the student's perceptions of the significant others (peers, teachers, parents) mentioned in the self-ratings. The items in the inventory consist of bipolar pairs of adjectives (for example, "relaxed" versus "nervous") on a four-point continuum; the student indicates proximity to one end or the other by marking one of the four points. The manual includes norms and information on validity and reliability. Generally, moderate to substantial correlations with other self-concept measures are reported, although information on the samples used to obtain the data is scanty. Compared with many other published self-concept measures, however, this measure shows an admirable amount of empirical work done to date. For research or evaluation studies involving elementary-age children, the Self-Perception Inventory is one measure that should be considered.

In the following pages, two illustrative self-concept measures designed for use with young children are described; the overview is presented in Table 19. These represent two different approaches in terms of theoretical basis and type of stimuli used. The brevity of this section reflects, in part, our general concern with the nature of the self-concept measures currently available; many of them lack the supporting materials necessary for a thorough review. A few additional measures that seemed promising were identified, but are not included here because they are not now available for distribution. Notable among them is the Pictorial Self-Concept Scale (PSC) for children in kindergarten through grade four (Bolea, Felker, and Barnes, 1971), a fifty-item measure in which children sort pictorial cards according to how similar the drawings are to themselves. (For a description of the measure, including results of initial validity studies, see the article by Bolea, Felker, and Barnes, 1971.)

Children's Self-Social Constructs Test (CSSCT). The preschool form of the CSSCT is one of three forms (the others being for older elementary-age children and adolescents) developed by Henderson, Long, and Ziller (undated). The test provides a nonverbal measure of several aspects of a child's conception of self in relation to others. The approach taken is relatively unique (Coller, 1971a). "In this method, a subject is presented with a booklet containing a series of symbolic arrays in which circles and other figures represent the self and/or other persons of importance. The subject responds to each task by arranging these symbols— by selecting a circle to represent the self or some other person from those presented, by drawing a circle to stand for himself or another, or by pasting a gummed circle representing the self onto the page with other symbols. From these arrangements, in which the subjects relates himself symbolically to a variety of social configurations, certain aspects of the person's conception of himself are inferred" (Henderson, Long, and Ziller, undated, p. 1).

The theoretical background for the CSSCT derives from the works of a variety of psychologists, social psychologists, and sociologists who contend that self-concept evolves through interpersonal relationships. Self-concept is thus described as thoughts about "self in relation to others," with its "essential nature considered to be relational" (Henderson, Long, and Ziller, undated, p. 3). Early social experiences, cultural expectancies and roles, and interpersonal relationships are also believed to be important in the shaping of self-concept. Building upon this theoretical foundation, the designers intended the CSSCT as a nonverbal test with emphasis on the self in relation to significant others.

The preschool form of the CSSCT is individually administered by a teacher or other examiner; no special training is required. It takes approximately ten minutes to administer the twenty-six item test, and perhaps an additional five minutes to score it. The test is designed for ages three through eight years. The tasks for the child are relatively simple, requiring no reading or verbal responses. To indicate his response, the child either points to it, circles it, or places a gummed label on it; the choice of a particular response mode is apparently at the discretion of the examiner.

The test has six subscales, most of which consist of several identical items

Table 19. Illustrative Self-Concept Measures in Early Childhood Education

Title and Date	Age Range	Administration	Scales or Scores	Source
Children's Self-Social Constructs Test: Preschool Form (Undated)	3 to 8 years	Individual; 10 minutes	Preference for Particular Others Self-Esteem Realism Size Identification with Particular Others Social Interest (or Dependency) Individuation or Minority Identification	Virginia Research Associates, Ltd. P.O. Box 5501 Charlottesville, Va. 22902
Self-Concept and Motivation Inventory (Preschool/Kindergarten Form Items: 1967; Manual and Early Elementary Form Items: 1968)	4 years to end of Kindergarten (Preschool/Kindergarten Form) Grades 1 to 3 (Early Elementary Form)	Group; 25 to 30 minutes	Self-Concept Role Expectations (Early Elementary only) Self-Adequacy (Early Elementary only) Motivation Achievement Needs Achievement Investment	Person-O-Metrics 20504 Williamsburg Rd. Dearborn Heights, Mich. 48127

scattered throughout the test. In other words, the same item is presented more than once. The tasks and scoring involved in each subscale are described below:

1. Preference (for Mother, Father, Friends, or Teacher): Six forced-choice items are included to measure the child's differential preference for significant others. Each item consists of two representational drawings of mother, father, friends, or teacher; all possible pairs of the four significant others are presented. The child is told who the drawings are supposed to be and then points to the one with whom he prefers to be. Scoring for the subscale entails tabulating the number of times, from zero to three, that each type of significant other is chosen. A relative ordering of the child's preferences for significant others is thus determined.

2. Self-Esteem: The four identical items in this subscale are based on the assumption that self-esteem is "derived from an accumulation of self-other comparisons on an evaluative dimension" (Henderson, Long, and Ziller, undated, p. 5). In each item, a column of five circles of equal size is shown to the child. The child is told that the circles represent children and is then asked to choose one circle to represent himself. Higher self-esteem is associated with higher circles on the page. The child receives a score between 5 (uppermost circle) and 1 (lowest circle), depending on the exact circle chosen. The four item scores are summed to obtain a total Self-Esteem score.

3. Realism Size: The two items in this subscale are designed to measure the child's acceptance of his physical self. For each item, an array of twelve circles—four each of three sizes—are shown to the child. The child is first asked to choose a circle to represent his father and then to choose one to represent himself. Based on the size of the circle chosen, the child receives a score from 1 (smallest circle) to 3 (largest circle). The two item scores are summed. Higher scores are associated with less realism for size.

4. Identification (with Mother, Father, Friends, or Teacher): Eight items are included to measure the extent to which the child identifies with significant others. Two identical items are presented for identification with each of the significant others—mother, father, friends, and teacher. Each item consists of a row of six circles, with the leftmost circle containing a representative drawing of the significant other. The child is told who that person is (mother, father, friends, or teacher) and then is asked to point to the circle that represents himself. Depending on the proximity of the chosen circle to the one containing the representative drawing, a score from 1 (nearest the picture) to 6 (farthest) is recorded. Lower scores thus are associated with closer proximity—that is, greater identification. Each pair of items is summed, producing four total scores for identification with mother, father, friends, and teacher, respectively.

5. Social Interest (or Dependency): The four items in this subscale measure the degree to which the child views himself as part of a group of children. Each item consists of three circles arranged triangularly. The child is told that the circles represent children and is then asked to point to the place on the page where he belongs. A score of 1 is awarded if he places himself within the triangle formed by the circles, while no points are given if he places himself outside

the triangle. A total Social Interest score is calculated by summing the four item scores, with higher total scores representing greater dependency or social interest.

6. Individuation or Minority Identification: In this subscale, the extent to which the child perceives himself as similar to or different from other persons is assessed. According to the authors, "majority identification is presumed to reflect a degree of security accompanied by depersonalization, minority identification to involve less security but greater personalization" (Henderson, Long, and Ziller, undated, p. 7). Two identical items comprise the subscale. A box with ten circles is presented—seven plain circles and three shaded circles. On the right side of the box are two additional circles, one plain and one shaded. The child is told that the circles in the box represent other children and is asked to choose one of the two circles to the right of the box to represent himself. A score of 1 is given if the child chooses the minority (shaded) circle; a score of 0 if he chooses the majority (plain) circle. Summing the two item scores yields a total subscale score, with a higher score representing greater individuation or minority identification.

Evidence for the construct validity of the three forms of the CSSCT is summarized in the manual. Several of the studies cited dealt with the validity of the preschool form. In two separate investigations of sex, race, class, and age differences (Long and Henderson, 1968, 1970), the CSSCT was administered to groups of entering first-graders in rural Southern communities. In the 1968 study, seventy-two black children in Head Start programs were compared with the same number of white, middle-class children; in the 1970 study, 192 children (half of them white, half black; half girls, half boys, half middle-class, half lower-class) were tested. In both studies, the black children had significantly lower Otis IQ scores and less preschool/kindergarten education than the white children. Results showed significant differences (favoring the white, middle-class children) on preference for fathers, scores for self-esteem, realism size, and identification with fathers. Teachers' ratings of classroom behavior were obtained for black children only in the 1968 sample; when the twelve boys and twelve girls with the highest ratings were compared with the twelve boys and girls with the lowest ratings on each subscale score, significant differences (favoring the children with the high teacher ratings) were found on self-esteem and identification with teacher. Boys' scores reflected significantly less identification with mother and with teacher than did girls' scores for the black sample. Correlations between CSSCT subscale scores and chronological age, amount of preschool education, birth order, and number of siblings were zero to low.

The CSSCT was also field-tested by a Head Start Social Emotional Task Force prior to the 1969–70 Head Start national evaluation (Boger and Knight, 1969). About forty four- and five-year-old children in an urban Head Start program were given the test. Significantly lower scores for the black children were found for realism size and for identification with mother, father, and friends.

As to reliability, no stability coefficients are reported in the manual. However, split-half reliability coefficients for the preschool form, based on ninety-six first-graders, are reported. The coefficients ranged from .48 to .85, with a median of .74. The internal consistency coefficients reported by Boger and Knight (1969) were slightly lower (median coefficient was .57).

The usability features of the CSSCT are weak. No norms or other aids to interpretation are provided in the manual. Meaningful interpretation of individual scores is not possible. Boger and Knight (1969) noted that the CSSCT appeared to be too long for the children tested, as they became restless during the last quarter to third of the test.

The CSSCT represents a unique, nonverbal method for measurement of self-concept and related self-social constructs. However, Wylie (1974) questioned the CSSCT authors' contention that this approach avoids or minimizes variations in word interpretation, which weaken the validity of self-report measures; she pointed out that there is no evidence that children interpret the nonverbal symbols more uniformly than they interpret words or phrases in a self-report measure. More important, the validity data reported thus far are inconclusive. Differences between racial and social class groups on CSSCT subscale scores were confounded with differences on intelligence and preschool/kindergarten educational experiences. Additional validation is needed; in particular, data on the relationships between CSSCT subscale scores and other indexes of self-concept and social behavior are required. The reliability technical data also require attention. The internal consistency coefficients are somewhat misleading, given the repetition of identical items within subscales. Coefficients of stability would be more applicable as reliability indicators. In general, then, use of the CSSCT should be restricted to research studies until further empirical work, including determination of norms, is conducted.

Self-Concept and Motivation Inventory (SCAMIN). Also called What Face Would You Wear?, SCAMIN was designed as a measure of academic self-concept and motivation (Milchus, Farrah, and Reitz, 1968). Four forms are available: preschool/kindergarten, early elementary, later elementary, and secondary. Only the first two forms—appropriate for ages four through kindergarten and grades one through three, respectively—are discussed here.

According to its authors, the SCAMIN measures two elements of academic self-concept as well as two elements of academic motivation, as indicated in the definitions below:

1. Academic Self-Concept: how a child views his role as a school learner; the sum of his experiences, perceptions, attitudes, and feelings about school and schoolwork.
   a. Role Expectations: "the positive acceptance of the aspirations and demands that the student thinks others—significant others—expect of him."
   b. Self-Adequacy: "the positive regard with which a student views his present and future probabilities of success."
2. Academic Motivation: a child's expressed need to achieve a goal in school, with a moderate avoidance of failure.
   a. Achievement Needs: "the positive regard with which a student perceives the intrinsic and extrinsic rewards of learning and performing in school."

   b. Achievement Investment: "the awareness and concern toward shunning the embarrassment and sanctions which are associated with failure in school" (Milchus, Farrah, and Reitz, 1968, p. 1).

Administration of the SCAMIN requires a minimum of twenty-five minutes. It is group-administered, orally, by the teacher. No special training is required for administration or scoring. In response to each question, children mark their answer sheets by blackening the nose of the face that best expresses how they feel or would react in the situation described to them. One happy face, one neutral face, and one sad face are presented for each question on the preschool/kindergarten form, while five faces—ranging from very sad to very happy—serve as response choices on the early elementary form.

The two forms were constructed in similar fashion. Items were written to fit specifications defined by a factorial matrix, in which the four subscales (Role Expectations, Self-Adequacy, Achievement Needs, and Achievement Investment) were crossed with six sources of support climate (teachers, parents, peers and siblings, self, school climate, and academic climate). Twenty-four items, one for each of the cells in the matrix, were written for each form. For example, one item was generated to measure the child's role expectations in regard to his teacher, another to measure his self-adequacy in regard to his parents, and so on. Items were written by teachers enrolled in graduate classes (Milchus, 1977).

Each question is read by the teacher and begins with, "What face would you wear if . . . ?" The situations and behaviors represented are ones familiar to school children, such as demonstrating skills to others, being evaluated by teachers or parents, relating to peers, and learning new information. Each item is scored from 1 to 3 (preschool/kindergarten) or 1 to 5 (early elementary); higher scores indicate a greater degree of the construct measured.

Scoring the early elementary form of the SCAMIN involves summing the six item scores for each subscale (Role Expectations, Self-Adequacy, Achievement Needs, and Achievement Investment). Total Self-Concept and Motivation scores are obtained by summing the two subscale scores pertinent to each. The scoring for the preschool/kindergarten form is similar, except that Self-Concept is not broken down into the two subscales. Thus, on it, three scores are obtained: Self-Concept, Achievement Needs, and Achievement Investment. As with the early elementary form, a Motivation score can be obtained by summing the scores for the latter two subscales.

Information on the validity of SCAMIN is minimal. Readers must obtain a supplementary document (Milchus, 1977) to receive any information on validity. The data presented there are insufficiently described, with very few details on sample sizes and characteristics, or testing conditions. Several factorial studies are cited. Results of one study identified three of the four factors on the early elementary form, while another confirmed all four factors. In other studies alluded to, SCAMIN scores were used in regression equations to predict the success of elementary school students with computer-assisted instruction and to predict first-grade reading success. In both cases, SCAMIN scores apparently had low correlations with the dependent variables. Additional uses of SCAMIN referred to were in program evaluation efforts; again, the information is so scanty (including incomplete references) that little can be determined about the validity of the measure.

The reliability of SCAMIN is given no more attention than the validity. In the supplementary document, a split-half coefficient of .79 is reported for the preschool/kindergarten Self-Concept subscale. For the early elementary form, a stability coefficient for total SCAMIN scores of .77 is given (Milchus, 1977).

Tables of norms are included in the manuals. To establish the norms, approximately 1,000 students were given each form. The students in the samples were located in urban, suburban, and ghetto areas of Los Angeles, and a large proportion were minority students (Milchus, 1977). In the preschool/ kindergarten manual, the table of norms for the Achievement Needs and Achievement Investment subscales contain raw score transformations to "high," "middle," or "low"; the norms for the Self-Concept subscale are expressed as stanine scores. One table in the early elementary manual presents norms for grade one; another gives the norms for grades two and three. In both cases, norms are expressed as stanine scores for each of the four subscales. For individual interpretation of scores beginning in third grade, profile analysis is recommended (Milchus, Farrah, and Reitz, 1968). Five profiles are possible, each one marked by a particular combination of high, medium, or low subscale scores. The five profiles are Anxiety, Denial, Protection, Security, and Placid.

The usefulness of SCAMIN is weakened by the lack of validity and reliability information, the incomplete and scattered descriptions of construction procedures and empirical work, and the lack of nationally representative norms. Considering the strong emphasis in the manual on individual interpretation of scores, the lack of validity and reliability evidence for the separate subscales and profiles is especially serious. Shepard (1978) reviewed SCAMIN and criticized its lack of validity. She emphasized the need for construct validation—both concurrent and discriminant (see Chapter Three). She recommended that, without validity data, its use be restricted to research or program evaluation studies, in which the intent would be to look at differences between experimental and control groups or at changes in group scores over time.

The format of SCAMIN is one that should appeal to young children. It is relatively quick and easy to administer and score. Acceptable validity and reliability data and more representative norms are needed, however, to enhance its usefulness.

Illustrative Measures of Social Skills and Competencies

In this section, several measures of children's social skills and competencies are considered. The focus is on children's social interactions with others— adults and peers—in typical settings such as home and school. As is true with the self-concept measures, many constructs subsumed under this category could also be viewed as aspects of personality. Unlike those measures in the section on personality, however, the ones in this section were designed primarily as measures of social skills or competencies.

White and Watts (1973) conducted an extensive observational study to learn more about the range and nature of social competencies in very young children. They arrived at a list of abilities that they believed differentiated more competent from less competent children:

1. Ability to get and maintain the attention of adults in socially acceptable ways.
2. Ability to use adults as resources—that is, to obtain something (information, assistance, food) by verbally requesting it, demanding it, or physically demonstrating a need for it.
3. Ability to express affection or hostility to adults through verbal or physical means.
4. Ability to lead and follow peers—that is, to both give and follow suggestions, take and follow the lead of others, and so forth.
5. Ability to express both affection and hostility to peers through verbal or physical means.
6. Ability to exhibit interpersonal competition.
7. Ability to show pride in one's accomplishments, including things one has created.
8. Ability to act out a typical adult activity or verbally express a desire to grow up.

In a general sense, the measures presented here are concerned with the abilities listed above. They represent several different measurement techniques, including sociometry and structured interviews. Most common, however, are rating scales or checklists completed by persons familiar with the child, such as parents or teachers. Two measures discussed later in this section, the Bristol Social Adjustment Guides (Stott, 1972) and the California Preschool Social Competency Scales (Levine, Elzey, and Lewis, 1969), are of this type. Two similar measures, not included in this section but noteworthy, are the Stamp Behavior Study Technique or BST (Stamp, 1972) and the Devereux Elementary School Behavior Rating Scale or DESB (Spivack and Swift, 1967).

The BST, an essentially multiple-choice rating scale used by preschool and kindergarten teachers following direct observation, measures a child's development of social skills in twelve areas: people, selfhood, demands of others, expression of demands on others, coping with frustration, coping with stress, coping with realistic fears, need for approval, communication, physical health, use of powers, and general behavior. The measure is reported to have multiple uses in helping teachers, counselors, and psychologists to understand child behavior and to identify "potentially disturbed" children. The BST underwent a careful development process, including the obtaining of extensive empirical data to substantiate the scoring system. However, only partial evidence is reported for its validity and reliability, and no detailed norms are provided.

The DESB, also a rating scale, is intended for use by elementary teachers and measures behavioral difficulties assumed to interfere with successful academic performance. The forty-seven behaviors measured by the DESB are categorized into eleven areas: classroom disturbance, impatience, disrespect-defiance, external blame, achievement anxiety, external reliance, comprehension, inattentive-withdrawn, irrelevant-responsiveness, creative initiative, and need for closeness to teachers. Data on validity and reliability are reported in a separate publication (Swift and Spivack, 1968). Correlations between DESB subscale scores and classroom achievement grades were obtained for almost 1,000 children in grades one through six; the coefficients ranged from low to substantial and varied across grade level. While the DESB is not applicable to many early childhood settings, it has been used with kindergartners and early grade school children, and related data are available.

Walker (1973) and Guthrie (1971) listed additional measures of social skills for use with young children. While the four measures now described are illustrative of much of the work done in this area, interested readers may also want to consult these two compendiums. An overview of the four measures in this section is presented in Table 20.

Bristol Social Adjustment Guides (BSAG). The 1970 edition of the BSAG (Stott, 1972) is a revision of the original 1956 edition. The BSAG "provides a means of detecting and assessing behavior disturbances (maladjustment) in children aged five to sixteen years within a school setting" (Stott, 1972, p. 3). Teachers rate their students on a variety of dimensions by choosing and underlining words in the Guides that describe the students' behaviors. Two forms are available—one for rating boys and the other for rating girls—but the only difference is the use of appropriate pronouns (that is, "she" versus "he," and so on). Five uses are claimed for the BSAG:

1. To provide information to clinicians.
2. To aid guidance counselors and social workers in understanding reasons for learning disability.
3. To measure effects of special treatments, such as placement in a special school or class, or to measure changes over time in children's behavior.
4. To prepare teachers to recognize maladjustment and adopt professional attitudes toward "bad" behavior.
5. To study relationships between maladjustment and genetic or environmental variables.

The BSAG is designed to be completed by a teacher who is familiar with the child's ways of behaving; at least one month of contact with the child is recommended prior to using the BSAG. No special training is required of the teacher who completes the rating scale. Approximately ten to twenty minutes are needed to rate one child.

The BSAG measures five core syndromes, considered to be handicaps or impairments to adaptive behavior: unforthcomingness (fearful of new tasks and strange situations), withdrawal, depression, inconsequence (failure to restrain first impulse), and hostility. No overall score for maladjustment is provided. Rather, two main scores are yielded: an "Unract" score representing the under-

Table 20. Illustrative Measures of Social Skills and Competencies in Early Childhood Education

Title and Date	Age Range	Admin-istration	Scales or Scores	Source
Bristol Social Adjustment Guides (1970: Items; 1972: Manual)	5 to 16 years	Individual; 10 to 20 minutes	Unforthcomingness Withdrawal Depression Nonsyndromic Underreaction Total Underreaction (Unract) Inconsequence Hostility Nonsyndromic Overreaction Peer Maladaptiveness Total Overreaction (Ovract) Neurological	Educational & Industrial Testing Service San Diego, Calif. 92107
California Preschool Social Competency Scale (1969)	2½ to 5½ years	Individual; time required not stated (our estimate is 10 to 15 minutes)	Social Competency	Consulting Psychologists Press, Inc. 577 College Ave. Palo Alto, Calif. 94306

Test	Age Range	Administration	Measure	Source
Minnesota Sociometric Status Test (1965)	Preschool and Kindergarten	Individual; 7 to 8 minutes per child (entire group must be tested)	Sociometric Status	S. G. Moore Institute of Child Development University of Minnesota Minneapolis, Minn. 55455
Vineland Social Maturity Scale (1953: Manual; 1965: Items and Condensed Manual)	Birth to Maturity	Individual; time required not stated (our estimate is 30 minutes)	Social Quotient	American Guidance Science, Inc. Publishers' Bldg. Circle Pines, Minn. 55014

reacting mode of maladjustment and an "Ovract" score indicating the over-reacting mode of maladjustment. The Unract scale consists of three core syndromes—unforthcomingness, withdrawal, and depression—as well as an "associated grouping" of nonsyndromic underreaction items. The items in the latter grouping are not specific to any of the three core syndromes for Unract but are closely related to the underreaction construct. Similarly, the Ovract scale consists of the other two core syndromes—inconsequence and hostility—as well as an associated grouping of items categorized as nonsyndromic overreaction (including items related to delinquency, peer-group deviance, and defiance of social norms). In addition, the Ovract scale draws on items from a peer-maladaptiveness associated grouping (including items related to aggression, domineering, lack of control, and unpopularity). Finally, a separate neurological scale is used to identify behavior problems based on neurological malfunctioning. In sum, then, there are eleven possible scores yielded by the BSAG. Scores on Unforthcomingness, Withdrawal, Depression, and Nonsyndromic Under-reaction are summed to yield a Total Underreaction, or Unract, score. Similarly, scores for Inconsequence, Hostility, Nonsyndromic Overreaction, and Peer-Maladaptiveness are added to produce a Total Overreaction, or Ovract, score. The Neurological scale produces the eleventh score.

The original 1956 edition of the BSAG was constructed by obtaining descriptions from large numbers of teachers of the characteristics of children who were not acting in their own best interests, not interacting effectively with their environment, or creating bad situations for themselves. Systematic observation by trained observers within classrooms and general school settings yielded supplemental descriptive information. Based on empirical tryouts with maladjusted and normal children, a pool of 133 items were selected and classified into nine syndromic groupings (Walker, 1973). Based on over 2,500 BSAG ratings collected in 1970 for children ages five through fourteen, the measure was revised. Some of the original items were deleted, and empirical analyses produced the present set of syndromic and associated groupings.

Each form of the BSAG consists of thirty-three sets of phrases descriptive of children's behavior, categorized into seven areas: interaction with teacher, school work, games and play, attitudes toward other children, personal ways, physique, and school achievement. For each of the seven categories, from one to eleven sets of phrases are presented. Each set is further labeled to orient the rater to the situation. For example, four sets of phrases are provided for the ratings of behavior under "school work": paying attention in class, working by himself (herself), engaging in manual tasks or free activity, and facing new learning tasks. The actual phrases within each of the four sets give variants of children's responses to the defined situation. For example, under "paying attention in class," the teacher may note any of the following: that the child attends well, attends only to nonwork stimuli or activities, is apathetic, is extremely quiet and gives no indication of whether attending or not, or is a daydreamer. The rater underlines as many phrases as apply, but leaves the entire set unmarked if none apply. Scoring the BSAG can be done by the teacher using transparent templates that yield scores on the five core syndromes, three associated groupings, and

Neurological scale. Scores are recorded on a diagnostic form, and the Unract and Ovract scores are computed.

Validation of the BSAG involved investigations of the relationships of maladjustment with poor health, multiple impairment, motor impairment, and delinquency. (In Chapter Eight, the Test or Motor Impairment, also developed by Stott, is described.) Information in the manual on the size and characteristics of the samples used in these studies is limited, but the samples apparently were drawn from the 1970 revision sample. Unfortunately, the nature and extent of the resulting relationships are only partially reported in the manual. The author stated, however, that the five core syndromes and the Ovract and Unract scores were associated with morbidity, frequency of health-related impairments, severity of motor impairment, and number of delinquent offenses.

Internal consistency (Cronbach's Alpha) reliability estimates were obtained from the 1970 sample. The estimates for the five core syndromes, associated groupings, and the Neurological scale ranged from .45 to .83; the median estimate was .67. Reliability estimates for total Unract and Ovract scales were .83 and .91, respectively. To obtain coefficients of stability, teachers completed a second BSAG one year later for two randomly selected subsamples (n's not given). Coefficients of stability are not reported. The scores from the second ratings were lower (indicating less maladjustment) than those from the first ratings, with the boys' scores decreasing more than the girls'. According to the author, this decrease was probably due to teachers' increased sensitivity and attention to maladjusted behaviors following the first ratings, and subsequent improvement by the children.

Norms for the BSAG are based on the 1970 sample. Although analyses of these data showed differences according to socioeconomic status, rural-urban distinctions, age, and sex of the children rated, the norms are broken down by sex only. The tables of norms in the manual present frequency distributions for raw scores on the syndromic and total scales, as well as percentile ranks. In addition, cut-off scores for gauging degree of severity on the five syndromic and total scores are given, presumably for diagnostic purposes. For example, for the Unract scores, cut-off scores are given for five diagnostic categories: (1) stability and near-stability, (2) mild underreaction, (3) appreciable underreaction; (4) maladjusted underreaction, and (5) severe maladjusted underreaction.

The usability of the BSAG is hampered by the vague descriptions of validation procedures and results, and by lack of validation in terms of other indicators of maladjustment (such as ratings by psychologists or scores on other socioemotional measures). Especially serious is the lack of empirical evidence for the validity of the diagnostic categories, since the measure is intended primarily for use in individual, rather than group, assessment. Considering the extensive work conducted during development and revision of the BSAG, it is unfortunate that sufficient validity data are not provided. Its use should be restricted to investigation of group differences or changes over time. Further, as one reviewer noted, the Guides "appear to have a great deal to offer in helping the everyday observer sharpen his observations of children" (Morgan, 1965, p. 159).

California Preschool Social Competency Scale (CPSCS). The purpose of the

CPSCS is "to measure the adequacy of preschool children's interpersonal behavior and the degree to which they assume social responsibility" (Levine, Elzey, and Lewis, 1969, p. 3). The measure can be used with children two and a half to five and a half years old. The CPSCS is a thirty-item rating scale to be completed by a child's teacher or someone who has had an opportunity to observe the child in a variety of situations. Although no time limits or estimates are given, completing the scale would probably take about ten to fifteen minutes. According to its authors, the CPSCS was developed primarily for use by preschool teachers. In addition, they viewed it as useful for measuring the effects of instructional intervention and environmental variables on children's development at various ages, and for predicting academic achievement (Levine, Elzey, and Lewis, 1969).

Each of the thirty items elicits a rating of the child's competence in a specific behavioral area. In order to make the rating, the rater must have actually observed the child in the situation or behavioral area listed. The thirty behavioral areas include a wide range of activities, such as accepting changes in routine, greeting a new child, reporting accidents, following instructions, communicating wants, sharing, accepting limits set by adults, and seeking help. Four descriptive statements, representing varying degrees of social competence, are presented as possible responses for each behavioral area. The rater circles the number of the option that best characterizes the child's "typical" performance. Several of the sets of options speak to the frequency with which the child demonstrates competence. For example, the rater indicates how often (hardly ever, sometimes, frequently, or nearly always) the child accepts changes in routine without resistance or becoming upset. To aid the rater in making the appropriate choice, the manual contains additional definitions of terms and explanations of the levels of activity for some of the items.

Development of the CPSCS began with observing children's interactions in a variety of preschools and holding discussions with preschool personnel to identify behaviors for inclusion in the scale. The information gathered directly, along with reviews of the literature and of existing social behavior measures for preschoolers, led to specific criteria that each item had to meet. An item had to (1) involve a behavior observable in the preschool setting, (2) be applicable to both boys and girls, (3) allow specification of four unidimensional levels of competence, (4) minimize the use of value judgments in determining competence, and (5) be independent of any particular cultural orientations. A pool of items was generated that met these criteria, and these items were then judged by early childhood educators and teachers enrolled in early childhood graduate programs. Each item was judged in terms of importance, clarity, relevance for children in the target age group, and differentiation among the four levels of competence provided as response choices. These judgments led to the composition of an initial scale of thirty-four items, which was then pretested in many California preschools. Item analyses of the data resulted in eliminating a few items and revising others.

The four levels of each item are scored in terms of the implied child competence. The lowest level of competence is assigned a score of 1, and so forth, with the highest level of competence given a score of 4. To obtain the overall Social Competency score, the ratings for the thirty items are summed. Thus, raw scores can range from 30 to 120 (low to high competence) and can be converted to percentile ranks by referencing the tables of norms in the manual.

The CPSCS manual contains no mention of criterion-related or construct validity. However, Walker (1973) referred to the use of the CPSCS in the fall 1970 Head Start Planned Variation Study and reported that correlations with other tests were generally low. The largest correlation, .39, was with the Cooperative Preschool Inventory (described in Chapter Five). In addition, some of the items were judged to be culturally biased by Walker, Bane, and Bryk (1973).

Interrater reliability coefficients are reported in the manual. Data from three separate studies, conducted with fifteen, twenty-four, and seventy-one children, compared ratings made by multiple judges, such as teachers, assistant teachers, program directors, and consultants. The coefficients ranged from .75 to .86, with a median of .78. In addition, for the norming sample ($n = 800$), split-half coefficients were computed separately by age, sex, and parents' occupational level and ranged from .90 to .98. Walker (1973) reported a split-half coefficient of .96 for the Head Start Planned Variation sample of nearly 4,000 children. However, Walker also noted extensive variation among teachers in their ratings, a finding that led her and others to "recommend that CPSCS scores not be aggregated across classrooms for summative evaluation analyses" (Walker, 1973, p. 262).

The norms for the CPSCS were obtained from ratings of 800 children. Representing all geographic regions of the country, the sample approximated the proportion of preschool-age children in the major urban areas for each geographic region. Fifty children in each of sixteen age-by-sex-by-occupational level categories comprised the norming sample; "occupational level" was either high or low, depending on the occupation of the major wage-earner in the family. Percentile norms are presented in the manual for each of four age groups, each broken down further by sex and occupational level.

Several features of the CPSCS enhance its usability: it is easily and quickly administered and scored, and the scores are relatively simple to interpret. The norms were developed very carefully and are sufficient for most users— although the absence of normative data beyond the target age groups and of breakdowns by ethnicity may weaken the measure's usefulness in some settings. The inclusion in the manual of interrater reliability data is another noteworthy feature; the estimates are adequate, although small sample sizes and Walker's findings preclude a strong conclusion about the consistency across raters. Further, coefficients of stability would add critical information not now provided.

The most serious criticism of the CPSCS is the lack of construct or criterion-related validity evidence. Although the content validity evidence is fairly good, due to the care taken during development, it alone does not suffice. The use of the CPSCS for the intended purposes of the developers is not warranted without validation for those purposes. Reviewers of the measure have criticized the CPSCS for the lack of validity data, as well as for the middle-class view of competency that it apparently represents (Calfee, 1978; Lytton, 1978). The measure should be considered a research edition until further validity evidence becomes available.

Minnesota Sociometric Status Test (MSST). First described in the literature a number of years ago (Moore and Updegraff, 1964), the Minnesota Sociometric Status Test is an unpublished measure available from the first author. It "was developed to obtain measures of peer acceptance and peer rejection of young children attending nursery schools, daycare centers, and other group programs" (Moore, 1973, p. 1). The MSST uses sociometric procedures to study interrelations among group members and, specifically, to determine how each child is perceived by the group. (Sociometric techniques are discussed in Chapter Twelve.)

The test is individually administered by a teacher or other examiner; no special training is required. All children in a class or group are interviewed in turn, with each interview taking seven or eight minutes. Using a picture board that includes a head-and-shoulder photograph of each member of the peer group, the child indicates three members of the group he especially likes and then three members he does not like very much. Actually, he is asked six separate questions—three for his "likes" and three for his "dislikes." Moore (1973) claimed several advantages for the MSST's picture-interview format over alternate approaches to eliciting children's sociometric preferences. For example, she saw this method as a more economical, and more likely to elicit feelings of peer admiration, than observational methods—the latter because a child may admire another child but not interact with him unless the admiration is mutual.

The MSST is an adaptation of two earlier sociometric measures—the Dunnington and the McCandless-Marshall Sociometric Status Test (Walker, 1973). Asking children to make both positive and negative choices represents the major difference between this measure and the McCandless-Marshall test (which only elicited positive, or "liked," choices). The addition of the negative choices was made to distinguish the social isolates (unchosen children) from the disliked children (those children whose behaviors are actually noxious to their peers).

The MSST should be administered after most children in a particular group are well acquainted with each other; for classes that start in the fall, a spring administration is recommended. Prior to the administration, the picture board must be assembled. Instructions for photographing the children are included in the manual; the photographer (presumably the teacher or other examiner) is encouraged to obtain pictures with similarity in head size and facial expression (which should be relatively neutral) and is given tips on reducing the children's apprehension or reticence about the picture-taking experience. The resulting pictures are mounted on a board or cardboard in such a way that they can be moved around between interviews (to reduce possible bias due to position). The names of the children can be placed by their pictures to aid an examiner who might be unfamiliar with the group. Relatively simple interview procedures are detailed in the manual; the child is asked, three times, to point to or name a child he likes, and then is asked to repeat the process with three children he does not like very well. The names of the children chosen are recorded.

Several ways are given for scoring the MSST. The seemingly most common procedure for determining a child's sociometric status is to subtract the total number of times he was his peers' disliked choice from the total number of times he was chosen as a liked child. To eliminate negative scores for some children, a constant would then be added to each child's score. Weighting of the choices—according to whether they were first, second, or third choices—is also possible, but does not enhance group interpretation. Moore (1973) reported that correlations between weighted and unweighted scores for six different groups were high, ranging from .92 to .98; that is, weighting does not yield significantly different rankings of children.) Scoring can also consist of totaling only the positive (liked) or only the negative (disliked) choices. For example, the latter might be preferred if the primary purpose for using the test was to identify children with social problems. Yet another scoring alternative is to add the positive and negative scores for each child, yielding an "impact" score. A high impact score (that is, many positive and/or negative nominations) would imply that the child was having substantial social impact on his peers, whereas a low score would suggest minimal social impact. This scoring technique, then, might serve to differentiate the extroverted, influential, and well-known children from the introverted and shy children. Apparently, the teacher or examiner is left to decide which scoring alternative(s) to use and also, as discussed later, how to interpret and use the sociometric data obtained.

Several validation studies (primarily criterion-related) have been conducted on the MSST. Moore and Updegraff (1964) observed three groups of children during free play and recorded nurturance-giving, peer-oriented dependence, and adult-oriented dependence. Sociometric status scores correlated low to moderate with nurturance-giving (.20, .49, and .29 for the three groups) and with peer-oriented dependence (.14, .35, and .40). However, sociometric status was unrelated to adult-oriented dependence except for the very young children (for whom the correlation was −.55). In other words, giving nurturance to classmates and exhibiting peer-oriented dependence tended to be associated with greater popularity, while being dependent on adults was unrelated to popularity among older preschoolers and possibly even interfered with achieving a high status among the younger preschoolers. A further finding from this study was that age and sex were not related to sociometric popularity, although both sexes tended to make positive choices of same-sex peers and negative choices of opposite-sex peers.

In other validation studies (Charlesworth and Hartup, 1967; Hartup, Glazer, and Charlesworth, 1967), classroom observations were conducted of children's use of both positive and negative social reinforcement. For three replications, correlations between positive sociometric scores (total number of "liked" choices) and use of positive social reinforcement were .70, .67, and .61. Correlations between negative sociometric scores (total number of "disliked" choices) and use of negative social reinforcement were .28, .73, and .80. In yet another study, Moore (1967) correlated sociometric scores with peer judgments of other social characteristics, obtained by having each child respond orally to thirty statements on a Peer Perception of Social Behavior scale. Sociometric scores were found to relate to three (of five) clusters of statements: friendly interaction (correlations ranging from .24 to .48); aggression ($-.21$ to $-.78$); and compliance in routines (.21 to .67).

The reliability of the MSST has also been examined (Moore and Updegraff, 1964). Coefficients of stability for three groups of children, ranging in size from eighteen to twenty-four, were determined by correlating sociometric status scores obtained over intervals of from one to two weeks. Coefficients ranged from .52 to .78, with higher estimates for the older children. Split-half reliability estimates, apparently not stepped-up, were also calculated on four groups of children. Each child's score was split into two half-scores by randomly dividing the judgments of his peer group in half and then summing the ratings he received within each subgroup. Correlating the resultant sets of half-scores yielded coefficients of .27, .34, .61, and .70.

No norms are provided in the manual. Of course, this sociometric procedure yields direct information on each child, and therefore norms are not needed to enhance interpretation for the individual child. At the same time, norms based on defined classroom groups—norms that detail the expected proportions of different statuses (isolates, those chosen as liked by one or more classmates, and so forth) within the defined type of classroom group—might allow interpretations of something like the "social health" of the class. Also absent from the manual, unfortunately, are other aids to interpreting and using the scores obtained. Although resourceful teachers might devise ways to use MSST results to enhance the interactions in their classrooms and the development of both individuals and the total group, it would be fitting for the MSST manual to address the topics of interpretation and use, and at some length.

In all, the technical validity and reliability data on the MSST are at least moderately supportive. The measure is easy to administer. However, the manual's silence on interpreting and using the scores obtained limits the MSST's usability. Potential users of the MSST should examine Chapter Twelve and the measurement texts cited there for guidance on making appropriate use of sociometric data. In general, sociometric data can provide insights into the social psychology of a group of children, but such data should be carefully and conservatively interpreted.

Vineland Social Maturity Scale (VSMS). The Vineland Social Maturity Scale was first published over forty years ago (Doll, 1935). The current edition (Doll, 1965) is not greatly different from the earlier one. The purpose of the scale is to measure social maturity and responsibility in persons from birth to maturity: "The scale provides a definite outline of detailed performances in respect to which children show a progressive capacity for looking after themselves and for participating in those activities which lead toward ultimate independence as adults" (Doll, 1965, p. 1). Although the VSMS was not designed exclusively for use with young children, we include it here because of its common use with children in the preschool and early elementary age range.

The Vineland consists of 117 items divided into eight categories of social maturity: self-help general, self-help eating, self-help dressing, self-direction, occupation, communication, locomotion, and socialization. The items are ordered according to developmental age progression, from shortly after birth to age twenty-five plus, and connote increasing freedom from the need for assistance or supervision. Each item deals with a particular aspect of social ability, such as following instructions, eating with a spoon, initiating play activities, buttoning a coat, going about the neighborhood unattended, using a pencil to write with, and the like. Purportedly, the items measure only aspects of social ability (social participation, self-direction, self-sufficiency, and so on) and not such factors as personality, achievement, intelligence, or skill; further, specific effects due to training, economic opportunity, habit, or incentive are reportedly not reflected in the scale (Doll, 1965).

The VSMS consists of an individually administered, untimed interview. The interviewer rates the subject on the items after obtaining information from one or more persons intimately familiar with the subject, such as a close relative or teacher. It is acceptable to interview the subject himself (if he is at least five years old), but the information obtained should be verified by interviewing an independent informer or by observing the subject's actual behavior on a subset of items.

The VSMS manual describes only briefly the interview procedures. More detailed instructions are presented in a book, *The Measurement of Social Competence* (Doll, 1953). Training in the interview technique is essential. Qualifications for interviewers are extensive: "the examiner must be broadly experienced in general techniques of clinical psychological casework or the equivalent in similar disciplines" (Doll, 1953, p. 266). After determining the subject's age, general abilities, special handicaps, and similar general information, the interviewer begins to question the informant on items well below the subject's anticipated final score. For each item, the interviewer must ascertain if the subject actually exhibits the behavior, the extent to which he exhibits it, and so on.

Scoring the items also requires the skills of a trained professional. According to his status on the behavior specified in the item, the subject receives one of six possible scores:

1. +: The behavior is habitually performed.
2. +F: The behavior formerly was performed successfully but is not now because of physical restraint or lack of opportunity.
3. +NO: The behavior has not been performed because of lack of opportunity but presumably could be learned easily and performed habitually.
4. +/−: The behavior is in a transitional or emergent state and occasionally is performed successfully.
5. −: The behavior has never, or rarely or only under unusual incentive or great pressure, been performed successfully.
6. −NO: The behavior has not been performed and there has been no opportunity, but presumably it could not be performed even if the opportunity were provided.

The first and second scores (+ and +F) represent full credit on the item, as does the third (+NO) if it occurs in a continuous string of plus scores (no credit is given if +NO occurs in a string of minus scores, while half credit is given if it falls among mixed plus and minus scores for surrounding items). The fourth score (+/−) receives half credit, while the last two (− and −NO) result in no credit.

Testing continues until the examiner has recorded "at least two consecutive minus scores in each category [of social maturity] appropriate to the range of application" (Doll, 1965, p. 13). A basal score is then determined—equivalent to the highest numbered item passed at the end of the continuous string of pluses recorded for the subject. To the basal score are added additional scattered credits and half-credits for items passed, at least in part, beyond the basal score. The resulting total score is converted to a Social Age (SA) score by referencing a table in the manual; the SA score expresses the chronological age at which the subject's social performance would be typical. A Social Quotient (SQ) is then calculated by dividing SA by Life Age (LA), or chronological age, of the subject and multiplying by 100. That is, SQ = (SA/LA)100. Note the marked similarity between the SQ and the ratio IQ formerly employed by some intelligence tests, such as the Stanford-Binet. The usefulness of the SQ must be questioned because of methodological problems associated with such ratio scores (see Chapter Two).

The major validation study was conducted with institutionalized mentally retarded children in New Jersey in 1939–40. The study was primarily descriptive: the VSMS scores of several hundred institutionalized children were obtained and compared, descriptively, with the norms established for normal children. The institutionalized children demonstrated far less social maturity than that reported for normal children. The correlation between VSMS Social Age scores and Binet Mental Age scores was high, namely .84 (Doll, 1953). Social Age correlated moderately (about .50) with chronological age for children fourteen and under; for older children, the relationship was zero. In other studies with children from the same population, VSMS scores were correlated with independent rankings of the children's social maturity by supervisors and directors at the institution. The rank-order correlation coefficients reported—not all were reported—were high, .85 to .95. Other studies (summarized in Doll, 1953) involved using the VSMS with various types of handicapped child and in diverse settings. An additional validation study is reported in Walker (1973). Using 165 preschool- and kindergarten-age children, LeVinson (1961) found a correlation of −.03 between VSMS SQs and adjustment ratings of clinicians.

The reliability of the VSMS was reported for the norming sample of 250 subjects examined twice with a time interval between interviews of almost two years (Doll, 1953). The subjects ranged in age from just after birth to twenty-four years. The correlation between SA scores for the two testings was .98; the average SA increment was 1.95 years. The VSMS was used again for almost 80 percent of the original 250 subjects after an additional time lapse of over one year. The correlation between the second and third SA scores was .97; between the first and third, .94. Reliability estimates are not reported separately by age group, and data pertaining to interrater reliability are not provided.

The norming sample consisted of 620 normal subjects, 10 females and 10 males at each age-level (or year-group) from just after birth to thirty years. All subjects lived in Vineland, New Jersey, in 1936, the year of the standardization. A single examiner conducted all the interviews, generally with the subjects' mothers. The resulting data yielded item-age norms—that is, the average age when the behavior detailed in the item could be performed. The data also were used to produce the table for converting total VSMS scores to SA scores (Doll, 1953).

Reviewers of the VSMS and the associated book noted that the scale was actually a clinical interview tool and cautioned that examiners with clinical psychological training were required for accurate administration and interpretation; further, they considered the norming sample inadequate because of its restricted geographical nature and its inclusion of only twenty persons at each age level (Kolstoe, 1954; Krugman, 1956; Shaffer, 1954). Others commented on the limited nature of the validation sample (retarded children) and the resulting lack of data on the last fourth of the test items—those corresponding to average chronological ages of fifteen to adulthood (Cruickshank, 1954; and Pedrini and Pedrini, 1966). Given its emphasis on items measuring age-appropriate behaviors for the very young or preschool child, the VSMS has been considered by some to be more valid and useful for that age group (Krugman, 1956; and Pedrini and Pedrini, 1966).

In the hands of a competent, experienced clinician the VSMS can very likely provide supplemental information for identifying social maturity levels. However, the scale has several shortcomings. First, the interviewing and scoring procedures rely heavily on the subjective impressions of the examiner and wrong conclusions could easily be drawn. Second, the VSMS relies almost exclusively on "reported" behavior, rather than any direct measure or observation of the subject actually performing the behavior. Third, the norms are based on insufficient numbers of children and are outdated and unrepresentative. Fourth, and most important, the validity of the instrument is not firmly established. Although some validity evidence is presented, it is based heavily on descriptive studies of mentally retarded and institutionalized children. The very high correlation between Binet Mental Age and Vineland Social Age for institutionalized children (Doll, 1953) causes one to wonder if separate constructs are being assessed for that group, while the absence of any relationship between clinicians' adjustment ratings and Vineland Social Quotients (LeVinson, 1961) is disquieting. The critical validity information that is lacking is data on the relationships between VSMS scores and other indicators of social maturity and responsibility for both normal and special categories of children.

Two measures closely related to the VSMS deserve mention. The Preschool Attainment Record (PAR), also developed by Doll (1966), utilizes the same type of item and interview procedures as the VSMS. The PAR measures a child's development in three general areas, each composed of two or three categories of behavior: physical area (ambulation and manipulation); social area (rapport, communication, and responsibility); and intellectual area (information, ideation, and creativity). For each of the eight categories, there is one item per six-month age interval, from one half through seven years. The measure is currently available only as a research edition. Norms are not reported in the manual and apparently are not yet available. A few validity and reliability studies were reported by Walker (1973); generally, however, the PAR appears to still be in a development phase.

The second related measure is the Developmental Profile (Alpern and Boll, 1972). Reportedly designed as a replacement for the VSMS (Hunt, 1978a), this measure assesses the developmental levels of children from birth through age twelve in five areas: physical skill, self-help, social competence, academic skills, and communicative ability. Parental interviews are held to obtain scores for the items in each subscale. Hunt (1978a) reviewed the measure and noted that reliability data suggest high test-retest and interrater reliability and that the standardization population reflected important national demographic variables. Some validity data also have been reported, but further work is needed to establish the Developmental Profile as a valid screening measure in the five areas it encompasses.

Illustrative Measures of Attitudes and Preferences

In the past, measures of children's attitudes and preferences have covered a wide range of topics. Currently, much societal interest centers on racial attitudes and sex-role preferences. Our selection of illustrative measures reflects these current concerns.

Attitudes have been studied extensively, and a variety of definitions are available. According to Khan and Weiss, "attitudes are selectively acquired and integrated through learning and experience . . . they are enduring dispositions indicating response consistency . . . positive or negative affect toward a social or psychological object represents the salient characteristic of an attitude" (1973, p. 761). *Attitudes* are thus considered to be learned, emotionally toned predispositions to react in a consistent manner toward objects, people, ideas, or situations. Attitudes are typically inferred from one's behavior, and direct measurement of attitudes is considerably more difficult than measurement of skills or cognitive knowledge. The difficulties involved in affective measurement of young children, cited in the early part of this chapter, clearly apply to the assessment of children's attitudes.

Preferences are closely related to attitudes. A word often used in conjunction with preferences is *interests,* defined as "reflections of attractiveness and aversions in behavior, of feelings of pleasantness and unpleasantness, likes and dislikes" (Remmers, Gage, and Rummel, 1965, p. 308). Attitudes toward a task, object, or situation are considered to underlie interests or preferences (Emmerich, 1968); stated differently, preferences and interests are usually conceived of as being less internalized than attitudes.

Although much has been written about the assessment of students' attitudes toward school, there are few school-related attitude measures for very young children. Only one such measure is listed in Walker (1973), and even that one is not available commercially. Our search failed to locate any widely used measure of attitudes toward school for young children, although it did identify subtests of other measures that relate to school attitudes. The CIRCUS battery, developed recently by Educational Testing Service and discussed in Chapter Five, contains two subtests that deal with children's preferences and attitudes toward school-related activities. Things I Like is a self-report scale that uses pictures to measure children's relative preferences for verbal or nonverbal activities and for individual or group activities; it is available at Level B only (late kindergarten and early first grade). The Activities Inventory, available at both Levels A (preschool and early kindergarten) and B and somewhat different for each, is a rating scale used by teachers to rate children's participation in various types of activities, such as physical, motor, language, music, and art activities. The categories of ratings for each activity include such matters as the frequency with which the child engages in the activity, the level of complexity of the child's activity, the amount of structure preferred by the child, the amount of adult help sought during the activity, and the kind and size of peer group the child prefers when engaging in the activity. Normative data and interpretation aids are included in the user's guides and manuals for these measures, but only limited validity information appears. Another measure, the Primary Academic Sentiment Scale, or PASS (Thompson, 1968, discussed earlier in this chapter in the section on personality measures), contains a subscale on academic sentiment or academic motivation, which also partially relates to attitudes toward school.

The measures now discussed use the self-report technique. The stimuli and response modes vary, but generally involve pictures and oral descriptions presented to the child, who then points to, marks, or verbally indicates his choice. Table 21, presents an overview of the measures included in this section.

It Scale for Children (ITSC). The It Scale for Children (Brown, 1956) is a measure of sex-role preference developed for five- and six-year-olds. *Sex-role preference* refers to the preferential responses of a child to sex-typed objects and activities. The child conveys his own role preference by indicating the activities or objects that "It," a child-figure drawing of indeterminate sex, would prefer. The It-figure was built into the test in an attempt to avoid eliciting either conforming or socially desirable responses from the child. "In using It the assumption is made that the child will project himself or herself into the It-figure on the basis of his or her own sex-role preference, and will attribute to It the child's own role preference. Thus, a girl who basically prefers the masculine role will tend to attribute this role to It, while the girl who prefers the feminine role will project such a preference to It, and the girl who is ambivalent or confused in sex-role preference will tend to give reponses indicating a mixture of both masculine and feminine components" (Brown, 1956, p. 5).

The ITSC is individually administered and untimed, requiring approximately ten minutes per child. No special training for examiners is required. The measure consists of thirty-six three-by-four inch picture cards depicting various activities, figures, and objects commonly associated with masculine or feminine roles. Presentation of the pictures is divided into three sections. First, sixteen

Table 21. Illustrative Measures of Attitudes and Preferences in Early Childhood Education

Title and Date	Age Range	Administration	Scales or Scores	Source
It Scale for Children (1956)	5 and 6 years	Individual; 10 minutes	Sex-Role Preference	Psychological Test Specialists Box 1441 Missoula, Mont. 59801
Preschool Racial Attitude Measure II (PRAM) and Color Meaning Test II (CMT) (1975)	3 to 9 years	Individual; 20 minutes for PRAM; 15 minutes for CMT	PRAM: Racial Attitude Sex-Role Attitude CMT: Color (Black/White) Attitude	J. E. Williams Dept. of Psychology Wake Forest University Winston-Salem, N.C. 27107
Sex Stereotype Measure II (SSM) and Sex Attitude Measure (SAM) (1976)	Preschool to Grade 6	Individual or group; 20 to 30 minutes for SSM; 15 to 25 minutes for SAM	SSM: Female Stereotype Male Stereotype Total Sex-Role Stereotype SAM: Female Positive Male Negative Total Sex Attitude	J. E. Williams

pictures of toys are presented, eight that portray typical male toys (tractor, train, and so on) and eight that depict typical female toys (doll, purse, and the like). The child is asked to make eight choices for It—that is, to choose the toys that It would like best. Second, a series of eight paired pictures is presented, such as an Indian princess and an Indian chief; men's shoes and women's shoes; building tools and baking articles; and so forth. As each pair is shown, the child chooses the one picture that represents what It would rather be, do, play with, or work with. Finally, pictures of four children—a girl, a boy, a girlish boy (that is, a boy dressed as a girl), and a boyish girl (a girl dressed as a boy)—are displayed. The child chooses the one that It would rather be. In all three sections of the ITSC, the male and female items are alternated during presentation.

Each section is scored separately before the total score is calculated. The score for the first section, the toy pictures, is determined by awarding one point for each male toy chosen and zero for each female toy chosen; the maximum score possible, therefore, is a score of 8. For the second section (the paired pictures), 8 points are given each time the child chooses the male activity, object, or figure; thus, 64 points could be scored in all. For the third section, the child receives 12 points for choosing the boy, 8 points for choosing the girlish boy, 4 points for the boyish girl, and 0 points for the girl. The total ITSC score, the sum of the three section scores, can range from 0 to 84. Higher scores indicate greater male preference, while lower scores reflect greater female preference. A score in the mid-range (around 42) represents an intermediate preference between feminine and masculine roles.

Content validity of the ITSC was claimed on the basis of item selection. Brown (1956) noted that items selected were based on the contrasting behavior patterns identified with the male and female social roles in this society.

> Thus, the kinds of objects and activities typical for boys in contrast to girls and vice versa, along with the more obvious differences between adult masculine and feminine roles to which the child is continually exposed—these considerations formed the basis for the content of the ITSC. In our culture, for example, boys normally play with trucks and trains, wear shirts and trousers, and grow up to use shaving articles; whereas girls typically play with dolls and dishes, wear dresses, and grow up to use cosmetics. Preferences for such male or female items are assumed to be indicative of preference for aspects of the masculine or feminine roles. Similarly, a boy who expresses a desire to be a girl, or a girl to be a boy, indicates a corresponding opposite sex-role preference. These examples illustrate what may be termed the operational validity of the ITSC [Brown, 1956, pp. 4–5].

The ITSC was piloted with seventy-eight male and sixty-eight female kindergarten children (median age of five years, ten months), primarily from middle-class homes, who were enrolled in a Denver public elementary school in the 1950s. Data from these children are presented in the manual as validity evidence. Briefly, the findings were:

1. Large, significant differences between boys' and girls' total scores.
2. Significantly greater male preference among boys than female preference among girls.
3. Greater prestige and value attributed to the male toys and activities than to the female ones, as evidenced by the fact that girls were more prone to choose the male items than boys were to choose the female items.
4. No significant differences in scores among children when grouped into upper-middle, middle, and lower-middle class groupings.

Further, when the children were asked to give It a name at the conclusion of the testing, 85 percent of the boys, but only 45 percent of the girls, gave a name consistent with their own sex.

Other investigations of the ITSC have shown the male sex-role preference among boys to be more rigid than the female preference among girls (Hall and Keith, 1964), and the sex-role preferences of second-born preschoolers to be influenced by the sex of older siblings (Bigner, 1972). Several researchers have questioned the claimed neuter status of It, and findings from a variety of studies tend to suggest that It can easily be viewed as masculine rather than neuter by both boys and girls (Brown, 1962; Hartup and Zook, 1960; Lefkowitz, 1962; and Schell and Silber, 1968). In two studies of racial differences (Summers and Felker, 1970; Thompson and McCandless, 1970), ITSC scores of white preschoolers were found to be different from those of black preschoolers, with white girls more likely to attribute male characteristics to It than black girls. When ITSC scores were correlated with two teacher rating scales, the hypothesis that development of sex-role preference precedes the development of sex-role adoption was supported (Thompson and McCandless, 1970).

The manual includes coefficients of stability as evidence of ITSC reliability. Based on a one-month interval, coefficients of .69 for the boys and .82 for the girls were obtained. Varying the standard procedures by ascribing to It the sex or name of the child taking the test produced slightly higher coefficients for three- and four-year-olds (Hartup and Zook, 1960).

Although the data from the normative sample are well described in the manual in terms of summary statistics, no conversion tables are included. This weakens the interpretability of ITSC scores. Even if such tables were available, however, the circumscribed nature of the sample and, especially, its dated quality, render it atypical for most present-day uses.

The validity of the ITSC has not been clearly established, despite its use in a variety of studies. The assumption that the child really identifies with, and projects himself into, It is suspect; as several of the studies cited above suggested, It is more likely to be seen as boy-like than as of indeterminate sex. A second feature not yet validated pertains to the masculine-feminine continuum represented by the test stimuli; Harriman (1965) noted the subtle, elusive nature of sex roles and the lack of substantiating data for the validity of the sex-role distinctions upon which the measure is based. Considering society's de-emphasis of many sex-role distinctions during the last ten years, especially in regard to children and their play and school activities, this lack of validation is quite serious.

Although the ITSC represents an interesting, simple approach to the measurement of sex-role preference, it is clearly in need of updating and additional validation, and should be considered a research edition until that is accomplished. Also, it could serve as a useful prototype for guiding others in the development of this general type of measure.

Preschool Racial Attitude Measure II (PRAM) and Color Meaning Test II (CMT). The Preschool Racial Attitude Measure and the Color Meaning Test were originally developed in 1967 (Williams and Roberson, 1967); the revised versions (PRAM II and CMT II) became available eight years later (Williams, Best, and Associates, 1975). PRAM was designed to measure the attitudes of the preschool child toward Euro-American (white) and Afro-American (black) persons, as well as the child's awareness of sex-typed behaviors. CMT was developed to assess the child's attitudes toward the colors black and white. Although PRAM II and CMT II are distinct tests and can be used separately, the CMT was developed as a companion to the PRAM and the two tests share many features and some materials. Many users will probably want to consider them as a package to be used conjointly.

Both PRAM II and CMT II are picture-story techniques. Children's attitudes are measured according to their responses (choices of pictures) to simple evaluative adjectives contained in short stories told to them by the examiner. Children who consistently select one type of picture in response to adjectives with positive evaluative connotations, and the other type of picture when responding to negative adjectives, are said to hold a positive attitude toward the former and a negative attitude toward the latter. Both PRAM II and CMT II are individually administered (in about twenty and fifteen minutes, respectively) to children ages three to nine. A teacher or other examiner can administer the test without any special training.

The PRAM II test materials consist of thirty-six eight-by-ten inch colored photographs and accompanying stories. Twenty-four of the pictures and stories are used to measure racial attitudes, while the remaining twelve are for sex-role assessment. Each of the twenty-four racial-attitude photographs shows two human figures who are identical in all respects (sex, age, position, hair color, and so on) except skin color. Similarly, the twelve sex-role photographs each show a male and female figure, identical in race, age, and pose; six of the photographs show a white male and female and six show a black male and female. Every third photograph in the total set of thirty-six is a sex-role photograph.

The CMT II test materials include twelve eight-by-ten inch colored photographs and twenty-four stories. Two animals (horses, dogs, cows, sheep, and so on), identical in all respects except body color, are depicted in each photograph. Each picture is used twice; that is, it is used as the stimulus for two of the stories.

The twenty-four racial-attitude PRAM II stories and the CMT II stories are similar. Each story contains three to five short sentences, describing a person or animal in terms of a positive or negative evaluative adjective and illustrating how the person or animal acts to exemplify the adjective. The twenty-four positive and negative evaluative adjectives, used in both PRAM II and CMT II, are:

Positive Evaluative Adjectives	*Negative Evaluative Adjectives*
clean	dirty
good	bad
kind	mean
nice	naughty
pretty	ugly
smart	stupid
friendly	cruel
happy	sad
healthy	sick
helpful	selfish
right	wrong
wonderful	unfriendly

To administer the PRAM II or CMT II, the examiner shows the child a photograph while reading the associated story aloud. The child is then asked to choose the one figure in the photograph that fits the description in the story, and the examiner records the child's choice. An alternate way of administering the tests is to use a "teaching machine" (Behavioral Control Institute, Model SR 400), in which smaller (five by seven inches) photographs are presented along with the tape-recorded stories. The child chooses a figure for each story by pressing a button under the selected figure. Responses are recorded and scores produced by the machine.

The PRAM II racial-attitude items and the CMT II items are scored by awarding one point for the selection of the white figure in response to stories with positive adjectives, and one point for the selection of the black figure in reponse to stories with negative adjectives. The racial attitude total score for the PRAM II and the total CMT II score have a range of 0 to 24, broken down into five score ranges; high scores (17 to 24) indicate a pro-Euro/anti-Afro bias, middle scores (10 to 14) indicate no bias, and low scores (0 to 7) indicate a pro-Afro/anti-Euro bias. Scores of 15 or 16 and of 8 or 9 are considered evidence of probable pro-Euro/anti-Afro bias and probable pro-Afro/anti-Euro bias, respectively. The twelve sex-role items on the PRAM II are scored by giving one point for each conventional sex-appropriate response. Total sex-role scores thus range from 0 to 12, with high scores indicating high sex-role awareness and middle scores (around 6) indicating no sex-role awareness. Scoring of both the PRAM II and the CMT II is facilitated by record and scoring sheets, which include keys for assignment of points to item responses.

A list of thirty-three studies employing PRAM I and II and CMT I and II procedures is included in the recent test manuals. In two studies (O'Reilly, 1971; and Williams and Roberson, 1967), the relationships between PRAM racial attitude scores and race of children were studied; findings indicated that white children demonstrated greater pro-Euro/anti-Afro bias than black children. Race of examiner was shown to influence children's PRAM II racial attitude scores (Williams and others, 1975; Williams, Best, and Boswell, 1975); both black and white children obtained higher scores (indicative of pro-Euro/anti-Afro bias) when tested by white examiners. In another study (Best, 1972), however, no evidence of effects due to race of examiner were found when sixty white preschool children were administered the test by both white and black examiners. No relationships between PRAM racial attitude scores and sex, age, or IQ of the children tested have been found. In the CMT II standardization study, CMT II scores correlated .14 with chronological age and .27 with Peabody Picture Vocabulary Test scores for black and white children combined (Williams, Best, and Associates, 1975).

Other studies with the PRAM procedures have shown that laboratory training procedures can modify preschoolers' expressed racial attitudes (Edwards and Williams, 1970; McMurtry and Williams, 1972; and Williams and Edwards, 1969). White preschool children were found to demonstrate less of a pro-Euro/anti-Afro bias on the PRAM following attempted modification of their evaluations of the colors black and white (via training using reinforcement principles). The CMT II has not been studied as extensively as the racial-attitude portion of the PRAM II, although it was employed in some of the modification studies. CMT II scores were found to correlate moderately (about .40) with PRAM II racial attitude scores and with a measure of fear of darkness (Boswell and Williams, 1975).

In regard to the sex-role portion of PRAM II, the manual indicated that "the sex role score has been shown to be a useful measure of general conceptual development, correlating positively with both age and IQ among preschool children" (Williams, Best, and Associates, 1975, p. 14). No further information on the source for these statements, or other validation information, is given.

Reliability data for the sex-role portion of the PRAM II are not reported, but data are given in the manual for the racial-attitude portion of the PRAM II and for the CMT II. Split-half internal consistency reliability coefficients were calculated for the PRAM II racial-attitude items, based on responses of nearly 400 children. Correlations were calculated separately for black and white children as well as combined, and according to several different ways of splitting the test in half. Coefficients were substantial, ranging from .53 to .76 and with a median at .68. The various ways of splitting the test did not show significant fluctuations in coefficients, nor were there large differences according to race of the children. Internal consistency of the CMT II was calculated in similar ways, using the 320 subjects from its standardization sample. A coefficient of .63 (for the total sample, presumably) was found, regardless of the type of split used.

A coefficient of stability is also reported for the PRAM II racial attitude scores. Fifty-seven children (about half of them black and half of them white), with an average age of about fifty-seven months, were tested twice with an interval of twelve months. The correlation between the two sets of total scores was .55. The coefficient of stability and equivalence, based on the correlation between different half-scores over the twelve-month interval, was .28.

The standardization sample for PRAM II consisted of 272 children located in Winston-Salem, North Carolina, in 1970–72. The children ranged in age from thirty-seven to eighty-five months; the average age was sixty-five months. Approximately equal numbers of white female, white male, black female, and black male children were tested. The race of the examiners was balanced by having half the children in each race-sex group tested by white female examiners and half tested by black female examiners. The frequency distributions and mean PRAM II racial attitude scores for children in each group, as well as the percentage of children in each of five score ranges, are given in the manual. No such data are given for the sex-role scores.

Similar procedures were used for the CMT II. In 1972–73, 320 North Carolina children, ranging in age from forty to ninety-one months (average age was sixty-one months) were tested. No children scored in the 0 to 6 range, the range indicative of pro-Afro/anti-Euro bias.

The norms for both PRAM II and CMT II are representative of only one geographic locale and, in this sense, are restrictive. Further, the way in which the normative data are presented in the manual is cumbersome for use in interpretation of scores. Percentile ranks could be calculated from the data, but are not presented directly.

The PRAM II and CMT II could be useful in research studies, but their utility for other purposes is limited by the lack of strong validity data. The correspondence between racial attitude scores on these measures and other indexes of racial attitudes or behaviors has yet to be documented.

Sex Stereotype Measure II (SSM) and Sex Attitude Measure (SAM). The Sex Stereotype Measure II (SSM), a revision of an earlier measure, was developed "to assess children's knowledge of adult-defined, conventional sex-trait stereotypes"; the Sex Attitude Measure (SAM) was developed "to assess children's attitudes or evaluative bias toward male and female persons, independent of their stereotype knowledge" (Williams, Best, and Associates, 1976, p. 1). The measures were developed by the same persons who developed PRAM II and CMT II, and all four measures have common features.

Both SSM II and SAM consist of pictures and associated stories. The thirty-two SSM II stories represent adult-defined traits descriptive of male and female stereotypes (Williams and Bennett, 1975). The twenty-four SAM stories contain the positive and negative evaluative adjectives used in both PRAM II and CMT II. The use of third-person singular pronouns is avoided in all stories. The stimulus figures are identical for the SSM II and SAM: pairs of human figure silhouettes, one male and one female.

Each measure can be individually or group-administered; the former is recommended for young children and the latter for children who possess adequate reading skills. The SSM II and SAM require approximately twenty and fifteen minutes for individual administration, respectively; group administration requires slightly more time. SAM is ordinarily administered after SSM II. It is recommended that both female and male examiners be used—randomly assigned to children if the measures are individually administered, and as a team if group-administered. No special training is required for the examiners.

The thirty-two SSM II stories are short (two or three sentences) and begin with "One of these people. . . ." The descriptions that follow are behavioral or personological descriptors, such as talkative, ambitious, gentle, and stern. Half of the stories contain descriptors stereotypic of females, while the other half are stereotypic of males. The adjectives used in the original SSM I were selected from the Adjective Check List or ACL (Gough and Heilbrun, 1965) on the basis of data from white college students who judged the ACL items as being more representative of either males or females (Williams and Bennett, 1975). The revision of SSM I to product SSM II involved lengthening the test by adding more items identified by another group of college students as being male- or female-stereotypic (Williams and Best, 1977).

After the child is read the stimulus sentences for each item (or reads them himself, if the test is group-administered), he chooses either the male or female figure as the person whom he thinks would demonstrate the behavior or trait described. Scoring yields three summary scores: a Female Stereotypic score, a Male Stereotypic score, and a Total Sex-Role Stereotype score. The Female Stereotypic score is computed by tabulating the number of times the child chooses the female figure in response to stories containing conventional female stereotype activities or traits; the Male Stereotypic score is computed by tabulating the number of times the child chooses the male figure for male-stereotype stories. Each score can range from 0 to 16. The Total Stereotype score is the sum of the Female and Male Stereotype scores and can range from 0 to 32. High scores (19 to 32) indicate consistent knowledge of conventional sex-trait stereotypes, and low scores (0 to 13) indicate reversal of conventional sex stereotypes. Scores in the 14 to 18 range are considered indicative of no consistent knowledge of sex stereotypes.

The SAM test materials consist of twenty-four of the pictures used in SSM II, and accompanying short stories. The stories are identical to those used in the racial-attitude portion of PRAM II, with minor changes to accommodate the change in stimulus figures from two of the same sex to two of different sex. The child chooses either the male or female figure in response to each story. Each item is scored 0 or 1, with 1 awarded if the child chooses the female figure in response to a positive adjective or the male figure in response to a negative adjective. Total Female Positive and Male Negative scores can be found by totaling the item scores for the positive and negative adjectives separately. The Total Sex Attitude score is the sum of all item scores, with the maximum possible being

24. The guide for interpretation of the individual child's score, as presented in the manual, is similar to that for PRAM II:

Score Range	Interpretation
17–24	definite pro-female/anti-male bias
15–16	probable pro-female/anti-male bias
10–14	no bias
8–9	probable pro-male/anti-female bias
0–7	definite pro-male/anti-female bias

The validity and reliability of the SSM II and the SAM are not addressed explicitly in the manual, although data from the standardization sample are presented. For the SSM II, these data show total SSM II scores increasing as age increases, and Male Stereotypic SSM II scores higher than Female Stereotypic scores at all ages tested. Analysis of SAM standardization data yielded no systematic score increases according to age. No significant differences according to the sex of the examiner were found for either measure, although such an effect had been found with fourth-grade children in an earlier study using the SSM I (Williams, Bennett, and Best, 1975).

A separate technical report gives additional information about the SSM II (Williams, Best, and Davis, 1977). In one investigation summarized in the technical report, the relationships between SSM II scores and scores on the California Test of Mental Maturity and the Metropolitan Math and Language Achievement Tests were examined. Ninety-six black and white children were administered the IQ and achievement tests in the second grade and the SSM II in the third grade. The highest correlation (.34) was between SSM II and the IQ scores for the total sample. The correlation for black children was only .19, while that for white children was .31. Achievement correlated .14 with SSM II for each racial group, and .20 for the total sample. Other studies summarized were ones in which the effects of variant procedures (such as repeating each story using both male and female third-person singular pronouns versus using the standard third-person plural pronouns) on SSM II scores were measured. No major differences were found under several such variant procedures. Still other studies, cross-sectional rather than longitudinal, reaffirmed the developmental nature of sex-stereotype knowledge, although some differences in developmental trends were shown for black and white adolescents. Finally, the scores of two groups of black third-graders were compared to determine the effects of the two types of picture stimulus on black children's scores. One group was given the standard pictures and told they were pictures of white persons; another group saw the same silhouettes with Afro hair styles added and was told they were pictures of black persons. No significant differences between the scores of the two groups were found. When these data were combined and compared with scores of white third-graders, however, the white children were seen to have significantly higher total stereotype scores.

The SSM II has also been used in cross-cultural studies of children's knowledge of sex stereotypes. The nature of the sex stereotypes learned by children in the United States, England, and Ireland has been shown to be similar, although the rate of learning was somewhat slower among the children in Ireland (Best and others, 1977).

Both the SSM II and the SAM were standardized on a sample of 196 white children enrolled in preschool/kindergarten and elementary schools in Winston-Salem, North Carolina in 1975–76. The average age of the sixty preschoolers was four years, eleven months. The elementary group consisted of eighty-eight third-graders and forty-eight sixth-graders. Half of the children in each age group were male and half were female. Examiners of both sexes were used to test the children. Tables in the manual include average subscale and total scores, broken down by children's age and sex of examiner. Transformed scores, such as percentile rank, are not given.

While the SSM II and SAM are interesting, appealing measures and relatively easy to administer and score, work remains to be done to produce more representative norms that include children of different races. The reliability of both remains uninvestigated, as does the validity of the SAM. The data available for the SSM II serve primarily to confirm an age-related trend in children's knowledge of typical sex-role attributes and behaviors. Further research is needed to determine the relationships of SSM II and SAM scores with other measures of children's attitudes and behaviors related to sex roles and to determine the differences in sex-role knowledge and attitudes among children of various races.

The SSM II and SAM appear to be developed largely for research purposes, especially cross-cultural research. When additional empirical evidence become available, they may also prove useful for other purposes.

Chapter 8

=====

Psychomotor
Measures

Much of what goes on in the world of the young child involves movement. This is true for the newborn child (see Lipsitt, 1971) and becomes increasingly obvious as the child advances in age.

> With the start of walking, the world of the child expands rapidly. Quite literally, he goes anywhere and everywhere paths are open to him. Since he has increasing amounts of energy available as he grows older and much of this energy is directed into gross motor activity, he needs a safe and, if possible, spacious place to play. In the years from two to six, all of the usual locomotor patterns are perfected and a variety of eye-hand coordinations are learned. The latter are more dependent upon opportunity than the former and are almost certainly more influenced by instruction and encouragement. The child will talk and run, for example, push furniture about and climb onto it in the ordinary course of development. He does not learn to catch or bounce balls nor to strike or bat them without help [Espenschade and Eckert, 1967, p. 105].

A child's everyday activities frequently are based on, or even dominated by, movement (Ellis, 1973; Herron and Sutton-Smith, 1971). Further, the changes in motor response and skill in basic motor control between the ages of two and eight are phenomenal. Individual differences between children on motor performance are pronounced. Thus, it is appropriate that we examine psychomotor measures.

The psychomotor domain represents the third and last principal area into which we have classified early childhood education measures. Since a variety of meanings have been attached to words commonly used in discussing the domain, depending on people's orientation and training, we begin by defining *psychomotor*. The definitions by Singer and by Krathwohl are relevant to our concerns here.

> Activities that are primarily movement-oriented and that emphasize overt physical responses bear the label *psychomotor*. The psychomotor domain is concerned with bodily movement and/or control. Such behaviors when performed in a general way represent a movement pattern or patterns, and when highly specific and task-refined indicate a skill or sequence of skills. They include the following kinds of behaviors, all of which could be interrelated or any of which could be independent.
> - Contacting, manipulating, and/or moving an object.
> - Controlling the body of objects, as in balancing.
> - Moving and/or controlling the body or parts of the body in space with timing in a brief or long *act* or *sequence* under predictable and/or unpredictable situations [Singer, 1975, p. 23].

Krathwohl, Bloom, and Masia (1964), while principally engaged in detailing an affective domain taxonomy (see Chapter Seven), noted that the psychomotor domain was concerned primarily with some muscular or motor skills, some manipulation of objects, or some act requiring neuromuscular coordination. However, if one considers neuromuscular coordination as the link between nerve impulse and muscle operation, then such coordination need not be regarded separately since both motor and manipulative skills require it.

Several taxonomies for the psychomotor domain have been proposed. Four different but overlapping schemes described in Singer (1972a) included classifying (1) by complexity from simple perception to automatic performance, (2) by task based on the results of an empirically derived performance assessment, (3) by process based on information, and (4) by the type of performance that is required of the subject. Somewhat better known is the taxonomy suggested by Harrow (1972). Defining *psychomotor behavior* as observable voluntary human motion, she sketched a six-level taxonomy. Level 1, *reflex movements,* involves actions elicited without conscious volition, such as stretching, flexing, and making postural adjustments. (The inclusion of this level does not match the "voluntary" aspect of the psychomotor definition; possibly Harrow included reflex movements principally to lay a foundation for Level 2 behaviors.) Level 2, *basic fundamental movements,* consists of combinations of reflex movements that represent more complex skilled movements, either locomotor (such as walking or climbing), nonlocomotor (pushing or swaying), or manipulative (handling or grasping). Level 3, *perceptual abilities,* involves making discriminations that are kinesthetic (maintaining balance during a handstand), visual (tracking a moving object), auditory (identifying sounds of musical instruments), tactile (differentiating coins solely by touch), or coordinated across several senses (catching a ball). Of course, voluntary human motion seemingly would always require a perceptual base—that is, sensory input. Level 4 of the taxonomy, *physical abilities,* includes endurance (distance running and swimming), strength (lifting), flexibility (touching one's toes), and agility (dodging and tumbling). Level 5, *skilled movements,* represents an elaboration of Level 2 (illustrative behaviors are dancing, painting, and handwriting). Level 6, *nondiscursive communication,* is made up of expressive movement (gestures and facial expressions designed to communicate) and interpretive movement (rhythmic movements created by the child).

Although the measures in this chapter can all be classified somewhere in the psychomotor domain, remember that extensive overlap and interplay exist between the cognitive, affective, and psychomotor domains. A familiar example is represented by the sportscaster's lengthy analysis of the psychological states of competing athletes or teams. The perfecting of many psychomotor skills requires extensive practice—not likely to occur without strong motivation, which is both affective and cognitive in nature. The close relationship between psychomotor and cognitive behavior has been discussed extensively by Cratty (1969, 1971a, 1973a), Gallahue (1976), and Singer (1968, 1972a,b). Several of the illustrations involve young children. For instance, Cratty (1971a, 1973a) described a number of active games designed to improve children's memorization, categorization, communication, problem solving, and evaluation.

The interrelationship of the three domains can also be observed at a more theoretical level. Many theorists have remarked on the inextricability of the domains in the behavior of very young children. Best known is Piaget, who identified the sensorimotor stage, the first two years of life during which action and "thought" and motive intertwine. In a more general theoretical orientation, the information processing interpretation of skill acquisition (Fitts, 1964, 1965; Posner and Keele, 1973), three phases of skill learning are proposed. In the first (cognitive) phase, the student conceptualizes the skill to be performed. In the second (organizing) phase, the skill is actually practiced. In the third (perfecting) phase, the skill is gradually improved over time. (The second and third phases are closer to the usual conceptions of psychomotor skill acquisition.) A good way to visualize these three phases in the motor learning of young children is by considering the process of learning to ride a bicycle.

Another theoretical formulation of the interaction of domains is Cratty's (1971b, 1973b) model of the multiple variables that influence a single motor performance act. He classified such variables at three levels. At the first, basic behavioral supports, he included aspiration level, general arousal level, muscular tension, and ability to analyze tasks. At the second level, ability traits and personal tendencies, Cratty grouped relevant perceptual abilities, strength, reaction time, movement speed, flexibility, and manual abilities. Variables unique to the performance act constituted the third level, such as prior practice on similar tasks, motivation specific to the task, emotional climate, instructions, and number of spectators. For early childhood education, "number of spectators" obviously would seldom apply, unless we witness counterparts of Little League Baseball and Pee-Wee Football springing up in preschool! More appropriately, this concept might be thought of as reactions by parents, teachers, and peers to the young child's attempts to acquire motor skills. Cratty pointed out that educators could change third-level variables more easily than those at the initial two levels. Germane to the discussion here is the pronounced mix of cognitive, affective, and psychomotor variables incorporated in Cratty's model.

In this chapter, we have excluded large blocks of psychomotor tests. As before, we generally have not included tests that are principally used in clinical settings, preferring instead measures more directly pertinent to educational activities. Another category also excluded for the most part involves tests that deal with just visual perception, or just auditory discrimination, or the like. This decision was reached because of the large number of such instruments and because some of the comprehensive tests presented later include perceptual subtests in them (as did some of the developmental screening tests reviewed in Chapter Six). An exception was made, though, in the case of the Marianne Frostig Developmental Test of Visual Perception, which warranted inclusion because of its wide use and its group administration feature.

Nature and Status of Psychomotor Measures

In terms of education-related measures, the psychomotor domain seems like the poor stepsister compared to the other domains (especially the cognitive). Relatively few psychomotor measures exist that bear directly on educational matters. The reasons for this situation are not clear. One possible reason might be that psychologists simply have been more interested in developing cognitive and affective measures. A second possible explanation is that there is less public demand for reports on how well school children are developing and performing in psychomotor areas than there is for comparable reports on cognitive performance, such as reading, arithmetic, and language skills. At the same time, most communities are known for their avid support of school athletic teams and their singular attention to the win-loss record of each team—a vivid measure, indeed! Yet this focus overlooks the great majority of school children and circumvents a balanced approach to psychomotor measurement.

The foregoing is not meant to imply that elementary schools have failed to develop and implement substantial physical activity programs. It appears that considerable progress has been made in this regard. Still, extensive measurement of psychomotor performance, for either the planning of future physical activities or reporting pupil progress, is not a salient characteristic of such programs. Possibly it is not clear what aspects of motor performance need to be measured for future program planning and comprehensive reporting. At the preschool level, physical activity curriculums have appeared with increased frequency of late, but the use of measurement for planning and reporting functions has not been addressed directly, for the most part.

The relative lack of psychomotor measures in education is reflected in a recent survey of the frequency of use and the quality of measures used in federally sponsored research on children and adolescents (Heyneman and Mintz, 1977). Over 3,500 research proposals involving young persons that were funded by federal sources in fiscal year 1975 were examined to determine what measures were used and how often. Cognitive measures, primarily intelligence, achievement, and reading tests, accounted for over 70 percent of all instruments used. Affective measures, especially character and personality tests, registered above 20 percent. Depending on one's definition of *psychomotor,* the proportion of psychomotor measures used was somewhere above 3 percent but less than 6 percent. As we have defined the psychomotor domain here, the lower estimate is probably realistic. (Incidentally, Heyneman and Mintz used the Center for the Study of Evaluation's ratings of measurement validity and normed technical excellence as indexes of psychometric quality [see the source book section following Chapter Twelve for a more complete discussion of the Center's procedures]. Generally, they found positive and statistically significant relationships between frequency of use and quality rating, especially for achievement tests. However, such relationships were not in evidence for reading and personality measures.)

Although the study cited involved only federally supported research and included young persons of all ages, its finding of less frequent psychomotor test usage probably applies also to early childhood education settings. Some qualification is necessary, however. Instruments that assess psychomotor development are more likely to be used in early childhood education settings than in schools for older children. Some early childhood educators even put primary emphasis on psychomotor objectives. Still, this orientation has not been accompanied by an extensive test development effort. For the most part, existing measures survey psychomotor development in general and are not specific to psychomotor activities or curriculums that one might find in early education settings. As more books appear that focus on movement education for preschoolers (such as Cratty, 1973a; Flinchum, 1975; Sinclair, 1973), possibly more attention will be given to specific measures.

It is of some significance to the status of psychomotor measures in early childhood education that the compensatory education movement, as it hit its stride in the decade following 1965, did not place great emphasis on psychomotor behaviors and outcomes. True, some attention was given to the perceptual abilities, fine motor skills, and physical characteristics of children from poor families. However, any such attention was overshadowed by the attention given to the children's present or future cognitive performance in school (and their health, particularly in Head Start). Attitudes, self-concept, motivation, and other affective outcomes were also frequently targeted as highly relevant objectives for compensatory programs. The low profile of psychomotor objectives in such programs was possibly less of an oversight than it was a reflection of the reality that the majority of children from impoverished homes exhibited satisfactory physical development and psychomotor performance. The compensatory education movement served to stimulate new test development and revisions of existing measures, but this activity was most pronounced for cognitive measures and least apparent in the psychomotor domain. With the increasing federal and state legislation aimed at the handicapped child in the mid 1970s, it is possible that more instruments assessing psychomotor performance will appear.

It is also of substantial interest that Mediax Associates, Inc., currently assisting the federal Administration for Children, Youth, and Families in their effort to locate or develop a new collection of measures to evaluate the effects of Head Start nationally, has placed great emphasis on the domain of Health and Physical Development (Taub and others, 1979). The domain is conceptualized as consisting of five closely interrelated domains—medical, dental, nutritional, gross motor development, and fine motor development. The decision to highlight this domain was due to its importance in the *Head Start Program Performance Standards* (Administration for Children, Youth, and Families, 1975) and to the great frequency with which parents, teachers, and scholars identified desirable attainments for young children that related to health and physical development.

Categorization of Psychomotor Measures

Somewhat distinct from the earlier-described taxonomic attempts to order motor behaviors are several common approaches used in categorizing psychomotor measures. Three such schemes are addressed here: (1) listings of numerous motor activities or tasks, (2) schemes centering on the distinction between fine motor and gross motor skills, and (3) at an even more general level, types of typical performance measure.

Lists of Motor Activities or Tasks. This first approach is characterized by lists of motor behaviors and, usually, some indication of the age at which such behaviors normally appear. The work of Espenschade and Eckert (1967) provides one such listing, all the way from infancy to old age. A related work, specific to ages two to six years, has been published by Sinclair (1973). She selected twenty-five movement tasks that she considered fundamental to the complex motor activities of play, work, and the movement arts. She believed that the tasks represented a good movement curriculum for young children. Only commonly available materials and equipment were required. The tasks were discussed in detail in terms of their elements, how to judge success, and at what ages (between two and six) success and also a "basic pattern" might be expected. The tasks used were ascending stairs, bouncing on a board, bouncing a large ball, carrying, catching, climbing a ladder, creeping, descending stairs, figure-8-run, forward roll, galloping, hanging, hitting, hopping, kicking, pulling, pushing, running, running high jumps, skipping, sliding, standing broad jump, throwing a small ball, walking, and walking a beam.

To better understand this approach, consider the elaboration of the skipping movement task. Prescribed elements include: alternates feet evenly, uses arms for balance, uses limbs in opposition, makes contact on balls of feet, moves in direct path, displays uneven but steady rhythm (short-long), uses symmetrical skip (alike on both sides), and can skip over the prescribed distance of twenty to thirty feet. Success or achievement is judged when the above elements are displayed for four or more successive skips, usually by age four and a half. The basic pattern is achieved when the child uses a steady, rhythmic skip for twenty feet, a skill normally demonstrated by age six.

In this connection, it is fitting to note that discrepancies are frequently found in the age norms for many motor tasks. As one compares ages on lists such as those described above with ages set on measures like the Denver Developmental Screening Test, the Learning Accomplishment Profile, and similar instruments (Chapter Six), considerable variability in expected performance age can be noted for the same task. There are several possible reasons for such discrepancies. First, the tasks may not be identical, even though they sound the same. One or another might require or permit some variation that makes the task easier or more difficult. There also might be minor differences in the materials used. Second, the standards of judging a performance as satisfactory might vary with the specific instruments or with the specific examiners involved. Third, the normative samples could be considerably different. Samples too frequently represent just a single geographic locale. There also might be a considerable time period—many years—between the dates when the sampling data for various lists and measures are collected.

Gross and Fine Motor Categorizations. A second common means of categorizing psychomotor behaviors, and therefore their associated measures, is by differentiating them as either gross motor or fine motor. Such category systems imply that psychomotor skills can be neatly divided into those involving large muscle groups (*gross*) or those employing smaller muscles (*fine* or *manipulative*). Cratty (1973b) rightly observed that such a distinction was misleadingly simple, and suggested the addition of an intermediate point. Thus, *gross* might be used for movements in which the total body changed position in space, *intermediate* for movements involving the limbs, and *fine* only for small movements such as those made by the hands or fingers. Cratty noted that skills might be placed along a gross-fine continuum. However, he expressed concern that such classification would still be oversimplified. For example, even skills normally classified as gross, such as balancing, also involve rather fine adjustments of muscles in the feet and ankles. Or, conversely, an individual performing a fine motor task for an extended time period, such as writing or painting, often complains of backache or similar discomfort. Experiments have shown that considerable activity takes place in the larger muscle groups during such "fine motor" activities. From the sports world, Cratty observed that a basketball player executing a jump shot had to jump high (gross) but release the ball with a "light touch" (fine).

Nevertheless, for many purposes—including measurement—the gross-fine motor distinction is useful. For example, in writing on the measurement of learning in preschool education, Kamii (1971) divided objectives in the perceptual-motor area into those involving either gross or fine motor coordination. She proceeded to detail procedures and criteria that could be used to measure and evaluate gross motor objectives such as walking and jumping and fine motor objectives such as cutting with scissors and drawing a line between two narrowly spaced parallel lines. The procedural technique that she illustrated could be applied to many other motor objectives, and the gross-fine motor distinction provides a convenient organizational framework. Some actual procedures for measuring gross and fine motor capabilities are now presented.

Gross motor skills: A typical gross motor scale was developed by Cratty (1969) and also was reported in Cratty and Martin (1969). It has been used by Cratty with normal (ages four to eleven), neurologically handicapped, and retarded children. Six tests are included: (1) body perception, (2) gross agility, (3) balance, (4) locomotor agility, (5) ball throwing, and (6) ball tracking.

In the body perception test, the child must follow ten sets of directions. On four of these, the examiner demonstrates varying reclined positions, which the child then imitates. The other six items concern discriminating left-right and identifying body parts (for example, "Touch your left elbow with your right"). One point is given for each of the ten tasks performed correctly.

The gross agility test measures how accurately and quickly the child can move his total body in two tasks. On the first, the child lies on his back. Then the examiner asks him to "see how fast you can stand up and face me." The child earns up to five points, depending on his quickness and directness of movement. The second task requires the child to kneel on one knee at a time and then to stand on one leg at a time. Up to five points can be scored on the untimed task depending on how accurately and steadily the movement is completed. Using the hands for balance lowers the score earned.

The balance test measures the child's ability to maintain a steady, upright position in space while the availability of visual cues and his use of arms are varied. A ten point maximum is set. The first four points are earned according to how.long the child can balance on one foot (such as one point for one second, or four points for over six seconds). Then the examiner makes the task more difficult by requiring the child either to fold his arms across his chest, to close his eyes, to shift to his nonpreferred foot, or to perform some combination thereof. The more difficult positions must be held for over five seconds.

The fourth gross motor test, locomotor agility, differs from the gross agility test in that the child must move his whole body over some distance. Again, the maximum score is ten points. The child must crawl, walk, jump forward, jump backward, or hop to earn the initial five points. A four-by-six foot mat is then marked with two rows of six one-foot squares, forming a six-by-two rectangle of twelve squares. To earn additional points, the child is required to jump (and later hop) so as to land only on certain squares, much as in hopscotch.

The ball throwing test measures the child's ability to effectively and accurately throw an eight-inch rubber ball. The first five points are awarded on the basis of throwing form—that is, how well the child imitates the examiner's one-handed overhand throwing movement. Only one point is given if the child simply pushes the ball with his hands or feet, while five points result if the child throws one-handed overhand with a weight shift forward of the body and with a simultaneous step of the opposite foot. Intermediate points are awarded similarly. Throwing accuracy forms the basis for earning the second five points. A target two feet square is sketched on a four-by-six foot mat. The child stands fifteen feet from the mat and attempts to hit the target with the ball, and points are awarded consistent with accuracy.

The ball tracking test requires the child to anticipate and to react to a moving ball. From a distance of ten feet, the examiner bounces an eight and a half inch rubber ball once so that it reaches the child chest-high. This occurs five times, with the child receiving one point for each successful catch. In the second phase of the test, a rubber softball is hung on a string so that it is level with the child's chin and at a distance equal to the length of the child's arm. The ball is then swung back and forth in front of the child, who must touch it as it passes by. This sequence occurs five times, with the child getting one point for each successful touch.

Cratty provides norm tables on the six tests by sex and for various groups of children. Intercorrelations among the six tests for normal children are moderate (centering around .50), suggesting that they are addressing a common gross motor capability.

Fine motor skills: An example of the measurement of fine motor performance is Connolly and Elliott's (1972) observation and recording of the spontaneous use of a paintbrush by forty-nine nursery school children, ages three to five. The focus of their work was the functioning of the children's hands during nonstructured painting sessions; that is, children were neither told to paint certain pictures nor in a specific manner. Children stood at easels to paint. The observer took a position five feet behind the child and to the side of the child's dominant hand. Each child was observed on four separate occasions, with approximately twenty-five observations made at each session. Each observation required the recording of four variables: hand used to hold the brush, grip employed, movement of the arm and body, and stroke produced on the paper.

The findings of this study provided much information about the development of this fine motor skill. For example, with regard to handedness, over 95 percent of the children used either the right or left hand rather than using both hands simultaneously. There was a marked tendency in the direction of right-handedness, with only 10 percent of the children displaying a preference for the left hand. Older children were more likely to make exclusive use of one hand or the other. In terms of grip, "precision" grips were much more in evidence than "power" grips. Precision grips involved opposition of the thumb and a spreading of the fingers, while power grips involved a clamping or clenching action of the fingers into the palm without thumb opposition. The adult grip, a precision grip, was used three quarters of the time by the children, especially older ones. With regard to movement of body parts during painting, movements of shoulder and elbow joints together were most frequent, accounting for over half the movements observed. Shoulder joint movements were the next most common, making up over one quarter of the movements seen; especially in evidence were lateral arm sweeps. Wrist joint movements were observed with 15 percent frequency. Strokes produced on the paper were most often vertical straight lines (over 50 percent), with horizontal ones (over 22 percent) the second most common. Older children drew more horizontal straight lines. Curved lines were drawn with only 7 percent frequency, while dots were made about 10 percent of the time. The remaining 10 percent of the strokes were right or left oblique straight lines. In all, Connolly and Elliott provided substantial information on hand function during the painting effort by young children.

A second example of the measurement of fine motor performance is inherent in the work, once again, of Cratty and Martin (1969). They investigated and reported on the drawing of standard shapes by young children—an early and important fine motor skill. Nearly 200 children, ages four to eight, were used in the norming effort. Each child was worked with individually and watched as the examiner sketched a standard geometric drawing, a complex aggregate of shapes (top of Figure 7). The examiner drew one shape at a time, starting with the large center square. The child was told to draw the shape exactly as the examiner had. Then the examiner would draw the next shape, and

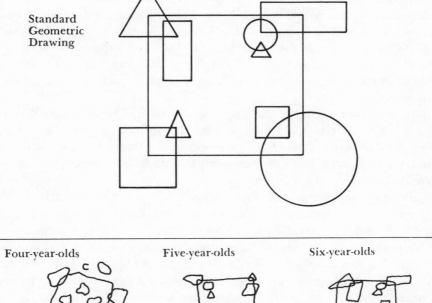

Standard
Geometric
Drawing

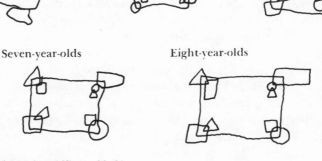

Four-year-olds   Five-year-olds   Six-year-olds

Seven-year-olds   Eight-year-olds

Source: Cratty and Martin, 1967, pp. 80–81.

**Figure 7. Standard Geometric Drawing (Stimulus)
and Typical Drawings of It by Children Ages Four to Eight.**

the process was repeated for all ten shapes. The examiner invariably did well on the demonstration sketches, thanks to a specially marked ditto sheet with the standard drawing reversed (mirror-image) on its back side to allow tracing. The child, however, used a blank sheet of paper. In the lower part of Figure 7, typical drawings for the five age groups are depicted. The four-year-olds did not overlap their figures but drew them separately. Their inability to produce triangles and rectangles was obvious; most of their figures appeared as squared circles or, if you prefer, rounded squares. Further, their placement of the shapes was jumbled, at best. Marked improvement with increasing age was obvious, with six-year-olds placing the shapes in reasonable correspondence with the standard drawing. Eight-year-olds usually performed the drawing task quite well. Cratty and Martin also reported interesting data on how each age group drew each shape in terms of starting point, whether drawn clockwise or counterclockwise, and whether drawn continuously.

Certain cognitive measures treated in Chapter Five used tasks similar to the drawing exercise just described. Let us note three of them, as further examples of ways in which fine motor competence is measured. First, recall that one of the performance tests of the Wechsler Preschool and Primary Scale of Intelligence is the Geometric Design test. On it, the child must copy a series of ten simple geometric shapes and designs with a colored pencil. Scoring is based on accuracy of reproduction.

The second example, the Copying test on the Metropolitan Readiness Tests, is less similar to the Cratty and Martin technique than the Geometric Design test. However, it may tap fine motor ability that is more directly school-related. On its Level I (beginning or middle of kindergarten), the teacher writes the child's name, and the child then copies it. The teacher rates the child's effort high, above average, average, below average, or low on the basis of how well the model provided by the teacher is reproduced, especially with regard to general appearance and legibility. Given the pronounced variability in length of children's names and in difficulty of formation depending on the particular letter, it is curious that this Level I task was not standardized by having the children all copy the same word. Such a practice would also avoid overestimating the writing skill of the child who has spent an inordinate amount of time practicing how to write his name. On Level II (end of kindergarten or beginning of first grade), the child must copy the printed sentence "The funny cat jumps." The teacher uses the same five ratings and criteria as on Level I when scoring the child's printing.

The third example of a fine motor measure from Chapter Five is Circus' Copy What You See, billed as a measure of perceptual-motor coordination. In the Level A version (preschool and early kindergarten), the child is presented with fifteen single letters and numbers and is instructed to "copy what you see" in the spaces directly beneath each of them. No ability to name the letters or numbers is required. Three of the items require circular lines (such as 0 and 8), six require straight lines (7 and W), and six require a combination of circular and straight lines (f and B). Different items are used on Level B (late kindergarten and first grade) because, during preliminary tryouts, those on Level A turned out to be too easy for older children. Level B of Copy What You See consists of fifteen geometric forms that the child must copy. Scoring on both levels is similar, with guides used to assign 0 to 4 points to each item based on accuracy of reproduction. Internal consistency (Alpha) reliabilities observed for Level A were .90 and .87 for the nursery school and kindergarten samples, respectively, while for Level B and the first-grade sample Alpha was .83.

One important reason, among many, that attention is directed toward young children's fine motor capabilities (such as those addressed in the three measures described) is their potential importance in handwriting. Very soon in their school lives, and increasingly so thereafter, children must learn to write, usually in printing first, and then cursive. Strangely, our search for tests of handwriting turned up very little. For example, the Buros' *Mental Measurements Yearbook* series contains only a scattering of handwriting measures (none in the Seventh Yearbook and only two in the Eighth). Further, very little seems to be available for children under the age of six years.

For the interested reader, however, three scales for evaluating handwriting in somewhat older children (older than the age focus of this book) will be noted. The PPP Writing Test (Levine, Fineman, and Donlon, 1973) is designed as a measure of near-point copying ability. Intended for children ages six to twelve, the untimed measure is part of the Prescriptive Profile Procedure for Children with Learning Disabilities. Administration can be individual or group. The child must copy shapes and partial letters, lower- and upper-case printed letters, lower- and upper-case cursive letters, single and multiple numerals, single words (two to six letters in length), a standard printed sentence, and a standard cursive sentence. Scoring is on the basis of the adequacy of the child's reproductions. A diagnostic handwriting chart, listing many common errors that can be circled, is also used to further specify an individual child's handwriting illegibilities. The PPP Writing Test also incorporates elements of a handwriting subtest that is part of the Durrell Analysis of Reading Difficulty (Durrell, 1955). Unfortunately, no reliability or validity information, and only sketchy norms, are provided for the PPP.

The other two handwriting scales are similar to each other in format. The Ayres Measuring Scale for Handwriting (Ayres, 1940) was originally published in 1912 and renormed in 1940. It is frequently called the "Gettysburg Edition" because students familiarize themselves with the first three lines of Lincoln's Gettysburg Address by reading and copying it. Once familiar with the material, the students are given two minutes to write it in ink on ruled paper. Each child's handwriting sample is compared with eight models (varying in their quality of writing) to find a match; it is recommended that this procedure be done twice to help assure scoring reliability. The rate of writing in words per minute is also determined. Sketchy norms are provided for grades two to eight in terms of both quality and rate of writing. However, no reliability or validity information is reported.

The other instrument, the Evaluation Scales for Handwriting (Zaner-

Bloser, 1979) consists of eight large scoring guides, one for each of the first seven grades and the last one for grade eight and above. The guides for grades one and two are in printed letters, while those for grades three on are in cursive. To administer the measure, the teacher writes on a ruled chalkboard a model of the stimulus sentence. For example, the grade one and two sentences are "I wrote my name upon the sand" and "I asked a tiger to tea," respectively (How else would you dare ask a tiger to tea?). The students practice writing the sentence once on lined paper and then, using their best handwriting, write the sentence again. In scoring, five elements are considered: letter formation, vertical strokes, spacing, alignment and proportion, and line quality (each judged either satisfactory or needing improvement). The teacher can also compare the student's sentence with five example sentences provided for each grade's scoring guides. Based on this comparison and the number of elements needing improvement, the teacher rates each child's handwriting sample excellent, good, average, fair, or poor (none or one, two, three, four, or five elements needing improvement, respectively). The example sentences were obtained by taking mid-year samples of children's writing, 500 children at each grade level. The samples were divided by Zaner-Bloser penmen into the five categories according to the quality of handwriting. A sample sentence was then selected as representative of each rating category for each grade level and became the example sentence for that level of proficiency. No validity or reliability information is provided with the scales.

Our intuition suggests to us that the decade of the 1980s will see some increase in emphasis on children's handwriting, as part of a more general swing toward basic subject matter. With careful longitudinal investigations, it would be possible to determine the extent to which performance on fine motor tasks by children four and five years old predicted later handwriting abilities. If substantial predictive validity could be achieved, it might then be possible to identify early young children who would benefit from systematic work on skills related to handwriting.

Typical Performance Measures. A third common means of categorizing psychomotor behaviors is by the typical performance measures used to describe many psychomotor activities. These measures are derived primarily from persons working in the motor learning area and have been summarized by Drowatzky (1975). The typical performance measures include (1) amount of response, (2) latency of response, (3) rate of response, (4) errors, (5) reminiscence, (6) trials, and (7) retention. Each of these is now discussed, with typical examples for school-aged children; when possible, applications involving even younger children are presented.

Amount of response is commonly used to measure motor performance. For some types of motor performance, number of repetitions might be used as the indicator amount—for example, number of push-ups, sit-ups, chin-ups, deep-knee bends, and so forth. For other types of performance, amount of response might be expressed in terms of endurance—for example, distance run, jumped, or swum. Although a greater amount of response is frequently associated with better performance, this is not always the case. Drowatzky pointed out that improved performance is sometimes accompanied by more appropriate, efficient movements, with extraneous and uneconomical movements eliminated and a smaller amount of response overall, as in handball. In early childhood education, many measures based on amount of response can be identified. Thus, one might record the distance that a ball is thrown or kicked by a child, the distance run, the number of times that a ball is bounced, the amount of weight lifted, the height jumped, strength of grip, and so on.

Latency of response refers to the time that elapses between the presentation of a stimulus and the initiation of a response. This is commonly referred to as *reaction time.* The concept is familiar to us from driving an automobile—reaction time is the time it takes us to apply pressure to the brake pedal after some event signals the need to stop quickly. Although latency of response is an important indicator of performance, it properly should be thought of as indicating the quickness of response rather than its strength or amount. Reaction time in early childhood education is exemplified well on the Kansas Reflection-Impulsivity Scale for Preschoolers or KRISP (Wright, 1971) and the Matching Familiar Figures Test or MFFT (Kagan, 1965) for older children; both measures were mentioned briefly in Chapter Five. They are used to identify reflective children and impulsive children in situations involving response uncertainty. On the two tests, the task for the child is to select from several similar drawings the one that is identical to a designated stimulus drawing. The alternative response drawings are similar enough that considerable doubt as to the correct response is present. Two measures are recorded for each child: (1) the number of errors made and (2) the time it takes the child to indicate his first answer. The time taken fits well the latency of response definition above, although it is probably more a cognitive than a psychomotor measure. Of course, other reaction time measures might be developed for use with young children, like the time it takes them to indicate that a light has changed from red to green, to press a button after a particular sound or signal is given, or to brake a bicycle after a signal to stop appears.

Rate of response is another measure frequently utilized in connection with psychomotor performance. Speed is frequently used as a measure when a behavioral response is lodged in a person's repertoire so firmly that errors are unlikely. Rate can also be used to measure the influence of external factors on performance—a more appropriate use, probably, than its use as an indicator of initial learning or acquisition. Many of the amount-of-response measures suggested above for early childhood education might also be expressed as rates. Thus, one can easily conceive of rates of walking, running, or swimming, or the number of times that a ball is bounced in thirty seconds. Rates could easily be applied to various calisthenics, like the number of jumping jacks done in one minute. Performance on other psychomotor tasks could also be appropriately expressed as rate measures, such as the time taken to tie shoes or to button jackets. Recalling that rates can be used to chart the influence of external factors on performance, note that one might ask the child to tie the shoe or button the jacket in the dark and then determine any apparent effect in terms of the new rate recorded. Or one might determine the rate of walking a ten-foot balance board when it is on the ground and then recalculate the rate when the board is elevated six inches above the ground.

The use of *errors* as a measure is not confined to the psychomotor domain, of course. Further, more than just the number of errors often can be noted, such as the location and kind of error. It is obvious that looking at number of correct responses (as an indication of amount of response) yields essentially the same information as considering the number of errors; however, kind and location of errors can yield additional data valuable for interpretation. In early childhood education, an error measure might be applied to walking a ten-foot balance board, three inches wide. Records might be made of the number of times the child stepped off the board (errors), the location on the board of errors that were made, and whether the child stepped off to the right or left of the board. An error measure would also be appropriate on a test of throwing accuracy, such as throwing bean bags from a distance at a target placed flat on the ground. In addition to number of misses (errors), other relevant measures might include degree of error (that is, how far from the target), location of error (right, left, over, or short), frequency of error at the start versus the end of the throwing session, and so forth.

The final three typical performance measures presented by Drowatzky—reminiscence, trials, and retention—have fewer specific applications to early childhood education. All three have enjoyed their greatest use in psychological laboratory studies. *Reminiscence* pertains to the improved performance that is observed on some tasks if a period of rest is allowed after extensive practice. The usual interpretation is that fatigue sets in during a long practice session and has a gradually increasing negative effect on performance. After rest, the effects of fatigue dissipate, and improved performance is observed on the task. We are unaware if studies have been done on reminiscence and learning to ride a bicycle, but we assume that acquiring such a skill is affected by fatigue. If so, a five-year-old might practice diligently all day one Saturday, not ride for a week, and yet display better riding form on the first ride a week later than he did at the end of the full day of practice. The second measure, the *number of trials* taken to achieve criterion performance, would be illustrated by recording the number of trials a six-year-old took to execute a satisfactory dive from the edge of a swimming pool. That is, on which trial was a satisfactory dive—proper form, suitable arch, no "belly-flop," legs together, and so forth—first exhibited? *Retention* applies to the amount of a skill retained after a period of time. Another way retention is sometimes expressed is in terms of *savings*. The number of trials (or time period) taken to relearn a skill that was previously mastered is subtracted from the original number of trials (or length of time) taken, and the result is then divided by the original number of trials (or time) to determine the savings. For example, extending the previous diving example, if Johnny initially takes fifty trials to exhibit criterion performance and then, after a six-month layoff, takes only twenty trials to reach criterion, the savings is 60 percent (fifty minus twenty, divided by fifty).

Our discussion of typical performance measures leads us to three concluding, fairly important points about psychomotor measures in early childhood education. First, when measuring certain behaviors, it may at times be judicious to use several of the performance measures described, rather than just one. For example, if one plans to measure the distance run in an endurance test, it is a simple matter to add rate of running as a companion measure. Second, note that psychomotor performance lends itself well to the formation of explicit instructional (or behavioral) objectives (Goodwin and Klausmeier, 1975; Harrow, 1972). This is because psychomotor behaviors are, in the main, readily observable and because criteria for evaluating the adequacy of performance are relatively easy to specify. For example, "With a running start, the child will high jump over a bar set at one third of his height," or "Thrown an eight-inch rubber playground ball five times from a distance of ten feet, the child will catch it on three or more occasions." Early childhood educators could, with relative ease, develop relevant psychomotor tests for local use by establishing behavioral objectives and using Drowatzky's list of performance measures to select and specify appropriate criterion measures for the objectives. Third, it should be noted that observation is an eminently suitable procedure for measurement in the psychomotor domain. Several of the psychomotor measures discussed either involve observation directly or easily could if slightly reconceptualized. The use of mechanical observation means, particularly movies and videotape, is widespread in the measurement of physical performance (for example, see Flinchum, 1975, pp. 10–15).

Illustrative Psychomotor Measures

Before examining several psychomotor tests in detail, let us elaborate upon the motor aspects of four measures previously discussed in Chapter Six—namely, the Comprehensive Identification Process (CIP), the Denver Developmental Screening Test (DDST), the Developmental Indicators for the Assessment of Learning (DIAL), and the Learning Accomplishment Profile (LAP). These developmental surveys contain substantial psychomotor elements.

On the CIP, some ratings of motor performance are made on the Observation of Behavior Form and on the Parent Interview Form. Perhaps more pertinent, the Child Interviewer's Record Form includes age-graded items in both fine motor and gross motor development. Fine and gross motor tasks are grouped separately by half-year age intervals with five items each at each interval. In general, the items are very diverse and change substantially from interval to interval. Illustrative fine motor tasks are: turning a door knob, building block towers, unwrapping a small piece of candy, buttoning a button, copying shapes, cutting paper with scissors, and touching the thumb to various fingers on the hand. Sample gross motor items include: balancing on one foot, walking backward, walking up and down stairs, throwing a large ball, walking on tiptoes, walking a line, kicking a ball, hopping. The interviewer begins a child on age-appropriate items and marks "+" for success on the task, "0" for inability to perform the task, and "R" if the child refuses to attempt the task. Based on the number and age level of the child's +'s and 0's, an overall rating is made for each area (fine and gross motor) of pass, refer or rescreen, or evaluate.

Looking again at the DDST (Figure 6), note that separate gross motor and fine motor sectors are included and together make up about half the total test. Gross motor tasks for children aged eighteen months to six years include many behaviors measured in the CIP or already mentioned earlier in this chapter, such as walking up steps, kicking, throwing, balancing and hopping on one foot, pedaling, jumping, heel-to-toe front and backward walks, and catching a ball. Some fine motor-adaptive items for the same age range are building towers and a bridge with cubes, copying or reproducing geometric figures, and drawing a man. In yet a third sector, personal-social, additional DDST items require motor performance, such as playing, removing garments, buttoning, dressing, and the like.

DIAL also incorporates both gross motor and fine motor abilities as two of its four skill areas. The specific items in each motor area were listed briefly in Chapter Six. Of the seven DIAL gross motor items, five are similar to those in the CIP and the DDST (throwing, catching, jumping, hopping, and balancing), while standing still and skipping represent new types of item. Five of DIAL's fine motor items are similar to those on the CIP and the DDST (building, cutting, touching fingers, copying shapes, and copying letters), while two are dissimilar (matching shapes and clapping hands). Also, it will be recalled that performance on DIAL items results in points that are converted to scaled scores from 0 to 3, while CIP and DDST items are simply scored pass or fail.

Of the LAP's six assessment areas, two are directly pertinent to the psychomotor domain (the gross and fine motor areas), while two others contain some relevant items (the social and self-help areas). In the gross motor area, the LAP includes practically all the DIAL or DDST items or highly similar ones (except standing still) and also assesses diverse movements (similar to the CIP) such as squatting, skipping, climbing, running, jumping rope, dancing to music, roller-skating, and jumping from a height of one foot and landing on toes only. Fine motor items on the LAP are also similar to those on the DIAL and the DDST, but, like the CIP selection, more extensive in that they also include turning book pages and door handles, manipulating clay, fitting blocks or pegs into a form board, operating an egg beater, painting, picking up small objects such as pins and thread, driving nails, stringing beads, printing simple words, imitating certain ways of folding a paper, and lacing shoes. The LAP also contains a substantial number of tasks involving writing. When LAP is compared with the DDST in social skills and self-help areas, the same pattern is evident; the LAP includes most of the DDST items, or similar ones, and also provides numerous additional ones. In social skills, the LAP has additional items such as carrying a tray and building with blocks; in the self-help area, items include drinking, using utensils, cutting, and grooming. The reader might want to review Chapter Six to recall the positive features and limitations of the CIP, the DDST, the DIAL, and the LAP.

The instruments now discussed differ from the four just cited in that they focus exclusively on psychomotor and perceptual areas. Further, as contrasted with the DIAL, the LAP, and to a lesser extent, the CIP and the DDST, some of them require specialized training for proper administration, scoring, and interpretation. The measures to be reviewed are listed alphabetically in Table 22.

Developmental Test of Visual-Motor Integration (VMI). The purpose of the VMI (Beery, 1967a; Beery and Buktenica, 1967) is to measure the integration of visual perception and motor behavior in young children. The child's ability to draw a series of twenty-four increasingly difficult geometric forms and shapes is examined. For illustration, the first form is simply a vertical line, while the last one is made by drawing two triangles with double-line outlines and positioning them one-over-the-other to form a six-pointed star (called, by Beery, the three-dimensional star). Children taking the test are allowed only one try on each form and erasing is not permitted. The student test booklet and instructions have been carefully designed to avoid several previous difficulties with geometric form reproduction—such as transparency of the paper used, impressions made on the following about-to-be-used pages, and the child turning the test booklet and, in effect, changing the stimulus figure and the task. Thus, the twenty-four stimulus forms are contained in a booklet of heavy green paper. The child begins on the last page and works toward the front of the booklet. The forms are arranged three-to-a-page and appear in a horizontal row across the top of the long axis of the paper. The child makes his reproduction attempt just below the stimulus form and is instructed to keep the test booklet directly in front of his body and not tilted. Similarly, the examiner is directed to "keep both the test booklet and the child's body centered and squared with the table throughout testing" (Beery, 1967a, p. 14). The test of twenty-four items is known as the long form and is declared suitable for ages two to fifteen. A short form, identical to the long except containing only the fifteen easiest items, is available for children ages two to eight.

Administration of the VMI appears straightforward, quick (about fifteen minutes), and easily manageable by the alert teacher. Although group administration is clearly possible, no information is provided about appropriate size groups at each age level. More important, scoring instructions, though detailed, may be inadequate even for the experienced examiner as they introduce a degree of subjectivity into the scoring process. Chissom (1972a) pointed out that developmental trend examples and scoring criteria are given for judging each reproduction "pass" or "fail," but also noted the ambiguity and subjectivity inherent in directions like "If there is any doubt whether a form should be marked 'passed' or 'failed' after the criteria have been studied, mark as 'passed'" (Beery, 1967a, p. 17). The child's raw score is determined by totaling the number of forms completed up to the point of three consecutive failures and subtracting the number of forms failed up to the same point. The raw score is converted to a VMI age equivalent.

The VMI is proposed as a tool for educational assessment. However, validity information for this particular purpose is not included in the manual. General information on validity is given in the manual (Beery, 1967a), and sev-

Table 22. Illustrative Psychomotor Measures in Early Childhood Education

Title and Date	Age Range	Admin-istration	Scales or Scores	Source
Developmental Test of Visual-Motor Integration (1967)	2 to 15 years	Individual or Group; time required not stated (our estimate is 15 minutes)	Visual-Motor Integration Age Equivalent	Follett Publishing Co. 201 N. Wells St. Chicago, Ill. 60606
Frostig Movement Skills Test Battery (1972)	6 to 12 years	Individual, 25 minutes; Small Group, 45 minutes	Hand-Eye Coordination Visually Guided Movement Flexibility Strength Balance	Consulting Psychologists Press Palo Alto, Calif. 94306
Marianne Frostig Developmental Test of Visual Perception (Items: 1961; Norms: 1963; Manual: 1966)	3 to 8 years	Individual, 30 to 45 minutes; Group, 40 minutes to 1 hour	Eye-Motor Coordination Figure-Ground Discrimination Form constancy Position in Space Spatial Relations	Consulting Psychologists Press

Purdue Perceptual-Motor Survey (1966)	6 to 10 years	Individual; time required not stated (our estimate is 20 to 30 minutes)	Balance and Postural Flexibility Body Image and Differentiation Perceptual-Motor Match Ocular Control Form Perception	Charles Merrill Publishing 1300 Alum Creek Dr. Columbus, Ohio 43216
Southern California Sensory Integration Tests (1972)	4 to 8 years (4 to 10 years for a few subtests)	Individual; 1¼ to 1½ hours	Seventeen measures of perception and psychomotor performance (see text)	Western Psychological Services 12031 Wilshire Blvd. Los Angeles, Calif. 90025
Test of Motor Impairment (1972)	5 to 13 years	Individual; 20 to 40 minutes	Balance Upper Limb Coordination Whole Body Coordination Manual Dexterity Simultaneous Movement	Brook Educational Publishers Ltd. P.O. Box 1171 Guelph, Ontario Canada

eral studies are mentioned in a back-up monograph (Beery, 1967b), but both presentations tend to be disorganized, indirect, and limited. For example, the correlation between VMI scores and chronological age across the two-to-fifteen age range was reported as .89, but this is really just evidence of the items' developmental sequence. Most studies reported deal with concurrent criterion-related validity, but several involve small or atypical samples (mentally retarded or institutionalized or both). In one larger study of almost 200 students from first, fourth, and seventh grades, the correlation between VMI scores and mental age was found to decrease from .59 to .38 from first to seventh grades. In the manual, it was further noted: "The VMI correlations with reading achievement in the first grade are higher than those between IQ and reading achievement. Scores are related more to integrative functions than to individual functions, which suggests that the VMI is a measure of a child's coordinating abilities. Scores of kindergarten and mentally retarded children have improved following perceptual-motor training" (Beery, 1967a, p. 11). Much emphasis was placed on attempting to establish that the VMI measured the integration of the visual and the motor functions, rather than either separately. Still, external criteria of visual-motor integration were not frequently referred to, and predictive validity was not addressed. In all, the information on validity seems tangential, and the potential user receives few clues as to the VMI's validity for the stated purpose of educational assessment. (Many of these validity concerns, and others, were expressed by Leton, 1978, and Rice, 1978.)

Reliability information does not appear in the manual, and that in the monograph is of limited utility. Internal consistency was reported to be .93 for one large sample, while it was .78 for a first-grade group. Stability reliability tended to be reported for small groups or mentally retarded children. An exception was a two-week test-retest reliability of .87 for girls and .83 for boys, involving 171 children in all. Since the entire age range was used, however, these correlations are spuriously high. Interrater reliabilities reported from two studies were high, although one study involved just ten mentally retarded children, while the other was only partially described.

With respect to usability, a table is provided in the manual for converting the child's raw score (from 1 to 24 correct) to a VMI age equivalent in years and months, with separate conversions for males and females. The norming group is described in the monograph rather than the manual. Over 1,000 children were involved, ages three to fourteen, although only 28 of these made up the three-year-old group. Three samples—middle-class suburban, lower-middle-class urban, and rural—all from Illinois, were used. A collection of IQ data and a brief comparison with previous performance on the VMI caused Beery to describe the normative group as "representative." However, considering the sample, its method of selection, its geographical narrowness, and its inadequate description in terms of socioeconomic status and ethnic composition, the user remains quite uncertain about its representativeness.

Apparently, the VMI is used quite widely. We believe, however, that substantial work needs to be done on the measure's validity, reliability, and norming.

Further, a single comprehensive and organized manual should be prepared to replace the present manual and monograph. With such efforts, especially with regard to validity, the appropriateness of the VMI for different purposes should become clearer.

Frostig Movement Skills Test Battery. Designed for children aged six to twelve years, the Frostig Movement Skills Test Battery has been made available only in an experimental edition (Orpet, 1972). Its purpose is to assess the sensorimotor development and motor skills of young children so that appropriate remedial action can be taken when deficiencies are found. It can be given individually in twenty-five minutes or to groups of three to four children in forty-five (by utilizing common demonstrations). The manual does not specify what training is required to administer the test, although it does call for the examiner to be thoroughly familiar with the administration and scoring procedures and to follow the standardized methods precisely. Examination of the test procedures suggests that only moderate amounts of training (say, one to two days with supervised practice administrations) would be necessary for most examiners.

The Frostig battery consists of twelve subtests that relate to five abilities:

Order of Administration of Subtests	*Abilities*
1. Bead Stringing	
2. Fist/Edge/Palm	1. Hand-eye Coordination
3. Block Transfer	
4. Bean Bag Target Throw	2. Visually Guided Movement
5. Sitting/Bending/Reaching	3. Flexibility
6. Standing Broad Jump	
7. Shuttle Run	
8. Changing Body Position	4. Strength
9. Sit-ups	
12. Chair Push-ups	
10. Walking Board	
11a. One Foot Balance, Eyes Open	5. Balance
11b. One Foot Balance, Eyes Closed	

The subtests are listed in their order of administration except for Chair Push-ups, which is given last.

A brief explanation of each subtest, grouped by ability, is in order. On Bead Stringing, purportedly a test of bilateral eye-hand coordination and dexterity, the child is presented with eighteen wooden beads, one-half inch square and of the same color, and an eighteen-inch round shoelace with a plastic tip to prevent fraying on one end and a knot tied twelve inches from the tip to stop the beads. After receiving a demonstration, the child strings the beads as quickly as possible. The performance is timed. The child's raw score is the number of beads on the string at the end of thirty seconds, or, if the task is completed earlier, the child is given a score from 19 (for a time of twenty-eight or twenty-nine seconds) to 27 (for a time of twenty seconds). The Fist/Edge/Palm subtest reportedly measures unilateral coordination and motor sequencing. The child forms three sequential positions with his hand — (1) making a fist, (2) extending the fingers while resting the edge of the hand on the table, and (3) placing the hand palm down on the table. Together, the three positions constitute one cycle. The child repeats the cycle as fast as possible for twenty seconds using the preferred hand. Then the task is switched to the other hand for twenty seconds. The child's raw score is the number of correct cycles for the two hands combined. The Block Transfer measure is designed as a test of eye-hand and fine motor coordination that entails crossing the midline of the body. Eighteen single-color, one-inch square wooden blocks and a wide form board are used. On one end of the board, across its narrow dimension and to the left of the child, are three rows of six holes, each one and one-sixteenth inch square. The blocks are placed on the smooth end of the board, about twenty inches to the right of the child. The child is seated and must transfer the blocks, one at a time using his preferred hand, to the recessed holes on the left side of the board. The performance is timed, with raw scores determined as on the bead stringing task.

The visually guided movement ability is assessed using the Bean Bag Target Throw, a test devised to measure visual-motor coordination, aiming, and accuracy. An eighteen-inch square, multicolored target is mounted on a wall, its bottom edge four feet above the floor. The center five-inch square of the target is one color; it is surrounded by an eleven-inch square of a second color, while the remainder (from eleven to eighteen inches) is a third color. According to the manual, red and green should not be used. Without any practice and from a distance of ten feet, the child throws a series of fifteen bean bags overhand at the target. To determine the raw score, three points are given for each hit in the five-inch square, two points for each hit in the eleven-inch colored area, and one point for each hit in the eighteen-inch colored area.

Flexibility is also assessed using a single subtest, namely Sitting/Bending/Reaching. The child sits on the floor with his legs extended and heels six inches apart. A meter stick is placed on the floor between his legs, the zero end toward his body and the thirty-centimeter mark even with his heels. Without bending his knees, the child bends forward and reaches on the floor between his feet as far as possible. Three trials are allowed. The raw score recorded is the farthest point on the centimeter stick reached by the child's fingertips on any of the three trials — 30 centimeters if he can just reach his heels, and less or more if he cannot reach them or can reach beyond them.

Five subtests contribute to assessing strength. On the Standing Broad Jump, a measure of leg strength, three trials are permitted. The raw score is the distance of the best jump, in centimeters, from the restraining line to the heel nearest the line after the jump. The Shuttle Run is a measure of running and stopping speed as well as of changing direction. Two circles are drawn twenty feet apart, and three bean bags are placed in one of them. The child starts from the empty circle with his back turned. On signal, he turns, runs to the far circle, picks up a bag, returns and places the bag in the empty circle, and continues until all three bags are in the starting-point circle. The raw score is the number of seconds required to complete the task. Changing Body Position examines the child's speed and agility in moving from a standing to lying to standing position. Starting from a standing position, the child lies on his stomach with his face touching the floor. Then the child returns to the standing position with knees straight. This cycle is repeated. The child's raw score is twice the number of cycles completed in twenty seconds; that is, one point is given for each change of position. In the Sit-ups subtest, a measure of abdominal muscle strength, the child lies on his back, fingers interlocked behind his head, and knees bent at a ninety-degree angle. With the examiner holding his feet on the floor, the child sits up and touches both elbows to his knees, then returns to the starting position. The raw score is the number of sit-ups completed in thirty seconds. The final strength measure is Chair Push-ups, designed to assess arm and shoulder strength. The child places his hands on the near corners of a chair and assumes a leaning position. On signal, he lowers his body, flexing at the elbows until his chest touches the near edge of the chair. The child then resumes the starting position and continues. The raw score consists of the number of push-ups performed in twenty seconds.

The first measure of balance is the Walking Board, which utilizes two boards, twelve feet long and standing four to five inches above the floor. The child first has two trials on the wide (three and five-eighths inches) board, walking in heel-to-toe fashion with hands on his hips. On each trial, the score is the number of steps taken by the child until he loses his balance or removes his hands from his hips, up to a maximum of twelve per trial. The child then takes two trials on the narrow (one and five-eighths inches) board, with identical procedures and scoring. The maximum score possible is 48 (two boards, two trials per board, and twelve points per trial). On the One Foot Balance subtest, the child stands on the preferred foot, with hands on hips and the top of his other foot placed behind the knee of the opposite (balancing) leg. This is done first with eyes open and then with eyes closed. The performance is timed until the child touches the other foot to the floor, removes either hand from his hips, or otherwise loses his balance. Two raw scores are recorded: the number of seconds balance is maintained, up to thirty, with eyes open, and balance time with eyes closed, up to a maximum of twenty seconds.

The thirteen raw scores (one for each of the subtests except the One Foot Balance, which yields two) are each converted to scale scores (mean of 10, standard deviation of 3) using age appropriate tables, separate for males and females. Scale scores for the subtests making up a single ability are averaged to produce mean scale scores for each of the five abilities. Similarly, all thirteen scale scores are averaged to determine a composite mean scale score for the entire battery.

The only type of validity addressed by the Frostig Movement Skills Test

Battery is factorial. Related factor matrices for each age group are reported to justify the grouping of the various subtests under the five abilities. Unfortunately, no intercorrelation matrix showing the relationships of all the subtests with each other is presented. The omission of criterion-related validity is serious. Statements in the manual such as "The experimental battery was not validated by correlating it with a criterion variable, such as an existing test, because an adequate criterion measure was deemed not to exist" (Orpet, 1972, p. 3) are of small comfort to the conscientious potential user. Conspicuously absent are comparisons between the test's assessments of children's movement skills and analogous assessments made by well-trained clinicians.

Reliability information is also scanty. All that is reported are the lower-bound estimates of reliability based upon the communalities (common factor variance) from the factor analysis for each of seven age groups (aged six to twelve years). These ranged from .44 to .88, with fourteen of the ninety-one communalities less than .60. However, these figures serve only as estimates of internal consistency and, although substantial overall, are low enough on occasion to be disturbing. The absence of stability and interscorer reliabilities is regrettable.

Although the manual contains elaborate tables for converting raw to scale scores, the standardization process was limited. The sample is not fully described, but enough information is provided to create concerns about its representativeness. In all, over 700 children from a single Southern California elementary school were used, somewhat over 100 for each age group, six to twelve years. No further description is provided except that all the children were Caucasian. The lack of information on the sample, such as the children's socioeconomic status, and its narrow geographic and ethnic composition seriously limit its usefulness.

The recency of the Frostig Movement Skills Test Battery apparently has precluded extensive reviews of it. Some leniency for its shortcomings is warranted given its "experimental edition" label. Nonetheless, it is clear that extensive work is required on validity, reliability, and norming if future editions of the battery are to achieve an important place in assessing young children's psychomotor abilities. These sentiments were echoed, for the most part, in recent reviews by Oakland (1978) and Rosen (1978).

Marianne Frostig Developmental Test of Visual Perception (DTVP). Of all the measures discussed in this chapter, the DTVP (Frostig, 1966; Frostig and others, 1964) clearly stands as the one most closely related to a perceptual ability. Its inclusion was prompted by its wide use and by its authors' stated intent to select and develop motor and perceptual subtests relevant to school performance. The DTVP's purpose is to measure several perceptual skills related to vision so that warranted remediation activities can be implemented. The measure is suggested as a screening device for preschoolers through first-graders, and as a clinical evaluative instrument for older children having learning difficulties. The manual clearly specifies training needed for administering the test. Classroom teachers presumably could give the test to all but severely handicapped and disturbed children if the teachers first underwent the moderate to substantial training suggested in the manual and if they had access to a school psychologist as questions arose.

Designed for children three to eight years old, the test can be given to an individual in thirty to forty-five minutes, and to groups in forty to sixty minutes. Optimum group sizes are specified, such as two to four nursery school children aged four to five years or twelve to sixteen first-graders. According to the manual, the DTVP measures "five operationally defined perceptual skills," each by a separate subtest. The subtests are in a single booklet in which the child writes with an eraserless pencil or, if a preschooler, a sharpened crayon. Erasures are not allowed.

On the Eye-Motor Coordination subtest (sixteen items), the child draws straight and curved lines between increasingly narrow boundaries or draws straight lines between two or three small stimulus figures. Points are lost if the child's line touches or (especially) goes outside the boundaries, if the line is broken, or if it extends too far beyond or does not touch the beginning and stopping stimulus figures. In the Figure-Ground Discrimination subtest (eight items), the child must discriminate between intersecting shapes by outlining the one(s) designated and must find and outline hidden figures (kites and eggs). The raw score earned depends on the clarity of outlining the specified figures and on the number of kites or eggs found and correctly outlined. The third subtest, Form Constancy (seventeen items), requires discrimination of circles and squares that appear in different positions, shadings, and sizes from other shapes on the same page. A child's raw score is the number of circles and squares clearly outlined minus any other shapes marked. On the Position in Space subtest (eight items), the child must mark whichever figure in a series of identically shaped stimulus figures is positioned differently than the other four. On the second part of the same subtest, the child must select from four figures the one that is positioned the same as a designated stimulus figure. Raw scores vary from 0 to 8, depending on the number of correct differentiations made. The final subtest, Spatial Relations (eight items), entails copying given stimulus patterns by drawing lines to link dots. The raw score is the number of patterns satisfactorily reproduced.

Scoring procedures, overall, seem quite straightforward and clear. Tables are provided in the manual to convert a raw score on any of the five subtests to a perceptual age (the performance of the average child of a given age group for that particular subtest). Further, Frostig defines a scale score as the child's perceptual age divided by his chronological age multiplied by ten. Tables are provided at quarter-year intervals of chronological age that directly convert raw scores to scale scores; the same tables permit expressing the sum of a child's five scale scores as a perceptual quotient. The perceptual quotient is a deviation score utilizing constant percentiles for each age group. That is, perceptual quotients of 125, 110, 100, 90, and 75 are equivalent to the 95th, 75th, 50th, 25th, and 5th percentile ranks, respectively, regardless of chronological age reference group.

Considerable validity information is presented in the DTVP manual. In several correlational studies, modest criterion-related validity was exhibited (see reviews by Austin, 1965, Chissom, 1972b, and Mann, 1972). For example, the DTVP was given in July to twenty-five children, mostly five years old, and eight earned visual perceptual quotients of or below 90 (that is, at or below the 25th percentile). The following October, the children were rated for reading achievement. Only one of the eight scoring at or below 90 had begun to read, while only one of the other seventeen (scoring above 90) had been displaying reading difficulties. Other studies showed correlations of .40 to .50 between DTVP scores and beginning reading scores. However, little is presented in the manual that validates the Frostig for identifying or predicting specific reading difficulties. In another manual-reported study, less directly related, teacher ratings of the classroom adjustment, motor coordination, and intellectual functioning of over 300 kindergarten children correlated .44, .50, and .50, respectively, with the youngsters' perceptual quotients on the DTVP. (Unfortunately, the test authors do not report the intercorrelations between the three teacher ratings.) Other studies contained in the manual indicate that the Frostig does discriminate between normal and neurologically impaired children. It is important to note that the bulk of the validity studies reported involve just the overall perceptual quotient, and not any one of the five separate subtests.

One aspect of the DTVP's validity deserves special mention. The manual indicates that Frostig, based on her experience and the work of others, postulated that the five abilities (represented by the five subtests) developed "relatively independently" and were of "particular relevance to school performance." Further, separate conversion tables and sets of derived scores are provided for each of the subtests. However, factor analytic studies of the DTVP typically find it to be a single-factor test, especially for preschoolers through second-graders (Chissom, 1972b; Mann, 1972). To describe the test as measuring five separate visual perception skills is misleading given the factor analyses conducted to date.

The reliability of the five separate subtests leaves much to be desired, as evidenced by the low reliability coefficients. Two-week coefficients of stability for thirty-five first-graders and thirty-seven second-graders ranged from .42 (Figure-Ground Discrimination) to .80 (Form Constancy), with .80 stability for the perceptual quotient. In a second study, trained nonpsychologists were used as administrators to ascertain two-week stability coefficients for fifty-five kindergartners and seventy-two first-graders. Raw score correlations ranged from .33 (Eye-Motor Coordination) to .83 (Form Constancy), with a median coefficient of .60 observed. For scale scores, a median coefficient of .56 was in evidence, with a .69 stability calculated for perceptual quotients. In yet a third study, perceptual quotient stability over a three-week interval for fifty children having learning difficulties was reported as .98 (however, the test was given individually by the same trained psychologist). Internal consistency reliabilities (split-half) were also reported for four large age groups. The reliabilities were highest for five-year-olds and lowest for eight-year-olds. Perceptual quotient internal consistencies were the most creditable of those reported, being .89, .88, .82, and .78 for children aged five, six, seven, and eight, respectively. Subtest internal consistencies for the four age groups ranged from .35 to .96 with a median coefficient of

.71. In all, reliabilities for subtests were much too frequently on the low side, while perceptual quotient reliability fared better.

Although the Frostig DTVP has enjoyed wide use, its usability can be questioned. The normative sample consisted of over 2,100 children, ages three to nine. The public school portion of the sample was described as "overwhelmingly middle class" (93 percent) by the test authors themselves, who also indicated that the preschool portion defied reliable socioeconomic classification. However, the public school sample was also overwhelmingly unrepresentative in terms of geographic region (coming totally from Southern California) and ethnicity (containing a few Mexican-American children, still fewer Oriental children, and no black children). Further, the norms provided are not differentiated by sex. The DTVP's utility is also limited by the lack of information on how to interpret resulting scores. Little is elaborated in the manual beyond the already discussed cutoff point of perceptual quotients of 90 for kindergarten children, below which a child should receive perceptual training (a training program and materials are available from Frostig). An additional potential difficulty with the DTVP is the introduction of the perceptual quotient concept without full and adequate information on its nature. The furnishing of separate booklets—one for the administration and scoring of the Frostig and one for more technical data—is frustrating at times. In all, the Frostig DTVP has shown applicability and some utility for many types of child, and the perceptual quotient has displayed some predictive power. With additional careful work on validity, reliability, and norming, however, the Frostig (and especially its subtests) might be upgraded from an adequate measure of general visual perception to a substantial diagnostic instrument linked closely to remedial techniques for improving school performance.

Purdue Perceptual-Motor Survey (PPMS). Although the authors of the PPMS indicated that the measure was not designed for diagnosis, they also stated that its purpose was to identify children lacking in perceptual-motor abilities necessary for acquiring academic skills and to designate problem areas for remediation (Roach and Kephart, 1966). Many persons would label such activities *diagnostic,* as we did in Chapter Two. (In fact, many of the tests described in this chapter have a diagnostic orientation.) Developed for children six to ten years old, the PPMS is given individually. The manual does not say how much time is required for administration, but we would guess twenty to thirty minutes. It is unclear what role the authors of the PPMS intended classroom teachers to play in administering, scoring, and interpreting the measure. Although they professedly sought items easy to administer and scoring criteria simple and clear enough that little training would be necessary, they also implied that clinicians would give the test. Our impression is that modest training (say one to three days under supervision) would permit most teachers to administer, and possibly even score, the PPMS satisfactorily. However, acquiring adequate interpretation skills would probably require substantial additional training, especially since the manual provides little material on interpretation of specific ratings or profiles of ratings.

Five major areas of performance and eleven subtests comprise the PPMS.

On each subtest, the child performs a task or series of tasks and his performance is rated from 4 (high) to 1 (low). For the performance area of Balance and Postural Flexibility, two subtests exist. The Walking Board subtest uses an eight- to twelve-foot board, slightly elevated off the floor. The child walks the wide side of the board (three and five eighths inches) forward, then backward, then sideways; he receives a 1-to-4 rating for each mode based on the balance displayed. On the PPMS, unlike the Frostig Movement Skills Test Battery, neither hands-on-hips nor heel-to-toe walking is required and no narrow side board is walked. The Jumping subtest is also intended as a measure of balance and posture. Eight tasks are included. On the first, the child jumps forward using both feet simultaneously (bilateral activity). The second task requires the child to stand on his right foot and jump forward landing on the same foot, while task three switches to the left foot (unilateral activity). The next three tasks are described as regular alternating patterns, namely skipping, hopping on alternate feet, and hopping twice on one foot and then twice on the other. Tasks seven and eight entail irregular alternating patterns. Seven requires the child to repeat a sequence of hopping twice on the right foot and once on the left, while eight switches to double hops with the left foot and single hops with the right. A single 1-to-4 rating is made as a summary judgment of performance on all eight tasks.

Five PPMS subtests are grouped together in the performance area of Body Image and Differentiation. In Identification of Body Parts, apparently related to subsequent development of space localization, the child must touch his shoulders, hips, head, ankles, ears, feet, eyes, elbows, and mouth. A single summary rating is given. The Imitation of Movements subtest measures neuromuscular control and the translation of visual clues into motor movement. It includes seventeen sequential positions of the arms, much as a Navy seaman sending semaphore signals using flags and arm movements. The examiner demonstrates each position and the child, facing the examiner, imitates it. A rating of 4 is given if the child imitates all the patterns promptly, consistently, and surely, with movements the exact duplicate of the examiner's. A 3 rating is given for the same high-quality performance if the child's movements are the mirror image of the examiner's. Obstacle Course, a measure of spatial reactions to objects in the environment, consists of three tasks for which a single rating is made. The child must step over a stick set at knee level, duck under a stick set just below shoulder height, and move sideways between the stick and the wall without touching either. On the Kraus-Weber subtest, the child must perform two tasks, which purportedly correlate well with school achievement. The child lies on his stomach, clasps his hands behind his head, and lifts his head, shoulders, and chest off the floor for ten seconds. Then the child reverses this procedure and, still lying on his stomach with his head resting on the floor, raises his legs about ten inches off the floor and holds this position for ten seconds. Both positions must be performed well and held ten seconds for a 4 rating. The fifth measure in the Body Image and Differentiation block is Angels-in-the-Snow. The child lies on his back, arms at his sides, and goes through a few practice movements— moving his arms in a wide arc until they are directly above his head and moving his legs wide apart while keeping his heels on the floor. Ten movements are then directed and the child moves sequentially his right arm, left arm, right leg, left leg, both arms, both legs, left arm and leg, right arm and leg, right arm and left leg, and left arm and right leg, returning after each to the starting position.

Two subtests are grouped under the area of Perceptual-Motor Match. Four tasks make up the Chalkboard subtest, a measure of the child's ability to perform motor tasks using visual clues as feedback for control. Using his preferred hand, the child must draw a large circle (twenty to twenty-four inches in diameter) directly in front of him on the chalkboard and, in so doing, must cross the midline of his body. Further, right-handers should draw the circle counterclockwise, while left-handers should draw it clockwise. On the second task, two large circles are drawn simultaneously, one with each hand. Again, directionality is important (right-handed children are expected to draw the right-hand circle counterclockwise and the left-hand circle clockwise; for left-handed children, directions are reversed). The third task requires the child to draw a lateral line between two X's twenty-four to thirty inches apart at shoulder height. Noted especially are midline problems, like shifting the chalk to the other hand midway or walking while drawing to complete the line. On task four, two X's are drawn above the child's head and he must simultaneously draw two vertical lines to the bottom of the chalkboard. Midline problems are at times noted by a bowing apart of the lines. The Rhythmic Writing subtest, another Perceptual-Motor Match test, measures the child's performance on a continuous copying task. Poor performance purportedly may be characteristic of children having problems of visual-motor translation or directionality. The examiner writes the first of eight motifs on the chalkboard, a regular pattern of connected open boxes, and instructs the child to make one exactly like it. The other seven motifs are then presented, one at a time. They include a wavy smooth line, and then several series of lower-case letters written in cursive: e's, alternating l's and m's, alternating m's and n's, b's, p's, and alternating b's and p's. Three aspects of the child's performance are rated separately: rhythm (smoothness of the flow of the writing movement), reproduction (accuracy), and orientation (straightness of the horizontal line of writing).

Ocular Control, the ability to establish and maintain visual contact with a target, is assessed because of its presumed relationship to the acquisition of reading skills. On the Ocular Pursuit subtest, the examiner uses a penlight and moves it through a pattern about twenty inches from the child's face. The child receives separate ratings on each of four tasks: pursuit of a penlight pattern by both eyes, by the right eye, by the left eye, and convergence (the ability to use both eyes to triangulate on the penlight as it is moved from twenty inches away to four inches from the face).

Visual Achievement Forms, the eleventh and last PPMS subtest, is also called "developmental drawings" and is used to measure the performance area of Form Perception. The basic task is very similar to the Developmental Test of Visual-Motor Integration presented earlier. However, only seven stimulus figures on cards are used (not twenty-four), the child is allowed to slant his paper and also the stimulus cards, and erasing and correction are permitted. The seven stimuli are a circle, a cross, a square, a triangle, a rectangle with interior diagonal lines, a vertical diamond, and a horizontal diamond. As each card is presented, the child is instructed to "Make one like this" and also to leave room on the paper for the other figures. Two ratings are made: one for the form of the figures, and the other for their organization and size on the page.

Attempts to validate the measure centered on the PPMS performances of an achieving group and a nonachieving group of students. The achieving group of 200 was formed by randomly selecting 50 children from grades one through four in an Indiana elementary school. The nonachieving group consisted of 97 children, also from grades one through four, who had been referred to a clinic because of general nonachievement in the classroom; it is unclear if they were from the same school as the 200 or from another school or schools. Neither group contained mentally retarded or physically handicapped children. Chi-square analyses were used for each rated task on each subtest to show that children passing each task (ratings of 3 and 4) tended to be in the achieving group, while those failing (ratings of 1 and 2) tended to be in the nonachieving group. Intercorrelations of performance on all the items and subtests were generally low (mostly in the .10 to .30 range) except for the much higher intercorrelations of the Ocular Pursuit items. These low correlations prompted the test authors to suggest that the PPMS was measuring several perceptual-motor behaviors with minimum overlap. However, since subtest reliability is not reported, it is not clear to what extent the low intercorrelations may have resulted from low subtest reliability. Further, Jamison (1972) cited factor analytic work suggesting that the PPMS items are not appropriately grouped and that the factors are not stable across grades.

Concurrent validity was also addressed in the manual. Teachers assigned ratings on overall academic performance to the achieving group of 200 students; possible ratings were 5, 4, 3, and 2—that is, superior, high average, average, or low average, respectively. The 97 nonachieving students were automatically assigned a rating of 1. These ratings correlated substantially (.65) with total PPMS scores. We have three main reservations about this procedure. Most important, the 97 nonachievers automatically given ratings of 1 were not rated by teachers, except quite indirectly. Examination of the pertinent table in the manual (Roach and Kephart, 1966, p. 27) reveals that if the nonachieving group were not considered, the correlation between total PPMS score and teacher rating (5 through 2) would be considerably lower; that is, the PPMS scores do not differentiate levels of achievement as clearly in the 200-student group. For example, among the 45 low-average achievers (by teacher rating), 16 had PPMS total scores from 81 to 100, 15 had scores from 66 to 80, and 14 had scores from 41 to 65. (The range of PPMS scores for the full group of 200 achieving students was 41 to 105.) A second reservation concerns the apparent circularity involved in using teacher judgment as an external criterion when attempting to validate a test that is designed as an advance over teacher judgment for identifying students with certain problems. A third reservation stems from the simple observation that other existing tests, such as intelligence or readiness measures, would produce comparable correlations with teacher ratings of student achievement.

Two final points concerning the validity of the PPMS deserve mention. First, the test authors looked at the socioeconomic status (SES) of the normative sample in hopes of establishing some relationship between SES and total PPMS scores. Using just head of household's occupation, they formed the normative sample into six SES groups: I — Professional; II — Semi-Professional; III — Farmers; IV — Clerks; Service and Office Workers; V — Skilled Labor; and VI — Unskilled Labor. They found groups IV and V had total PPMS scores significantly higher than group VI, with the other three higher SES groups performing in between the extremes set by IV/V and VI. Roach and Kephart (1966) believed that the explanation for these observed differences might lie in the parental demands placed on children for either physical exercise or sports participation in the various SES groups. They also advised that additional study was needed.

Second, and more important, recall that the PPMS was designed to identify children deficient in the perceptual-motor abilities necessary to achieve satisfactorily in schools. Yet the validation effort failed to establish that such identification occurs; no use was made of external criteria such as clinical examination or judgment. Rather, the effort jumped to achievement criteria, overlooking the validation of the important intermediate link.

Reliability of the PPMS was addressed by computing a one-week coefficient of stability on a random sample of 30 children from the normative sample (achieving group of 200). All grades were represented, and different examiners were used on the retest. A high coefficient of .95 was reported and is nothing short of amazing given the change in examiners and the low specificity of scoring instructions. However, it is misleading for several reasons. First, the mixing of grades—and thus increased variability of performance—in the retest probably resulted in some inflating of the coefficient over those coefficients probable for each grade separately or for grades one and two combined and grades three and four combined. Second, the coefficient used total PPMS scores only; fairly stable total scores could mask relatively changeable subtest scores. In general, the lack of any reliability data for subtests is distressing. Third, the test-retest period was quite brief and an additional coefficient computed over a longer interval would have been informative and almost certainly lower. Finally, no low-achieving children were included in the sample used to examine stability.

The usability of the PPMS, apart from the foregoing reservations about validity and reliability, is limited. The normative sample came from a single school (bespeaking severe geographic unrepresentativeness), and the school population is only partially described. No conversion tables for major performance areas, subtests, or individual tasks are provided in the manual—although an indefatigable user could interpret scores by using the means and standard deviations reported for each task for each of the four grades. Separate means and standard deviations are not, however, reported by sex, apparently because total scores for boys and girls were not significantly different. Still, the reader is left to guess if significant differences between sexes were found on subtests. The authors suggested that a total PPMS cutoff score of 65 effectively separates achievers from nonachievers, but this seems a rather limited aid to interpretation given the extensive individually administered test on which it is based. Additional limitations in the interpretation of PPMS performance have been indicated by Landis (1972a).

Compared with most other measures discussed in this chapter, the PPMS appears quite weak in the usability-interpretation area. Although it addresses validity and reliability more extensively than several of the other measures, the procedures and content of these efforts leave considerable room for improvement.

Southern California Sensory Integration Tests (SCSIT). This battery contains seventeen subtests related to perception and psychomotor performance, many of which had been published and used prior to their incorporation in the SCSIT in 1972. The stated purpose of the SCSIT is "to detect and to determine the nature of sensory integrative dysfunction" so as "to understand the perceptual-motor and related deficits in children with learning and behavior disorders" (Ayres, 1972, p. 1). Our inclusion of the SCSIT here is somewhat unusual in that the instrument has several clinical aspects; however, the educational relationships clearly implied by "learning and behavior disorders" prompted us to review it.

The training suggested for administering and interpreting the battery is extensive; the tester is expected to know statistical and psychometric concepts, understand sensory integration dysfunction, and give twenty tests under expert supervision. Designed for children four to eight years old (or to ten on a few subtests), the SCSIT is individually administered. The total time required is one and a quarter to one and a half hours. Because of its length, two separate sessions are sometimes used. Although measures similar to several of the SCSIT subtests have been described earlier, other SCSIT subtests are unique. The seventeen subtests, and the child's task on each, are listed below:

Subtest	*Child's Task*
1. Space Visualization (Thirty items)	1. Selects from two blocks the one that will correctly fit into a shaped hole.
2. Figure-Ground Perception (Sixteen items)	2. Selects from six pictorial responses the three that are identical to three stimulus pictures.
3. Position in Space (Thirty items)	3. Selects picture or design that matches a stimulus figure; attempts to remember stimulus figures (presented for three seconds) and then to select a set that matches the stimulus figures.

4. Design Copying
   (Thirteen items)

4. Connects dots to reproduce pattern of stimulus figure (like the Spatial Relations subtest on the Frostig DTVP).

5. Motor Accuracy
   (One item)

5. Traces a printed black line design with preferred, and then other, hand.

6. Kinesthesia (Ten items)

6. Attempts to reposition his index finger exactly on the spot where the examiner had previously placed it; does not use eyes throughout and alternates hands.

7. Manual Form Perception
   (Twelve items)

7. Feels block in hand (cannot see block as hand is behind screen) and selects picture of block held; alternates hands.

8. Finger Identification
   (Sixteen items)

8. Attempts to identify the finger(s) touched by the examiner's finger or the eraser end of a pencil (child's hands are screened from view during touching by examiner).

9. Graphesthesia
   (Twelve items)

9. Attempts to reproduce the design on the back of his hand that the examiner previously drew there (child's hands are screened from view during drawing by examiner, and the examiner is cautioned not to draw so forcefully as to cause "blanched or dented skin").

10. Localization of Tactile Stimuli
    (Twelve items)

10. Attempts to touch the spot on his hand or arm that the examiner touches with a ballpoint pen (child's hands and arms are screened from view throughout).

11. Double Tactile Stimuli
    Perception (Sixteen items)

11. Attempts to touch the spot(s) on his hands or cheeks that the examiner touches with the end of one or two pencils (child's back is to the examiner, but eyes are open).

12. Imitation of Postures
    (Twelve items)

12. Attempts to imitate (mirror image) the examiner's posture using arms and hands (child and examiner are seated facing each other).

13. Crossing Midline of Body (Eight items, repeated three times)

13. Attempts to imitate (mirror image) the examiner's hand movements to the eyes and ears on the same and opposite sides of the body from the hands (child and examiner are seated facing each other).

14. Bilateral Motor Coordination (Eight items)

14. Attempts to imitate (mirror image) the examiner's pattern and sequence of slapping the right or left thigh with the same-side hand or clapping (child and examiner stand facing each other).

15. Right-Left Discrimination (Ten items)

15. Attempts to follow examiner's commands or to answer examiner's questions involving right-left discriminations (child and examiner are seated facing each other).

16. Standing Balance: Eyes Open (One item)

16. With eyes open and without losing balance, stands on one foot at a time, for as long as possible (up to 180 seconds for each foot).

17. Standing Balance: Eyes Closed (One item)

17. Identical to the previous test except that eyes are closed (these last two subtests are similar to the One Foot Balance, Eyes Open and Closed subtest of the Frostig Movement Skills Test Battery).

In all, the measure represents quite a long test, although the first three subtests are terminated after five errors are made. Raw scores on each subtest are converted to standard z-scores (sometimes after adjustment for time taken or other factors) via extensive tables.

Although no section on the validity of the SCSIT is contained in the manual, rather lengthy passages are included on the theoretical foundation and factor analyses of the measure. On the basis of the analyses, Ayres stated that the SCSIT can assist in identifying four types of sensory integrative disorder: (1) limited form and space perception, (2) apraxia (low capacity for motor planning and executing), (3) impaired postural and bilateral integration, and (4) tactile defensiveness (low scores on tactile perception tests and defensive reactions to certain types of tactile stimulus). The manual's discussions of the factor analyses of the theoretical model and test score interpretation, which unfortunately are not uniformly clear, reveal the clinical orientation of the measure. The absence of criterion-related validity in the manual is particularly distressing. It is curious why Ayres chose to ignore such a section. Portions of the SCSIT were in print earlier, and reviews of them (see Gaines, 1972; Kephart, 1972a, b; Landis, 1972b; Proger, 1970) made it clear that, in some cases at least, additional validity information of varying quality could have been presented. The emphasis on factor analysis in the current manual has a hollow ring when presented without substantiating concurrent and predictive validity studies and information. Such omissions of criterion-related validity are particularly serious given the diagnostic purpose of the SCSIT.

On the subject of reliability the SCSIT manual contains considerable information. Coefficients of stability for an unspecified test-retest interval are presented for each year group in the norming sample. Associated standard errors of measurement are also included. The exception to this pattern was the Motor Accuracy subtest, for which internal consistency reliabilities, mostly in the .80s and ranging from .67 to .94, were reported for various age groups, along with standard errors of measurement. Nearly perfect (.998) interrater reliability also was reported for this subtest; no other interrater reliabilities were presented.

Generally, the stability coefficients reported could be described as only moderate. They were low (predominantly in the .30s or less) in the case of the following subtests: Graphesthesia, Double Tactile Stimuli (especially low), Crossing Midline of Body, Right-Left Discrimination, and Standing Balance: Eyes Closed; and they were only somewhat higher for Figure-Ground Perception and Localization of Tactile Stimuli. The author discussed these correlations at some length and noted the reduced variance on some of the subtests (thus making substantial test-retest correlations highly unlikely). Further, she "hypothesized that the very nature of the neurophysiological processes which are under attempted measurement by some of the SCSIT is unstable when compared to the usual psychologically measured parameters" (Ayres, 1972, p. 50). Be that as it may, the low reliability of performance on many of the SCSIT subtests must remain a source of considerable discomfort to the conscientious user.

The normative sample consisted primarily of children four to eight years old. For the first four subtests, dealing with visual perception and design copying, children four to ten years old were used. In the manual, it is stated that "the geographic and socioeconomic levels of metropolitan Los Angeles and surrounding areas were represented" (Ayres, 1972, p. 48). However, the descriptive information specified is insufficient to permit the potential user to estimate the representativeness of the sample and its appropriateness in the situation at hand. Tables to convert raw to standard scores are provided, usually at half-year age intervals. Since Ayres administered different subtest combinations to different groups of children, the number of females (or males) in each half-year norming group varied widely (from thirteen to seventy), but commonly totaled forty to fifty. One table is included that indicates separate means and standard deviations for males and females for those subtests and age groups that were marked by statistically significant differences between sexes. However, none of the conversion tables provide separate male and female data.

The SCSIT battery contains some unusual tasks for the young child. At present, however, it seems to have only limited utility for early childhood educators (a view likely to be supported by Reed, 1978, and Westman, 1978). The principal concern is its insufficient attention to validity. Both reliability and norming could also be improved. The manual tends to be on the technical side (understandably, considering the technical nature of the measure), and this further reduces the usefulness of the measure for educators of young children. Even in the hands of a skilled clinician, it seems that the SCSIT might often be speculative and provocative rather than definitive and prescriptive.

Test of Motor Impairment. The purpose of the Test of Motor Impairment (Stott, Moyes, and Henderson, 1972) is to detect impairment of motor function indicative of possible neurological dysfunction. The authors have suggested several ways of using the measure: for screening; for individual assessment; for correlating with other types of handicap having possible neurological determinants, such as behavior disturbances; and for researching aspects of motor function and dysfunction (Henderson and Stott, 1977). Designed for children five to thirteen years old, it is given individually in twenty minutes if the child is found to be normal and up to forty minutes if some impairment is suspected (necessitating more extensive testing). Although the manual is silent on the matter of administration qualifications, it would seem that most alert teachers, with some supervised practice, could administer and score the Test of Motor Impairment. However, detailed interpretation would be quite another matter—that is, interpretation beyond a global judgment of either "probably normal" or "probably impaired."

The Test of Motor Impairment represents a fairly recent revision of the Oseretsky Tests of Motor Proficiency, first published in Russia in 1923. An English adaptation was sponsored by Doll in 1946, and nearly a decade later a new version of the test, thoroughly revised and restandardized, was published as the Lincoln-Oseretsky Motor Development Scale (Sloan, 1955). Judging from the reviews, the Lincoln-Oseretsky was better regarded than the earlier Oseretsky adaptation (see Espenschade, 1953, 1959). It was also considerably shorter, retaining only thirty-six of the original eighty-five items. The conception of Oseretsky, and then Sloan, apparently was to determine a motor age for the child tested, much in the "mental age" tradition of Binet. Thus, on Sloan's Lincoln-Oseretsky, the thirty-six items were ordered by difficulty, the child earned a total point score based on which and how well items were passed, and tables were entered by sex and chronological age in years to convert total points to a percentile rank.

We have decided to focus on the Test of Motor Impairment because of its considerably more recent development and norming and because it apparently is being used with increasing frequency. Although it consists of more items than the Lincoln-Oseretsky (forty-five versus thirty-six), it requires less time because no attempt is made to determine an exact motor age. Rather, the test is used merely to differentiate children who are probably normal in motor development from those who are probably impaired. Thus, a child is given a set of five items (representing five categories of motor functioning, discussed presently) typically passed by children his age. If he passes all five full items (earning a score of 0, that is, no impairment) or fails in only part of one item (earning a score of 1, that is, failing with only one hand or one foot), he is considered normal in motor development and no further testing occurs. For each full item failed at his age level, he is given two points. Further, under the standard test procedure, a child with an initial score of 2 or higher is also tested on all the items at the next-lower age level until he passes all items at a given level. (A shortened test procedure exists in which the child is tested at the next-lower age level only on those categories of items initially failed; however, the short procedure is recommended only when the group tested is very large.) An overall Motor Impairment score of 6 or higher (that is, failing a total of three or more full items) characterized the lowest 10 to 15 percent of the normative distribution and was thus considered by the test authors as indicative of definite motor impairment. Our hope is that a future revision of the Test of Motor Impairment might also include normative tables to convert performance to percentile ranks or some other indicator of degree of motor coordination or proficiency.

The test of Motor Impairment is also unusual in at least three other regards. First, on most items, two or three trials are permitted, and, on a few, up to ten trials are allowed (such as the ball-catching items and the ball-throwing accuracy item). Second, attempts are made to limit the influence of cognitive and emotional factors by making the tasks simple (so as to be understood by children of IQ 50 and over), by allowing examiners great latitude in giving instructions to ensure that the child understands the requirements of each task, by reducing any demands on the child to solve complex problems or to remember elaborate instructions, and by avoiding items that might frighten the child (such as the original Oseretsky item of running and jumping onto a chair). Third, it is unusual for a "revision" because it departs markedly from the parent Oseretsky measure. Only 35 percent of the items (sixteen out of forty-five) on the Test of Motor Impairment were derived from the original Oseretsky, and most of these were either incorporated at new age levels or provided with new scoring criteria. The substantial dissimilarity between the final items on the Test of Motor Impairment and those on Sloan's Lincoln-Oseretsky is striking given that both measures began development from the original Oseretsky. An even more recent variation of the Oseretsky has just been released, the Bruininks-Oseretsky Test of Motor Proficiency (Bruininks, 1978), but information on its reception and use is still limited.

The five categories of motor functioning purportedly addressed by the Test of Motor Impairment are:

1. Balance (control and balance of the body while immobile).
2. Upper Limb Coordination (control and coordination of the upper limbs).
3. Whole Body Coordination (control and coordination of the body while in motion).
4. Manual Dexterity (manual adeptness with emphasis on speed).
5. Simultaneous Movement (manual adeptness with emphasis on simultaneous movement and precision).

These categories represent five of the six areas on the original Oseretsky. For each age level, a single item is provided for each category.

The items for each category at each of the age levels relevant to the focus of this book are presented in Table 23. Though not shown in the table, the same pattern of single items for each category is followed for ages nine, ten, eleven-twelve, and thirteen plus. Note too that, although the test is appropriate only for five- to thirteen-year-old children, items at a sub-five age level are included for five-year-olds who fail one or more items at the five-year level. Note that many items in Table 23 involve testing both hands or both feet, particularly in the Balance and Manual Dexterity categories. Different criteria are sometimes set depending on the hand or foot used, and these appear in the table separated by a slash line. For example, on the Placing Pegs in Board item (manual dexterity for seven-year-olds), only seventeen seconds are allowed for the child's preferred hand while a twenty-one second ceiling is set for the other hand.

Validity for the Test of Motor Impairment takes three principal forms. First, sufficient information is provided about the selection and tryout of items through four revisions to allow the reader to judge the adequacy of that process. In general, it seemed carefully done and resulted in appropriate percentages of children passing each item at every age level. Second, several studies reported in the manual addressed criterion-related validity. In one, teachers first identified sixty six- to eight-year-olds they thought showed motor impairment. A matched group of sixty children were then selected. All 120 children were then rated by the teachers for motor functioning in the five categories and also were given the Test of Motor Impairment by an external administrator. The initial selection by the teachers, their detailed assessments, and the test results all were substantially to highly related. For example, the total disagreement between the teachers' detailed assessments and the test results was less than 18 percent. Again, as we have noted previously, although such substantial relationships support the validity of the measure, they are at the same time somewhat disquieting inasmuch as the test is supposed to be a better detector of motor impairment than human (in this case, teacher) judgment. Other studies demonstrated quite convincingly a substantial relationship between test scores and both ill health and various types of behavior disturbance. For example, motor-impaired children as identified by the Test of Motor Impairment showed over three times the incidence of maladjustment that well-coordinated children exhibited (on the basis of an adjustment scale completed by teachers). The most pronounced difference involved *inconsequence*, defined as overreaction characterized by the failure to inhibit first responses—quite close to *hyperactivity* as currently used. Third, and probably most closely linked to validation, almost 90 percent of the children described as impaired on the basis of the test received that designation because of poor performance in more than one category of motor functioning on the test.

A relationship between scores on the Test of Motor Impairment and socio-economic status was found similar to the one between Purdue Perceptual-Motor Survey scores and SES. That is, after establishing four SES levels—upper, middle, lower-middle, and lower—Stott, Moyes, and Henderson (1972) reported greatest motor impairment in the lower SES group and least impairment in the lower-middle SES group. While primarily pointing out the need for additional studies, they described the motor superiority of the lower-middle or skilled manual worker group as "hard to explain by any accepted theory of human development" (Stott, Moyes, and Henderson, 1972, p. 29). They suggested that the greater motor impairment of the lower SES group might be due to malnutrition or adverse environment.

The treatment of reliability in the Test of Motor Impairment manual is neither comprehensive nor systematic. Although four studies were reported, each with sizable coefficients, all of them involved stability over short time periods (two days to four weeks) and fairly small groups of children (fifteen to thirty-nine). In one study, done during the third revision, and separately for each year-group, only test categories I and III were used as only they were considered final. When retest examiners were changed and actual balance times correlated, stability coefficients primarily in the high .90s were observed for category I. On category III, percentage of agreement varied from 79 to 100 percent and averaged nearly 95 percent (yet chance agreement was high given the substantial pass rate). Still, only a small sample was used (three children retested in each of the eight year-groups). In a second study, fifteen motor-impaired children were retested after two weeks. Percentages of agreement were 91, 96, 84, 78, and 100 for categories I through V, respectively. It was not stated if the retesting was done by the same or different examiners, nor what ages the children represented. The third study, using different examiners on retest, involved between twenty-eight and thirty-nine six- to eight-year-old children for each category of items. The overall correlation was .71 over a two-week interval, while average impairment scores of 7.5 and 7.8 were observed on the two occasions. However, this study involved only the second revision of the test and coefficients for separate ages were not reported. The final study entailed a variable two-to-four week interval, twenty-four children six to eight years old, and probably the same test examiner on both occasions (although this is not specified). A correlation of .93 was reported, but separate coefficients for each age are missing. In all, the reliability data indicate substantial stability but still must be considered scattered and incomplete. If a systematic effort to establish reliability on the current version of the measure resulted in comparable coefficients for each separate age group, the test user could be more confident about the reliability of performances observed.

The usability of the Test of Motor Impairment in terms of normative sample appears less than satisfactory. The sample came from a single industrial city in Ontario, so it was, at the outset, geographically constrained. Sampling procedures followed within the city seemed appropriate. Thirty-one schools were divided into four socioeconomic groups and subjects were drawn proportionately therefrom. In all, the sample included over 800 children between their sixth and fifteenth birthdays (no mention of the source of the five-year-old sample is made) who were born on the fifteenth or sixteenth day of any month. Additional descriptive information about the sample is needed to allow the user to determine the representativeness of its demographic characteristics. No norm tables are provided as such, since a Motor Impairment score of 6 or more results in a decision of "probably impaired" for both boys and girls. Sex differences

Table 23. Items on Test of Motor Impairment by Category of Motor Functioning and Age Level

			Age Level (in years)				
Category of Motor Functioning	*Sub-5*	*5*	*6*	*7*	*8*		
I. Balance	Heel-Toe Balance (Standing heel-to-toe and later switching foot position, must maintain balance for 10/8 seconds; 2 trials for each foot position.)	Toe Balance (Standing on tiptoes, must maintain balance for 10 seconds; 3 trials.)	One-Leg Balance (Standing on one leg and testing each leg, must maintain balance for 15 seconds; 3 trials for each leg.)	One-Leg Balance, Arms Raised (Standing on one leg, raising arms above head, and testing each leg, must maintain balance for 20 seconds; 2 trials for each leg.)	Stork Balance (Standing on one leg, placing the other foot on the knee, and testing each leg, must maintain balance for 20 seconds; 2 trials for each leg.)		
II. Upper Limb Coordination	Bridge of Rods (Must build a bridge from three short, square rods; 3 trials.)	Bouncing Two-Hand Catch (Must bounce a tennis ball on the floor and cleanly catch it in two hands at least 4 times out of 10 trials.)	Bouncing One-Hand Catch (Testing each hand, must bounce a tennis ball on the floor and cleanly catch it in one hand at least 8/5 times out of 10 trials for each hand.)	Spiral of Holes (Testing each hand, must poke a pencil through a track of holes in a wooden board in 23½/28½ seconds; 2 trials for each hand.)	Catching Off Wall (Must throw a tennis ball underarm against a wall and cleanly catch it in two hands at least 4 times out of 10 trials.)		

III. Whole Body Coordination	Jump and Clap (Must jump and clap once at face level before landing; 3 trials.)	High Jump (Must jump over a cord set at just below knee height; 3 trials.)	Hopping Forward (Standing on one foot and testing each foot, must hop forward for 5 yards without letting the free foot touch the floor; 2 trials for each leg.)	Heel-Toe Walk (Must walk heel-to-toe along a line, completing at least 10 steps; 3 trials.)	Sideways Jumping (Moving in each of two directions and landing inside marked areas, must jump sideways 3 times with feet together; 2 trials in each direction.)
IV. Manual Dexterity	12-Pin Board (Testing each hand, must pick up and place 10 holed squares one at a time onto a pin board in 20/22 seconds; 2 trials for each hand.)	Posting Coins (Testing each hand, must pick up and place 12 coins one at a time into a slotted bank box in 18/20 seconds; 2 trials for each hand.)	Threading Beads (Must thread 8 cube-shaped beads onto lace in 25 seconds; 3 trials.)	Placing Pegs in Board (Testing each hand, must pick up and place 10 pegs one at a time into holes on a board in 17/21 seconds; 3 trials for each hand.)	Lacing Board (Must thread a lace through a series of holes in a wooden board in 16 seconds; 3 trials.)
V. Simultaneous Movement	Simultaneous Matchsticks (Must pick up matchsticks with both hands and simultaneously drop them in box, handling 10 matchsticks in 10 seconds; 3 trials.)	Simultaneous Markers (Must pick up markers with both hands and simultaneously drop them in box, handling 16 markers in 12 seconds; 3 trials.)	Circle Trace (Must trace a continuous circular path with a pen without crossing the boundary more than twice; 3 trials.)	Fingertip Touching (Testing each hand and using the thumb of the same hand, must touch each fingertip separately in the order 5, 4, 3, 2, 2, 3, 4, 5; 2 trials for each hand.)	Bead-on-Board Balance (Testing each hand, must balance a bead on a rectangular block held vertically with one hand while walking 10 yards; 3 trials for each hand.)

were found in the norming sample and reported, but apparently were not considered large enough to warrant separate cutoff scores. There is a notable absence of interpretation information in the manual, although considerable rationale for, and background information about, the development of the test are provided.

Some additional minor criticisms of small consequence can be made. For example, in at least one case (the first item for sub-five), the illustrative picture does not correspond well to the task description. However, in all, the Test of Motor Impairment shows considerable promise (also note the generally favorable review by Pauker, 1978). With additional attention to validity and a comprehensive study to establish reliability, the test's stature could be enhanced notably. A more representative sample would also be desirable. If the test authors were to decide that their test might take on another function in addition to identifying likely motor impairment—namely, measuring motor development—then possibly the Test of Motor Impairment and Development could be christened. That is, while norming with a more representative sample, they might do the additional testing necessary to prepare tables to convert the maximum performance of any child to a percentile rank. Thus, the present scoring procedure and process to determine likely impairment status could be maintained. Further, if a user wanted to do the additional testing necessary to establish a child's maximum motor performance, the child's effort could be interpreted using specific norm tables.

Before concluding this chapter on the psychomotor domain, we would like to alert the reader to the existence of a rather extensive number of other psychomotor measures, most often less well known, or locally developed, or both. One collection of such measures, also mentioned in the section on source books, is *Testing for Impaired, Disabled and Handicapped Individuals* (American Alliance for Health, Physical Education, and Recreation, undated). A large number of instruments are briefly described in the book, including physical fitness tests, psychomotor (perceptual-motor) scales, and developmental profiles. Although the information presented frequently is insufficient to permit final instrument selection decisions, the descriptions are sufficiently detailed to allow determination of scales to obtain for further study and possible use. Thus, as an example, the entry for the Hughes Basic Gross Motor Assessment or BGMA (Hughes, 1975) contains the following: a description of what is measured (static balance, gross motor coordination, dynamic balance, fundamental movement and locomotor skill, and eye-hand coordination), how it is measured, information on the administration of the test, comments, and the address where the BGMA may be obtained. (Unlike many measures in the psychomotor domain, the Hughes BGMA places emphasis on recording exactly how various tasks are performed, noting a child's "poor-form adjustments," and scoring on the basis of any such adjustments made.) The book also contains some valuable summary charts comparing areas measured by different instruments. In all, the book describes about fifty published and ten locally developed measures.

Chapter 9

=====

Conceptual Frameworks
for Evaluation

=====

As indicated in the opening chapter, the principal focuses of this book are measurement and evaluation as they pertain to early childhood education. *Measurement* was defined as the process of determining, through observation or testing, an individual's behaviors or traits or a program's characteristics, and then assigning a number, score, or rating to that determination. As such, measurement involves numbers, scales, constructs, validity, and reliability. *Evaluation* was defined as the process of judging the worth of something—frequently in terms of its adequacy, costs, or effectiveness. Most often evaluated in early childhood education are programs, educational procedures and products, and individual performance. As noted earlier, much meaningful evaluation is comparative, although some judgments are made according to a selected standard or criterion. Therefore, evaluation concerns values, measurement, criteria, needs, bias control, and cost analysis. Since measurement is an important component of evaluation, the credibility of an evaluation is directly related to the quality of any measures used.

In Chapters Two through Eight, we focused on basic measurement concepts, observation, and specific early childhood measures. At this point, the spotlight is shifted toward evaluation. In Chapters Nine through Twelve, we examine conceptual frameworks for evaluation, evaluation of individuals' performance in early education settings, examples of program evaluations, and contributions from other fields to early childhood program evaluation. Since measurement is normally an integral part of evaluation, there is some interweaving of evaluation and measurement themes in these four final chapters. For example, many of the contributions to evaluation from other disciplines, noted in Chapter Twelve, are measures and measurement techniques.

Chapters on educational evaluation would have been much simpler to write fifteen to twenty years ago. As late as the early 1960s, evaluation of educational programs had not been addressed on any broad, systematic basis. This is not to imply that evaluation was absent from the educational scene prior to 1960. On the contrary, evaluation concerns have been repeatedly aired during this century, as Merwin (1969) noted in his historical review of changing concepts in educational evaluation. However, up to 1960, the emphasis was primarily on the measurement of individual performance, on the appropriateness of various rating, grading, and marking procedures, and on the accreditation of schools. In the 1960s, interest in educational evaluation, especially program evaluation, was spurred by federal legislation requiring evaluation as one condition for the initiation and continued funding of new educational programs under the Elementary and Secondary Education Act of 1965. Since that time, educational evaluation has been the focus of considerable developmental work and debate.

An excellent sign of the increasing maturity of this field is its attempt to develop standards to govern evaluations. Since 1975, a broadly representative committee has been operating to draft a set of standards for evaluation analogous to the well-known *Standards for Educational and Psychological Tests* (American Psychological Association, 1974). The committee has produced a draft copy of the *Standards for Evaluations of Educational Programs, Projects, and Materials* (Joint Committee on Standards for Educational Evaluation, 1978) and hopes to release a final document by 1980. Currently, the evaluation standards are conceptualized in four areas:

1. Accuracy standards, which examine whether the evaluation was technically adequate and produced sound information.
2. Utility standards, which concern the usefulness of the evaluation—the extent to which it is informative, timely, and influential—for various audiences.
3. Propriety standards, which consider the legality, ethics, and regard for human welfare evidenced by the evaluation.
4. Feasibility standards, which address the practicality, political viability, and cost effectiveness of the evaluation.

Such standards would do much to improve the practice of educational evaluation, and thereby to increase its effectiveness.

In this chapter, seven conceptual frameworks for the conduct of educational evaluations are reviewed. The chapter offers an overview of the highlights of this recent development activity as well as a short summary of earlier work on educational evaluation. Since an in-depth treatment of this broad field is impossible in a single chapter, we provide ample references for the reader who wishes to pursue a selected topic in greater depth. As a further aid to our readers, we repeatedly focus on possible applications of the evaluation frameworks to early childhood education.

As the conceptual frameworks are examined, the reader will be reminded that evaluations can have diverse purposes, as implied in Chapter One. Anderson and Ball have provided an intriguing list of six major purposes for program evaluation and noted that such purposes are not necessarily mutually exclusive:

1. To contribute to decisions about program installation;
2. To contribute to decisions about program continuation, expansion, or "certification";
3. To contribute to decisions about program modification;
4. To obtain evidence to rally support for a program;
5. To obtain evidence to rally opposition to a program; and
6. To contribute to the understanding of basic psychological, social, and other processes [Anderson and Ball, 1978, pp. 3–4].

The various frameworks now considered have varying utility for the several purposes listed.

In our review of most of the conceptual frameworks, we found Worthen and Sanders' book (1973) on educational evaluation a valuable reference and are indebted to them. The applications of the various frameworks to early childhood education, however, represent a totally new effort, at least to the best of our knowledge. The frameworks were drafted by their various developers to address program evaluation, and, by and large, this chapter concerns program evaluation. However, several of the sections on early childhood applications involve measurement of individuals and thus are not necessarily specific to program evaluation.

Accreditation Framework

Accreditation has been defined as "the process by which a program or institution is recognized as being in conformity with some agreed-upon standard" (Anderson, Ball, Murphy, and Associates, 1975, p. 4). The conceptual framework of accreditation is embodied in the work of organizations such as the National Council for Accreditation of Teacher Education (1970) or NCATE and the six regional associations for the accreditation of secondary schools and colleges, such as the North Central Association of Colleges and Secondary Schools or NCA (National Study of Secondary School Evaluation, 1969). Accreditation represents one of the earliest types of systematic evaluation activity affecting large numbers of American schools; for example, NCA was formed in 1895 and was actively working on accreditation matters by the early 1900s.

The main purpose of the accreditation framework is to identify deficiencies in secondary schools or teacher-education institutions with regard to their preparation of students or professional school personnel, such as guidance counselors, administrators, or teachers. Historically, elementary schools have not been subject to accreditation, although one of the six regional associations is exploring such a possibility (Commission on Elementary Schools, 1971). In accreditation, emphasis is placed on the educative processes employed, with special attention to subject matter offered, teaching-learning procedures used, and resources provided. Standards for assessing the adequacy of the institution for the most part are derived from judgments made by groups of persons considered to be expert in secondary and higher education. Periodically, the standards are updated and revised. Frequently, the standards are stated as minimum levels (such as levels of degrees held by faculty, adequate library resources, and the like) assumed to be necessary for satisfactory program operation.

The accreditation process follows a typical pattern. A secondary school or institution of higher education comes up for accreditation periodically (usually every seven to ten years). The initial activity in accreditation is an involved self-study by the institution, using the standards set by the accrediting body. These standards tend to be fairly detailed and comprehensive. For example, the NCATE standards systematically consider aspects of curriculum, faculty, student policies (including admission and retention processes), resources and facilities, and graduate follow-up, program review, and planning. The six regional accreditation agencies use standards covering educational philosophy and objectives, curriculums, student activities, faculty, administration, guidance services, facilities, and media resources and services.

The second accreditation activity is an extensive on-site visit conducted by a team of experts (professional colleagues). Guided by the standards, the team considers the self-study results, observes the program in operation, interviews officials, faculty, students, and relevant others, and examines the resources and facilities supporting the program. A period of team deliberation follows, and then a report is written. If major deficiencies are noted, accreditation is withheld. Withholding of accreditation ordinarily creates considerable pressure on the institution to remedy the conditions judged substandard.

Advantages and Limitations. Several advantages are claimed for the accreditation approach to evaluation. First, the required self-study encourages self-improvement. Second, accreditation can be implemented quite easily. Third, there is a relatively short time period between the on-site visit and the delivery of the evaluative report. Fourth, the range of variables that can be examined is wide.

Limitations also can be noted. A major one involves the lack of evidence that the standards established via professional judgment are linked to effective school practices. A second, related, concern is the uncertain replicability of the process. Would a second accreditation team, operating independently, reach conclusions similar to those of a first team? Would the team be equally competent and fair? In other words, the nature of the many personal judgments integral to accreditation is questionable. A third limitation is the concentration on the processes of education and the relative lack of attention to outcomes, such as student learning. Finally, the accreditation framework is oriented toward assuring that a program has achieved at least a minimum level on each standard. Such an orientation can lead to some insensitivity to degrees of program quality above the established minimum floor.

Application to Early Childhood Education. Two existing applications of the accreditation framework to early childhood education can be cited. The most obvious one is the accreditation process required for institutions preparing teachers of young children. A second application can be found in the state licensing of daycare and preschool centers. Although licensing departs in some ways from accreditation, many similarities exist. The process followed by the childcare licensing unit of the Colorado Department of Social Services is typical. Centers intending to operate in the state must make an initial application. Representatives of three agencies visit the center: the local fire department, to inspect for compliance with fire regulations; the state health department, to approve sanitation facilities, food preparation areas, and the like; and the state licensing unit, to examine the qualifications of personnel, the building space and equipment, the record-keeping capability, and similar features of the center. The center cannot operate until all three agencies grant approval. Family daycare homes, serving six or fewer children in a private residence, also must be licensed to operate in Colorado; a visit by the licensing unit is required (no visit by fire or health officials is mandated). After the initial approval, the center's or daycare home's license must be renewed annually. The renewal process entails a visit by the state licensing unit. Standards used in the initial and subsequent evaluative processes eventuate from group meetings of childcare experts, practitioners in centers, and parents. The standards are reviewed by an advisory committee to the state licensing unit and ultimately must be approved by the Colorado State Board of Social Services.

A third potential application of the accreditation framework rests on the likely appeal of its self-study feature to persons who work with young children in educational settings. Providing for an extended period of self-study under competent guidance might serve to reduce the threat that often accompanies evaluation. Further, a close examination by a competent team of a program's self-study efforts and its actual operations could lead to program improvement. Although we envision considerable acceptance by early childhood educators of self-study and, to a lesser extent, of visitation teams, this acceptance in no way reduces the limitations of accreditation just detailed. Our belief is that the accreditation framework cannot serve as a fully effective evaluation strategy until empirical evidence is assembled that first links the standards used to effective teaching procedures and desirable student outcomes, and second demonstrates an acceptable degree of objectivity by visiting teams and a substantial replicability of the outcomes of the visitation process.

Tyler's Objective-Attainment Framework

Ralph Tyler was an early contributor to the literature on educational evaluation. During the 1930s, he served as Research Director for the Eight-year Study of schools conducted by the Commission on the Relation of School and

College. Later, Tyler and his associates presented and elaborated their conceptual framework, intended primarily for curriculum evaluation, in a series of writings (Smith and Tyler, 1942; Tyler, 1942; and Tyler, 1951).

The Tylerian framework concentrates on delineation of objectives for students and on measurement to ascertain the extent to which objectives are attained. The essentials of the framework are embodied in seven procedural steps (Tyler, 1942):

1. Formulate a statement of objectives. This initial step requires a determination of the broad goals of the school program.
2. Classify the objectives. This step entails development of a classification scheme of types of objective, which in turn helps assure even coverage and some parallelism in format.
3. Define objectives in behavioral terms. Stating objectives as observable student behaviors has become the central feature of this framework. Tyler himself, however, held less stringent standards for the specificity of behavioral objectives than do some contemporary evaluators (such as Popham, 1975).
4. Identify situations in which attainment of objectives might be assessed. Once noted, these become potential test situations for gathering evidence bearing on the achievement of objectives. Tyler indicated that such an activity, conscientiously implemented, should lead to a much wider range of situations than had commonly been utilized.
5. Select or develop measures and try them out. This step involves the examination of standardized tests, questionnaires, and other measures and, frequently, development of new measures to assess certain objectives. Then, a preliminary tryout of the measures is suggested.
6. Refine and improve the more promising appraisal methods. Based on the preliminary tryout results, potentially valuable measures are developed further and their operating characteristics are more closely examined.
7. Collect and interpret data. This final step entails administering the measures, scoring or describing the results, and interpreting the findings. Interpretation centers on a comparison of the student performance data with the previously established behavioral objectives.

The emphases of the Tyler framework clearly lie in the explicit statements of behavioral objectives and the measurement of such objectives. This centering on outcomes—specific student behaviors—is in sharp contrast to the accreditation framework, which focuses on the process of instruction. The Tyler framework emphasizes measurement; pre-test data are used to determine entry levels of behavior and post-test data to assess the effects of instruction. Comparison of these data should indicate to decision makers the extent to which designated behavioral objectives were attained via a given curriculum unit or course. Note that student performance is being compared with prespecified objectives rather than with performance under some competing curriculum.

More recent pronouncements by Tyler extend the role of behavioral outcomes in evaluation. For example, Tyler identified student learning as the most direct and valid means of evaluating teachers (Tyler, 1958). In a related area, he supported accountability efforts (discussed later in this chapter) that rely on criterion-referenced measures to assess student learning (Tyler, 1971). As chairman of the National Assessment of Educational Progress (NAEP)—a large project, initiated in the mid 1960s, that conducts a national sampling of young persons at four age levels to measure their cognitive and affective behaviors in ten subject areas (Womer, 1970)—Tyler continued to emphasize specific student outcomes.

Two more recent conceptual frameworks for evaluation also focus on the attainment of behavioral objectives. Hammond (1973) used local personnel and consultant evaluators to assess the effectiveness of innovative programs by comparing obtained performance data with specified behavioral objectives. Compared with Tyler, Hammond concentrated more on instructional and institutional dimensions of programs—that is, their processes—in terms of their possible effects on objective-related performance. Metfessel and Michael's framework (1967) closely approximated that of Tyler. An important contribution by Metfessel and Michael was an extensive list of different types of criterion measures that might be used to ascertain a program's attainment of objectives.

Advantages and Limitations. A major advantage claimed by proponents of the Tyler evaluation scheme is the focus on unambiguous behavioral objectives (this feature can also be viewed as a limitation, as is soon noted). Such explicitness is assumed to enhance the efficiency and effectiveness of instruction. A second advantage is the systematic examination of the congruence between established objectives and actual student performance. A third advantage derives from current definitions of behavioral objectives. One required component of a complete behavioral objective is detailed criteria for assessing the adequacy of the behavior exhibited. Therefore, once the objective is prespecified in adequate terms, it is relatively easy to appraise the extent to which it is attained. A final merit is that educators are given key roles in the evaluative process, such as specifying objectives and measuring relevant outcomes.

Since the Tylerian conceptual framework concentrates heavily on behavioral objectives, it is not surprising that the three most often mentioned limitations all relate to these objectives. One limitation cited is that the focus on behavioral objectives ignores the appraisal of important educational processes or antecedent conditions. The framework is inappropriate for evaluating processes directly, or equipment, or organization plans, or anything that is not clearly and directly linked to the specified objectives. A second limitation, pointed out by Glass (1969), among others, is that many significant educational outcomes are not manifested until some time after instruction has ceased. Therefore, evaluation must involve measurement of proxy behaviors—those that take the place of the ultimate objectives, which cannot immediately or economically or ethically be observed. Satisfactory performance of a proxy behavior is only circumstantial evidence that satisfactory performance would occur later on the ultimate objectives. A third limitation concerns the lack of attention given to the worth or value of the objectives. Common charges leveled at behavioral objectives are their tendencies to be trivial, to involve only behaviors that are easily measured, and to squash creativity. (For a full discussion of the merits and limitations of explicit instructional or behavioral objectives, see Goodwin and Klausmeier, 1975.)

Application to Early Childhood Education. There is a sizable group of early childhood educators, although probably not a majority, who advocate the use of behavioral objectives with young children. Their support of this methodology results primarily from instructional design considerations rather than from an evaluation orientation. Two early childhood education program models, both well known and utilized in Head Start and Follow Through evaluations (see Chapter Twelve), are characterized by their explicit specification of behavioral objectives for students. The Behavior Analysis Classroom (Bushell, 1973), developed at the University of Kansas, employs behavioral objectives, programmed or highly structured academic materials, and an active token reinforcement system. The second model, the Academically Oriented or Direct Instruction Model, was initiated at the University of Illinois (Bereiter and Engelmann, 1966) and further developed at the University of Oregon (Becker and Engelmann, 1973). Now known as DISTAR (Science Research Associates, 1972), the model emphasizes behavioral objectives embodied in detailed materials for teaching language, arithmetic, and reading; direct instruction by the teacher in a pattern drill format; and active involvement of small groups of children via choral responding. For these highly structured models, the Tylerian evaluation framework might well be appropriate. However, many other educational models for young children do not use explicit instructional objectives, and many of the persons sponsoring these models would be uncomfortable with the Tylerian evaluation approach. Some of the least structured models (as described in Chapter Eleven) probably view prespecification of detailed outcomes for children as counterproductive.

Be aware that although the Kansas and Oregon models incorporate the use of behavioral objectives, these objectives essentially are provided for the program user. In the Tylerian evaluation framework, educators formulate, classify, and "behaviorize" objectives appropriate for their students. Although there is nothing wrong with selecting a packaged curriculum program, note that such a practice detracts from an important advantage of the Tylerian framework—that is, the active involvement of educators in specifying objectives.

Another aspect of the Tyler framework has application to early childhood education. In many educational settings, including those for young children, adults in charge have given insufficient attention to the child outcomes desired. Although considered extreme by some, the explicitness of objectives required in the Tylerian scheme does alert educators to the fact that objectives are often poorly defined, "fuzzy," or not consciously formulated at all. For example, judging from their staunch dedication to the task, some teachers have as their primary objective "covering" a subject by completing the textbook, even though Hawkins (as noted in Duckworth, 1973) has pointed out the wiser practice of "uncovering" a subject. For such teachers to carefully conceptualize the outcomes they intend for students—whether in a strict behavioral format or not—would seem desirable.

Other potential applications to early childhood education of the Tyler approach can be imagined. For example, allegiance to the framework might prompt educators to develop or to locate and examine the objectives for preschool and the early grades. One source of such objectives is the Instructional Objectives Exchange (P.O. Box 24095, Los Angeles 90024), a repository bank and clearinghouse for behaviorally stated objectives. Such objectives could then be used to determine entry and terminal performance by students. If desired, the student performance data could be treated as pre- and post-measurements in keeping with the Tyler design.

It seems important to reaffirm the inapplicability of the Tyler framework for those early childhood educators whose own personal beliefs are incompatible with the philosophical message of the framework. We believe that serious attempts to follow Tyler's advice on evaluating teachers—by appraising their students' performance on behavioral objectives—would be strongly resisted by most early childhood educators, and with good reason (see Chapter Ten).

Stake's Countenance Framework

Robert Stake, a psychometrician, has written extensively on evaluation in education. In addition to the countenance framework discussed here, we later consider his responsive framework. Both these approaches and most of Stake's other pronouncements on evaluation are of relatively recent origin.

The countenance framework is so named because it was detailed in an article entitled "The Countenance of Educational Evaluation" (Stake, 1967). In the article, Stake encouraged the educator to examine the full countenance (appearance) of evaluation and to recognize the distinction between informal evaluation (based on casual observation, implicit objectives, intuitive norms, and subjective judgment) and formal evaluation. He then specified the characteristics of formal (or objective) evaluation.

To be adequately evaluated and understood, an educational program has to be both fully described and fully judged. This dual emphasis on description and judgment is the salient feature of formal evaluation via the countenance framework. Stake believed that although either description or judgment was valuable in its own right, both were requisite in conducting a complete evaluation. In Figure 8, the graphic representation of the scheme, the centrality of these two processes is apparent in the full description and judgment matrices (upper and lower halves of the figure, respectively).

Stake intended the layout of his framework (Figure 8) as a guide to the measurement and interpretation activities in a formal evaluative undertaking. His examples made it clear that the evaluator should collect data and statements for all twelve cells in the matrices. An elaboration of the terms appearing in Figure 8 is in order to clarify the likely nature of the cell entries. One dimension of the figure, cutting across both the description and judgment matrices, repre-

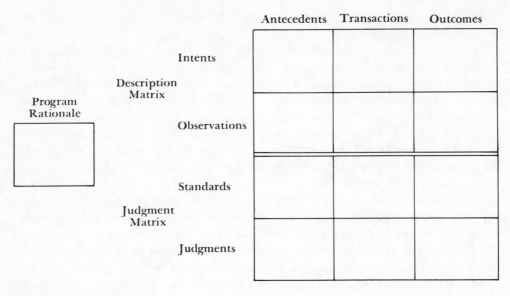

Source: Stake, 1967, p. 529.

**Figure 8. Layout of Required Data and Statements for a
Complete Evaluation of an Educational Program.**

sents three sequential clusters of information that should be tapped: antecedents, transactions, and outcomes. *Antecedents* are conditions existing prior to the operation of the program, such as student knowledge or age, which may relate to outcomes. (Tyler's student entry levels would be considered antecedents.) *Transactions* are the activities or succession of engagements that constitute the program. As such, they are processes and include all that goes on during the program. *Outcomes* are defined as the effects of the program, whether achievements, attitudes, motivation levels, or other effects. The accreditation framework emphasized process, and Tyler focused on outcomes primarily and on antecedent student behaviors secondarily. Stake, however, incorporated all three clusters into his framework to stimulate plans for a comprehensive data collection, not to subdivide such a collection, and to highlight his belief that inordinate emphasis was too commonly placed on outcomes.

The second dimension in Figure 8 concerns intents and observations (in the description matrix) and standards and judgments (in the judgment matrix). Each of these four subclassifications is considered in the light of relevant antecedents, transactions, and outcomes. *Intents* represent the goals or objectives of the program designers, operators, and participants. For example, they would include the program developer's plans for the type of student to be included, the operator's intended demonstrations or coverage of subject matter, the principal's anticipations about student outcomes, the students' own expectations about likely transactions and outcomes, and so forth. The intents should be listed and described. If key participants have difficulty expressing their objectives, it is the evaluator's task to assist them and to transform their intentions and expectations into data. *Observations* constitute the other half of the description matrix. They include combinations of the many types of measure we described extensively in earlier chapters of this book (also see the review of measurement techniques in evaluation by Sjogren, 1970). The evaluator must make decisions about which program antecedents, transactions, and outcomes to observe and measure; resources for observation are typically limited.

In the judgment matrix, *standards* are essentially bench marks of performance available for reference. Stake noted the appropriateness of both absolute and relative standards for evaluation purposes. Absolute standards tend to be formulated by experts and other interested groups (such as societal spokesmen, parents, or teachers) who set a desired level of performance, or a desired environment, or a desired quality of something related to that which is being evaluated. The expert opinion is usually based, at least in part, on empirically generated knowledge. A formalized, absolute standard would establish acceptable and meritorious levels for antecedents, transactions, and outcomes. Relative standards are derived by comparing the program to be evaluated with characteristics and outcomes of alternate programs. Stake expressed concern about the frequent unavailability in education of explicit, absolute standards (although informal, subjective standards abound). Relative standards are not commonly employed, since well-controlled comparative evaluations are infrequently conducted in education (see Chapter Twelve). *Judgments* involve determining whether or not a standard has been met. If no standard is available, one must be estimated. If several standards are available, the evaluator must decide how to weight them and which to give most credence to. Methods of gathering judgment data have been detailed by Stake (1970a). For example, the evaluator can seek judgments from a designated group using instrumentation such as a survey, the Q-technique, or the semantic differential; these judgments are then aggregated.

Once data are collected relevant to the twelve cells, and once the program rationale has been explicated, the evaluator can process the data. Descriptive evaluation data (again, the upper half of Figure 8) are processed in two principal ways: (1) by locating the contingencies (relationships) among antecedents, transactions, and outcomes, and (2) by determining the congruence between intents and observations. During program planning, a logical chain of relationships should have been formulated between intended antecedents, transactions, and outcomes; these relationships, that is, among the data cells in the first row of Figure 8, can be examined. In logical analysis, essentially a before-the-fact "armchair" technique, one looks for cogent arguments linking antecedents, transactions, and outcomes. Further, empirical relationships among antecedents, transactions, and outcomes actually observed—the second row of Figure 8—can be scrutinized. Congruence is determined by comparing intended antecedents, transactions, and outcomes with those in fact observed. In terms of Figure 8, the data in the first row of cells are compared with the data in the corresponding cells in the second row. Complete congruency—a perfect match between intentions and what actually happens—seldom occurs. Once the descriptive matrix data have been processed, the evaluator can consider them in terms of data in the judgment matrix. That is, the intended and observed data can be compared with absolute standards of excellence or with data generated from an alternate program or programs, establishing a relative standard. Such comparisons then are judged either directly by the evaluator or by relevant groups (parents, teachers, students, administrators, and the like) with the evaluator collecting and processing the judgment data (Stake, 1970a). The evaluator then prepares a report with recommendations, or possibly several types of report for different audiences.

Advantages and Limitations. A principal advantage of the countenance framework is its comprehensive and thorough scope. By including intents, observations, standards, and judgments—not just for outcomes but also for antecedents and transactions—the framework creates a panoramic, rather than a microscopic, view of the program being evaluated. A related advantage is the advocacy of a systematic method for ordering descriptive and judgmental data and for examining relationships between them. A third positive feature of Stake's scheme is its insistence on fairly explicit standards for use in making judgments and its provision for utilizing either absolute or relative standards. In his countenance model (1967) and elsewhere (1970a), Stake made valuable contributions toward a better understanding of the role of judgments in evaluation. The generalizability of the framework constitutes a fourth advantage. It could be used with virtually all programs and for several types of evaluation, such as formative and summative (as discussed next in relation to Scriven's framework). It also could be used for purposes other than program evaluation, such as staff evaluation. A fifth desirable characteristic of Stake's framework is its recognition that an evaluation can be of interest to several audiences and that the need might exist to fashion multiple evaluation reports.

Two limitations in the countenance framework derive from methodological inadequacies. One shortcoming is the lack of well-developed methods to obtain the data and information required in the matrices, particularly in regard to intents and judgments; a second is the lack of methods for determining which standards and whose judgments should be given priority. A third bothersome aspect of the framework is the definitional overlap between some aspects of the evaluation design matrices. For instance, the distinctions between standards and judgments are not always clear. A final limitation derives from the extensive scope of the countenance framework. If full description and full judgment are implemented, the evaluation could become excessively complex and costly.

Application to Early Childhood Education. One purpose of the cells in the countenance framework matrices is to serve as collection points for program data and information. The following brief description of an early childhood situation illustrates how such a function could be applied. Suppose that a preschool, located near a busy intersection used by most students, is planning to conduct a two and a half hour safety program on five consecutive days. The purpose of the program is to teach the students to cross the intersection only when the "Walk" light is on.

Intents:

- Antecedents: During the week prior to the program, fifteen (one fourth) of the preschoolers at least once did not wait for the "Walk" light to cross the intersection (as measured unobtrusively). Sporadic teacher warnings seemed ineffective.
- Transactions: The program was planned over the course of one week; discussions and guest speakers from the police department and the local hospital were intended.
- Outcomes: The objective was to eliminate any crossing of the intersection except when the "Walk" light was on.

Observations:

- Antecedents: Eight students were sick for the week and missed the entire program; the other students had at least three program sessions, and most had all five.
- Transactions: The program ran long some days but not others and, in total, was about two and a half hours. Discussions seemed spirited. The police department official gave an interesting talk and showed an informative movie; the hospital was not able to send a speaker.
- Outcomes: In the week following the program, six of the students (10 percent) at least once did not wait for the "Walk" light (as measured unobtrusively); half of these were students who had missed the program.

Standards:

- Antecedents: Although the teachers expected young children to be absent periodically, they also believed that any important instruction missed should be "made up."
- Transactions: The teachers expected that the discussions and talks would be clear enough, and the key safety rules repeated often enough, for all the students to understand them.
- Outcomes: The preschool director, teachers, and aides all agreed that every student had to follow this safety procedure.

Judgments:

- Antecedents: Retrospectively, the teachers judged that the material was important enough that it should be "made up" by the students who missed it.
- Transactions: The teachers judged the discussions good and the police representative's talk and movie very good; comments from some students made the teachers feel that a good addition to the program would be practice sessions with students actually crossing the intersection.
- Outcomes: The director, teachers, and aides judged the improved crossing behavior encouraging and believed it was due to the program.

Based on this data and information, the director and teachers decided to reschedule much of the program for students who had missed it and also for those few who continued to walk against the light. They also decided to periodically monitor student's behavior at the crossing and to activate the program again if unsafe crossing increased. Obviously, in the example provided, the data and information entered in each cell by no means exhausted the supply of relevant entries. In an actual evaluation, multiple entries in most cells would be the rule.

A second possible application to early childhood education concerns the processing of information and data on standards and judgments. Readers well acquainted with the field of early childhood education are aware that there are, in the first place, widely varying opinions about the necessity for such preschool programs for young children. And, among those supporting the programs, there are varying beliefs as to appropriate student participants, essential teacher preparation, effective instructional procedures, desirable student outcomes, and the like. If knowledgeable evaluators move toward developing even better methodologies for determining standards and formulating judgments, early childhood education could benefit substantially. Such procedural advances could help explicate the varying beliefs concerning the education of young children and the types and proportions of persons holding such beliefs. The resultant standards and judgment processing strategies could be used in the evaluation of diverse types of program.

Another application of the framework to early childhood education, more obvious than the previous one and already available, is in program planning. In fact, such an application could be made to any educational program. The framework's comprehensive view of the program makes it highly appropriate to planning. For example, if a new preschool is being designed, intentions could be detailed (such as type and number of participating students and teachers, appropriate learning activities, and desired student and staff outcomes), observations could be planned, standards could be located or developed, and criteria and personnel for making judgments could be identified. If the program designers give careful attention to all those elements suggested by the systematic and comprehensive framework, and to their interrelationships, then the probability for the development of a complete, well-integrated program is high.

Scriven's Frameless Framework

Michael Scriven, a philosopher, has strongly influenced the field of educational evaluation. Although his work has taken the form of a series of insights rather than that of a formal evaluation framework, the collected pronouncements provide substantial information on conducting an evaluation. We have dubbed Scriven's work the *frameless framework* and have included several of his more salient observations. Many aspects of Scriven's work are compatible with Stake's countenance framework, just presented. In fact, Worthen and Sanders (1973) classified the approaches of both Scriven and Stake as *judgmental strategies,* as did Popham (1975) in a slightly different manner. Although Stake concentrated more on measurement than did Scriven, both men indeed emphasized judgment as central in the evaluation process.

An important distinction was made by Scriven (1967) between the *goals* and *roles* of evaluation. The single goal of an evaluation is determination of the value or merit of whatever is being evaluated. This determination, which involves judgment, is required in order to answer a certain type of question, such as "Does this curriculum result in better student performances than that curriculum?" or "Is the use of aides in preschool classes worth their cost?" (In question are the value of the curriculum and the value of the aides, respectively.) Although the goal of evaluation is the assignment of value, the roles that evaluation can take in education are highly variable. For example, evaluation could have the role of assisting in developing curriculums, in improving teacher performance, in purchasing equipment, in determining local support for an upcoming bond issue, and on and on. To help classify such diverse undertakings, Scriven proposed two basic roles—formative and summative.

The key to understanding these roles lies in the meaning of the terms themselves. *Formative evaluation* focuses on programs in operation or products under development, determines the merit of certain of their features (such as their durability, attention-holding power, efficiency, and so forth), and feeds data back into the cycle to reform the program or product. In essence, a series of judgments are made about a program or product as it is being formed or developed. These judgments, via the formative evaluation process, influence the nature of the program or product that ultimately results. *Summative evaluation* involves judging the overall worth of a program or product, usually at an end or critical decision point. Thus, a completed instructional program might be summatively evaluated to determine if it is worthy of continuation or should be terminated. One of us (Goodwin, 1974) presented some oversimplified, but clarifying, distinctions between formative and summative evaluation; in somewhat modified form, these distinctions are now listed.

Feature	Formative Evaluation	Summative Evaluation
Principal purpose	Developmental improvement of a program or product	Judgement of the overall worth of a program or product
Schedule of use	Continual; data fed back into developmental cycle	Normally when program completed or product finished; or at go-no go, fund-no fund decision point
Evaluative style	Rigorous, systematic, diagnostic	Rigorous, systematic, comparative or using absolute standards
Normal evaluators	Internal staff or supportive consultants hired by program or product developers	External, nonpartisan personnel
Consumers of evaluation results	Program designers and staff, product developers, "insiders"	Market consumers, funding agencies, "outsiders"

In regard to the "normal evaluators" distinction above, Scriven also described professional and amateur evaluation. Noting that "professional evaluators may simply exude a kind of skeptical spirit that dampens the creative fires of a productive group" (1967, p. 45), Scriven advised that programs just beginning engage in amateur (or self) evaluation (recall the discussion of Issue 7 in Chapter One). In all, the formative and summative concepts of evaluation have been used energetically (for example, see Airasian, 1974; Baker, 1974; and Bloom, Hastings, and Madaus, 1971).

Another important contribution by Scriven (1967) was his insistence that *goals be evaluated.* The merit of the goals or objectives of a program must themselves be assessed, along with the achievement of the goals. Of what significance would it be if trivial or inappropriate goals have been achieved? In Scriven's words, "it is obvious that if the goals aren't worth achieving then it is uninteresting how well they are achieved. . . . Thus evaluation proper must include, as an equal partner with the measuring of performance against goals, procedures for the evaluation of the goals" (1967, p. 52). Following Scriven's dictum, it is conceivable that evaluations would sometimes find goals inappropriate or worthless. This is a good argument for evaluating goals before the project begins.

Scriven's amorphous framework is also noteworthy in its encouragement of *comparative evaluations.* Believing that decisions must often be made between competing alternatives—such as Curriculum A or B or Products R, S, or T—Scriven (1967) advocated direct comparison as a logical means to provide information bearing on such decisions. Others have disagreed. For example, Cronbach (1963) pointed out that comparative evaluations would only identify the more (or most) effective alternative and would not shed light on why the alternative was more effective. Scriven countered (much as we did in considering Issue 14 in Chapter One) that causal explanation was not an evaluative function and that the more effective alternative could be adopted without knowing why it was more effective. (Later objections to comparative evaluations and use of control groups have been voiced, such as those by Guba and Stufflebeam, 1968; these are mentioned later in connection with Stufflebeam's framework and are treated more fully in Chapter Twelve.)

Although Scriven advocated comparative evaluations using experimental or quasi-experimental designs (see Chapter Twelve), he realistically noted that such approaches are not always possible. Accordingly, he formulated the *Modus Operandi Method* (Scriven, 1974). This approach, according to Scriven, derives from investigative techniques used by historians, anthropologists, detectives, and electronics troubleshooters. The term *modus operandi (MO)* is commonly used to denote a distinctive operating pattern followed habitually by a particular criminal.

Use of the method in evaluation begins with the observance of a particularly significant phenomenon, either positive or negative. Two questions arise: What caused the phenomenon? and, especially, Could the cause have been the program or intervention that is being evaluated? Scriven suggested, "The MO of a particular cause is an associated configuration of events, processes, or properties, usually in time sequence, which can often be described as the *characteristic causal chain* (or certain distinctive features of this chain) connecting the cause with the effect" (1974, p. 71). The evaluator's task involves looking for such a chain of occurrences—an MO—between the program or intervention being evaluated and the observed phenomenon, that is, the effect of interest. If a complete chain or MO can be discerned, then the program or intervention becomes the probable cause. The evaluator also has the responsibility to check for other complete MOs; more than one probable cause might exist for the observed phenomenon of interest, resulting in probable co-causes. The Modus Operandi Method yields results that are probabilistic rather than definitive; nevertheless, its use in educational evaluation seems warranted when more conclusive means (such as controlled experimentation—see Chapter Twelve) are inappropriate or not feasible. Popham characterized the Modus Operandi Method as "intriguing" and suggested that it could "bring out the latent Sherlock Holmes in all of us" (1975, p. 30).

Another element in Scriven's frameless framework is his distinction between intrinsic and payoff evaluation. *Intrinsic evaluation* is an approach for examining educational processes, personnel, or programs by evaluating their goals, content, teacher operations, attitude, grading procedures, or the like; emphasis is on evaluating the means used to reach certain ends. *Payoff evaluation* is a procedure that focuses on the effects of a process, personnel, or a program. These would usually be effects on students, although not always (for example, in evaluating the effects of an inservice program on teachers). Payoff evaluation concentrates on the ends rather than the means. Intrinsic and payoff evaluation correspond closely to Stake's evaluation of transactions and outcomes, respectively. Intrinsic evaluation can take a formative role (such as judging the sequencing of content in a program) or a summative one (judging the final content materials). Payoff evaluation can also be formative (as in judging student performance after an early version of a program, or at an interim point in a program, and informing developers of the judgments) or summative (judging the final effects of a fully developed program). Although Scriven opined that payoff evaluation was more valuable, he also recognized the merit of intrinsic evaluation.

Another useful procedure suggested by Scriven (1974) was *goal-free evaluation*. The typical evaluation might be labeled *goal based;* that is, the evaluation effort centers on the goals or objectives of a program and on the extent to which the goals have been attained. For example, a common practice since the mid 1960s has been the use of external teams that periodically make on-site evaluation visits to a federal- or state-funded project. The normal operating procedure for such teams began with their requesting the goals of the project and asking for the project staffs' opinion on the current attainment status of each goal. Scriven served on many such teams and was strongly impressed by the extensive influence of the stated goals on the nature and direction of the evaluation visit. Reflecting on this situation, he was concerned that such goal-based evaluations lured the evaluator into adopting so narrow a perspective that other important project effects, either positive or negative, might not be noted. To counteract this phenomenon, Scriven proposed goal-free evaluation, in which the evaluator receives neither a statement of project goals nor staff rhetoric on progress toward goal attainment. Rather, he searches for the effects of the project, whether intended or unanticipated, and evaluates them. "The less the external evaluator hears about the goals of the project, the less tunnel vision will develop, the more attention will be paid to *looking* for actual effects (rather than *checking* on alleged effects). . . . The value of goal-free evaluation does not lie in picking up what everyone already 'knows,' but in noticing something that everyone else has overlooked, or in producing a novel overall perspective" (Scriven, 1974, pp. 36, 38). Stated differently and more colorfully, "The goal-free evaluator is a hunter out alone and goes over the ground very carefully, looking for signs of any kind of game, setting speculative snares when in doubt. The goal-based evaluator, given a map that supposedly shows the main game trails, finds it hard to work quite so hard in the rest of the jungle" (Scriven, 1973, p. 327).

Goal-free evaluation has aroused extensive reactions (see Scriven, 1974, pp. 43–67). In replying to these concerns, Scriven has further elaborated the concept. For example, he did not envision goal-free evaluation as a replacement for goal-based effort but as a powerful adjunct procedure. Thus, a project might be evaluated using (independently) both goal-based and goal-free approaches. He further made clear that he was not abandoning his earlier position that it was important to evaluate goals; such a practice was appropriate, he believed, in such situations as the determination of which proposals to fund. Scriven also explained that the goal-free method could be used both in formative and, especially, in summative roles.

The several procedural suggestions recounted above represent just a sampling of Scriven's pronouncements regarding evaluation. Recall from Chapter One that he also introduced the concept of the "cheapy competitor" and elaborated the notion of cost-free evaluation. Another contribution has been a systematic Checklist for the Evaluation of Products, Producers, and Proposals, including rating criteria and reporting procedures like the Product Evaluation Profile (Scriven, 1974). In all, Scriven's frameless framework contains numerous concepts of importance for educational evaluation.

Advantages and Limitations. A major advantage of Scriven's framework is its consistent insistence that the goal and principal characteristic of evaluation is the determination of value or merit. Not all the framework authors examined here agree with Scriven on this point. We do, however, and we find the definition a reassuring landmark in the definitional jungle of evaluation terms. A second merit is the emphasis on the evaluation of the goals or objectives of an endeavor as a critical venture in its own right. If such a practice were more frequently employed, it could well reduce the number of contenders for the "Golden Fleece Award" periodically given by a United States senator to that research project he considers most trivial and most wasteful of federal spending. (Note that many congressional ventures could qualify for an analogous "Taxpayers' Fleece Award.") A third contribution of the frameless framework is the several useful distinctions that have been provided for educators and evaluators alike—the most influential of which has probably been the distinction between the formative and summative roles of evaluation. The provocative nature of much of Scriven's work constitutes a fourth advantage. His writings on goal-free evaluation, "cheapy competitors," cost-free evaluation, the Modus Operandi Method—to name but a few—have stimulated the field and led to productive dialogue. A final advantage is the wide applicability of most of Scriven's work to diverse areas of education and to diverse types of evaluation.

A principal limitation of Scriven's framework lies in its frameless character. Scriven has not chosen to incorporate his concepts into a single, comprehensive unit. As individual concepts, Scriven's pronouncements have had a large effect; if they were tied together in an integrated scheme, their impact might be greater yet. A related limitation is the overlap between concepts, with some ambiguity about the intended relationships between, say, formative-summative, intrinsic-payoff, amateur-professional, and so forth. A third shortcoming in the framework is the absence of methodology to implement several of the proposed concepts. Scriven provided creditable rationales for most of the types of evaluation he identified, but the enabling methodology was often unspecified. For example, he stressed the importance of assessing the validity of judgments, but no methodology was detailed (this deficiency also was partly present in Stake's countenance framework). A second example is goal-free evaluation—the rationale provided was elaborate, but several of the enabling methodological procedures were given scant attention.

Application to Early Childhood Education. An immediate application of Scriven's recommendations to early childhood settings might be the serious evaluation of program objectives. The organizers and staff of a preschool should believe in the value of the school's goals and should have substantial supporting rationales. Goals judged of little value should be eliminated. Such a practice should help establish consistency in staff purpose and possibly enhance staff morale. Further, having a prepared statement listing the goals of the school as well as explicit reasons why the goals are worthwhile should facilitate communication with parents, both those with children enrolled in the preschool and those considering enrollment.

A less obvious application might involve goal-free evaluation. Imagine a preschool, well established in a community, with a director and staff who are reasonably confident that it is accomplishing its stated goals. Although the school undergoes an annual visit from state officials to check that minimal standards are met, it has never received a thorough external evaluation. The director and her advisory board decide to commission a three-day evaluation of the goal-free type. A well-regarded evaluator, unfamiliar with the program and the staff, is contacted and agrees to the task. The evaluator, in turn, recruits additional unbiased team members—a preschool director-teacher, a parent of young children, and an educational psychologist. Without knowing the goals of the preschool or receiving staff reports on them, the team observes operations for three days, interviews children, parents, and staff, and reviews school records and materials. The team's report provides the preschool staff with considerable information—it confirms effects on some of the school's preset goals, but not on all of them, and it identifies other apparent but unanticipated effects, both positive and negative.

A third potential application of the frameless framework to early childhood education might be the institution of formative evaluation. Recall from our discussion of Issue 16 in Chapter One that evaluation commonly inspires anxiety. If evaluation could be presented as an ongoing process designed to improve the program, it might be welcomed with less trepidation. Accordingly, a preschool or any organization working with young children on educational pursuits might hire a formative evaluator or consultant, or designate one staff member to perform that role. Decisions by the full staff about which questions most need answering would give direction to the formative evaluation efforts. Data and information collected could be fed back to program staff, providing timely answers to questions of immediate concern and steering activities in promising directions.

A substantial list has been prepared containing suggested procedures for the formative evaluation of early childhood education programs; a second list includes formative evaluation suggestions for programs preparing personnel to work in early childhood settings (Goodwin, 1974, pp. 224–230). Sample procedures based in part on the first list (for various early childhood education program areas) are relevant here and are noted briefly below:

Program Area	*Suggested Formative Evaluation Procedures*
Goals/objectives of program	1. Assess the merit of the program's goals and the probability that the intended program activities will stimulate their attainment.
	2. Ascertain if objectives are stated so that measurement of progress is possible.
	3. Evaluate intended measures' appropriateness for determining attainment of objectives.
Recruitment of students for program	4. Poll parents (via interview or questionnaire) on how they learned of the program and why they selected it.
	5. Vary recruitment techniques systematically in different randomly selected sections of areas served; record outcomes in terms of student enrollments and eventual student success.
	6. Evaluate attractiveness, conciseness, and effectiveness of brochure describing program.
Program content and methods of instruction	7. Initiate "follow-in" activities to compare success in the program of groups of students (characterized by sex, age, developmental level, competence, personality, and source of recruitment).
	8. Vary instructional methods systematically, such as sensory modality emphasized (Goodwin and Klaus-

meier, 1975), and assess method effectiveness in terms of student attentiveness, outcomes, and the like.

9. Vary instructional materials systematically; observe student preferences, attentiveness, and outcomes.

10. Observe students' preferred reinforcers.

11. Record proportions of school day characterized by child talk and child initiation as distinct from adult talk and adult initiation.

12. Observe attention span of children during different activities and various instructional techniques; determine "holding power" of certain activities and techniques; match difficult content with activities and techniques having greater holding power.

13. Measure student progress periodically on attaining objectives; revise and reformulate objectives or instruction accordingly.

Program staff involvement

14. Assist staff to set personal goals; periodically discuss and record progress in some fashion.

15. Require each staff member to keep a daily log; monitor its content to determine amount and type of involvement; examine patterns of involvement with the staff member.

16. Provide format in which staff opinion on program policies, plans, methods, and the like can be presented and recorded; repeat the process periodically and note trends in staff opinion and involvement.

Program-parent rapport

17. Vary procedures systematically for informing different (randomly formed) groups of parents of children's progress; ascertain effectiveness of procedures.

18. Provide format for receiving and recording input on program from parents or parent advisory committee; repeat the process periodically and note trends in parental opinion.

19. Vary procedures systematically for effecting liaison with randomly selected parents on home educational activities; ascertain the extent to which such activities are stimulated and their apparent effects on students.

Program long-range effects

20. Initiate "follow-up" studies to ascertain success and adjustment of former students (characterized as in number 7 above and by success in the program) in later educational settings; use "blind" raters when possible, such as teachers unaware of children's previous preschool experience.

The procedures listed above are, obviously, suggestive rather than definitive. Many other procedures could be detailed. In every case, though, the procedures selected will depend on the exact context of the program and on formative evaluation priorities.

Another fairly obvious application of Scriven's framework to early childhood education is the use of his "cheapy competitor" strategy. Most of the readers of this book who have worked in early childhood educational settings probably have already engaged in "cheapy competitor" evaluation strategies, although only implicitly. For example, the staff of a preschool might know that they need numerous sets of objects with which students can practice their categorization and classification skills. After examining several expensive, commercially available sets, the staff decides to find or bring in readily available real-world "junk" (boxes of buttons, magazine pictures, utensils, articles of clothing, seashells, leaves, insects, and the like) instead. This decision resulted from the implicit use of the "cheapy competitor" strategy and the belief that the home-variety collections would be as effective as the commercial sets in helping students attain the targeted skills. A conscious decision to systematically evaluate planned activities and expenditures in terms of available "cheapy competitors" could serve well most early childhood programs.

Several other applications of Scriven's work to early childhood education could be noted, but space limitations have caused us to conclude by mentioning his emphasis on comparative evaluations. As noted in Issue 12 in Chapter One, we consider the use of comparative evaluations in education a valuable, but underused, methodology. Scriven's endorsement of the method, and Stake's generally positive attitude toward it, give us hope that it will be increasingly common, especially for local, formative evaluation efforts. Several contributions to the design of comparative evaluations can be traced to classical experimental design, such as utilizing comparison or control groups. These contributions are detailed in Chapter Twelve.

Stufflebeam's CIPP Framework

Daniel Stufflebeam, a Professor of Education and now Director of the Evaluation Center at Western Michigan University, developed the CIPP evaluation framework (1968). Early development and revisions of the scheme were influenced by Egon Guba and the Phi Delta Kappa National Study Committee on Evaluation (Stufflebeam and others, 1971). The framework was initially designed to assist school personnel in evaluating their federal projects. "Serving decision making in change efforts was and is the most unique characteristic of the model. It has been extended recently, however, to provide information both for decision making and accountability in change efforts" (Stufflebeam, 1974a, p. 117). Given this pronounced emphasis on decision making, it is not surprising that Stufflebeam defined evaluation as "the process of delineating, obtaining, and providing useful information for judging decision alternatives" (1974a,

p. 121) or, more simply, as "the science of providing information for decision making (1968, p. 19).

Stufflebeam and others (1971) approached the development of their framework by criticizing what they saw to be the weaknesses of other available approaches to educational evaluation. Specifically, they believed that evaluation should not be conducted via, or equated to, professional judgment (as in accreditation), a standardized test/measurement orientation (Tyler's framework), or experimental design methods. Though we agree with aspects of their interpretations, we view their analysis and criticism of experimental design and related critiques (Guba and Stufflebeam, 1968) as ill-advised and misleading, and, at times, incorrect. (This issue is considered in Chapter Twelve.) The merits of CIPP might have been advanced without alleging deficiencies in other schemes.

In the CIPP framework, four types of evaluation—context, input, process, and product (hence the acronym CIPP)—were identified to serve four classes of decisions—planning, structuring, implementing, and recycling. In Table 24, these basic elements of the framework are presented for two roles of evaluation, decision making and accountability. The table is self-explanatory. It should be noted that evaluation is viewed as a system—that is, as a cyclical, continuous process with new information frequently becoming available. This information influences upcoming decisions and also serves as feedback allowing the reexamination of earlier decisions.

Using Stufflebeam's definition of evaluation and the concepts in the table as guides, the evaluator designs the CIPP evaluation. He takes three procedural steps—delineating, obtaining, and providing—for each of the four cells in the decision-making or accountability column in the table, depending on the role being fulfilled. For example, for context evaluation serving a decision-making role, the evaluator takes the following steps:

1. Determines what questions will be addressed, thereby *delineating* the priority information needed by the decision maker.
2. Determines how the needed information will be secured, *obtaining* the information using varied measures and analysis techniques.
3. Determines how the obtained information will be reported, thus *providing* information to the decision maker in highly useful form.

Depending on the scope of the evaluation, the same three steps would be followed for input evaluation, and so forth. Stufflebeam provided three criteria for assessing the resulting evaluation designs and reports: (1) technical adequacy (validity, reliability, and objectivity of the information), (2) utility (relevance, scope, timeliness, importance, pervasiveness, and credibility of the evaluation), and (3) cost-effectiveness.

In all, then, Stufflebeam viewed the purposes of evaluation as either obtaining information for the decision maker or recording information for accountability, or both. This position is in dramatic contrast to the purposes of

Table 24. The CIPP Framework: Characteristics of Context, Input, Process, and Product Evaluation as Related to Decision-Making and Accountability Roles

Type of Evaluation	Roles of Evaluation		
	Decision Making	*Accountability*	
Context	Serves planning decisions; involves choosing objectives. Entails identifying underlying problems, high-priority needs, unused resources, and available opportunities.	Provides a record of plans made and those ideas rejected. Documents existing problems, needs, resources, and opportunities, and relates them to the objectives selected and to those rejected.	
Input	Serves structuring or programming decisions; involves formulating a project to achieve objectives. Entails designing and analyzing alternative procedures for attaining objectives.	Provides a record of project design selected and those designs rejected. Documents strengths and weaknesses of alternative project designs and relates them to the established objectives.	
Process	Serves implementing decisions; involves putting a program into operation and implementing a project design. Entails initiating and monitoring project operations.	Provides a record of project implementation, including decisions en route. Documents activities that actually occur in the course of the project and relates them to each other and to the flow of the project.	
Product	Serves recycling decisions; involves analyzing and reacting to project results. Entails identifying and measuring project results.	Provides a record of project outcomes and recycling decisions. Documents outcomes and relates them to modification, continuation, and termination decisions.	

Source: Based on Stufflebeam, 1974a, pp. 121–123.

evaluation envisioned by Stake and Scriven. Both of the latter maintained that evaluation must involve an active judgmental process, with the evaluator making judgments or processing judgments of significant groups. In Stufflebeam's framework, there is much less emphasis on judgment; those important judgments that do occur are typically made by the decision maker on the basis of information provided or recorded through evaluation. In a sense, the CIPP framework includes the description matrix of Stake's countenance approach (Figure 8) but not the judgment matrix. Stufflebeam (1974a) also labeled the decision-making evaluation role *proactive* and likened it to Scriven's formative evaluation. Overlooking Scriven's greater emphasis on judgment, the analogy appears close. In similar fashion, Stufflebeam termed CIPP's accountability role as *retroactive* and therefore like summative evaluation (Stufflebeam, 1971, 1974a). To better interpret this presumed resemblance, a brief explanation of accountability is in order.

As mentioned in our discussion of the Tyler framework, accountability is a recent trend in education. Definitions of it have varied widely (Anderson, Ball, Murphy, and Associates, 1975; Baker, 1973; Glass, 1972; Lessinger, 1970, 1973; McDonald, 1973; Sciara and Jantz, 1972; and Stake, 1973). For example, some writers refer to accountability when discussing performance contracting (a private business firm contracts with a school to bring about specified performances, usually achievement test gains in basic skills, and gets paid only for those students displaying the prespecified performance). Others consider accountability to be embodied in the voucher system (parents receive vouchers from the state, shop for an appropriate educational institution for their children, and pay the selected school using the voucher). However, such practices contain only some elements related to accountability. It is clear, though, that the focus of most of the accountability pronouncements is on holding the school or the teacher responsible (accountable) for student learning.

To get an idea of Stufflebeam's conception of how the CIPP framework fulfills the accountability role of evaluation, let us take another look at Table 24. Its distinctive feature—the recording of project information, including decisions made—does provide a valuable and extensive base for several accountability-like activities. Still, what to do with the information to implement accountability is vague. How is it determined that a given teacher or principal has or has not been accountable? Does the decision maker simply let the information filter through the system until a decision forms? Do external, objective evaluators help the decision maker decide? What standards are used to ascertain sufficient or insufficient accountability? What redress is available to the consumer if the teacher or principal is considered unaccountable? Who decides on the type and amount of redress? How? If one accepts Stufflebeam's interpretation of accountability as "the ability to describe and defend past decisions and actions" (1974a, p. 135), then CIPP serves well the accountability evaluation role. On balance, though, most conceptions of accountability are considerably wider in scope than his and would no doubt have to establish or seek out productive ways to use the CIPP information base to fully implement accountability.

Two final topics relevant to Stufflebeam's work are the CSE (Center for Study of Evaluation) framework and meta-evaluation. The *CSE framework* (Alkin, 1969) is considered only briefly here because of its similarity to CIPP. For example, the CSE definition of evaluation closely paralleled that used in CIPP: "Evaluation is the process of ascertaining the decision areas of concern, selecting appropriate information, and collecting and analyzing information in order to report summary data useful to decision makers in selecting among alternatives" (Alkin, 1969, p. 2). Alkin proposed five types of evaluation to facilitate decision making in five different areas.

1. Systems or needs assessment, resulting in problem selection decisions; similar to CIPP's context evaluation.
2. Program planning, leading to program selection decisions; analogous to CIPP's input evaluation.
3. Program implementation, leading to program modification decisions; most closely related to CIPP's process evaluation.
4. Program improvement or progress evaluation, also leading to program modification decisions.
5. Outcome evaluation, leading to program certification or adoption decisions; similar to CIPP's product evaluation.

The CIPP and CSE frameworks are highly similar, although the CSE framework is more closely tied to specified decision areas. CSE also uniquely adds evaluation of products along the way as an important part of process evaluation.

Meta-evaluation was a term introduced by Scriven (1969) to indicate the evaluation of evaluation studies. Stufflebeam elaborated the concept further: "Good evaluation requires that evaluation efforts themselves be evaluated. Many things can and often do go wrong in evaluation work. Accordingly, it is necessary to check evaluations for problems such as bias, technical error, administrative difficulties, and misuse. Such checks are needed both to improve ongoing evaluation activities and to assess the merits of completed evaluation efforts" (1974b, p. 1). Stufflebeam then presented classes of problems that needed to be addressed by meta-evaluation methodology, a logical structure for designing meta-evaluation studies, and five meta-evaluation designs. A related concept, *secondary evaluation*, was elaborated by Cook (1974), who also attempted a classification of secondary analysis models. A secondary evaluation is the systematic reevaluation of the reports or data generated in a primary evaluation; Scriven (1976) viewed secondary evaluation as a special case of meta-evaluation. Some secondary evaluations are considered in Chapter Eleven.

Advantages and Limitations. A principal advantage of the CIPP framework is its scope and comprehensiveness. In terms of documenting intentions and observing most aspects of a program, the CIPP approach is similar to Stake's countenance framework. A second positive feature is the recognition that evaluation can take place at any stage of a program. In other words, evaluation can appropriately concern context or input or process or product or all of these—

there is no inordinate emphasis, for example, on just process or on just out-comes. A third advantage is that relationships between CIPP's four types of evaluation are addressed and built into the framework. Thus, CIPP can be operationalized as a systems approach to evaluation, providing a continuous cycle of information to influence decisions and to serve as feedback on the apparent effects of previous decisions. A fourth attractive feature of CIPP, at least in the view of many, is the extensive service function that is performed for administrators and decision makers. The CIPP (and CSE) framework requires that the information provided through evaluation have utility for the decision maker; in fact, the decision maker often plays a key role in shaping the evalua-tion activities that occur. A fifth advantage accrues from Stufflebeam's attempt to tie CIPP to emerging concepts of importance to educational decision makers. Most notable, of course, has been his relating of CIPP to accountability (Stufflebeam, 1971, 1974a).

A major limitation of the CIPP framework is its avoidance of valuing and judging. Matters involving judgment are largely unspecified; apparently most important judgments are to be made by the decision maker after inspecting the information collected through evaluation. The second and third limitations de-rive from the initial one. That is, the evaluator is reduced to the role of a technician, merely providing information to the decision maker and not making or processing judgments about it. Also, some activities viewed by CIPP as evaluation—such as identifying problems, priority needs, untapped resources, and available opportunities in context evaluation—would be considered merely descriptive from other perspectives. Certainly, both Scriven and Stake would label such description, in the absence of valuing and judging, as "nonevaluative." A fourth shortcoming is the framework's lack of specificity about the decision-making process. With the hub of the approach being the decision maker and his or her activities, the relative absence in CIPP of description about that central process and its associated methodological features is disturbing. Another limita-tion of CIPP, and one that it shares with Stake's countenance framework, is its likelihood of being complex and expensive if fully implemented. A final weak-ness of CIPP, at least from our viewpoint, is its previously noted attempt at self-justification by, at times, unfairly criticizing other approaches to evaluation.

Application to Early Childhood Education. The comprehensive scope of the CIPP framework establishes the foundation for valuable applications to early childhood education in program planning. The CIPP emphases on collecting information on needs, resources, program alternatives, and the like, and provid-ing it in usable form for the decision maker, make the framework an appropriate one for program planning. CIPP would be particularly well-suited to the plan-ning of a new program "from scratch." For example, education officials in a rural area might decide via context evaluation that a preschool opportunity for area children is a high-priority need, that several untapped resources exist to meet such a need, and that certain types of preschool objective should be em-phasized. Then, via input evaluation and assistance from early education consul-tants, they review a variety of alternative programs for achieving the established objectives and, ultimately, select the program with greatest promise. Information obtained subsequently via process and product evaluations allows the officials to make decisions involving implementation and also permits them to reappraise earlier decisions. The CIPP framework serves well both early and continuing program planning.

CIPP also has application to program documentation in early childhood education. Users of CIPP are expected to keep records of the information obtained, the decisions made, and supporting rationale, during all four stages of program activity (context, input, process, and product). These applications of CIPP to program planning and documentation are not unlike those derived from the countenance framework. In CIPP, however, greater attention is given to recording and documenting. In this regard, the CIPP framework incorporates program evaluation considerations from other fields, such as anthropology (see Chapter Twelve). Although documenting program decisions, activities, and even outcomes represents a valuable contribution of CIPP to early childhood education, it is far from obvious that this documentation constitutes accountability (CIPP's purported retroactive role). Rather, a data base is recorded that might be utilized in accountability. In general, however, CIPP's relevance to applications such as program planning and documentation is easily and directly established by reviewing the entries in Table 24 and reconceptualizing them in an early childhood education context.

A predominant feature of the CIPP framework is the requirement that any information provided have utility for the decision maker. In early childhood education settings in which the administrator or other decision maker has a real need for substantial amounts of information bearing on upcoming decisions, the CIPP can have fruitful applications. For example, if an administrator is running a program for students from several distinct environmental settings and, concomitantly, different value orientations, then he or she may feel special needs for information related to each objective contemplated, to each alternative instructional method considered, and so forth. Similarly, an administrator new to a preschool or other early childhood education program may have pronounced needs for information bearing on a large number of approaching decisions. Another illustration could well be any program that is "under fire," necessitating that the administrator take pains to assure that all future decisions in sensitive areas are based on substantial information and that the reasons for rejecting alternatives are carefully documented.

Provus' Discrepancy Framework

Malcolm Provus, primarily during the period when he served as Director of Research for the Pittsburgh Public Schools, developed the discrepancy framework for evaluating school programs (1969, 1971, 1972). He considered the principal purpose of evaluation to be determining whether to improve, maintain, or terminate a program. He defined evaluation as "the process of agreeing upon program standards, determining whether a discrepancy exists between some aspect of the program and the standards governing that aspect of the program, and using discrepancy information to identify the weaknesses of the program" (Provus, 1969, p. 245). As will be noted, the discrepancy approach represents a hybrid of several of the frameworks already presented.

The discrepancy framework derives its name from its attention to comparing actual performance with set standards. Discrepancies identified become feedback for program developers and decision makers. In each of five evaluation stages, performance is compared to some standard:

Stage and Performance	Standard
1. Program definition and design (input, process, and output components).	Design criteria for programs (comprehensiveness, internal and external consistency).
2. Program installation.	Designed input and process components.
3. Program interim products.	Designed process and output components.
4. Program terminal products.	Designed output components.
5. Program cost comparison.	Costs of other programs yielding same product.

Several features of the framework require elaboration. In Stage 1, the evaluation and program staffs work together to design a feasible program. In fact, a team approach is advocated in the framework, with evaluators, developers, researchers, and others all making contributions. All program components—input, process or transaction (Provus acknowledged Stake's influence here), and intended output—are considered a "comprehensive blueprint" of the new program proposed. The influence of Tyler is apparent in Provus' framework; although recognizing the need for some flexibility, Provus indicated that behaviorally stated program objectives were essential for most purposes. Once the program is designed, it is compared with design criteria representing the standard for the first stage. Provus suggested that this Stage 1 comparison be conducted at a panel meeting, attended by the program director, the program evaluator, a program content consultant, and other persons from the school system's research and evaluation offices; each panel member would play an important role in applying the design criteria. The comprehensiveness criterion is assessed by determining if the design is complete, specific, and stated in usable form. Internal consistency is judged by noting the feasibility of the proposed relationships between program components. For example, are activities planned for students of sufficient intensity to change expected input levels on key variables (such as most district students below the national average in mathematics skill) to desired output levels (that is, most students at or above the national average in mathematics performance)? External consistency is judged by determining the compatibility of the proposed program with other programs already operating in the school system. The program design, in terms of its input, process, and output components, must either be terminated (a possibility in any of the five stages) or refined to the point where no discrepancies exist between it and the design criteria. The first stage is critical—if a program design is approved, it becomes the standard for judging the next three stages.

Stages 2, 3, and 4 involve program installation, interim products, and final products. (In terms of its first four stages, the discrepancy framework has many similarities with both the CIPP and CSE approaches to decision management and facilitation.) In Stage 2, the evaluator compares the actual program inputs and processes with those intended in the design, noting both congruences and discrepancies. Based on the comparison and discrepancies found (if any), one of four decisions is made: (1) terminate, (2) proceed with no changes, (3) alter the performance (inputs and processes, in this case), or (4) revise the standards. In Stage 3, interim products, the initial effects of the program and "enabling" objectives are assessed (such as whether student behavior is changing in the desired manner). During this stage, the evaluator proceeds much like Scriven's formative evaluator, Stufflebeam's (CIPP's) process evaluator, or Alkin's (CSE's) progress evaluator; much interaction with the program staff is necessary. The comparison between actual and intended processes and outputs is made, with information on noted discrepancies guiding decision makers, who again must determine whether to terminate, proceed, alter performance, or revise standards. In Stage 4, the principal question addressed is whether the program is achieving its terminal objectives. The salient comparison is made between the designed outputs and the actual outcome behaviors displayed. Provus believed that experimental design had utility for evaluating a program in Stage 4; in earlier stages, he feared that its use would be premature and too conservative for the developing program. As he noted, "According to the evaluation strategy advanced in this paper, experimental design is irrelevant to evaluation until a program is in its final stages of development. When an evaluation is properly conceived and conducted, it has the power to sound the death knell of a project long before it reaches stability and maturity. Evidence as to excessive cost, inconsistency, unreliability, or the incompatibility of a project at various stages in its development will provide a sound base from which to estimate its probable success at various points in time" (Provus, 1969, pp. 282–283).

Stage 5 in the discrepancy framework, program cost comparison, represents an element not explicated in the frameworks already presented. It consists of comparing the costs of the now completely developed program with the costs of other programs yielding similar outcomes. Provus listed this cost-benefit analysis as an optional stage in his 1969 paper; by 1972, he called it the "ultimate rational step" in program assessment. However, even in 1972, he noted the absence of enabling information and methodology. Provus also wisely observed that such cost comparisons were academic unless the programs compared were sufficiently well defined to be replicable. In effect, cost-benefit analysis as endorsed by Provus has certain similarities to Scriven's cheapy competitor strategy. An essential difference, however, is that cost-benefit analysis (at least as Provus conceived it) is carried out at the conclusion of program development, while cheapy competitors are sought before the development cycle begins.

The hybrid nature of the discrepancy framework becomes obvious when one examines the links to the work of Tyler, Stake, Scriven, Stufflebeam, and Alkin. Overall, however, Provus' approach is most directly related to the work of the latter two. Like CIPP and CSE, the discrepancy framework centers on the decision maker. After Stages 1 through 4, a decision must be made to terminate, to proceed, to alter performance, or to revise standards; after Stage 5, a decision must be made about relative cost-effectiveness.

Advantages and Limitations. From the standpoint of many educators, the primary advantage of the discrepancy framework is that it includes explicit suggestions. Enough "how to" passages are provided to permit viewing the approach as a practical guide for evaluating and providing information for decision makers. A second positive feature, for many, is the flexibility allowed — performance objectives and standards are self-generated and can be changed relatively easily. A third advantage rests in the team approach to evaluation and development. Although the evaluator and his staff maintain some independence, they also work closely and communicate often with the program director and development staff. In most cases, the evaluators and developers report to the same decision maker, and agreement from all parties is sought before many actions are taken. This closeness and rapport might permit the evaluator access to new information from developers that otherwise would be suppressed. Generally, Provus viewed evaluation and development as highly compatible (others, such as Scriven, would consider such compatibility likely and desirable only during formative evaluation). A fourth desirable feature of the discrepancy framework is its advocacy of en route assessment with evaluation appropriate at any stage. The inclusion of the cost-benefit stage represents another advantage, even though the probability of actually conducting such analyses remains small.

Limitations of the framework are related to certain of the claimed advantages. The personnel needed to staff the team would be difficult to find and, once found, expensive to employ. Second, the cost in time, if the approach is fully implemented, would be extensive. A third limitation, linked to the flexibility of the discrepancy method, involves the general inadequacy of the procedures for establishing credible standards. The setting of standards during the design phase (Stage 1) is principally done by in-house staff, with limited external judgment involved. Then, if performance does not meet the standards set, one option is to revise the standards. This process is essentially circular, and one should not become too comfortable with standards so easily shifted. A final limitation is the potential loss of objectivity of the evaluation; the closeness and rapport between developers and evaluators could cloud objective assessment by the evaluator.

Application to Early Childhood Education. An important application of the discrepancy framework to early childhood education programs might be the establishment of standards during the design phase. The standards, which primarily represent judgments by persons directly associated with the program, also serve to create explicit in-house expectations about inputs, processes, and outputs. Thus, the staff "goes on record" in terms of desirable inputs, intended processes, and hoped-for outputs. When the staff of an early childhood education program (or any program, for that matter) establishes such internal standards, it has, in effect, set goals or objectives toward which it can work and by means of which it can measure progress. The very process of determining explicitly what constitutes program success (an activity often overlooked) can conceivably have a strong positive influence on program progress.

The team approach implied in the discrepancy framework also has potential application to early childhood education, especially in formative evaluation efforts. Most persons attracted to the field would probably prefer being part of an evaluation team rather than being targeted by an evaluator as a high-priority data source. Participation in a joint effort could help program staff better appreciate the potential for improvement offered by a viable formative evaluation. Of course, it would be unusual for an early childhood education activity, such as a preschool, to have full-time evaluators and developers on staff (although this does occur on some special projects, often externally funded). Nevertheless, the program might well have part-time access to evaluators and developers through a central agency, such as a school district office or a regional support center.

The cost-benefit stage of the discrepancy framework offers another possible application. It is most unlikely that early childhood education programs will be immune from close scrutiny with regard to costs. Certainly a common concern about many intervention programs is the high costs of operating with pupil-teacher ratios of five or ten to one. Careful cost-benefit analysis would be of substantial value in the early childhood field. Cost-benefit procedures in education have been described, but usually their limitations are also noted (Hartley, 1969; House, 1973b; Kelly, 1973; and Kraft, 1974). For example, Kraft reported a cost-effectiveness evaluation of a vocational-technical education program, but noted the difficulty of determining personal and social outcome measures, and benefits to society as a whole. In all, the enabling methodology for the application of cost-benefit analysis to education remains relatively undeveloped.

Finally, an actual application of the discrepancy framework, which at least indirectly affects early childhood education, should be mentioned. Commencing in 1972, the Division of Personnel Preparation, Bureau of Education for the Handicapped, U.S. Office of Education, funded the Evaluation Resource Center (ERC) at the University of Virginia to provide technical assistance in evaluation to programs preparing persons to work with the handicapped. ERC decided to base this support service on the Provus discrepancy framework. Technical assistance to aid these programs in evaluating their training efforts has been delivered to program personnel (often in colleges or universities) in the form of instructional materials, workshop sessions, and follow-up services all based on the discrepancy framework. These personnel, in turn, have conducted their programs, evaluated them, and influenced thousands of students in training. A substantial number of the trained students now work in educational settings with handicapped children.

Stake's Responsive Framework

Robert Stake, whose countenance framework was presented earlier in this chapter, also developed the so-called responsive approach to educational evaluation (1975). Stake perceived the two frameworks as compatible; in fact, he proposed using the countenance layout of required data and statements (Figure 8) in a responsive context. Stake's countenance framework focused on the information deserving attention in evaluation (that is, its content structure) and on the key role of judgment in evaluations. In contrast, his responsive framework centered on the process of evaluation (that is, its functional structure), with emphasis on the roles played by the evaluator's clients and audiences.

Stake described "preordinate" evaluation as a coherent, systematic study of whether or not prespecified objectives were achieved (similar to the Tylerian framework); he considered this type of evaluation appropriate when it was important to know if certain goals had been reached or if predetermined issues were to be investigated. Although recognizing the legitimacy of preordinate evaluation, he was concerned that too often it caused an undue concentration on student performance (outcome) data and resulted in evaluations and related reports that lacked utility and missed the essence of much that had actually occurred (Braskamp and Morrison, 1975). As a result, the evaluation too often had no influence. If it was reported inappropriately, it might be misunderstood or ignored. If it was highly critical of the client's program, it might be rejected out of hand. Interesting cases of client resistance to evaluation findings have been reported (Carter, 1973; Goodwin, 1971), and Davis (1964) contended that evaluation studies usually make the client look bad. (Many evaluators seem to conceive of their role as principally finding out what is wrong with a program, and thus make little or no effort to look for positive program features or outcomes. It is as if they believe that they must turn up significant negative features to justify their role. Evaluators of this ilk have all of the charm and many of the "moves" of some Internal Revenue Service auditors.)

Stake designed the responsive framework to meet legitimate evaluation needs in certain situations that were not well suited to the preordinate approach. (Many of his examples are drawn from contractual work he did in evaluating the arts in education.) As House (1976) and Stake himself (1975) noted, responsive evaluation has a distinct service flavor—it attempts to be useful to persons in and around the program, especially the clients commissioning the evaluation. "During an evaluation study, a substantial amount of time may be spent learning about the information needs of the persons for whom the evaluation is being done. The evaluator should have a good sense of whom he is working for and their concerns" (Stake, 1975, p. 13). Similarly, the responsive evaluator must know the interests and language of other important audiences for the evaluation and must meet their information requirements. In general, the responsive approach relies primarily on natural communication.

The responsive evaluator is more concerned with what is actually taking place in a program than with intentions. He guards against forming preconceived notions of what constitutes project success. Rather than focusing on preset program objectives, the evaluator stays alert to issues, problems, and potential problems. The issues and problems help guide the conduct of the evaluation, although other issues and problems emerging during the evaluation may also be given priority by the evaluator. These characteristics of the responsive framework prompted Macdonald (1974) to praise it while finding fault with most other approaches.

With a preliminary conception of issues and problems, the responsive evaluator conceives a general plan of operations, usually featuring observations. Rather than a formal observational measurement system (as described in Chapter Four), Stake envisioned observation as the recording of naturally occurring responses to actual happenings. Nor is the evaluator the only observer and interpreter—he enlists the aid of students, teachers, administrators, central school office personnel, community persons, and others as observers, depending on the issues involved and the audiences to be served. With repeated observation and numerous "natural" observers, Stake expected an increase in data reliability. Another major data collection strategy is informal interviewing. Occasionally, the responsive evaluator might decide that the use of tests or similar measuring instruments is appropriate. The observation, interview, and other data allow the evaluator to prepare (often with the help of some of the observer cadre) brief narratives, portrayals of people and events, product displays, graphs, and similar items. The evaluator solicits reactions from various key persons (such as project staff, authority figures, and audience representatives) to help assure the quality of these documents. In general, Stake anticipated that the more natural, informal approach to data collection would yield information of greater use to the evaluation's several audiences—even if at the expense of a reduction in measurement precision.

During data collection, the responsive evaluator operates much differently than most preordinate evaluators. Overall, the responsive evaluator follows "a less interventionist and a more responsive approach. The principal stimuli can be the activities of the program, including the responses of students and subsequent dialogues. . . .The evaluator would pick and choose what to observe, what to record, what to feed back. He would not be passive. For clarification and extension, he would ask for additional opportunities to observe, and would gradually assume more of a stimulus responsibility, conveying to clients and audiences his impressions, portrayals, and reports. He might go further and provoke these communicants with unexpected issues or recommendations. His decisions would depend on how the program (its plan, its process, its products) stimulated him" (Stake, 1975, p. 21).

With all the data and information collected, appropriate reporting occupies center stage. Stake emphasized that the reporting process should make the program seem real—even "come to life"—for the designated audience. "We need a reporting procedure for facilitating vicarious experience. We need to portray complexity and convey the holistic impression, the mood, even the mystery of the experience. The program staff or people in the community may be uncertain, and the audiences should feel that uncertainty. Among the better evangelists, anthropologists, and dramatists are those who have developed the art of story telling. More ambiguity rather than less may be needed in our reports. Oversimplification obfuscates" (Stake, 1975, p. 23).

The reporting procedures used will be varied, depending on the report's content and audience. They may be informal (talks, for example), written (short or long reports), or presented via electronic media (such as movies, slides, audio or videotapes). Potential audiences for evaluation reports include participants (or their parents or sponsoring institutions), program staff, administrative staff and directors of the unit in which the program is housed, the community at large, other institutions considering adopting the program, funding agencies, and policy makers (Bracht, 1975). Further, Stake made it clear that the evaluation reports should contain the varying value perspectives of program successes and failures held by different groups. Although not excluded from judging, the responsive evaluator appears more as a processor of judgment data and a reporter of the differing judgments made by significant groups. Examples of reports that exemplify responsive evaluation are available (Brauner, 1974; Smith and Pohland, 1974; Stake and Gjerde, 1974).

Elsewhere (Braskamp and Morrison, 1975), Stake visualized the responsive evaluator as a civil servant (rather than a philosopher commenting on the civil scene), as an arranger and facilitator (rather than a consultant or a conscience), and as a promoter of internal (rather than external) authority. The major contribution of the evaluator is helping persons discover ideas, answers, and solutions within their own minds. One might be tempted, on the basis of these pronouncements, to view the responsive evaluator as someone who must be all things to all people, who rarely judges and takes care not to judge harshly. But Stake pointed out that responsive evaluation can sometimes lead to the raising of hard questions, since the responsive evaluator carries the responsibilities of discovering the best and worst in the program and of fully informing the various audiences of his findings. His judgments should also be reported, along with the standards and processes employed in reaching them.

Advantages and Limitations. A principal advantage of the responsive framework is its utilitarian orientation. Its focus on the concerns of the client commissioning the evaluation and on those of the program staff highlight this orientation, as does the attention given to appropriate reporting for several audiences. This emphasis on utility and service could improve the evaluation report's chances of having an impact on the client, the staff, or audiences, rather than being filed away permanently, never again to see the light of day. A second, and related, advantage is the appropriateness of the responsive approach for segments of education that might otherwise shun evaluation, or even be hostile to it. Thus, persons in subject fields such as art and music might view the responsive framework as suitable for evaluating their work with young children, as might preschool directors conducting less structured programs (those described in Chapter Eleven as "gooey"), who may have an aversion to trappings such as specific behavioral objectives and paper-and-pencil tests. A third desirable characteristic of the framework is its goal-free tone. The responsive evaluator does not get too immersed in intended objectives and in measured outcomes. Rather, his participant posture and attention to project events as they occur allow him a good vantage point for observing actual effects, whether intended or not. A final advantage of the responsive evaluation framework is its establishment of links to other fields and orientations. For example, as will be noted in Chapter Twelve, the responsive orientation has much in common with anthropological methodology and reporting, and with "illumination evaluation."

Limitations of the responsive framework also can be noted. One involves the lack of detailed methodological procedures. Responsive evaluation is more an orientation or attitude than it is a set of procedures. The lack of specific methodology could lead to rather ambiguous operational features. Second, the unspecified nature of the method and its flexibility—to some degree, it is a heartfelt recording by the evaluator of his impressions of the program—cause one to question the reliability of the process. To what extent would two responsive evaluators, independently observing the same program events and conducting interviews of the same people, make and report similar observations? A final limitation may be the most important. It seems possible that an evaluator following this framework could become too responsive, possibly even therapeutic. True responsiveness might be purchased at the cost of evaluator objectivity, and there might be a fine line distinguishing a responsive evaluator from a subservient one. For some reason, we visualize the true responsive evaluator as much like the Koala bear that most of us have seen on television commercials where the Koala expresses dissatisfaction with Qantas Airlines for bringing so many tourists to Australia. We note the Koala's fine and sensitive eyes for careful observation, his large cupped ears for active listening, and his soft, fuzzy-wuzzy overall appearance, which conveys security, support, and succor. We see the Koala holding on to a branch part way up the eucalyptus tree, slowly munching on a leaf, and trying to amuse and humor anyone in the audience who might have an interest in him. The Koala may be tailless, but he more than compensates by producing tale after tale, appropriately varied for any given audience, about the program of interest. Rather than be anti-Qantas, our Koala-like evaluator is more likely to be anti-quantitative. But then, this portrayal of the responsive evaluator as a Koala bear may seem, to some people, more a strength than a limitation—they may point out, for example, that one can do worse than be a clinger to eucalyptus trees.

Application to Early Childhood Education. Reflection on the responsive evaluation framework results in several possible applications to early childhood education. One rather obvious application lies in the direct use of the framework for early childhood program evaluation. More than any of the approaches previously discussed, except possibly the self-study feature of the accreditation framework, the responsive orientation to evaluation matches well the personality characteristics of a substantial portion of early childhood educators. This is particularly the case for educators advocating more open, less structured approaches to helping young children develop and learn (see Evans, 1975, pp.

291–325). They like the idea of sensitivity to ongoing events and challenge the importance of the more traditional student outcome measures. For example, proponents of the Educational Development Center model for early education would find much to identify with in the responsive evaluation orientation.

A second potential application of the responsive framework might be in evaluating certain nonacademic subject areas engaged in by young children. Many early childhood programs contain moderate or even heavy emphasis on art, crafts, music, dance, and the like. As noted, one stimulus for the development of the responsive framework was Stake's desire to more appropriately evaluate programs in the arts. The responsive evaluator should manifest the sensitivity required to work well with adults deeply immersed in the arts, to observe relevant events, and to record both the nature of the activities and the possible outcomes reached by children. In all, the framework is more compatible with such areas of activity than are other evaluation approaches.

A third application suggested by a responsive evaluation stance relates to the one just mentioned. Eisner (1969) believed that specific behavioral objectives (such as those proposed in Tyler's objective-based measurement framework or in preordinate evaluation as defined by Stake) had two serious limitations: (1) they overestimated the degree to which student outcomes were predictable and (2) they were not well suited to those outcomes involving creative production. Accordingly, Eisner advocated the recognition of an additional type of objective, namely, the *expressive objective*, which he defined as the outcome of an educational encounter. The salient characteristics of such objectives are as follows:

1. Expressive objective outcomes are not predetermined as are behavioral objectives. Rather, outcomes for expressive objectives are believed to be unpredictable to some extent and may be only vaguely formed in the mind of the teacher.
2. Expressive objectives identify educational encounters with potential for richly influencing students. The encounter itself is detailed, rather than expected behavioral changes in students.
3. Expressive objectives do not focus on the acquisition of the known as do most behavioral objectives. Instead, they emphasize the modification and elaboration of the known or even the production of the new.
4. Expressive objectives are evaluated after the fact—that is, after the educational encounter has been observed and the outcomes recorded. A fruitful encounter is likely to produce many outcomes, different for individual students, and seldom predictable before the fact.

The compatibility between expressive objectives and responsive evaluation is obvious, especially in view of the fourth characteristic above. The early childhood teacher might plan educational encounters for her charges—such as visiting a zoo or a farm, riding a bus or a train, viewing babies at the hospital nursery, or the like—and then use ideas from the responsive framework to observe, record, and evaluate the resulting encounter and the possible outcomes experienced by students. Note that this methodological package—that is, expressive objectives plus a responsive evaluation orientation—could have considerable use in early childhood education for some evaluation purposes. For other purposes, the Tylerian approach, utilizing behavioral objectives, would be methodologically appropriate. The two frameworks address different requirements, and both could be used in the evaluation of a single program.

Selecting an Evaluation Scheme

The seven frameworks described in this chapter advocate varying methodologies of program evaluation. Although seldom directly contradictory, the frameworks do have different emphases and operational implications, as was apparent in the suggested applications to early childhood education. (Incidentally, the applications that were detailed represent only a small sample of those that might have been described.) Given this variability, how should the early childhood educator or evaluator select the most appropriate framework?

In a limited number of cases, there may be a good match between the particular program to be evaluated and the principal orientation of one of the frameworks. Selecting the appropriate conceptual framework is then not too difficult. The potential user should, of course, study the references cited for the framework chosen in order to obtain a more complete understanding than that provided by the brief sketches contained in this chapter.

Much more often, at least in our experience, a single framework is not selected and systematically used as written. On occasion, a given framework is extensively modified. Even more frequently, an eclectic spirit reigns, with the evaluator choosing and implementing features from several frameworks. There is nothing inappropriate about the latter practice. A carefully designed eclectic evaluation can be very effective. Our view is shared by Popham.

> Although it is sensible for educational evaluators to inform themselves of the nature of educational evaluation models, they should not get too caught up in that enticing but enervating game known as *comparative model meshing*. Some people take great delight in seeing how Model X differs from Model Q and is ever so slightly like the seventy-ninth stage of Model Z. This kind of model comparison may represent a pleasant avocation for the retired educational evaluator; although fruitless, it also appears harmless. . . . Instead of engaging in a game of "sames and differents," the educational evaluator should become sufficiently conversant with the available models of evaluation to decide which, if any, to employ. Often, a more eclectic approach will be adopted whereby one selectively draws from the several available models those procedures or constructs that appear most helpful [Popham, 1975, p. 21].

The merit of the frameworks does not necessarily lie in their implementation during program evaluation. Using one or more frameworks during the early planning of program operations can also be beneficial. Such an exercise helps define project intentions and encourages a logical analysis of the means proposed for realizing them. It can also alert the program staff or evaluator to the need for early data collection, such as pertinent premeasures.

The frameworks represent a good starting point for planning an evaluation of an early childhood program. Additional ideas on planning an effective evaluation can be found in basic evaluation primers such as Anderson and Ball (1978), Popham (1975), and Worthen and Sanders (1973). Evaluation plans invariably involve determination of relevant variables and measures. In addition to the material in Chapters Two through Eight and the source book section, the long lists of potentially important variables provided by the Association for Supervision and Curriculum Development, Early Childhood Council (1971), Messick and Barrows (1972), and Metfessel and Michael (1967) should be scanned to ensure appropriate coverage in the evaluation plan.

Gephart (undated) expressed a not uncommon dissatisfaction with the proliferation of educational evaluation models. He suggested that the frameworks were more alike than different and proposed a three-by-five structure or matrix for classifying and (more importantly) synthesizing the existing models. He hoped that such a synthesis would permit the evaluation field to move away from unproductive discussions belaboring the merits and limitations of specific frameworks, thereby releasing resources and energy to address other problems and attain new accomplishments in evaluation. The first dimension of the matrix was conceived of as a continuum of evaluation models denoting relationships to decision making:

1. Perhaps associated with decision making (for example, when evaluation is equated with measurement—inappropriately, in our view).
2. Serving decision making (for example, Gephart placed here Tyler's objective-attainment, Stake's countenance, Stufflebeam's CIPP, and Provus' discrepancy frameworks and Scriven's formative-summative distinction).
3. Encompassing decision making (for example, the accreditation framework and Scriven's goal-free evaluation).

Thus, Gephart suggested reducing the number of evaluation models to three general types. The second dimension of the matrix consisted of five categories for describing each type of model: (1) its general nature; (2) characteristics of problems for which it is an appropriate strategy; (3) activities and events making up the evaluation process; (4) products or outcomes realized from the evaluation; and (5) the criteria useful in assessing the quality of the evaluation conducted.

Although Gephart's major point is well-taken—that is, that the existing frameworks overlap in various ways—we believe that his structural matrix masks or distorts important distinctions between the approaches and that such reductionism does not advance the discipline. Quite possibly a heuristic synthesis will, in time, be forthcoming, but our preliminary attempts at generating such a scheme were not very satisfying. Our view persists that careful reflection on the many elements in the conceptual frameworks and in the sources detailed in this chapter, particularly if done early, can result in the identification of important areas to be addressed in the evaluation of a particular program. Additional considerations relevant to evaluation planning are presented in the next three chapters.

In concluding this initial chapter on evaluation, we should like to note that some writers, such as Weber (1970), have been notably pessimistic about the prospects for effective evaluation of early childhood programs. We can agree with some specific points raised by Weber, such as the disappointing supply of quality affective measures. However, we remain optimistic about the value of evaluation for such programs and about the likelihood of its increased use.

Chapter 10

===========

Evaluation of Individuals' Performance

===========

In the evaluation of any program, it is almost inevitable that certain aspects of the effort will involve evaluation of individuals' performance and even attitudes or other relevant characteristics. At the same time, the evaluation of individuals in early childhood education has many facets, some of which would not ordinarily be central features of program evaluation. It is for this reason that we devote a separate chapter to the evaluation of individuals. We consider three categories of individuals here: children, parents, and staff of early childhood education settings. Greater attention is given to parents and staff than to children simply because the latter have been the focus of most of the previous chapters. We have purposely called this chapter "Evaluation of Individuals' Performance" rather than "Evaluation of Individuals" to emphasize that it is particular characteristics that are being evaluated—such as children's performance in school, parents' involvement in educational efforts, or staff's competence in particular roles—and not persons per se. Obviously, the uniqueness and the intrinsic worth of individuals are beyond evaluation.

Child Evaluation

Material pertaining to child measurement and evaluation has been presented throughout this book. For example, many of the issues raised in Chapter

One and all the measures described in Chapters Four through Eight were child-related. At the same time, there is a need to consider somewhat broader questions to fit these already presented pieces into a total evaluation perspective. Two such encompassing and integrating questions are now briefly examined—namely, why conduct child evaluation in early childhood education, and how?

Why Conduct Child Evaluation? There is little reason to measure children in a number of cognitive, affective, and psychomotor areas if the data thus generated are not used. One purpose for such measurement, and an important one, is to evaluate educational programs for young children. Another purpose is to test hypotheses in research investigations. A third purpose, and surely most important to early childhood education, is to provide information that can be used to facilitate young children's learning and development. As Hess and Croft remarked, "From the teacher's point of view, the most significant functions of evaluation procedures are to diagnose growth patterns and achievement levels of her class and establish learning objectives for both individual children and the group" (1972, p. 316). Several sources detail procedures to use in diagnosing specific learning difficulties that young children are having (for example, see Brophy, Good, and Nedler, 1975, pp. 235–261). This last purpose can also include special efforts, such as identifying the perceptually or physically handicapped child so that appropriate instruction can be planned and implemented.

It is this third purpose—using evaluation to facilitate learning and development—that we focus on in this section. When early childhood educators systematically and professionally undertake evaluation for such a purpose, important advantages accrue to them and to children in their programs. Hendrick (1975, p. 282) has identified several such advantages; we paraphrase them below:

1. Providing the educator with an increased understanding of each child.
2. Increasing the quality and specificity of the curriculum (by directing it toward particular skills in light of assessed strengths and weaknesses).
3. Improving the morale of the educator (by recording the early and later behavior of children and providing evidence of progress).
4. Vitalizing the process of reporting to parents (by providing detailed assessments on their child).
5. Serving as a valuable data base for reporting to funding agencies and governing agencies.

To these five advantages we would add an overriding benefit—namely, increasing the educator's satisfaction that an active effort has been made to facilitate the learning and nurture the development of each child in the program. (Also see Smith, Neisworth, and Greer, 1978.)

How to Conduct Child Evaluation. Despite the several advantages cited above, it can be noted that many early childhood education programs, perhaps the majority of them, continue to approach measurement and evaluation casually, if at all. Assessment of young children is an area steeped in controversy; to a lesser extent, recording and reporting children's progress also involves controversy. "Assessing, recording, and reporting children's progress is one of the most controversial aspects of program development for young children. Generally speaking, the controversy concerns: (1) the purposes of evaluation and the methods used in the assessment; (2) the staff time spent in recording children's progress, the possibility of records negatively typecasting children, and the indiscriminate release and use of information about children (and their families); and (3) the problem of 'what' and 'how much' to communicate to parents who are not professionally trained in interpreting assessment results and who are emotionally involved in their children's development. Although there are not clear-cut answers, the assessing, recording, and reporting of children's progress serve as a basis for many worthwhile functions such as planning and implementing all services of the early childhood program, guiding the development of each child, and communicating with parents, the public, and the regulatory agencies" (Decker and Decker, 1976, p. 155). These three processes—assessing, recording, and reporting—are now examined.

Assessing: Assessment has already received considerable attention. In Chapters Four through Eight, different types of measure were described— observational, unobtrusive, and published instruments covering a wide spectrum. Further, Chapters Two and Three discussed concepts important for determining the merit of such measures. There is no need to review those presentations here. Instead, we offer some general advice on the use of such measures in child evaluation. The following list of principles builds upon ideas from Brophy, Good, and Nedler (1975, pp. 216–217) and Hendrick (1975, pp. 282–284).

1. Establish a relaxed, informal situation to ensure that children are comfortable rather than anxious during assessment.
2. Utilize multiple measures that match the important objectives of the program—cognitive, affective, and psychomotor.
3. Utilize measures with a range of difficulty levels, including assessment of higher-order skills.
4. Present tasks to children in a standard way; during the individual testing of many children, any variation in assessment procedures by the teacher can reduce the comparability and meaning of the data obtained.
5. Avoid the "getting-better-and-better" syndrome; if assessing the same child several times during the year, the teacher may be biased toward viewing the child's behavior and performance as improved with each assessment when, in fact, this is not always the case.
6. Conduct evaluations on a timely, reasonable schedule; somewhere between the extremes of once-a-year evaluation, which is usually too little, and "continuous" evaluation, which is usually unfeasible, a balance should be sought that encourages evaluation at those times during the year when data can affect instructional planning and decision making.
7. Treat data obtained on children confidentially and professionally; data on

children, whether based directly on their performances or secured from reports of parents or others, should be used for its intended purpose of facilitating their learning and development.

Assessment of children's performance in educational settings is the theme of a large number of books on measurement and evaluation (such as Ahmann and Glock, 1975; Bloom, Hastings, and Madaus, 1971; Gronlund, 1976; Mehrens and Lehmann, 1978; Noll and Scannell, 1972; Payne, 1974; Smith, Neisworth, and Greer, 1978; Stanley and Hopkins, 1972; Ten Brink, 1974; Thorndike and Hagen, 1977; and Tuckman, 1975). Although such texts give only limited attention to the evaluation of very young children, many of the principles and procedures they present for school-aged students might be cautiously extrapolated downward for application to younger children.

In terms of student assessment, the *Handbook on Formative and Summative Evaluation of Student Learning* (Bloom, Hastings, and Madaus, 1971) is particularly noteworthy. The authors adapted Scriven's concepts of formative and summative evaluation of programs (Chapter Nine) to the evaluation of student learning. For them, formative evaluation yielded the data necessary to facilitate individual student progress toward defined objectives. Summative evaluation assessed the achievement of more general objectives at the end of the entire course or some substantial portion of it. Secondary purposes of summative evaluation were to report to administrators and parents and to grade students. To illustrate these concepts in early childhood education, formative evaluation would be involved in trying to ascertain why Susan has had continuing difficulty in understanding and producing appropriately words of relative location or position (above, behind, below, between, over, under, in, out, and the like). Summative evaluation would be used to assess Susan's overall language usage and comprehension, including both her receptive and productive language.

Bloom and his colleagues presented their ideas in a schematic model reproduced in Figure 9. Although a full elaboration of their model would require more space than we have available, four essential points should be noted. First, the model suggests the relationships between formative and summative evaluation, as well as relationships between them and other assessment and instructional processes. Second, the model reflects the view that the evaluation of student performance is a comprehensive and systematic process. Third, the scope of the model reveals that appropriate student evaluation is a time-consuming process, but (in Bloom, Hastings, and Madaus' perspective and ours) critically worthwhile in light of its vital role in facilitating learning and improving programs.

The fourth point to note about the model is its prescription of essential elements for effective evaluation. This prescriptive quality is woven throughout the model but is most apparent in the table of specifications for outcomes. The table implies that the program director will follow a process of first explicating objectives and content and then conducting appropriate assessments of students for many of the resulting content-objectives' intersections. (This process is

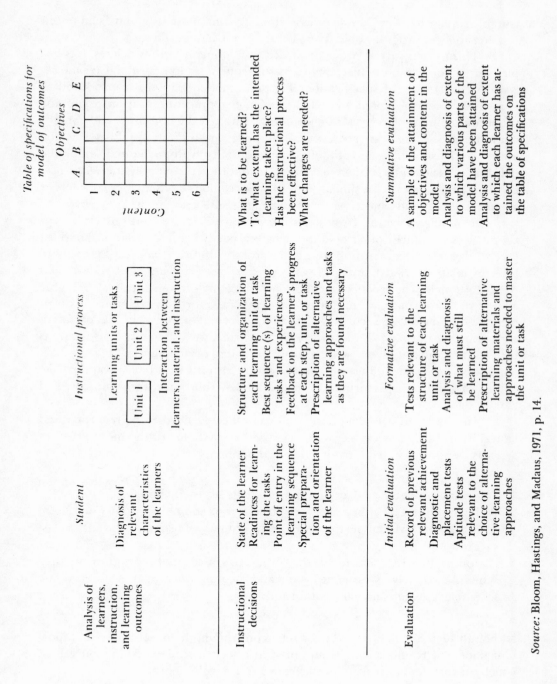

Figure 9. Model for Student Evaluation Showing the Relationships Among Evaluation, Instructional Decisions, and the Analysis of Learners, Instruction, and Learning Outcomes.

Source: Bloom, Hastings, and Madaus, 1971, p. 14.

roughly similar to our example of assessing the content of a standardized test in relation to local program objectives, Figure 4 in Chapter Three.)

This prescriptive process, proposed by Bloom and his associates, was implemented for certain subject fields in subsequent chapters of the *Handbook*. Kamii's (1971) table of specifications for preschool education is reproduced as Figure 10. She elaborated in detail assessment procedures appropriate for numerous content-objectives' intersections. Although the objectives and content might be expected to vary somewhat from program to program, this systematic approach to assessment and student evaluation, if fully implemented, should be helpful in facilitating student learning. In another chapter in the *Handbook*, Cazden (1971) presented a similar table of specifications detailing her concepts of suitable content and objectives for early language development.

Recording: Turning from assessing to recording, we find ourselves with only a limited number of observations to offer, partly because this topic has been given relatively little attention in the literature. Educators vary dramatically in their inclination toward, and their effectiveness at, recording evaluation-linked data. Both major camps of early childhood educators—those endorsing a highly structured approach and those favoring a more open, unstructured orientation—advocate recording data on children, although they are partial to different types of data. Educators from programs with structured orientations lean toward quantitative and diagnostic data, test performances, and the like, while open-program educators prefer more narrative and observational accounts of children's performances, collections of children's work samples, and similar data.

In any event, the data and products collected need to be recorded and stored in an easily retrievable, well-organized form. Some of the more effective systems we have observed involve three components:

1. Individual folders for data on, and products of, each child.
2. A file organized by either program objectives or content (or sometimes both) for data on individual performance and summary statistics for the entire class or group.
3. A comprehensive outline of the program's assessment program, with a schedule of likely assessment events and a column in which to enter a date when each event is actually conducted.

Although such detailed recording is time-consuming, the ready access to important data that results strongly supports an effective student-evaluation effort, which, in turn, enhances student learning and development.

Reporting: Reporting to administration, funding agencies, or parents has been widely written about with regard to elementary and secondary schools but not with regard to preschool educational settings. Nevertheless, certain principles and procedures that would probably be effective can be derived from the

Objectives

Figure 10. Table of Specifications for Preschool Education Showing Objectives (Affective, Perceptual-Motor, Cognitive) and Content.

Content	Socio-emotional								Perceptual-motor		Cognitive		Logical knowledge					Representation	
	A Dependence on the teacher	B Inner controls	C Interaction: quantity	D Interaction: quality	E Comfort in school	F Achievement motivation	G Curiosity	H Creativity	I Gross motor coordination	J Fine motor coordination	K Physical knowledge	L Social knowledge	M Classification	N Seriation	O Number	P Space	Q Time	R Symbols	S Language: signs
1. The self																			
2. Body parts																			
3. Members of the class																			
4. Members of the family																			
5. Community roles																			
6. Playground equipment																			
7. Foods																			
8. Clothes																			
9. Furniture																			
10. Houses and buildings																			
11. Tools																			
12. Kitchen utensils																			
13. Vehicles																			
14. Animals																			
15. Plants																			
16. Art materials (paint)																			
17. Toys (balls)																			
18. Colors																			
19. Sizes																			
20. Shapes																			

Source: Kamii, 1971, p. 284.

literature involving older students. In the brief remarks that follow, we concentrate on reporting to parents. Policy boards, advisory groups, and funding agencies typically have their own expectations and set their own regulations (often idiosyncratic and almost always exhausting) in terms of required reports on children and program progress.

Reporting to parents involves two major considerations: *content* (what is reported) and *process* (how the content is reported). Content performance reported to parents can involve a large number of areas that have been evaluated. A good indication of the range of areas that might be addressed during such reports is provided by Brodinsky (1972). Surveying a national sample of school districts at the start of the 1970s, he found over 120 skills, attitudes, and achievements reported on for kindergartners. He grouped these into thirteen areas. In order of items listed under each, from most to least, these areas were reading readiness, work habits, language development, mathematics, social maturity, health-safety-physical education, science, art, eye-hand coordination, general well-being, identity, music, and perception of direction. It would seem that the typical preschool's report to parents would include many of these same areas.

Data collected by Brodinsky also related to the delivery systems used in reporting to parents—that is, how the information is conveyed to parents. Several national trends in the early 1970s were noted by him, namely:

1. An intermingling of innovative reporting procedures with traditional report cards, often with both coexisting in the same school.
2. An increase in efforts to personalize and individualize grading at the elementary school level.
3. An increase in the use of computerized cards at the secondary school level, posing barriers to providing individualized information.
4. An increase in the variety of report forms and formats, with widespread agreement that grading and reporting should be used to promote understanding rather than to reward, punish, or establish a student's rank in school.

More specific to the age group of interest here, Brodinsky noted the following trends and emphases in kindergarten through grade three:

1. Parent-teacher conference is the goal universally accepted and is spreading widely in actual use.
2. Emphasis is on assessing stage of development rather than on formal grades or ratings; "failing" grades are practically eliminated.
3. Checklists, narrative reports, letters to parents are three commonly used media.
4. The child as a citizen and the child as a scholar are not clearly distinguished; grades for achievement and grades for citizenship are frequently blurred.
5. Great diversity of forms and formats is found at this level.
6. Scattered attempts are made to involve the child in self-evaluation, with the help of the teacher [1972, p. 64].

Two factors, one general and one specific, cloud our estimate of current reporting procedures in early childhood education. The general factor is a relatively pronounced societal swing toward greater stress on basic skills (highlighted by President Carter's 1978 pronouncements on education). In some localities, growing support is found for fundamental schools that focus on (sometimes exclusively) reading, writing, and arithmetic. It is unclear whether the personalizing trends in reporting and grading noted by Brodinsky will reverse themselves with this current societal swing. The specific factor, alluded to earlier, is the uncertainty involved in extrapolating downward to programs for children five years old and younger. However, it appears most likely that parent-teacher conferences would be the predominant reporting vehicle used. Although we have little advice on the relative weight that should be given the child's cognitive, affective, and psychomotor development in such reporting conferences, we do believe that all three should be given substantial emphasis.

We also believe very strongly that programs purporting to nurture the development of young children should report to parents, and frequent face-to-face conferences seem a good way. Further, we encourage early childhood educators to provide specific data to the parents, such as the child's measured skill performances and his actual work samples. Direct, open communication channels between educator and parent are needed if the child is to be well served in both the school and the home.

Evaluation of Parent Involvement

Parent involvement and parent education are currently popular concepts in early childhood education in this country. That is, they generally are considered at least desirable and, by some, even essential (see Nedler and McAfee, 1979; and Grotberg, 1972). Although these concepts were emphasized as early as 1825 (see Stevens and King, 1976), they gained a new prominence in the mid 1960s, partly as a result of the new federal guidelines calling for parent participation or even employment in federally funded programs. Even prior to such federal pronouncements, however, many—probably a majority of—early childhood educators exhibited a deep and abiding belief in the importance of parent involvement. Most recent books on early childhood education contain at least one chapter on parent involvement, and some entire books address the topic (such as Nedler and McAfee, 1979).

Examination of the many different approaches or programs in early education reveals considerable diversity in type or degree of parent involvement. Some programs simply keep parents informed of scheduled activities and of their children's progress. Others seek to involve parents more deeply by conducting parent education classes, training parents in new skills, using parents as volunteers, or sharing decision making with parents. For example, Gordon (1972) examined six program models in the Head Start "Planned Variations" undertaking on several bases, including their parent involvement roles. He found pronounced variability in them, with his own model, the Florida Parent

Education Program, involving more diverse and more highly specified roles for parents.

In this section, we focus on the measurement and evaluation of parent involvement in early childhood education programs. To facilitate such a presentation, it is first necessary to structure somewhat the diverse field of parent involvement. In searching for an organizing theme, we were struck by the tendency of the sources consulted to list comparable roles or types of involvement for parents (see Association for Supervision and Curriculum Development, Early Childhood Council, 1971; Goodson and Hess, 1975; Gordon, 1970; and Nedler and McAfee, 1979). For example, Goodson and Hess (1975) adopted four focuses for their evaluative review of parent involvement in early childhood education programs: (1) parents as better parents, (2) parents as supporting resources for the programs, (3) parents as more potent teachers of their own children, and (4) parents as policy makers. Gordon (1970), reviewing compensatory education programs, conceptualized five levels of parent involvement, from minimal to high involvement: (1) receiver of information about the conduct of the program, (2) teacher of the child at home or outside the school setting, (3) program volunteer assisting in the classroom, organizing other parents, or the like, (4) worker trained and employed to do classroom activities, and (5) member of an advisory or policy-making board. Many points of similarity can be noted between Gordon's levels and the focuses of Goodson and Hess.

Based on the several sources noted and particularly on Gordon's work (although we do quibble some with his ordering of the levels), we treat the evaluation of parent involvement under the following headings (ordered generally in terms of increasing involvement in the program):

1. Parents as recipients of information about the program.
2. Parents as students in parent education programs (or even as teachers in the home).
3. Parents as volunteers in an early childhood education program.
4. Parents as members of a program advisory council.

For each of these topical areas, we examine instances of actual evaluation and measurement practices as well as some potentially relevant techniques. Evaluation of parents as paid staff members in a program is not considered here although it receives indirect attention in the last section of this chapter on staff evaluation; employing poor parents as program workers has been addressed by Chilman (1973). We also do not consider the typical evaluation procedures used in programs designed to change parent life-styles through therapy, extensive retraining for new employment, or other procedures; the reader interested in such parent-focused programs will want to consult Chilman (1973) or White and others (1973b).

Parents as Receivers of Program Information. Although this is the lowest level of parental involvement that we consider, it clearly represents an advance over receiving no program information at all. Closely related to this role of receiving information, of course, is that of supplying information requested by the program. It is normally hypothesized—although it has by no means been definitively established—that parent involvement is associated with positive parent attitudes toward the program or the school and that it signals a helpful, supportive influence on the child's academic future (Raizen and Bobrow, 1974). Therefore, most programs seek parent involvement on at least this initial level.

Diverse procedures are used by programs to provide information to parents. They include such techniques as sending work samples of the child, newsletters, or messages to the parent via mail or the child; telephoning the parent; scheduling orientations or program visitations for groups of parents; conducting home visits; reporting a child's progress via mail or at a conference; interacting considerably with parents when they bring the child to the program or pick him up; and preparing and disseminating pamphlets or a handbook describing principal program activities or the like.

Our general feeling is that evaluating the effectiveness of such procedures—in terms of resultant parental awareness of the program's activities or parental participation at scheduled events—is quite effectively done using a collection of unobtrusive measures (see Chapter Two). Thus, a record could be kept of parents' responsiveness to queries sent home, of parents' attendance at scheduled orientations and visitations, or of parent-initiated contacts with the program, indicating the mode of contact (that is, phone, written, or in person) and its content (such as a complaint, a request for information on a child's performance, or a cookie delivery). An unobtrusive measure to ascertain the extent to which a program newsletter or handbook was read might be to subtly ask individual parents an easy question about some obvious feature of the document.

Of course, evaluation could proceed using more direct, apparent techniques. Parents could be interviewed by phone or in person to determine their awareness of the program staff, activities, publications, or the like. More commonly, a questionnaire is sent to parents asking them to rate an orientation session, a prepared handbook, program staff, or some other program activity or product (for example, see Lally and Honig, 1977).

We have some real concerns in this topical area (and subsequent ones) about much of the evaluation data produced through use of interviews, questionnaires, and rating scales completed by parents (and less concern about unobtrusive measures or direct observation of parent behavior). Our concerns generally intensify if the interviews, questionnaires, or rating scales are administered by program staff. Even apart from the difficulty that staff have of being unbiased and objective about their own performance or program (especially if a very important or summative evaluation is underway), it is clear that parents (or respondents more generally) often try to be "good subjects"—that is, to respond with what they believe the information seeker wants to hear or read (for example, see Orne, 1962; Rosenthal, 1966; and Rosenthal and Rosnow, 1969). The net result may too often be that the parents bathe the program or specifics about it in too favorable an evaluative glow. We have similar reservations about parents' reports on how well their children perform certain program-related behaviors (as we did about the developmental survey items in Chapter Six that could be passed by parent report). The general difficulty that investigators have had with the accuracy of parent recall of earlier child behavior or experiences is well established (Jones, Reid, and Patterson, 1975; Wenar, 1961; and Yarrow, Campbell, and Burton, 1970).

These concerns notwithstanding, parents are a repository of considerable data about how they value a given program for their children, about their children's behavior and performance, and about the interactions between themselves and their children over education-related matters. Further, such data are important. Parents' attitudes are probably key determiners of their children's behavior and attitudes—for example, their expectations with regard to achievement (see Katkovsky, Preston, and Crandall, 1964). More generally, Collins (1977) and others (see Nedler and McAfee, 1979) have held that parents are the single most important influence on young children's early education and development. The assumed importance of parent attitudes and behaviors is sufficient reason to measure them as accurately as possible. (Note, however, that some recent investigations have questioned the presumed causative link between parents' attitudes and children's behavior; see Moss, 1967, Stolz, 1967, and Yarrow, Campbell, and Burton, 1968.) Having parents provide self-reports of their observations, attitudes, and behaviors generally is less preferred than making more direct measurements of the variables of interest. When parent reporting is to be used, it is probably best preceded by some instruction (such as training in observation, careful explication of the importance of factual reports, or the like).

At this first level of parent involvement, then, measurement and evaluation concerns center on the awareness of the parent about the program. The subsequent levels of involvement considered represent more active parental behavior.

Parents as Students in Parent Education Programs. This second level of parent involvement refers to activities designed to educate parents, usually about child growth and development or more effective home management practices, such as those affecting health or nutrition. Many early childhood education programs, as well as community programs for the poverty sector, have parent education components. In general, the goal of parent education projects is to impart knowledge to parents about the physical, social, economic, and emotional aspects of family life; such knowledge presumably will influence parents to adopt more effective childrearing practices (Goodson and Hess, 1975). The extensive number of such parent education efforts since the mid 1960s has probably contributed to the development of parenting courses in many secondary schools in this country.

Several delivery modes are used for parent education. Most common are parent discussion groups and lecture-demonstrations, or some combination of these. The formality of such endeavors varies widely. Less frequently used delivery means include printed materials (pamphlets, magazines, or books), audiovisual presentations (audiotapes and slides, movies, and commercial and educational television), and individual counseling (conferences with physicians, nurse practitioners, nurses, teachers, clergymen, social workers, counselors, or other professionals).

Evaluation of parent education programs has not, in the past, frequently occurred. When it has, its form has typically been recording, sometimes unobtrusively, the level of activity (as by noting the number of attendees, pamphlets distributed, or people counseled), with the usual judgment being the more, the better. A second typical form is parent or student ratings of the quality of the instruction received or suggestions for improvement. Although we view such activity-level data and ratings as important for evaluation, we consider other measures much more critical. Thus, at a very minimum, one would seek to determine to what extent parents had acquired the new knowledge that was made available to them. Locally designed or even standardized achievement tests might be used for this purpose, preferably as part of a rigorous evaluation design that controlled for potential invalidating sources (see Chapter Twelve); attitudes might also be assessed with the special care that we have alluded to previously.

If knowledge gains and attitude changes do result, an even more important step then would be to measure whether parents' behavior itself has been altered. This step optimally would involve observation of parents interacting with their children. For example, if the parent education course stressed the importance of certain types of parent-child communication, and if the parents generally acquired such knowledge and a favorable attitude toward its use, then the observation system might focus on parent-child communication. Certain unobtrusive indicators might also be examined. For example, if the parent education instruction emphasized health, the evaluator might note the incidence of physical examinations or other health checkups before and after the instruction, or the frequency of parent-promotion of exercise or other health-related activities. If nutrition were targeted, family food purchases might be observed unobtrusively. (Webb and others, 1966, suggested using garbage analysis for such purposes, but we have noted few persons willing to collect such pungent data.) Unfortunately, the lack of evaluation resources or other factors has severely limited direct measurement of parent behavior during or after parent education programs; further, some persons would question the ethical propriety of unobtrusively assessing parental practices.

Considerable attention has been given to developing effective parent education via discussion groups and the like (for example, see Auerbach, 1968; Lazar and Chapman, 1972; and Pickarts and Fargo, 1971). Pithy recommendations have been offered, like: use a skilled and sensitive group leader, focus in on specific topics, schedule a limited number of sessions at regular intervals, pay particular attention to scheduling sessions when parents are available, and so forth. Unfortunately, only limited evidence has been collected on the effectiveness of parent education programs. The scant evidence that is available derives primarily from programs for poor parents and, by and large, suggests that most parent education programs are not effective (Chilman, 1973; White and others,

1973b, d). The reviews by Chilman and White both noted the difficulty such programs had attracting and holding parents (especially fathers), the likely minimal impact of the programs (particularly on mothers facing survival questions related to housing, income, and safety), and the lack of strong evidence that parents' attitudes and behaviors changed as a result of such programs.

Somewhat distinct from parent education programs are books and materials designed to help parents nurture their child's development (for example, see Ahr and Simons, 1968). Even more distinctive are *parent training* endeavors, fairly intense efforts focused on helping the parent develop new skills that can be used in teaching the child at home. "Parent training projects offer skill training to adults, primarily mothers—either individually or in groups—to improve the family's function of cognitive stimulation of children. Parent training is distinct from parent education. . . . The techniques used in parent education strategies are intended mainly to inform; those used in parent training aim to impart new skills" (White and others, 1973b, p. 256). Such training takes place in the home, in a central place (such as an early education center), or both.

Elements that might profitably be incorporated in such training programs can be extracted from studies of childrearing practices and maternal teaching styles (such as those by Baumrind, 1967; Hess and Shipman, 1965; Streissguth and Bee, 1972; White and Watts, 1973; and Wiegerink and Weikart, 1967). For example, Baumrind found that parents of competent three- and four-year-olds required that their children perform maturely at their intellectual and social ability levels and communicated effectively and clearly with their children. White and Watts' in-home observations led them to conclude:

> Our most effective mothers do not devote the bulk of their day to rearing their young children. Most of them are far too busy to do so; several of them, in fact, have part-time jobs. What they seem to do, often without knowing exactly why, is to perform excellently the functions of designer and consultant. . . . They design a physical world, mainly in the home, that is beautifully suited to nurturing the burgeoning curiosity of the one- to three-year-old. It is full of small, manipulable, visually detailed objects, some of which were originally designed for young children (toys), others normally used for other purposes (plastic refrigerator containers, bottle caps, baby-food jars and covers, shoes, magazines, television and radio knobs, etc.). It contains things to climb, such as chairs, benches, sofas, and stairs. It has available materials to nurture more mature motor interests, such as tricycles, scooters, and structures with which to practice elementary gymnastics. It includes a rich variety of interesting things to look at, such as television, people, and the aforementioned types of physical objects.
>
> The child is encouraged in the vast majority of his explorations. When the child confronts an interesting or difficult situation, he often turns to his mother for help. Although usually working at some chore, she is generally nearby. He then goes to her and usually, but *not always*, is *responded to* by his mother with help or shared enthusiasm, plus, occasionally, an interesting, naturally related idea. These ten- to thirty-second interchanges are usually oriented around the child's interest of the moment rather than toward some need or interest of the mother.

These mothers very rarely spend five, ten, or twenty minutes teaching their one- to two-year-olds, but they get an enormous amount (in terms of frequency) of teaching in "on the fly," and usually at the child's instigation. Although they do volunteer comments opportunistically, they react mostly to overtures by the child [White and Watts, 1973, pp. 243–244].

Reviewing many of the programs and studies in the parent training and teaching area, Stevens and King were prompted to list both parental behaviors and environmental features likely to enrich children's cognitive development (1976, pp. 206–207). Paraphrased, these were:

Parent Behaviors Likely to Enrich Children's Cognitive Development
1. Praising appropriate behavior of the child.
2. Requesting verbal feedback from the child.
3. Labeling objects in the environment.
4. Noting relationships between environmental objects.
5. Interacting with the child verbally (extensively).
6. Interacting with the child in a variety of settings.
7. Avoiding intrusion into task performance by the child.

Parent Structuring of the Environment to Enhance Children's Cognitive Development
1. Structuring a novel, changing environment with varying levels of complexity.
2. Providing toys, materials, and manipulable objects that the child is free to act on.
3. Providing objects for examination (such as books).
4. Providing environmental objects and stimuli that the child can engage with or retreat from.
5. Establishing moderate noise stimulation.
6. Provisioning an environment responsive to the child.
7. Balancing the availability of materials and people in the child's environment.

Using such prescriptive guides and related ideas, a considerable number of parent training programs have been developed. (For listings of such programs, see Chilman, 1973; Day and Parker, 1977; Stevens and King, 1976; and White and others, 1973b.) Such programs have varied in their involvement of parents and in the specific treatments implemented. For example, in the Florida Parent Education Infant and Toddler Programs (Gordon, Guinagh, and Jester, 1977), a paraprofessional, who was also a parent in the community, made thirty- to sixty-minute weekly visits to homes and taught other parents ways to stimulate their infants at home. The child activities were based on Piagetian tasks. Two-year-old children in the project also attended a "learning center" in one of the homes two hours each week. Similarly, Karnes and Zehrbach (1977) used trained parent coordinators to instruct groups of ten to fifteen mothers at weekly meetings with emphasis on the mothers learning teaching strategies and constructing materials to stimulate their children's development. Even more important, in the program developers' view, were biweekly visits by the coordinators to each home in order to reinforce the strategies taught, to observe the appropriateness of the materials developed, and to address problems experienced by individual mothers. Somewhat different means to the same ends were embodied in the Mother-Child Home Program (Levenstein, 1977). Eight sessions were used to train toy demonstrators who, in turn, each visited project homes twice weekly and used toys and books to interact with a three- or four-year-old child while the child's mother and siblings looked on. The mother, then, was to play and read with the child outside of the weekly sessions. In the Parent-Child Toy Library Program (Nimnicht and others, 1972; and Nimnicht, Arango, and Adcock, 1977), parents of three- to eight-year-olds took part in a training course over an eight-week period. They practiced specific behaviors related to teaching their children and they learned how to use eight basic toys and games (such as sound cans, color lotto, a feely bag, and stacking squares). After completing the course, the parents could check out toys from the library for as long as desired. Many other parent training programs have been initiated, but those just described are representative. The federal Home Start Program could be considered, by and large, a parent training program (Home Start is more fully described in Chapter Eleven).

Evaluations of parent training programs can take, and have taken, several forms. Whether centralized instruction or home instruction of parents is involved, many of the suggestions made above for the evaluation of parent education programs apply, such as noting attendance (or appointments kept), parent ratings of the program, knowledge acquired, and the like. Most of the parent training programs do intend that parents will acquire and display new teaching skills in the home with the child, and this intention suggests important evaluation focuses. Three such focuses can be noted. First, the amount of stimulation for the child that is present in the home can be assessed (with the presumption that parents having undergone training will have improved the stimulation available). Ideas concerning possible approaches to such assessment are found in work by Bodin (1968) and, as described in Chapter Twelve under the measurement of classroom climate but also applicable to families, Moos (1975b). Even more pertinent are the Home Environment Scale or HES (High/Scope Educational Research Foundation, 1974) and the Inventory of Home Stimulation or STIM (Caldwell, 1968), parent questionnaire and interview procedures, respectively, that yield data on the home setting and parent-child interactions. For example, HES contains thirty-seven items in five areas concerning mother's involvement, mother's teaching, the child's participation in household tasks, the playthings available, and the books present. HES was used in a national evaluation of Home Start, while STIM was used variously, such as in the evaluation of the Family Development Research Program (Lally and Honig, 1977). It can be noted that such data on stimulation in the home could be relatively costly to obtain if in-home observers were utilized.

Second, parents can be directly measured or observed to ascertain the quality of the teaching skills they have acquired, how often they use them, what their attitudes are toward their new skills, and the like. For example, in the

National Home Start Program Evaluation (see Chapter Eleven) conducted by the High/Scope Educational Research Foundation and Abt Associates (Love and others, 1976), several observational measures of mother as teacher were used. In the Eight-Block Sort Task, the mother was observed and rated as she tried to teach her child how to sort the blocks. The same task, originally developed by Hess and Shipman (1965), was also used in the Planned Variation Head Start Evaluation and the ETS-Head Start Longitudinal Study. Gordon, Guinagh, and Jester (1977) administered a paper-and-pencil self-concept scale to the parents in their program, while Gilmer, Miller, and Gray (1970) examined mother's self-concept, level of aspiration, and ability to plan, organize, and implement a teaching strategy. Thus, the evaluation of parent training efforts can involve the direct measurement of parents' acquired teaching capabilities or changed attitudes, in terms of self-concept or perceived locus of control. Again, however, such data are usually relatively expensive to acquire.

The third focus for the evaluation of parent training programs can be assessment of the children's progress. This also is likely to be a costly procedure, somewhat less so if the children are accessible in groups in a central location. Nearly all parent training programs have children's improved cognitive performance as an objective, usually of first priority. Child measures typically used to evaluate attainment of this objective have been intelligence tests, such as the Binet, the Cattell, the Bayley, and the Peabody Picture Vocabulary Test. Interestingly, siblings of target children have sometimes been included in the assessment process. Another evaluation strategy is to chart later school performance and achievement or to let naive teachers (unaware of which children's parents were given the special training) who later have the children in class rate the performance of all the students to see if those whose parents were trained are distinguishable. Such a strategy has been used—with results generally favoring children whose parents had been trained (see Goodson and Hess, 1975)—and is markedly more definitive if a rigorous evaluation design is in place, including the use of randomly formed control groups as noted in Chapter Twelve.

Reviews of the effectiveness of parent training programs (Chilman, 1973; Goodson and Hess, 1975; and White and others, 1973b, d) have documented generally positive results. "Parent training for cognitive stimulation does produce useful, but often flawed, evaluation data. IQ or achievement score gains are usually statistically significant and of moderate magnitude. These gains decline somewhat with time but remain for at least a year or more. Trained paraprofessionals seem to be as effective as social workers or professional teachers in the parent training role. Variation in curriculum produces similar results. Important side benefits include possible IQ gains for younger siblings, less attenuation of gains, and employment opportunities for low-income parents when paraprofessionals are used" (White and others, 1973d, p. 26). Additionally, Goodson and Hess (1975) noted some evidence of an improved sense of personal efficacy in parents and more realistic developmental expectations for their children, improved parent-child interactions, and improved quality of the stimulation in the home. At the same time, many (including Chilman, 1973) have questioned the wisdom of the heavy evaluative emphasis on children's intelligence test score gains. Similarly, Goodson and Hess (1975) argued for an even wider view of the effects of parent training. They wondered about largely unanticipated side effects of such programs, both positive (more social interaction, increased desire by parents for further training, more contact with middle-class institutions, and increased opportunities for community activities) and negative (unexpected problems due to the program, such as some parents developing unrealistically high expectations for their children's school performance, or friction due to unmet program promises).

It is clear that most of the parent education projects, especially those involving parent training, were funded at substantial levels, as were their evaluations. Be that as it may, local small-scale efforts to implement parent education and parent training programs or components could probably develop effective evaluation procedures by adopting techniques used in the larger projects and by limiting or avoiding costly in-home observation. Note too that if a parent training program uses discernible activities or units (such as toys or books), records of the usage of each of them and attitudes of the parents and children toward them might well prove to be valuable data for a formative evaluation.

Parents as Program Volunteers. Most early childhood education programs utilize volunteers in various capacities, and the largest single group of volunteers tends to be parents with children in the program. (Note, however, that the following discussion applies to volunteers generally, whether parents, older students, senior citizens, or others.) Most writers in early childhood education favor an active volunteer program, and, in general, we agree. Nedler and McAfee (1979) observed three important advantages of having volunteers — (1) expanding available resources, (2) developing closer contact between parents or community members and program staff, and (3) enabling parents and others to directly contribute to children's education. However, they also appropriately noted that these advantages were partially counteracted by disadvantages — for example, the need for additional staff work to establish and maintain the volunteer program, and problems such as volunteer absenteeism, inconsistencies in dealing with children (possibly their own), and lapses in professional ethics.

The overriding purpose of most early education volunteer programs is to increase educational benefits for children. The chain linking a particular volunteer's activities to the presumed child benefits can be short (as when a parent directly tutors an individual child) or long (as when the volunteer maintains the grounds around a center so that program resources can be freed up for educational materials, teacher salaries, or the like). The tremendous diversity of possible volunteer activities is reflected in the following partial list (drawn in part from Brock, 1976; Nedler and McAfee, 1979; and Robison, 1977):

Activities Related to Other Volunteers or Parents
1. Coordinate, telephone, and encourage others to volunteer.
2. Raise funds to support the program.
3. Explain the program to the community at large.

4. Baby-sit so other parents can volunteer.
5. Accompany teacher on home visits.
6. Plan special events for the program.
7. Help prepare a handbook on community resources the program could use.
8. Help prepare a handbook on activities for volunteers, especially noting activities to be done with children.

Activities Related to Children More Directly
1. Make instructional materials.
2. Secure instructional materials from the community.
3. Serve as a resource person to program staff.
4. Serve as an interpreter for children or assist in the conduct of bilingual instruction.
5. Tutor children or help them review subjects.
6. Print stories as children tell them.
7. Work with children in varying size groups on special topics, educational games, or the like.
8. Help monitor children during art, lunch, rest period, recess, gardening, field trips, and other related activities.

Activities Related to the Educational Setting
1. Start plants and help in transplanting them in or around the classroom.
2. Help establish an outdoor learning center.
3. Help design and construct an outdoor play-development area.
4. Maintain and operate equipment (audiovisual, cooking, and similar equipment).
5. Help repair, paint, and maintain the classroom and the building housing it.
6. Help maintain the grounds outside the center or school.
7. Assist in the design and physical layout of the room.
8. Help prepare multicultural exhibits for display in the classroom.

This sampling of possible volunteer activities highlights the difficulty of prescribing general evaluation strategies for so diverse a collection. Clearly, however, most of the activities above suggest some rather immediate measurement and evaluation undertakings. For example, among the activities related to other volunteers and parents, the first could be evaluated by the incidence of participation, the second by the amount of money raised, and the third by the incidence of requests for program explanations and the reactions of the persons or groups receiving the explanations. The seventh and eighth activities could be evaluated by determining the usage rate and the perceived utility of the community resource handbook to program staff and of the activity handbook to volunteers. Similarly, some fairly direct evaluations could be made of the volunteer activities affecting children directly as well as those related to the general educational setting.

The sheer weight of recording all the activities of volunteers— documentation that would serve as a first, logical step in most evaluation strategies—prompts us to recommend that a program devise a system whereby volunteers record their efforts themselves. A specially prepared form could be utilized and, at a minimum, should require the recording of the name of the volunteer(s), the date, the activity, and its duration. Additionally, the volunteer could respond to checklist- or Likert-type items on the perceived value of the activity, on how well the volunteer liked doing it, on the volunteer's self-evaluation of her design and conduct of the activity, and so forth. (Forms that could be adapted appear in several sources; for example, see Brock, 1976, and Nedler and McAfee, 1979.) The forms could be turned in to a designated staff member, who could check their completeness and file them. Later analysis of the forms might be very revealing for both formative questions (for example, which activities were most and least regarded, or how many hours were contributed by each volunteer) and summative questions (what was the total resource input, in hours and estimated dollar equivalents, that the volunteers' contributions represented, or did the contributions of the volunteer program outweigh the "costs" in terms of staff time and inconveniences). Careful analysis of such forms over time, such as by charting the amount and kind of volunteerism during certain periods of the year or by noting possible trends in amount and kind of participation over longer time intervals, would probably yield helpful insights.

For a more general evaluation, volunteers could be asked to rate the volunteer program at set intervals, either via questionnaire ratings or interviews. Likewise, program staff should also rate the volunteer program. A comparison of these two collective perceptions would be in order; quite possibly, such a comparison could be better focused by also examining actual volunteer contributions, such as generated by the system of filed volunteer reports described above. Careful evaluation of a program's volunteer program could lead to constructive changes in its format and scope.

Parents as Advisory Board or Policy Board Members. This type of parental involvement is usually viewed as the most intense level, that is, where parents are most active. We agree if the criterion is the degree of parents' involvement in the direction of the program per se—that is, in advising on or setting program policy. However, if the criterion is the degree of involvement of the parents in direct educational exchanges with their children, then some parent training programs probably represent the most intense level of involvement.

In this discussion, we intended to treat advisory boards and policy boards as separate entities because, in concept, they are. An advisory board is meant to advise on all types of matters, possibly including policy, while a policy board is established to set policy. In practice, however, it appears that the line between giving advice and setting policy is often not a clear one. Additionally, and perplexing to us, there is a clear lack of definitive materials on both advisory and policy boards and almost no research on their effectiveness. Therefore, we have ended up treating them together, as both involve parents to some degree in the planning and conduct of programs. Further, the evaluation issues pertaining to both appear similar.

The scant literature on parent participation on advisory or policy boards is highly varied. A national survey of citizens' advisory committees established as adjuncts to school districts' boards of education and central administrations revealed their widespread existence and their diverse characteristics (Oldham, 1973). There are reflective, low-key pronouncements on the importance of parental involvement in planning (such as the newsletters of the Colorado Institute for Parent Involvement, 1235 York Street, Denver 80206) and, at the other extreme, calls for parents to assume a type of Old West vigilante control of their children's schools (for example, see Jones and Jones, 1976). There are also a number of testimonials about instances where extensive parent participation in planning and control did lead to positive outcomes (Davies, 1976). Goodson and Hess (1975) discussed the goal of parent power with its underlying assumption that changes in the curriculum due to parents' influence would result in better educational experiences for their children. They also noted that some programs assumed that a secondary outcome would be an increased sense of personal control for some parents, a change that possibly would be reflected in a more active, responsible attitude toward their children's education.

Chilman pointed out the recent origin of involving poor parents on such boards:

> The principle of including parents, particularly poor and minority group parents, on advisory and policy-making committees is rapidly being accepted at the federal level in the fields of education, welfare, and health. It is made mandatory in certain aspects of the legislation pertaining to these fields (such as Head Start and Follow Through) and became HEW policy in a number of programs concerning children and youth, including the daycare programs. Of course it has been an operating principle in the OEO programs since their inception in 1964. Such participation was one of the demands of the 1968 Poor People's Campaign, and it has been a very lively subject of contention in a number of our large cities, particularly in the fields of housing and education.
>
> The demand for citizen participation as policy makers and planners at neighborhood, city, county, state, and federal levels seems highly justified. But here again there is almost no research-based evidence for *how* such programs actually operate, let alone how *well* they operate . . . Problems abound; among them are those of how to elect or select representatives of the poor to serve on advisory committees. There are indications that in actuality only a very small proportion of poor people actually participate in social action groups and on committees and boards [Chilman, 1973, p. 445].

Chilman also noted that middle-class involvement in such roles was a fairly routine, although sometimes superficial, aspect of social service, health, and education agencies, and was fairly well-established historically.

Evaluation of parent involvement on such boards could take several forms. Who participates on the boards would clearly be of interest, as well as who participated in placing them there (the latter question taking on more meaning if the board members were elected by their constituents rather than selected by the program director). Other evaluative data that could be collected would be attendance at scheduled meetings and time devoted to the role between meetings.

Evaluation of advisory and policy boards' operations should probably address the questions of who exercises what power or influence and in what ways. LaCrosse described a situation that apparently occurs quite frequently: "Power sharing is definitely a two-way street. The administrator must believe that the people with whom he shares it are indeed trustworthy. The people trusted, on the other hand, must genuinely believe that they're being given power to use. There have been many mishaps when people are given power that they don't believe is really theirs. They subsequently test its limits, which panics the administrator to the point where he'll snatch it back quickly. Everyone is then locked into a vicious circle: 'See, I gave them power and they couldn't use it,' 'He gave us power but he didn't really mean it!'" (LaCrosse, 1975, p. 11).

Some aspects of the Comprehensive Coordinated Child Care Project in Denver vividly illustrated the situation depicted by LaCrosse; one of us was involved in the evaluation of the project (Goodwin and others, 1973). The project was intended to design a system for matching young children's needs with existing childcare facilities and resources. A project advisory board was formed, composed of seven parent representatives, six technical service representatives (professional staff from the University of Colorado Medical Center), and two medical school students. Its purposes were to advise the project staff on project policy and operation, to inform the project staff of parent concerns and desires, to provide the project staff with professional advice in the areas of psychological, social, and medical services, and to serve generally as an instrument of community participation.

The early months of the development of the project advisory board were not without problems of group dynamics and role definition of the board relative to the project and its staff. In her fall progress report, the project director indicated that these problems had produced a polarization in the board, with parent representatives on one side and project staff and service representatives on the other. According to the director, the project staff "was desperately wanting input from the board and participation in solving day-to-day problems to get the project as written on the road." The parents on the board seemed to desire more power and the freedom to change project priorities. As a result, exchanges between the factions became defensive and threatened to become openly hostile and antagonistic. The project staff perceived a need for some formal evaluation and recommendations on the question of the advisory board. At this point, the staff contracted with our (external) evaluation team to study the workings of the board and to make recommendations to the staff and the board.

Accordingly, we scheduled two observers to attend the three remaining fall meetings of the advisory board. One observer was briefed on the history of the board and the other was purposely kept naive. Although the two observers conducted their work independently at the meetings, they developed quite similar interpretations of the major interaction patterns being demonstrated. From the data generated, it was apparent that the board's meetings were dominated by the project staff, the board chairman (a service representative), and a single parent representative. The rest of the board primarily ended up as passive onlookers of this triangular interaction pattern. Legitimate parent concerns, when expressed, seemed to be met by the staff with either a patronizing, superficial response or a barrage of jargon (essentially, defensively toned technical justifications by the staff for actions already taken). Further, the evening hours of the meeting seemed inconvenient; several members came late and others left early. Based on the data, the evaluators made eight recommendations to the project director and the board, which were fairly well summarized in this concluding statement: "With all the safety afforded by our noninvolvement, we respectfully submit the following observation to the program staff: the advisory board is not threatening to run away with the project, and the advisory board members have more concerns than they have expressed, but they may hesitate to express them out of fear that their questions will be answered 'too competently.' If the advisory board were given the freedom to raise issues and questions and discuss them with little intervention from the project staff, the result would likely be a more cohesive, involved advisory board with a more satisfactory sense of its purpose and contribution" (Goodwin and others, 1973, Appendix H).

Six months later, two observers (one continuing and one new) again independently observed two advisory board meetings. In general, the board appeared to be operating very smoothly, with democratic participation much in evidence, project staff keeping a markedly lower profile than at the fall meetings, and meeting times perceived by the board members as satisfactory. Further, the evaluators used a mail survey to have each board member independently rank order six possible functions for the advisory board. The parent representatives, the technical service representatives, and the project staff all held highly similar perceptions of the role of the advisory board. Overall, the repeated, systematic, and intensive evaluation of the advisory board resulted in the documentation of the development of the board and, probably more important, in changes that improved the board's mode of operation.

Obviously, an evaluation strategy such as that described above required considerable resource expenditures. It is our opinion, however, that a conscientious advisory or policy board can often set up a scheme by which it can monitor and evaluate its own proceedings. Someone at the board meeting—a project assistant, a secretary, or some board member—could be assigned to keep track of certain key features of each meeting. For example, who does what percentage of the talking at the meetings? Who votes how on key issues? What is the response by the board as a whole to legitimate questions asked by any representative or by project staff themselves? Are motions proposed and voted upon that make it clear to project staff the advice that is being suggested (or the policy that is being established) by the board? Are there issues left hanging for which appropriate ad hoc subcommittees should be appointed? These and other questions could be answered for each board meeting if personnel were assigned the responsibility of doing some simple charting of what takes place at the meetings. Such data could be available to the entire board in its attempts to improve its own functional effectiveness. Although such a procedure would lack the objectivity inherent in the use of external evaluators or observers, it nonetheless could produce quite useful evaluation data. Note too that an enterprising board, although short of funds for evaluation purposes, could probably solicit a competent person to serve as an objective external observer of the board process—and some helpful formative evaluation data might result.

Staff Evaluation

When we speak of staff evaluation, we mean evaluation of the job-related characteristics of early childhood education personnel, including program directors, teachers, and supporting staff—child development associates, paraprofessionals, paid parent volunteers, and aides. Many authors have observed that teachers and other school personnel find evaluation extremely threatening (Bolton, 1973; Hess and Croft, 1972; and Wolf, 1973). It need not be, however, if the major purpose is formative rather than summative (see Chapter Nine), and if the staff are involved in the process. In this section, we first discuss reasons for conducting staff evaluation, and then present a variety of methods used to obtain evaluative data about staff performance.

Why Conduct Staff Evaluation? The two most common reasons given for evaluating staff are (1) to make administrative decisions about retention, salary, promotion, or tenure of staff, and (2) to facilitate improvement of the instructional process. The first reason is largely summative, involving judgments of overall worth, while the second is more formative and aimed at revision or modification of existing instructional strategies and programs. Related to the first purpose is the practice of holding teachers accountable for student learning, and measuring that learning as a means of evaluating teachers. Such outcome accountability is indeed threatening to the staff involved and, as others have pointed out, often unfair. Rosenshine and McGaw (1972) summarized the major difficulties involved in outcome accountability:

> First, let us look at differences of opinion on the relative importance of various outcomes. For example, although reading comprehension is commonly accepted as a major objective in education, different teachers emphasize different aspects of reading: some focus on reading for information; others teach critical thinking, literary style, or oral reading. But the standardized achievement tests in reading comprehension focus on the ability to learn new words in context, to synthesize new material, and to make inferences from unfamiliar texts. These differences between the reading outcomes emphasized by some teachers and the outcomes measured by the standardized reading tests may account for the claims of some teachers that the tests are not "valid."
>
> A second problem is that outcome accountability can be implemented only where trustworthy and accepted measures have been developed. Unfortunately, we are a long way from developing trustworthy measures of student confidence that he can manipulate the subject matter on his own, student belief that "doing" the subject matter has value, student persistence in the subject matter after instruction has stopped.... Nor do we have reliable measures of a student's self-esteem, his disposition to inquire into new problems, or his ability to make reasoned choices.... The concern for outcome accountability may result in concentrated work

on educational outcomes that are easily measured. The danger is that other valuable but less easily measured educational outcomes may be ignored or forgotten by educators and the public.

Third, in areas where trustworthy tests are available and there is reasonable consensus on ends, the problem of determining the amount of student learning for which a teacher is responsible is a statistical quagmire. The common goal, a year's progress in a year's time, means different things to a teacher whose class begins the year near or above grade level and a teacher whose class begins two or three years below grade level. The statistical procedures usually recommended for adjusting class growth scores to take into account initial differences have been shown to have serious shortcomings [Rosenshine and McGaw, 1972, p. 640].

We share Rosenshine and McGaw's view that outcome accountability is a poor procedure for staff evaluation. We do see, however, several useful purposes for staff evaluation, most of them formative. Improvement of instruction is certainly a worthwhile goal, and one that many staff readily accept. "Evaluation of instruction is required before systematic improvement can occur. It is necessary to establish a starting point from which to work. . . . Through [a] knowledge of strengths and weaknesses a teacher can improve his work. Usually, when a teacher views evaluation as a means to improve his instruction, he accepts it as a part of the teaching assignment" (Bolton, 1973, p. 99). Closely related to improvement of instruction as a purpose for staff evaluation is the promotion of individual growth and self-improvement. By being involved in the evaluation process—via self-evaluation, in part—staff members can continuously diagnose their own teaching and related activities, and work on individual growth and development.

Other purposes of staff evaluation include the modification of staff assignments (for example, changing workloads, making decisions about to whom and for what purposes release time should be allocated, and identifying needed in-service programs); legal protection of centers, schools, and staff members; and validation and improvement of staff selection processes (Bolton, 1973). Although these purposes may be less acceptable to staff than the instructional improvement purpose, they need not be resisted by staff—if the staff are involved in establishing specific purposes for evaluation activities, setting criteria, and interpreting resultant data. Further, the alternatives to systematic staff evaluation can be capricious and arbitrary. As Hess and Croft (1972) noted, evaluation of preschool programs and staff is inevitable; if it is not done formally (systematically), it is done by informal conversations among parents, other staff, administrators, and so on. If one or two administrators, advisory council members, or vocal community members are allowed to use subjective impressions about staff for purposes of dismissal, increases in student-teacher ratios, or reduction in funds for certain programs, the results can be devastating and unfair to the staff involved. Therefore, staff members should be encouraged to participate in evaluation planning and implementation for their own protection as well as for their personal growth and the improvement of their instructional strategies.

In planning staff evaluation, it is wise to consider the differences among individual staff members in terms of such factors as amount of experience, type of training, and individual goals. An example of a useful scheme for differentiating among staff members is Katz's (1972) developmental stages of preschool teaching. After examining the stages and changes preschool teachers evidence during their first years of professional experience, Katz identified four developmental stages. The first stage is *survival,* a time of anxiety and concern about daily classroom procedures, the safety and learning of the children, and one's own self-image. Having recently been given full responsibility for a group of small children, the preschool teacher in this stage needs special on-site support and advice. The second stage, *consolidation,* is usually reached by the end of the first year of teaching. In this stage, the teacher feels more organized and secure with the children and other staff and can begin to concentrate less on routine problems and more on curriculum changes and individualizing instruction. While the teacher continues to need support and guidance from more experienced colleagues, the major need is for advice centered around curriculum planning, program development, and use of community and agency resources. *Renewal* is the third stage, which generally occurs after several years of teaching. At this time, the teacher may become bored with the repetition of activities and projects, and start to seek challenges and new stimulations. Membership in professional associations, participation in in-service programs, working on curriculum committees, summer- course work, and visiting other programs are frequently helpful to the teacher in this stage. Some teachers may begin to specialize at this time, and desire more focused teaching assignments. Moving into Katz's final stage, *maturity,* the teacher views herself as a committed professional. A philosophy of education meaningful to that teacher has emerged. While still recognizing the need for continual professional growth and self-renewal, the mature teacher also aids newer teachers by providing information and offering advice and support. For self-renewal purposes, teachers in this stage may seek additional training and advanced educational degrees.

We have described Katz's developmental stages of preschool teachers in some detail to illustrate the individual differences that exist among staff members within any educational setting. Staff evaluation can be made especially meaningful if such differences are included in the planning and implementation of evaluations, as well as in the interpretation of data. To treat all teachers, or all staff, in a like manner would ignore an individual teacher's developmental stage, abilities, contributions, and needs. Regardless of the purpose of the evaluation, it can be enhanced if individual differences are taken into account.

How to Conduct Staff Evaluation. A variety of methods are available for the evaluation of staff in early childhood education settings. Most of these methods were first used in college settings, and then to some extent in secondary and elementary schools. When they were adapted for use with the staff of early childhood education programs, some modifications (although not major ones) became necessary. Several authors have written extensively on the pros and cons of various approaches to teacher evaluation (for example, see Glass, 1974; and

McNeil and Popham, 1973). For the most part, their arguments in favor of or against different approaches are applicable to early childhood program staff evaluation as well as to the evaluation of teachers at other educational levels.

Before a particular method is chosen for staff evaluation, several decisions must be made. As we discussed in the previous section, the purposes of staff evaluation can vary. An important first step in planning staff evaluation is to delineate the ultimate purpose(s) of the evaluation. Those conducting the evaluation could be sorely disappointed with the resultant data if they find that the data do not address any of these major purposes. To avoid this unfortunate situation, careful specification of the goals and objectives of the evaluation is necessary at an early stage.

Other important early decisions include the selection of evaluation criteria. "The first step [in the selection of criteria] is to determine whether all personnel should be evaluated by the same criteria and what criteria should be used in evaluating personnel performance. Generally speaking, personnel providing similar services should be evaluated using the same criteria, but personnel having dissimilar roles (for example, director and care-giver) should be evaluated using different criteria, although some evaluation items might be the same" (Decker and Decker, 1976, p. 51). As we pointed out in the previous section, a further breakdown of criteria for different individuals within similar roles can lead to even greater fairness and precision of evaluative information. For example, some criteria for preschool teachers in different developmental stages (in Katz's framework) could vary to correspond with the unique features of each stage, whereas other criteria could measure features common to all the stages.

Since establishing evaluation criteria is a critical element in the evaluation process, it is wise to obtain input from representatives of all concerned parties. Administrators, teachers, other staff members, parents, and advisory council members should be involved (to varying degrees, of course) in setting criteria. According to Decker and Decker (1976), four types of staff characteristics are frequently used as criteria in staff evaluation in early childhood education:

1. Physical characteristics (that is, physical health and vitality conducive to effective performance which the position demands);
2. Mental ability (that is, ability to conceptualize the philosophy of the program, the needs of the children and adults involved in the program, and the employee's role and the roles of others as they relate to his position);
3. Professional qualifications (that is, knowledge of methods and materials used in performing his role); and
4. Personal attributes (that is, enthusiasm, poise, ability to adjust to frustrations, and ability to cooperate with colleagues) [Decker and Decker, 1976, p. 52].

Other possible focuses for evaluation might include maintenance of a safe and healthy environment, interpersonal sensitivity, planning and evaluating child progress, working with parents to promote home-school unity in child progress, and classroom and behavior management (Robison, 1977). Many of these same focuses are stated in even more operational form in Honig's clever Twenty Question Game (1977).

Once the general areas for staff evaluation have been selected, criteria must be established. This is frequently a difficult and time-consuming aspect of the evaluation planning, and often is done in conjunction with the development of the evaluation instruments. Specifying staff behaviors and skills to be rated is usually of concern here, since most staff evaluations include assessment of the teaching process in addition to, or instead of, assessment of student outcomes. (As we noted earlier, use of student outcome data can produce misleading results, especially if the evaluation is intended to address accountability demands or is to be used for personnel promotion, retention or dismissal, or related decisions. Although student outcome data can be informative for several reasons, discussed later in this section, relying solely on such data is rarely sufficient in staff evaluation.)

Since assessment of staff effectiveness, either for formative or summative purposes, is one primary goal of most staff evaluations, it is relevant to consider briefly the relationships between process and outcome variables. A question frequently raised in conjunction with teacher evaluation, at all educational levels, is, "What teaching process variables are valid indicators of teaching effectiveness in terms of student outcomes?" Are there certain teacher behaviors, interpersonal skills, and organizational or management styles that result in positive cognitive and affective outcomes for students? Unfortunately, not a great deal is known about the relationships between classroom process and student outcome variables, especially at the early childhood level. Probably the most comprehensive summary to date of the known relationships between process and outcome or product variables is Dunkin and Biddle's *The Study of Teaching* (1974). A second useful source with information of this type is Brophy and Good's *Teacher-Student Relationships: Courses and Consequences* (1974). While it is beyond the scope of this book to discuss in detail the research findings summarized by these authors and others (see, for example, Goodwin and Klausmeier, 1975, pp. 142–172), it is important to note that many process variables used in assessing staff effectiveness have no clearly understood relationships (especially causal relationships) with student cognitive or affective outcomes. The same is true for presage, or predictive, variables such as intellectual ability, college grades, personal appearance, and other characteristics of staff members in early childhood education settings. The few teacher behaviors that have been found to relate to children's learning or classroom behaviors include clarity of presentations and explanations, task orientation, enthusiasm, and use of a variety of teacher-initiated activities (Rosenshine, 1971). Affective characteristics of teachers that probably influence children's cognitive and affective outcomes include warmth, friendliness, acceptance of students' ideas, and preference for nondirective classroom procedures (Ryans, 1960).

Lists of behaviors considered important for teachers of young children are available. These can be utilized in developing criteria and evaluation instruments for staff evaluation, although any particular staff evaluation program will undoubtedly require modifications (deletions, additions, changes) in such criteria lists. Prescott and Jones (1969) provided such a list based on their examinations of teacher-child interactions in fifty preschool centers in the Los Angeles area. They discovered, using factor analysis (see Chapter Two), four patterns of teacher behavior: (1) encouragement/restriction, (2) conformity to routine, (3) group teaching, and (4) independence. For each pattern, specific behaviors are presented that could be used in developing evaluation criteria and instruments. For example, the teacher who is encouraging rather than restrictive is one who expresses nonroutine encouragement to individuals; is concerned with teaching lessons in consideration, creativity, and experimentation; expresses pleasure, awe, and wonder; and so forth. The behaviors listed by Prescott and Jones or those by Honig (1977) previously mentioned could be very helpful in planning staff evaluation by aiding the planners to focus on specific behaviors considered important to them. Additional references of this type, not all research-based, will be cited in the following sections in which we present specific ways of evaluating staff. We have organized these sections according to the source of the evaluation data—that is, the type of persons or records providing the information. Note that the first six methods described involve ratings of some kind—often based on direct observation of staff performance. Ratings are the most widely used procedure for obtaining teacher evaluation data (Popham, 1975). What distinguishes the various rating methods presented below are the types of person making the ratings, the ways in which the ratings are made, and the level of involvement of the staff in the evaluation process.

Staff self-evaluation: Having staff members in early childhood education settings judge their own performance and identify their own areas of strengths and weaknesses is one approach to staff evaluation. This method is primarily aimed at improving the staff member's own performance; that is, it has a formative focus. This can be effected by having staff members fill out checklists evaluating their own performance on some type of scheduled basis (say three to four times annually). Such a procedure is limited, however, as the staff members get no direct feedback on their performance. Use of videotaped recordings of actual performance, subsequently judged by the staff person who was taped, is one way of facilitating such self-evaluation. Robison (1977) cited several behaviors and skills that can be videotaped and then self-evaluated: nonverbal behaviors, including the unconscious sending of negative messages to children; story reading skills, involving eye contact, showing pictures appropriately, voice modulation and production, articulation and phrasing; use of divergent questions; pacing of questions; behavior management skills; skills of differentiated initiatives and responses to individual children; responsiveness to individual children in a group without losing the group; and ascertaining children's cognitive levels, involving skills of eliciting actions, verbalizations, and reasons for actions, as well as probing for children's meanings. The videotaped segments could be discussed by the staff member with other staff, supervisors, or college teachers, in addition to, or instead of, being used for self-evaluation. Under these latter circumstances, the method becomes more participatory in nature.

If done constructively and carefully, self-evaluation can produce helpful information for staff. Unfortunately, however, results of research on the effects of self-viewing via videotape or film generally do not support the claim that this procedure results in better performance by teachers, unless information about the amount of departure from a desired standard, acceptable to the viewer, is also provided (Salomon and McDonald, 1970). In addition, with any type of self-rating, there is a tendency for the raters to overrate themselves, and the relationships between self-ratings and other criteria such as student ratings and student achievement have been found to be negligible (McNeil and Popham, 1973).

If intended mainly for self-improvement, self-evaluation can be valuable. It has the advantage of providing opportunity for self-improvement without external threat. In any comprehensive staff evaluation, however, self-evaluation should not be the sole source of data, because of the problems noted above. The cooperative evaluation method, described later in this section, utilizes some features of self-evaluation but also involves input from other sources.

Peer evaluation: Use of peers to evaluate staff members is a method employed only infrequently. It is one of the more threatening methods for staff-evaluation, unless the staff themselves choose this approach. The Center for Research on Learning and Teaching at the University of Michigan prepared a statement for their faculty that summarized the strengths and weaknesses of peer evaluation:

> Some of the arguments *for* peer evaluation are: teachers are better able to judge what's happening in the classroom than are administrators, who are "too removed" from the classroom problems; another teacher in the same area of specialization as the teacher being evaluated is better qualified in that subject matter than a principal, who must be all things to his staff; teachers will be more sympathetic to one another; it spreads the time-consuming burden of evaluating among more people. Arguments *against* peer evaluation include: it may create bad feeling among teachers, and conversely, is subject to distortion because of personal friendships or animosities; teachers don't like to pass judgment on their colleagues; it destroys teacher unity; there are practical administrative and monetary objections to it because of the need to train teachers and to release them from their regular duties to perform evaluations [Center for Research on Learning and Teaching, 1974].

Utilizing peers as part of an evaluation team—which also might include an administrator, a parent, an external observer, and so forth—is probably a better approach than using peers only. Further, if the peers are persons who hold similar positions in different settings (for example, teachers from different preschools), then this approach might seem less threatening.

Rather than having peers actually make evaluative judgments, a staff evaluation plan might include them as consultant-helpers afterwards. For example, staff members might work with each other to strengthen the weak areas of each that had been identified by the evaluation data. If viewed as a cooperative venture aimed at program improvement, this procedure could yield positive and productive changes in teaching and other staff behaviors.

Supervisor ratings: Staff evaluation by supervisors is a common occurrence. "Directors assess teachers and staff, head teachers assess assistants, aides and volunteers. Part of the job of each person in any hierarchy is a continuous appraisal of the performance and personal qualities of those for whose work they are responsible" (Hess and Croft, 1972, p. 294). The ways in which supervisors evaluate those whom they are responsible for varies. Generally, however, some type of rating form is used, often followed by a postevaluation conference between the supervisor and the staff member. The rating can be made via direct observation, specifically intended for evaluation purposes, or in a more general way, on the basis of prior informal visits and impressions. We prefer the use of direct observations, with more than one time period and several different days and visits used for this purpose; such procedures allow the supervisor to actually watch diverse performances by the staff member, and resultant evaluative judgments are less likely to be capricious or arbitrary.

Evaluation by supervisors can cause considerable stress for those being evaluated. Again, one way to reduce this stress is to involve the staff in the planning and criteria-setting. Scheduling several observations of staff, not just one or two, over a period of time should also help staff feel more comfortable with the process.

Devising an observation checklist or schedule that encompasses all relevant behaviors is important in this type of staff evaluation. The particular behaviors included will, of course, depend on the type of early childhood education program, the purposes of the evaluation, and the type of staff being rated. Bean and Clemes, in their *Elementary Principal's Handbook* (1978), offered the following list of teacher behaviors as a guide for principals in constructing rating scales or observation schedules for teacher evaluation. According to the authors, these factors have proven important in teacher performance and productivity.

1. Warmth
   a. The teacher provides positive reinforcement through praise, and pays close attention to what children say.
   b. The teacher makes physical contact with children by holding hands, hugging, touching, and so on—in ways appropriate to age and sex.
   c. The teacher uses humor frequently, especially in ways that do not disparage or shame children.
   d. The teacher makes frequent contact with individual children by a touch, a comment, eye contact, smiles, and so on.
   e. The teacher adjusts the style of contact, taking into account differences among children.
2. Clarity in communication
   a. The teacher gives directions that are understandable to children.
   b. The teacher makes clear, prior to a new task, what is going to happen, and how it should be done.

    c. The teacher makes frequent checks for feedback from children, asking them to repeat what they heard her say, clarifying that they understood, and seeks their opinions on events in the classroom.

    d. When the teacher asks a question, she leaves sufficient time for children to respond to her.

    e. When children respond, the teacher makes frequent use of paraphrasing to indicate her comprehension of what the child has said.

3. Classroom management

    a. Consequences for misbehavior are clarified to individuals and the class, and follow-through occurs.

    b. The teacher makes minimal use of threats when attempting to manage children.

    c. The classroom rules are clear to children, and frequently referred to.

    d. The noise level of the classroom is monitored by the teacher, and varies according to the activity.

    e. The teacher gets the class's attention when she requires it, and commands the children's interest in what she does and says.

4. Physical arrangements

    a. There is physical evidence of current activities that reinforce directives and the main principles being taught.

    b. The teacher maintains a standard of neatness, which is appropriate to the task at hand, and furthers the goals of the activity.

    c. The decorations and displays in the classroom stimulate interest and attention.

    d. The arrangement of desks and tables makes effective use of space, promotes effective grouping of children, and insures safety.

    e. Materials are easily accessible to children.

5. Productivity

    a. The teacher completes activities in the time and sequence that was defined.

    b. The teacher is able to specify short- and long-range goals, objectives, and activities (relative to the school's policies and curriculum), and is on target in accomplishing them.

    c. When teaching a lesson, the teacher has all materials required, in sufficient quantity to complete the task.

    d. There is available a variety of materials that serve the needs of children who are working at various levels of competence.

    e. The teacher has procedures that identify various competence levels.

    f. Administrative requirements are completed by the teacher on time, and at an appropriate standard [Bean and Clemes, 1978, pp. 23–24].

Another source the reader might wish to review in this connection is the Assessing the Behaviors of Caregivers observational checklist (Honig and Lally, 1975). Once a rough list has been constructed using sources such as those just noted, it will probably need modifying to match specific program and staff characteristics. This list at this point should be discussed, defined, and refined with staff and other relevant persons. As Popham (1975) pointed out, a major problem with supervisor ratings stems from the diverse perceptions that people have regarding what constitutes good teaching or good staff performance. Discussing discrepancies of this sort prior to deciding the final form of the evaluation instrument can reduce subsequent resistance to the evaluation's conclusions.

If the completed instrument is to be a rating form (see Chapter Two), response formats must be devised. These could follow a frequency continuum (for example, "never" to "almost always"), or an evaluative continuum (for example, "very poor" to "excellent"), depending, in part, on the type of behavior included and the ways in which statements are phrased. If the instrument is to be an observation schedule (Chapter Four), decisions must be made about the frequency with which behaviors will be observed and rated. A review of the several formal observational systems in Chapter Four, such as the Flanders Interaction Analysis procedure presented in Table 10, should provide guides for making such decisions. In any event, it is an excellent idea to try out and further refine an instrument of this type with several staff members before actually using it for staff evaluation.

In concluding this section, we present an example of a rating form that can be used for staff evaluation by supervisors. This form was developed by the Education Development Center (1977) for use with Follow Through teachers (but it clearly is also appropriate for preschools). Its items clearly reflect a focus on open education concepts. Although it was originally constructed for self-assessment by teachers, it could also obviously be used to obtain ratings by supervisors or external observers. It contains seventy items, divided into seven scales. For each item, a six-point response format is followed: 1 = Never; 2 = Infrequently; 3 = Occasionally; 4 = Moderately; 5 = Frequently; and 6 = Always.

Open Education Teacher Self-Assessment Form

Instruction —Guidance and Extension of Learning
I1. I give individual children small concentrated amounts of my time rather than giving my general attention to the children as a class all day.
I2. I encourage children's independence and exercise of real choice.
I3. I plan based on observation of and interaction with the children to inform myself of the needs, interests, and capabilities of individual children.
I4. I am thoughtful of the needs of the children and the activities in which they are engaged before making decisions about changing or extending activities.
I5. I use the child's interaction with materials, equipment, and his or her environment as the basis of my instruction.
I6. I avoid whole class assignments; instead, I extend the activities which the children have chosen, through conversation, introduction of related materials, direct instruction when warranted, and assignments appropriate to individual needs.
I7. My approach to learning is interdisciplinary; for example, the child is not expected to confine himself to a single subject.
I8. Activities arise from children's interests and responses to materials as extensions of prescribed curriculums.
I9. I keep in mind long-term goals for the children which guide me in extending children's involvement in activities.

Diagnosis of Learning Events

D1. In diagnosis, I pay attention not only to the correctness of a child's response or solution, but also to the understanding and reasoning processes which lead the child to the particular response or solution.

D2. To obtain diagnostic information, I take an involved interest in the specific work or concern of the child at the moment, through attentive, individualized observing and questioning which is immediate and experience based.

D3. I see errors as a valuable part of the learning process because they provide information which the child and I can use to further the child's learning.

D4. In diagnosis, I value the child's fantasy as an aid to understanding the child's concerns, interests, and motivations.

D5. When I group children, I base my grouping upon my own observations and judgment rather than only standardized tests and norms.

D6. Children do not always depend on my judgment; they are also encouraged to diagnose their progress through the materials they are working with.

Provisioning for Learning

P1. Manipulative materials are supplied in great diversity and range, and children work directly with them.

P2. Books are supplied in diversity and profusion, including reference books, children's literature, and "books" written by the children.

P3. The environment includes materials developed by the children and me, and common environmental materials (plant life, rocks, sand, water, pets, egg cartons, plastic bottles, and such).

P4. Materials are readily accessible to children.

P5. I gradually modify the content and arrangement of the classroom based upon diagnosis and evaluation of the children's needs and interests and their use of materials and space.

P6. I encourage children's use of materials in ways I had not foreseen and I help to move activity into useful and constructive channels.

P7. Each child has an individual space for his or her own personal storage, while the major portion of the classroom space is organized for use by all children.

P8. Activity areas provide for a variety of potential usage and allow for a range of ability levels.

P9. Children move freely about the room without asking permission.

P10. Given adequate supervision, children are encouraged to use other areas of the building, schoolyard, and neighborhood for educational purposes during the school day.

P11. Different activities generally go on simultaneously.

P12. Informal talking between children and exchanging of information and ideas is encouraged as contributing to learning.

P13. Children help one another.

P14. The day is divided into large blocks of time. Within each block of time many different activities may be occurring simultaneously.

P15. The children and I jointly determine individual work plans and schedules.

P16. Children generally work individually and in small groups, sometimes predetermined by me and other times by their own choice.

P17. I occasionally group children directed at specific immediate needs.

P18. I provide occasions when the whole group gathers for activities such as story or discussion, to share feelings, ideas, and activities which promote a sense of community and belonging to the group.

P19. The class is heterogeneous with regard to ability. Generally, groups are formed around interests or needs, not similarity of ability.

P20. I occasionally group children for lessons directed at specific immediate needs.

P21. I create a purposeful atmosphere to enable the children to use their time productively and to value their work and learning.

Evaluation of Diagnostic Information

E1. Observation of the child's interaction with materials, equipment, and other children is the basis of my evaluation of each individual's learning.

E2. Evaluation of a child's school experience is not accomplished by looking only at data collected in a single situation or series of experiences; that is, evaluation of the effect of a child's school experience covers a long range of time, more than a year.

E3. My record-keeping includes writing and compiling individual notes and progress reports chronicling the child's cognitive, emotional, and physical development.

E4. I collect samples of each child's work with which the child and I measure the child's progress.

Humaneness—Respect, Openness, and Warmth

H1. I respect each child's personal style of operating, thinking, and acting.

H2. I guide but rarely command.

H3. I value each child's activities and products as legitimate expressions of his or her interests.

H4. I demonstrate respect for each child's ideas by making use of them whenever possible.

H5. I respect each child's feelings by taking them seriously.

H6. Children feel free to express their feelings mindful of their mutual respect and consideration.

H7. I attempt to recognize each child's emotions with an understanding of that particular child and the circumstances.

H8. Conflict is recognized and worked out within the context of the group, and there is no abdication of responsible adult authority.

H9. The class and I develop clear guidelines and operate within them.

H10. The children and I create an atmosphere that promotes openness and trust among children and with me.

H11. Relationships are characterized by unsentimental warmth and affection.

H12. I base my evaluation of a child's work upon the capabilities of the particular child and circumstances operating at the time.

H13. I recognize and admit my limitations when I feel unable to give a child the help he or she needs.

H14. I promote a nonthreatening climate by helping children to accept mistakes as part of learning, not as measures of failure.

Seeking Opportunity to Promote Growth

S1. I seek information about new materials.

S2. I experiment with materials myself.

S3. I seek further information about the community and its physical and cultural resources.

S4. I make use of help from a supportive advisor.

S5. I enjoy ongoing communication with other teachers about children and learning.

S6. I attempt to know more about the children by getting to know their parents or relatives and their neighborhood.

Self-Perception of the Teacher

SP1. I view myself as an active experimenter in the process of creating and adapting ideas and materials.

SP2. I see myself as a continual learner who explores new ideas and possibilities both inside and outside the classroom.

SP3. I value the way I am teaching as an opportunity for my own personal and professional growth and change.

SP4. I feel comfortable with children taking the initiative in learning, making choices, and being independent of me.

SP5. I recognize my own habits and need for importance and recognition; I try to restrain myself from premature and insensitive intervention.

SP6. I see my own feelings as an acceptable part of the classroom experience.

SP7. I trust children's ability to operate effectively and learn in a framework not centered on me.

SP8. I see myself as one of many sources of knowledge and attention in the classroom.

SP9. My lesson plans reflect a broad spectrum of learning objectives which are not always scheduled within fixed time periods.

SP10. I trust myself as one who can facilitate learning within a structure which necessitates spontaneous responding to individuals and to a changing variety of situations [Educational Development Center, 1977].

Direct observation by external observers: Closely related to supervisor ratings as a means of staff evaluation is the use of external, or independent, observers as raters. On balance, this procedure probably yields more objective data than supervisors' ratings, since the observers are new to the setting and should hold few, if any, preconceived notions of the performance levels of the staff. But of course the external observers do not have the detailed knowledge of program objectives and staff roles that the supervisors have. External observers can offer insights and comments about strengths and weaknesses that those closely involved in the program might not identify. Nevertheless, their evaluations must focus on behaviors considered important to the administrators and staff if the data are to be meaningful to the program personnel.

When external observers are used, the observation process is often more systematic than when it is done "in-house." That is, the raters are trained and checked for interrater reliability (see Chapter Three); sometimes, in fact, external observers are collecting data for research purposes as well as to aid with staff evaluation. If external observers bring already developed schedules with them, the program director and staff should check them over to make sure that the criteria match those of the program.

Student ratings: The most frequently used method of evaluating teachers in colleges and universities is student ratings; at other educational levels, this approach is taken less often. The usual mode is to provide students with a rating form on which they anonymously rate their teachers in terms of such dimensions as communication, student contact, assignments, and effectiveness of teaching. The validity of student ratings in higher education has been studied extensively; generally, a moderate positive relationship between ratings by students and student achievement has been shown (Costin, Greenough, and Menges, 1971).

We have found no evidence of the use of written questionnaires for very young children for the purpose of staff evaluation. It would be possible to construct such a form, however—using happy-to-sad faces as response choices and having items about staff read aloud by a nonstaff person. Another approach, and we believe a more feasible one, would be to interview the children—at least a randomly selected sample of them. Children might be asked a series of pre-established questions based on criteria agreed upon by staff and administrators. Or, they could be asked to first describe what constitutes a "good teacher" and then to describe their own teacher. Hess and Croft (1972) presented the following assessments by preschool children of a good teacher's characteristics: "*A good teacher* holds you and reads to you, sings songs to you, doesn't slap you, pushes you high on a swing, goes to meetings, when you have a hurt finger she puts a band-aid on it right away, smiles at you, doesn't make you sit still or be quiet, wears pretty beads, lets you play with her hair, helps you, fixes bikes, doesn't get mad, works hard, builds with us, [and] makes you laugh" (Hess and Croft, 1972, p. 295). Information from students can make a valuable contribution to any staff evaluation, especially if obtained in conjunction with other data. Although young children's appraisals of staff will not be as clearly defined as appraisal by adults, the children's impressions are certainly relevant data that, as part of formative evaluation, could lead to suggestions for staff improvement.

Parent evaluation: Utilizing parents as a source for staff evaluation data is another possible, though frequently overlooked, alternative. As with student evaluations, parents' rating should be used in conjunction with other data.

Ratings by parents of staff effectiveness can be obtained in several ways. Rating forms, soliciting general impressions about the program staff, can be sent or mailed to parents. A more thorough approach involves observations by parents, with ratings made during or after their visits. A third possibility is interviews with parents, either immediately after they have visited the program or even without such visits. Some visitation, however, is preferred if the evaluation is to be as comprehensive as possible.

Parent evaluation of early childhood education programs is inevitable. Parents' opinions are reflected in increased or decreased enrollments, the reputation and image of the program, and parents' willingness to participate in parent conferences, program activities, and other meetings. Incorporating this informal but important parental evaluation network into a more formal evaluation system can help prevent problems before they occur. For example, if parents are systematically surveyed for evaluation data, their opinions of strengths and weaknesses do not have to be deciphered via such events as decreased enrollments. Further, an understanding of parents' perceptions of their children's educational needs and of what constitutes a "good program" is vitally important to the staff. Discrepancies between parents' and staff's perceptions and philosophies can be discussed once they are known.

Cooperative Appraisal Plan: A cooperative approach to evaluating staff has been implicit throughout this section. The Cooperative Appraisal Plan or CAP (Tomblin, 1976) integrates many cooperative features into a systematic evaluation process. CAP has been used and researched more extensively in industry than in education. In a study of the approach at the General Electric Company, Meyer, Kay, and French (1965) found that performance improved most when specific goals were established mutually rather than by the employer or the employee alone.

CAP consist of three phases; the staff member and the evaluator (usually the supervisor) participate in all three phases. In the first phase, *planning,* criteria are formulated. The criteria consist of objectives for the staff member for a certain period of time, usually a year. How the objectives will be measured is specified, as well as a time frame for the completion of each objective. Both the supervisor and the staff provide input. During the second phase, *operation,* the plan is carried out by the staff member. Evaluative data, as specified in the plan, are also collected. The data may consist of observer's reports, self-reports, questionnaire results, records of books read or courses completed, and so on. The third phase is termed *final evaluation.* At this time, the staff member presents collected data to the supervisor or evaluator at a conference; an evaluation report is agreed upon, written, and submitted to the district personnel office, advisory council, or other appropriate supervisory body. If agreement cannot be reached, the staff member may write and file a report separate from that of the supervisor's report.

Obviously, this approach incorporates elements of the methods discussed earlier, especially supervisor's ratings and self-evaluation. What makes it unique is the systematic cooperative spirit that infuses the entire process. Following CAP's guidelines aids those involved in the staff evaluation in participating as a team in the evaluative effort—from the very beginning until the final report is written and submitted.

Performance of children: Actual performance of children certainly comprises a relevant source of data about staff effectiveness. As we mentioned earlier, however, measurement and statistical problems abound in attempts to infer teacher effectiveness levels from student performance levels. Glass (1974) summarized the problems in using pupil gains to evaluate teachers, pointing out that standardized tests lack validity and fairness for many purposes, that teachers of highly intelligent children have a definite advantage with this evaluation approach over teachers of less bright children, that gain scores cannot be reliably measured by such tests, and that the process encourages, if not pressures, teachers to "teach to the test."

Although student learning gains are an unfair basis for accountability, children's performance data can be used in several meaningful ways in formative evaluation. One way involves observing children's behavior in conjunction with observing staff behavior. Children's affective responses to the staff, and their ways of interacting with the staff and each other, and other behavioral variables of this type, can be assessed by observing children in the classroom and on the playgrounds. An additional method involves analyzing the range and type of work products of the children; a content analysis of this sort, especially if done by an independent judge, might help the staff realize that certain objectives are being stressed more than others in the activities that individual staff are providing for the children.

Testing the staff: Administering a test to the staff is another option for staff evaluation. This is used less frequently than the methods described above for evaluating elementary and secondary school teachers (Masonis, 1976; and Tractenberg, 1973). The test can take several forms—for example, a written standardized test, a written essay test, or a performance test. The teaching performance test is an evaluation method advocated by McNeil and Popham (1973; also see Popham, 1975). The test requires the teacher to plan a brief lesson to promote learner mastery of a specific instructional objective given to the teacher. After preparing the lesson, the teacher instructs a small group of learners, usually for fifteen to twenty minutes. The students are then given a test, previously unseen by the teacher, that assesses mastery of the objectives; they are also asked to judge how interesting the lesson was, using some kind of rating form. Learners can be either children or adults, such as fellow teachers. Topics can be either novel or familiar; if familiar topics are used, the learners are pretested to identify sufficiently naive learners for the exercise (Popham, 1975).

Advantages cited for the method include the use of similar data for comparisons among teachers; meaningful comparison requires, of course, that extraneous conditions, such as teaching and preparation time, be kept constant for all teachers. Learners, too, must be comparable—a feature best achieved via random assignment of learners to teachers. The method obviously has a focus on summative, rather than formative, staff evaluation. For instructional improvement purposes, it does not yield the realistic data obtained by some of the other methods, such as videotaped recordings of actual performance, observer's reports, or students' and parents' ratings.

Glass (1974) criticized the use of teacher performance tests on several grounds, especially because of its focus on measuring narrow behavioral changes in students. "Is the teacher's ability to produce behavioral changes in pupils 'the real thing' about schooling? Hardly. Education is many 'real things.' Changing children's behavior is just one of them. Permitting children to grow in supportive and interesting environments is another. . . . We can currently conceive of, and recognize in particular instances, many more types of behavioral change than modern techniques can reliably measure" (Glass, 1974, p. 15). Further, Glass critiqued the studies conducted to date on the validity and reliability of the teacher performance test as an evaluation method. Generally, stability estimates (assessed by measuring the same teachers on different occasions) were low, and validity data lacking.

Unobtrusive measures: A final method for staff evaluation involves the use of unobtrusive measures. As described in Chapter Two, unobtrusive measures are less immediate, direct, and obvious to those being evaluated than are any of the other staff evaluation procedures already presented. The intent is to make inferences about behaviors, skills, attitudes, and so forth, from some other areas of behavior or attitude. Turnover rate among staff, eagerness of staff to sign contracts, students' attendance rates, students' apparent happiness, and students' use of staff-provided materials are examples of unobtrusive measures that might be used for staff evaluation purposes in early childhood education settings.

Although unobtrusive measures have the advantage of indirectness (that is, the staff do not know they are being observed or measured in some way and thus do not behave differently than normal for the sake of the evaluation), there are several obvious problems with this approach. Invasion of privacy can become an issue — for example, if staff records are used for evaluation purposes without the prior permission of the staff. A second problem involves the inferences that are drawn. "Unobtrusive measures are handicapped by the fact that the behavior observed or recorded is connected with other behavior only by inference. High teacher turnover rate *may* indicate low morale but may also indicate other conditions, such as a well-trained staff which is motivated to go for additional training or is hired away for promotions which the school itself could not provide. This type of measure is useful but should be interpreted cautiously with alternative interpretations kept in mind" (Hess and Croft, 1972, p. 302).

Multiple criteria and multiple methods in staff evaluation: Each of the ten methods presented above for staff evaluation has strengths and weaknesses. No one method can produce perfectly valid or reliable data, regardless of the purpose of the evaluation. Using multiple criteria and multiple methods is advised. For example, criteria for a staff evaluation might include specific behaviors of staff and of children, measured with supervisor's ratings; staff ratings made by parents and students; staff self-assessment and discussions with supervisors about perceived strengths and weaknesses, areas of job satisfaction and dissatisfaction, and so forth; and possibly collection of data on turnover rates. The particular criteria and methods used will depend on the purposes of the staff evaluation, but considering a diversity of criteria and methods will yield more balanced data than will focusing on just one method. As we stated several times throughout this section, staff evaluation — by other staff, parents, community members, personnel in other centers — is inevitable. It is much fairer and more meaningful to all concerned to conduct a systematic, carefully planned staff evaluation than to rely on unsystematically assessed, word-of-mouth opinions as the basis of judging the effectiveness of the staff or of providing suggestions for staff improvement.

Chapter *11*

Program Evaluations

O ur purpose in this chapter is to provide the reader with examples of actual program evaluations conducted in the field of early childhood education. The examples are intended to illustrate, on the one hand, the interplay between measurement and evaluation (involving many of the measures and concepts presented heretofore in the book) and, on the other hand, the relationships between both of these processes and the real world supports, constraints, and limitations that inevitably are encountered. Our focus includes the settings, the evaluation designs employed, the measures used, and the evaluation outcomes.

Selecting the evaluations to highlight was difficult. An extremely large number of evaluations have been conducted, as is readily apparent in most reviews (for example, see Bronfenbrenner, 1974; Gotts, 1973; Horowitz and Paden, 1973; Hunt, 1975; Mann, Harrell, and Hurt, 1976; White and others, 1973b; and Wolf and others, 1978). Since the mid 1960s, most of the evaluations of educational programs for young children have involved compensatory education. S. B. Anderson defined compensatory education as "a preventive and global (otherwise it would be *remedial*) intervention into the lives of people judged to have socioeconomic handicaps (physical handicaps would require *special* education) assumed to be predictive of unnecessarily limited school achievement and life chances" (1973, pp. 198–199). She pointed out that evaluations of compensatory education had to determine, first, whether the program did in fact compensate.

Our selection of evaluations to highlight in this chapter reflects this predominant emphasis in the field of compensatory program evaluation. Our original intentions to detail the evaluations of Head Start and Follow Through were modified when the massive literature concerning each was assembled. In the case of Head Start, a partial list of noteworthy evaluations, most of them national in scope, are presented chronologically below:

1. Westinghouse Learning Corporation/Ohio University: *The Impact of Head Start: An Evaluation of the Effects of Head Start on Children's Cognitive and Affective Development,* 1969.
2. Kirschner Associates: *A National Survey of the Impacts of Head Start Centers on Community Institutions,* 1970.
3. Stanford Research Institute: *Implementation of Planned Variation in Head Start: Preliminary Evaluations of Planned Variation in Head Start According to Follow Through Approaches (1969–1970),* 1971.
4. System Development Corporation: *Effects of Different Head Start Program Approaches on Children of Different Characteristics: Reports on Analysis of Data from 1966–67, 1967–68, and 1968–69 National Evaluations,* 1972.
5. Huron Institute: *The Quality of the Head Start Planned Variation Data,* 1973 (Walker, Bane, and Bryk).
6. Educational Testing Service: *Disadvantaged Children and Their First School Experiences, ETS–Head Start Longitudinal Study: Notable Early Characteristics of High and Low Achieving Black Low-SES Children,* 1976 (Shipman and others).
7. Abt Associates: *National Day Care Study. Second Annual Report, 1975–1976, Phase II Results and Phase III Design,* 1976.
8. High/Scope Educational Research Foundation/Abt Associates: *National Home Start Evaluation: Final Report,* 1976 (Love and others).
9. High/Scope Educational Research Foundation: *A Process Evaluation of Project Developmental Continuity: Draft Final Report of the PDC Feasibility Study, 1974–1977,* 1977 (Love and others).
10. Abt Associates: *A National Survey of Head Start Graduates and Their Peers,* 1978.
11. Applied Management Sciences: *Evaluation of the Process of Mainstreaming Handicapped Children into Project Head Start. Phase II, Draft Interim Report,* 1978.

Adding to the complexity of these diverse Head Start program evaluations are interpretive reviews from many different perspectives (such as Bissell, 1973; Gotts, 1973; Grotberg, 1969; Horowitz and Paden, 1973; Hunt, 1975; Mann, Harrell, and Hurt, 1976; McDill, McDill, and Sprehe, 1972; Rivlin and Timpane, 1975; Taub and others, 1979; White and others, 1973b; and Wolf and others, 1978). Complexity also arises from direct challenges of the evaluations, such as the Smith and Bissell (1970) challenge of the Westinghouse Learning Corporation/Ohio University evaluation of Head Start (also see the reply to the challenge by Cicirelli, Evans, and Schiller, 1970). Of course, some synthesis also results from these counter-interpretations and reviews. For example, reviewing most Head Start national evaluations, Taub and others (1979) found the measures used distributed among domains as follows:

Domain	Percentage
Cognitive-Perceptual Development	41
Socioemotional Development	30
Language Development	15
Medical, Dental, Nutritional, and Health Development	7
Psychomotor Development	6
Life-styles Development	1

Such overviews permit consideration of how well the measures used reflect the established Head Start goals. However, our overall judgment was that the complexity of the Head Start evaluation effort to date defied a succinct treatment here—instead, we opted to highlight just the Home Start evaluation.

Complexity also characterizes the Follow Through evaluations to date. The chronological list of selected national evaluation reports below represents just a small portion of all that have been written:

1. Stanford Research Institute: *Interim Evaluation of the National Follow Through Program 1969–1971. A Technical Report,* 1973 (Emrick, Sorenson, and Stearns).
2. Soar: *Final Report. Follow Through Classroom Process Measurement and Pupil Growth (1970–1971),* 1973.
3. Abt Associates: *Final Report. Education as Experimentation: Evaluation of the Follow Through Planned Variation Model,* Vol. 1, 1974 (Cline and others).
4. Stanford Research Institute: *Follow Through Classroom Observation Evaluation 1972–73,* 1974 (Stallings and Kaskowitz).
5. Abt Associates: *Final Report. Education as Experimentation: Evaluation of the Follow Through Planned Variation Model,* Vol. 2, 1975 (Cline and others).
6. RMC Research Corporation: *A Cost Analysis of Follow Through Projects,* 1977 (Rogers and others).
7. Abt Associates: *Education as Experimentation: A Planned Variation Model,* 1977 (Stebbins and others).

Although these reports are substantial (the last one listed consists of six separately bound documents making up four volumes—altogether about 2,100 pages), there are literally hundreds of additional reports and articles relevant to Follow Through. One extensive bibliographical list is found in Villaume and Haney (1977). Some evaluations have concerned the hoped-for benefits that were to be provided by the program continuity and linking that Follow Through afforded students from Head Start (see, for example, Weisberg and Haney, 1977). Further, as was true for Head Start, major evaluation findings in Follow

Through have been challenged. A recent example of this phenomenon occurred after the release of the Abt analysis of the Follow Through data (Stebbins and others, 1977); that is, a chain of diverse interpretations and counter-interpretations were soon forthcoming (Anderson and others, 1978; Becker, 1977; Bereiter and Kurland, 1978; Hodges, 1978; House and others, 1978; Mc-Lean, 1978; and Wisler, Burns, and Iwamoto, 1978). Within this diverse assemblage of reports and interpretations, we have selected the observational evaluation by Stallings and Kaskowitz (1974) to highlight.

In addition to our treatments of Home Start and Follow Through via focused evaluations within each, we also consider at some length the evaluations of Sesame Street (which also was intended primarily as a compensatory education effort). We then present briefly a few additional evaluations in early childhood education and some sources that review several relevant evaluations.

The Home Start Evaluation

The National Home Start Demonstration Program was launched early in 1972 under the auspices of the federal Office of Child Development (now the Administration for Children, Youth, and Families). Home Start was designed to provide comprehensive child development services for preschool children in their homes—and thus to demonstrate an alternative method for delivering services like those offered by Head Start, an essentially center-based effort. Home Start was to enhance mothers' skills for teaching and nurturing development of "their own children in the home. At the same time, comprehensive socioemotional, health, and nutritional objectives were adopted as part of the care program" (Love and others, 1976, p. 1). Along with the Home Start program, the Office of Child Development also funded a sizable evaluation project to operate concurrently. The evaluation was to chart the processes used in Home Start and to determine the program's effectiveness. The primary evaluation contract was awarded to the High/Scope Educational Research Foundation, while Abt Associates served as a subcontractor. The final report of the evaluation contractors (Love and others, 1976) served as the basic reference for most of the presentation that follows.

Home Start, like Head Start, was directed toward meeting the needs of low-income preschoolers and their families. Though benefits were clearly intended for the children, the project was to build on family strengths so that the delivery of many of these benefits would occur through parents. Funded for three years, Home Start operated at sixteen sites in the country. Each of the sixteen projects was capable of serving about eighty families at an annual budget of approximately $130,000 (somewhat over $100,000 provided from federal revenues and about $26,000 from local "matching" contributions). The typical staff for a project consisted of a director, three specialists (a nurse, a social service/ parent involvement coordinator, and either a home visitor supervisor or a child development specialist), seven home visitors, and a secretary-bookkeeper. The typical home visitor was about thirty-five years old, had some college work, and had previous job experience in some way related to her home visitor role. Each home visitor was responsible for about ten or eleven families, and each family received two ninety-minute visits monthly. In each family a focal child was designated; other siblings were involved in the home visit activities in 85 percent of the homes in which there were siblings. Although the home visits were the principal means of delivering services, there were also monthly meetings for children and/or parents, parent policy council meetings, and referrals to other community services.

The total family emphasis of Home Start was reflected in the nature of the home visit activities. Global estimates were that the home visitor spent one third of the typical visit interacting with the focal child, one third with the parent, and one third with both parent and child. Home visitors followed a four-component curriculum: education, health, nutrition, and social-psychological services. The proportional focus of home visit activities was charted as follows: 55 percent on education (child's school readiness and physical development, and parents' education and acquisition of child development knowledge); 24 percent on parental concerns and other services such as assistance in securing improved housing, employment, legal services, and counseling; 10 percent on the child's emotional development; 9 percent on family health and nutrition; and 2 percent on other concerns and topics.

Elaboration of the Evaluation Design. The evaluation design was established to accomplish three purposes:

1. To document and to measure the effects of Home Start on parents and children.
2. To compare the cost-effectiveness of Home Start with that of Head Start.
3. To examine and document Home Start implementation and operations with an eye toward explaining child and parent outcomes and making recommendations to improve program efficiency.

Thus, the evaluation was both summative (purposes 1 and 2) and formative (purpose 3).

These purposes influenced the design adopted. Six of the sixteen Home Start sites were selected to provide the summative evaluation data, while data from all sixteen sites were collected to address the third purpose. Although the six were not selected randomly but rather on the basis of site start-up delays, evaluation travel costs, and other factors, data from them verified their similarity to the other ten sites. At each of the six summative sites, twice as many families were recruited as could be enrolled. This overrecruitment permitted the random assignment of families either to Home Start or to a deferred-treatment control group. A pretest was given in Fall 1973, with other testing conducted after seven months (Spring 1974), twelve months (Fall 1974), and twenty months (Spring 1975). After serving as comparison groups for the 1973–74 Home Start families, the deferred-treatment control groups at each site began (in Fall 1974) to receive the Home Start program themselves. Evaluation activities during the final Home

Start year (1974–75) also included a comparison of the effects of one year and two years of Home Start involvement (using the two groups initially involved in the random assignment) and a replication study of the seven-month findings comparing Home Start and Head Start programs (using two new groups that began receiving each program in Fall 1974).

The comparisons intended to establish the differential effects of Head Start and Home Start were not as clear-cut as those involving Home Start versus no Home Start. Random assignment to either Head Start or Home Start was not possible at the four sites (of the six summative sites) involved in this comparison; rather, the comparison groups were simply obtained from the Head Start programs operating in the Home Start communities. Differences between the groups were apparent, with Head Start families generally appearing less rural and less disadvantaged. Further, the focus of the two programs differed: Home Start emphasized parenting skills to a greater degree, while Head Start provided an important indirect service—daycare—for working mothers. Cost data were collected over the entire three-year period (1972–1975) from both Home Start and Head Start projects.

Data collection was implemented primarily by using "community interviewers," paraprofessionals selected from the communities involved and trained in interviewing techniques. For control and Home Start families, testing and interviewing took place in the home, and for Head Start families and children, principally in centers. Procedures were used to monitor the psychometric qualities of the data collected. Various statistical analyses were performed including factor analyses, analyses of variance and covariance, and multivariate analyses of covariance and regression. Attrition was heavy over the two-year evaluation period, with retention of somewhat over 40 percent of each category of family (Home Start, original control, and Head Start); however, attrition appeared to have no differential effects on the nature of the families retained in each category.

Description of the Measures. The Home Start evaluators operated under several general criteria in selecting measures. "Completely new measures could not be developed, total testing time had to be reasonable, individual items had to interpretable, instruments had to measure national or local objectives, measures had to be appropriate to the population, tests and interviews had to be practical to administer, some measures should have been used in other evaluations, and the measures had to have good psychometric characteristics" (Love and others, 1976, p. 43). In accordance with these criteria, ten measures were used, and from them fifty-eight dependent variables were derived. The variables are depicted in Figure 11, listed by the originating measure and grouped into five child and four parent objective areas. A succinct description of each measuring instrument is in order.

The Preschool Inventory (PSI) is a shortened, thirty-two item version of the sixty-four item Cooperative Preschool Inventory described in Chapter Five. The PSI is a measure of achievement in areas frequently regarded as necessary for success in school, such as general knowledge and basic concepts. One reason

Figure 11. Home Start Evaluation: Matrix of Measuring Instruments by Objective Areas.

Measuring Instrument	Child Objective Area					Parent Objective Area			
	School Readiness	Physical Development	Socioemotional Development	Nutrition	Medical	Mother-Child Relationship	Mother as Teacher	Materials for Child in Home	Community Resource Use
Preschool Inventory (PSI)	Total Score								
Denver Developmental Screening Test (DDST)	Language Scale	Gross Motor and Fine Motor-Adaptive Scales	Personal-Social Scale						
Eight-Block Sort Task	Child Task and Child Talk Scores						6 Scores on Mother Behavior		
Schaefer Behavior Inventory (SBI)			Task Orientation, Extrov.-Introv., and Hostility-Tolerance Scales						
Pupil Observation Checklist (POCL)			Test Orientation and Sociability Scales						
Height and Weight		Height and Weight							
Child Food Intake Questionnaire				7 Food Group Scores, Total Nutrition and Vitamins					
Parent Interview (PI)					5 Scores on Immunizations, Doctor, and Dental				17 Scores on Resources Used and Locus of Control
Mother Behavior Observation Scale (MBOS)						Supportive and Punitive Scales			
Home Environment Scale (HES)						Mother Involvement and Household Tasks Scales	Mother Teaches Scale	Books and Playthings Scales	

Source: Love and others, 1976, pp. 50–53.

for using the PSI as a school readiness measure was its previous use in a national Head Start evaluation.

The Denver Developmental Screening Test (DDST) was detailed in Chapter Six. For Home Start purposes, only those DDST items discriminating for three- to six-year-olds were utilized, and a few items duplicated in the PSI were eliminated. Based on pilot testing, a few items were deleted, a few were revised, administration instructions were clarified, the Fine Motor-Adaptive Scale was reordered so as to be administered first (to help establish rapport with the child), and the Personal-Social Scale items were all answered by mother-report. The Language Scale was considered a measure of school readiness, the Gross and Fine Motor Scales as measures of physical development, and the Personal-Social Scale as a socioemotional development measure.

The Eight-Block Sort Task was briefly mentioned in Chapter Ten with regard to parent evaluation. Used in both the Head Start Planned Variation and ETS-Head Start Longitudinal Studies, the measure provides the opportunity to observe mother-child interactions in a teaching context (and serves as a verification of verbal parent reports on the Home Environment Scale subsequently described). The task consists of three stages. In the first, the community interviewer leads the mother through the block-sorting procedure in standardized fashion. In the second, the mother teaches the child with six mother-behavior variables observed by the interviewer:

1. Request talk: frequency with which a mother elicits child talk focused on relevant block-sorting dimensions.
2. Diagnostic: frequency with which a mother uses open-ended questions to elicit child thinking about the sorting problem.
3. Talk about: frequency with which a mother talks about relevant dimensions of the block-sorting task.
4. Interactions per minute: average number of shifts in conversation from mother to child and vice versa, per minute.
5. Mean length of string: average number of uninterrupted comments by a mother (that is, the extent of mother monologue).
6. Feedback: frequency of mother's reactions to child's comments or block placements, including acknowledgement, praise, encouragement, and corrections.

In the third stage, two child school readiness scores result: (1) the task score, indicating the child's ability to acquire the concepts taught by the mother, and (2) the talk score, conveying how many relevant comments the child makes while being taught to sort the blocks.

The Schaefer Behavior Inventory (SBI) is a rating scale consisting of fifteen descriptive statements, five items for each of three children socioemotional development variables. The mother reads the items and makes her ratings on a seven-point scale from "never" to "always," indicating how well each statement describes her child. A sample statement from each scale follows: (1) Task

Orientation Scale: "Stays with a job until he (she) finishes it"; (2) Extroversion-Introversion Scale: "Likes to take part in activities with others"; and (3) Hostility-Tolerance Scale: "Stays angry for a long time after an argument."

The Pupil Observation Checklist (POCL) is a nine-item rating scale filled out by the community interviewer after completing the testing and interviewing. Each item consists of bipolar adjectives, such as "quiet-talkative" and "resistive-cooperative," with a seven-point scale between. Scores on two scales result: (1) Test Orientation, involving the child's behavior during testing, and (2) Sociability, pertaining to the child's overall behavior.

Height and weight were measured directly by the community interviewer. These data were used as assessments of the child's physical development. Further, they were important in assessing the comparability of groups at the start of the evaluation, as "height and, to a lesser extent, weight are general indicators of physical growth, and large discrepancies from the norms may be related to nutritional status" (Love and others, 1976, p. 47).

The Child Food Intake Questionnaire was used to obtain a quantitative and qualitative index of food consumption. Mothers were asked to recall all the foods eaten by their child on the previous day. Mothers' estimates and interviewers' recordings were enhanced by using plastic child-size (two-ounce) beef patties, four- and eight-ounce glasses and ten-ounce bowls all marked at two-ounce intervals, and tablespoons. Mothers pointed to the markings to indicate how much of a certain food the child had eaten. The interviewer avoided mentioning particular foods or appropriate amounts thereof, although some probing was permitted when it seemed likely that certain additions had been overlooked (like milk on dry cereal or lettuce on sandwiches). From such information, the total number of servings was determined in each of the seven food groups (milk, meat, egg, vitamin-A vegetables, other vegetables, citrus fruits, and breads and cereals). A total nutrition score was also derived. A ninth score resulted from asking the mother whether or not the child took vitamins.

The Parent Interview (PI) yielded data pertaining to the child's medical history and the family's use of community resources. Medical care consisted of five variables: immunization since fall (yes or no), months since last doctor visit, reason for visit, and the same two questions with regard to the dentist. Mothers were quizzed on the use of fifteen community resources: welfare, food stamps, medicaid, food commodities, hospital, public health clinic, mental health clinic, family counseling, planned parenthood, daycare, recreational programs, legal aid, housing authority, state employment office, and job training programs. An organizational score was also determined by totaling the number of organizations that some family member belonged to (such as the Boy Scouts, Girl Scouts, 4-H Club, youth groups, parent-teacher organization, church group, social club, political organization, or the like). A final part of the interview concerned eight questions dealing with the parents' perceived locus of control; that is, did they believe themselves to be in command of their lives (internal locus of control) or heavily under the influence of outside forces and pressures (external locus of control).

The Mother Behavior Observation Scale (MBOS) consisted of ten items completed by the community interviewer after the last visit to a family. Each item of the observational checklist was checked in one of the three ways: "never," "once or twice," and "three times or more." Five and four MBOS items composed the Supportive and Punitive behavior scales, respectively. The tenth item involved the amount of child's artwork displayed in the home, but it belonged to neither scale and was not analyzed.

The tenth and final Home Start measure was the Home Environment Scale (HES), mentioned previously in Chapter Ten. A thirty-seven item questionnaire for parents, the HES yielded scores on five scales. Two scales concerned the mother-child relationship: the Mother Involvement Scale, which noted the frequency with which mothers spent time with their children on liked activities; and the Household Tasks Scale, which charted how frequently children helped their mothers with simple household chores. The Mother Teaches Scale ascertained the beginning reading and writing skills mothers were trying to teach their children. The final two scales involved materials for children found in the home—in one case, the number of children's books available (and frequency with which they were read to children) and, in the other, the number of ordinary playthings in the home.

In all, the fifty-eight variables from the ten measures constituted a wide array. All three domains—cognitive, affective, and psychomotor—were well represented, as were variables concerning both child and parent behavior. Further, a variety of types of measure was in evidence. Sufficient measures were incorporated to address the three purposes of the evaluation.

Evaluation Outcomes. In addition to findings related to each of the three evaluation purposes, the Home Start evaluators also provided some anecdotal evidence similar in nature to some aspects of the responsive evaluation framework (Chapter Nine) and the illumination and literary evaluation approaches (Chapter Twelve). For example, they noted that Home Start helped a Cleveland widow with six sons receive her General Equivalency Diploma, serve on the program's parent advisory council, and be elected as a ward committeewoman. In another illustration, they noted how a Utah father, partially paralyzed in a work accident, and his family were assisted by Home Start to establish new daily routines. For the most part, however, the results of the evaluation dealt with the three pre-established purposes.

With regard to the first purpose, it was found that Home Start was effective for both parents and children. Home Start mothers, after seven months of the program, were more likely than control group mothers to read stories to their children, to allow their children to help with household tasks, to teach reading and writing skills to their children, and to provide books and common playthings for their children's use. On the Eight-Block Sort Task, the Home Start mothers employed more thought-provoking questions, a higher rate of verbal interactions, and more talk focused on the task dimensions. Home Start children, after seven months, were significantly ahead of controls on the Preschool Inventory, the DDST Language Scale, the Eight-Block Child Talk Score, and

SBI Task Orientation. The Home Start children also were reportedly receiving better medical and dental care. No differences were noted in terms of immunizations, fine and gross motor development, and nutrition (although both Home Start and control children's diets were less nutritious than commonly recommended). Whereas some differences persisted to the twelve-month testing, several did not, quite possibly because the original "control" mothers and children had already started to receive Home Start at the time of the twelve-month testing. Outcomes for families in Home Start for two years were found to be similar to those for families in the program for just one year. Further, the effects of Home Start and Head Start on parents, and also on children, were generally found to be quite similar.

The cost-effectiveness of Home Start relative to Head Start was examined to accomplish the second purpose of the evaluation. In general, the two programs were found comparable in terms of effects on parents and children, while Home Start cost somewhat less (about $1,400 in federal funds annually per Home Start family as compared with slightly over $1,700 in federal expenditures per Head Start child). Thus, compared with Head Start, Home Start was judged to be a cost-effective use of public revenues.

The third evaluation purpose, essentially formative, involved documenting Home Start implementation activities and relating them to program outcomes. With regard to *program implementation,* the evaluators documented considerable variability in actual services delivered to families, in per family costs, and in the number of specialists employed by a project (which also affected program costs). Projects were seen as successful in obtaining local resources to support Home Start, averaging about 20 percent of the federal expenditure. Home visitors were perceived as being paid minimally for their work (slightly over $5,000 annually). The focus of Home Start visits shifted increasingly to parents over the demonstration period, although attempts to involve fathers in project activities were generally not as successful as efforts to encourage sibling participation. Supervision of home visitors was judged not completely adequate in some project sites, primarily because of insufficient monitoring personnel. A final program implementation finding was the relatively large number of low-cost (in terms of federal dollars) referrals made via Home Start to meet family needs. An annual average of seven referrals per family was observed, typically over half of these concerning the health of the focal child and over a quarter involving the social-psychological needs of the family. Referrals were also made for nutritional and educational reasons, but with less frequency.

In the more complicated area of *program relationships* (that is, relationships between activities, staff and program characteristics, and outcomes), several findings were offered. Home visitors with too large a "family load" (more than thirteen families) had difficulty maintaining a schedule of regular contacts, and this lack of consistency was shown to be related to lower school readiness scores for children. Also, fewer visits were made by home visitors with children of their own at home. Fewer visits were made to urban than to rural families, possibly because of the difficulty of scheduling regular visits to urban families. Fewer but longer visits were made to families with older focal children, while families with younger focal children received shorter, more frequent visits. An interesting relationship was observed between home visitor age, duration of employment, and home visit focus. "Older home visitors spent less time on educating the parent about the child than younger home visitors did (about a third less time with each ten-year interval). Older home visitors tended to adopt a 'grand-motherly' attitude and focused most of their attention on the child" (Love and others, 1976, p. 23). As time of employment increased, however, the older home visitor progressively devoted more time to educating the parent about the child, in keeping with the focus of Home Start. The evaluators also found no relationship between a particular specialist's expertise and the time spent on specific content areas by home visitors working with that specialist, nor any statistically significant relationship between the home visit emphasis on particular components and parent and child outcomes. Finally, infrequent visits, or visits quite short in duration, were found to be related to lower child performance on the Preschool Inventory and the DDST.

In all, the Home Start evaluation was quite exemplary in its approach to meeting the three evaluation purposes. An imaginative combination of evaluation design features and an adequate number of reasonably creditable measures helped assure the solidarity of the evaluation effort. Credible summative and formative findings resulted. Although the Home Start evaluation was well funded, several features of it should serve as valuable guides to those designing an evaluation with fewer supporting resources.

The Follow Through Classroom Observation Evaluation

For over a decade, much attention in early childhood education has been directed toward the national Follow Through program and its evaluation. "Follow Through, initiated in 1967, is a project for disadvantaged children from kindergarten through third grade. It is intended to be a comprehensive project offering educational, medical and dental, nutritional, social, and psychological services to children previously enrolled in Head Start. Follow Through uses a strategy of planned variation in approaches to early elementary education, and twenty different approaches are now being implemented in Follow Through sites throughout the nation. The Follow Through project represents a major test of the viability of exporting models, some of which have been effective in experimental sites, to other locations to be implemented by individuals other than initiators" (White and others, 1973b, p. 83). One principal purpose of Follow Through, then, was to extend the time period that school-disadvantaged children would receive special programs, thereby, it was hoped, maintaining and enhancing the effects of Head Start.

A technical history of the resulting Follow Through program and its evaluation called them both large, complex, and controversial (Haney, 1977). The (sometimes awkward and crisis-oriented) shifts in evaluation contractors were documented in the technical history, as were many of the issues in the complex data analyses that resulted. Despite the major effort that has gone into the evaluation of Follow Through, many of the findings remain controversial, as we indicated in the opening to this chapter. Further, the data available for analysis are extensive, and what one finds depends, in part, on which specific portion of the data is examined.

The specific data on which we focus resulted primarily from observations of Follow Through classrooms and associated testing during the 1972–73 school year. Our presentation here draws principally from three sources (Stallings, 1975; Stallings and Kaskowitz, 1974; and Villaume and Haney, 1977). Although additional analyses and interpretations of these evaluative data undoubtedly could be made, we have tended to report here only those central analyses and interpretations contained in the three sources just mentioned.

Like Head Start, Follow Through was funded under the Economic Opportunity Act, but it was administered by the U.S. Office of Education (via a delegation of authority from the Office of Economic Opportunity). In 1972, five years after its inception, twenty-two Follow Through program models or sponsors were operational (rather than twenty as indicated in the White quote above), each subscribing to somewhat different aspects of basic learning and development theories. (Even today most of the models continue to operate under Follow Through.) Half of the models were university-based, eight were associated with private research agencies, and the remaining three were community-developed. As described (see Stanford Research Institute, 1972), the twenty-two models varied considerably along several dimensions. This "planned variation" in curricular activities and instructional strategies was deliberate, and the participating communities or project sites (over 150 in all) had a wide choice of alternative programs from which to select. The planned variation approach also permitted the examination of the differential effectiveness of the various program models with the approximately 4,000 classrooms and 78,000 children involved.

The 1972–73 Follow Through Classroom Observation Evaluation, conducted by Stanford Research Institute, involved only seven of the twenty-two models. By and large, these seven sponsors were operating at more sites nationally than were the other models, and each of them had been implemented in at least five locations. Brief descriptions of each of them follow:

1. Behavior Analysis Classroom (University of Kansas): Based on Skinnerian principles of positive reinforcement, this approach uses a token exchange system. Children successfully completing learning activities receive tokens that can be exchanged for preferred activity participation or other reinforcements. This model utilizes explicit behavioral objectives, self-paced programmed materials in basic skill areas, and instructional teams (a teacher responsible for reading, a full-time aide for math, and two paid parent aides for spelling, handwriting, and individual tutoring).

2. Academically Oriented or Direct Instruction Model (University of Oregon; initially at the University of Illinois): Also based on positive reinforcement theory, this model uses praise and pleasurable activities as reinforcers, while unproductive behavior tends to be ignored. A teacher and two full-time

aides are involved. "Working very closely with a group of five or six pupils at a time, each teacher and aide employs the programmed materials in combination with frequent and persistent reinforcing responses, applying remedial measures where necessary, and proceeding only when the success of each child with a given instructional unit is demonstrated" (Stanford Research Institute, 1972, p. 47). Appropriate adult stimulus speech and child responses are explicitly specified in program-like materials for these structured drills in reading, arithmetic, and language. The essence of this program is embedded in the currently widespread DISTAR materials (Science Research Associates, 1972).

3. Responsive Education Program (Far West Laboratory for Educational Research and Development): Key elements in this model are a structured environment responsive to each individual child's needs and autotelic (self-rewarding) activities. The *autotelic principle* is that a child's learning is enhanced if the environment encourages risking, guessing, questioning, exploring, and discovering without harmful psychological effects. Feedback is to be received from both materials and human interactions. The child is self-paced and, within pre-established limits, is free to choose from learning centers, games, and other activities, all directed toward problem-solving skills, sensory discrimination, and language. A healthy self-concept and self-confidence are presumed to develop in such an environment. The model seeks active parent involvement.

4. Cognitively Oriented Curriculum Model (High/Scope Educational Research Foundation): Leaning most heavily on Piagetian theory, this approach stresses stage-relevant thinking. Greatest emphasis is on the active experience and involvement of the child, enhanced by detailed plans for classroom organization and activities. Each classroom contains three adults, a teacher and two aides or two teachers and an aide. They are supported at each site by a curriculum assistant trained by the Foundation staff, a project director, a parent program staff, and home visitors. The model uses an active home teaching component.

5. Tucson Early Education Model or TEEM (University of Arizona): TEEM represents a moderately open approach to early education. The curriculum emphasizes four developmental areas: (1) language competence, (2) intellectual base (such as attending, recalling, and evaluating alternatives), (3) motivational base (positive attitudes toward school and expectations of success), and (4) societal arts and skills (reading, writing, and math combined with social skills such as cooperation and planning). Simultaneously addressing all four developmental areas via a single functional setting is termed *orchestration*. Interaction, imitation, and social reinforcement are stressed, as is experience more generally.

6. Bank Street Model (Bank Street College of Education): With some leaning toward the British Infant School, the Bank Street approach intends to develop the "whole child" by supporting the child's active involvement and autonomy, by extending his world, and by sensitizing him to the meaning of his experiences. Heavy emphasis is placed on the processes of learning and developing. *Developmental interaction,* for Bank Street sponsors, denotes both the impor-

tance of interaction for a child's development and the intertwining of cognitive and affective development. Diagnostic teaching is encouraged, using tasks that simultaneously meet a child's needs and promote his cognitive and affective development (for example, through developing coping skills, using language to express ideas and feelings, experiencing creativity, and establishing a positive self-image). Academic skills are acquired in the larger context of planned activities organized around themes such as home, school, and community. Model sponsors believe that the open framework requires extensive planning. Parent involvement is supported.

7. EDC Open Education Model (Education Development Center): This final approach included in the evaluation is based on the British Infant School and on EDC's experience in school and curriculum reform. The child's active participation is considered essential, as is a setting chock-full of materials and problems to investigate. The room may be divided into interest areas for construction, reading, math, social studies, art, and music. In this remarkably open environment, children are unusually free to choose their own activities. Teachers are also active, leading children to extend and deepen their own projects, by using thoughtful responses, questions, and suggestions. Aides and other adults also have teaching roles, and parent involvement and responsibility are fostered. Schools are viewed as an important part of the larger community, and supportive links between school and community are sought. In EDC classrooms, greater emphasis is placed on processes and experiences than on outcomes. Nevertheless, desirable outcomes for children (and for teachers, too, for that matter) would include initiative, persistence, imagination, self-regard, openness to change, and other critical abilities.

The diversity of the seven approaches is marked. Although they vary on several dimensions, the one that has served most of our early childhood education students best has been the amount of structure in a model. By structure, we mean the degree of specificity of the model in terms of teacher behaviors, student behaviors, expected transactions, and expected outcomes. In the case of the seven models above, the first and second, the Behavior Analysis Classroom and the Academically Oriented or Direct Instruction Model, are clearly the most structured, while the third model listed, the Responsive Education Program, leans in this direction. The sixth and seventh models, Bank Street and EDC Open Education, are obviously the least structured. The fourth and fifth approaches fall somewhere between these extremes. Our students have also found helpful, for preliminary classification, the nonpejorative yet somewhat facetious labels of *pricklies* for the models high in structure and *gooeys* for those low. By and large, the prickly approaches tend to incorporate active measurement and testing, more rigid scheduling and drill, limited opportunity for children to follow their interests, external reinforcers, less active home-school relationships, and relatively less emphasis on affective outcomes. The gooey models, by contrast, are distinguished by the avoidance of formal testing, less rigid scheduling and no drill, extensive freedom for children to explore their interests, intrinsic motivation, more active home-school partnerships, and relatively more emphasis on affective outcomes. Although the prickly-gooey distinction or continuum is obviously overstated, it does serve to highlight the planned variation—that is, the great diversity of the educational approaches—involved in the Follow Through evaluation.

Elaboration of the Evaluation Design. The 1972–73 Follow Through Classroom Observation Evaluation had two major purposes: (1) to determine whether the sponsors could "export" their models and successfully implement them in diverse communities, and (2) to establish the relationship between the processes in any given model and the child outcomes that eventuated. These two general purposes were reflected in seven questions that the evaluation was to answer (Stallings, 1975):

1. Are processes observed in the classrooms consistent with their sponsors' intentions?
2. Are processes observed in a single sponsor's classrooms consistent within a site (which would contain several classrooms) and between sites?
3. Do the processes observed in sponsored classrooms differ on specified dimensions from those observed in comparison (non-Follow Through) classrooms?
4. How distinct are the seven Follow Through models from one another?
5. How do selected classroom processes relate to children's scores on cognitive and affective measures?
6. How do selected classroom processes relate to child behaviors such as independence, cooperation, and question asking?
7. How do selected classroom processes relate to children's school attendance?

The exportability-implementation purpose generated the first four evaluation questions, and the process-outcome purpose, the last three. It can be noted in the questions that, although Follow Through was designed to reinforce and continue all the services of Head Start (education, health, nutrition, and social-psychological), this evaluation centered heavily on education. Indeed, this was true for most Follow Through evaluations.

The evaluation sample consisted of 271 Follow Through classrooms. Up to four first-grade and four third-grade classrooms were observed in each of thirty-six sites (towns and cities), representing five sites for six of the models and six sites for TEEM. Sites were chosen on three criteria: (1) they were already scheduled to receive the Spring 1973 Follow Through testing, (2) they represented a balanced distribution (urban-rural, North-South) of each sponsor's sites, and (3) they included at least two sites that the sponsor considered well implemented. The resulting sample represented all geographic regions, urban and rural areas, and several ethnic and racial groups; over 70 percent of the sites had been operating for five years, while the others had had three or four years of implementation. Also, within each selected site, one first-grade and one third-grade non-Follow Through classrooms were also scheduled for observation for comparison purposes.

Within each classroom, adults were observed as well as four children. The latter were randomly selected from among those children who had received base line testing (that is, those children who previously had taken a Fall pretest upon entering the first year of the Follow Through program, usually in kindergarten although some programs began at first grade). Attrition was higher by third grade than first grade (as expected) and also varied extensively from site to site; this affected the proportion of the class that had base line scores and, thus, that was available for random selection. (For more detailed concerns about how this attrition may have affected sampling, see Villaume and Haney, 1977, p. 200). At those sites where base line data were not available, the evaluators selected the children for individual observation randomly from classroom rosters. Base line data were also available for a majority of the non-Follow Through classes.

To generate operational definitions of each model that could be used to assess the degree of model implementation at diverse sites, the following procedures were instituted. Stanford Research Institute (SRI) staff wrote descriptions of each model, which the sponsor reviewed; these were then revised accordingly. Variables were then identified that were available within the observation system (described in the next section) and that seemed to describe representative elements of each of the seven approaches. The sponsors were all involved in this process and identified those variables that were both important in their models and that could be expected to occur more (or less) frequently than in conventional classrooms. The resultant list, combined for all models, contained fifty-five critical variables. The number of these that had been selected as important by each sponsor ranged from sixteen for the Academically Oriented or Direct Instruction Model to twenty-eight for the Responsive Education Program. (For technical concerns about the reductionism involved in going from a vast potential list of variables down to just fifty-five, see Villaume and Haney, 1977, pp. 200–201.)

Each classroom, both Follow Through and non-Follow Through, was scheduled for three consecutive days of observation during Spring 1973. Data were generated that related to the critical variables mentioned above as well as to classroom processes more generally. Outcome test data on students—both cognitive and affective—were also collected in the same classrooms in Spring 1973 (the measures are described in the next section). The evaluation design, therefore, called for a series of comparisons based on these data sets and used a series of analyses (sometimes involving the comparison with non-Follow Through classrooms) to answer the seven evaluation questions initially posed.

Description of the Measures. Development of the Classroom Observation Instrument (COI) was begun in 1969, with assistance and input from sponsors. Designed to record classroom arrangements and events considered educationally significant by sponsors, the COI was a time sampling (category) formal observational method (see Table 9 in Chapter Four). A single observer used the COI over a three-day period in a given classroom. During each hour of the five-hour classroom day, the observer was to complete four observation sequences, each covering five minutes of classroom interactions. This scheme thus was expected to yield twenty sequences per day, and sixty over the three-day observation period. Any day that resulted in fewer than twelve sequences, owing to intervening events, was disregarded.

"A form of shorthand was used to record the continuous action and interaction of selected persons in the classrooms. On two of three days of observation, there was an adult focus; that is, the classroom adults were subjects of observation. On the remaining day, the four randomly selected children were the focus. Hence the data provided one set of measures of classroom process (adult focus) and one set of child behaviors (child focus) with the same set of categories, or codes" (Stallings, 1975, pp. 10–11). In no case were beginning teachers observed; most teachers had two to three years' experience with the sponsor's model.

When used in Spring 1973 the COI consisted of 602 variables (including the 55 critical variables identified by sponsors of the models) within five categories:

1. Classroom Summary Information (CSI) Variables: These seventeen variables were completed once daily and identified the sponsor, site, teacher, grade, observer, and so forth, as well as the number of children, teachers, aides, and volunteers present. Ratios of children to adults were noted, as was the total class duration.

2. Physical Environment Information (PEI) Variables: Also completed once daily, the forty-three PEI variables concerned seating arrangements, work-group patterns, and the presence and use of equipment and materials.

3. Classroom Check List (CCL) Variables: The CCL, together with the following two categories of variables, made up the five-minute observation sequence that was coded four times each hour. The CCL is referred to as a "snapshot" of the classroom, as it portrays the distribution of persons and all the activities engaged in at a given point in time. Using the 202 CCL variables, the observer recorded the activities occurring, the adult and child grouping patterns, the adult roles, the child involvement, and the materials and equipment used in academic activities. If several activities were occurring simultaneously, they were all recorded.

4. Preamble (PRE) Variables: The seventy-eight PRE variables were used to record what the preselected focus person was doing just before the five-minute sequence began; the focal person was identified, as was the size of the group interacting with that person, the activity initially engaged in, and any adult roles involved.

5. Five-Minute Observation (FMO) Variables: The 262 FMO variables represented two duplicate sets, one set used for adult focus and one for child focus. Essentially, the FMO variables were used to denote the activities and interactions engaged in by the focal adult (or child) during the five-minute observation sequence. A highly diverse coding scheme printed on the observation form permitted the observer to rapidly complete a frame (of who does what to whom and how). Seventy-two such frames were available for each five-minute observation sequence.

A seven-day training session on the use of the COI was conducted for seventy-two persons. Of these, sixty-three met the final criterion of coding a specimen videotape at a 70 percent or greater accuracy rate. These sixty-three were employed as observers, and nine additional persons were trained in a special session to replace those failing to meet the criterion. After about two weeks of actual observations using the COI, the observers received videotapes of twenty simulated classroom situations, each about twenty interaction frames long. They coded these interactions. Matrices were constructed for each observer, and by comparing these against a standard (an "expert" coding of the twenty simulated situations) observer accuracy and bias could be determined — bias in terms of overuse, underuse, or confusion of codes. Since the data generated by any single observer were coded as such and retrievable, it was possible to use the observer's accuracy rates in interpreting the data appropriately.

Varied child measures were used. The Wide Range Achievement Test (WRAT) was used as the base line measure, since a majority of children had taken it when they entered Follow Through. As its name implies, the first level of the WRAT is purportedly appropriate for children from five to twelve years old, and it measures skills in spelling, reading, and arithmetic.

The child outcome measures used as dependent variables included the following:

1. Metropolitan Achievement Test (MAT): This standardized test was used to measure the reading and mathematics achievement of both first- and third-graders. The MAT was selected for use in Follow Through because it covered several achievement areas, was reliable, and included children from low-income families in its norming sample. This test has many features similar to the Comprehensive Test of Basic Skills and the Stanford Early School Achievement Test, which are described in Chapter Five.

2. Coloured Progressive Matrices (Raven's): Stanford Research Institute included the Raven's, for third-graders only, as a measure of a child's problem-solving ability in visual perceptual tasks, although it was originally designed as a culture-fair nonverbal intelligence test. (The Raven's is mentioned briefly in Chapter Five).

3. Intellectual Achievement Responsibility Scale (IAR): As indicated in Chapter Seven, the IAR purports to measure whether a child takes responsibility for his successes (and failures) in school or attributes them to other people and external forces. SRI adapted the IAR by making the language simpler and used it with just third-graders. Two scales resulted, one related to a child's feelings of success and one to his feelings of failure. Items were scored so that higher scores on each scale indicated attributing successes and failures to internal forces.

4. Coopersmith Self-Esteem Inventory: As described in Chapter Seven, this fifty-eight item self-report measure purportedly assesses children's self-concept. It was used with third- graders only.

5. Attendance data were determined from school records.

Finally, six child dependent behaviors were derived from the COI previously described:

1. Independence: A child or group of children engaging in a task without an adult.
2. Task Persistence: A child engaging in self-instruction for at least five interaction frames.
3. Cooperation: Two or more children working on any joint task together without an adult.
4. Verbal Initiative: A child asking questions, instructing someone, commenting generally, engaging in task-related conversation, or providing feedback to other children.
5. Observed Self-Esteem: A child offering his opinion, making statements about his self-worth, or extending his response when asked questions.
6. Question Asking: A child asking questions to gain information.

Evaluation Outcomes. Many of the outcomes of the observational evaluation of Follow Through were derived from rather complicated statistical analyses, which are not detailed here. The reader interested in the specific features of the analyses should consult Stallings (1975) or Stallings and Kaskowitz (1974). Before we survey the outcomes, we should note that SRI conducted a preliminary analysis and found relatively high consistency (essentially day-to-day stability reliability, as defined in Chapter Two) in the processes observed in any given classroom over the three-day observation period. This consistency, observed in both Follow Through and non-Follow Through classrooms, led the SRI evaluators to conclude that the observation period was sufficiently long and the observation system sufficiently reliable to get a reasonably stable estimate of the classroom processes occurring.

The initial two evaluation questions concerned (1) the consistency of the classroom processes observed with each sponsor's stated intentions, and (2) for any given model, the consistency of the processes observed for that model's classrooms within a site and between sites. Recall that the sponsors had indicated those variables that were important to their particular models and that could be expected to occur more (or less) frequently than in conventional classrooms. The fifty-five critical variables defined in this way were observed in both Follow Through and non-Follow Through classrooms. For each variable denoted as critical by a given sponsor, a total (degree of) implementation score was calculated for each classroom at each of the sponsor's sites. Similarly, a total implementation score was determined for each non-Follow Through classroom using each sponsor's set of critical variables. The difference between each model's average implementation score and the average implementation score for the non-Follow Through classes was then tested for statistical significance. Each of the seven Follow Through models, at both first and third grades, was found to be significantly different from the comparison non-Follow Through classrooms. However, in relation to the second evaluation question, sizable differences in implementation scores were frequently found among the four classrooms for a given model at a site, and also between the average implementation scores for a given model's five or six sites. The between-site differences were subjected to statistical test. In the case of the Bank Street Model, neither its first- nor third-grade implementation scores were significantly different among sites. However, implementation score differences among sites did reach significance (1) for both the first- and third-grade sites of the Tucson Early Education, Cognitively Oriented Curriculum, and EDC Open Education models, (2) for the first-grade sites of the Direct Instruction and Behavior Analysis Classroom approaches, and (3) for the third-grade sites of the Responsive Education Program. Overall, then, models seemed well implemented compared to the sponsors' stated intentions, but most models still evidenced considerable variation in implementation from classroom to classroom and, especially, from site to site.

The analyses used to answer the third and fourth questions were closely related, and overlapped considerably. The third evaluation question involved whether the processes observed in Follow Through Model classrooms differed on specified dimensions from those observed in comparison non-Follow Through classrooms. While this question was addressed in part when answering the first question above, it also was addressed by using a classification procedure based on multivariate normal theory (described in Anderson, 1958). Four separate sets of COI data were used: designated PEI and CCL variables for first-grade classrooms and also for third-grade classrooms (to examine environmental components); and designated FMO variables for first-grade classrooms and also for third-grade classrooms (to assess interactions). For each grade and each set of variables, the most effective or "best" linear functions were determined for classifying classrooms by sponsor. These classification functions were used to match each classroom (including the comparison non-Follow Through classrooms) with the sponsor it was most likely to have come from. Of the 132 first-grade Follow Through classrooms, 83 percent were correctly classified on the environmental PEI and CCL variables, and 78 percent were correctly assigned via the interaction or FMO variables. For the 130 third-grade Follow Through classrooms, the comparable figures were 73 and 79 percent. The Behavior Analysis Classroom and Direct Instruction Model were least often misclassified; that is, they were more distinct than the other five models. The non-Follow Through classrooms were rarely classified as belonging to the Behavior Analysis Classroom or, in the case of the environmental variables, to the Cognitively Oriented Curriculum Model. However, almost 45 percent of the third-grade non-Follow Through classrooms were classified as most similar to the Direct Instruction Model.

The fourth evaluation question asked whether the seven Follow Through models were distinct from one another, a question at least partly answered in the classification of classrooms procedure just described. In this case, however, the basic statistical technique involved was discriminant function analysis (Cooley and Lohnes, 1962; and Rao, 1965). Four analyses were done using the same four sets of COI variables used in the classification endeavor. "With the possible exception of a 'degree of structure' dimension, the discriminant function on which the sponsors differed did not seem to represent abstract concepts, such as 'individualization of instruction' or 'child initiation' versus 'responsiveness,' but were dominated by one or two very specific classroom process variables, such as 'large group with aide/math' or 'adult reinforcement with token, academic.' One or two individual variables shared by one or two sponsors seemed to be the best discriminators" (Stallings, 1975, p. 46). More specifically, and not surprisingly given the classification analysis, the Behavior Analysis Classroom and Direct Instruction Model (the aforementioned "pricklies") tended to stand out as distinctive from the other five models. Villaume and Haney (1977) appropriately pointed out that had these four discriminant analyses also included the non-Follow Through classrooms, SRI would have had an additional opportunity to determine whether Follow Through classrooms could be discriminated from non-Follow Through classrooms. (Note also the concerns of Villaume and Haney concerning implementation.)

Reviewing the apparent answers to the four evaluation questions concerning exportation and implementation, SRI concluded that, save for minor exceptions, the seven Follow Through approaches were implemented as planned. Although we believe SRI overstated this conclusion, we do agree that intended implementation was substantial and certainly adequate enough to address the three remaining questions relating selected classroom processes to child measure and behaviors.

Several analyses were used in the attempts to answer the fifth, sixth, and seventh evaluation questions. However, the key analysis (the one reviewed here) used partial correlations and residual gain scores. The partial correlation technique allows the determination of the relationship between two variables, having controlled for or "partialed out" the influence of a third variable (Hopkins and Glass, 1978). In this case, SRI computed partial correlations between selected classroom processes and child outcomes, after having partialed out the influence of base line WRAT scores determined as children first entered Follow Through. Stated differently, the partial correlation technique was equivalent to holding constant children's entering WRAT scores. Similarly, the residual gain score analysis technique adjusted the children's outcome scores to compensate for differences observed in entering WRAT scores.

The fifth evaluation question asked how selected classroom processes were related to children's scores on cognitive and affective measures. The three cognitive measures were the total raw scores in reading and math on the Metropolitan Achievement Test (MAT) and the raw score on the Coloured Progressive Matrices (Raven's). The SRI evaluators found the following variables significantly related to higher reading achievement scores: longer school days, more class time spent in reading activity and in social studies, more systematic instruction (that is, the teacher provides information, asks a question, the child responds, and teacher provides immediate feedback, either guided direction if the response is wrong or some type of reward if correct), small group instruction in grade one (though a large group worked well in grade three), higher task persistence, and greater use of textbooks and programmed workbooks. On the residual gain score analysis, two models most likely to use these procedures—the Direct Instruction Model and the Behavior Analysis Classroom—showed the greatest adjusted reading gains of all seven models in both first- and third-grade classrooms. These two models also had larger adjusted gains than the non-Follow Through comparison classes in first-grade reading. (It is important to note that the Cognitively Oriented Curriculum Model had too few third-grade classrooms both tested and observed to be included in any of these third-grade analyses.)

In mathematics, SRI found better performance related to many of the same variables: longer school days, more class time spent in math activity, more systematic instruction, higher task persistence and greater independence, greater use of textbooks and programmed workbooks, and use of Cuisenaire rods and Montessori materials. At the first-grade level, the Behavior Analysis Classroom demonstrated the highest adjusted math scores of all models and the comparison non-Follow Through classrooms; at the third-grade level, the Direct Instruction Model achieved this same distinction.

On the Raven's (given only to third-graders and purported by SRI to be a measure of nonverbal perceptual problem solving), higher performance was associated with more flexible classrooms, more diverse classroom activities, a wider variety of instructional materials, more manipulation of materials, more self-selection of groups, more one-to-one interactions with adults, more open-ended questions by teachers, and more verbal initiative by students. As one would expect, given this list of environmental and interaction variables, children in the Direct Instruction and Behavior Analysis Classrooms did least well of all the models in terms of adjusted Raven's scores, while children in the Tucson Early Education and EDC Open Education Models fared best.

Affective outcomes for third-grade children were measured on the Coopersmith Self-Esteem Inventory and the Intellectual Achievement Responsibility Scale (IAR). On the Coopersmith, very few significant relationships were found with instructional variables; further, no significant differences were found between the average Coopersmith scores of the seven sponsor models and the non-Follow Through comparison classrooms. On the IAR, differences were found. Children in the more open, less structured models (our gooeys) took more responsibility—that is, displayed more internal locus of control—for their own academic success but not for their failure (except children in the EDC Open Education Model, who took responsibility for both their academic success and failures). Children in the highly structured models (our pricklies) tended to take responsibility for their academic failures, but attributed their successes to teacher skill or other external factors.

The sixth evaluation question involved examining the relationship between selected classroom processes and six child behaviors previously defined: independence, task persistence, cooperation, verbal initiative, observed self-esteem, and question asking. Independent behavior was related to classrooms where children had some opportunities to select seating and groups, where various activities were available, and where exploratory and audiovisual materials were available; children in the EDC Open Education Model and the Responsive Education Program evidenced more independent behavior. Task persistence was more often observed in classrooms using texts and workbooks and those providing one-to-one instruction; the Tucson Early Education Model and Behavior Analysis Classroom approaches had children with higher task persistence scores. Cooperative behavior was associated with classrooms having diverse activities, exploratory materials, and child-selection of groupings; this behavior was more frequently displayed in the EDC Open Education, Bank Street, and Cognitively Oriented Curriculum classrooms. Children displayed more verbal initiative in classrooms offering a diverse array of activities and materials and those where adults engaged in general conversation with them; not surprisingly, children in all five of the more open models displayed higher verbal initiative scores than students in the two highly structured models and those in the comparison non-Follow Through classrooms. Self-esteem was demonstrated by children more frequently in classrooms with diverse activities and exploratory academic materials, as well as in those where adults asked children questions in small groups; children in the Tucson Early Education and the Direct Instruction Models demonstrated higher observed self-esteem scores. More frequent question asking by children was associated with classrooms having more one-to-one relationships between children and adults, more adult responding to children's questions, and more general conversation between adults and children; such behavior occurred more often in children in the Responsive Education, Bank Street, Behavior Analysis, Cognitively Oriented Curriculum, and EDC Open Education models. In general, the relationships between the various models and the observed child behaviors were consonant with each model's operational features. Further, this particular analysis helped to highlight many of the differences in classroom processes, not only between Follow Through models but also between them and the more conventional non-Follow Through classrooms.

The final evaluation question examined the relationship between selected classroom processes and attendance. SRI found better attendance in the more open classrooms—that is, those with high rates of child independence, child questioning and adults responding, open-ended questioning, smiling and laughing, and individualized instruction. Poorer attendance was related to those classrooms with more large-group instruction, more direct academic questions by adults, frequent critical corrective feedback, and (in the third grade) more punishment. In general, lower absence rates were associated with the Responsive Education, Tucson Early Education, and Cognitively Oriented Curriculum Models.

In all, the SRI Follow Through Classroom Observation Evaluation represented an ambitious attempt to evaluate and relate processes and outcomes in early education. One must keep in mind that most of the findings were heavily dependent on correlational data (as distinct from experimental, that is, cause-and-effect, data). At the same time, the findings add much to the increasing pool of information concerning the evaluation of early education. If interpreted with due regard to the cautions suggested by Villaume and Haney (1977) and by

Stallings herself (1975; and Stallings and Kaskowitz, 1974), the two major conclusions reached by Stallings seem, for the most part, supportable: (1) that the various Follow Through models were transported and implemented with substantial success, and (2) that the various Follow Through models were exemplified by different classroom processes, which, in turn, related to achievement, other child behaviors, and attendance—with different models offering different advantages to their students, including some advantages not common in traditional classrooms.

The Sesame Street Evaluation

The best-known effort to use television as an educational medium for young children is "Sesame Street," produced by Children's Television Workshop (CTW) for children ages three to five (Stein and Friedrich, 1975). Following extensive planning—by experts in child development, preschool education, and television production (Lesser, 1974)—the show was first televised in November 1969. Support for the show came from a variety of public and private grants; such agencies and organizations as the National Center for Educational Research and Development, the National Institute of Child Health and Human Development, the U.S. Office of Economic Opportunity, the National Foundation on the Arts and Humanities, the Carnegie and Ford Foundations, the John and Mary Markle Foundation, and the Corporation for Public Broadcasting contributed funds initially totaling $8 million (McDill, McDill, and Sprehe, 1972). Two years later, in 1971, a second series, aimed at early elementary-age children, was first televised. Entitled "The Electric Company," this show focuses on instruction in reading skills (Liebert, Neale, and Davidson, 1973). Both shows have been evaluated extensively by staff of the Educational Testing Service (Ball and Bogatz, 1970a, b; Ball and Bogatz, 1973; Ball and others, 1974; Bogatz and Ball, 1971). In this section, we will deal with the evaluation of "Sesame Street"; for a complete description of the evaluation of "The Electric Company," see Ball and Bogatz (1973) and Ball and others (1974).

The most extensive description of the evolution of "Sesame Street" is in a book by Gerald Lesser (the chairman of the National Board of Advisors to CTW), *Children and Television: Lessons from Sesame Street* (1974). According to Lesser, "Sesame Street" was conceived as a supplementary educational experience intended to prepare children, especially disadvantaged children, for school. Specific cognitive skills were to be taught; particular emphasis was placed on attention-holding tactics, such as humor, fast movement, animation, and slapstick, to increase the likelihood that young children would watch and learn. Thus, the broad goal for CTW, as it began the development of "Sesame Street," was "to develop and telecast a daily, hour-long television show for preschool-aged children that would both entertain them and foster their intellectual and cultural development" (Ball and Bogatz, 1970a, p. 2).

The specific goals and objectives for the first year of "Sesame Street" were couched in behavioral terms and categorized into four general areas: (1) symbolic representation, (2) cognitive processes, (3) the physical environment, and (4) the social environment. Included in the first category, symbolic representation, were nineteen behavioral objectives related to the recognition of letters, numbers, and geometric forms and the performance of rudimentary operations involving these basic symbols. Cognitive processes, the second category, consisted of twenty-seven objectives pertaining to perceptual discriminations, relational concepts, classification, and sorting. Included here were problem-solving objectives, such as, "The child can suggest multiple solutions to simple problems" and "Given a set of suggested solutions to a simple problem, the child can select the most relevant, complete, or efficient" (Lesser, 1974, p. 68). The third category contained specific objectives related to the child's conception of the physical environment. Viewers were expected to learn general information about natural phenomena (for example, land, sky, water, city and country, plants and animals); certain processes that occur in nature (for example, reproduction, growth and development); certain interdependencies among natural phenomena (such as weather and seasons); and the ways in which humans explore and exploit the natural world (via machines, appliances, buildings). The final category, social environment, dealt with social units (self, family, groups, and institutions relevant to children) and social interactions. Some of the objectives here pertained to cooperation and sharing, recognizing fairness and unfairness, and recognizing differences in perspectives. (For the complete list of objectives, see Ball and Bogatz, 1970a, or Lesser, 1974.) During the first year of "Sesame Street," the simpler objectives—and primarily those concerning the cognitive processes—were stressed. The second year of operation saw an expansion of the show's goals to include the more difficult areas and to achieve wider curriculum coverage. For example, counting from one to ten, an objective covered during the first year, was extended to counting from one to twenty during the second year (Ball, 1974). In the years following the first two (for which the evaluations were conducted), the show has continued to expand and change and is now viewed internationally—although the basic objectives remain much the same.

Elaboration of the Evaluation Design. The principal sources used in this and the following sections were Ball and Bogatz (1970a, b) and Bogatz and Ball (1971). These sources make clear that the need for extensive evaluation of "Sesame Street" was recognized by the program developers during their initial planning for the show. A research group was set up within CTW to conduct formative evaluation; included among the tasks for this group were "writing the instructional goals of CTW; informing production staff of the needs, interests, and abilities of the target population; trying out specific materials as they were produced; and reporting on their impact with samples of four-year-old children" (Ball and Bogatz, 1970a, p. 3). To conduct the summative evaluation, CTW contracted with Educational Testing Service (ETS) during the early stages of program development. The principal evaluator from ETS was present at planning sessions, held throughout 1968; the evaluator's role at those sessions included helping to prepare the statements of goals for the first year's production. Our description of "Sesame Street's" evaluations in this and the following sections will focus on the summative work done by ETS. The use of an in-house group to conduct formative evaluation should not go unnoticed, however. This dual approach to evaluation—formative by persons integrally involved within the program, and summative by independent, external evaluators—is consistent with Scriven's approach to evaluation described in Chapter Nine.

ETS conducted summative evaluations of the overall impact of "Sesame Street" during its first two years of production. The major evaluation questions posed for the first year's study were these:

1. Do three- through five-year-old children who view "Sesame Street" at home or in classrooms learn more than comparable children who do not view the show?
2. Of those children who watch the show, what characterizes the children who learn most and least from the show?
3. Is the show effective among various subgroups of three- through five-year-old children—for example, boys and girls, lower- and middle-class children, heavy and light viewers, high- and low-achieving children?
4. Inasmuch as "Sesame Street" adopted a magazine-style format, what elements in the show seemed to be most effective in terms of attention holding and amount learned? [Ball and Bogatz, 1970a, p. 6].

These questions reflected an important concern of the evaluators—not just to discover whether viewers learned more than nonviewers but also to try to discover which children benefited most from the show and which features of the show more effectively facilitated learning. Further, unintended as well as intended outcomes were measured—as will become evident later when we discuss the measures used in the evaluation.

The evaluation of the second year of "Sesame Street" included a follow-up study of some of the first-year subjects (in particular, the at-home, disadvantaged children) as well as a replication of the first-year study in different sites. As noted earlier, CTW's goals for "Sesame Street" changed somewhat for the second year; the major goal areas remained the same, but specific objectives represented an extension and broadening of first-year objectives. The second-year evaluation included measurements related to the new objectives, as well as replications of first-year measures.

The sample for the first-year evaluation consisted of 943 children from five locales: Boston, Massachusetts; Durham, North Carolina; Philadelphia, Pennsylvania; Phoenix, Arizona; and a rural area in the northwestern section of California. Included were disadvantaged inner-city children, disadvantaged Spanish-speaking children, advantaged suburban-area children, and rural-area children. Overall, more boys than girls, and more lower-class than middle-class children, were involved. The children ranged in age from three to five, with the majority being four years old. The first stage of sampling, in which the five locales were identified, was not a random selection. Sites were chosen because they contained children of primary interest to CTW, with an emphasis on lower-SES, urban, black and white children in the South, Northeast, and West; lower-SES children in a rural area; and middle-SES children in an eastern city.

Following the selection of the five locales, specific neighborhoods and schools in each were identified. In each locale, except the rural area, the effects of viewing "Sesame Street" in two settings—home and preschool—were studied. Preschools, especially Head Start centers, were asked to participate in the evaluation study. Once permission was granted, the neighborhoods around those centers were canvassed (house by house) to obtain an at-home sample.

The preschool classes agreeing to participate were randomly assigned to either the viewing (or encouraged-to-view) condition or the nonviewing (or not-encouraged-to-view) condition. Viewing classes were provided with television sets. The children in the at-home samples were also randomly assigned, by block rather than individually, to viewing and nonviewing conditions. Because the program developers and evaluators feared, initially, that few children in the experimental group would watch the show (in part, because it was being delivered on educational television channels, for which lower-class audiences were known to be small), it was decided to assign two thirds of the at-home group to the viewing condition and only one-third to the nonviewing condition. The parents of the viewing group were told about "Sesame Street," given publicity material, and visited weekly by an ETS-trained staff member during telecasting time; the nonviewing group did not receive any of these treatments.

Effects of viewing the program on children's cognitive functioning were measured before and after the 1969–70 season; pretests and posttests were administered individually. A parent pretest questionnaire was used to obtain demographic information on the children and their home backgrounds. A parent posttest questionnaire was used to assess unintended side effects of viewing "Sesame Street," such as changes in parent-child interactions, as well as to measure the television viewing habits of the children. An important variable subsumed under the latter was, of course, how much time was actually spent in viewing "Sesame Street." Parents were paid for filling out pre- and postquestionnaires. For children in the viewing conditions, additional daily viewing records were kept by teachers and by parents. These records were picked up by ETS staff members during the weekly visits to children in the at-home and classroom viewing groups; designated subgroups of each were also observed by the visitors during times when "Sesame Street" was being televised. Visitors recorded information about the children's verbal, visual, and motor responses to particular segments of the show. A final component of the evaluation consisted of two separate content analyses of the show, carried out by the ETS evaluators. Content, processes, and production techniques were charted to provide CTW with precise information useful in subsequent production efforts.

One of the findings from the first-year study (described later in greater detail) was that children in the control (nonviewing or nonencouraged) groups did watch "Sesame Street," at least occasionally. Therefore, in the new sample for the second-year study, sites were chosen where the program was available only on cable or UHF television; reception capability was supplied to the viewing group but not to the control group. Another consideration in selecting the second-year sample was that it be comprised primarily of at-home urban disadvantaged children. Two locales were chosen: Winston-Salem, North Carolina, and Los Angeles, California. For the follow-up component of the second-year evaluation, the at-home disadvantaged children in Boston, Durham, and Phoenix were used. Children and parents in both samples (new and follow-up) were pretested in October and November, 1970, and posttested in May, 1971. Measures used, described in detail in the next section, represented replications of first-year measures as well as new measures designed for the second-year evaluation. Children in the follow-up sample continued in their viewing or non-viewing groups, as originally assigned before the first-year study. Children in the new sample were randomly assigned to those two groups as well; here, however, it bears re-emphasizing that the ETS evaluators had control over reception of the show. That is, UHF adaptors or cables were installed for the viewing group but not for the control groups.

Description of the Measures. The measures used to assess children's learning outcomes were developed by ETS specifically for the "Sesame Street" evaluation. The development procedures were lengthy and included piloting the measures during the summer before the evaluation was implemented. Twelve tests, many of which contained two or more subtests, were constructed for the first-year study. A basic format was common to all of them: (1) graphic representations were presented to the child individually (by a trained administrator), (2) each representation was described to the child (for example, "Here is a bear, here is a bear, and here is a bear"); and (3) the child was asked to respond (for example, to point to the biggest bear).

The major tests and subtests developed for the first-year study were as follows:

1. Body Parts Test (42 items)
   a. Pointing to Body Parts
   b. Naming Body Parts
   c. Function of Body Parts (pointing response)
   d. Function of Body Parts (verbal response)
2. Letters Test (51 items)
   a. Recognizing Letters
   b. Naming Capital Letters
   c. Naming Lower-Case Letters
   d. Matching Letters in Words
   e. Recognizing Letters in Words
   f. Initial Sounds
   g. Reading Words
   h. Reciting Alphabet
3. Forms Test (8 items)
   a. Recognizing Forms
   b. Naming Forms
4. Numbers Test (44 items)
   a. Recognizing Numbers
   b. Naming Numbers

    c. Numerosity
    d. Counting
    e. Addition and Subtraction
    f. Counting from 1 to 20
5. Matching Letters, Numbers, and Forms (11 items)
6. Relational Terms Test (17 items)
    a. Amount Relationships
    b. Size Relationships
    c. Position Relationships
7. Sorting Skills (6 items)
    a. Sorting by Number
    b. Sorting by Function
8. Classification Skills Test (24 items)
    a. Classification by Size
    b. Classification by Form
    c. Classification by Number
    d. Classification by Function
9. Puzzles Test (10 items)
10. What's Wrong Here? (1 item)
11. Hidden Triangles (10 items)
12. Which Comes First? (12 items)

A substantial number of the first-year "Sesame Street" goals were assessed in this battery. Reliability estimates (Alpha) were obtained for the subtests from the pretest; these were generally moderate to high, ranging from .17 (Initial Sounds, and Size Relationships) to .93 (Naming Capital Letters), with a median of .66. The pretest battery took an average of two hours to administer. The posttest battery was much the same as the pretest battery, except that some items were eliminated since they had not functioned well in the pretest. Further, tests 11 and 12 (in the above list) were developed for the posttest to obtain greater coverage of the problem solving goal area; Hidden Triangles required the child to point to one of four pictures that had an equilateral triangle embedded in it, while Which Comes First entailed pointing to that picture (of three or four) that was first (or last) in a sequence of events represented. On the average, posttest administration required one and a half hours.

The children's measures used in the second year's evaluation of "Sesame Street" "were built on the successes and experiences of the first year's efforts. . . . The second year's evaluation had two emphases. These were to follow some of the children involved in the first-year study and to study the effects of the new show on children who had not viewed the first season. This necessitated a three-fold purpose for the tests: new items and tests needed to be developed to assess new goals of the show; old items and tests needed to be included to ascertain the effectiveness of old goals on new 'Sesame Street' viewers; and new items and tests needed to be developed to assess some of the goals of the first year that either were not assessed then or whose assessment was inconclusive" (Bogatz and Ball, 1971, pp. 35, 39).

The test format used in the first-year study was continued. Revisions and additions to original tests were subjected to review and pilot testing prior to actual use. Attitude assessment (especially attitudes toward school and related activities), an area added for the second-year study, required the most extensive new development work.

The tests and subtests used in the second-year study were as follows:

1. General Knowledge Test (30 items)
   a. Naming Body Parts
   b. Function of Body Parts
   c. Naming Forms
   d. Recognizing Forms
   e. Roles of Community Members
2. Letters Test (56 items)
   a. Matching by Form
   b. Matching by Position
   c. Recognizing Letters
   d. Naming Letters
   e. Letters' Sounds
   f. Initial Sounds
   g. Decoding
   h. Reading Words
   i. Left-Right
   j. Alphabet Recitation
3. Numbers Test (49 items)
   a. Recognizing Numbers
   b. Naming Numbers
   c. Enumeration
   d. Conservation
   e. Counting Strategies
   f. Number/Numeral Correspondence
   g. Addition and Subtraction
   h. Counting from 1 to 30
4. Relational Terms Test (17 items)
5. Classification Test (24 items)
   a. Classification
   b. Double Classification
6. Sorting Test (16 items)
7. Parts of Whole Test (10 items)
8. Emotions and Attitudes Test (25 items)
   a. Emotion
   b. Attitude to School
   c. Attitude to Others
   d. Attitude to Race of Others

An additional children's test used in both studies was the Peabody Picture Vocabulary Test or PPVT (described in Chapter Five). This was given as part of the pretest battery to all first-study children, primarily to enable the researchers to describe the sample and compare it with samples from other studies. In the second study, the PPVT was given as both a pretest and a posttest, to measure the effects of "Sesame Street" in terms of scores on that test as well as on ETS' own tests. Thus, the PPVT was included to measure unintended side effects of "Sesame Street"—since the show's stated goals had never included increasing IQ or vocabulary (White and others, 1973b).

Parent questionnaires were also developed by ETS for use in the "Sesame Street" evaluations. These questionnaires were much the same for the first- and second-year studies. The pretest questionnaire assessed parental level of aspiration for the child, parental attitudes toward education, affluence indexes, pre-"Sesame Street" television viewing habits of the child, SES of the family, and "intellectual climate" in the home. Some questions—those related to SES and intellectual climate—dealt with such factors as numbers and type of possessions owned, educational and occupational levels of the parents, number of persons living in the home, mobility of family during the last three years, and number and type of books read yearly and magazines read regularly. The parents' post-test questionnaire included some items from the pretest, such as those dealing with parental levels of aspiration for their children and mother-child interactions. Television viewing habits of children since the prequestionnaires were of major concern on the postquestionnaire, and several questions dealt with viewing habits in regard to "Sesame Street" as well as other shows.

Six indexes were developed by grouping items on the parent questionnaires:

1. Parent Expectation Index (dealing with parents' levels of aspiration for their children).
2. Child Affluence Index (a measure of the children's personal possessions).
3. Educational Uses Index (a measure of the extent to which children were exposed to educational facilities outside the home).
4. Parent Affluence Index (dealing with material affluence in the home).
5. Socioeconomic Status Index (primarily an index of educational levels of the parents).
6. School Expectation Index (a measure of how successful the parents feel their children will be in school).

In addition to the questions on the postquestionnaires regarding viewing habits, parents of children in the first study's at-home viewing groups filled out daily "Sesame Street Records." Amount of time spent watching "Sesame Street" was recorded according to the following scale:

0 = Child watched little or none of the show.
1 = Child watched about half (30 minutes) of the show.

2 = Child watched all or almost all of the show.

3 = Child watched all of one show and all or parts of a second showing (if applicable) that day.

Similar records were kept by teachers of the first study's classroom viewing groups. For each child in the class, the teacher recorded "Sesame Street" viewing according to a three-point scale:

0 = Child was absent or present but watched little of the show.

1 = Child watched only about half (30 minutes) of the show.

2 = Child watched all or almost all of the show.

Additional viewing records included "TV Guide" questionnaires, which all parents completed about once a month. A list of television shows was presented, and the parents indicated which shows the child watched on a particular day and how many times a given show was watched that day. (This record was the only type of child viewing record, in addition to parent postquestionnaires, used in the second study.)

Overall amount-of-viewing scores were calculated by combining and weighting responses from the various viewing records. In the first study, children were divided into quartiles on the basis of composite scores:

- Q1 (Quartile 1) = Children who never or only rarely (about once per week) watched the show.
- Q2 (Quartile 2) = Children who watched, on the average, two to three times per week.
- Q3 (Quartile 3) = Children who watched four to five times per week, on the average.
- Q4 (Quartile 4) = Children who watched more than five times per week, on the average.

Additional measures used in the "Sesame Street" evaluation included (1) observation records (first study), completed by regular ETS visitors and concerned with children's verbal, visual, and motor reactions to various segments, major characters, animation, and so on, (2) teacher questionnaires (first study), dealing with teachers' attitudes toward the show and their use of the show in the classroom, and (3) teacher ranking questionnaires (second study), used by teachers of follow-up children to rank children in terms of readiness for school.

Readers interested in complete details of all measures used in the two evaluations should consult the Ball and Bogatz (1970a) report of the first-year study and the Bogatz and Ball (1971) report of the second-year study.

Evaluation Outcomes. The extensive data collected for the "Sesame Street" evaluations were analyzed in several ways. The first-year study, particularly, yielded data on a variety of subgroups. The results will be described here separately for the two evaluations.

First-year evaluation outcomes: One of the major questions posed for this evaluation was "Do 'Sesame Street' viewers differ from nonviewers in their learning?" However, as we mentioned previously, this intended comparison was not feasible since most subjects in the control group watched the show, at least occasionally. Instead, the sample was divided into the four quartiles noted according to amount of viewing. Change scores—differences between pretest and posttest scores—became the dependent variables for the analyses.

For the total sample (all 943 children), the children in the highest viewing quartile performed better on all the tests than children in the lower quartiles. Although the positive effects of viewing held for all tests, the gains on some—for example, the Letters, Numbers, and Classification tests—were more dramatic than on others, such as the Body Parts Test. It must be noted, however, that the average pretest scores within each quartile also varied, with the children in the Q4 (those who watched the most) scoring highest on all pretests and those in Q1 scoring lowest. Still, the gain scores were greatest for the Q4 children.

Consistent with other major evaluation questions, subsequent analyses involved investigating the effects of viewing "Sesame Street" on separate subgroups of the total sample. A subgroup of prime concern to CTW and ETS was the school-disadvantaged—since the show had originally been developed specifically with that group in mind. Of the total sample, 731 were considered to be from disadvantaged backgrounds. These children tended to watch the program less often than the advantaged group. Nevertheless, when gain scores were broken down according to amount of viewing, the gain scores of the disadvantaged showed the same type of pattern as those of the total sample. The Q4 children made the greatest gains; amount of gain decreased with each quartile. These differences were found for both the at-home groups and the classroom groups, and for both boys and girls. Although the amount of viewing did not differ greatly according to age, gain scores did. The three-year-olds on Q4 had higher average gain scores than four-year-olds in Q1, Q2, and Q3, and higher than five-year-olds in Q1 and Q2. When these results were examined for each test and subtest separately, it was found that they were most pronounced on tests of specific knowledge and skills. That is, as would be expected, the goals that were indirectly taught were better learned by five-year-olds, while the three-year-olds made their most dramatic learning gains in terms of goals that were directly taught.

The effects of amount of viewing were further isolated, more sharply, by the Age Cohorts Study. This study involved a comparison of pretest scores for one subgroup with the posttest scores of another subgroup. The two subgroups were the same chronological age (between fifty-three and fifty-eight months), of comparable mental age (as determined by PPVT scores), and resident in the same communities at the time of comparison. This was, therefore, an attempt to control the two groups in terms of age, IQ, and home background; the difference between them was that the first subgroup had not yet viewed the show, whereas the second subgroup had. Large differences were found, with the Q3 and Q4 children from the second subgroup (which had already viewed "Sesame

Street") exhibiting much higher scores than comparable children from the first subgroup. Further, Q1 children in the second subgroup differed only slightly from Q1 children in the first subgroup.

Separate analyses for the advantaged children showed substantial gains from pretest to posttest (again with greater gains for children who had watched the show with greater frequency), although the gains were smaller than those for the disadvantaged. Analyses for Spanish-speaking children were somewhat hampered by small numbers; there were fewer than fifty Spanish-speaking children in the study, and less than half of them fell in the frequent-viewing quartiles. Nevertheless, gains were extremely high for the frequent-viewing Spanish-speaking children.

Other outcomes from the first-year evaluation included generally positive reactions from the teachers whose classes participated, although "they were divided in their opinions about the appropriateness of its use in the classroom. Some felt strongly that the show took up valuable time that could better be given to other activities; others felt that it was a worthwhile addition to the school day" (Ball and Bogatz, 1970b, p. 11). In terms of findings involving parents, it was revealed that the children in Q4 tended to have mothers who watched the show with them. These mothers also tended to hold somewhat higher expectations for their children than parents of less frequent viewers. From observational data collected throughout the study, visual attentiveness to all characters and production techniques was found to be high among all subgroups. The more popular characters (for example, Ernie, Susan, and Big Bird) were identified. Through content analyses, animation was found to be associated with goal areas in which gains were especially high. These observational and content analysis findings were of a somewhat more formative nature than other findings; that is, they were directed toward the CTW production staff for use in later programming decisions.

Second-year evaluation outcomes: The more rigorous controls on the viewing habits of the children in the new sample for this evaluation made it possible to compare the experimental (encouraged-to-view) and control (not-encouraged-to-view) children. Of the experimental children, 93 percent viewed "Sesame Street"; of the control, 65 percent did not.

The results essentially reinforced those from the first-year study. Children in the new sample who viewed the show improved more than those who did not. Age and sex of child did not differentially affect the results. A slight negative correlation between SES and total gain score (−.24) for the encouraged children suggested that the show's greatest impact may be for those from the most disadvantaged backgrounds. (Note, however, that the relatively homogeneous nature of the sample—all low SES—would tend to attenuate the size of this correlation over what it might be with more heterogeneous samples.)

The scores for a subgroup of Spanish-background children, in both experimental and control groups, were analyzed separately. Unfortunately, most of the control children in this subgroup did not maintain their control status—that is, almost all of them tended to watch the show. The comparison of the few nonviewers with the viewers yielded nonsignificant differences. As the evaluators pointed out, however, "It would seem that a definitive answer to the question of the impact of 'Sesame Street' on Spanish-background children is not yet available" (Bogatz and Ball, 1971, p. 172).

The children in the follow-up component of the second-year study continued to show learning gains. Almost all these children had become viewers by the second year, making comparisons according to amount of viewing difficult. In a Follow-Up Age Cohorts Study, similar to the first-year Age Cohorts Study, two second-year effects of "Sesame Street" were noted: (1) second-year children learned more from new goal areas during the second year than they did from repetitions of original goal areas, and (2) second-year children showed more positive attitudes toward school and toward race of others than did the newer viewers.

Three types of unintended outcome were also investigated in the second-year study. First, it was found that the child's viewing of "Sesame Street" showed no relationships with parental expectations for the child, parental attitudes toward education, or the child's television viewing habits. Second, no different attitude effects were found for the experimental and control groups in the new samples (although effects for the follow-up group were found, as cited above). Third, significant differences on PPVT scores, favoring the viewers, were discovered.

In summary, the two ETS evaluations of "Sesame Street" produced positive findings, especially in regard to learning outcomes of disadvantaged viewers. McDill, McDill, and Sprehe, in their review of the "Sesame Street" evaluations, stated:

> Compared with findings from evaluation research on other compensatory education programs, Sesame Street appears encouraging. Findings to date are considerably positive and relate directly to amount of viewing time. In addition, the test results suggest that transfer of learning is an outcome of the program. In attempting to account for Sesame Street's apparent success, one turns most immediately to the method of preparation of program segments. The program staff, buttressed by eminent educational consultants, adopted and maintained an openly experimental approach to their materials. The staff took the viewpoint that their target group was a difficult audience to reach, one which was highly selective in viewing and which had a very short span of attention. They therefore felt that conventional assumptions concerning TV programming for children could not be expected to hold true, and they must find out from the children themselves whether or not the materials were interesting and educational. . . . Future evaluations would benefit from refining the principal explanatory variable utilized in the ETS study, "amount of viewing time." The adequacy of the operational definition of the variable could be questioned since there is no knowledge of factors such as circumstantional distractions which might affect quality of viewing. . . . Nevertheless, the ETS results lead to the tentative conclusion that Sesame Street is one of the more efficacious compensatory education programs [McDill, McDill, and Sprehe, 1972, pp. 169–170).

In the years following the two ETS evaluations of "Sesame Street," secondary analyses of the ETS data were performed by another group of researchers (Cook and others, 1975). These analyses revealed smaller viewer impacts of the show than the original analyses did—findings that the ETS evaluators criticized and rejected (see the concluding chapter by Ball and Bogatz in Cook and others, 1975). Interested readers will find this work stimulating and thought-provoking. However, our assessment of the ETS evaluations is consistent with that of McDill, McDill, and Sprehe (quoted above). We applaud the careful, comprehensive work done by ETS—and hope that other evaluators will take up where they left off on the evaluation of this show, and refine their approach for other evaluations in early childhood education.

Other Evaluation Examples

We now describe two other examples of program evaluation in early childhood education. Both evaluations were somewhat less expansive and less costly than the Home Start, Follow Through, and "Sesame Street" evaluations already detailed. We follow the same pattern here as earlier in the chapter; that is, we describe the project, elaborate the evaluation design, describe the measures, and present the evaluation outcomes. However, these two presentations are relatively succinct, and the interested reader will want to examine the source documents on each evaluation to enrich the basic description provided here. Additional examples of early childhood program evaluations are available in many sources, such as the edited books by Day and Parker (1977), Ryan (1974), and Stanley (1972b, 1973). The final discussion in this section concerns reviews of many other evaluations of programs for young children and their families. The brief descriptions of those reviews should make it apparent that evaluation is widespread in early childhood education.

The Four Preschool Programs Evaluation. This project concerned a comparative evaluation of four different preschool models, including a three-year longitudinal follow-up (Miller and Dyer, 1975). Initiated in 1968 as part of the Louisville, Kentucky, Head Start program, the evaluation examined the differential effects of these models:

1. The Direct Instruction or Academically Oriented Preschool Model, as initially developed by Bereiter and Engelmann (1966) and as described in the Follow Through Classroom Observation Evaluation in this chapter.

2. The Darcee Early Intervention Program (Gray and others, 1966) developed at George Peabody College in Nashville, Tennessee. This approach attempts to remedy the linguistic and conceptual deficiencies of school-disadvantaged children and to develop in them positive attitudes toward academic achievement. Children are grouped into small, homogeneous units and receive fairly direct, sequenced instruction from teachers and rewards for good performance. Home visits and parent training are also emphasized.

3. The Montessori Program (see Montessori, 1964), generally representing the traditional Montessori approach. This model focuses on development of

the senses, conceptual development, character development, and competence in everyday activities. Structured materials are used to present much of the program and reinforce desired behaviors; teachers organize the environment but give little direct instruction. As distinct from the first two approaches, Montessori does little grouping for instruction, does not emphasize language, and does not use direct teacher reinforcement. Rather, children develop the self-discipline to work alone, to select learning tasks, to clean up after themselves, and generally to operate from an intrinsic motivation base.

4. The Traditional Head Start Program (Office of Economic Opportunity, 1965), with emphasis on child development generally. As alluded to in the description of the evaluation of Home Start in this chapter, Head Start addresses broad goal areas including intellectual, social, and physical development, as well as nutrition and health. Little formal grouping is used, and children are allowed considerable freedom, within limits. There is little attention to the sequence of instruction; sensory stimulation tends to be emphasized.

Two major purposes were set for the evaluation: (1) to determine the differences between the four programs and any dimensions on which they could be ordered, and (2) to determine both the immediate and long-range impact of the four programs on children's intellectual, social, perceptual, and motivational development. The experimental design called for random assignment of four-year-olds (within each of four target areas) to all-day prekindergarten classes, each of which was to implement one of the four program approaches. However, only two Montessori teachers could be obtained, so in two target areas the random assignment involved just the other three models. In all, then, the fourteen experimental classes enrolled over 200 children, primarily black, and operated during the 1968–69 school year; there were four classes each for the Direct Instruction, Darcee, and Traditional Head Start approaches and two for the Montessori model. A low-income control group of thirty-four children was also obtained from the same geographic areas (unfortunately, however, it was not formed via the initial random procedures).

After eight weeks of class, the experimental and control children were pretested on a battery of measures. Five times during the year, the experimental classes were monitored and videotaped; also, teachers provided the evaluators with records on attendance, parent contacts, and class visitors. In April and May of 1969, all children were posttested on the original battery and also given additional tests.

The original design called for following children from these fourteen classes and from the control group longitudinally as they undertook kindergarten, first, and second grade. However, these intentions had to change when the City of Louisville inaugurated the Behavior Analysis Classroom Follow Through approach (as described earlier in this chapter) in one of the target areas in Fall 1969. Four of the original experimental classrooms, one representing each of the four models, entered kindergarten Behavior Analysis Classrooms, while children from all other classrooms and the control group entered Louisville's regular kindergarten program. Since none of the original control students entered a

Behavior Analysis Classroom, a second control group was formed from children in the Behavior Analysis kindergarten who had had no prekindergarten class experience. To implement the longitudinal feature of the evaluation, some videotape monitoring of kindergarten and first-grade classes was done (but not of any second-grade classes), and all groups of children were tested in April or May of each year through Spring 1972, when they completed the second grade.

Measurement was used extensively in the evaluation. For charting the classroom processes, two separate observation systems were used. One system was designed to code teacher behavior only—that is, all the teacher's acts as recorded on videotape—by utilizing an adaptation of Bales' Interaction Process Analysis (1950). The second observational scheme consisted of a time sampling sign procedure (see Chapter Four) and was used for in-class monitoring of activities, group size, media used, and the like. Observer reliability was established for each system.

The battery of pretests used in the Fall of 1968 included the Stanford-Binet and the Cooperative Preschool Inventory (CPI), both described in Chapter Five. Also included were four subtests from the Cincinnati Autonomy Test Battery (Banta, 1970), as listed below (the first three were included as motivational measures, and the fourth as a perceptual measure):

1. The Curiosity Box, designed to measure the tendency to explore, investigate, manipulate, and discover in relation to novel stimuli.
2. The Replacement Puzzle, intended to measure both persistence and resistance to distraction.
3. The Dog and Bone Test, purported to measure the tendency to generate alternative solutions to problems.
4. The Early Childhood Embedded Figures Test, designed to assess perceptual field independence (that is, the tendency to separate an item from the context or field in which it exists).

Based on their observations of experimental children, teachers filled out a twenty-item rating scale, the Behavior Inventory (Hess and others, 1966). The face sheet of the Binet, which allows examiners to rate children on their behavior during the exam, was also used as a rating scale.

In Spring 1969, the measures above were given as posttests. Five additional tests were also used as posttests. Two of these, the Basic Concept Inventory (BCI) and the Peabody Picture Vocabulary Test (PPVT), are described in Chapter Five. Two others, the Parallel Sentence Production and Expressive Vocabulary Inventory (Stern, 1968), were language measures to determine preschoolers' mastery of English. The final posttest was a locally developed arithmetic test. Many of the Spring 1969 measures were repeated as the children were tested in the Springs of 1970, 1971, and 1972. However, the Expressive Vocabulary Inventory and the PPVT were given only after prekindergarten (Spring 1969), while the CPI, Embedded Figures, and arithmetic tests were given only through kindergarten (Spring 1970). The Metropolitan Readiness Test (see Chapter Five) was added as a Spring 1970 measure, while the California Achievement Test was given after first and second grades. The BCI was given through first grade, but not after second grade.

Outcomes related to the first evaluation purpose—determining the four programs' differences and dimensions—were similar to those found in the SRI Follow Through Classroom Observation Evaluation described earlier in this chapter. That is, via the observation systems used and subsequent data analyses, the four programs were found to be distinct in terms of both teacher and child behaviors, and in predictable directions. For example, the Direct Instruction Model was often characterized by teacher modeling of academic information, and Montessori by manipulation of materials. Results on more complex dimensions were also predictable, for the most part. For instance, "teacher-directed and fast-paced" tended to identify the Direct Instruction and Darcee Models, while Montessori and Traditional tended to cluster as "child-centered and slow-paced."

The second evaluation purpose was to examine the immediate and long-range effects of the four programs on children's development. It was determined that the four programs did have different effects on children, both immediately and over the three-year follow-up (regardless of what programs they had in kindergarten, first, and second grade). After the prekindergarten year, the children in the experimental programs scored significantly higher on the Binet than did the controls. Further, on most of the cognitive instruments, there was a relatively consistent ordering of programs, from high to low performance, namely: Direct Instruction, Darcee, Montessori, Traditional, and Control. Such consistent patterns were not in evidence on the motivation measures, but the average scores for all four experimental programs on the Replacement Puzzle (task persistence and resistance to distraction) were markedly above the mean score for control students. On the Behavior Inventory, none of the four programs was consistently low on any of the ratings, and significant between-class variations on average ratings were noted for both the four Direct Instruction and the four Traditional classes. On the Binet face sheet ratings, the Direct Instruction and Traditional program students received, on average, better ratings than students in other programs.

In terms of longitudinal effects over the ensuing three-year period, the results were not nearly so encouraging for advocates of early childhood education. Most of those prekindergarten program effects (as compared with the control) that were still distinguishable tended to be in noncognitive areas, and then only for selected programs. Students from all four programs declined in IQ over the follow-up period (especially girls), with the decline most dramatic for children in the program that had shown the greatest gains initially (the Direct Instruction Model). Although Montessori appeared to be the best program for boys on the basis of second-grade achievement, even they were just at grade level (although they were still above the control students), and the grade-to-grade trend was a downward one. Concerns over the noncomparability of control students might be raised (for example, they more often appeared to be from two-parent families), but generally the results contained little encouragement that the early intervention had had lasting effects. In the longitudinal study, it was also shown that certain combinations of prekindergarten programs and later schooling emphases were better than others for maintaining achievement gains. For example, Direct Instruction (in prekindergarten) and Behavior Analysis Classroom (in later grades) appeared a more effective combination than Direct Instruction and subsequent regular classrooms, while Darcee and regular classrooms appeared a more effective combination than Darcee and Behavior Analysis Classroom. Miller and Dyer (1975), among their several conclusions, questioned the alluring simplicity of raising IQ as a solution for enhancing later school achievement. They also recommended careful study of the sequencing of educational experiences, given the intriguing outcomes of the prekindergarten and kindergarten model combinations. We would agree.

The California State Preschool Program Evaluation. This evaluation was conducted by evaluators at the Center for the Study of Evaluation (CSE), a research and development center at the University of California at Los Angeles. The overall purpose of the evaluation was to assess the effectiveness of the California State Preschool Program "in meeting its goal of improving the performance, motivation, and productivity in school of educationally disadvantaged children" (Hoepfner and Fink, 1975, p. 1).

The California State Preschool Program was begun in 1965. At that time, the California legislature appropriated funds, including some federal funds, for the statewide program. The program was founded on the legislature's belief that preschool experiences for children from low-income or disadvantaged families would enhance their performance, motivation, and productivity in kindergarten and elementary school. In 1973, the legislature enacted another law calling for an evaluative study of the program's effects. This evaluation was conceived of primarily as a retrospective study—that is, a post hoc analysis of early elementary motivation, performance, and productivity of the Preschool Program's "graduates." CSE was awarded the contract for the evaluation. Our summary of the evaluation is based on CSE's evaluation (Hoepfner and Fink, 1975).

The specific evaluation question that guided the work of the CSE group was "Do children who previously experienced the State Preschool Program for at least one year show significantly improved performance, motivation, and productivity in their subsequent elementary schools when compared with children who have either experienced other preschool programs (like the California Children's Centers) or who have not experienced a traceable institutionalized preschool program?" (Hoepfner and Fink, 1975, pp. 6–7). Since interactions between preschool and early elementary school experiences were also considered potentially important in comparing Preschool Program children with non-Preschool Program children, the enrichment provided by the elementary schools in which the evaluation study children were enrolled was included as a factor in the evaluation design. Each elementary school was categorized as either low or high in enrichment, depending on the number of state or federally funded enrichment programs operating in that school.

A further evaluation concern was the differential effectiveness of the various program emphases and approaches known to exist in the California State Preschool Programs. To examine this, CSE first asked each agency involved in the study to classify itself according to its main educational purpose: psychomotor development, preacademic skills, socialization and interaction skills, attitude to school and learning, or self-concept development. It then became possible to make comparisons on dependent variables between the different types of program.

Three categories of children who had formerly attended the Preschool Program were involved in the evaluation: children currently in kindergarten, first grade, and second grade (1972–73, 1971–72, and 1970–71 Preschool Program attendees, respectively). Using a complicated, multi-stage sampling procedure, the CSE evaluators obtained a representative sample of forty-two State Preschool agencies—those administrative units that had received funds for conducting one or more Preschool Programs. The forty-two agencies represented all sections of California and were concentrated in the state's major population centers, Los Angeles and San Francisco. Once the agencies had been chosen, 148 elementary schools attended by Preschool Program graduates were selected to participate in the evaluation. Selection criteria for the schools included numbers of former Preschool Program children enrolled, as well as the representativeness of the schools' respective agencies in terms of enrollment size and racial and ethnic composition.

The comparison groups were selected after the Preschool Program sample was determined. That is, within each participating elementary school, the former Preschool Program children were first identified. Then, in each class, children who had attended California Children's Centers were identified. These daycare centers were designed for children of AFDC (Aide to Families with Dependent Children) parents and had an educational component; children who had attended these centers were selected as a comparison group for this evaluation "because the Centers offer the largest single alternative institutionalized preschool experience for California children" (Hoepfner and Fink, 1975, p. 37). Further, a group of "No-Program" children was randomly selected in each class. Some of the children in this comparison group most likely had experienced some preschool program, although their experiences were different from either the Preschool Program or the California Children's Centers; CSE was not able to identify the precise nature of the No-Program students' preschool experiences because such identification would have required questioning the parents—a procedure considered too costly in time and money for this evaluation. In each class, eligibility for any child's participation, regardless of group, also rested on the availability of at least one piece of evaluative information (detailed below). A final restriction was that the number of children selected for the two comparison groups in any given class could not exceed the number of Preschool Program children eligible for the study; that is, the number of Preschool Program children with evaluative information in each class determined the maximum number chosen for the two comparison groups in that class. The total number of children who participated was over 6,000, with approximately 2,400 kinder-gartners, 1,100 first-graders, and 2,800 second-graders. Preschool graduates were most heavily represented (over 3,000 in all), with about half that number in each of the two comparison groups.

Since the overall purpose of this evaluation was to study the performance, motivation, and productivity outcomes of the Preschool Program, the children's measures were of those three types—performance measures (1 and 2), motivation measures (3 and 4), and productivity measures (5):

1. Entry Level Test: Developed by the California State Department of Education, the Entry Level Test contains five subparts related to reading readiness: Immediate Recall, Letter Recognition, Auditory Discrimination, Visual Discrimination, and Language Development. This test had been administered to entering first-graders in California schools in the Fall of 1973; scores for first-graders in the Preschool Program evaluation were obtained from the company that maintained the statewide computer bank of scores.

2. Cooperative Primary Test—Reading: This test, published by Educational Testing Service in 1965, served as the performance measure for second-graders on the evaluation. Scores were obtained from students' records in the schools. The test had been administered to all first-graders in the state in the Spring of 1973; thus, although it was used as a second-grade performance measure in this evaluation, scores actually represented end-of-first-grade performance. (Note that no kindergarten performance measure was used in the evaluation.)

3. Attitude to School Questionnaire: Consistent with the California Legislature's objectives for the evaluation, CSE elected to define motivation in terms of attitudes toward school, especially toward the academic component of schooling. Developed by CSE staff in 1970, this group-administered measure of academic sentiment has separate forms for boys and girls. The children are presented with drawings and oral descriptions of school-related activities; they express their attitudes by circling a happy, neutral, or sad face for each item. All children—kindergartners, and first- and second-graders—in the sample were administered this measure by their teachers.

4. Attendance Rate: Considered an unobtrusive measure of motivation and interest in school, attendance rates during the Fall 1973 semester were obtained from school records.

5. Student Productivity Index: This teacher rating form was a slightly modified version of the Schaefer Behavior Inventory used in the Home Start Evaluation (described above). The five items concerning task-orientation in the classroom were rated on the seven-point scale from "never" to "always." Each teacher completed the scale for each study child. The CSE evaluators chose this as a measure of productivity "since the ability to attend to a task and follow it through to completion may be considered to be a logical and necessary first step in the production of educationally valuable products" (Hoepfner and Fink, 1975, p. 51). Obviously this logic can be questioned.

In addition to the children's measures, CSE used two other instruments, both of which they developed for this evaluation: the Preschool Agency Purpose Survey and the Enrichment Checklist. The former was used to obtain data on the preceding three years. As mentioned earlier, each agency rank-ordered five emphases in terms of its own program's focus. Each agency completed the Survey for each of the three years, 1970–71, 1971–72, and 1972–73. The Enrichment Checklist was developed to collect data on the number of state- and federally funded enrichment programs in each elementary school. Schools were then categorized as "low enrichment" (zero to two programs) or "high enrichment" (three or more such programs).

Prior to analyzing the data, the CSE evaluators specifically stated what interpretation would be made for various types of finding:

1. If significantly higher performance, motivation, or productivity of Preschool Program students resulted as compared with Children's Center or No-Program children, the Preschool Program would be judged a "definite success" for those outcome areas showing the significant differences.
2. If no significant differences on any or all children's measures resulted, the program would be judged a "probable success" for those outcome areas.
3. If significantly higher scores for either or both comparison groups resulted, as compared with the Preschool Program group, the program would be judged a "definite failure" for those outcome areas.

Outcomes of the analysis of *performance* data were (1) no significant differences among first-grade groups on Entry Level Test scores, as well as no significant interactions between groups and enrichment levels, and (2) no significant differences in second-grade groups on Cooperative Primary Test-Reading scores when all three groups were compared, although the Preschool Program second-graders were significantly lower than the No-Program second-graders when just those two groups were compared. Further, the second-grade analyses revealed significant differences favoring the children in Low Enrichment schools over those in High Enrichment schools.

Regarding the *motivation* measures, no significant differences were found in the comparison of Attitude to School scores for the three groups, nor for just the two groups (Preschool Program versus No-Program). However, higher scores for children in Low Enrichment schools, as compared with those in High Enrichment schools, were found for kindergartners and first-graders. The only significant finding for attendance rates occurred when all three kindergarten groups were compared; Children's Center kindergartners showed significantly lower absenteeism than Preschool Program or No-Program kindergartners.

Analysis of *productivity* scores revealed that Preschool Program children were significantly less productive than the No-Program children at each grade level. When all three groups were compared, however, no significant differences were found. Enrichment showed no effects or interactions.

To compare the various Preschool Program agencies on the three outcome dimensions, the intent was to group the agencies into clusters according to their major purposes (as indicated on the Preschool Agency Purpose Survey). However, 98 percent of the agencies had ranked the self-concept purpose either first or second in importance, rendering discrimination by major purpose impractical. Self-concept was then disregarded by the CSE evaluators, and the agencies were grouped according to the rankings they had given to the other four purposes. Three types of agency resulted: (1) emphasis on preacademic skills (twenty agencies), (2) emphasis on socialization and interaction skills (eleven agencies), and (3) emphasis on attitudes toward school and learning (eleven agencies). When average scores for these three types were compared, no significant differences were found on either the first- or second-grade performance measures, leading to the conclusion that Preschools' purposes had no influence on later student performance. Likewise, no significant differences were found on the Student Productivity Index scores or on the Attitude to School scores. However, tests for differences in attendance rates among the types of Preschool yielded significant findings at the kindergarten and first-grade levels. Preschools concentrating on social and interaction skills (first grade) or attitudes toward school and learning (kindergarten) had better attendance rates than those emphasizing preacademic skills (a finding comparable to one in the Follow Through Classroom Observation Evaluation).

The overall conclusions of the evaluators, in keeping with the aforementioned preestablished criteria for program success, included the following:

1. That children who attended the California Preschool Program probably show improved performance and motivation, but probably not improved productivity.
2. That high-enrichment schools were frequently shown to have detrimental effects, but that this finding could be attributed in part to a nonrepresentative sample of schools with varying enrichments.
3. That no one type of Preschool purpose related consistently to improved performance, motivation, or productivity.

The CSE evaluation of the California State Preschool Program paid exemplary attention to details (such as in the sampling) and to documenting the rationale for its actions. Nevertheless, there were several troublesome aspects of the evaluation that consumers of the evaluation should take into account. First, the lack of control over the three comparison groups, via random assignment or some post hoc control through such methods as analysis of covariance, threatened the validity of any cause-effect conclusions. That is, the Preschool Program children were different in many systematic ways from children in the other two groups—especially in their greater disadvantagement. Second, since the evaluation involved only retrospective analyses, no documentation was available regarding what actually went on in the Preschool Program classes. Such documentation is obviously valuable for fully describing the program and suggesting possible explanations for outcome results. Third, only selected types of outcome variable—performance, motivation, and productivity—were examined. Yet almost all the agencies involved in the evaluation ranked self-concept development as first or second in importance. This deviation of the agencies' prime purpose from the legislature's expectation is interesting in itself. It also suggests a need to consider other dimensions—such as those related to self-concept development—to effect a comprehensive evaluation of the program.

Reviews of Other Evaluations. For those readers who are attempting to locate a particular type of evaluation to guide their own evaluations or studies, we now present brief descriptions of five reviews surveying hundreds of evaluations related to early childhood education. In places, the reviews overlap (that is, they consider the same evaluations). Although the reviews by no means chart all the evaluations that have been conducted, they are reasonably comprehensive in scope and thus provide an appropriate starting point for readers seeking direction to groups of other evaluations.

The first of these reviews, *Federal Programs for Young Children: Review and Recommendations,* is undoubtedly the most comprehensive and has been referred to extensively throughout this book. Dubbed by some "The Yellow Peril" (apparently on account of its length and its bright yellow cover), the four-volume work was completed by Sheldon White and his colleagues (1973a, b, c, d). Volume 1 of the document, *Goals and Standards of Public Programs for Children,* gives the purpose and the design of the study, a history of the evolution of public programs for children, a review of early experience and critical periods, a long treatise on predicting adult characteristics from child characteristics, and material on health care for children. The second volume, *Review of Evaluation Data for Federally Sponsored Projects for Children,* is particularly germane to our purpose here, as it surveys evaluations in five domains: (1) Early Elementary Education, (2) Preschool Projects, (3) Day Care Projects, (4) Family Intervention Projects, and (5) Health Care Programs. The third volume, *Recommendations for Federal Program Planning,* contains separate recommendations for preschool and for day-care, as well as suggestions on program emphases in terms of education, family involvement, and health. Two consistent themes in the recommendations are individualizing services and working with, rather than around, the family. Thus, with regard to preschool programs, especially Head Start, the recommended courses of action include: (1) shifting Head Start away from its center-based orientation and broadening its focus to include most aspects of child development; (2) implementing widespread screening programs; and (3) providing individualized services for handicapped children, including training of their parents. The final volume, *Summary,* rounds out this valuable resource document.

A second source of reviews, completed about the same time as the White series, is "The Effectiveness of Environmental Intervention Programs" (Horowitz and Paden, 1973), an article contained in the third *Review of Child Development Research.* In this article, Horowitz and Paden provided an excellent concise review of the historical foundations and basic issues surrounding intervention (as distinct from enrichment). For example, they elaborated on the critical issue of the social implications of successful intervention: "the matter is one of striking the delicate balance between preventive intervention and cultural annihilation. Uncritically perpetrating a deficit model may involve the unwitting destruction of a struggling cultural identity" (Horowitz and Paden, 1973, p. 393). They examined the evaluations of infant intervention projects, Head Start, Follow Through, and a series of other projects. Their conclusions generally matched those already presented in this chapter. Placing these conclusions in the larger social context of intervention represented an important contribution.

The third review document is *A Report on Longitudinal Evaluations of Preschool Programs: Is Early Intervention Effective?* (Bronfenbrenner, 1974). It surveyed many of the same studies examined in the first two reviews described above, but apparently had access to some later data. Bronfenbrenner also examined important methodological issues related to the quality of the data in the evaluative studies and the confidence that one could place in them. He derived a rationale (correctly, from our perspective) for weighting most heavily evaluations using randomly formed experimental and control groups. The conclusions of his review generally reinforced outcomes already reviewed in this chapter. For example, he noted immediate cognitive gains for children in most special programs but then, over time, a gradual decline in this advantage over control children. However, he also noted, "children who were involved in an intensive program of parent intervention during and, especially, prior to their enrollment in preschool or school, achieved greater and more enduring gains in the group program" (Bronfenbrenner, 1974, p. 53).

The final two reviews, more recent than the first three detailed, both suggest that there are long-term beneficial outcomes from early childhood intervention programs. In the first of these, *Found: Long Term Gains From Early Intervention* (Brown, 1978), the results of ninety-six major studies on the impacts of early intervention programs, especially Head Start, are summarized. Many of these studies were initiated in the 1960s; collectively they represent extensive amounts of data collected over many years. Data from these efforts have provided evidence for long-term effects, especially late-developing gains (also known as "sleeper effects"), in the areas of intelligence, achievement, and emotional adjustments. Like Bronfenbrenner, Brown concluded from this series of studies that early involvement or training of parents appeared especially efficacious.

The final review (closely related to the fourth) is represented by two overlapping documents: *The Persistence of Preschool Effects* (Lazar and others, 1977) and *Lasting Effects after Preschool* (Lazar and Darlington, 1978). These reports involved a detailed examination of the longitudinal evaluations of fourteen infant and preschool programs. The programs and evaluations were conducted by well-known names in the field of early childhood education—namely, Kuno

Beller, Cynthia and Martin Deutsch, Ira Gordon, Susan Gray, Merle Karnes, Phyllis Levenstein, Louise Miller, Francis Palmer, David Weikart, Myron Woolman, and Edward Zigler. The reports documented lasting effects, favoring the program children over control children in terms of the following variables:

1. Less frequent assignment to special education classes.
2. Less frequent retention in grade—that is, failing a grade.
3. Significantly higher achievement scores in mathematics as of the fourth grade (where most data were available) and a similar but nonsignificant trend in reading achievement scores.
4. Significantly higher IQ scores for children in some programs up through age twelve, but not thereafter.
5. More frequent giving of achievement-type reasons for being proud of themselves.

No differences were found in the use of child welfare services by treated and control families.

These last two reviews concentrated on "high-quality" early education programs, that is, programs in which a consistent, rational approach to nurturing young children's development was systematically implemented, evaluated, refined, and improved. The findings summarized in the two reviews lead us to believe that such quality, and attempts to achieve it, are essential if programs for young children are to be effective. They reinforce our conviction that high-quality early childhood education programs can increase the range and quality of children's life alternatives.

Chapter 12

Contributions from Other Fields

That there is immense variability in early childhood education programs becomes obvious as one visits programs across the country or reads descriptions of them. This diversity can be appreciated, at least in part, by scanning the numerous federal programs for young children described by White and his colleagues (1973a, b). To measure and evaluate well such a complex assortment of programs, there is need for a broad array of measures and evaluation designs. Those presented so far in this book have mostly been the work of professionals in the field of education. However, other fields have also made contributions to educational measurement and evaluation, such as data collection methodologies, unique measures, and reporting formats. This chapter contains a review of many such contributions and notes their application to early childhood education programs.

To encourage the use of measurement and evaluation in early childhood education, we have deliberately presented broad conceptualizations of appropriate measures, of suitable conceptual frameworks for evaluation, and (in this chapter) of diverse contributions from other fields. Our rationale is that this variety of possible measures and designs might attract more early childhood educators than a limited number of "recommended" measures and "endorsed" designs, which would often be ill-fitting at best and suspect at worst. Over a quarter-century ago, Homans expressed a similar view: "People who write about methodology often forget that it is a matter of strategy, not of morals. There are neither good nor bad methods but only methods that are more or less effective under particular circumstances in reaching objectives on the way to a distant goal" (1949, p. 330).

The contributions described in this chapter often represent the intersection of a given field of study, such as sociology, with education. At first glance, the reader might be surprised to find no section titled "Contributions from Psychology," although ecological psychology is represented. This is not an oversight—rather, the influence of psychology, particularly educational and developmental psychology, permeates much of the material in earlier chapters. Further, the initial section on classical experimental design and also a subsection on applied behavioral analysis are principally drawn from psychology. Thus, psychological influences have already been well represented, although certainly not exhausted; other important areas are highlighted in *Psychological Processes in Early Education* (Hom and Robinson, 1977). The contributions now listed are a small subset of all those that might be detailed. Nevertheless, they enrich the available supply of measures and evaluation designs.

Contributions from Classical Experimental Design

In Chapter One (especially with regard to Issue 12) and elsewhere in the book, we presented previews of our position that experimental design procedures are often appropriate for conducting evaluations. This position is not a new one for us (for example, see Goodwin, 1966, 1974). Still, experimental design deserves attention here because, in our estimation, its employment in educational evaluation has been relatively limited and its potential benefits remain unrealized by many educators. The brief treatment here, however, serves only as an introduction to the topic. Persons intending to conduct evaluations using experimental design procedures will want to consult more comprehensive source books (such as Bennett and Lumsdaine, 1975; Campbell and Stanley, 1963; Kerlinger, 1973; or Riecken and Boruch, 1974).

Essential Elements of Experimental Design. An experimental design is in effect when "one or more *treatments* (programs) are administered to some set of persons (or other units) *drawn at random* from a specified population" and when "observations (or measurements) are made to learn how (or how much) some relevant aspect of their behavior following treatment differs from like behavior on the part of an untreated or *control group* also drawn at random from the same population" (Riecken and Boruch, 1974, p. 3). Put more simply, the purpose of an experiment is to test whether particular treatments have any effects and to estimate the size of the effects. Several terms in this definition require amplification.

A *treatment,* in this context, is the program to be evaluated. It represents an intervention into the natural scheme of things. Examples of a treatment would include a special type of daycare program, a particular preschool model for facilitating children's learning, a method for motivating children to learn, "Sesame Street," a new approach for teaching reading, or the like. In a research experiment, as distinct from an evaluation, the term analogous to treatment is *active independent variable,* the variable actively manipulated by the experimenter and the presumed cause of any effects later found via observation or measurement of one or more *dependent variables* or outcome measures (Kerlinger, 1973). Available design and statistical techniques also permit determining if a treatment is differentially effective for various categories of children. For example, if the treatment were a special type of daycare program, it would be possible to determine the program's differential effects on boys and girls, or on children from low and middle socioeconomic-status homes, or on two- and four-year-olds, or on countless other variables. In research experiment terminology, variables of this latter type are built into the study design as *attribute independent variables* (also referred to as *classificatory* or *status variables*); they simply are determined or measured by the experimenter rather than being manipulated (Kerlinger, 1973).

Another essential element in experimental design is a *control group*—a group that does not receive the special program (or treatment). In some cases, the control group receives no special attention at all but simply keeps on with the status quo; in others, it receives a placebo or dummy treatment (such as a sugar pill in a medical experiment to determine the effect of a new drug) or some other minimal activity (Riecken and Boruch, 1974). In the daily routine of a preschool, for instance, the treatment group might be given fifteen minutes of special instruction in problem solving, while the control group receives an extra fifteen minutes of play period with no problem solving instruction. Inclusion of a control group is necessary to allow inferences about whether the observed treatment effect would have occurred even if no treatment had been administered, and to provide a no-treatment base line from which to measure the size of treatment effects. One modification of the treatment and control group paradigm is to utilize more than one treatment group and no control group—and then compare the effects evidenced by the several treatment groups. This modification, usually called *comparative evaluation* and alluded to in both Chapters One and Nine, has some attractive features—it allows comparison of treatments, it ensures that no students are "left out," as no control group is formed, and so forth. Comparative evaluations, nevertheless, yield more valuable information when a control group is also included—that is, when multiple treatment groups plus a control group are utilized in the design.

The final essential element in using experimental design principles in evaluation is forming groups *at random.* If one is to conclude with some confidence that a treatment causes certain effects (as distinct from their being caused by outside events, normal growth, testing effects, or whatever), then it is important that the treatment group(s) and the control group be as equivalent as possible before the treatment activity is initiated. A preferred way to achieve this before-the-fact equivalence is by randomly assigning persons from the same "pool" to either the treatment group(s) or the control group. (In comparative evaluations with no control group, persons should be assigned randomly to the various treatment groups.) The central principle involved in randomization is that each person has the same chance of being assigned to any given group.

For example, consider the most basic case involving simple random assignment. Assume that sixty kindergarten students are available for a study to test the effectiveness of a new physical exercise procedure on their physical prowess and development. Giving all sixty students the new procedure would make it logically impossible to determine the procedure's effects with any certainty. Rather, using a chance procedure such as a table of random numbers, each student is assigned randomly to either the treatment group or the control group, with the only restriction being that each group ultimately contain thirty students. The special physical exercise procedure is then used with the treatment group and outcome measures for both the treatment and control groups are examined to determine treatment effects. Although the two groups as initially formed will be different in some respects, they will be as equivalent as one would expect by chance. The probability of randomly forming more nearly equivalent groups increases as the size of the groups increases. Note too that "attribute independent variables" could be built into the evaluation design prior to random assignment. For example, the sixty children might first be formed into two groups of thirty girls and thirty boys. The girls would then be randomly assigned, fifteen to the treatment group and fifteen to the control group. A similar procedure would be used with the boys. This procedure (stratified, rather than simple, random assignment) results in equal numbers of each sex in each group and permits determining the differential effects of the treatment for girls and for boys. Note that additional attribute variables, such as age or initial agility, might also be added to the evaluation design.

Forming groups randomly probably is the most resisted aspect of experimental design (Houston, 1972; Stanley, 1972a). Most human beings believe that they can form more equivalent groups (using "matching" and other techniques) than can chance principles; but such beliefs are basically incorrect. The logic behind random assignment cannot be fully explicated here, but is well elaborated elsewhere (for example, see Riecken and Boruch, 1974). The major contribution of classical experimental design to evaluation methodology is increasing the probability of establishing cause-and-effect relationships—that is, of estimating accurately the effects of the treatment (or cause). Basic to this contribution is the random formation of groups so as to minimize threats to both the internal and external validity of the evaluation (fuller explanations of these concepts appear in Bracht and Glass, 1968; Campbell and Stanley, 1963; Houston, 1972; and Kerlinger, 1973). When it is impossible or simply not feasible to form groups randomly, some less desirable but still valuable procedures are available. For instance, statistical procedures exist "to make groups comparable," such as using a measure taken prior to the evaluation, possibly a child competency score or a pretest score, as a covariate in the design. Also available are quasi-experimental designs, which approximate certain features of true experimental designs but also have limitations (Campbell and Boruch, 1975; Campbell and Stanley, 1963; Messick and Barrows, 1972; and Stevens and King, 1976).

Debate over Experimental Design. There has been much opposition to the use of classical experimental design procedures for evaluation. Several writers have been critical of such a practice for a variety of reasons (for example, see Guba, 1969; Guba and Stufflebeam, 1968; Guttentag, 1973; Parlett and Hamilton, 1976; and Stufflebeam, 1968). In Chapter One, we considered two of the reasons, specifically high costs and ethical questions such as the appropriateness of denying the treatment to control students (Issues 6 and 12, respectively); we also presented rebuttals to these charges. Other common objectives to the use of experimental design in evaluation include the following:

1. Objections that there is only a remote possibility of being able to form groups randomly for real-world evaluation purposes. Accordingly, the use of experimental design may be viewed as ideal but impractical, ill-suited, or even impossible.
2. Objections that classical experimental design methodology results in establishing strict controlled conditions that represent a marked departure from reality. Guba (1969) termed this characteristic *laboratory antisepsis.* Parlett and Hamilton contended that "strict control is rarely followed. To attempt to simulate laboratory conditions by manipulating educational personnel not only is dubious ethically, but also leads to gross administrative and personal inconvenience. Even if a situation could be so unnervingly controlled, its artificiality would render the exercise irrelevant: rarely can 'tidy' results be generalized to an 'untidy' reality" (1976, p. 143).
3. Objections that experimental design procedures are outcome-oriented and, therefore, that they prevent midstream redefinition and continuous refinement. This charge assumes that a treatment must remain fixed during the full experimental period and that any developmental changes in the treatment must be suppressed.
4. Objections that experimental design often relies on using large samples to permit making statistical generalizations and, in so doing, becomes "insensitive to local perturbations and unusual effects" (Parlett and Hamilton, 1976). This concern relates to the second objection above—if strict controls cannot be maintained in an experimental-design evaluation, one compensatory procedure is to increase the number of students treated in the study. In Parlett and Hamilton's view, the evaluator using controlled experimental design is damned either way—whether using strict controls that lead to distortions of reality or using large samples that mask individuality and breed insensitivity.
5. Objections that classic design methodology seeks only data that are quantitative and objectively generated. This quantitative orientation, it is charged, causes the evaluator to disregard data that are subjective, impressionistic, or anecdotal even though such information could help place the evaluation findings in proper perspective.

These five objections to the use of classical experimental design in evaluation, as well as many others, have been countered most effectively by Boruch (1976). His basic tactic was to cite examples of evaluations that effectively used experimental design methodology. Worthen and Sanders (1973) have also challenged the objections. Specific rebuttals to the five objections, based principally on Boruch's work, are as follows:

1. The objection that randomization is infeasible is countered by noting the large number of evaluations that have been conducted using such procedures; Boruch provided a bibliography of over 200 such evaluations. He also noted new practices being studied that might reduce public resistance to randomization, such as a program candidate's assigning himself randomly to a program condition rather than being assigned by program staff (Hendricks and Wortman, 1975).

2. The charge of artificiality is parried similarly by examining the wide variety of real-world settings in which evaluations using experimental design have been carried out. Thus, field experiments have been used to evaluate programs in education, economics, rehabilitation, police training, delinquency and criminal reform, medicine, fertility control, and so on (Boruch, 1976; and Gilbert, Light, and Mosteller, 1975). In Boruch's words, "Given the number, quality, and variety of field experiments which we have been able to identify, the general contention that experiments are impractical is a bit underwhelming" (1976, p. 162). Further, expecting that all studies will fall neatly into two ordered piles—either experimental-manipulative-interventionist or naturalistic—is unrealistic and simplistic; rather, there are degrees of control exercised in both investigation paradigms (Willems, 1969).

3. The objection that experimental design procedures make program redefinition and refinement impossible is based on a fixed-treatment assumption and the belief that only final outcome measures are relevant. Several examples exist in which experimental design methods were used in the sequential development of a program, such as the audio-bus project (Goodwin and Sanders, 1971) described in Chapter One. The assumption, therefore, is misleading and not inherent in experimental design. Programs can be evaluated using a series of small interim experimental studies—treatments often are modified moderately during such a process.

4. The concern that large samples result in insensitivity to local conditions and unusual effects is situation-specific. That is, controlled experimental designs in evaluation need not necessarily result in large samples; if large groups are contemplated, then sensitivity to local conditions and unusual effects can be achieved if adequate resources are available for monitoring (this is the case regardless of the particular methodology used). Note too that no inherent incompatibility exists between experimental design and observational procedures; both could be well used in complementary roles on the same evaluation.

5. The objection that experimental design methods ignore subjective, impressionistic, and anecdotal data is also situation-specific and not inherent in such design methods. It is true that experimental methodology requires systematic and reliable information, but this can be quantitative or qualitative or both

(Boruch, 1976). Many evaluations using experimental design and also considering narrative and impressionistic information were identified by Boruch.

Several of these objections apparently stem from a narrow conception of experimental design as necessarily rigid, laboratory-bound, long-range, and artificial. In all, the objections discussed in this section appear weak and easily countered. This conclusion on our part should not imply that we endorse the exclusive use of experimental design in conducting evaluations. But we do consider experimental design a legitimate and effective methodology for many evaluation purposes.

Application to Early Childhood Education. As long as experimental design is treated as a flexible method, the prospects for its application to the evaluation of early childhood education programs are excellent. Numerous possible applications come to mind. However, we consider it unnecessary to bombard the reader with a barrage of examples of such applications. In earlier chapters, we have already provided material closely related to such applications (such as several of the twenty suggested formative evaluation procedures listed in connection with Scriven's frameless framework in Chapter Nine). Further, a number of controlled-experiment approaches to evaluation were examined in Chapter Eleven, such as the Home Start Evaluation. Rather, we will offer here a single example that should help the reader visualize the wide applicability of the method.

Suppose that two kindergarten teachers decided to combine their classes and to work as a team. Together, they had fifty-four youngsters in the morning and another fifty-four in the afternoon. The morning and afternoon groups contained children of about the same age, from primarily lower-middle class homes, and (as luck would have it—at least for this example) an equal number of boys and girls. Early in the school year, the teachers became interested in what effect systematic home instruction by parents might have on student academic performance. They introduced the idea at a parent meeting and found the parents enthusiastic and supportive.

With the help of a consultant, an evaluation was planned based on experimental design methodology. It was first determined that parents might be most effective at helping their children in mathematics and language. Then, all 108 children were given three pretests in mid October—the mathematics, language, and general concepts tests of the Tests of Basic Experiences (TOBE), Form K. Further, raw scores on the general concepts test were used to divide the fifty-four girls into three performance groups—high, average, and low—of eighteen girls each. A similar process was followed for the boys. This resulted in dividing the kindergartners into six groups of eighteen students each: high, average, and low girls; and high, average, and low boys. The eighteen students in each of these blocks were then randomly assigned to one of three groups: Treatment 1: parent assistance in mathematics; Treatment 2: parent assistance in language; or Control: parent assistance in art. Thus, thirty-six children ended up in each of these final three groups, and each group contained six children of each "type" (that is, six high girls, six high boys, six average girls, and so forth).

For the next sixteen school weeks, the thirty-six children in the first treatment group received mathematics worksheets that they carried home. The worksheets were designed to provide each parent-child dyad with about fifteen to twenty minutes of shared math instruction every evening. Analogous procedures were established for the second treatment group, with daily language worksheets, and for control group children who received daily art worksheets. During the sixteen-week period, the teachers kept anecdotal records related to the children's behavior during math, language, and art instruction. They also recorded children's scores on unit tests in math and language. In early March, at the end of the sixteen weeks, all 108 again took the TOBE mathematics, language, and general concepts tests, but this time from Level L. The children's attitudes toward mathematics, language, and art were also assessed, as were both their and their parents' attitudes toward the home instruction sheets. Attitude instruments were developed by the evaluation consultant.

Analyses of the resulting data revealed that children receiving parental assistance in mathematics outperformed the other two groups, and by a statistically significant amount ($p < .01$), on the mathematics test. (Statistical significance indicates the probability [p] that an obtained difference occurred by chance. The evaluator sets a level of significance or probability level, usually .05 or .01. If the obtained difference between the means of the groups is small, the difference could have occurred easily by chance and is not statistically significant. If the obtained difference is large enough to be statistically significant at the .05 level, it indicates that a difference as large as the one obtained would occur by chance only five times out of a hundred. In this case, the math group did best on the TOBE math test and by enough points that the difference observed would have occurred by chance only one time in a hundred.) Children receiving parental assistance in language did better on the language test than the other two groups, but the difference was not quite large enough to reach statistical significance (at the .05 level). Both treatment groups outperformed the control group on the general concepts test (and at a statistically significant level).

Students in high groups consistently outperformed those in average groups, who in turn did better than those in low groups. No differences between boys and girls were noted except on the language test, on which "average" girls receiving the home language worksheets profited much more than "average" boys. These results, overall, were consistent with the children's performance on the sequential unit tests that had been given during the sixteen-week period. On the attitude instruments, students generally displayed more favorable attitudes toward the subject areas that their parents had assisted them in, but the differences reached a statistically significant level ($p < .05$) only in the case of art (that is, control group students expressed significantly more positive attitudes toward art than did students in either treatment group). Both children and parents expressed very positive attitudes toward the program. Based on these results, the teachers commenced using worksheets in all three areas, alternating so that only one worksheet was sent home daily.

To set this example in more formal terms, note that the active independent variable had three levels: parental assistance in math, language, or art (control group). Two attribute independent variables were built into the design: sex and initial general concepts level. The design involved multiple dependent variables: the TOBE mathematics, language, and general concepts tests (also given as pretests); tests of children's attitudes toward math, language, and art; and tests of children's and parents' attitudes toward the program. Further, en route measures were collected, unit tests as well as relevant anecdotal records. In all, this example should serve to demonstrate the limitless applications of the experimental design method to the evaluation of early childhood education programs.

Contributions from Sociology

Sociology, as a behavioral science, is naturally concerned in many ways with young children and their behavior. A number of writers have addressed sociological aspects of early childhood education (such as King, 1973; King and Kerber, 1968; and Margolin, 1974), although sociological influences on measurement and evaluation are only tangentially considered. Explanations of the relevance of sociology to early childhood education have usually taken a form similar to that below:

> The child is not isolated; from birth he is part of a family, a neighborhood, a subculture, all existing within the broad general culture of his country. Recognition of this fact is the basis for a new approach to early childhood education now needed in the burgeoning classrooms of preschools, kindergartens, and Head Start Child Development Centers across America today. . . . A sociological approach to the study of childhood will have as its central concept socialization. Socialization is the process of the individual's interaction with others in the human group. Hand in hand with the concept of socialization goes the process of enculturation. Enculturation takes place within the socialization process, as the individual is fitted into his culture by accepting as his own the norms, values, and attitudes of the groups with which he interacts. . . . One cannot write about socialization and education today without taking into consideration our shrinking world and the revolutions now taking place in mass communication. Contemporary writers in education, psychology, sociology, and anthropology point continually to the effects on young children of television, high mobility, family disintegration, desegregation, civil rights movements, and the threats of global war. A sociology of early childhood education must take account of these trends [King and Kerber, 1968, p. 13].

Rather than attempt to survey the numerous links between sociology and measurement and evaluation in early childhood education, we will note a few basic concepts in sociology and some methodological contributions from that field.

Any number of sociological concepts or areas of study have direct relevance to early childhood education and therefore also have implications for measurement and evaluation. For example, the various roles that a young child takes—son or daughter, sibling, friend, student, and so on—all carry expectations of various kinds. Both the roles and the expectations can be described, and to some extent behaviors or attitudes related to them can be measured. A second relevant sociological concept, implied by the earlier King and Kerber quote, is that of the socializer-socializee relationship. Often this is viewed as the parent-child or guardian-child relationship, while at times it might involve teacher-child, significant adult-child, or child-child relations and interactions. These relationships are important to study, and measurement and evaluation quickly come into play. A third important sociological focus is the family. An excellent review of federal family intervention projects (White and others, 1973b) highlighted the integral use of measurement and evaluation to determine the effects and worth of such efforts. Family intervention projects are programs for families, such as parent education, parent training, family social casework, and parent therapy; they are designed to improve family life, thereby providing for optimal child development. (Evaluation of parent involvement in early childhood education was treated in Chapter Ten.)

A major concept probably creditable to sociology, social psychology, and economics jointly is socioeconomic status (SES). This concept is a pervasive one in early childhood education, and hence in the field's measurement and evaluation efforts. Extensive references to SES have been made in several previous chapters of this book. SES correlates well with student characteristics such as academic achievement, school motivation, IQ scores, and the like.

Methodological contributions from sociology have involved both evaluation procedures and, especially, measures. Developed evaluation procedures have principally been related to data collection methods, involving the use of questionnaires, interviews, and other survey techniques. With regard to measures, Bonjean, Hill, and McLemore (1970) clearly demonstrated the tendency of sociologists to develop specific measures for a given research or evaluation study rather than use existing measures. They surveyed four key sociology journals over an eleven-year period and found reference to over 2,000 measures in seventy-eight conceptual areas (such as crime and delinquency, family interpersonal relations, and behavior and interaction in small groups). Nearly three fourths of the 2,000 measures were used in only one study, while only one measure out of every forty-four was used in more than five studies. Thus, sociologists have contributed numerous new measures, many of which are applicable to young children. Sociologists have also taken active roles in the identification of social indicators and unobtrusive measures (Bouchard, 1976; Denzin, 1970; and Webb and others, 1966).

Measurement of Socioeconomic Status. Sociologists have been especially diligent in devising ways to assess SES. Such procedures are quite variable. Some methods involve assessing the home environment—examining its size and location, the presence or absence of certain items (such as books, newspapers, magazines, refrigerators, television sets, vacuum cleaners, telephones, and so on), and typical family activities or travel. Examples of such efforts include the American Home Scale (Kerr and Remmers, 1942), the Home Index (Gough, 1971a, b), and the Living Room Check List (Laumann and House, 1970). (Because of the "easy-credit" nature of today's society, the validity of some of these approaches has begun to be questioned.)

More common measures of SES involve some combination of occupational level, educational level, amount and/or source of income, and type of residence. One widely used and elaborate procedure is the Index of Status Characteristics or ISC (Warner, Meeker, and Eells, 1949). Four factors make up the ISC—occupation, source of income, housing, and dwelling area—and each is rated on a seven-point scale. For example, the occupation scale runs from professional (rated 1) to unskilled worker (rated 7). To derive a total ISC score, ratings on the four factors are multiplied by 4, 3, 3, and 2, respectively; that is, occupation is weighted twice as much as dwelling area. Total ISC scores are then converted to one of five social class ratings: upper (12 to 22), upper-middle (23 to 37), lower-middle (38 to 51), upper-lower (52 to 66), and lower-lower (67 to 84). Thus, if a family received the middle rating of 4 on each factor, its total ISC score would be 48 (4 × 4 plus 3 × 4 plus 3 × 4 plus 2 × 4), and its social class rating would be lower-middle.

Since information on residences is often difficult (and sometimes sensitive) to obtain, many evaluators and researchers prefer Hollingshead's Two-Factor Index of Social Position (Hollingshead and Redlich, 1957). This SES index considers just occupational and educational level of the household head, each on a seven-point scale. The occupational level is multiplied by 7 and the educational level by 4 to yield an Index of Social Position (ISP). (Occupation has typically been the single best predictor of SES.) ISPs are converted to one of five social class levels: I (11 to 17), II (18 to 27), III (28 to 43), IV (44 to 60), and V (61 to 77). Thus, a plumber (5) who is a high-school graduate (4) receives an ISP of 51 (7 × 5 plus 4 × 4), and a IV social class index. A nurse (2) who is a college graduate (2) has an ISP of 22 (7 × 2 plus 4 × 2) and is in social class II.

Two additional and more recent indexes of a similar nature are available. The National Opinion Research Center (NORC) at the University of Chicago has published a scale of the perceived social standings of occupations (Siegel, 1971). The NORC prestige scale contains ratings for over 400 occupational categories from the 1970 U.S. Census code. Ratings vary widely, such as physician (82), college and university teachers (78), actors (55), mail carriers (42), sign painters (30), garage workers and gas station attendants (22), freight and material handlers (17), cleaners and charwomen (12), and bootblacks (9). The second scale, the Standard International Occupational Prestige Scale (Treiman, 1977) likewise provides ratings of occupations but is based on data from over fifty countries. This scale, expressed in a standard metric for each country, ranged approximately from 0 to 100 (apparently the NORC scale had a similar range). The international scale ratings, valuable in cross-cultural evaluative research, are generally similar to the NORC ratings; some notable and curious exceptions (with the NORC rating given first) include dental hygienists (61–44), preschool and kindergarten teachers (60–49), funeral directors (52–34), college administrators (61–86), and midwives (23–34). Evaluators of early childhood education programs needing to determine SES to refine their findings should find these scales and ratings valuable.

Recall too, from Chapter Five, the System of Multicultural Pluralistic Assessment (SOMPA). One set of measures in SOMPA involves Sociocultural

Scales—via parent interview, SES, family size, family structure, and urban accul-
turation scores are determined. These four scores are converted (using separate
norm tables for "Anglo, Black, and Latino" children) and then are combined to
yield adjustment factors. The adjustments are used to modify obtained WISC-R
scores, resulting in an Estimated Learning Potential (that is, for a given child,
modified Verbal, Performance, and Full Scale IQs are determined). The
SOMPA Sociocultural Scales clearly derive from sociology. Actively adjusting
obtained scores on the basis of sociological and environmental considerations
represents a new twist in measurement. It remains to be seen whether such a
practice will become widespread.

  Sociometric Techniques. Another of sociology's contributions to measurement is the sociometric technique for studying the interrelationships among
members of a group. The basic premise underlying sociometry is that the morale
and efficiency of a group are in large part determined by its informal organization, based on interpersonal feelings. Introduced in *Who Shall Survive* (Moreno,
1934), sociometry has been developed principally by sociologists and social
psychologists. In Chapter Seven, we presented information on one sociometric
measure, the Minnesota Sociometric Status Test. Other sociometric measures
have also been used with preschoolers and kindergartners (for example, see
Northway, 1969a, b).

  Three basic sociometric techniques have been developed: (1) nomination,
(2) guess who, and (3) placement. All of them work better if confidentiality of
response is assured and if the group members have been together sufficiently
long to know each other well. In *nomination,* each child names a given number of
children whom he likes, wants to sit next to, wants to play with, or the like. The
Minnesota Sociometric Status Test used this procedure. Issues surrounding the
nominating procedure include whether the children's choices are actually implemented (that is, whether they influence changes in the class seating pattern or
assignments for play or project activity) and whether young children also should
be asked to make negative selections (such as on the Minnesota where they are
asked to name three children whom they dislike). Gronlund addressed both
issues:

> The choices should be actually used to organize or rearrange
> groups. More spontaneous and truthful responses can be expected where
> the pupils know that their choices will be put into effect.
>   There is some disagreement among sociometric experts concerning
> the desirability of asking pupils to name also those whom they would not
> want as a companion. The arguments in favor of such negative choices are
> that rejected pupils can be identified and helped, and that interpersonal
> friction can be avoided in arranging groups. The counterargument is that
> such questions make pupils more conscious of their feelings of rejection
> and that this may disturb both group morale and the emotional develop-
> ment of pupils. The safest procedure seems to be to avoid the use of
> negative choices unless they are absolutely essential to the purpose for
> which the technique is being used. Where their use is essential, the ap-
> proach should be casual and the pupils permitted, rather than required, to
> make such choices [Gronlund, 1976, p. 458].

The *guess who* technique, like nomination, is frequently used, possibly because of its simplicity. Peer judgments are obtained by asking a student to indicate which classmate or classmates (if any) match brief descriptive statements. For example, "Guess who is usually sad?"; "Guess who is usually friendly and nice to everybody?"; and "Guess who is most active in games?" With young children, the statements can be read to each child individually and his responses recorded; with older children, written responses suffice.

The least used sociometric technique is *placement.* In it, a situation is described either pictorially or verbally and respondents are asked to place group members in the positions described in the situation. For example, the school playground might be sketched to scale, and the child is asked to indicate where (on the sketch) each classmate would usually be located.

Data from the two more common sociometric techniques, nomination and guess who, typically are first put in tabular or matrix form. With children's names on one axis and the various nomination or guess who categories on the other, entries are made to indicate when a particular child was nominated or guessed. Often the data are then presented visually in either a sociogram or target diagram. A *sociogram* ordinarily contains separate symbols for boys and girls (such as squares and circles), and each symbol is numbered or lettered to represent a particular boy or girl. Lines are used to connect symbols of children who name or guess each other, with arrowheads usually pointing toward the person selected. A *target diagram* also uses symbols like those of a sociogram, and sometimes arrows too, but differs in format from the sociogram in that it consists of a series of concentric circles like a target. Girls are typically placed in half of the target, boys in the other half. Frequently chosen children are placed in the center circle or bull's-eye; children selected moderately often appear in the middle rings; and rarely chosen ones are positioned in the outer circle. Of course, many variations of sociograms and target diagrams are possible, as well as visual displays that combine the two approaches.

A simple example will help illustrate the applicability of sociometric techniques to early childhood education. Suppose a teacher has just taken over a morning kindergarten class at midyear. The social relationships and friendship patterns in the small class of sixteen children are not entirely clear to her. She decides to use a sociometric nomination technique as one way of learning the social structure of the classroom. Since the class is gearing up for an extended project—simulating an American colonial village within the classroom—she asks each child individually to name the student he or she would like to work with on the project and also to indicate a second choice, if possible.

The responses given appear in Table 25. The number 1 indicates a first choice and 2 a second choice. For example, Ann chose Olive first and Iris second. Two children, Eve and Jay, did not make any choice at all. The other fourteen children all had first choices, and nine of them also indicated second choices. At the bottom of the table are indicated the total times each child was chosen, as well as whether the choices were first or second. Frequently chosen children were Iris, Paul, and Bob, with 5, 4, and 3 choices, respectively. Five children—Eve, Gail, Kay, Jay, and Ned—were not selected at all.

Table 25. Choices of Work Partners by Kindergarten Children

Choosers	Chosen Students															
	Ann	Cindy	Eve	Gail	Iris	Kay	Marie	Olive	Bob	Dave	Fred	Herb	Jay	Lee	Ned	Paul
Ann (A)	—				2			1								
Cindy (C)		—			1		2									
Eve (E)		1	—													
Gail (G)				—	1											
Iris (I)		1			—							2				
Kay (K)					1	—										
Marie (M)							—									
Olive (O)	1							—				2				
Bob (B)									—	2						1
Dave (D)									1	—						2
Fred (F)											—			1		
Herb (H)					2				2			—				
Jay (J)													—			
Lee (L)											1			—		1
Ned (N)										2					—	1
Paul (P)									1							—
First Choices	1	2	0	0	3	0	0	1	2	0	1	0	0	1	0	3
Second Choices	0	0	0	0	2	0	1	0	1	2	0	2	0	0	0	1
Total Choices	1	2	0	0	5	0	1	1	3	2	1	2	0	1	0	4

A sociogram of the data in Table 25 was constructed by the teacher to better reveal likely social patterns in the classroom. Readily apparent in Figure 12 are the *stars* (the frequently chosen children), such as Bob, Paul, and particularly Iris. The *isolates* (unchosen children) are also easily identified, especially Eve and Jay, who also made no choices of their own. The *fringers* or *neglectees* (infrequently chosen children) can also be spotted, such as Ann, Olive, Fred, and Lee, although they are paired up and so "have each other." The possible mutual admiration between Bob, Paul, and Dave shows up in the diagram, suggesting to the teacher that the three boys may represent a *clique*. Herb occupies a unique position in that he was the only student chosen by a member of the opposite sex—both Iris and Olive made him their second choice—although no boy chose him. After studying the sociogram, the teacher grouped the children about as they wished for the project, taking care to place isolates carefully. She also decided that she would actively seek ways to increase the interaction between boys and girls in the class and between the less chosen and more frequently chosen students. This illustrative sociogram, although purposely simple, indicates the relative ease and marked utility of sociometry.

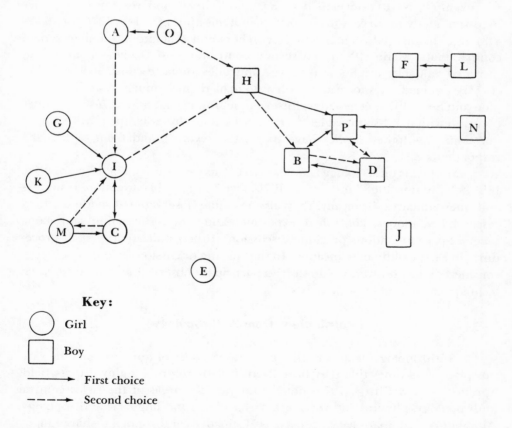

Figure 12. Sociogram Depicting Choices of Work Partners by Kindergarten Children.

Sociometry, sociograms, and target diagrams could be put to excellent use in early childhood education as one aid to understanding the social relationships existing in a school class or other grouping of youngsters. Detailed explanations of the method and sample sociograms and target diagrams can be found in several texts (Gronlund, 1976; Noll and Scannell, 1972; Stanley and Hopkins, 1972; Ten Brink, 1974; and Thorndike and Hagen, 1977). The apparent ease of using sociometric techniques should not lead one to expect that the interpretation of results is routine. Other sources of data should also be examined and considerable care taken in interpreting sociometric data.

Other Sociological Methods. Sociology has made a number of other contributions to measurement and evaluation methodology. Sociological data collection methods are of particular interest. For example, Lin (1976) and Mann (1968) detailed the documentary-historical method for extracting data from census data, archives of various types, official files, archeological evidence, personal diaries, eyewitness accounts, propaganda literature, and similar sources. Other sources have addressed the issue of how to conduct an effective survey, especially by questionnaire (a common sociological method used frequently in evaluation). For example, NORC developed many sample items and response categories used frequently in surveys (over forty such items appear in Lin, 1976, pp. 395–413) and encouraged their use by researchers and evaluators to enhance data comparability. Mann (1968) and several contributors to Denzin's book (1970) provided valuable insights into survey and questionnaire construction. Robin (1973) examined ways to secure returns to mailed questionnaires, as did Champion and Sear (1973). The latter, for example, found that higher response rates occurred with hand-stamped letters (rather than machine-stamped), with longer questionnaires (other studies have found the reverse), and from higher-SES respondents.

Most texts on sociological methods (such as Cochrane, 1973; Denzin, 1970; Lin, 1976; Mann, 1968; and Smith, 1975) give considerable attention to surveys and questionnaires. Typically, they also examine observational methods, field research techniques, controlled experimentation, and simulation and game theory. Space limitations preclude discussion of their utilization of such procedures in early childhood education. In the ensuing discussion on anthropological considerations, however, we do discuss participant observation, a field research technique also used by sociologists.

Contributions from Anthropology

Anthropology deals with the comparative study of humans in all the various places and times that they have lived. It is therefore a highly diverse field. Spradley and McCurdy (1975) noted four primary areas of the field: cultural anthropology, physical anthropology, archaeology, and linguistic anthropology. Although its comparative approach is distinctive, anthropology shares many boundaries with other fields, especially sociology. Early anthropological work usually focused on primitive or peasant societies; today, however, some anthropologists study urban cultures or subcultures. Hence, in some content and methodological areas, the dividing lines between anthropology and sociology have become blurred.

Anthropological Methodology a la Malinowski. Certain anthropological research methods, especially those involving data sources and data collection, have potential application to educational evaluation. An excellent way to get a feel for such methods is to review salient features of two of Malinowski's classics, *Argonauts of the Western Pacific* and *Coral Gardens and Their Magic,* originally published in 1922 and 1935, respectively. Living among and studying the natives on the Trobriand Islands off the eastern end of New Guinea for several years, Malinowski gave considerable attention to methodology. For example, he believed that an effective ethnographer must live for a considerable time period right among the people being studied. As he said of the Trobriand Islander: "If you want to know him, you must meet him in his yam gardens, among his palm groves or in his taro fields. You must see him digging his black or brown soil among the white outcrops of dead coral and building the fence, which surrounds his garden with a 'magical wall' of prismatic structures and triangular supports. You must follow him when, in the cool of the day, he watches the seed rise and develop within the precincts of the 'magical wall,' which at first gleams like gold among the green of the new growth and then shows bronzed or grey under the rich garland of yam foliage" (Malinowski, 1965, p. xix). Even beyond this "living in" arrangement, the anthropologist must actively pursue relevant data: "But the ethnographer has not only to spread his nets in the right place and wait for what will fall into them. He must be an active huntsman, and drive his quarry into them and follow it up to its most inaccessible lairs" (Malinowski, 1961, p. 8). He also believed that the ethnographer should be well schooled in theory, not to be burdened with preconceived ideas of what he would find but rather to be aware of "foreshadowed problems" that might require elaboration and clarification.

In Malinowski's opinion, data of three types, each with methodogical implications, should be produced by the ethnographer:

1. Data on the *organization and anatomy* of the group being studied. Malinowski believed that "each [cultural] phenomenon ought to be studied through the broadest range possible of its concrete manifestations, each studied by an exhaustive survey of detailed examples" (1961, p. 17). The enthnographer was to integrate the examples with documents either found or constructed, such as a social constitution, a genealogical chart showing kinship relations, or other similar overview tables or charts. This method of concrete, statistical documentation, as Malinowski called it, should result in a clear outline of cultural phenomena—a "firm skeleton" of the group's life—disentangling the laws and regularities from the irrelevances.
2. Data on the *imponderabilia of actual life* in the studied group. Here detailed observation was called for, possibly recorded in an ethnographic diary or through photographs. "Living in the village with no other business but to follow native life, one sees the customs, ceremonies, and transactions over and

over again, one has examples of their beliefs as they are actually lived through, and the full body and blood of actual native life fills out soon the skeleton of abstract constructions" (Malinowski, 1961, p. 18).
3. Data on the group members' *feelings, opinions, typical utterances,* characteristic narratives, folklore, and the like, as evidence of group thinking, attitudes, and values.

   These three types of data were to be used by the ethnographer to describe, understand, and sense the essence of the group being studied. In interpreting the data, and frequently when generating them, the ethnographer made use of *informants,* group members who were talked to regularly. Informants could be used in several roles. If particularly observant and skilled in conversation, they might be used to report events unseen by the ethnographer or to help analyze some group events. The informants might serve as their group's representatives or typical respondents to the ethnographer's questions or even act as census takers. Malinowski believed that the three types of data and the use of informants should lead to a final goal: "to grasp the native's point of view, his relation to life, to realize *his* vision of *his* world" (1961, p. 25). In the preface to Malinowski's book, Sir James Fraser put it well by noting Malinowski's drive to take full account of the complexity of human nature and to see it "in the round and not in the flat."

   The methods endorsed by Malinowski represent a sharp departure from much we have already presented in this book. Instead of remaining detached and aloof to retain objectivity, the anthropologist immerses himself in a culture, takes an active participatory role, and tries to remain objective despite this immersion and participation. Rather than focusing on test performance to intuit a person's learning or attitudes or to estimate the effects of an event, the anthropologist is more likely to ask for persons' opinions directly, or to ask trusted informants for their interpretations. In this regard, Malinowski struck an early blow for what is coming to be called the *constructiveness approach* (Magoon, 1977). In essence, this view assumes that persons or groups being studied or evaluated are knowing beings and that their knowledge has "a complex set of referents and meanings that also must be taken into account when the scientist is studying human actions or behavior. A second assumption, independent of the first, is that the locus of control over much so-called intelligent behavior resides initially with the subjects themselves" (Magoon, 1977, p. 652). Malinowski justified fairly well a philosophical base for his research orientation and for its associated methods. Modern-day anthropologists owe much to his insight and methods, although they now also use additional techniques such as life histories or autobiographies of some group members, case studies of individuals, and even projective tests and questionnaires (Spradley and McCurdy, 1975).

   Documentation and Degree of Observer Participation. Two aspects of the anthropological perspective deserve elaboration because of their close relationship to evaluation. Anthropology's emphasis on careful documentation clearly yields much data for various evaluation purposes. This emphasis on documentation is similar to that found in the CIPP evaluation framework (Chapter Nine). The feasibility of the anthropological participant-observer role for evaluation (or for research efforts) remains a perplexing issue. This issue principally concerns the objectivity of the evaluator, essentially the issue raised about Stake's responsive evaluator (Chapter Nine). That other issues also arise was made clear in McCall's and Simmons' edited book (1969) on participant observation. From that source, Gold's (1969) article on field observation roles highlighted several trade-offs as one moved along the continuum from complete observer to complete participant. For example, the field worker in the complete observer role has the advantages of being detached, which should enhance objectivity, and of taking little self-risk. Limitations he encounters are the danger of ethnocentrism, a lack of meaningful interactions with informants, and the danger of misunderstanding the observed events or people (in this connection, *The Silent Language*, Hall, 1959, is very relevant). By contrast, the field worker in the role of complete participant has the benefits of becoming privy to information that might otherwise be denied him and of having significant interactions with informants (as they perceive him as "one of them" and not as an observer at all). At the same time, the field worker risks "going native," which would reduce his objectivity and render his reporting suspect; further, if he conceals his research or evaluation purpose, the complete participant may face an ethical dilemma.

An actual example is enlightening. Everhart (1977) spent two years in a junior high school as an observer-evaluator and found his role shifting from observer to friend, especially becoming a friend to his student informants. He believed he obtained qualitatively different data as a friend than he had obtained as a stranger. The liability he found in being a friend, however, was "the propensity for the observer to lose his sensitivity, for his senses to be dulled, and for him to be less aware of the significance of everyday behavior. He may be too intimately involved with his informants, thereby unable to order their world in a way any different from their own ordering" (Everhart, 1977, p. 14).

Mann (1968) provided a different perspective on observer participation. For four different observational methods of obtaining data on people, he characterized the observer's control of, and participation in, the research or evaluation situation:

Principal Methodology	*Control of Situation*	*Direct Participation by Observer*
Laboratory observation of contrived situation	Maximum	Minimum
Interview	Maximum	Maximum
Naturalistic observation such as child watching	Minimum	Minimum
Participant observation	Minimum	Maximum

Of course, these principal methodologies are not mutually exclusive, and those of an anthropological persuasion might at times use all but the laboratory observation. It is obvious, too, that "participant observation" might take quite different forms in varying situations—for example, with respect to the amount of direct observer participation.

Application to Educational Research and Evaluation. Anthropology's influence on educational research and evaluation is apparent in a small but growing number of methodological pronouncements and reported research and evaluations (for example, see Everhart, 1975; the comprehensive table in Magoon, 1977; and Wolcott, 1976). Space limitations permit us to review only a few examples from research and evaluation. Specifically, we focus on the work of Philip Jackson and that of Louis Smith and his colleagues, and then describe the illuminative and literary approaches to evaluation.

Jackson (1968, 1974) spent much time observing in elementary schools, using a more naturalistic than participatory style. He noted that the process was more conducive to hypothesis development than to hypothesis testing (others, such as Lutz and Ramsey, 1974, have agreed). Further, he believed that many school and teaching practices of long standing were probably quite useful even though they might be only weakly defended as customary or traditional practices. "But even custom and tradition are functional, as every anthropologist knows, in the maintenance of a social institution. The baring of what might be thought of as the tacit rationale underlying many current practices may be one of the chief contributions of naturalistic studies to the field of education. We need help in seeing that many apparently senseless ways of doing things in schools are not so senseless at all" (Jackson, 1974, p. 90). Jackson also indicated that his research and similar efforts allowed him to reach two inescapable conclusions: first, that schools and their operations were "incredibly complex," and second, that educators are unaware of "the tangle of forces in which they are enmeshed. As a consequence, they often are lured by simplified schemes and the promise of miracle cures for our educational ailments" (Jackson, 1974, p. 86). Elsewhere, this irrational belief in miracle cures has been dubbed *miracle monomania* (Goodwin and Klausmeier, 1975).

Using a similar combination of anthropological and sociological methods, Henry (1971) observed in classrooms of school-disadvantaged children. Skillfully, he used his observations to note the vulnerability of students and teachers alike, to question Piaget's pronouncements on egocentrism in young children's language, and to describe "readiness for triggering" (the tendency of American school children to become excited and feverish while engaging in almost any school activity that is not held under strict teacher control).

A more directly anthropological study, mentioned at the conclusion of Chapter Four, centered on a class of seventh-graders in a slum school (Smith, 1967; and Smith and Geoffrey, 1968). For one semester, Smith, an educational psychologist, observed the class taught by Geoffrey:

> Any endeavor is partially known by its label. This research, in its broadest scope, used the technique of direct observation of an ongoing, naturalistic situation. To say that we collected 'anecdotal records' of the

events of the classroom casts the project in a mildly disreputable and trivial light. Such a label makes our work seem much less important than our own feelings reflected at the time. Consequently, when one of our colleagues suggested that we were engaged in the 'microethnography of the classroom,' we knew immediately that this was what we were doing, that it was high-sounding and important. Beyond the emotional quality of the label, it does suggest two other points of importance. First, we were, as we have indicated, trying to describe carefully the small social system. Secondly, we pursued our problem quite consciously as a social anthropologist might have done [Smith and Geoffrey, 1968, p. 3].

Of greatest relevance here are the components of Smith and Geoffrey's microethnographic methodology. Uniquely, both external and internal observers were used. Smith served as an external, nonparticipating observer, while Geoffrey was very much an internal or participant observer, briefly recording significant events as he actually taught the class. This arrangement produced two perspectives on the functioning of the class. In addition to Geoffrey's sketchy notes, Smith kept three kinds of record: (1) longhand descriptions of classroom events with inferences and interpretive comments bracketed off for easy identification; (2) field note summaries of the observations and interpretations, including reflections on broader school events, initially taped by Smith as he drove to and from school each day; and (3) documents such as classroom materials, occasional work samples, sociometric and other test results, parent notes, and the like. Using this data base, and their unique outsider-insider perspectives, Smith and Geoffrey constructed a vivid portrayal of the functioning of the class, generated provocative hypotheses to guide future studies, and commented generously on their classroom analysis methodology. Their debt to Malinowski was apparent as they wrote of foreshadowed problems, and they were fascinated by the vividness and concreteness of the raw data.

Smith also used a distinctive anthropological technique, the field study, to evaluate the introduction of computer-assisted instruction (CAI) into an isolated rural school district (Smith and Pohland, 1974). Recalling Malinowski's dedicated observation of the Trobriand Islanders in Melanesia, Smith and Pohland noted: "So it was with CAI. Our Melanesia was the Rural Mountains; the school children of the region our Trobrianders. Our yam gardens were the classrooms, and our palm groves and taro fields the broom closets, special rooms, and odd corners that housed the teletype terminals. We, too, noted the 'magical wall of prismatic structures and triangular supports' that enclosed CAI. In the broadest sense that 'wall' was the culture of the region itself" (1974, p. 6). The field study methodology involved specification of foreshadowed problems, long observation periods (especially of children at the teletype terminals), field notes, informal interviews, and documents (including computer printouts of machine-child interactions).

Actually, three types of evaluation were utilized with the CAI program. In addition to the anthropologically oriented field study, experimental design procedures (assessing academic achievement via pre- and post-tests and control groups) and survey methods (assessing attitudes of students, teachers, and parents) also were used. Data generated in the field study resulted in two major findings. First, it was documented that the CAI program was beset with technical problems and ran only sporadically throughout the school year. The frustration that resulted was captured well in the case of a young girl erroneously instructed by the computer to "Cry again" (instead of "Try again"), whereupon she told her teacher, "I could just cry again and again." Second, the field study results indicated major variance among the teachers in their use of the CAI program to complement their regular in-class math instruction. This variance was partly due to the undependability of the CAI equipment, but also reflected many teachers' inability or reluctance to break from textbook-centered teaching of math and considerable in-class drill (even though CAI was supposed to be used for drill). Several other teachers abandoned the traditional drill and text approach and creatively approached math as a discovery process.

Smith and Pohland also addressed anthropological field work at a more general level. For example, they classified their study and five other field studies in terms of their emphasis on description via narration, generation of theory, testing of theory, and quantification of data. Five of the six studies placed high emphasis on descriptive narrative; Smith and Pohland's description of CAI is very concrete and, at the same time, elaborate. Less, but still considerable, emphasis on theory generation was noted in the field studies, with even less emphasis yet on theory testing and data quantification (Smith and Pohland rated their own field study as "low emphasis" on these last two criteria). In all, Smith and Pohland's study stands as a provocative application of anthropological methods to educational evaluation. Note too that certain features of this evaluation match well Stake's responsive evaluation framework (Chapter Nine) and his recent endorsement of a case study approach (Stake, 1978). Interested readers also should note the recent *Case Studies in Science Education* (Stake and Easley, 1978; also see Denny, 1978 a, b).

Parlett and Hamilton (1976) have proposed an *illuminative evaluation approach* to assessing innovations; the approach is distinctively anthropological and, to a considerable extent, is also aligned with Stake's responsive evaluation orientation. Under this paradigm, the overriding purpose of evaluation is to illuminate problems, issues, and significant program features, rather than to judge worth. Evaluation is conceived as flexible, attentive to program uniqueness, and focused on description and interpretation rather than on measurement, prediction, and comparison. Believing that an innovative program cannot be separated from the total learning milieu and instructional system in which it is embedded, the proponents of illuminative evaluation refuse to treat the program as a self-contained phenomenon. "At the outset, the researcher is concerned to familiarize himself thoroughly with the day-to-day reality of the setting or settings that he is studying. In this he is similar to social anthropologists or to natural historians. Like them he makes no attempt to manipulate, control, or eliminate situational variables, but takes as given the complex scene he encounters. His chief task is to unravel it, isolate its significant features, delineate cycles of cause and effect, and comprehend relationships between beliefs and practices and between organizational patterns and the responses of individuals. Since illuminative evaluation concentrates on examining the innovation as an integral part of the learning milieu, there is a definite emphasis both on observation at the classroom level and on interviewing participating instructors and students" (Parlett and Hamilton, 1976, p. 147).

An illuminative evaluation process typically consists of three stages: the evaluator (1) observes, (2) inquires further into phenomena selected for sustained and intensive inquiry, and (3) then seeks to explain. The process results in the assembly of an information profile containing four types of datum: (1) documentary and background, (2) observational, (3) interview, and (4) questionnaire and test. During the process, considerable emphasis is placed on the evaluator's use of intellectual prowess and interpretative insight. Since much of the data collection contemplated involves interaction with program staff and participants, the evaluator must also possess interpersonal skills.

Not as distinctly anthropological as illuminative evaluation, the *literary evaluation approach* nevertheless exhibits some similar characteristics, particularly in terms of emphasizing full narrative reports. Numerical data tend to be avoided for the most part; rather, the evaluation report is written in a nontechnical, highly descriptive, and highly interpretive style. To our knowledge, no one has detailed the essentials of a literary evaluation approach. However, in the AERA Monograph Series on Curriculum Evaluation, a literary or narrative evaluation example was provided, "The First Probe" (Brauner, 1974). In a vivid and almost novelistic style, Brauner described an extended outing for over fifty "college graduates with a common interest in architecture." The outing involved a number of high-intensity experiences: being isolated in the wilderness for several days with no provisions for food or shelter; examining in depth both a small port town and a large urban city; establishing a social and cultural center in a large abandoned kiln; and the like. Evaluative statements were woven into the narrative account. Reacting to the evaluation report, Sjogren observed:

> Brauner's style is literary and quite interpretive. No objective numerical data are presented, but my reading of it convinced me that some very important outcomes were achieved by the participants in the experience. I doubt that these outcomes were ever stated in behavioral terms. . . . Perhaps the style of some educational programs is such that a particular type of evaluation should be used. Would another type of evaluation in this setting have been so intrusive as to seriously inhibit the program itself? After reading the paper, I wondered what would have happened if somebody had insisted on pre- and posttesting or questionnaires or had forced any structuring of the program through its evaluation. The style and content of the Brauner paper would be useful for certain audiences. Those planning a similar program would gain much useful information. The participants could use it for reflection, the sponsors for deciding whether promises were kept. The literary style makes more interesting reading than the technical style and may be read with understanding by a lay audience. The danger of the literary style is apparent, however. Certainly overinterpretation can occur. The many qualifications that would be inserted by the technical writer are often absent in literary efforts [Sjogren, 1974, p. 3].

Another example of a literary evaluation report, although containing some questionnaire results, appeared in a series of articles published in the *Los Angeles Times* (Greenwood, McCurdy, and Durant, 1973). In typical journalistic form, the articles described, interpreted, and evaluated student life at an urban high school.

Eisner (1972), who affirmed a need for something like the literary approach to evaluation, examined the procedures and techniques of art criticism and proposed them as a complement to quantitative evaluation procedures. He indicated that two skills were needed to be a competent critic:

> First, he must have developed highly refined visual sensibilities; that is, he must be able to see the elements that constitute a whole and their interplay. Second, he must be capable of rendering his perceptions into a language that makes it possible for others less perceptive than he to see qualities and aspects of the work that they would otherwise overlook. The critic, like a good teacher or book, directs attention to the subtle, he points out and articulates, he vivifies perception.
>
> This vivification of perception which it is the critic's office to further is carried out by a particular use of language. It is quite clear that our discourse is not as differentiated as our sensibilities. We experience more than we can describe. Thus, what the critic must do is not to attempt to replicate the visual, dramatic, or musical work verbally, but to provide a rendering of them through the use of poetic language. The vehicles the critic employs are suggestion, simile, and metaphor. These poetic vehicles carry the viewer to a heightened perception of the phenomena [Eisner, 1972, pp. 585–586].

It would seem that persons using the literary evaluation method do embody much that Eisner envisioned. Although their levels of experience and skill in the area being evaluated often might not match the levels expected in art critics, their inclination toward poetic language is obvious.

The potential applications of anthropological methods to evaluation in early childhood education are rather obvious and will not be belabored here. However, recall from Chapter Four the suggestion that Smith and Geoffrey's participant-nonparticipant observer team might have considerable utility in early childhood evaluation. Note further that the less formal give-and-take between evaluator and subject and the emphasis on long-term intensive involvement (both implied in the anthropological orientation) are in harmony with the outlook of many early childhood educators.

A final important bond between anthropology and early childhood education is the importance for each of cross-cultural investigations. Anthropology relies heavily on cross-cultural comparisons. Similarly, early childhood education is increasingly adopting a cross-cultural perspective, with regard to both program characteristics (Austin, 1976) and developmental characteristics of children (Glick, 1975). It would seem that evaluations for early childhood education programs could be designed more sensitively if the design team had an adequate appreciation of cross-cultural information. For example, take an actual anthropological study conducted in a Mexican village (Lewis, 1951). A commonly held assumption by most segments of our society is that thinking is a desirable activity—and certainly not detrimental, unless engaged in to a point of extreme fatigue. Likewise, "thinking hard" while taking a test or engaging in analogous mental performance is usually considered an appropriate challenge for children and adults. Contrast this view to one observed in Tepoztlan, Mexico, as children were given individual psychological tests: "The children did not enjoy being the center of attention in the testing situation. They were shy, ill at ease, and unaccustomed to taking tests involving much talking, and they soon became weary with the effort of expressing themselves. There is a general feeling in the village that it is not good for a person to study or think too much, and the many questions were *molestia* (a bother). One mother objected to the continuation of a test on the grounds that *se calienta la cabeza,* that is, the child's head would get too hot from thinking so much" (Lewis, 1951, pp. 307–308). Being aware that such an attitude might exist in some parents, particularly in certain American subcultures, could make an evaluator significantly more perceptive and sensitive when, say, interviewing parents or developing questionnaires to be responded to by parents. Overall, anthropological considerations could serve to render many evaluations in early childhood education more effective.

Contributions from Ecological and Environmental Psychology

Ecological psychology has been defined as "the branch of psychology that deals with the behavior and psychological situations of designated persons under natural conditions, that is, without input from the investigator" (Barker, 1978, p. 49). In Chapter Four, "Observational Measurement," we introduced field studies of this persuasion conducted by Barker, Wright, Gump, and others, all of whom had some relationship with the Midwest Psychological Field Station in Oskaloosa, Kansas (Barker, 1963, 1968, 1978). These studies featured lengthy specimen records of behavior as it occurred in natural settings, such as a seven-year-old boy's activities during a single day (Barker and Wright, 1951) and the daily routine established in six third-grade classrooms (Gump, 1969).

Environmental psychology has been defined by Proshansky, Ittelson, and Rivlin (somewhat reluctantly, because of the newness of the field and the absence of any well-defined theory) as "the study of human behavior in relation to the man-ordered and man-defined environment" (1970, p. 5). In their edited book (1970), they considered environmental psychology studies from four areas: (1) basic psychological processes (such as perception, cognition, learning, and emotion) in relation to the environment; (2) individual needs in the organization of the environment (such as privacy and territoriality); (3) social interactions and institutions in relation to environmental design; and (4) environmental planning. The multidisciplinary nature of environmental psychology is striking; for example, in Proshansky, Ittelson, and Rivlin's edited book, contributions are made by psychologists, sociologists, anthropologists, psychiatrists, biologists, geographers, designers, and architects.

We consider ecological and environmental psychology together in this section since their similarities appear more pronounced then their differences. Both focus on the environmental context of human behavior. Both are new fields of study, which borrow heavily from existing disciplines (this is especially true for environmental psychology). Both make use of observational measurement, although this is more a predominant methodology in ecological psychology. Both are included here for the same important contribution to evaluation in early childhood education—their emphasis on the influence of environment on behavior and on assessing environmental settings. Note too that both fields address well societal areas that currently are of great concern—conservation of plant and animal life; pollution of water, air, and urban areas; the scarcity of many natural resources; and the quality-of-life "trade-offs" that invariably seem to accompany technological "progress" and resulting environmental change.

Full coverage of the contributions from these two fields is not feasible. Rather, we consider the assessment of settings, the assessment of climate, and the application of the field's methodology in education. In the following discussion, somewhat greater emphasis is placed on environmental psychology as several aspects of ecological psychology overlap with content already presented in Chapter Four.

Measurement of Places and Settings. Psychology traditionally has emphasized the measurement of individuals' characteristics and, less frequently, characteristics of groups. Relatively little attention has been given to measuring settings or climates.

> At long last, the assessment of environments is beginning to gain its proper share of scientific investigation. That the systematic description of environments has previously received disproportionately less attention than the description of persons has been consistently noted in critical reviews of psychological assessment. . . . Places are similar to persons in being complex, multidimensional entities. Indeed, adaptation of concepts and techniques from the field of personality assessment offers a tremendous methodological resource for the assessment of environments.
>
> In studies of the interplay between human behavior and the everyday physical environment, comprehensive, standard techniques must be available for assessing systematic variation in environments as well as in behaviors. Research on environmental description and evaluation seeks to identify not only what environments are preferred or not preferred by various observers, but also what descriptive responses of the observers mediate their preferences and, most pertinently, what specific environmental characteristics are associated with both descriptive and evaluative appraisals [Craik, 1971, p. 40].

In his comprehensive review of the assessment of settings, Craik (1971) identified five focal points for such assessment:

1. The physical and spatial properties of places (such as characteristics of flood plains, drought regions, and camp sites).
2. The organization of material artifacts of places (like the furnishings or decor in a home).

3. The traits of places (for example, the nature of buildings or rooms).
4. The behavioral attributes of places, that is, the stable activity patterns of humans that tend to occur in a given place (such as their holding power or capability of attracting persons and keeping them, the variety and frequency of behaviors occurring there, and the like).
5. The institutional attributes of places (like climate or spirit).

Craik provided numerous examples of each approach to assessing places, and the interested reader is directed to his review and related schemes, such as Bersoff's psychosituational assessment (1973). Note that many of the works in ecological psychology (such as Barker, 1968, 1969, 1978; Barker and Wright, 1951; Gump, 1969; and Willems and Raush, 1969) fit nicely under Craik's fourth category. His second and third categories were introduced earlier in the chapter in the form of the socioeconomic status measures that assessed the home environment in terms of the presence or absence of specified items, and the home's location and size. At the conclusion of this section on ecological and environmental psychology, we present a number of examples of assessments of educational settings, each of which can be related to one or more of Craik's categories.

Wolf (1966) has provided an interesting new perspective on environmental assessment, as well as an accompanying methodology. He conceptualized the environment as being composed of multiple subenvironments, each influencing the development of a specific characteristic. Thus, different subenvironments were conceived for the development of intelligence, achievement, independence, stature, and so forth. He also determined to assess these subenvironments, not in terms of parents' education, occupation, income, and the like, but in terms of what parents did in their interactions with their children. Focusing on the subenvironments for the development of academic achievement and of general intelligence, he scoured the research literature in child development, learning theory, motivation, and psychometry for variables probably related to each characteristic. Those identified for the academic achievement subenvironment were the following:

1. The atmosphere created for achievement motivation.
2. The opportunities established for verbal development.
3. The assistance given in overcoming academic difficulties.
4. The activity level of individuals in the environment.
5. The intellectual level in the environment.
6. The work habits expected of the individual.

In similar fashion, three general intelligence subenvironment variables were identified:

1. The stimulation supplied for intellectual development.
2. The opportunities established for, and emphasis on, verbal development.
3. The provision for learning in varied situations.

For each of these variables, Wolf again examined the research literature and developed a list of process (interaction) characteristics detailing specific parent behaviors. For example, for "the atmosphere created for achievement motivation," he listed the following process characteristics: "the parental aspirations for the child's education; the parents' own aspirations; parental concern for academic achievement; the social press in the home for academic achievement; the rewards accorded academic accomplishments; parental knowledge of the educational progress of the child; and the preparations made for the attainment of educational goals" (Wolf, 1966, p. 494). In a related manner, "the opportunities established for, and emphasis on, verbal development" was particularized as: "the emphasis on use of language in a variety of situations; the opportunities provided for enlarging vocabulary; parental emphasis on correctness of usage; and the quality of language models available" (Wolf, 1966, p. 495).

The resulting parent behaviors were specific enough to be measurable and were built into a structured interview to be responded to by the mother or by both parents. In the interviews, a persistent theme was avoiding what parents *were* while concentrating on what parents *actually did* with their children as related to the variables making up academic achievement and general intelligence. Starting with all the fifth-graders in a midwestern community, Wolf used a stratified random sampling plan to select sixty homes for interviewing—homes representative of, and proportional to, each social class grouping in the United States. Each home received two total subenvironmental ratings—one for academic achievement and one for general intelligence. Then, achievement and intelligence test scores for the sixty fifth-graders whose homes were visited were obtained from the school files. The correlation observed between the intelligence subenvironment ratings and the students' intelligence scores was .69, while the academic achievement subenvironment ratings and students' achievement scores correlated .80. These very substantial correlations are considerably higher than those typically observed between socioeconomic status and intelligence and achievement test performance. Wolf concluded, "as we make use of the conception that a single physical environment may consist of a number of subenvironments and seek to develop measurement procedures that capture the operant social and psychological conditions and processes in an environment, we should be able to greatly increase our understanding of the process of how individual characteristics are developed and maintained. Only when we have such understanding can we develop more adequate theories of behavior, and only then can we determine how particular characteristics can be maintained or altered" (1966, p. 502).

Measurement of Climate. Assessing the climate of an institution or organization (essentially, Craik's fifth category) is exemplified well in some recent work. The start of a theoretical base underlying classroom climates and learning environments has appeared (Walberg, 1977), as have reviews and descriptions of instruments available to assess climate (Anderson and Walberg, 1974; Craik, 1971; Moos, 1973, 1975a, b; Nielsen and Kirk, 1974; and Walberg, 1974).

Moos (1973) lauded the pioneering efforts of Barker and his associates to demonstrate that behavior settings could have pervasive effects on individuals. Unlike them, however, Moos (1975a, b) developed and used questionnaire methods rather than observation. He assessed the unique "personalities" of four types of environment: treatment (hospital and community psychiatric programs); total institution (correctional institutions and military training units); community setting (social, task-oriented, and therapeutic groups; work milieus; and families); and educational (university student groups living in dormitories, sororities, and fraternities; and junior high and high school classrooms). Within these environments, Moos charted several subscales and aggregated them to make statements about the relationship, personal development, and system maintenance and change dimensions present. For example, Trickett and Moos (1973) used the Classroom Environment Scale to contrast the climates in two high school classes; one class was found higher on the involvement, affiliation, and teacher support subscales (the relationship dimension), lower in task orientation and competition (the personal development dimension), and lower in order and organization, rule clarity, and teacher control, but much higher in innovation (the system maintenance and change dimension). More recently, Moos (1978) has examined the social environments of 200 secondary school classes. Cluster analysis (a technique similar to factor analysis) differentiated five types of class—those oriented toward control, innovation, affiliation, task, and competition—each with associated patterns of student satisfaction and mood, and teacher satisfaction. (See also Moos, 1979.) Moos has not extended his investigations to younger children (to our knowledge), possibly because of the likely requirement for substantial methodological alterations.

Nielsen and Kirk (1974), examining measures of classroom climate, noted the predominance of two methodologies: observational and questionnaire. They reviewed numerous observation systems, such as the Climate Index (Withall, 1949), the Observation Schedule and Record or OSCAR (Medley and Mitzel, 1958), and the Interaction Analysis System (Flanders, 1968), which we included in Chapter Four. They also surveyed numerous self-report questionnaires, including the above-mentioned Classroom Environment Scale (Trickett and Moos, 1973) and the Elementary School Environment Survey (Sinclair, 1969). While noting some advances in measuring classroom climate, Nielsen and Kirk generally were concerned about the insufficient validation of several of the climate indexes and, particularly, about the failure of the developers to relate outcomes on their climate measures to cognitive achievement and attitude development in classrooms. Other questionnaire measures of note that deal with classroom conditions are the following:

1. The Learning Environment Inventory or LEI (Anderson, 1971), a 105-item instrument with fifteen subscales designed for secondary students.
2. The Class Activities Questionnaire (Steele, House, and Kerins, 1971), which is similar to the LEI and which uniquely measures classroom emphasis on the several levels of Bloom's cognitive taxonomy (1956).
3. My Class Inventory (G. J. Anderson, 1973), a scaled-down version of the LEI

that contains forty-five items and five subscales (friction, competitiveness, difficulty, satisfaction, and cohesiveness) and is appropriate for six- to twelve-year-old students.

A somewhat different approach to climate is a rating scale to measure *social weather,* the overall social treatment given an individual (Simpson, 1963). Ratings are made in three component areas, each composed of three subscales:

1. Warmth, the emotional tone expressed toward the child (Acceptance, Affectionateness, and Approval subscales).
2. Tendance, the direct efforts made for the child (Attention, Assistance, and Communication subscales).
3. Indulgence, the range of freedom allowed the child (Adaption, Privilege, and Choice subscales).

Simpson found that the social weather of six preschoolers differed from that of six school-age children in most behavior settings that they shared.

Walberg and Thomas (1972) conducted a study illustrative of those measuring social climate, a study highly pertinent to early childhood education. It compared open education classes in Great Britain and the United States with each other and with traditional U.S. classes. Explicit statements specifying open classroom characteristics were drawn from open education publications and sent to twenty-nine prominent open educators, who could agree or disagree with the statements and suggest changes. Fifty statements that survived this expert review and that described behaviors that could be readily observed in classrooms were used to build an observation rating scale and a parallel teacher questionnaire.

About twenty classrooms of each type (U.S. open, Great Britain open, and U.S. traditional) were deliberately selected to include major cities, suburban areas, and small towns, with equivalent representation of lower- and middle-class schools for each of the three types. Only classes for five- to seven-year-old children were included in the sample. Trained observers recorded multiple classroom sessions for each site, and teachers at each site responded to the questionnaire. These measures yielded the climate patterns displayed in Figure 13; questionnaire results are on the left side of the figure, and observation data are plotted on the right. The vertical 0 line represents the average data for the U.S. traditional classes, while the horizontal scale shows differences between group means in standard deviation units. The figure demonstrates the following:

1. The questionnaire and observation methodologies yielded, for the most part, comparable data (that is, the patterns on the left and right of the figure are similar).
2. The open classes in Great Britain and the United States were highly similar in terms of climate, especially on the observation criteria.

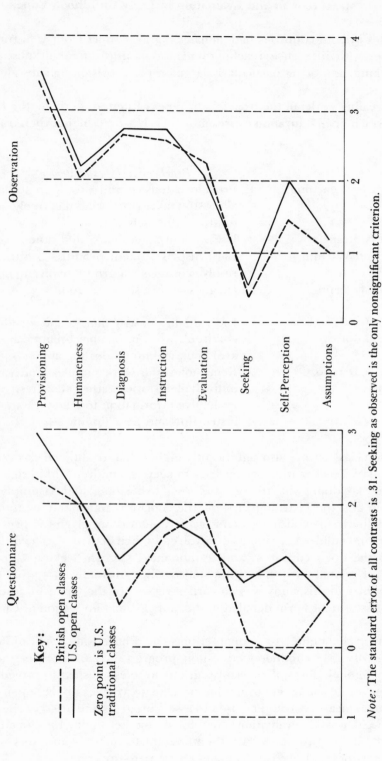

Note: The standard error of all contrasts is .31. Seeking as observed is the only nonsignificant criterion.

Source: Walberg and Thomas, 1972, p. 206.

Figure 13. Standardized Contrasts of Classroom Climates Found in U.S. and British Open Education Classes with Those Found in Traditional Classes.

3. Open classes in both countries had climates highly distinct from U.S. traditional classes, with differences reaching statistical significance for all subscales except Seeking, and being particularly large on the Provisioning subscale.

It is revealing to detail the practices or types of item underlying the five subscales on which open education classes most clearly scored higher than traditional classes:

Theme or Subscale	*Practices or Types of Item*
1. Provisioning for Learning	1. Provide extensive and diverse materials; allow students to move and talk freely, and to group themselves.
2. Humaneness, Respect, Openness, and Warmth	2. Use student-made books and other materials; display student products profusely; resolve conflicts via group involvement.
3. Diagnosis of Learning Events	3. Diagnose via close observation.
4. Instruction, Guidance, and Extension of Learning	4. Individualize instruction; avoid dividing children's work into subject-matter areas; avoid curriculum guides for direction.
5. Evaluation of Diagnostic Information	5. Keep notes and work samples, and write individual histories rather than test; use evaluative information to guide classroom instruction and provisioning.

Open education classes were also significantly higher than traditional classes on Self-Perception of Teacher (the teacher tries to keep all children within sight to ensure that they are doing what they are supposed to be doing) and Assumptions about Children and the Learning Process (the climate is warm and accepting, behavior guidelines are explicit, academic achievement is not given top priority by the teacher, and children are intensely involved in their activities). The difference between the open education and traditional classes on Seeking Opportunities for Professional Growth was not statistically significant. (Note that the questionnaire used in this study was an earlier version of the Open Education Teacher Self-Assessment Form detailed in the Staff Evaluation section of Chapter Ten.)

Measuring climate in educational settings could have wide application in the evaluation of early childhood education programs, as the Walberg and Thomas study implies. Thus, if special programs were established to provide a particular type of learning environment or climate (for example, open or humane), climate measures could be used to assess progress and areas of special strength and weakness. Or evaluation might focus on determining the climate in many early childhood programs, and then attempt to match youngsters with special characteristics and needs to climate-appropriate programs.

Application to Educational Settings. We now present, in brief form, a number of examples of actual and potential applications of ecological and environmental psychology to early childhood education. In some cases, the examples actually involved young children—in other cases, we cite the example and note its potential application in early childhood settings. Note that most of the applications fall under Craik's (1971) fourth category, the behavioral attributes of places.

Barker and Gump (1964), comparing students' experiences in large and small high schools, found more varieties of instruction in large schools but no clear evidence that average students experienced a broader range of academic classes. Students in large schools participated slightly more often in out-of-class activities, but students in small schools clearly experienced a larger variety of participation. The latter students performed in twice as many responsible positions (because the school setting was undermanned), reported a greater sense of responsibility for school affairs, and reported experiencing more direct satisfaction from meeting challenges, developing competence, and establishing close cooperation with peers. These outcomes would not have been predicted easily. An obvious application would be to examine analogous behaviors for young children in large and small daycare centers, preschools, elementary schools, and the like.

One such application has been made to large and small daycare centers (Prescott, 1970; and Prescott and Jones, 1967). A random sample of fifty full-day care centers, public and private, were observed. Compared with small centers, large centers of over sixty children placed more emphasis on rules and routine guidance, exhibited more teacher control and restraint (over twice the amount found in small centers), offered little participation in wide age-range groups, provided limited opportunities for play and child-initiation, and stimulated little interest or enthusiastic involvement by children. It was concluded: "In the early years a child's experience and personal resources are too limited for him to benefit from care which is impersonal and highly rule-oriented or from care which communicates sharp discrepancies between the home and the daycare center. The establishment of the large center is an unimaginative solution to a need that requires a diversity of alternatives which can guarantee rich, personal child-rearing environments" (Prescott, 1970, p. 2). More recent work of a similar nature has been conducted (Prescott, and others, 1975).

Kelly (1969), using ecological psychology methods, studied two similar-size high schools, one "constant" with less than 10 percent of the entrants leaving during the school year and one "fluid" with 42 percent leaving. Three observation sites, and the behaviors recorded in each, were hallways (size and amount of group membership, dress, and general behavior), cafeterias (behavior during lunch, such as table-hopping, and the proportion of males and females at each table), and the main office (number of faculty and students entering the main office and the proportion of these that went into the principal's private office). Different behavior was observed in the two school environments. Behavior in the constant school was characterized by small groups (two to four), uniform dress and grooming, restrained and "low-level commentary" speech, sedate movement, small groups and little table-hopping at lunch, and relatively infrequent entrance into the offices (range of 1 to 15 persons entering the main office in the three-minute observation periods). The fluid school featured larger groupings, considerable variability in dress, make-up, and hair style, noisy and active communication (or none at all), active movement, varying group membership at lunch with much noise and table-hopping, and frequent office entrance (a range of 30 to 110 entrances into the main office in the three-minute observation periods). The "new kid in school" differences were noteworthy. In the constant school, new students received the silent treatment—they had to conform to the prevailing norms before being accepted, although acceptance was facilitated if they possessed a visible competence or skill in short supply. In the fluid school, new students were greeted enthusiastically by an informal committee of the "welcome-wagon" variety that provided "inside" information on the school's operation and encouraged newcomers to participate in various or innovative activities. Of interest are the patterns of behavior that might emerge in early childhood educational settings that were constant or fluid.

Procedures exist for evaluating the use of different types of building space. Working from an environmental psychology orientation, Sommer (1970) used observations and questionnaires to investigate spaces within university libraries in terms of their desirable and undesirable features as study areas. Both social or psychological factors and physical factors were identified and measured. Factors found desirable were adequate table size, good table arrangement, more quiet, and sufficient internal lighting, while leading undesirable factors were distractions and activity, and noise. Libraries, schools, and other environments have also been studied by Mehrabian (1976), who offered ideas on better utilization of such space. For example, he caustically observed, "Those who call for a rigid, Spartan, no-nonsense school environment are in effect urging that an unpreferred environment be used to promote the performance of unpreferred tasks" (Mehrabian, 1976, p. 153); he recommended, instead, making the school environment pleasant and "sufficiently loaded" (that is, stimulating, unrestrictive, and pleasant). McLean (1975) devised a number of procedures, observational and rating, to evaluate "the quality of a school as a place where the arts might thrive." He categorized four areas or themes for evaluation of a school's support of the arts: environment (quantity, diversity, excellence, originality, and vitality); workspace (suitability, accessibility, and quantity and quality of equipment and supplies); output (quantity, diversity, excellence, and originality); and internal and external support (teachers, rewards, exhibitions, and participation). Spaces designed for educational use by young children could be evaluated using procedures analogous to those of Sommer, Mehrabian, and McLean.

Several approaches to the evaluation of buildings themselves, often schools, have been reviewed by Canter (1975). With regard to teacher satisfaction with a building, he noted a Scottish study that demonstrated a sharp, steady reduction in satisfaction during the five years after a new building was occupied. However, satisfaction increased proportional to the changes made in the building after it was built. (In this regard, also see Richardson, 1970.) Canter identified three principal factors involved in the teachers' reactions, all related to their classrooms: overall atmospheric quality (satisfaction with the classroom, its lighting, view, heating, and ventilation); position (centrality, convenience, and isolation); and freedom from noise and distractions. More generally, Canter found evaluations focusing on some combination of eight building aspects: esthetic quality, friendliness, organization, potency (that is, rugged or delicate), space, ornateness, neatness, and size. Such evaluations usually involved taking persons to buildings that were to be rated or evaluated, or providing a simulation of the building by using models, slides, photographs, or some other mediated means (for example, see Ittelson and others, 1974; and Winkel and Sasanoff, 1970). From his work, Canter speculated that three key processes were involved in preferences for buildings:

1. The existing environmental context has a marked influence upon preferences in the direction of preference for the existing environment.
2. The role of the person within the building influences his environmental preferences.
3. The degree to which a person is able to act upon and modify a building may well influence his preference for it [Canter, 1975, p. 178].

Obviously, buildings designed for young children's educational programs could be evaluated in similar ways, using the perceptions of child development and educational experts, teachers of young children, and the children themselves. The latter's perceptions might be particularly insightful. This was the case with Margie, an urban elementary school black confidante of Coles (1969); she talked candidly about "those places they call schools," and her testimony underscored the bleakness of many schools.

Environmental and ecological psychologists have also studied the influence of various class settings and conditions on behavior. Gump's (1969) analysis of activities in third-grade classrooms, described more fully in Chapter Four, is a good case in point (and, more generally, see Gump, 1975). Lott and Sommer (1973) examined how college students seated themselves in relation to a person of higher, lower, or equal social status. Richardson (1970) presented ideas and informal observations on classroom furniture arrangement and classroom rituals and related them to student behavior and learning. This marked influence of environmental setting on behavior has been demonstrated in early childhood education by Shure (1963) and Prescott, Jones, and Kritchevsky (1971).

Shure charted the psychological ecology of a nursery school using a time-sampling (categories) observation procedure. She examined the free play period behavior in five areas of the room; in order of frequency of total use, from greatest to least, the areas were: (1) block, (2) art, (3) games, (4) doll, and (5) book. The preferential order for girls was 2, 1, 4, 3, 5 and for boys 1, 2, 3, 4, 5. Large numbers of children moved in and out of the doll and games areas, while the book area evidenced only limited movement. Boys' activity was most often irrelevant in the art area and doll corner (that is, their behavior often did not involve art or dolls even though they were in areas so designated), while girls' was frequently irrelevant in the block area. The doll and block areas exhibited the greatest amount of social interaction between children. Other findings by Shure similarly demonstrated that the various play areas elicited markedly different child behaviors and usage rates.

Prescott, Jones, and Kritchevsky (1971), in a continuing effort to describe a child's experienced environment, observed two- to five-year-olds in three settings: group daycare centers (half having open-structure programs and half closed), family daycare homes, and middle-class homes where the children attended morning nursery school (these children were observed both at home and in school). Their ambitious study is too broad in scope to present fully here. Of particular note, however, were the findings that children in closed-structure group daycare centers spent about a quarter of their time in official transitions (that is, teacher-directed shifting from one activity to another), over twice the amount evidenced for children in open-structure centers. Also, activities were much more likely to be initiated by the teachers in the closed-structure programs, and adults in such programs intervened frequently. In open-structure centers, children were twice as likely to spontaneously initiate activities, and were less subject to adult intervention. Also of note were several observational measures of physical spaces developed in the study, such as a seclusion-intrusion measure and a softness rating. For example, the softness rating is determined by noting the presence or absence of eleven setting features:

1. Child/adult cozy furniture: rockers, couches, lawn swings, etc.;
2. Large rug or full carpeting indoors;
3. Grass which children can be on;
4. Sand which children can be in, either a box or area;
5. Dirt to dig in;
6. Animals which can be held (usually guinea pigs);
7. Single sling swings;
8. Play dough;
9. Water as an activity;
10. Very messy materials such as finger paint, clay, mud; and
11. "Laps," teachers holding children [Prescott, Jones, and Kritchevsky, 1971, p. 24].

Softness ratings discriminated the seven open- from the seven closed-structure daycare center settings. All open centers had child/adult cozy furniture; none of the closed centers did. All open centers provided messy materials and single sling swings, while only one and two closed centers, respectively, did. In terms of live animals to cuddle, six of the seven open centers maintained guinea pigs, while only one closed center had an animal (a rabbit, but off-limits for holding). Such measures to describe early childhood education settings seem particularly promising, as do other measures that assess children's differential behavior in various settings. A good example of the latter is the *focusing unit,* an observational measure of a young child's attending behavior in diverse naturalistic settings (Brown, 1974).

Children's play behavior outside their dwellings has also been studied (White, 1970), as has playground behavior. Hayward, Rothenberg, and Beasley (1973) studied school-age children's behavior on three types of urban playground: traditional—containing slides, swings, seesaws, and the like; designed—incorporating discrete sliding and swinging elements and joining them into a continuous sculpture based on sand; and adventure or junk—featuring old tires, packing crates, scrap lumber, and assorted discarded materials from which the children construct their own environment. Dependent measures were frequency of use, type of use (behaviors displayed and equipment used), and time spent and level of mastery achieved. Three complementary types of datum were collected: (1) specimen records of randomly selected children, tape-recorded by observers, (2) behavioral maps sketched by observers at regular time intervals, and (3) interviews of randomly selected children as they were leaving the playground. *Behavioral mapping,* a technique not discussed heretofore, is a spatial approach to observation in which specific persons or events are recorded or tracked on a scale-drawn map of the locale being observed. A visual diagram results that suggests relationships between aspects of the environment and behavior therein. Behavioral maps have four uses: (1) description of a setting, (2) comparison of settings, (3) derivation of general principles of the use of space, and (4) prediction of behavior in a new facility in advance of occupancy or even prior to actual construction (Ittelson and others, 1974; and Ittelson, Rivlin, and Proshansky, 1970).

In the study cited above by Hayward and his colleagues, maps were made of the three playgrounds. Every twenty minutes, an observer entered on the map a symbol showing each child's specific location on the playground, the child's age and sex, the activity being engaged in, and the apparent grouping of participants. Analyses of all the data revealed that type of playground largely determined the nature of activities that occurred. Children were not very imaginative or inventive in using the traditional or designed playgrounds. In summarizing Hayward's study, Ittelson and his associates noted: "the kinds of activities engaged in stemmed directly from the available equipment and materials. Loose parts such as dirt, sand, water, boards, and crafts materials were important to school-aged children and allowed for stimulating and involved interaction with the world around them. Further, the creative potential of a place was seen to be important in fostering social as well as environmental interaction. Where there were more materials that could be combined or changed, there was also more peer-group interaction and more responsive communication" (Ittelson and others, 1974, p. 238). Ittellson and his colleagues also correctly cautioned the reader that some confounding may have been present in the study; since children were not randomly assigned to playgrounds, certain pre-existing characteristics of children may have prompted them to seek out a particular type of playground.

Caplan (1977) investigated the effects of social density on playground behavior. A daycare center serving about fifty children, ages two and a half to eight, was utilized. Its designed playground was conceptualized as six distinct areas, each dominated by a piece of equipment: the sandpit complex, the swings, the tower complex, the pipe and tire complex, the climbers, and the sidewalk. Caplan systematically varied the social density of children on the playground—half of the time, ten children randomly selected for a given day were allowed on the playground, while, the other half of the time, the full center population of thirty to fifty children used the playground. Patterns of behavior usage under the two conditions of social density were observed. Under the high-density, large-group condition, proportionately more language activity and social interaction were noted, as well as a slight increase in aggressive behavior. Under the low-density, small-group condition, proportionately more interaction with the environment took place. Like Hayward and his colleagues, Caplan noted little shaping of the designed playground environment by the children. She found the sandpit complex most used and the sidewalk least used under both high- and low-density conditions. The less popular areas of the playground appeared to serve as overflow receptacles, as their proportional use increased under the high-density condition. Other investigations of the effects of social density on children's behavior have been made; for example, Hutt and Vaizey (1966) used checklists, tape recordings, and 8mm motion pictures to determine that normal children showed more aggressive behavior in using a playroom only when group size got large. Lofthouse (1978) examined the effects of spatial density (that is, room size) on kindergartners.

Before concluding this overview of contributions from environmental and ecological psychology, we should note the use of cognitive maps in the assessment of environments. Different from behavioral maps, *cognitive* or *mental maps* are images or pictures of settings that people have in their minds. Cognitive maps,which were first described by the learning psychologist Tolman (1948), allow persons to remain oriented and to know how to get around. A typical procedure used by environmental psychologists is to have persons sketch maps of an area (say, a city or portion thereof) and then describe their trips through it. Meaning is sought in terms of what features of the setting are salient enough to warrant inclusion in an individual's sketch. This procedure has been used to study human perceptions of urban areas—how such perceptions develop, how they vary from person to person, and how they influence behavior. Applications of the methodology can be seen in the "Journey-to-Work Game" (Golledge and Zannaras, 1973), in *The Image of the City* (Lynch, 1960), and in "A Walk Around the Block" (Lynch and Rivkin, 1970). To our knowledge, cognitive map methods have not yet been used with very young children. Their cognitive maps of a preschool, a first-grade class, or other educational setting might be very provocative and, in combination with other data, might make an effective component of a setting's measured profile. (Also see Siegel and White, 1975.)

In all, we believe (as do Weinberg and Moore, 1975) that ecological and environmental psychology offer potentially valuable contributions to evaluation and measurement in early childhood education programs; this belief explains, in part, the considerable attention given both fields here. Their principal focus on measuring and evaluating settings suggests innumerable applications to early childhood. Further, assessing settings for young children might appeal more to many early childhood educators than assessing children themselves. Our position is that assessing both settings *and* children offers the best chance of facilitating their learning and development.

Considerations from Other Sources

Considerations from several other sources have also influenced measurement and evaluation in early childhood education. Some of these are discussed briefly below. The brevity of treatment reflects our space limitations rather than the potential importance of such considerations. Interested readers are encouraged to pursue these topics through the cited works and their bibliographies.

Ethology. Originating within zoology, ethology initially focused on the study of animals in their natural habitats. More recently, attention has shifted to humans, including young children (Hutt and Hutt, 1970; Jones, 1972b; Tinbergen, 1972; and Vandenberg, 1978). The etholgical approach is distinguished by the following characteristics: "(1) emphasis on the use of a large variety of simple observable features of behavior as the raw data; (2) emphasis on description and a hypothesis-generating, natural history phase as the starting point of a study; (3) a distrust of major categories of behavior whose meaning and reality have not been made clear; (4) belief in the usefulness of an evolutionary framework for determining which kinds of questions need to be asked about behavior" (Jones, 1972a, pp. 4–5). Thus, in its study of human behavior, ethology complements psychology. Like ecological psychology, ethology relies principally on observation and focuses on what people do "naturally." The emphases on sticking close to the raw data, on avoiding inferences, and on viewing behavior within an evolutionary perspective also distinguish ethology. In his edited book on ethology and child behavior, Jones (1972b) justified ethology as a field in its own right but also took the opportunity to criticize certain methods (such as rating scales and interviews) used by sister fields.

Ethology has made important contributions to describing and measuring child development processes. The topics considered by the authors contributing to Jones' book (1972b) on ethology illustrate the nature of such endeavors: human nonverbal communication, play and social interaction patterns of preschoolers, categories of child-child interaction, social development in nursery school children (with emphasis on introduction to the group), reactions of preschoolers to a strange observer, observations of mother-infant interactions, attachment behavior of toddlers out-of-doors, behavior of children and their mothers at separation and greeting, social behavior of normal and problem children, comparative aspects of mother-child contact, and the evolution and ontogeny of hand function (specifically, three- to five-year-olds' holding and using of a paintbrush). The last illustration was described in Chapter Eight as an example of measuring fine motor performance of young children. Another instance of ethological work was considered in Chapter Four—recall Jones' (1971) excellent study of young children's facial expressions (Figure 5).

An important measurable concept from ethology that first surfaced in studies of spacing behavior in lower animals has been termed *interpersonal spacing*. Horowitz, Duff, and Stratton (1970) found that personal space needs existed and hypothesized a body–buffer zone, an internal projection of body image to include the space immediately around oneself. Noting that schizophrenic persons would not approach another person or an inanimate object (a hatrack) as closely as would normal persons, Horowitz and his colleagues conjectured that the schizophrenic had a larger body–buffer zone.

Related work summarized by McGrew (1974) is more relevant to our purposes here. McGrew reported on a continuing series of ethological studies examining the interpersonal spacing of preschoolers. Three- and four-year-old children in a Scottish nursery school were observed in the playroom during free play period. In one study, the *nearest neighbor technique* was used to determine if the children spaced themselves randomly or not. The technique required a record for each of the twenty children of the three other children nearest him at a given point in time. An observer recorded this information at random times until about seventy observations had been made for each child. Resulting analyses revealed that the spacing was highly nonrandom. The children tended more often to be near other children of the same sex and of similar age. In another study, McGrew used a form of behavioral mapping methodology to demonstrate that older children, experienced in the workings of the nursery school, were more often in close proximity to other children, while newcomers to the school were more frequently alone and near the periphery of the room during free play. In other reported studies, McGrew examined children's interpersonal spacing as influenced by social density (varying group size, as did Caplan, 1977) and by spatial density (varying room size, as did Lofthouse, 1978); he also compared his interpersonal spacing measures with results from sociometric measures and noted a correlation of .40.

Applied Behavioral Analysis. In the opening section of this chapter, we examined contributions to program evaluation from classical experimental design, a methodology more generally used in research. An additional source of ideas that can be used in evaluation (and also in research, for that matter) is the relatively new field of applied behavioral analysis. Related to experimental psychology, the field has grown rapidly since midcentury and has drawn heavily on work by Skinner (1948, 1953, 1954, 1957, 1968, and 1971).

Two basic paradigms used in applied behavioral analysis are the reversal and multiple base line techniques (Baer, Wolf, and Risley, 1968), which have acquired numerous variations (for example, see Ciminero, 1977, and Risley and Baer, 1973). In the *reversal technique,* a behavior is measured over time to establish how frequently it normally occurs (that is, to establish a base line). Then some experimental variable is introduced (some program or treatment is initiated). "The behavior continues to be measured, to see if the variable will produce a behavioral change. If it does, the experimental variable is discontinued or altered, to see if the behavioral change just brought about depends on it. If so, the behavioral change should be lost or diminished (thus the term 'reversal'). The experimental variable then is applied again, to see if the behavioral change can be recovered. If it can, it is pursued further, since this is applied research and the behavioral change sought is an important one. It may be reversed briefly again, and yet again, if the setting in which the behavior takes place allows further reversals" (Baer, Wolf, and Risley, 1968, p. 94).

In many settings, however, it is not feasible or permissible to engineer continued reversals. The second procedure, the *multiple base line technique*, circumvents the feasibility-permissibility issue. A number of behaviors are identified and measured over time to establish multiple base lines. "The experimenter then applies an experimental variable to one of the behaviors, produces a change in it, and perhaps notes little or no change in the other base lines. If so, rather than reversing the just-produced change, he instead applies the experimental variable to one of the other, as yet unchanged, responses. If it changes at that point, evidence is accruing that the experimental variable is indeed effective, and that the prior change was not simply a matter of coincidence. The variable then may be applied to still another response, and so on" (Baer, Wolf, and Risley, 1968, p. 94).

The applied behavioral analysis approach, therefore, involves systematic measurement before, during, and after some carefully monitored treatment or program (the "experimental variable" in the quotes above) is introduced. In the reversal technique, additional series of "durings" and "afters" increase the certainty of one's judgments about the effectiveness of the treatment. In the multiple base line procedure, the certainty about the treatment's effectiveness increases as additional behaviors are altered in desired directions. In a very real sense, the applied behavioral analysis paradigm thus provides a viable alternative to classical experimental design. Note also that there tends to be little use of inferential statistics and no requirement for a control group in the behavioral analysis procedure (although both could be incorporated to advantage). In Chapter Four, the work of Friedrich and Stein (1973) was cited as a sign time sampling observational method to determine the effects on children of viewing various television shows, either prosocial, aggressive, or neutral. That study combined features of both classical experimental design and applied behavioral analysis, although no reversals were used.

Variations of the applied behavioral analysis method have been used extensively in research investigations and in evaluations. Evaluations have been conducted of a program to train mentally retarded adolescents to brush their teeth (Horner and Keilitz, 1975), a curriculum "package" to train volunteers to canvass community residents (Fawcett, Miller, and Braukman, 1977), children's use of particular toys (Quilitch, Christophersen, and Risley, 1977), and a parent advice package for family shopping trips, designed to reduce child disruptions and to increase positive child-parent interactions (Clark and others, 1977). Procedures developed in applied behavioral analysis are used to evaluate treatment effects in diverse fields, including numerous educational settings (for example, see Ciminero, Calhoun, and Adams, 1977; Essa, 1978; Gambrill, 1977; and Risley, 1978). Such procedures are also manifest in the emerging use of single-case methodology (see Hersen and Barlow, 1976). Reviews of such work will alert the reader to many potential applications of such techniques to evaluation in early childhood education.

Law: The Adversary Model. Recently, there has been an attempt to apply procedures from law, and to a lesser extent from formal debate, to educational evaluation. This has been termed the *judicial model* (Wolf, 1975) or the *adversary model* or *proceeding* (Anderson, Ball, Murphy, and Associates, 1975; Kourilsky, 1973; Levine, 1973; Owens, 1973; Popham, 1975; and Scriven, 1976). Although specifics vary depending on the particular source consulted, the salient feature of the model (or, more appropriately, "framework," as the term was used in Chapter Nine) is the use of two evaluators or evaluation teams—one to present the positive features of a proposal or program and one to set forth the negative aspects. In some interpretations of the framework, the pro-evaluator and con-evaluator actually collect data, testimonials from experts and users, and the like; in others, they are viewed as interpreters and synthesizers of data collected by some impartial group. In either event, the two adversaries meet in open forum and present their cases to either a hearing officer, a small panel of judges, or even a "jury." Ground rules are established, such as allowable procedures for introducing and evaluating evidence or cross-examining witnesses, but in general these are conceptualized more informally and flexibly than in a court of law. The hearing officer, or judges, or jury hears both cases presented and then renders a decision or opinion on the major issue(s) involved.

The most common argument for the use of the adversary framework is that a program or proposal will be evaluated more fairly if different evaluators are charged with presenting its best and its worst aspects. Wolf noted this advantage and others: "Perhaps the most compelling reason for using legal methodology is that it offers a useful system of evidentiary rules and procedures aimed at producing alternative inferences from data prior to the rendering of judgment. In adapting and modifying certain procedures, evaluators can develop a clear set of issues upon which to focus the inquiry, rely on human testimony more than other evaluation approaches do, present a balanced view of the evidence (by employing two evaluation teams exploring the different sides of the issues), and, finally, structure the deliberations of the decision-making group" (1975, p. 185). Wolf, a proponent of a comprehensive, start-to-finish adversary evaluation mode, identified four major steps in implementing the judicial approach: (1) generating possible issues, (2) selecting salient issues for the hearing, (3) preparing arguments (collecting testimony, synthesizing data, and identifying witnesses), and (4) conducting the hearing itself.

Only a limited number of evaluations using the adversary model have come to our attention:

1. In 1970 in Hawaii, a hypothetical issue—whether public schools in the state should adopt *Man: A Course of Study*—was considered by a hearing officer and three judges (Owens, 1973).
2. In 1971 in St. Paul, Minnesota, Stake and Gjerde (1974) presented two evalua-

tion statements, one by an advocate and one by an adversary, summarizing reactions to a summer program for talented secondary school students. However, no hearing or trial was held and the statements were merely appended to the overall evaluation report with the implication that final judgment was left to the reader; in all, the evaluation better exemplified the responsive approach (Chapter Nine).

3. In 1975 in Bloomington, Indiana, Wolf (1975) and others took part in a six-month adversary evaluation of Indiana University's attempt to reform and revitalize its teacher education program; a two-day hearing before thirteen "jurists" culminated the effort. (Shortly after the Bloomington evaluation, Wolf apparently also used the adversary framework to evaluate an alternative high school in Indianapolis.)

4. In 1976 and 1977 in Hawaii, two four-person evaluation teams used the adversary approach to examine a large-scale team-teaching program for kindergarten through grade three (Popham and Carlson, 1977).

Estimates of the value of the adversary framework have ranged from skeptical to enthusiastic. Various assessments have been made of the value of the methodology in the four cases above: in the same respective numerical order they are: (1) "strong potential" but with limitations (Owens, 1973); (2) "admirably done" (Scriven, 1976); (3) "exceedingly promising" (Wolf, 1975); "needs improvement" and "holds great promise" (Arnstein, 1975); and (4) "not worth much" (Popham and Carlson, 1977). Wolf (1975) presented the positive case well: "The major strengths of the model appeared to be the use and exploration of human testimony, providing for a variety of perspectives to be displayed, the illumination of biases that were operating, and use of a wide array of data. Perhaps most significantly, it provided a deliberative framework for decisions" (1975, p. 187). Although Wolf also noted some "cautions," the impression conveyed was that they could be guarded against relatively easily.

Popham and Carlson (1977), however, after their experiences on the advocate team for the Hawaii team-teaching project, were much less charitable in their assessment of the adversary framework. They listed six "deep dark deficits" for it: (1) disparities in the skill and prowess of adversaries, (2) fallible arbiters or judges, (3) inordinate confidence in the model's potency (here, they quoted an eminent lawyer's denigration of amateurs' use of legal methodology to achieve "a quaint fantasy of technical closure"), (4) difficulties in stating issues or propositions to allow adversary resolution, (5) opportunities for biased decision makers to use adversary proceedings as a smoke screen to justify their predetermined decisions, and (6) excessive costs. Although they suggested remedies for most of the deficits, Popham and Carlson in sum viewed the adversary model as having a few real benefits, many imaginary benefits, and far too many deficits.

Our impression is that the jury is still out on the worth of the adversary approach, and that a long deadlock is conceivable. With sufficient resources (that is, funds and time), the adversary approach might allow important, deliberate reflection on varying interpretations of data on the quality and nature of a program. This reflection might then lead to accurate judgments and sensible decisions. At the same time, the merit of the approach over cheaper alternatives has not been clearly demonstrated. Evaluation efforts of early childhood education programs would probably do well to experiment with small-scope, less-expensive versions of the adversary strategy before committing extensive evaluation resources to it.

Political Considerations. When addressing Issue 9 in Chapter One ("Are most evaluations merely whitewashes?"), we alluded to the significant influence that political considerations can have on evaluation. Cohen noted two salient political aspects of evaluation:

> There is one sense in which any educational evaluation ought to be regarded as political. Evaluation is a mechanism with which the character of an educational enterprise can be explored and expressed. These enterprises are managed by people, and they take place in institutions; therefore, any judgment on their nature or results has at least a potential political impact—it can contribute to changing power relationships. This is true whether the evaluation concerns a small curriculum reform program in a rural school (if the program is judged ineffective the director might lose influence or be demoted), or a teacher training program in a university (if it is judged a success its sponsors might get greater authority). . . .
>
> There is another sense in which evaluation is political, for some programs explicitly aim to redistribute resources or power; although this includes such things as school consolidation, social action programs are the best recent example. They were established by a political institution (Congress) as part of an effort to change the operating priorities of state and local governments and thus to change not only the balance of power within American education but also the relative status of economic and racial groups within the society [Cohen, 1970, pp. 214–215].

Other aspects of politics' interrelations with evaluation have been surveyed by House (1972, 1976).

Brickell directs a large nonprofit corporation that contracts to do evaluations, principally with local, state, and federal governments. In a candid article (Brickell, 1976), he revealed a number of illustrations of how political influence was used on him and his organization and caused them to modify their evaluation findings or report. Speaking as "a well-riddled target of political factors," he cited a case in which area superintendents in a large school district that had employed him to evaluate the use of paraprofessionals told him and his staff to file a positive report as the paraprofessionals would not be given up. In another example, agencies being evaluated wanted most negative findings in reports either tempered or eliminated; depending on the political situation, Brickell's organization either complied in full, in part, or not at all (in the latter case jeopardizing receipt of subsequent evaluation contracts from that agency).

> Are there external political factors that influence the role and methodology of evaluation? You bet there are. And they are powerful.
> Because the seeking, the winning, and the exercising of power are a prominent part of life within an institution as well as between institutions,

internal evaluation staffs are just as subject to political influences as external evaluation staffs. Perhaps you have noticed that.

Sometimes political forces control the populations we can sample.
Sometimes they limit the data we can gather. Sometimes they shape our
instruments. Sometimes they influence the designs we can use. Sometimes
they guide our interpretations. Sometimes they shape our recommendations. Sometimes they touch the wording of our reports. And they always
influence the impact of what we recommend.

I think I have never written an evaluation report without being conscious of the fact that what I say will be used in the winning and the
exercising of power, that my findings are going to be lined up on one side
or the other of a contest that somebody else has already set up, and that
jobs are on the line—maybe my own job [Brickell, 1976, p. 5].

One might conjecture that evaluation in early childhood education would
be relatively or totally immune from such political influence. After all, the programs are for young children, and ethics would dictate an active, impartial, and
unbiased search for the "truth" to make such programs as effective as possible
and to allocate scarce resources optimally. Such a conjecture would be dramatically in error. In fact, recent government programs for young children—like
Head Start, Follow Through, and Title I of the Elementary and Secondary
Education Act (ESEA)—have provided vivid examples of politics' impact on
evaluation (for example, see Cohen, 1970; and Williams and Evans, 1972).

It is impossible to eliminate the influence of politics on evaluation. However, the alert evaluator can estimate the political factors bearing on any particular evaluation. Popham (1975) provided two primary ways for the evaluator to
cope with the reality of political influence. First, the evaluator should be aware
that judgments and decisions will be made on several factors in addition to any
evaluation results. Second, the evaluator can attempt to detect any vested interests and describe such interests in the evaluation report itself. The discovery
of political factors should not automatically suggest collusion, dishonesty, or unethical practices. Rather it should serve as a reminder that evaluation is "intimately involved with negotiations and relationships between people"(House,
1973a, p. 43).

Needs Assessment and the Delphi Technique. In the past decade, considerable
emphasis has been placed on needs assessment in education: "The process by
which one identifies needs and decides upon priorities among them has been
termed *needs assessment.* In the context of education and training programs, a
need may be defined as a condition in which there is a discrepancy between an
acceptable state of affairs and an *observed* state of affairs. Needs assessment may be
applied to individuals, groups, or institutions" (Anderson, Ball, Murphy, and Associates, 1975, p. 254). The typical procedure in needs assessment is: (1) identifying important goal areas, (2) selecting or developing measures relevant to the
goal areas, (3) establishing acceptable performance on the measures, (4) administering the measures, and (5) comparing actual performance levels with the pre-
established acceptable levels to determine needs. Some less formal procedures
also have been interpreted as needs assessment. In effect, needs assessment is a

vital step in an educational unit's efforts to set educational priorities (Stake and Gooler, 1971). Procedural kits have been developed to facilitate the needs assessment process (for example, see Center for the Study of Evaluation, 1973).

A technique used to forecast future trends has relevance here, for it could be used to estimate future needs. The Delphi Technique (Cyphert and Gant, 1971; and Linstone and Turoff, 1975) was first developed about a quarter-century ago to estimate the effects of a massive atomic attack on the United States (Helmar, 1975). Since then, its use has grown markedly. It is a method for reaching consensus among individuals (often experts in a given field) while controlling extraneous factors that often influence group judgments.

> Traditionally, the method for achieving consensus is a round-table discussion among individuals who arrive at a group position. There are a number of objections to this procedure. The final position, usually a compromise, is often derived under the undue influence of certain psychological factors, such as specious persuasion by the group member with the greatest supposed authority or even merely the loudest voice, an unwillingness to abandon publicly expressed opinions, and the bandwagon effect of majority opinion. In contrast, with the Delphi Technique an attempt is made to overcome these factors by not bringing the participants together in one place and by not reporting individual opinions. This eliminates committee activity and replaces it with a carefully designed program of sequential interrogations . . . interspersed with information and opinion feedback [Cyphert and Gant, 1971, p. 272].

Two distinct Delphi forms exist. The more common or conventional Delphi form uses a paper-and-pencil questionnaire. "In this situation a small monitor team designs a questionnaire which is sent to a larger respondent group. After the questionnaire is returned the monitor team summarizes the results and, based upon the results, develops a new questionnaire for the respondent group. The respondent group is usually given at least one opportunity to reevaluate its original answers based upon examination of the group response" (Linstone and Turoff, 1975, p. 5). In the second and newer form, a computer replaces the monitor team, compiles group results, and much more rapidly provides feedback to the respondent group. Both forms eventually result in the respondent groups' best estimate of what the future will produce on the selected issues.

In early childhood education, needs assessment has obvious applications, such as determining the need for a preschool program in a given area or setting subject-matter (reading, math) or process-oriented (thinking, measuring) curriculum priorities in the early grades. The Delphi Technique also could be effectively used, such as by polling experts to estimate future childcare needs, to predict societal requirements for preschool settings in terms of number and type, and the like.

Open Education. The graph in Figure 13, earlier in this chapter, showed a marked difference in climate between traditional and open education classrooms. The distinctness of the open education orientation (see Chapter Eleven) has prompted open educators to challenge many existing measurement and evaluation procedures and to propose others. The tone of such challenges and the nature of the open education evaluation proposals are well expressed in a series of documents emanating from the North Dakota Study Group on Evaluation (Carini, 1975; Engel, 1975; Feiman, 1975; Hein, 1975; and Patton, 1975) and from the Education Development Center (De Rivera, 1973; Standardized Testing in America, 1977).

Several challenges that were detailed involved the limitations and inappropriateness of standardized tests for open education (especially see Hein, 1975). Interestingly, limitations of standardized tests are also of great concern to more conventional educator-evaluators, as Worthen and Sanders document (1973, pp. 280–285); they also considered procedures to overcome such limitations. Other challenges by the open educators were directed at evaluation via the classical experimental design paradigm.

Alternatives proposed by those oriented toward open education are largely measures and evaluation procedures that we have already discussed. Thus, instead of standardized tests, they propose extensive observation, work samples, documentation of naturally occurring events during the educational endeavor, and other process-oriented measures (such as using a project historian to record salient program events). Instead of classical experimental design for evaluation, they propose procedures similar to a combination of the responsive framework (Chapter Nine) and anthropological methods (presented earlier in this chapter). As Patton noted, "the alternative paradigm relies on field techniques from an anthropological rather than natural science tradition, techniques such as participant observation, in-depth interviewing, detailed description, and qualitative field notes" (1975, p. 8).

Overall, these major objections and concerns of the open educators appear well met by their own work and by the increasing supply of alternative measurement and evaluation strategies. At the same time, the belief of open educators that funding agencies and decision makers continue to be partial to more traditional measures and evaluation is well-founded. Our own position is that both perspectives on measurement and evaluation—the open and the traditional—have led to important contributions. In our opinion, educational measurement and evaluation have been enriched by the differing perspectives.

Source Books of Early Childhood Measures

The measurement of traits, attitudes, or behaviors of young children is often an integral part of operating an early childhood education program. The descriptions of measurement concepts and techniques in this book are intended to help the reader understand how the measurement process works. Still, when one is faced with the reality of designing an assessment program or an evaluation, the task of actually finding or developing adequate measures can seem formidable. It need not be, however. A tremendous number of instruments have been developed for assessment, evaluation, and research purposes, and many of these can be obtained easily—either for direct use or for use as models for the construction of new instruments. To aid the teacher, program director, counselor, or anyone in need of tests and measures of a certain type, several useful source books and compendiums are available. Knowing what these source books consist of and how to use them can greatly reduce the amount of time spent in searching for instruments or constructing them from scratch. The purpose of this section is to describe the contents of several such references and to recommend some procedures that can facilitate their efficient and effective use.

The available source books differ in several respects: the domain(s) covered, the ages for which the tests and measures are applicable, the amount and type of descriptive and evaluative information provided for the instruments,

516

and the type of source—commercial or noncommercial—from which the instruments can be obtained. Several of the source books and articles considered are concerned only with published measures, others deal exclusively with unpublished measures, and still others include some of both types. In nearly all cases, the tests and instruments cited can be obtained either from commercial publishers, from the authors directly, or from the original journal article in which the instrument is presented. Finding data on the reliability, validity, and use of the instruments is not always so simple—and for some measures it may be impossible. The availability of such information is usually reported in the source books or compendiums. This in itself is an extremely useful feature of these works, for it can aid the potential user in deciding whether or not further investigation of a measure would be worthwhile.

The problem of locating suitable measures for a particular purpose is only partially solved by these source books. A survey of the possible instruments quickly reveals their dearth of supportive reliability and validity evidence and nationally representative norms. This situation is lamented in the introductory section of most of the major source books. Walker (1973), for example, notes that the standardization, reliability, and validity studies that are conducted on tests designed for use with young children typically are based on small, selective samples that render the resulting data of limited value. Hoepfner, Stern, and Nummedal, whose source books include their own ratings on such criteria as normed technical excellence and measurement validity, likewise acknowledged the underdeveloped state of the art, although they also expressed some hope for improvement. "It is quite likely that the ratings reported here will be extremely disappointing to those who expect a list of ready-made tests to answer all of their evaluation questions. Unfortunately, the state of the art cannot yet offer any panaceas. However, balancing the rather dismal picture presented by the bulk of the published tests, it should be noted that there is tremendous ferment in the fields of assessment of young children. Many measurement specialists, supported by large grants from public and private sources, are energetically engaged in the development of more precise tools to assess the outcomes of various types of intervention programs" (1971, p. v).

Oscar Buros, who devoted over thirty-five years to preparing bibliographies of critical reviews on published tests of all types, perhaps realized more fully than anyone else the extent to which test development and data-based documentation could be improved. "Test publishers continue to market tests which do not begin to meet the standards of the rank and file of MMY [Mental Measurements Yearbook] and journal reviewers. At least half of the tests currently on the market should never have been published. Exaggerated, false, or unsubstantiated claims are the rule rather than the exception. Test users are becoming more discriminating, but not nearly fast enough. It is still true, as I said over ten years ago in *Tests in Print,* that 'at present no matter how poor a test may be, if it is nicely packaged and if it promises to do all sorts of things which no test can do, the test will find many gullible buyers'" (1972, pp. xxvii–xxviii). From Buros' comments in the *Eighth Mental Measurements Yearbook,* published in 1978 shortly after his death, it is clear that his evaluation of published tests generally remained severe.

Seasoned, sage, and systematic use of the source books discussed here can help reduce the number of "gullible buyers." Most of the authors have organized their test presentations in similar ways, including descriptive information (such as title, author, publisher, appropriate age range, cost, length, format) and critical comments for each instrument. The critical comments usually consist of information about the sufficiency of reliability, validity, and normative data and, in some cases, additional evaluative remarks about the worth of the measure. The source books can serve test users in several ways: by helping them identify and locate already-developed instruments; by offering summaries of research results on specific tests; and by providing evaluations, usually by testing or subject-area specialists, on the usefulness of specific tests for the purposes for which they were developed. Thus, the kind of information that the potential user of a test looks for in the manual can usually be found in these source books, eliminating the necessity of ordering specimen sets or examination copies of all tests being considered for a particular use.

Four source books are treated in detail in this section. Buros' *Mental Measurements Yearbooks* and *Tests in Print* are frequently the volumes of choice for the initial search for tests and for locating critical reviews of published tests; the books in this series offer the most comprehensive coverage of published tests dating back to the 1930s. Although not specifically oriented to early childhood education, Buros' volumes constitute such a major source of descriptive and critical information for test users that they are considered to be as important for early childhood educators as the source books prepared specifically for that field. The other three reference works considered in detail here are directly related to the assessment of young children. Walker's *Socioemotional Measures for Preschool and Kindergarten Children* (1973) includes both published and unpublished measures for the assessment of behaviors, traits, and attitudes defined as part of the affective domain. Johnson and Bommarito's *Tests and Measurements in Child Development: Handbook I* (1971) and Johnson's *Tests and Measurements in Child Development: Handbook II* (1976) together list over 1,000 instruments for use in measuring variables of all types related to infancy, childhood, and adolescence. The majority of the cited tests and measures are not commercially published but are available from authors or in professional journals. The fourth compendium given special attention here is two volumes of the series produced by Hoepfner and others at the Center for the Study of Evaluation (CSE) at the University of California at Los Angeles. The *CSE-ECRC Preschool/Kindergarten Test Evaluations* (Hoepfner, Stern, and Nummedal, 1971) and the *CSE Elementary School Test Evaluations* (Hoepfner and others, 1976) contain evaluative ratings of published tests that are listed according to educational goals they address.

For each of the four works presented in the first section, a hypothetical example is given showing why and how the source might be used. The example follows a description of the source's content and organizational scheme. As the reader reviews these four sources and examples of their use, some overlap in the instruments included in them will be noted. However, each source is also unique in some ways. Taken together, the four provide a fairly comprehensive picture of the assessment devices available to early childhood educators and evaluators. The only type of measurement technique not given full coverage in any of these four source books is observational measurement. The most useful compendium of observational schedules for use with young children, *Measures of Maturation: An Anthology of Early Childhood Observation Instruments* (Boyer, Simon, and Karafin, 1973), was introduced in Chapter Four and is mentioned just briefly in the second part of this section.

This second part is an annotated bibliography of other source books and articles that contain references to measures for young children. These works are, for the most part, not concerned primarily or solely with tests and instruments for the assessment of children below age eight, or they furnish information on only one assessment domain. For these sources, detailed examples of potential uses are not given. However, a discussion of the content and organization of each, including a delineation of the subparts applicable to early childhood education, is provided.

Our purpose is not only to inform the reader about these references, but to encourage their use—especially in locating critical reviews of tests. Careful selection of measures with optimal validity and reliability will greatly enhance the usefulness of the data gathered.

Buros' *Mental Measurements Yearbooks* and *Tests in Print*

Description. The eight editions of the *Mental Measurements Yearbook* (MMY) and the two volumes of *Tests in Print* (TIP) contain more information about published tests than any other source. With the publication of the first Yearbook in 1938, Buros embarked on a lifelong effort to provide facts, critical reviews, and bibliographies pertaining to all tests published in English-speaking countries; eight Yearbooks have been produced to date, the most recent in 1978. These Yearbooks are, for the most part, supplemental to each other; each contains information on tests published since the last Yearbook. *Tests in Print I* and *II* (TIP I and TIP II), published in 1961 and 1974, respectively, are master indexes to the Yearbooks. In addition, a series of lengthy monographs specific to certain subject areas and types of test (English, Foreign Language, Mathematics, Reading, Science, Social Studies, Intelligence Tests, and Personality Tests) have been published since 1975, each containing names and reviews of the relevant tests in the Yearbooks.

This discussion will focus on the two most current books in the series—the Eighth MMY and TIP II. This is not meant to imply, however, that the earlier Yearbooks are obsolete; on the contrary, as will be pointed out, each Yearbook offers unique information, and earlier Yearbooks will often be required in the search for information on particular tests.

The objectives for the *Eighth Yearbook* are the same as for earlier volumes:

1. To print information about tests published in English-speaking countries.
2. To provide critical test reviews, written by testing and subject-area specialists.
3. To offer comprehensive bibliographies on construction, validity, and use of the published instruments.
4. To reprint evaluative excerpts of test reviews originally published in professional journals.
5. To provide lists of new and revised books on testing, along with portions of published reviews of those books.

This two-volume Yearbook contains listings for 1,184 tests, most of which are accompanied by reviews: there are 140 excerpts of reviews that appeared in professional journals and 898 reviews prepared specifically for the Yearbook. In addition, over 17,000 bibliographical references for the tests are included. The tests are listed alphabetically, by title, within fifteen major categories: Achievement Batteries, English, Fine Arts, Foreign Languages, Intelligence, Mathematics, Miscellaneous, Multi-Aptitude Batteries, Personality, Reading, Science, Sensory-Motor, Social Studies, Speech and Hearing, and Vocations. Most of these categories include several subcategories, resulting in a total of 80 subcategories. The tests in this Yearbook are, for the most part, ones that were published between 1971 and mid 1977. A few selected older tests—ones that are widely used or referred to often in published literature—are also listed and reviewed, even though they are mentioned in earlier Yearbooks.

Six indexes, in addition to the Table of Contents, aid the reader in locating specific material. Most helpful for locating tests of certain types are the Index of Test Titles and the Scanning Index. The former includes listings of tests by key words in the titles as well as by the official titles, and by acronyms for some widely used tests; the latter is an expanded Table of Contents, with the names of all tests listed by category or subcategory. The other indexes are the Periodical Directory and Index, which lists the journals from which test and book reviews were excerpted; the Publishers Directory and Index, which gives the addresses of the publishers of tests and books cited in the Yearbook; the Index of Book Titles, which includes the names of all books on testing that are listed and reviewed; and the Index of Names, a compendium of names and roles (for example, reviewer, test author, book author) of all persons mentioned in the text.

Tests in Print II supplements the *Mental Measurements Yearbooks* by serving as a master index to all the Yearbooks. It is, for the most part, an updated version of *Tests in Print I,* rather than an addendum. TIP II contains over 16,000 citations, organized into several sections: a bibliography of all published English tests; a classified index to the material in the first seven Yearbooks; bibliographies on the construction, validity, and use of some of the tests; a list of tests that have gone out of print since TIP I (1961); a cumulative index of names, with references, for each test; indexes of the titles of all in-print and out-of-print tests in the first seven Yearbooks, as well as a similar index of names; a directory of publishers' names, addresses, and corresponding tests; a classified scanning index of tests, organized according to subcategories and including a description of each test's intended population; and a reprinting of the APA-AERA-NCME 1974 *Standards for Educational and Psychological Tests.* (See Chapter Three for a discussion of the *Standards.*) The primary purpose of TIP II "is to direct readers to the MMY test reviews, the excerpted test reviews from journals, and to the professional literature on the construction, use, and validity of the tests being considered" (Buros, 1974, p. xxii).

The information that is presented for each test cited in the bibliographical test section of TIP II is as follows: title; characteristics of the intended population, including appropriate age; copyright date(s); acronym, if any; any pertinent special comments, such as in regard to restrictive uses, available separate subtests, administration sites, and so on; number and description of part scores, if any; factual critical statements, such as, "no manual," if any; author; publisher; adaptations for foreign use, if any; closing asterisk indicating that the test entry was prepared from a first-hand examination of the test, if it was; cross-references within TIP II; references to entries in other volumes in the Buros series and references to journal articles and other published works in which the test's properties are discussed. The lists of references are the most important aspect of TIP II insofar as they direct the reader to critical reviews and additional information about the test.

The information in MMY is similar to that in TIP II except that each test entry is much longer; the critical review(s) for each test follow the brief descriptive information. These reviews were either prepared specifically for Buros by testing and subject-area specialists or were excerpted by Buros from professional journals.

Use. One of the most common uses of the volumes in the *Mental Measurements Yearbooks* and *Tests in Print* series is that of gaining quick access to critical review(s) of a specific test or a few tests in a specific area. The source books are also useful for other purposes: surveying the field of available tests of a certain type as part of an initial selection process; locating bibliographical references for a test so as to do in-depth study of its construction, use, or validity; and so forth. We have decided not to take the reader through the process of initially locating or choosing a test because of the extensive duplication of material from the source books that that would entail. It should be noted, however, that Buros' volumes are frequently the first reference books to be searched during the quest for possible tests to use for a particular purpose.

Our example of the use of the Buros' works involves a school psychologist working for a large metropolitan school district. A year ago, he served on a committee of school district personnel that wrote and submitted a proposal to Title IV-C, Elementary and Secondary Education Act (ESEA), for money to institute a special innovative program for gifted children in the district. The program was subsequently funded, its purpose being to supplement the regular school day with special classes for gifted children in kindergarten through the third grade. The first task that the project staff—which includes our school psychologist—faces is identifying "gifted" children in grades K–3.

The psychologist plans to use several different types of datum during a preliminary screening, including teacher referrals, intelligence test scores, achievement test scores, and parent questionnaire results. He will then make ratings, based on personal interviews with the children identified by the preliminary screening and, possibly, on additional intelligence and creativity test results. The purpose of the ratings is to help the staff make the final selections.

To collect the data for the rough screening phase, the psychologist needs an intelligence test that can be quickly and easily administered to all the K–3 children (about 1,500) in the district. He wants a test that requires a minimum amount of testing time, that can be administered by teachers and teacher aides, and that is appropriate for use with this age group. Of course, the test must also have sufficient reliability and validity. The Quick Test has been suggested to the psychologist as a suitable intelligence test for this purpose. Since he is not familiar with this measure, he goes to Buros' volumes to investigate it. Starting with the most recent volume in the series, the *Eighth Mental Measurements Yearbook*, and already knowing the title of the test, he turns to the Index of Test Titles. There he learns that the Quick Test can be found on page 324 and that its reference number is 225. These test reference numbers in the body of the Yearbook (in the "Tests and Reviews" section) are ordered consecutively, and appear in the upper outside margins of the pages. Under reference number 225, the following information is given for the Quick Test (Buros, 1978, p. 324):

> *The Quick Test.* Ages 2 and over; 1958–62; QT; picture vocabulary; individual; Forms 1, 2, 3, ('58, 1 card); provisional manual ('62, 54 pages); instruction cardboard ('62, 1 page); item cardboard ('62, 1 page, includes words for all 3 forms); record-norms sheet ('62, 2 pages); norms for combinations of 2 or 3 forms also presented; $16 per set of testing materials including all 3 forms, 100 record sheets, and manual; $10 per 100 record-norms sheets; $5 per manual; cash orders postpaid; specimen set not available (manual illustrates all materials); (3–10) minutes; R. B. Ammons and C. H. Ammons; Psychologist Test Specialists.*
>
> See T2:522 (15 references); for excerpted reviews by Peter F. Merenda and B. Semeonoff, see 7:422 (30 references); for reviews by Boyd R. McCandless and Ellen V. Piers, see 6:534 (3 references).

References

1–3. See 6:534.

4–33. See 7:422.

34–48. See T2:522; also includes a cumulative name index to the first 48 references, 2 reviews, and 2 excerpts for this test.

49. McCartin, Rose Amata, and Meyers, C. E. "An Exploration of Six Semantic Factors at First Grade." *Multi Behav Res* 1(1):74–94 Ja '66.* (PA 41:1415)

50. Braginsky, Dorothea D., and Braginsky, Benjamin M. "The Intelligent Behavior of Mental Retardates: A Study of Their Manipulation of Intelligence Test Scores." *J Personality* 40(4):558–63 D '72.* (PA 50:3170)   [References continue through number 81].

The citing in the Eighth Yearbook informs the psychologist that the test is designed for use with children two years and older, that it was published and copyrighted between 1958 and 1962, that *QT* is its acronym, and that it was developed by Ammons and Ammons and published by Psychological Test Specialists. The asterisk denotes that this entry was prepared after a direct examination of the test materials. The remainder of the entry consists of references to reviews of the test in other MMY volumes and references to journal articles that deal with the construction, use, or validity of the test. References cited here are ones not previously listed in other MMY volumes (and therefore ones published since the 1974 Tests in Print II).

The second paragraph in the entry is of most concern to the psychologist at this point. The numbers 6:534 and 7:422 refer to entry numbers in the Sixth and Seventh editions of MMY, respectively. Entry 422 in the Seventh Yearbook is found in the same way that the 225 in the Eighth was found, and it contains the same initial identifying information as was printed in the Eighth. In addition, two excerpted critical reviews of the Quick Test are presented, as well as references 4 through 33. The critical reviews are reproduced below (Buros, 1972, pp. 761–762):

> *Brit J Psychol 55:117 F '64. B. Semeonoff.* * essentially a shortened version of the . . . *Full Range Picture Vocabulary Test* * Each of its three "forms" is represented by a card bearing four line drawings. The subject is required to say, for each of 50 words associated with a given card, which of the four pictures "best fits it." The purpose of the test is to provide a means of "quick screening of verbal intelligence in practical situations." Separate norms (in the form of "I.Q." conversions) are provided for each form separately, any pair, or all three together. The idea is an attractive one, but the material published is open to criticism. Three points, in order of increasing seriousness, are as follows: First, the drawings are crude—though seldom really ambiguous. Secondly, some of the attributions of meaning, and the cues on which they rest, are highly dubious. Thus, *celerity* is regarded as appropriate to a picture of a restaurant because the waitress is "bending over in her hurry." Again, in the same picture the diner very definitely looks *bovine*—another of the key words, for which the correct choice is a drawing showing a cow by a stream, because, the manual says, this "is the only drawing with a cow on it." Thirdly, and finally, the method seems positively to encourage acceptance of loose use of language. Whether this is inherent in the method would seem to rest on further experiment with better pictures. Here everything seems to have been sacrificed to convenience, and one cannot help feeling that the validities claimed for the test and its parent FRPV (which are considerable) must have been achieved in spite of rather than because of their characteristic features.*
>
> *Ed & Psychol Meas 25:268–71 sp '65. Peter F. Merenda.* [Review of the Provisional Manual.] This excellent monograph . . . is . . . a provisional manual . . . [and] . . . a combination of *(a)* an exposition on the merits of brief screening devices for estimating a wide range of human intellectual abilities; *(b)* a plea to critics of short psychological tests to consider factors other than brevity in their evaluation of such instruments; and *(c)* a review and summary of the professional literature reporting a great scope of

research findings with the *QT* and its parent test—*The Full-Range Picture Vocabulary Test (FRPV)*. * the authors . . . maintain that they have found that reasonably intelligent adults with no formal training in testing can learn to administer the *QT* efficiently and that with some additional training such persons can be taught to interpret it adequately. They go on to say that it is better to train non-psychologists to administer and interpret these tests adequately rather than unrealistically to expect untrained persons to do absolutely no testing! In line with this reasoning, they have simplified the presentation of directions and materials in this manual. Such statements will undoubtedly elicit some strong negative reactions on the part of the authors' professional colleagues, but this reviewer for one, on the basis of his own personal experiences, is willing to agree with Ammons and Ammons. * the controversial nature of the contents of much of this provisional manual for the *QT* is deemed inevitable. There will be those who will undoubtedly be greatly concerned about the brevity of the tests, the relatively small samples utilized in the normative, reliability, and validity research, and the rather high correlation coefficients reported which suggest spuriousness. To these critics, and to all users or potential users of the *QT*, this reviewer can only advise others to consult the basic research literature on the *QT* to which the authors make repeated reference in the monograph. Of course, this reviewer is not necessarily willing to accept all the findings reported in the monograph at face value. Nevertheless, the data and arguments presented by Ammons and Ammons are both impressive and seemingly convincing. Therefore, they cannot be blindly ignored! If the *QT* is only partly as good as the data and findings reported in this provisional manual seem to imply, then the authors will have made an outstanding and lasting contribution to the field of psychological testing. It is necessary, however, for the discriminating user and researcher to go beyond the data reported herein and, as the authors themselves suggest, conduct his own research with the *QT*.

For reviews by Boyd R. McCandless and Ellen V. Piers, see 6:534.

The asterisks that appear in various places in the reviews signify breaks in the reading resulting from Buros' decision to reproduce selected sections of previously published journal reviews. In order to keep the reviews in MMY short, only the most relevant comments—those pertaining to descriptions, reliability, use, validity, norms, and critical suggestions for potential users—are printed in MMY.

Since this test was reviewed in the Sixth Yearbook as well as the Seventh, the psychologist will check the entry in that volume also. The reviews that appear there are different from the ones in the Seventh, since the Yearbooks are supplemental but not repetitious in terms of reviews included. Entry 534 in the Sixth MMY contains two reviews solicited specifically for that Yearbook.

Tests in Print II (TIP II), published in 1974, does not contain reviews. Rather, it serves as a cumulative referencing index for previous MMY volumes and provides updates on journal references. Since there was a several-year gap between the publication of the Seventh Yearbook and TIP II, the psychologist could find additional references for the Quick Test by also checking TIP II (in this case fifteen, references 34 through 48).

The amount of information the psychologist obtains from the three Yearbooks and TIP II is sufficiently promising to prompt him to order a specimen set of the test materials for examination. The impression he gains from the Buros reviews is that the test can be quickly and easily administered by untrained persons, and that the available research results have led reviewers, generally, to describe it as "adequate" as a large-scale screening device but probably less valuable than competing intelligence tests for other purposes. The psychologist tentatively plans (pending examination of the specimen set and consultation with teachers) to use the Quick Test as one assessment technique in the first phase of his selection procedure, but to supplement his data-bank in the final selection phase with scores from another intelligence test, probably the Stanford-Binet or the Wechsler.

Walker's *Socioemotional Measures*

Description. Walker's handbook is a useful source for identifying published and unpublished measures for children ages three to six. The book contains information on 143 measures categorized as belonging to the *socioemotional domain,* a term intended to include all "social and emotional behaviors that may be separable, unseparable, or overlapping" (Walker, 1973, p. 4). (We consistently have termed this domain *affective;* see Chapter Seven.) The domain is subdivided into six parts: attitudes; general personality and emotional adjustment; interests or preferences; personality or behavior traits; self-concept; and social skills or competency.

The tests and measures cited by Walker were located after an exhaustive search for references in both published and unpublished materials. The materials searched were as follows:

1. Issues of ninety-two English-language educational and psychological journals published between 1966 and 1972.
2. Evaluation reports of federally funded early childhood programs.
3. Annotated bibliographies of published and unpublished tests (for example, Coller, 1971a, b).
4. Several of the standard textbooks on tests and measures.
5. Johnson and Bommarito's *Tests and Measurements in Child Development: Handbook I,* 1971.
6. The *CSE-ECRC Preschool/Kindergarten Test Evaluations,* edited by Hoepfner, Stern, and Nummedal, 1971.
7. Buros' *Fifth* (1959), *Sixth* (1965), and *Seventh* (1972) *Mental Measurements Yearbooks* and *Personality Tests and Reviews* (1970).
8. *Mirrors for Behavior II: An Anthology of Observation Instruments,* edited by Simon and Boyer, 1970.

From this set of materials, Walker chose for inclusion any measure that belonged to the affective domain and that was designed for use with children ages three to six. Instruments developed exclusively for brain-damaged, physically handicapped, or mentally retarded children were not included unless also used with normal children. Other types of measure that do not appear in this book include creativity, cognitive-style, and coping measures; special screening devices; cognitive batteries that include, only secondarily, an affective test; measures of environmental "perception or conception"; and measures that deal primarily with mother-child interaction or with classroom processes.

Each of the entries is categorized as belonging to one of the six subparts of the affective domain. In the case of tests that consist of several separate subscales, the test is usually classified in the one area under which it is predominantly subsumed; in a few such cases, however, the subscales—if they clearly measure different aspects of the domain—are classified separately.

Each test or measure is identified by the name given it by the developer; in the case of instruments described in journal articles but not named, Walker supplied names. The publication or copyright date, if available, is included in parentheses after the name. The additional information provided for each test consists of the following, when available: the author of the instrument; the age range for which the instrument is appropriate; the measurement technique that is used (for example, projective, unobtrusive, rating scale, observational, self-report, situational); sources in which the instrument is described (for example, journal articles, other handbooks or references); address from which the instrument can be obtained; a description of the instrument, including specification of the variables assessed, administration and scoring procedures, examples of items, administrator training required, special uses; information regarding what norms are available; information on results of validity studies; and evidence of reliability. This source book would be a useful starting place for any person interested in measuring affective variables pertaining to young children. It provides, first of all, a relatively compact and organized view of what tests and measures have been developed in this area. Of more importance is its use as a guide to obtaining copies of actual instruments and to obtaining some information about validity, reliability, use, and norms.

Use. As an example of the use to which Walker's handbook might be put, let us take the case of a kindergarten teacher who wants to measure the "learner self-concept" of her pupils at the beginning of the academic year. After examining the school's records, she knows that about half of her pupils have previously spent one year in a preschool; the other half have had no formal schooling to date. All of the students come from middle-income families and none of them are bilingual. Her reason for wanting to measure learner self-concept is twofold: she would like to know if there is any difference between the group that has had formal schooling and the group that has not in the way they perceive themselves as learners; and she would like to examine individual differences among all the children in her class, in order to identify those pupils who may have negative self-images as learners.

Reading the introductory chapters and the Table of Contents in *Socioemotional Measures for Preschool and Kindergarten Children,* the teacher notes that there is an entire section devoted to tests and measures of self-concept. She also pays close attention to caveats provided there regarding the dearth of validity information for most self-concept instruments and the lack of correspondence across instruments, even though identical names are given to the variables being assessed. Knowing that titles alone may not convey sufficient information about the content of the measures, she reads the eighteen entries in the Self-Concept chapter. She identifies five measures that deserve further attention, since they all include (under "Description of Measure") some mention of the assessment of school- and learning-related self-concept. Further, none of them appear to rely on vocabulary or reading skills, which is important to the teacher because she does not want to bias the test results in favor of those children who read or who have had some schooling. The titles of the five measures are as follows: Self-Concept and Motivation Inventory: Preschool-Kindergarten Form (or SCAMIN); Faces Scale; Learner Self-Concept Test; Perception Score Sheet; and Self-Concept Interview. The entry for the first measure listed—the SCAMIN, which was also discussed in Chapter Seven—is here reproduced (Walker, 1973, p. 249):

Self-Concept and Motivation Inventory:
Preschool-Kindergarten Form
(Also Called What Face Would You Wear?)

Authors: G. A. Farrah, N. J. Milchus, and W. Reitz.
Age Range: Preschool to kindergarten.
Measurement Technique: Self-report, semiprojective inventory.
Sources in Which Measure Described: See Coller (1971b).
Address from Which Measure Can Be Obtained: Person-O-Metrics, 20504 Williamsburg Road, Dearborn Heights, Mich. 48127.
Description of Measure: This group-administered test, paced for twenty-five to thirty minutes, measures self-concept with regard to school (role expectation, achievement needs, failure avoidance, and self-adequacy). A child responds to questions by marking with a crayon on faces with expressions such as happy and sad. Two forms for elementary grades and high school are also available. No training is needed to administer the test.
Norms: Grade-level quartile norms for 300 to 500 children are available (Coller, 1971b).
Validity: Not available.
Reliability: The reliability coefficient for the preschool-kindergarten form was .79 (sample size and type of coefficient not given) (Coller, 1971b).

In order to compare the five tests, the teacher constructs a chart that has, as its row headings, those aspects of the instruments that are important selection criteria for her: appropriateness of the age range, relevance of the variables being assessed for her purposes, ease of administration, norms, reliability, and validity. The column headings for her chart consist of the titles of the five tests. She then puts a +, −, or *n.a.* (not available) in each cell, to indicate if the criterion is met for each aspect (for example, adequate reliability has been demonstrated) or if the information is not, according to Walker, available. In some cells, her scoring is supplemented with explanatory remarks. Her chart is presented in Figure 14.

Figure 14. Comparison Matrix for Self-Concept Measures.

Criteria for Selection	Title of Measure				
	SCAMIN	Faces Scale	Learner Self-Concept Test	Perception Score Sheet	Self-Concept Interview
Appropriateness of Age Range[a]	+	− (probably for too advanced an age)	+	− (probably for too advanced an age)	− (probably for too advanced an age)
Relevance of Variables Assessed	+	− (only partly measures *learner* self-concept)	+	− (only partly measures *learner* self-concept)	+ to − (the "peers" subtest may not be relevant)
Ease of Administration	+	+	+	− (trained raters are necessary)	− (administrator training necessary)
Appropriateness of Norms	+? (need more information)	n.a.	n.a.	n.a.	n.a.

Evidence of Reliability	+? (need more information)	– (better evidence for K and grade 1 than for grades 2 and 3; weak overall)	n.a.	n.a. (factor analyses are questionable evidence of reliability)	n.a.
Evidence of Validity	n.a.	+ to – (generally low)	+ to – (generally low)	+? (need more information)	+ to – (conflicting results reported)

[a]Since the children to be measured are just now *entering* kindergarten, the appropriate age range would be preschool or preschool to kindergarten; that is, kindergarten is the *maximum* age range for an appropriate measure.

The teacher quickly eliminates the Faces Scale, the Perception Score Sheet, and the Self-Concept Interview from further consideration because the age range appropriateness is crucial to her. She then decides to order specimen sets of both the SCAMIN and the Learner Self-Concept Test, since neither has a clear advantage over the other. For both measures, the information on norms and reliability is either incomplete or not available. Although the evidence in support of the validity of the Learner Self-Concept Test is weak, the lack of any validity data at all for the other measure is a very serious shortcoming. Examination of the test manuals and forms, together with a review of the information listed under "Sources in which measure described" for each measure should permit this teacher to decide which one to use with her class—or perhaps prompt her to continue searching for another measure.

Johnson's *Tests and Measurements in Child Development*

Description. Two comprehensive source books of measures for young children have recently become available: *Tests and Measurements in Child Development: Handbook I* (Johnson and Bommarito, 1971) and a two-volume *Handbook II* (Johnson, 1976). These two handbooks are nonoverlapping guides to unpublished (sometimes referred to as "fugitive") measures of child behavior and development. The first Handbook contains descriptions of over 300 measures developed or used, primarily for research purposes, from 1956 to 1965; they were located through a search of fifty-three professional journals in the fields of education, psychology, and psychiatry. The second Handbook is the product of a continued search, covering the years 1966 through 1974, for the same kinds of measure. This Handbook, which consists of two volumes and includes descriptions of over 900 measures, represents a search through 148 journals. Whereas the first Handbook had twelve years as its maximum age for measures to be included, the second Handbook extends the maximum age to eighteen.

Measures were selected for inclusion according to six criteria:

1. The appropriate age range for the measure is birth to age twelve for Handbook I, and birth to age eighteen for Handbook II.
2. The measure is available for use—either through referencing a journal or other publication in which the entire measure appears or through contacting the author(s) for copies.
3. The measure is unpublished—in other words, it is not sold commercially by an established publisher.
4. Sufficient supplementary materials, especially administration and scoring instructions, accompany the measure so that it can be used effectively by persons other than the author(s).
5. The measure is long enough so that norms can be established and validity and reliability evidence can be obtained. (In some cases, such information is avail-

able, but for many measures the user would want to gather data for these purposes.)

6. Special laboratory equipment is not required for the use of the measure.

The measures in both Handbooks are classified according to content area, or, in other words, the type of variable predominantly measured by the instrument. The classification schemes for the two Handbooks are very similar. Handbook I is organized into ten major categories; Handbook II includes those same ten categories and adds an eleventh. Several of the major categories are subdivided to permit focusing on specific variables. The classification schemes are presented in Table 26. (Only modifications in Handbook II are cited; otherwise, the same categories and subcategories that are listed for Handbook I are also included in Handbook II.)

A brief description of each category and subcategory is found in the introductory chapters of both Handbooks and at the beginning of each major section of Handbook II. These descriptions define the categories and subcategories by listing the specific types of measure included in each. The format used for description of each measure is basically the same for the two Handbooks. For each measure, the following information is presented: author; appropriate age range; the specific variable(s) being assessed; the measurement technique used; the source from which the measure may be obtained; a description of the measure, which includes additional details on the variable(s) measured, the administration and scoring procedures, procedures used for the development of the instrument, available norms, length, special considerations, comments about usability, and sample items; results of any studies already completed on the reliability and validity of the measure; and a bibliography, in which journal articles or other references to the measure or its use are cited.

Use. Most of the measures in the Handbooks were developed for research purposes. They are, for the most part, intended for the assessment of groups of children rather than for individual diagnostic purposes. The variables they purportedly measure tend to be specific characteristics of children or of their environment; very few are "broad-based academic aptitude tests" (Johnson, 1976, p. 11). Testing specialists, child psychologists, researchers concerned with child behavior and development, and evaluators of many types of educational program will find these source books especially useful. Since the measures selected by Johnson and Bommarito are "unpublished," none of them are reviewed in Buros' *Mental Measurements Yearbook.* Therefore, this reference is a great time-saver in locating "fugitive" tests and measures and in obtaining syntheses of research studies on their reliability and validity.

A Table of Contents and a Subject Index are provided in both Handbooks; the user can start at either place in order to locate certain types of instrument. The Subject Index, however, provides more specific descriptors than the Table of Contents and includes a cross-referencing of measures by variable; that is, any measure that purports to assess a variable will be referenced for that variable, even if it is not the primary variable measured. This Index,

Table 26. Classification Schemes for Handbooks on Tests and Measurements in Child Development

Handbook I (1971)	_Changes in Handbook II (1976)_
Category 1: Cognition	
1-a: Intelligence and School Readiness	1-a: Intelligence, Readiness, and Maturation
1-b: Language and Number Skills	
1-c: Specific Achievements	
1-d: Cognitive Style and Cognitive Processes	
1-e: Miscellaneous	
Category 2: Personality and Emotional Characteristics	
2-a: Personality—General	
2-b: Personality Variables	
2-c: Personality Adjustment	
2-d: Anxiety	
Category 3: Perceptions of Environment	
3-a: Attitudes Toward Adults	3-a: Perceptions of Adults
3-b: Attitudes Toward Peers	3-b: Perceptions of Peers
3-c: Other Factors	3-c: Other Environmental Perceptions and Characteristics
Category 4: Self-Concept	
Category 5: Environment	
5-a: Quality of Mothering	5: Quality of Caregiving and Home Environment (no subscales)
5-b: Child-Rearing Practices	
5-c: Attitudes, Primarily of Parents, Toward School	

Category 6: Motor Skills, Brain Injury, and Sensory Perception

6-a: Motor Skills
6-b: Brain Injury
6-c: Sensory Perception

Category 7: Physical Attributes

Category 8: Miscellaneous Attitudes and Interests

Category 9: Social Behavior

Category 10: Unclassified

6: Motor Skills and Sensory Perception

(6-b eliminated)

8: Attitudes and Interests
8-a: Attitudes Toward School
8-b: Miscellaneous Attitudes and Interests

10: Vocational
11: Unclassified

then, is the more useful entry point if the user has identified specific variables for measurement.

As an example of how to use the two Handbooks, we will follow the procedures an evaluator would use in locating instruments to measure anxiety in preschool children. The services of this evaluator have been contracted for by the coordinator of early childhood education in a large school district. The district has implemented two types of preschool program in various schools, and one difference between the two programs is the amount of rest-period time allotted during the day for the children. The hypothesis that is to be tested is whether additional rest periods reduce anxiety in preschoolers.

The evaluator has both Handbooks available to aid in identifying measures of anxiety for this age group. She notes that one subcategory in the Table of Contents of both Handbooks is labeled *anxiety*. She also notes that several additional instruments listed (by page number) in the Subject Index deal with this variable. To ensure that she does not overlook any potentially useful instrument, she checks all of the references under "anxiety" in the Subject Index. She follows the same procedure for both Handbooks, since the second Handbook is supplemental to the first.

Even though there are over twenty measures cited in the two books as being concerned in some way with anxiety, only one—listed in the first Handbook—appears to be appropriate for this age group. The entry for this measure, The Anxiety Scale, is here reproduced (Johnson and Bommarito, 1971, pp. 238–239):

The Anxiety Scale

> *Author:* Jerry D. Alpern.
> *Age:* Preschool.
> *Variable:* Personality-anxiety.
> *Type of Measure:* Modified interview.
> *Source from Which the Measure May Be Obtained:* See Alpern (1959).
> *Description of Measure:* The Anxiety Scale is a modified interview consisting of seventy-nine items which the subject responds to by placing a steel ball in one of two boxes, one contiguous to and represented by a "happy" face of a child of the same sex as the subject, the other contiguous to and represented by a "sad" face of the same-sex child. The interview is composed of three types of items: those designed to elicit "happy" responses; those designed to elicit "sad" responses; and those constructed to elicit either a "happy" or "sad" response depending on the experience of the individual. The anxiety scores were derived from this last group of items (ambiguous items). The first ten items of the measure included six "happy" and four "sad" ambiguous items. The other sixty-nine items consisted of alternating ambiguous and unambiguous items, beginning with ambiguous item 11.
>
> In administering the measure, the examiner calls attention to the "happy box" and points out that there is a picture of a happy boy (or girl) by a period. He does the same for the "sad box" and then instructs the child to put the marble in whatever box he wants to after he hears the question.

Four scores are derived from the Anxiety Scale: (1) the total "sad response" score, which is the number of times the child makes a sad response to the ambiguous interview items; (2) the "speed score," which is the child's main latency on the ambiguous items, latency being defined as the time elapsed between the presentation of the item or question and response; (3) "latency score"; a basal response time was determined for each child by getting the average of the latency time on the thirty-four unambiguous items. The latency score, then, is the difference between the mean latency time on the thirty-five ambiguous items and the basal time mentioned above. (4) "Variance score," which is simply the variance of the latency times on the ambiguous items.

While reliabilities are not high and validity is not demonstrated in the form of significant correlations between any of the four anxiety scale scores and either of the two criteria, teachers' ranking of anxiety and a motor task, the test procedure used and the pool of items for the anxiety measure may be of interest to other researchers. Low reliability should be expected in view of the fact that the age range of the subjects was from 3 years 3 months to 5 years 1 month in the original sample.

Reliability and Validity: Test-retest reliabilities on the four anxiety scores, for the younger group (chronological ages 3 years 3 months to 3 years 11 months) range from −.14 to .46. For the older group, with chronological ages from 3 years 11 months to 5 years 1 month, the reliabilities ranged from .57 to .89. None of the anxiety scale scores correlated significantly with teachers' rankings of anxiety. There was also no significant relationship between performance on a motor task and any of the anxiety scale scores.

Bibliography: Alpern, J. D. "The Relationship of an Objective Measure of Anxiety for Pre-School Aged Children to Two Criterion Measures." Unpublished master's thesis, State University of Iowa, 1959.

The evaluator is dismayed somewhat at the lack of other potential instruments to use in her study. She should, of course, check other sources in addition to Handbooks I and II, for example, Buros' *Tests in Print II.* The Anxiety Scale does deal with the particular personality characteristic she is interested in, and it is appropriate for her subjects in terms of age. However, the lack of validity evidence is disturbing, as are the seemingly time-consuming administration and scoring procedures. While not totally satisfied with the measure as described, she decides to examine it more carefully by securing a copy from the source given. She may, after seeing the items, decide to construct her own anxiety measure based to some extent on the format and content of this one.

CSE Preschool/Kindergarten and Elementary School Test Evaluations

Description. Two volumes in the Center for the Study of Evaluation's (CSE) Test Evaluation Series that contain lists of published tests for young children are the *CSE/ECRC Preschool/Kindergarten Test Evaluations* (Hoepfner, Stern, and Nummedal, 1971) and *CSE Elementary School Test Evaluations* (Hoepfner and others, 1976). The tests in these two volumes are categorized according to educational objectives. Ratings on four dimensions—measurement validity, examinee appropriateness, administrative usability, and normed technical excellence—are given for each test. The books are intended primarily for persons interested in evaluating educational programs by measuring specified affective and cognitive outcomes. A secondary purpose of the books is to encourage development of tests in areas for which no instrumentation exists, and even to suggest specific criteria for constructing such tests.

Prior to the categorization and rating of tests according to educational goals, a classification system was established for the goals. The staff at CSE, in conjunction with teachers, supervisors, and other school personnel, outlined the goals for preschool/kindergarten education and for elementary education. The taxonomies of goals are similar but not identical for the two volumes. The Taxonomy of Goals of Preschool/Kindergarten Education consists of seventy-nine goals classified under four major headings: the affective domain, the intellectual domain, the psychomotor domain, and the subject achievement domain. The taxonomy for elementary school education is comprised of 150 goals subsumed under fourteen major headings: affective and personality traits, arts and crafts, career education, cognitive and intellectual skills, foreign language, language arts, mathematics, music, perceptual and motor skills, physical education and health education, reading, religion and ethics, science, and social studies. The list of goals in the preschool/kindergarten volume includes operational descriptions of children's behaviors indicative of mastery.

All published tests that appeared to qualify as measuring instruments for one or more goals were obtained by the CSE staff and categorized, according to publishers' claims, into appropriate age categories: preschool (thirty to fifty-nine months) or kindergarten (sixty to seventy-two months) for the preschool/kindergarten volume; grades one, two, three and four, or five and six for the elementary-level volume. The next step involved a classification of tests in terms of the predominant goal measured by each scale or subscale. This categorization was achieved by examining the test items to determine which goal was most directly addressed. Approximately 150 tests were located and rated for the preschool/kindergarten volume; over 800 tests were included in the elementary school collection. Many measures contained multiple scales, which were separately evaluated. Clinical or projective measures were not included, since the focus of the books is on presenting tests suitable for use by teachers, principals, and directors of special educational programs, rather than for use by psychologists.

An evaluation system—the MEAN Evaluation System—was created in order to obtain consistent and relatively objective ratings of the tests. MEAN is an acronym for the four major criteria against which the tests were judged: measurement validity, examinee appropriateness, administrative usability, and normed technical excellence. Specific aspects of each criterion were delineated, and points were assigned to each test according to the extent of agreement with desirable properties. Letter grades, based on the number of acquired points, were then awarded on each of the four criteria. The judges included a psychometrist, several experienced teachers, and graduate students with degrees in statistics, counseling and guidance, psychological measurement, and educational and developmental psychology.

The assignments of points were made according to a specific procedure that reflected the authors' priorities for criteria and aspects of criteria. Points were assigned for the preschool/kindergarten volume as follows:

1. Measurement validity (0 to 15 points)
   a. Evidence of construct and content validity (0 to 10 points)
   b. Evidence for predictive or concurrent validity (0 to 5 points)
2. Examine appropriateness (0 to 15 points)
   a. Appropriateness of test content for target age group (0 to 4 points)
   b. Appropriateness of instructions for target age group (0 to 4 points)
   c. Effectiveness of usage of Gestalt visual principles in format (0 to 2 points)
   d. Quality of illustrations and print (0 to 2 points)
   e. Appropriateness of pacing (0 to 1 point)
   f. Standardization of auditory presentation (0 to 1 point)
   g. Simplicity and directness of response recording procedures for examinees (0 to 1 point)
3. Administrative usability (0 to 15 points)
   a. Ease and convenience of administration (0 to 2 points, depending on size of group to which test can be administered)
   b. Required training for administrator (0 to 1 point, with "no training required" receiving 1 point)
   c. Required time for administration (0 to 1 point, with 1 point awarded to tests requiring twenty minutes or less)
   d. Ease and objectivity of scoring procedures (0 to 2 points)
   e. Adequacy of norm range for score interpretation (0 to 1 point)
   f. Simplicity and clarity of interpretation of scoring system (0 to 1 point)
   g. Simplicity and clarity of conversion from raw to normed scores (0 to 2 points)
   h. Adequacy of normative groups (0 to 1 point)
   i. Qualifications required of score interpreter (0 to 1 point)
   j. Adequacy of tables and charts in manuals to aid in decision making on basis of scores (0 to 3 points)
4. Normed technical excellence (0 to 15 points)
   a. Evidence of adequate stability (test-retest) reliability (0 to 3 points)
   b. Evidence of adequate internal-consistency reliability (0 to 3 points)
   c. Evidence of adequate alternate-form reliability (0 to 3 points)
   d. Reliability of conditions under which normed scores were obtained (0 to 1 point)
   e. Adequacy of range of coverage of test scores (0 to 3 points)
   f. Presentation of well-graduated normative scores (0 to 2 points)

Each test subsequently received four letter grades, one for each criterion. The letter grades were G (Good), F (Fail), and P (Poor), determined as follows:

Grade   *Point Range (Preschool/Kindergarten)*

Good   11 to 15 points
Fair   6 to 10 points
Poor   Less than 6 points

The MEAN Evaluation System used for rating tests and subtests in the elementary volume differed somewhat from the one used for the preschool/kindergarten tests and subtests. In general, the elementary MEAN system provided a more elaborate breakdown of subcategories within the four major categories. However, the point range for each of the four major categories remained the same—0 to 15 points. The assignment of letter grades for each category was made according to the following breakdown:

Grade   *Point Range (Elementary)*

Good   12 to 15 points
Fair   8 to 11 points
Poor   Less than 8 points

The authors' goal in preparing these source books was to provide compendiums of rated instruments for use in evaluation by educators who do not necessarily have technical expertise in measurement. Furthermore, the MEAN Evaluation System reflects the relative importance placed on various aspects of criteria by CSE. The user is appropriately cautioned against misinterpretation of the tests' ratings: "Should the goals of the reader not coincide with those of the Center, then the MEAN evaluations should be interpreted with different emphasis" (Hoepfner and others, 1976, p. xxxiii).

In order to aid the user in locating tests for specific needs, the volumes include a complete list of the educational objectives for each major age category of examinee. Each volume also includes a test-name index and a list of the names and addresses of the publisher and distributors of the measures cited. An additional aid to the user of the preschool/kindergarten volume is the inclusion of the names of individually administered tests and rating instruments, coded so that the user will recognize them as such. These codes alert the reader to expect low evaluations of the individual tests on most dimensions, since their very nature generally renders them less efficient for evaluation purposes.

Use. One attractive feature of these source books is the ease with which they can be used. It is essential, however, that the reader first peruse the introductory sections where the taxonomies are presented and the rationales for procedures used in the MEAN system are explained.

As an example of why and how one might use the CSE test information, consider the case of a Head Start director who would like to assess the familiarity of a group of preschool children with basic arithmetic concepts. The group is comprised of thirty preschoolers who are nearing the conclusion of one year at a Head Start Center. The curriculum for the past year for these children did not include formal instruction in arithmetic; nevertheless, the children were exposed indirectly to basic arithmetic concepts through many of their activities. The director is interested in determining how much knowledge they may have acquired in this indirect fashion.

Reading the introduction to *CSE-ECRC Preschool/Kindergarten Test Evaluations* and examining the list of educational goals under which tests are categorized, the director notes that one section of goals in the subject achievement domain is related to mathematics. That part of the taxonomy is reproduced below (Hoepfner, Stern, and Nummedal, 1971, p. xiv):

13. Mathematics

   A. Counting and Operations with Integers
      Recites numbers correctly and in order; relates counted numbers to numerosity of things; adds and subtracts whole numbers; checks answers.
   B. Comprehension of Sets in Mathematics
      Recognizes sets and understands set membership; performs basic set operations.
   C. Comprehension of Numbers in Mathematics
      Identifies and discriminates numbers and numerals; knows cardinal and ordinal numbers and the number line; knows odd and even numbers.
   D. Comprehension of Equality and Inequality in Mathematics
      Understands basic ideas of numerical equality and inequality; understands ideas of parts of things and how they relate to the whole; familiarity with fractional terminology.
   E. Arithmetic Problem Solving
      Solves simple problems of everyday life; learns names of coins and value relationships; develops an interest in problem solving.
   F. Measurement Reading and Making
      Understands concepts of length, volume, weight, time, and temperature, and how to measure them.
   G. Geometric Vocabulary and Recognition
      Recognizes names, basic geometric shapes and components; understands the concept of closed figures, curved and straight; makes basic comparisons among geometric shapes.

Since the outline of goals in this volume covers both preschool and kindergarten education, not all of these mathematics goals will be appropriate for the preschool level. For the purposes of the assessment this director wishes to carry out, tests related to goals "A" and "C" are most applicable.

In order to find the names and ratings of tests classified under these goals, the director pages through the first part of the volume (the pre school section). There the goals are numbered and ordered as they are in the general listing in the introduction. The preschool-level tests subsumed under the Mathematics goals are few in number; in fact, there are no tests listed for any of the Mathematics goals except "A." (This emphasizes either the lack of instrumentation for some educational objectives or the inappropriateness of the goals for the age level, or both.) A reproduction of the Mathematics-Preschool test section appears in Figure 15.

Checking again in the introduction, the director realizes that the symbol "o" represents an individually administered test, and the symbol "*" represents a rating scale. The director eliminates all tests cited under "A" that are preceded with an "o" since time is not available to administer a test individually to thirty children. She is also not particularly interested in using a rating scale, but does not want to exclude it as a possibility until she has checked other options. Unfortunately, there is only one other test cited under "A"—the Screening Test of Academic Readiness. Studying the ratings this test received on the aspects of the criteria, she is reasonably well satisfied with its ratings on administrative procedures, but she is disappointed in the lack of normative data. Another serious shortcoming of the test is its mediocre ratings on the dimension of examinee appropriateness. She is concerned that the items and instructions may be too difficult for her group of students. It appears, too, that the format may be too complicated and unclear for these children. Since the one other possible measure—the Preschool Attainment Record—is a rating scale, she does not have to be concerned about these "examinee appropriateness" aspects. However, this instrument also received very low ratings on other dimensions. Considering the problems with both measures, as well as the lack of measures for goal "C," the director decides her best course of action may be to construct her own test (with the assistance of other Head Start personnel and preschool teachers). Before making such a decision, she will order specimen sets of both the Preschool Attainment Record and the Screening Test of Academic Readiness. The latter, in particular, should help her in the construction of a new test—if she decides on that course of action—by suggesting types of item and by serving as a guide or model. Until she actually looks at the measures, she will be uncertain of their appropriateness for her group. The letters in parentheses following the names of the instruments are code names for the publishers. Turning to the Index of Publishers and Distributors at the back of the book, she finds the complete name and address for the publishers of the two instruments. She will write to each in order to obtain examination copies of these measures.

Other Sources of Early Childhood Measures

Following is an annotated bibliography of other sources of measures appropriate for evaluation and research in early childhood education. The sources vary in type—some are books, while others are journal articles or manuscripts located through the ERIC (Educational Research Information Clearinghouse) retrieval system. Some of these sources are concerned solely with particular assessment domains (for example, perceptual-motor development). Others are more general in scope, containing measures for various age groups. Generally, the sources cited here will not be used as frequently by early childhood educators and evaluators as the four source books described earlier, but they all do have some relevance to the field. The search for appropriate measures to use in a particular assessment is often more productive when several sources are perused. The sources listed here are organized alphabetically by author, or by title if no author is given for the entry. Full bibliographical citations are given in the References.

American Alliance for Health, Physical Education, and Recreation's Annotated Bibliography on Perceptual-Motor Development (1973). This 122-page monograph consists of four bibliographical sections: references for general readings on perception, learning, and development; lists of works by six specific authors; a bibliography organized by subject area (Auditory Perception and Movement, Body Image and Movement, and so forth); and references for materials on perceptual-motor programs, tests, and films. This final section is especially helpful for locating assessment instruments in the perceptual-motor domain.

The names and descriptions of tests are included in a subsection entitled "Tests, Programs, and Material Sources," which is organized alphabetically by title. The list was compiled from responses to letters sent to organizations and publishing companies requesting information on materials in the field of perception and perceptual-motor development. In addition to the tests cited, other materials, such as training and teaching guides, are also referenced. For each entry, information is presented to aid the reader in obtaining the most appropriate materials for his needs: author; title; publisher or sponsoring organization; cost; and a brief description, which, in the case of a test, includes reliability and validity findings, norms and standardization information, the ages for which the test is appropriate, administration procedures, and additional references. Over thirty tests are discussed; the majority are screening devices for the detection of visual and auditory impairments. Most are appropriate for children of at least four or five years, although a few are appropriate for use with younger children.

A few additional assessment instruments are described in a chart that follows the bibliography. For these measures, information is given on the intended purpose, age level, number of items, equipment needed, administrative ease, and distributors.

American Alliance for Health, Physical Education, and Recreation's Testing for Impaired, Disabled, and Handicapped Individuals (undated). This monograph (previously mentioned in Chapter Eight) contains over a hundred pages and overlaps to some extent with the *Annotated Bibliography on Perceptual-Motor Development;* both monographs are published by the same organization. The purpose of the guide is to provide information about instruments for use with impaired, disabled, and handicapped persons so that appropriate decisions can be made in selecting measures for prescriptive and diagnostic purposes.

In an opening section, an introduction to the value and uses of testing is provided. Then four types of measure are considered in separate chapters: physical fitness tests; motor ability, perceptual-motor development, and

Educational Objective Test Name	Measurement Validity		Examinee Appropriateness				
	Content and Construct	Concurrent and Predictive	Compre-hension		Format		
			Content	Instructions	Visual Organization	Quality of print/ Illustrations	Auditory Presentation
Rating Range	0-10	0-5	0-4	0-4	0-2	0-2	0-1
13. Mathematics							
A. Counting and Operations with Integers							
Detroit Tests of Learning Aptitude Number Ability (BMC)	6	0	2	3	1	2	0
Pictorial Test of Intelligence Size and Number (HMC)	4	1	2	3	2	2	0
Preschool Attainment Record Ideation (AGS)	3	0					
Preschool Inventory Concept Activation – Numerical (ETS)	4	0	2	2	1	1	0
School Readiness Survey Number Concepts (CPP)	4	0	2	1	0	1	0
Screening Test of Academic Readiness Numbers (PII)	4	0	2	2	1	1	0
Valett Developmental Survey of Basic Learning Abilities Conceptual Development (OPP)	3	0	3	3	1	1	0
Wechsler Preschool and Primary Scale of Intelligence Arithmetic (PC)	6	0	3	3	2	2	0
B. Comprehension of Sets in Mathematics							
C. Comprehension of Numbers in Mathematics							
D. Comprehension of Equality and Inequality in Mathematics							
E. Arithmetic Problem Solving							
F. Measurement Reading and Making							
G. Geometric Vocabulary and Recognition							

Source: Hoepfner, Stern, and Nummedal, 1971, pp. 8–9.

Figure 15. Preschool Test Evaluation.

		Administrative Usability										Normed Technical Excellence						Total Grades
Format		Administration			Scoring	Interpretation						Stability	Internal Consistency	Alternate Form	Replicability of Administrative Conditions	Range of Coverage	Gradation of Scores	
Time and Pacing	Recording Responses	Administration Test	Training of Administrator	Administration Time	Scoring	Norm Range	Score Interpretation	Score Conversion	Norm Groups	Score Interpreter	Can Decisions Be Made?	Stability	Internal Consistency	Alternate Form	Replicability of Administrative Conditions	Range of Coverage	Gradation of Scores	
0-1	0-1	0-2	0-1	0-1	0-2	0-1	0-1	0-2	0-1	0-1	0-3	0-3	0-3	0-3	0-1	0-3	0-2	Good-Fair-Poor
1	1	0	0	1	2	0	1	2	0	0	1	0	0	0	0	2	2	F F F P
1	1	0	1	1	2	0	1	2	0	1	1	0	0	0	0	2	1	P G F P
		0	1	1	0	0	1	1	0	1	1	0	0	0	0	0	1	P – F P
1	1	0	1	1	1	0	0	0	0	1	0	0	0	0	0	0	0	P F P P
1	1	0	1	1	2	0	1	2	0	1	3	0	0	0	0	1	1	P F G P
1	1	2	1	1	1	0	1	2	0	1	1	0	0	0	0	0	1	P F F P
1	1	0	1	0	0	0	0	0	0	1	1	0	0	0	0	0	0	P F P P
1	1	0	0	1	2	0	1	2	0	0	1	0	2	0	0	2	1	F G F P

Figure 15. Preschool Test Evaluation. (Continued)

psychomotor tests; developmental profiles; and locally developed assessment devices. In all, about sixty measures are included. Information presented on each measure includes the source, what is measured, how it is measured, notes concerning test administration, and comments. Helpful summary charts are also presented for each chapter in the form of matrices that show which tests measure specific characteristics. The monograph quite likely falls short of its goal of enabling final selection decisions, as adequate information cannot be conveyed in so encapsulated a form. Still, the basic information presented on each measure and the summary charts permit determination of which scales to secure for detailed study and possible use.

Beatty's Improving Educational Assessment and An Inventory of Measures of Affective Behavior (1969). The second section of this book—the "Inventory of Measures of Affective Behavior"—contains information on 133 published and unpublished measures. The measures are categorized as follows: attitude scales, creativity, interaction, miscellaneous, motivation, personality, readiness, and self-concept. For each scale or test, a narrative description provides information about the variables measured, the availability of norms, the evidence for reliability and validity, the content and format, and the author and source. In many cases, but not all, the age range for which the measure was designed is included in the description.

Only a modest number of the 133 measures cited appear to be appropriate for children in the two-to-eight year age range. This source book is informative, in a general sense, to someone interested in the types of affective measure obtainable. However, one must read entire entries to learn the age range intended and, even then, the information is not always presented. Therefore, although this source might turn up an appropriate measure on occasion, it is not particularly useful for persons wishing to measure attitudes and personality traits in very young children; Walker (1973), previously noted, is clearly more appropriate.

Bonjean, Hill, and McLemore's Sociological Measurements: An Inventory of Scales and Indices (1967). This volume contains an extensive bibliography of published works (primarily journal articles) that include references to sociological scales and indexes. The authors examined all the issues of four sociology journals—*American Journal of Sociology, American Sociological Review, Social Forces, and Sociology*—from January 1954 through December 1965 to locate measures of sociological variables used in research studies. They then categorized all the measures into seventy-eight conceptual classes. The bibliographical citation for each measure is listed under the conceptual class of primary membership (with the author's use of the measure being the criterion for placement) and is cross-referenced as well in other classes if the measure has been used for other purposes. The conceptual classes are listed in alphabetical order; the categories (measures) in each class are similarly organized.

No specific facts about the measures are available in this volume for most of the 2,080 scales and indexes that are referenced. Exceptions to this rule are the forty-seven measures for which five or more uses or citations were found in published works; these measures are described in detail within the relevant conceptual class and under the appropriate category. The description includes content and format of the instrument, scoring and administration procedures, references for published reviews (in Buros' *Mental Measurements Yearbook,* for example), and a reproduction of the instrument itself unless it is a commercially published one.

The seventy-eight conceptual classes are listed both in the Table of Contents and in the Introduction to the book. In addition, an Index of Topics and an Index of Names are included following the bibliographies. It is relatively easy, therefore, to find references for measures of specific variables.

The book is designed primarily to meet the needs of researchers interested in measuring sociological variables. The user must go to the articles referenced to find the instrument or further information about obtaining it. For this reason, it is not as "quick" a source book as some others for persons wishing merely to locate instruments. However, it does cover the sociological area quite thoroughly.

For the researcher or evaluator working in the field of early childhood education, many of the variables under which references are subsumed will be of interest. For example, twenty of the categories that fall into the conceptual class "Family: Interpersonal Relationships and Authority" are concerned with child-rearing practices. Many other categories also appear to deal with infancy and childhood, although the user would have to locate the bibliographical references to actually confirm this.

Boyer, Simon, and Karafin's Measures of Maturation: An Anthology of Early Childhood Observation Instruments (1973). This three-volume anthology contains seventy-three observation systems for recording behaviors of infants and young children. The systems are presented alphabetically by author. A detailed description is given of each, including rationale and purpose, dimensions of the system, instructions for coding, results of related research with the system, and references. Two summary charts precede each description. The first specifies the subjects of the observation, their ages, the number of children recorded, the setting for the observation, the data collection procedures, the required collection/coding staff, the coding units, and the uses of the system as reported by the author. The second presents details about the content dimensions that are focused on in the system. All of the information in the two charts is repeated for all seventy-three systems in a set of tables at the beginning of Volume I. There the reader can obtain a summarization of the contents, methods, subjects, and so on, for all seventy-three systems.

The categorization scheme used by Boyer, Simon, and Karafin to distinguish among the content dimensions of the systems includes the following broad categories: Individual, Social Contact, and Physical Environment. Each category is subdivided according to such variables as type of trait or behavior assessed and person(s) with whom the child interacts. For example, one subsection of the Individual category dimension is labeled Psychomotor, which is further subdivided into six categories: Facial Expression, Body Activity, Level of Activity, Nervous Habits, Body Orientation, and Sensory Perceptions.

Although most of the systems were designed for research purposes, some other uses (in the evaluation of programs, for example) are noted for several systems. The systems should certainly be valuable in examining and evaluating ongoing activities in early childhood education settings of almost all types.

Cattell and Warburton's Objective Personality and Motivation Tests (1967). This book reflects the authors' strong belief in the advantages of measuring and studying personality and motivation by means of objective tests rather than projective tests such as the Rorschach. The book is divided into two major sections. The first several chapters deal with measurement theory and test categorization and construction; following this section is a compendium of over 600 objective tests of personality. The first section is directed to students of test theory, while the second is intended primarily for researchers and other professional psychologists and educators who need to identify tests for use in applied settings. Although few of the instruments in the compendium are applicable for use with children under six, a substantial number are listed as appropriate for children age six and older.

The description of each test is complete with title, type, age range, alternate forms, derived factors, underlying theory, sample items, administration procedures, and so on. Six indexes aid the reader using the compendium. For example, the reader can locate tests of certain variables by using the Variables Titles Index or can find a specific test's entry by using the Titles Index.

Chun, Cobb, and French's Measures for Psychological Assessment (1975). This work represents a massive compilation effort. It provides a comprehensive bibliography of all measures of mental health and related variables found through a search of twenty-six measurement-related journals in psychology and sociology from 1960 to 1970. The types of measure selected for inclusion are as follows: mental health measures; measures of individual traits and moods (other than intelligence or aptitude), behaviors, and some attitudes; measures of interpersonal relationships; and measures of group characteristics, such as social structure and norms.

The book consists of two main sections. The Primary References section includes the title of each measure, a reference to the original source, key words descriptive of the measure's content, and reference numbers for the Applications section. The Applications section contains listings of journal articles that deal with uses of, and research related to, the measures, other than the original source for a measure. By using both sections, one can locate all articles pertaining to a particular instrument. In addition, an Author Index and a Descriptor Index are included. The latter is organized by descriptive key words, and thus would be the place to start if one were interested in locating measures of a specific variable.

This source is useful to researchers and evaluators, although it is not directly applicable to measurements in early childhood education. It is well organized and easy to use. One drawback is that the appropriate age range for measures must be inferred from the descriptors for each measure. The volume should not be overlooked, however, in the search for useful measures of the selected variables (mental health, attitude, social awareness, interpersonal relationships) for the assessment of young children.

Clarke's Physical and Motor Tests in the Medford Boys' Growth Study (1971). In this suspected male-chauvinist treatise, Clarke reports on the purpose, procedures, and results of the twelve-year (1956 through 1968) Medford Boys' Growth Study. The subjects for the study—several hundred boys from ages seven through eighteen—were measured annually on the following dimensions: physical maturity, physique type, body size, muscular strength and endurance, and motor and athletic ability. The same instruments were used repeatedly, yielding informative longitudinal data. Some measures were developed specifically for the project and some were already available. For each instrument used, the following facts and data are given, when applicable: a description of the measure; the origin of the measure; revisions of and insights into the measure resulting from its use in the study; inter-age correlation; growth patterns and variability; relationships with other measures in the same category; and relationships with other measures in other categories.

The instruments described in this book should be of interest, generally, to educators interested in the assessment of the psychomotor domain; in the context of early childhood education, specifically, most of the instruments are appropriate for use with children in the upper age range (seven and eight years).

Coller's The Assessment of "Self-Concept" in Early Childhood Education (1971b). Coller accomplished three tasks in this paper. He reviewed the self-concept literature, differentiating between the self-as-subject and self-as-object definitions; he briefly discussed fifty assessment instruments for measuring self-concept in young children; and he offered suggestions to enhance future evaluation efforts in this area. The fifty measures he described include checklists, multiple-choice tests, Q-sorts, rating scales, and other measurement techniques. He concluded his discussion with a few general remarks on the status of self-concept assessment—warning the reader that most of the measures "assess fundamentally different things regarding self-concept" (1971b, p. 58) and that the "bulk of currently available self-concept tests is not very useful in the evaluation of self-concept curricula" (1971b, p. 64).

This is an excellent source for names and reviews of self-concept instruments for children below age six. Coller's treatment of the field is perceptive and his criticisms are justified. Very few of the available self-concept measures are supported with substantial evidence of reliability and validity.

Comrey, Backer, and Glaser's A Sourcebook for Mental Health Measures (1973). Over 1,000 psychological measures related to mental health are described in this source book. The measures are classified into forty-five groupings of measures that share a common purpose, character, or both. The groupings cover a wide range of topics, from alcoholism to vocational tests. Titles of the groups aid the reader in identifying age-appropriate (adult versus child) sections.

Locating the measures involved an extensive search. One approach taken was to identify possible authors of measures by examining references in *Psychological Abstracts* for the years 1969–1971; membership lists for professional organizations such as the Psychometric Society, lists of National Institute of Mental Health (NIMH) grant projects funded during 1968–1971, faculty rosters for universities and colleges, and so forth. The search procedures yielded thousands of names of persons who might have developed measures pertinent to mental health research. Letters were sent to these individuals, requesting information about any measures developed by themselves or others they knew about; excluded from the request was information about popular instruments available from commercial publishers.

An abstract, limited to a maximum of 300 words, was prepared for each of the suitable measures obtained. Each measure included in the source book is identified by title, name and address of author(s), and source. In the abstract that follows, the measure is briefly described in terms of such features as content, measurement technique, development procedures, age range, and validity and reliability evidence, if available. Although many of the measures pertain to adults or adolescents, there are several sections with measures (of personality and educational adjustment, for example) appropriate for use with young children. This source book is one that should be especially helpful if mental health measures are required for use in research studies.

Educational Testing Service's Head Start Test Collection. At its main office in Princeton, New Jersey, Educational Testing Service (ETS) maintains an extensive library of tests and other measurement devices, called the Test Collection. Established to serve as an archive of testing materials, it also provides up-to-date information on tests and related services for potential users engaged in education, research, advisory services, or related pursuits. Over 10,000 instruments are currently on file. On-site access to the Test Collection materials is provided for qualified persons, whether directly affiliated with ETS or not. It is also possible to have specific questions answered by writing or phoning the Test Collection staff.

One segment of the Test Collection that is of particular interest to early childhood educators is the Head Start Test Collection. This consists of eight short publications, most of them annotated bibliographies. Fortunately for anyone interested in these documents, they are also available through the ERIC Document Reproduction Service, Computer Microfilm International Corporation, P.O. Box 190, Arlington, VA, 22210, either in hard copy ($1.50 each) or microfiche ($.75 each). The eight bibliographies currently available, and their ERIC accession numbers, are:

1. Assessing the Attitudes of Young Children Toward School (A State-of-the-Art Paper) (ED 056 086)
2. Language Development Tests: An Annotated Bibliography (ED 056 082)
3. Measures of Infant Development: An Annotated Bibliography (ED 058 326)
4. Measures of Social Skills: An Annotated Bibliography (ED 056 085)
5. School Readiness Measures: An Annotated Bibliography (ED 056 083)
6. Self-Concept Measures: An Annotated Bibliography (ED 051 305)
7. Self-Concept Measures: Revised 1973 (ED 086 737)
8. Tests for Spanish-Speaking Children: An Annotated Bibliography (ED 056 084)

Goolsby and Darby's Bibliography of Instrumentation Methodology and Procedures for Measurement in Early Childhood Learning (1969). This bibliography is not annotated and will most likely not be as useful in instrumentation selection procedures as some of the other available sources. However, it is included here because of its potential usefulness to evaluators and researchers who are attempting to design early childhood evaluation studies. The bibliography is the product of a literature review conducted during the first phase of the University of Georgia's evaluation program in early childhood education. Reports, books, articles, and selected tests published or available during the 1960–1968 period are cited. One section of the monograph—Experimental Instruments Found in the Current Literature—contains thirty-seven references, organized by type of test: achievement, mental ability, personality, and teacher assessment. Another section lists thirty-eight Standardized Instruments Appropriate for Measurement of Young Children. These, too, are organized by type, such as achievement, creativity, mental ability, personality, readiness, social maturity, and visual perception. However, no descriptive information or evaluative comments are available in this bibliography.

Hoepfner and Others' Tests of Higher-Order Cognitive, Affective, and Interpersonal Skills (1972). This manual, like the two Hoepfner and others' CSE Test Evaluation Series, conveys information on instruments available in a particular area (here, higher-order cognitive, affective, and interpersonal skill areas), and ratings on the quality and usefulness of those instruments. Several features of this volume distinguish it from the others in the Series: it resulted from a joint effort of the CSE staff and the Humanizing Learning Program of the Research for Better Schools (RBS), which is developing a skill-oriented curriculum to integrate intellectual, affective, and interpersonal skills; its primary classification is by type of instrument rather than by age of examinees; and its test ratings are based on an evaluation scheme slightly different from the MEAN system used in the other volumes. The criteria for the evaluation system, VENTURE, that was implemented for this volume, were as follows: validity, examinee appropriateness, normed excellence, teaching feedback, usability, retest potential, and ethical propriety.

In all, 2,600 published and unpublished scales and subscales that measure variables in the three domains of interest are listed. The classification scheme is a complex one. There are a total of 429 subcategories: 69 for tests in the higher-order cognitive dimension, 240 for tests in the affective domain, and 120 for tests that measure interpersonal skills. Each subcategory represents a combination of a specific content area and a specific type of assessment device. For example, an instrument that is classified, first of all, under the content area of Relations with Authorities at Home (Interpersonal Domain) is further categorized according to one of the following measurement techniques: descriptive self-report, speculative self-report, judgmental self-report, descriptive other-report, speculative other-report, judgmental other-report, contrived-situation behavioral measure, or actual-situation behavioral measure. The dearth or lack of instruments for many of the categories, as well as the low VENTURE ratings assigned to most measures that were located, paints a rather dismal picture. The authors commented on this situation in the introduction to the volume:

> In conclusion, it should be noted that, in the opinion of the CSE staff, the "state of the art," as it is presented here, leaves much to be desired. In terms of quantity, of the 429 categories in the three classification schemes, 183 (43%) contain 10 or fewer instruments. In addition, the quality of the instruments, as expressed by their VENTURE evaluations, is predominantly poor to fair. . . . the average ratings [for categories] for Validity, Normed excellence, Teaching feedback, and Retest potential are uniformly poor, while the ratings for Examinee appropriateness and Usability are predominantly fair, with good ratings on these two criteria occurring most frequently in the Interpersonal domain and least frequently in the Higher-Order Cognitive domain. In short, much work remains to be done, both in developing instruments where none now exist and in improving the quality of those instruments which have already been developed [Hoepfner and others, 1972, p. xxii].

The scales and subscales are identified in tabular form by name, form, other category assignments (if any), the applicable age range, and the source; numerical ratings on the seven VENTURE criteria then appear, followed by seven corresponding letter grades (G, F, or P, representing Good, Fair, or Poor, respectively). The point assignment for the criteria was made according to predetermined specifications, with points awarded on the extent to which specific aspects of the criteria were met. The reader should be aware that, as was true for the other CSE volumes, the VENTURE ratings are based on the goals and priorities of the CSE and RBS staffs. Before using the volume, the reader should familiarize himself with those goals and priorities.

Only a portion of the instruments are applicable for use at primary and preprimary levels. To locate instruments for certain ages, one must turn to the category of interest and then look for that age group under Age or Educational Level.

Lake, Miles, and Earle's Measuring Human Behavior (1973). This book focuses on measurement instruments for the "social functioning" domain. According to the authors, social functioning refers "to the properties of the individual (cognitive/perceptual, motivational, and overt behavioral) as he or she takes part in social interaction, and to the properties of the immediate social system involved (dyads, small groups, organizations)" (Lake, Miles, and Earle, 1973, p. xiii). Only a few measures described and critiqued in this book are intended for use with young children. Nevertheless, those few instruments that are appropriate for program evaluation or research in early childhood education are given comprehensive treatment. The stringent criteria employed for selection of measures for inclusion in this anthology, together with the integration of all available information in the descriptions of the measures, make this a highly useful set of measures and reviews. An additional attractive feature of this volume is the description and critique of twenty other compendiums of instruments, such as Johnson and Bommarito's *Handbook* and Buros' *Sixth Mental Measurements Yearbook.*

The 84 instruments listed and described were selected from about 300 measures of social functioning located by the authors. The criteria for inclusion were: measurement of some aspect of social functioning; development based on an underlying theory or conceptual scheme; evidence shown of substantial developmental work undertaken during the construction phase; appearance of being "interesting" and "potentially useful"; existence of reviews in other published works; availability to users; and availability of relatively current data on reliability and validity.

The measures are organized alphabetically by title. Each entry conforms to the following outline: title; author; availability (that is, where and how to obtain the measure); variables measured; description of format; administration and scoring procedures; a history of the development of the measure, including findings from reliability and validity studies; critique; general comment; and references. The critique and general comment sections are particularly useful; the former includes mention of possible problems with fakeability (that is, the ease with which scores can be "faked") of the instrument and susceptibility to response-set bias, while the latter succinctly considers the usefulness of the measure. Further, each measure is accompanied by one or more key words, called *uniterms,* which reference the variables being assessed and other pertinent features of the instrument, such as appropriate age. A Uniterm Index lists all key words and the measures or compendiums that deal with them. Unfortunately, the key word *child* in the Uniterm Index is followed by only six numbered references to instruments in the text. Other instruments should be of interest to test developers working with the young age group, however, as they can suggest formats and content for various assessment areas. The information contained in this volume is so comprehensive that the book should be included among the source books used by almost any evaluator or test developer.

Mardell and Goldenberg's Learning Disabilities/Early Childhood Research Project (1972). The major purpose of this paper is to describe the Developmental Indicators for the Assessment of Learning (DIAL), devised by the Early Childhood Research Project to identify pre-kindergarten children with potential learning disabilities. In the process of constructing the DIAL system, the authors evaluated over 900 instruments against the following set of standards: appropriate for children aged two and a half to five and a half years; individually administered; requiring a maximum administration time of no more than thirty minutes; low cost; assessing a wide range of behaviors; involving no labeling other than "high risk"; usable by paraprofessionals. According to the authors, none of the 900 measures they reviewed met all the criteria—a finding that induced them to develop DIAL. (DIAL is described in Chapter Six.)

An appendix contains critiques of 90 of the instruments considered. In the critiques, the administrative procedures, measurement techniques, performance areas assessed, and the applicability to young children are reviewed. This section should be helpful to persons trying to locate suitable screening devices for use with young children.

Robinson and Shaver's Measures of Social Psychological Attitudes (1973). This volume is the third in a series of handbooks on attitude measures by Robinson. The book is intended for three different audiences: researchers in psychology, sociology, and political science; students of research methodology; and non-researchers in relevant content areas, such as social commentators, political analysts, and journalists. Some chapters are also applicable to educational research and evaluation, and some instruments therein are applicable to early childhood settings. These include chapters on the measurement of self-esteem and related constructs, and internal-external locus of control. Other chapters deal with measures of life satisfaction and happiness; alienation and anomie; authoritarianism, dogmatism, and related constructs; other sociopolitical variables, such as radicalism-conservatism; values; general attitudes toward people; religious attitudes; and a few methodological factors, such as response-set factors. Each chapter has an introduction in which the focus is explained, the constructs are defined, measurement problems are explicated, and so on. The instruments are then presented.

The 126 instruments described and critiqued in this volume were obtained from a variety of sources: *Psychological Abstracts, Journal of Abnormal and Social Psychology, Journal of Social Psychology, Journal of Applied Psychology, Sociometry, American Sociological Review, Public Opinion Quarterly, American Political Science Review,* dissertations identified through *Dissertation Abstracts,* papers presented (and personal contact with researchers) at several annual meetings of professional associations, and other compendiums. Each instrument is reviewed thoroughly. Both descriptive and evaluative information are furnished. The title, author, variables measured, format, target population, scoring schemes, norming procedures, reliability and validity evidence, critical comments pertaining to use and effectiveness, and references are conveyed in the entries for most of the scales. In addition, the entire scale or sections therefrom are reprinted immediately following each entry.

The handbook is best used for locating scales by variable first, and then searching for ones applicable to the age group being studied. Only some sections pertain to measurement of social attitudes of young children; the nature of the variables in other sections precludes use with very young children. The scales that are included are given full coverage, and their actual reproduction is an extremely attractive feature of this handbook.

Shaw and Wright's Scales for the Measurement of Attitudes (1967). More than 175 scales, designed for the measurement of attitudes toward ten broadly categorized social referents, are presented in this volume. The referents are as follows: social practices, social issues and problems, international issues, abstract concepts (such as education, the law, and school courses), political and religious systems, ethnic and national groups, significant others (such as family members and educational workers), and social institutions. Each category is subdivided into from two to seven more specific attitudinal areas.

The scales were chosen for inclusion because, in the opinion of the authors, they possessed at least minimum reliability and validity and met minimum standards for construction. Nevertheless, the authors warned against the use of many of them for purposes other than research and group testing, because of lack of sufficient validity data, standardization, and so forth.

The scales are described in detail. For each one, information regarding the source, method of construction, reliability, validity, development sample, and number and type of items is given. In addition, actual items and administration and scoring directions are included. Three background chapters—pertaining to the measurement of attitudes, generally; the use and characteristics of attitude scales; and recommendations for improvement of attitudinal measurement—provide useful additional information.

Although few of the included scales have as their intended subject population primary or preprimary children, several relate to family and school life and others might be adapted for use with young children. Anyone interested in the study of perceptions of social institutions and interpersonal relationships involving young children would find this volume helpful.

Stott and Ball's Infant and Preschool Mental Tests: Review and Evaluation (1965). The intent of Stott and Ball was to present a "comprehensive evaluation of the present state of infant and preschool mental testing in the United States" (1965, p. 2). The monograph consists of several related sections: a review of the literature on the concept of intelligence and its measurement, especially as they relate to infants and preschoolers; a discussion of the development of tests and scales for the measurement of intelligence in infants and young children; the results of the authors' questionnaire survey of current practices in intelligence testing, with emphases on the relative frequency and intended purposes of use of different instruments, users' judgments of adequacy of the instruments, and their opinions on needed changes; and a comparison of five commonly used infant and preschool scales in terms of factor structure. Elaborating on the second section of the paper, brief descriptions of most of the commercially available instruments are given. The information in these descriptions includes mention of the variables being assessed and short summaries of the results of studies dealing with the reliability and validity of the instruments. Finally, note that the five measures treated in the fourth section of the paper are the Cattell Infant Scale, the California First-Year Mental Scale, the Gesell Developmental Schedule, the Merrill-Palmer Scale, and the Stanford-Binet Scale. Potential users of any of these scales should find this section helpful in better understanding the dimensions of the tests.

Although the monograph is quite technical, it should prove useful to psychometrists and persons who must select an instrument for the measurement of intelligence in infants and young children.

Straus' Family Measurement Techniques (1969). Representing several different measurement techniques, 319 instruments are abstracted in this volume. All of the instruments were developed for "quantitatively expressing the properties of the family or the behavior of people in family roles" (Straus, 1969, p. 3).

Referenced in the abstracts are 84 sociological and psychological journals published from 1935 to 1965. To be included in the volume, a measure had to meet three criteria: it had to consist of at least three items; it had to measure variables related to a family role; and it had to be available to readers, either through a commercial publisher or through the National Auxiliary Publication Service (NAPS). Straus gave details in his introduction of the procedure to use to order a copy of an instrument from NAPS.

The measures are arranged alphabetically by author's name. The information presented for each measure was obtained via the original source and any subsequent references to it in the published literature. Each of the following details are given, when available, for each measure cited: the name and author; the variables measured; a description of the content, format, administration and scoring procedures; a sample item; evidence of validity; the procedures used and the characteristics and size of the standardization and validation samples; evidence of reliability; length (time and number of items); norms; source from which the measure may be obtained; and references. The volume concludes with an Index of Test Titles, an Author Index, and a Subject Index. The latter is the preferred starting place to locate measures of specific aspects of family life as it is quite detailed and there is no content-related categorization in the text itself.

A substantial number of the instruments listed pertain to child-parent or child-family interactions, the adjustment of the child to family life, and so on. This is a useful compendium for investigations related to the infant's or young child's role in the family and family relationships. Given the current high interest in aspects of parental involvement in early childhood education, measures in the general area addressed by this source book may be of increasing importance and relevance.

Thomas' Psychological Assessment Instruments for Use With Human Infants (1970). This paper provides a review and integration of the literature on intelligence tests for infants. Nine instruments, both American and European, are reviewed in depth, with pertinent research of several decades summarized. Instrument selection involved two criteria: establishing an appropriate age range (through two years of age) and making a serious attempt to quantify infant behaviors. The nine instruments selected were: Cattell Infant Intelligence Scale; Gesell Developmental Schedules; Griffiths Mental Development Scale; Burnet and Lezine Scale; Bayley's Scales; Northwestern Intelligence Tests; Graham's Behavior Tests for Newborns; Prechtl's Neurological Examination; and Flint's Infant Security Scale.

The information provided for each instrument consists of the following: a description of variables assessed; the age levels for use; the format and administration procedures; a description of any subscales; the author and dates of the development and revisions; the languages in which it is available, and procedures for securing it if not commercially available; and standardization procedures, including a description of samples. Research studies on the validity and reliability of each instrument are also summarized. The paper is generally descriptive and objective, with only a brief comparative evaluative statement by the author at the conclusion of each instrument's section. Following the in-depth treatment of the nine measures, a few less-used instruments are mentioned. These tend to be very early scales that are no longer very popular, or relatively recent scales still in need of substantiating research. The final section of the paper is a discussion and summary of the "state of the art" in infant assessment.

This source should be especially useful to psychologists or psychometrists interested in infant intelligence testing. The list of references cited is extensive, and the integration of research findings in the body of the paper provides an excellent overview for each of the nine instruments.

Wylie's The Self-Concept (1974). One of Wylie's intentions in writing this book was to improve the quality of future self-concept research. Consequently, the book is largely methodological—offering chapters on theoretical issues, research designs applicable to valuations of self-concept theories, measurement techniques, and so forth. In two of the chapters, a few selected instruments designed for the measurement of self-concept and related variables are described and critiqued. No attempt is made to discuss all of the available instruments; rather, Wylie selected a few to focus on according to several criteria: frequency of use and representation of a variety of theoretical positions; aspects of self-concept assessed; and formats. The instruments that are covered in detail include such widely used tests as the Coopersmith Self-Esteem Inventory and the Piers-Harris Children's Self-Concept Scale. The treatments are comprehensive, including results of research studies on the scales.

The volume should be especially useful to researchers interested in the self-concept domain and to researchers and evaluators interested in constructing self-concept measures. However, it is not the place to initiate a search for existing instruments, as only a few are mentioned.

Concluding Remarks. The source books and articles highlighted in this section represent a broad range of sources of measures available for evaluation and research in early childhood education. Obviously, not all sources could be included here. We have identified the major reference works useful for identifying and locating instruments for use with young children. Each source cited includes its own set of bibliographical references—which can aid the interested user in exploring the assessment domains in greater detail.

References

Abert, J. G., and Kamrass, M. (Eds.). *Social Experiments and Social Program Evaluation.* Cambridge, Mass.: Ballinger, 1974.

Abt Associates. *National Day Care Study. Second Annual Report, 1975–1976, Phase II Results and Phase III Design.* Cambridge, Mass.: Abt Associates, 1976.

Abt Associates. *A National Survey of Head Start Graduates and Their Peers.* Cambridge, Mass.: Abt Associates, 1978.

Adkins, D. C., and Ballif, B. L. *Final Report: Motivation to Achieve in School.* Report to Office of Economic Opportunity. Honolulu: Education Research and Development Center, University of Hawaii, 1970. (Also available in ERIC, ED 037771.)

Adkins, D. C., and Ballif, B. L. "A New Approach to Response Sets in Analysis of a Test of Motivation to Achieve." *Educational and Psychological Measurement,* 1972, *32,* 559–577.

Adkins, D. C., and Ballif, B. L. *Animal Crackers: A Test of Motivation to Achieve: Examiner's Manual.* Monterey, Calif.: CTB/McGraw-Hill, 1973.

Administration for Children, Youth, and Families. *Head Start Program Performance Standards.* Washington, D.C.: U.S. Department of Health, Education, and Welfare, 1975.

Ahmann, J. S., and Glock, M. D. *Evaluating Pupil Growth: Principles of Tests and Measurements.* Boston: Allyn & Bacon, 1975.

Ahr, A. E., and Simons, B. *Parent Handbook: Developing Your Child's Skills and Abilities at Home.* Skokie, Ill.: Priority Innovations, 1968.

Airasian, P. W. "Designing Summative Evaluation Studies at the Local Level." In W. J. Popham (Ed.), *Evaluation in Education: Current Applications.* Berkeley, Calif.: McCutchan, 1974.

Alkin, M. C. "Evaluation Theory Development." *Evaluation Comment,* 1969, *2* (1), 2–7.

Allport, G. W. *Pattern and Growth in Personality.* New York: Holt, Rinehart and Winston, 1961.

Almy, M. *Ways of Studying Children: A Manual for Teachers.* New York: Teachers College Press, 1959.

Almy, M. *The Early Childhood Educator at Work.* New York: McGraw-Hill, 1975.

Alpern, G. D., and Boll, T. J. *Developmental Profile.* Aspen, Colo.: Psychological Development Publications, 1972.

Ambron, S. R. "Review of Circus." In O. K. Buros (Ed.), *The Eighth Mental Measurements Yearbook.* Vol. 1. Highland Park, N.J.: Gryphon Press, 1978.

American Alliance for Health, Physical Education, and Recreation. *Annotated Bibliography on Perceptual-Motor Development.* Washington, D.C.: American Alliance for Health, Physical Education, and Recreation, 1973.

American Alliance for Health, Physical Education, and Recreation. *Testing for Impaired, Disabled, and Handicapped Individuals.* Washington, D.C.: American Alliance for Health, Physical Education, and Recreation, Undated.

American Psychological Association. *Standards for Educational and Psychological Tests.* Washington, D.C.: American Psychological Association, 1974.

Ammons, R. B., and Ammons, C. H. "The Quick Test (QT): Provisional Manual." *Psychological Reports,* 1962, *11,* 111–161.

Ammons, R. B., and Ammons, H. S. *The Full-Range Picture Vocabulary Test.* New Orleans: R. B. Ammons, 1948.

Anastasi, A. "Review of Goodenough-Harris Drawing Test." In O. K. Buros (Ed.), *The Seventh Mental Measurements Yearbook.* Vol. 1. Highland Park, N.J.: Gryphon Press, 1972.

Anastasi, A. *Psychological Testing.* (4th ed.) New York: Macmillan, 1976.

Anderson, G. J. "Effects of Course Content and Teacher Sex on the Social Climate of Learning." *American Educational Research Journal,* 1971, *8* (4), 649–663.

Anderson, G. J. *The Assessment of Learning Environments: A Manual for the Learning Environment Inventory and the My Class Inventory.* (2nd ed.) Halifax, Nova Scotia: Atlantic Institute of Education, 1973.

Anderson, G. J., and Walberg, H. J. "Learning Environments." In H. J. Walberg (Ed.), *Evaluating Educational Performance.* Berkeley, Calif.: McCutchan, 1974.

Anderson, R. B., and others. "Pardon Us, But What Was the Question Again?: A Response to the Critique of the Follow Through Evaluation." *Harvard Educational Review,* 1978, *48* (2), 161–170.

Anderson, R. P. "Review of the Comprehensive Identification Process." In O. K. Buros (Ed.), *The Eighth Mental Measurements Yearbook.* Vol. 1. Highland Park, N.J.: Gryphon Press, 1978.

Anderson, S. B. "Educational Compensation and Evaluation: A Critique." In J. C. Stanley (Ed.), *Compensatory Education for Children, Ages 2 to 8: Recent Studies of Educational Intervention.* Baltimore, Md.: Johns Hopkins University Press, 1973.

Anderson, S. B., and Ball, S. *The Profession and Practice of Program Evaluation.* San Francisco: Jossey-Bass, 1978.

Anderson, S. B., Ball, S., Murphy, R. T., and Associates. *Encyclopedia of Educational Evaluation: Concepts and Techniques for Evaluating Education and Training Programs.* San Francisco: Jossey-Bass, 1975.

Anderson, S. B., and Messick, S. "Social Competency in Young Children." *Developmental Psychology,* 1974, *10,* 282–293.

Anderson, S. B., Messick, S., and Hartshorne, N. *Priorities and Directions for Research and Development Related to Measurement of Young Children.* Princeton, N.J.: Educational Testing Service, 1972.

Anderson, T. W. *An Introduction to Multivariate Statistical Analysis.* New York: Wiley, 1958.

Appleton, T., Clifton, R., and Goldberg, S. "The Development of Behavioral Competence in Infancy." In F. D. Horowitz (Ed.), *Review of Child Development Research.* Vol. 4. Chicago: University of Chicago Press, 1975.

Applied Management Sciences. *Evaluation of the Process of Mainstreaming Handicapped Children into Project Head Start: Phase II, Draft Interim Report.* Washington, D.C.: Administration for Children, Youth, and Families, 1978.

Arnstein, G. "Trial by Jury: A New Evaluation Model. II. The Outcome." *Phi Delta Kappan,* 1975, *57* (3), 188–190.

Arthur, G. *The Arthur Adaptation of the Leiter International Performance Scale: Manual.* Chicago: Stoelting, 1952.

Association for Supervision and Curriculum Development, Early Childhood Council. "Guidelines for the Analysis and Description of Early Childhood Education Programs." *Educational Leadership,* 1971, *28* (8), 812–820.

Auerbach, A. B. *Parents Learn Through Discussion: Principles and Practices of Parent Group Discussion.* New York: Wiley, 1968.

Austin, G. R. *Early Childhood Education: An International Perspective.* New York: Academic Press, 1976.

Austin, M. C. "Review of the Marianne Frostig Developmental Test of Visual Perception, Third Edition." In O. K. Buros (Ed.), *The Sixth Mental Measurements Yearbook.* Highland Park, N.J.: Gryphon Press, 1965.

Ayers, J. D. "Review of the Concept Assessment Kit—Conservation." In O. K. Buros (Ed.), *The Seventh Mental Measurements Yearbook.* Vol. 1. Highland Park, N.J.: Gryphon Press, 1972.

Ayres, A. J. *Southern California Sensory Integration Tests: Manual.* Los Angeles: Western Psychological Services, 1972.

Ayres, L. P. *Ayres Measuring Scale for Handwriting.* Iowa City: Bureau of Educational Research and Service, University of Iowa, 1940.

Baer, D. M., Wolf, M. M., and Risley, T. R. "Some Current Dimensions of Applied Behavioral Analysis." *Journal of Applied Behavioral Analysis,* 1968, *1* (1), 91–97.

Baird, L. L. "Review of Torrance Tests of Creative Thinking." In O. K. Buros

(Ed.), *The Seventh Mental Measurements Yearbook.* Vol. 1. Highland Park, N.J.: Gryphon Press, 1972.

Baker, E. L. "Opening Accountability: A Story in Two Parts." *Evaluation Comment,* 1973, *4* (1), 7–8.

Baker, E. L. "Formative Evaluation of Instruction." In W. J. Popham (Ed.), *Evaluation in Education: Current Applications.* Berkeley, Calif.: McCutchan, 1974.

Bales, R. F. *Interaction Process Analysis.* Cambridge, Mass.: Addison-Wesley, 1950.

Ball, S. *Assessing the Attitudes of Young Children Toward School.* Princeton, N.J.: Educational Testing Service, 1971.

Ball, S. " 'Sesame Street': A Case Study of an Evaluation." In J. G. Abert and M. Kamrass (Eds.), *Social Experiments and Social Program Evaluation.* Cambridge, Mass.: Ballinger, 1974.

Ball, S., and Bogatz, G. A. *The First Year of Sesame Street: An Evaluation.* Princeton, N.J.: Educational Testing Service, 1970a.

Ball, S., and Bogatz, G. A. *A Summary of the Major Findings in "The First Year of Sesame Street: An Evaluation."* Princeton, N.J.: Educational Testing Service, 1970b.

Ball, S., and Bogatz, G. A. *Reading with Television: An Evaluation of The Electric Company.* Vols. 1 and 2. Princeton, N.J.: Educational Testing Service, 1973.

Ball, S., and others. *Reading with Television: A Follow-Up Evaluation of "The Electric Company."* Princeton, N.J.: Educational Testing Service, 1974.

Banta, T. J. "Tests for the Evaluation of Early Childhood Education: The Cincinnati Autonomy Test Battery (CATB)." In J. Hellmuth (Ed.), *Cognitive Studies.* Vol. 1. New York: Brunner/Mazel, 1970.

Barker, R. G. (Ed.). *The Stream of Behavior.* New York: Appleton-Century-Crofts, 1963.

Barker, R. G. *Ecological Psychology: Concepts and Methods for Studying the Environment of Human Behavior.* Stanford, Calif.: Stanford University Press, 1968.

Barker, R. G. "Wanted: An Eco-Behavioral Science." In E. P. Willems and H. L. Raush (Eds.), *Naturalistic Viewpoints in Psychological Research.* New York: Holt, Rinehart and Winston, 1969.

Barker, R. G. *Habitats, Environments, and Human Behavior: Studies in Ecological Psychology and Eco-Behavioral Science.* San Francisco: Jossey-Bass, 1978.

Barker, R. G., and Gump, P. V. (Eds.). *Big School, Small School.* Stanford, Calif.: Stanford University Press, 1964.

Barker, R. G., and Wright, H. F. *One Boy's Day.* New York: Harper & Row, 1951.

Barron, F. *Creative Person and Creative Process.* New York: Holt, Rinehart and Winston, 1969.

Baumrind, D. "Child Care Practices Anteceding Three Patterns of Preschool Behavior." *Genetic Psychology Monographs.* 1967, *75,* 43–88.

Bayley, N. *Bayley Scales of Infant Development.* New York: Psychological Corporation, 1969.

Bean, R., and Clemes, H. *Elementary Principal's Handbook: New Approaches to Administrative Action.* West Nyack, N.Y.: Parker, 1978.

Beatty, W. H. *Improving Educational Assessment and An Inventory of Measures of*

Affective Behavior. Washington, D.C.: Association for Supervision and Curriculum Development, 1969.

Becker, W. C. "Teaching Reading and Language to the Disadvantaged—What We Have Learned from Field Research." *Harvard Educational Review,* 1977, *47* (4), 518–543.

Becker, W. C., and Engelmann, S. *Summary Analysis of Four-Year Data on Achievement and Teaching Progress with 7,000 Children in 20 Projects.* Follow Through Technical Report 73–1. Eugene: University of Oregon, 1973.

Beery, K. E. *Developmental Test of Visual-Motor Integration: Administration and Scoring Manual.* Chicago: Follett, 1967a.

Beery, K. E. *Visual-Motor Integration: Monograph.* Chicago: Follett, 1967b.

Beery, K. E., and Buktenica, N. A. *Developmental Test of Visual-Motor Integration: Student Test Booklet.* Chicago: Follett, 1967.

Beller, E. K. "Teaching Styles and Their Effects on Problem-Solving Behavior in Head Start Programs." In E. Grotberg (Ed.), *Critical Issues in Research Related to Disadvantaged Children.* Princeton, N.J.: Educational Testing Service, 1969.

Bennett, C. A., and Lumsdaine, A. A. (Eds.). *Evaluation and Experiment: Some Critical Issues in Assessing Social Programs.* New York: Academic Press, 1975.

Bennett, G. K., Seashore, H. G., and Wesman, A. G. *Manual for the Differential Aptitude Tests, Forms S and T.* (5th ed.) New York: Psychological Corporation, 1974.

Bentler, P. M. "Review of the Piers-Harris Children's Self-Concept Scale (The Way I Feel About Myself)." In O. K. Buros (Ed.), *The Seventh Mental Measurements Yearbook.* Vol. 1. Highland Park, N.J.: Gryphon Press, 1972.

Bentley, R. J., Washington, E. D., and Young, J. C. "Judging the Educational Progress of Young Children: Some Cautions." *Young Children,* 1973, *29,* 5–18.

Bereiter, C., and Engelmann, S. *Teaching Disadvantaged Children in the Preschool.* Englewood Cliffs, N.J.: Prentice-Hall, 1966.

Bereiter, C., and Kurland, M. "Were Some Follow Through Models More Effective than Others?" Paper presented at the annual meeting of the American Educational Research Association, Toronto, Canada, March 1978.

Bersoff, D. N. "Silk Purses into Sows' Ears: The Decline of Psychological Testing and a Suggestion for its Redemption." *American Psychologist,* 1973, *28,* 892–899.

Best, D. L. "Race of Examiner Effects on the Racial Attitude Responses of Preschool Children." Unpublished master's thesis, Wake Forest University, 1972.

Best, D. L., and others. "Development of Sex-Trait Stereotypes Among Young Children." *Child Development,* 1977, *48,* 806–819.

Bigner, J. J. "Sibling Influence on Sex-Role Preference of Young Children." *Journal of Genetic Psychology,* 1972, *121,* 271–282.

Bijou, S. W., and others. "Methodology for Experimental Studies of Young Children in Natural Settings." *Psychological Record,* 1969, *19,* 177–210.

Bissell, J. S. "Planned Variation in Head Start and Follow Through." In J. C. Stanley (Ed.), *Compensatory Education for Children, Ages 2 to 8: Recent Studies of Educational Intervention.* Baltimore, Md.: Johns Hopkins University Press, 1973.

Blank, M., Rose, S. A., and Berlin, L. J. *Preschool Language Assessment Instrument: The Language of Learning in Practice.* (Experimental ed.) New York: Grune & Stratton, 1978a.

Blank, M., Rose, S. A., and Berlin, L. J. *The Language of Learning: The Preschool Years.* New York: Grune & Stratton, 1978b.

Bloom, B. S. (Ed.). *Taxonomy of Educational Objectives. Handbook I: Cognitive Domain.* New York: McKay, 1956.

Bloom, B. S. *Stability and Change in Human Characteristics.* New York: Wiley, 1964.

Bloom, B. S., Hastings, J. T., and Madaus, G. F. (Eds.). *Handbook on Formative and Summative Evaluation of Student Learning.* New York: McGraw-Hill, 1971.

Bloom, L. "Language Development." In F. D. Horowitz (Ed.), *Review of Child Development Research.* Vol. 4. Chicago: University of Chicago Press, 1975.

Bodin, A. M. "Conjoint Family Assessment: An Evolving Field." In P. McReynolds (Ed.), *Advances in Psychological Assessment.* Vol. 1. Palo Alto, Calif.: Science and Behavior Books, 1968.

Boehm, A. E. *Boehm Test of Basic Concepts: Manual.* New York: Psychological Corporation, 1971.

Boehm, A. E., and Slater, B. R. *Cognitive Skills Assessment Battery: Interpretive Manual.* (Preliminary ed.) New York: Teachers College Press, 1974.

Boehm, A. E., and Weinberg, R. A. *The Classroom Observer: A Guide for Developing Observation Skills.* New York: Teachers College Press, 1977.

Bogatz, G. A., and Ball, S. *The Second Year of "Sesame Street": A Continuing Evaluation.* Vols. 1 and 2. Princeton, N.J.: Educational Testing Service, 1971.

Boger, R. P., and Knight, S. S. *Social-Emotional Task Force: Final Report.* East Lansing: Head Start Evaluation and Research Center, Michigan State University, and the Merrill-Palmer Institute, 1969. (Also available in ERIC, ED 033744.)

Bolea, A. S., Felker, D. W., and Barnes, M. D. "A Pictorial Self-Concept Scale for Children in K–4." *Journal of Educational Measurement,* 1971, *8*(3), 223–224.

Bolton, D. L. *Selection and Evaluation of Teachers.* Berkeley, Calif.: McCutchan, 1973.

Bonjean, C. M., Hill, R. J., and McLemore, S. D. *Sociological Measurement: An Inventory of Scales and Indices.* San Francisco: Chandler, 1967.

Bonjean, C. M., Hill, R. J., and McLemore, S. D. "Continuities in Sociological Measurement." In N. K. Denzin (Ed.), *Sociological Methods: A Sourcebook.* Chicago: Aldine, 1970.

Boruch, R. F. "On Common Contentions about Randomized Field Experiments." In G. V. Glass (Ed.), *Evaluation Studies Review Annual.* Vol. 1. Beverly Hills, Calif.: Sage Publications, 1976.

Boswell, D. A., and Williams, J. E. "Correlates of Race and Color Bias among Preschool Children." *Psychological Reports,* 1975, *36,* 147–154.

Bouchard, T. J., Jr. "Current Conceptions of Intelligence and Their Implications for Assessment." In P. McReynolds (Ed.), *Advances in Psychological Assessment.* Vol. 1. Palo Alto, Calif.: Science and Behavior Books, 1968.

Bouchard, T. J., Jr. "Unobtrusive Measures: An Inventory of Uses." *Sociological Methods and Research,* 1976, *4* (3), 267–300.

Boyer, E. G., Simon, A., and Karafin, G. R. (Eds.). *Measures of Maturation: An*

Anthology of Early Childhood Observation Instruments. Philadelphia: Research for Better Schools, 1973.

Bracht, G. H. "Planning Evaluation Studies." In R. A. Weinberg and S. G. Moore (Eds.), *Evaluation of Educational Programs for Young Children.* Washington, D.C.: Child Development Associate Consortium, 1975.

Bracht, G. H., and Glass, G. V. "The External Validity of Experiments." *American Educational Research Journal,* 1968, *5,* 437–474.

Bradley, R. H., and Caldwell, B. M. "Issues and Procedures in Testing Young Children." *ERIC/TM Report No. 37,* 1974.

Brandt, R. M. *Studying Behavior in Natural Settings.* New York: Holt, Rinehart and Winston, 1972.

Brannigan, C. R., and Humphries, D. A. "Human Non-Verbal Behaviour, A Means of Communication." In N. G. B. Jones (Ed.), *Ethological Studies of Child Behaviour.* Cambridge, England: Cambridge University Press, 1972.

Braskamp, L., and Morrison, J. "An Interview with Robert Stake on Responsive Evaluation." In R. E. Stake (Ed.), *Evaluating the Arts in Education: A Responsive Approach.* Columbus, Ohio: Merrill, 1975.

Brauner, C. J. "The First Probe." In D. D. Sjogren (Ed.), *Four Evaluation Examples: Anthropological, Economic, Narrative, and Portrayal.* AERA Monograph Series on Curriculum Evaluation No. 7. Skokie, Ill.: Rand McNally, 1974.

Brazelton, T. B. *Neonatal Behavioral Assessment Scale.* Philadelphia: Lippincott, 1973.

Brickell, H. M. "The Influence of External Political Factors on the Role and Methodology of Evaluation." *Evaluation Comment,* 1976, *5* (2), 1–6.

Bridgeman, B., and Shipman, V. C. "Preschool Measures of Self-Esteem and Achievement Motivation as Predictors of Third-Grade Achievement." *Journal of Educational Psychology,* 1978, *70* (1), 17–28.

Brock, H. C. *Parent Volunteer Programs in Early Childhood Education: A Practical Guide.* Hamden, Conn.: Linnet Books, Shoe String Press, 1976.

Brodinsky, B. (Ed.). *Grading and Reporting: Current Trends in School Policies and Programs.* Arlington, Va.: National School Public Relations Association, 1972.

Bronfenbrenner, U. *A Report on Longitudinal Evaluations of Preschool Programs.* Vol. 2: *Is Early Intervention Effective?* Washington, D.C.: Department of Health, Education, and Welfare, 1974.

Brophy, J. E., and Good, T. L. *Teacher-Student Relationships: Causes and Consequences.* New York: Holt, Rinehart and Winston, 1974.

Brophy, J. E., Good, T. L., and Nedler, S. E. *Teaching in the Preschool.* New York: Harper & Row, 1975.

Brown, B. *Brown-IDS Self-Concept Referents Test.* New York: Institute for Developmental Studies, New York University, Undated.

Brown, B. (Ed.). *Found: Long-Term Gains from Early Intervention.* Boulder, Colo.: Westview Press, 1978.

Brown, C. E. "The Development and Use of a Naturalistic Observation Instrument for Assessing Attending Behavior of 3-, 4-, and 5-Year-Olds." Unpublished doctoral dissertation, University of Colorado, 1974.

Brown, D. G. "Sex-Role Preference in Young Children." *Psychological Monographs,* 1956, *70* (14, Whole No. 421).

Brown, D. G. "Sex-Role Preference in Children: Methodological Problems." *Psychological Reports,* 1962, *11,* 477–478.

Bruininks, R. H. *Bruininks-Oseretsky Test of Motor Proficiency.* Circle Pines, Minn.: American Guidance Service, 1978.

Bruner, J. S. *The Process of Education.* New York: Vintage Books, 1960.

Buros, O. K. (Ed.) *The Mental Measurements Yearbook* (First through Eighth). Highland Park, N.J.: Gryphon Press: First, 1938; Second, 1940; Third, 1949; Fourth, 1953; Fifth, 1959; Sixth, 1965; Seventh, 1972; Eighth, 1978.

Buros, O. K. (Ed.). *Tests in Print: A Comprehensive Bibliography of Tests for Use in Education, Psychology, and Industry* (I and II). Highland Park, N.J.: Gryphon Press: I, 1961; II, 1974.

Buros, O. K. (Ed.). *Personality Tests and Reviews.* Highland Park, N.J.: Gryphon Press, 1970.

Bushell, D., Jr. "The Behavior Analysis Classroom." In B. Spodek (Ed.), *Early Childhood Education.* Englewood Cliffs, N.J.: Prentice-Hall, 1973.

Caldwell, B. M. *Inventory of Home Stimulation.* Little Rock, Ark.: Center for Early Development and Education (Kramer School), 1968.

Calfee, R. C. "Review of California Preschool Social Competency Scale." In O. K. Buros (Ed.), *The Eighth Mental Measurements Yearbook.* Vol. 1. Highland Park, N.J.: Gryphon Press, 1978.

Camp, B. W., and others. "Preschool Developmental Testing in Prediction of School Problems." *Clinical Pediatrics,* 1977, *16* (3), 257–263.

Campbell, D. T. "Reforms as Experiments." *American Psychologist,* 1969, *24,* 409–429.

Campbell, D. T., and Boruch, R. F. "Making the Case for Randomized Assignment to Treatments by Considering the Alternatives: Six Ways in Which Quasi-Experimental Evaluations in Compensatory Education Tend to Underestimate Effects." In C. A. Bennett and A. A. Lumsdaine (Eds.), *Evaluation and Experiment: Some Critical Issues in Assessing Social Programs.* New York: Academic Press, 1975.

Campbell, D. T., and Fiske, D. W. "Convergent and Discriminant Validation by the Multitrait-Multimethod Matrix." *Psychological Bulletin,* 1959, *56,* 81–105.

Campbell, D. T., and Stanley, J. S. *Experimental and Quasi-Experimental Designs for Research.* Skokie, Ill.: Rand McNally, 1963.

Canter, D. "Buildings in Use." In D. Canter and P. Stringer (Eds.), *Environmental Interaction: Psychological Approaches to Our Physical Surroundings.* New York: International Universities Press, 1975.

Caplan, A. "The Relationship between Playground Architecture, Social Density, and the Behavior of Young Children." Unpublished master's thesis, University of Colorado, 1977.

Carini, P. F. *Observation and Description: An Alternative Methodology for the Investigation of Human Phenomena.* Grand Forks: North Dakota Study Group on Evaluation, University of North Dakota, 1975.

Carroll, J. B. "Review of the Illinois Test of Psycholinguistic Abilities, Revised Edition." In O. K. Buros (Ed.), *The Seventh Mental Measurements Yearbook.* Vol. 1. Highland Park, N.J.: Gryphon Press, 1972.

Carroll, J. L., and Laming, L. R. "Giftedness and Creativity: Recent Attempts at Definition: A Literature Review." *Gifted Child Quarterly,* 1974, *18,* 85–96.

Carter, R. K. "Clients' Resistance to Negative Findings." In E. R. House (Ed.), *School Evaluation: The Politics and Process.* Berkeley, Calif.: McCutchan, 1973.

Cartwright, C. A., and Cartwright, G. P. *Developing Observation Skills.* New York: McGraw-Hill, 1974.

Cashen, V. M., and Ramseyer, G. C. "The Use of Separate Answer Sheets by Primary Age Children." *Journal of Educational Measurement,* 1969, *6* (3), 155–157.

Cassel, R. N. *The Child Behavior Rating Scale Manual.* Los Angeles: Western Psychological Services, 1962.

Cattell, P. *The Measurement of Intelligence of Infants and Young Children.* (Revised ed.) New York: Psychological Corporation, 1960.

Cattell, R. B. *Handbook for the Individual or Group Culture Fair (or Free) Intelligence Test, Scale 1.* Champaign, Ill.: Institute for Personality and Ability Testing, 1962.

Cattell, R. B., and Warburton, F. *Objective Personality and Motivation Tests.* Urbana: University of Illinois Press, 1967.

Cazden, C. B. "Evaluation of Learning in Preschool Education: Early Language Development." In B. S. Bloom, J. T. Hastings, and G. F. Madaus (Eds.), *Handbook on Formative and Summative Evaluation of Student Learning.* New York: McGraw-Hill, 1971.

Cazden, C. B. "Review of the Stanford Early School Achievement Test." In O. K. Buros (Ed.), *The Eighth Mental Measurements Yearbook.* Vol. 1. Highland Park, N.J.: Gryphon Press, 1978.

Center for Research on Learning and Teaching. "Memo To The Faculty." Memo No. 53. Ann Arbor: University of Michigan, 1974.

Center for the Study of Evaluation. *CSE Elementary School Evaluation Kit: Needs Assessment.* Boston: Allyn & Bacon, 1973.

Champion, P. J., and Sear, A. M. "Questionnaire Response Rates: A Methodological Analysis." In R. Cochrane (Ed.), *Advances in Social Research: A Book of Readings in Research Methods.* London, England: Constable, 1973.

Charlesworth, R., and Hartup, W. W. "Positive Social Reinforcement in the Nursery School Peer Group." *Child Development,* 1967, *38,* 993–1002.

Chase, C. I. "Review of the Illinois Test of Psycholinguistic Abilities, Revised Edition." In O. K. Buros (Ed.), *The Seventh Mental Measurements Yearbook.* Vol. 1. Highland Park, N.J.: Gryphon Press, 1972.

Chase, J. H. "Street Games of New York City." *Pedagogical Seminary.* 1905, *12,* 503–504.

Chilman, C. S. "Programs for Disadvantaged Parents." In B. M. Caldwell and H. M. Ricciuti (Eds.), *Review of Child Development Research.* Vol. 4. Chicago: University of Chicago Press, 1973.

Chissom, B. S. "Review of the Developmental Test of Visual-Motor Integration." In O. K. Buros (Ed.), *The Seventh Mental Measurements Yearbook.* Vol. 2. Highland Park, N.J.: Gryphon Press, 1972a.

Chissom, B. S. "Review of the Marianne Frostig Developmental Test of Visual Perception, Third Edition." In O. K. Buros (Ed.), *The Seventh Mental Measurements Yearbook.* Vol. 2. Highland Park, N.J.: Gryphon Press, 1972b.

Chomsky, N. *Language and the Mind.* (Enlarged ed.) New York: Harcourt Brace Jovanovich, 1972.

Chun, K., Cobb, S., and French, J. R. P., Jr. *Measures for Psychological Assessment: A Guide to 3,000 Original Sources and Their Applications.* Ann Arbor: Survey Research Center of the Institute for Social Research, University of Michigan, 1975.

Cicirelli, V. G., Evans, J. W., and Schiller, J. S. "The Impact of Head Start: A Reply to the Report Analysis." *Harvard Educational Review,* 1970, *40* (1), 105–129.

Ciminero, A. R. "Behavioral Assessment: An Overview." In A. R. Ciminero, K. S. Calhoun, and H. E. Adams (Eds.), *Handbook of Behavioral Assessment.* New York: Wiley, 1977.

Ciminero, A. R., Calhoun, K. S., and Adams, H. E. (Eds.). *Handbook of Behavioral Assessment.* New York: Wiley, 1977.

Circus Manual and Technical Report. Princeton, N.J.: Educational Testing Service, 1974–1975.

Circus Manual and Technical Report. (Teacher's ed.) Reading, Mass.: Addison-Wesley Testing Service, 1976.

Clark, H. B., and others. "A Parent Advice Package for Family Shopping Trips: Development and Evaluation." *Journal of Applied Behavioral Analysis,* 1977, *10* (4), 605–624.

Clarke, A. M., and Clarke, A. D. B. (Eds.). *Early Experience: Myth and Evidence.* New York: Free Press, 1976.

Clarke, H. *Physical and Motor Tests in the Medford Boys' Growth Study.* Englewood Cliffs, N.J.: Prentice-Hall, 1971.

Cline, M. G., and others. *Final Report. Education as Experimentation: Evaluation of the Follow Through Planned Variation Model. Volume I A: Early Effects of Follow Through and Volume I B: Monographs.* Cambridge, Mass.: Abt Associates, 1974.

Cline, M. G., and others. *Final Report. Education as Experimentation: Evaluation of the Follow Through Planned Variation Model. Volume II A: Two-Year Effects of Follow Through and Volume II B: Monographs and Appendices.* Cambridge, Mass.: Abt Associates, 1975.

Cochrane, R. (Ed.). *Advances in Social Research: A Book of Readings in Research Methods.* London, England: Constable, 1973.

Cohen, D. K. "Politics and Research: Evaluation of Social Action Programs in Education." *Review of Educational Research,* 1970, *40* (2), 213–238.

Cole, M., and Bruner, J. S. "Cultural Differences and Inferences about Psychological Processes." *American Psychologist,* 1971, *26,* 867–876.

Coles, G. S. "The Learning Disabilities Test Battery: Empirical and Social Issues." *Harvard Educational Review,* 1978, *48* (3), 313–340.

Coles, R. "Those Places They Call Schools." *Harvard Educational Review,* 1969, *39* (4), 46–57.

Coley, I. L. *Pediatric Assessment of Self-Care Activities.* St. Louis: Mosby, 1978.

Collard, R. R. "Review of the Bayley Scales of Infant Development." In O. K. Buros (Ed.), *The Seventh Mental Measurements Yearbook.* Vol. 1. Highland Park, N.J.: Gryphon Press, 1972.

Coller, A. R. *Self-Concept Measures: An Annotated Bibliography.* Princeton, N.J.: Educational Testing Service, 1971a.

Coller, A. R. *The Assessment of "Self-Concept" in Early Childhood Education.* Urbana, Ill.: ERIC Clearinghouse on Early Childhood Education, 1971b. (Also available in ERIC, ED 050822.)

Collins, R. C. *Children and Society: Child Development and Public Policy.* Unpublished paper. Washington, D. C.: Administration for Children, Youth, and Families, 1977.

Commission on Elementary Schools. *A Guide to the Evaluation and Accreditation of Elementary Schools.* Atlanta: Southern Association of Schools and Colleges, 1971.

Comprehensive Tests of Basic Skills. (Expanded ed.) Technical Bulletin No. 1. Monterey, Calif.: CTB/McGraw-Hill, 1974.

Comrey, A. L., Backer, T. E., and Glaser, E. M. *A Sourcebook for Mental Health Measures.* Los Angeles: Human Interaction Research Institute, 1973.

Connolly, K., and Bruner, J. S. (Eds.). *The Growth of Competence.* New York: Academic Press, 1974.

Connolly, K., and Elliott, J. "The Evolution and Ontogeny of Hand Function." In N. G. B. Jones (Ed.), *Ethological Studies of Child Behavior.* Cambridge, England: Cambridge University Press, 1972.

Connolly, K., and Smith, P. K. "Reactions of Preschool Children to a Strange Observer." In N. G. B. Jones (Ed.), *Ethological Studies of Child Behavior.* Cambridge, England: Cambridge University Press, 1972.

Cook, T. D. "The Potential and Limitations of Secondary Evaluations." In M. W. Apple, M. J. Subkoviak, and H. S. Lufler, Jr. (Eds.), *Educational Evaluation: Analysis and Responsibility.* Berkeley, Calif.: McCutchan, 1974.

Cook, T. D., and others. *"Sesame Street" Revisited.* New York: Sage Publications, 1975.

Cook, T. D., and others (Eds.). *Evaluation Studies: Review Annual.* Vol. 3. Beverly Hills, Calif.: Sage Publications, 1978.

Cooley, W. W., and Lohnes, P. R. *Multivariate Procedures for the Behavioral Sciences.* New York: Wiley, 1962.

Cooley, W. W., and Lohnes, P. R. *Evaluation Research in Education.* New York: Wiley, 1976.

Cooperative Preschool Inventory Handbook. (Revised ed.) Reading, Mass.: Addison-Wesley, 1970.

Coopersmith, S. *The Antecedents of Self-Esteem.* San Francisco: W. H. Freeman, 1967.

Corman, H. H., and Escalona, S. K. "Stages of Sensorimotor Development: A Replication Study." *Merrill-Palmer Quarterly,* 1969, *15,* 351–361.

Costin, F., Greenough, W. T., and Menges, R. J. "Student Ratings of College Teaching: Reliability, Validity, and Usefulness." *Review of Educational Research,* 1971, *41,* 511–535.

Craik, K. H. "The Assessment of Places." In P. McReynolds (Ed.), *Advances in Psychological Assessment.* Vol. 2. Palo Alto, Calif.: Science and Behavior Books, 1971.

Crandall, V. C., Katkovsky, W., and Crandall, V. J. "Children's Beliefs in Their Own Control of Reinforcements in Intellectual-Academic Achievement Situations." *Child Development,* 1965, *36* (1), 91–109.

Cratty, B. J. *Perceptual-Motor Behavior and Educational Processes.* Springfield, Ill.: Thomas, 1969.

Cratty, B. J. *Active Learning: Games to Enhance Academic Abilities.* Englewood Cliffs, N.J.: Prentice-Hall, 1971a.

Cratty, B. J. *Human Behavior: Exploring Educational Processes.* Wolfe City, Tex.: University Press, 1971b.

Cratty, B. J. *Intelligence in Action: Physical Activities for Enhancing Intellectual Abilities.* Englewood Cliffs, N.J.: Prentice-Hall, 1973a.

Cratty, B. J. *Teaching Motor Skills.* Englewood Cliffs, N.J.: Prentice-Hall, 1973b.

Cratty, B. J., and Martin, M. M. *Perceptual-Motor Efficiency in Children.* Philadelphia: Lea & Febiger, 1969.

Crockenberg, S. B. "Creativity Tests: A Boon or Boondoggle for Education?" *Review of Educational Research,* 1972, *42* (1), 27–45.

Cronbach, L. J. "Coefficient Alpha and the Internal Structure of Tests." *Psychometrika,* 1951, *16,* 297–334.

Cronbach, L. J. "Course Improvement through Evaluation." *Teachers College Record,* 1963, *64* (8), 672–683.

Cronbach, L. J. "Intelligence? Creativity? A Parsimonious Reinterpretation of the Wallach-Kogan Data." *American Educational Research Journal,* 1968, *5* (4), 491–512.

Cronbach, L. J. *Essentials of Psychological Testing.* (3rd ed.) New York: Harper & Row, 1970.

Cronbach, L. J. "Review of the BITCH Test (Black Intelligence Test of Cultural Homogeneity)." In O. K. Buros (Ed.), *The Eighth Mental Measurements Yearbook.* Vol. 1. Highland Park, N.J.: Gryphon Press, 1978.

Cronbach, L. J., and others. *The Dependability of Behavioral Measurements: Theory of Generalizability for Scores and Profiles.* New York: Wiley, 1972.

Cruickshank, W. M. "Review of the Measurement of Social Competence: A Manual for the Vineland Social Maturity Scale." *Exceptional Children,* 1954, *20,* 362–363.

Cruickshank, W. M. *The Brain-Injured Child in Home, School, and Community.* Syracuse, N.Y.: Syracuse University Press, 1967.

Cyphert, F. R., and Gant, W. L. "The Delphi Technique: A Case Study." *Phi Delta Kappan,* 1971, *52* (5), 272–273.

Dahl, T. A. "Review of the Boehm Test of Basic Concepts." *Measurement and Evaluation in Guidance,* 1973, *6* (1), 63–65.

Damarin, F. "Review of the Bayley Scales of Infant Development." In O. K. Buros

(Ed.), *The Eighth Mental Measurements Yearbook.* Vol. 1. Highland Park, N.J.: Gryphon Press, 1978a.

Damarin, F. "Review of the Cattell Infant Intelligence Scale." In O. K. Buros (Ed.), *The Eighth Mental Measurements Yearbook.* Vol. 1. Highland Park, N.J.: Gryphon Press, 1978b.

Damon, W. *The Social World of the Child.* San Francisco: Jossey-Bass, 1977.

Datta, L. "Review of the Peabody Picture Vocabulary Test." In W. K. Frankenburg and B. W. Camp (Eds.), *Pediatric Screening Tests.* Springfield, Ill.: Thomas, 1975a.

Datta, L. "Review of the Slosson Intelligence Test." In W. K. Frankenburg and B. W. Camp (Eds.), *Pediatric Screening Tests.* Springfield, Ill.: Thomas, 1975b.

Davidson, J. B., and others. *Directory of Developmental Screening Instruments.* Minneapolis: Project SEARCH, Minneapolis Public Schools, 1977.

Davies, D. (Ed.). *Schools Where Parents Make a Difference.* Boston: Institute for Responsive Education, 1976.

Davis, G. A. *Psychology of Problem Solving: Theory and Practice.* New York: Basic Books, 1973.

Davis, J. A. "Great Books and Small Groups: An Informal History of a National Survey." In P. E. Hammond (Ed.), *Sociologists at Work.* New York: Basic Books, 1964.

Dawe, H. C. "An Analysis of Two Hundred Quarrels of Preschool Children." *Child Development,* 1934, *5,* 139–157.

Day, M. C., and Parker, R. K. (Eds.). *The Preschool in Action: Exploring Early Childhood Programs.* (2nd ed.) Boston: Allyn & Bacon, 1977.

De Avila, E. A., and Havassy, B. E. "Piagetian Alternative to IQ: Mexican American Study." In N. Hobbs and others (Eds.), *Issues in the Classification of Children: A Sourcebook on Categories, Labels, and Their Consequences.* Vol. 2. San Francisco: Jossey-Bass, 1975.

De Avila, E. A., Struthers, J. A., and Randall, D. L. "A Group Measure of the Piagetian Concepts of Conservation and Egocentricity." *Canadian Journal of Behavioural Science,* 1969, *1* (4), 263–272.

Decker, C. A., and Decker, J. R. *Planning and Administering Early Childhood Programs.* Columbus, Ohio: Merrill, 1976.

Dellas, M., and Gaier, E. L. "Identification of Creativity: The Individual." *Psychological Bulletin,* 1970, *73,* 55–73.

Denny, T. *Some Still Do: River Acres, Texas.* Evaluation Report No. 3. Kalamazoo: Evaluation Center, College of Education, Western Michigan University, 1978a.

Denny, T. "Story Telling and Educational Understanding." Occasional Paper No. 12. Kalamazoo: Evaluation Center, College of Education, Western Michigan University, 1978b.

Denzin, N. K. *The Research Act.* Chicago: Aldine, 1970.

De Rivera, M. "Academic Achievement Tests and the Survival of Open Education." *EDC News,* 1973, Issue No. 2, 7–9.

Deutsch, M. "Facilitating Development in the Preschool Child: Social and

Psychological Perspectives." In F. M. Hechinger (Ed.), *Preschool Education Today*. Garden City, N.Y.: Doubleday, 1966.

De Vries, R. "Relationships Among Piagetian, IQ, and Achievement Assessments." *Child Development,* 1974, *45,* 746–756.

De Vries, R., and Kohlberg, L. "Review of the Concept Assessment Kit—Conservation." *Journal of Educational Measurement,* 1969, *6* (4), 263–266.

Diamond, E. E. "Review of the Tests of Basic Experiences." In O. K. Buros (Ed.), *The Eighth Mental Measurements Yearbook.* Vol. 1. Highland Park, N.J.: Gryphon Press, 1978.

Dickie, J., and Bagur, J. S. "Considerations for the Study of Language in Young Low-Income Minority Group Children." *Merrill-Palmer Quarterly,* 1972, *18* (1), 25–38.

Divoky, D. "Early Childhood Education: Who's Doing What to Whom, and Why?" *Learning,* 1976, *5* (4), 12–17, 20–21.

Doll, E. A. "The Vineland Social Maturity Scale: Manual of Directions." *Training School Bulletin,* 1935, *32,* 1–7, 25–32, 48–55, 68–74.

Doll, E. A. (Ed.). *The Oseretsky Tests of Motor Proficiency.* Minneapolis: American Guidance Service, 1946.

Doll, E. A. *The Measurement of Social Competence: A Manual for the Vineland Social Maturity Scale.* Circle Pines, Minn.: American Guidance Service, 1953.

Doll, E. A. *Vineland Social Maturity Scale: Condensed Manual of Directions.* Circle Pines, Minn.: American Guidance Service, 1965.

Doll, E. A. *Preschool Attainment Record Manual.* (Research ed.) Circle Pines, Minn.: American Guidance Service, 1966.

Drowatzky, J. N. *Motor Learning: Principles and Practices.* Minneapolis: Burgess, 1975.

Duckworth, E. "The Having of Wonderful Ideas." In M. Schwebel and J. Raph (Eds.), *Piaget in the Classroom.* New York: Basic Books, 1973.

Dudek, S. Z., Lester, E. P., and Goldberg, J. S. "Relationship of Piaget Measures to Standard Intelligence and Motor Scales." *Perceptual and Motor Skills,* 1969, *28,* 351–362.

Dunkin, M. J., and Biddle, B. J. *The Study of Teaching.* New York: Holt, Rinehart and Winston, 1974.

Dunn, J. A. "Review of the Child Behavior Rating Scale." In O. K. Buros (Ed.), *The Seventh Mental Measurements Yearbook.* Vol. 1. Highland Park, N.J.: Gryphon Press, 1972.

Dunn, L. M. *Peabody Picture Vocabulary Test: Manual.* Circle Pines, Minn.: American Guidance Service, 1965.

Durrell, D. D. *Durrell Analysis of Reading Difficulty.* (New ed.) New York: Harcourt Brace Jovanovich, 1955.

Dyer, C. O. "Construct Validity of Self-Concept by a Multitrait-Multimethod Analysis." Unpublished doctoral dissertation, University of Michigan, 1963.

Dyer, H. S. "Testing Little Children—Some Old Problems in New Settings." Technical Paper. Storrs: National Leadership Institute, Teacher Education/Early Childhood, University of Connecticut, 1971.

Eaves, R. C., and McLaughlin, P. "A Systems Approach for the Assessment of the Child and His Environment: Getting Back to Basics." *Journal of Special Education,* 1977, *11* (1), 99–111.

Education Development Center. *Open Education Teacher/Classroom Assessment Form.* Newton, Mass.: Education Development Center, 1979.

Educational Testing Service. *Disadvantaged Children and Their First School Experiences: ETS–Head Start Longitudinal Study. Theoretical Considerations and Measurement Strategies.* Princeton, N.J.: Educational Testing Service, 1968. (Also available in ERIC, ED 037486.)

Edwards, C. D., and Williams, J. E. "Generalization Between Evaluative Words Associated with Racial Figures in Preschool Children." *Journal of Experimental Research in Personality,* 1970, *4,* 144–155.

Eichorn, D. H. "Review of the Wechsler Preschool and Primary Scale of Intelligence." In O. K. Buros (Ed.), *The Seventh Mental Measurements* Yearbook. Vol. 1. Highland Park, N.J.: Gryphon Press, 1972.

Eichorn, D. H. "Review of the Slosson Intelligence Test." In W. K. Frankenburg and B. W. Camp (Eds.), *Pediatric Screening Tests.* Springfield, Ill.: Thomas, 1975.

Eisner, E. W. "Instructional and Expressive Educational Objectives: Their Formulation and Use in Curriculum." In R. E. Stake (Ed.), *Instructional Objectives.* AERA Monograph Series on Curriculum Evaluation No. 3. Skokie, Ill.: Rand McNally, 1969.

Eisner, E. W. "Emerging Models for Educational Evaluation." *School Review,* 1972, *80,* 573–590.

Elkind, D. "Two Approaches to Intelligence: Piagetian and Psychometric." In D. R. Green, M. P. Ford, and G. B. Flamer (Eds.), *Measurement and Piaget.* New York: McGraw-Hill, 1971.

Ellis, M. J. *Why People Play.* Englewood Cliffs, N.J.: Prentice-Hall, 1973.

Emmerich, W. "Children's Personal and Social Development." In Educational Testing Service, *Disadvantaged Children and Their First School Experiences: ETS–Head Start Longitudinal Study. Theoretical Considerations and Measurement Strategies.* Princeton, N.J.: Educational Testing Service, 1968.

Emrick, J. A., Sorenson, P., and Stearns, M. S. *Interim Evaluation of the National Follow Through Program 1969–1971: A Technical Report.* Menlo Park, Calif.: Stanford Research Institute, 1973.

Engel, B. S. *A Handbook on Documentation.* Grand Forks: North Dakota Study Group on Evaluation, University of North Dakota, 1975.

Engelmann, S. *The Basic Concept Inventory: Teacher's Manual.* (Field research ed.) Chicago: Follett, 1967.

Ernhart, C. B. "Review of the Goodenough-Harris Drawing Test." In W. K. Frankenburg and B. W. Camp (Eds.), *Pediatric Screening Tests.* Springfield, Ill.: Thomas, 1975a.

Ernhart, C. B. "Review of the Quick Test." In W. K. Frankenburg and B. W. Camp (Eds.), *Pediatric Screening Tests.* Springfield, Ill.: Thomas, 1975b.

Escalona, S. K., and Corman, H. H. *Albert Einstein Scales of Sensorimotor Development.* New York: Department of Psychiatry, Albert Einstein College of Medicine, 1969.

Espenschade, A. S. "Review of the Oseretsky Tests of Motor Proficiency: A Translation from the Portuguese Adaptation." In O. K. Buros (Eds.), *The Fourth Mental Measurements Yearbook.* Highland Park, N.J.: Gryphon Press, 1953.

Espenschade, A. S. "Review of the Lincoln-Oseretsky Motor Development Scale." In O. K. Buros (Ed.), *The Fifth Mental Measurements Yearbook.* Highland Park, N.J.: Gryphon Press, 1959.

Espenschade, A. S., and Eckert, H. M. *Motor Development.* Columbus, Ohio: Merrill, 1967.

Essa, E. L. "The Preschool: Setting for Applied Behavior Analysis Research." *Review of Educational Research,* 1978, *48* (4), 537–575.

Evans, E. D. "Measurement Practices in Early Childhood Education." In R. W. Colvin and E. M. Zaffiro (Eds.), *Preschool Education: A Handbook for the Training of Early Childhood Educators.* New York: Springer-Verlag, 1974.

Evans, E. D. *Contemporary Influences in Early Childhood Education.* (2nd ed.) New York: Holt, Rinehart and Winston, 1975.

Everhart, R. B. "Problems of Doing Fieldwork in Educational Evaluation." *Human Organization,* 1975, *34,* 205–215.

Everhart, R. B. "Between Stranger and Friend: Some Consequences of 'Long-Term' Fieldwork in Schools." *American Educational Research Journal,* 1977, *14* (1), 1–15.

Farnham-Diggory, S. *Learning Disabilities: A Psychological Perspective.* Cambridge, Mass.: Harvard University Press, 1978.

Fawcett, S. B., Miller, L. K., and Braukman, C. J. "An Evaluation of a Training Package for Community Canvassing Behaviors." *Journal of Applied Behavioral Analysis,* 1977, *10* (3), 504.

Feiman, S. *Teacher Curriculum Work Center: A Descriptive Study.* Grand Forks: North Dakota Study Group on Evaluation, University of North Dakota, 1975.

Finlayson, H. M. "Children's Road Behavior and Personality." *British Journal of Educational Psychology,* 1972, *42,* 225–232.

Fitts, P. M. "Perceptual Motor Skill Learning." In A. W. Melton (Ed.), *Categories of Human Learning.* New York: Academic Press, 1964.

Fitts, P. M. "Factors in Complex Skill Training." In R. Glaser (Ed.), *Training Research and Education.* New York: Wiley, 1965.

Flanders, N. A. "Interaction Analysis and Inservice Training." In H. J. Klausmeier and G. T. O'Hearn (Eds.), *Research and Development Toward the Improvement of Education.* Madison, Wis.: Dembar Educational Research Services, 1968.

Flanders, N. A. "Teacher Effectiveness." In R. L. Ebel (Ed.), *Encyclopedia of Educational Research.* New York: Macmillan, 1969.

Flaugher, R. L. "The Many Definitions of Test Bias." *American Psychologist,* 1978, *33* (7), 671–679.

Flinchum, B. M. *Motor Development in Early Childhood: A Guide for Movement Education with Ages 2 to 6.* Saint Louis: Mosby, 1975.

Forteza, J. A. "Algunos Problemas Referentes a La Medida de La Creatividad." *Revista de Psicologia General y Aplicada,* 1974, *29,* 1033–1055.

Frank, L. K. "Evaluation of Educational Programs." *Young Children,* 1969, *24,* 167–174.

Frankenburg, W. K., and Camp, B. W. (Eds.). *Pediatric Screening Tests.* Springfield, Ill.: Thomas, 1975.

Frankenburg, W. K., Camp, B. W., and Van Natta, P. A. "Validity of the Denver Developmental Screening Test." *Child Development,* 1971, *42,* 475–485.

Frankenburg, W. K., Goldstein, A., and Camp, B. W. "The Revised Denver Developmental Screening Test: Its Accuracy as a Screening Instrument." *Journal of Pediatrics,* 1971, *79* (6), 988–995.

Frankenburg, W. K., and others. "Reliability and Stability of the Denver Developmental Screening Test." *Child Development,* 1971, *42,* 1315–1325.

Frankenburg, W. K., and others. *Denver Developmental Screening Test: Revised Reference Manual.* Denver, Colo.: LADOCA Foundation, 1975.

Freides, D. "Review of the Wechsler Intelligence Scale for Children—Revised." In O. K. Buros (Ed.), *The Eighth Mental Measurements Yearbook.* Vol. 1. Highland Park, N.J.: Gryphon Press, 1978.

French, J. L. "Review of the Cooperative Preschool Inventory." In O. K. Buros (Ed.), *The Seventh Mental Measurements Yearbook.* Vol. 1. Highland Park, N.J.: Gryphon Press, 1972.

Frick, T., and Semmel, M. I. "Observer Agreement and Reliabilities of Classroom Observational Measures." *Review of Educational Research,* 1978, *48* (1), 157–184.

Friedlander, B. Z., and others. "Time-Sampling Analysis of Infants' Natural Language Environments in the Home." *Child Development,* 1972, *43,* 730–740.

Friedrich, L. K., and Stein, A. H. "Aggressive and Prosocial Television Programs and the Natural Behavior of Preschool Children." *Monographs of the Society for Research on Child Development,* 1973, *38* (4, Serial No. 151).

Fromberg, D. P. *Early Childhood Education: A Perceptual Models Curriculum.* New York: Wiley, 1977.

Frostig, M. *Marianne Frostig Developmental Test of Visual Perception: Administration and Scoring Manual.* (3rd ed.) Palo Alto, Calif.: Consulting Psychologists Press, 1966.

Frostig, M., and others. *Marianne Frostig Developmental Test of Visual Perception, Third Edition: 1963 Standardization.* Palo Alto, Calif.: Consulting Psychologists Press, 1964.

Gaines, R. "Review of the Southern California Figure-Ground Visual Perception Test." In O. K. Buros (Ed.), *The Seventh Mental Measurements Yearbook.* Vol. 2. Highland Park, N.J.: Gryphon Press, 1972.

Gallagher, J. J., and Bradley, R. H. "Early Identification of Developmental Difficulties." In I. J. Gordon (Ed.), *Early Childhood Education,* 71st Yearbook, Part 2. National Society for the Study of Education. Chicago: University of Chicago Press, 1972.

Gallahue, D. L. *Motor Development and Movement Experiences for Young Children.* New York: Wiley, 1976.

Gambrill, E. D. *Behavior Modification: Handbook of Assessment, Intervention, and Evaluation.* San Francisco: Jossey-Bass, 1977.

Gephart, W. J. "Evaluation: Past, Present, and Future." Occasional Paper No. 17. Bloomington, Ind.: Phi Delta Kappa Research Service Center, Undated.

Gesell, A., and Amatruda, C. S. *Developmental Diagnosis.* (2nd ed.) New York: Hoeber, 1947.

Getzels, J. W., and Dillon, J. T. "The Nature of Giftedness and the Education of the Gifted." In R. M. W. Travers (Ed.), *Second Handbook of Research on Teaching.* Skokie, Ill.: Rand McNally, 1973.

Getzels, J. W., and Jackson, P. W. *Creativity and Intelligence: Explorations with Gifted Students.* New York: Wiley, 1962.

Gilbert, J. P., Light, R. J., and Mosteller, F. "Assessing Social Innovations: An Empirical Base for Policy." In C. A. Bennett and A. A. Lumsdaine (Eds.), *Evaluation and Experiment: Some Critical Issues in Assessing Social Programs.* New York: Academic Press, 1975.

Gilmer, B., Miller, J. O., and Gray, S. W. *Intervention with Mothers and Young Children: A Study of Intra-Family Effects.* Nashville, Tenn.: George Peabody College for Teachers, 1970.

Glass, G. V. "The Growth of Evaluation Methodology." Mimeo. Boulder: Laboratory of Educational Research, University of Colorado, 1969.

Glass, G. V. "The Many Faces of Educational Accountability." *Phi Delta Kappan,* 1972, *53,* 636–639.

Glass, G. V. "Teacher Effectiveness." In H. J. Walberg (Ed.), *Evaluating Educational Performance: A Sourcebook of Methods, Instruments, and Examples.* Berkeley, Calif.: McCutchan, 1974.

Glass, G. V. (Ed.). *Evaluation Studies: Review Annual.* Vol. 1. Beverly Hills, Calif.: Sage Publications, 1976.

Glass, G. V. "Standards and Criteria." Occasional Paper No. 10. Kalamazoo: Evaluation Center, College of Education, Western Michigan University, 1977. (Also published in the *Journal of Educational Measurement,* 1978, *15* (4), 237–261.)

Glass, G. V. "Postscript to 'Standards and Criteria'." Paper presented at the Winter Conference on Measurement and Methodology of the Center for the Study of Evaluation, University of California, Los Angeles, January 1978.

Glass, G. V., and Stanley, J. C. *Statistical Methods in Education and Psychology.* Englewood Cliffs, N.J.: Prentice-Hall, 1970.

Glick, J. "Some Problems in the Evaluation of Preschool Intervention Programs." In R. D. Hess and R. M. Bear (Eds.), *Early Education: Current Theory, Research, and Action.* Chicago: Aldine, 1968.

Glick, J. "Cognitive Development in Cross-Cultural Perspective." In F. D. Horowitz (Ed.), *Review of Child Development Research.* Vol. 4. Chicago: University of Chicago Press, 1975.

Glucksberg, S., Krauss, R., and Higgins, E. T. "The Development of Referential Communication Skills." In F. D. Horowitz (Ed.), *Review of Child Development Research.* Vol. 4. Chicago: University of Chicago Press, 1975.

Gold, R. L. "Roles in Sociological Field Observations." In G. J. McCall and J. L. Simmons (Eds.), *Issues in Participant Observation: Text and Reader.* Reading, Mass.: Addison-Wesley, 1969.

Goldberg, L. R. "A Historical Survey of Personality Scales and Inventories." In P. McReynolds (Ed.), *Advances in Psychological Assessment.* Vol. 2. Palo Alto, Calif.: Science and Behavior Books, 1971.

Goldschmid, M. L., and Bentler, P. M. *Manual: Concept Assessment Kit — Conservation.* San Diego, Calif.: Educational and Industrial Testing Service, 1968a.

Goldschmid, M. L., and Bentler, P. M. "The Dimensions and Measurement of Conservation." *Child Development,* 1968b, *39,* 787–802.

Goldstein, H., and others. "Schools." In N. Hobbs (ed.), *Issues in the Classification of Children: A Sourcebook on Categories, Labels, and Their Consequences.* Vol. 2. San Francisco: Jossey-Bass, 1975.

Golledge, R. G., and Zannaras, G. "Cognitive Approaches to the Analysis of Human Spatial Behavior." In W. H. Ittelson (Ed.), *Environment and Cognition.* New York: Seminar Press, 1973.

Goodenough, F. L. *Measurement of Intelligence by Drawings.* New York: Harcourt Brace Jovanovich, 1926.

Goodlad, J. I., Klein, M. F., and Novotney, J. M. *Early Schooling in the United States.* New York: McGraw-Hill, 1973.

Goodson, B. D., and Hess, R. D. *Parents as Teachers of Young Children: An Evaluative Review of Some Contemporary Concepts and Programs.* Stanford, Calif.: School of Education, Stanford University, 1975.

Goodwin, W. L. "Project Models and the Use of Controlled Experiments in School Settings." In H. J. Klausmeier and others (Eds.), *Project Models: Maximizing Opportunities for Development and Experimentation in Learning in the Schools.* Occasional Paper No. 3. Madison: Research and Development Center for Cognitive Learning, University of Wisconsin, 1966.

Goodwin, W. L. "A Summary Report on the Evaluation of Performance Contracts." In A. R. Olson and W. M. Vining (Eds.), *Report on the Educational Achievement Act, FY 1971.* Denver: Colorado Department of Education, 1971.

Goodwin, W. L. "Evaluation in Early Childhood Education." In R. W. Colvin and E. M. Zaffiro (Eds.), *Preschool Education: A Handbook for the Training of Early Childhood Educators.* New York: Springer-Verlag, 1974.

Goodwin, W. L. "Review of Circus." In O. K. Buros (Ed.), *The Eighth Mental Measurements Yearbook.* Vol. 1. Highland Park, N.J.: Gryphon Press, 1978a.

Goodwin, W. L. "The Measurement of Children's Motivation as a Program Outcome." Unpublished manuscript. Westport, Conn.: Mediax Associates, 1978b.

Goodwin, W. L., and Klausmeier, H. J. *Facilitating Student Learning: An Introduction to Educational Psychology.* New York: Harper & Row, 1975.

Goodwin, W. L., and Sanders, J. R. "The Effects on Pupil Performance of Presentations Made on an Audio-Bus." Research Paper No. 52. Boulder: Laboratory of Educational Research, University of Colorado, 1971.

Goodwin, W. L., and others. *Incremental Summative Evaluation of the Comprehensive Coordinated Child Care Project.* Boulder: Laboratory of Educational Research, University of Colorado, 1973.

Goolsby, T., Jr., and Darby, B. *A Bibliography of Instrumentation Methodology and Procedures for Measurement in Early Childhood Learning.* Athens: Research and Development Center in Educational Stimulation, University of Georgia, 1969. (Also available in ERIC, ED 046978.)

Gordon, I. J. *Studying the Child in School.* New York: Wiley, 1966.

Gordon, I. J. *Parental Involvement in Compensatory Education.* Urbana: ERIC Clearinghouse on Early Childhood Education, University of Illinois Press, 1970.

Gordon, I. J. "An Instructional Theory Approach to the Analysis of Selected Early Childhood Programs." In I. J. Gordon (Ed.), *Early Childhood Education,* 71st Yearbook, Part 2. National Society for the Study of Education. Chicago: University of Chicago Press, 1972.

Gordon, I. J., Guinagh, B., and Jester, R. E. "The Florida Parent Education Infant and Toddler Programs." In M. C. Day and R. K. Parker (Eds.), *The Preschool in Action: Exploring Early Childhood Programs.* (2nd ed.) Boston: Allyn & Bacon, 1977.

Gordon, I. J., and Jester, R. E. "Techniques of Observing Teaching in Early Childhood and Outcomes of Particular Procedures." In R. M. W. Travers (Ed.), *Second Handbook of Research on Teaching.* Skokie, Ill.: Rand McNally, 1973.

Gotts, E. E. "Head Start Research, Development, and Evaluation." In J. L. Frost (Ed.), *Revisiting Early Childhood Education: Readings.* New York: Holt, Rinehart and Winston, 1973.

Gough, H. G. "A Cluster Analysis of Home Index Status Items." *Psychological Reports,* 1971a, *28,* 923–929.

Gough, H. G. "Socioeconomic Status as Related to High School Graduation and College Attendance." *Psychology in the Schools,* 1971b, *7,* 226–231.

Gough, H. G., and Heilbrun, A. B. *Adjective Check List Manual.* Palo Alto, Calif.: Consulting Psychologists Press, 1965.

Gray, S. W., and others. *Before First Grade.* New York: Teachers College Press, 1966.

Green, D. R., Ford, M. P., and Flamer, G. B. (Eds.). *Measurement and Piaget.* New York: McGraw-Hill, 1971.

Greenwood, N., McCurdy, J., and Durant, C. "Hamilton High: The Changing Urban School." *Los Angeles Times,* 1973.

Grill, J. J. "Review of the Developmental Indicators for the Assessment of Learning." In O. K. Buros (Ed.), *The Eighth Mental Measurements Yearbook.* Vol. 1. Highland Park, N.J.: Gryphon Press, 1978.

Gronlund, N. E. *Measurement and Evaluation in Teaching.* (3rd ed.) New York: Macmillan, 1976.

Grotberg, E. H. *Review of Research of Project Head Start: 1965 to 1969.* Washington, D.C.: Office of Child Development, 1969. (Also available in ERIC, ED 028308.)

Grotberg, E. H. "Institutional Responsibilities for Early Childhood Education." In I. J. Gordon (Ed.), *Early Childhood Education,* 71st Yearbook, Part 2. National Society for the Study of Education. Chicago: University of Chicago Press, 1972.

Guba, E. G. "The Failure of Educational Evaluation." *Educational Technology,* 1969, *9* (5), 29–38.

Guba, E. G., and Stufflebeam, D. L. "Evaluation: The Process of Stimulating, Aiding, and Abetting Insightful Action." Paper presented at the 2nd Phi Delta Kappa National Symposium for Professors of Educational Research, Boulder, Colo., November 1968.

Guilford, J. P. "Creativity." *American Psychologist,* 1950, *5,* 444–454.

Guilford, J. P. *The Nature of Human Intelligence.* New York: McGraw-Hill, 1967.

Guilford, J. P. "Varieties of Creative Giftedness, Their Measurement and Development." *Gifted Child Quarterly,* 1975, *19,* 107–121.

Guilford, J. P., and Hoepfner, R. *The Analysis of Intelligence.* New York: McGraw-Hill, 1971.

Gulliksen, H. *Theory of Mental Tests.* New York: Wiley, 1950.

Gump, P. V. "Intra-Setting Analysis: The Third Grade Classroom as a Special but Instructive Case." In E. P. Willems and H. L. Raush (Eds.), *Naturalistic Viewpoints in Psychological Research.* New York: Holt, Rinehart and Winston, 1969.

Gump, P. V. "Ecological Psychology and Children." In E. M. Hetherington (Ed.), *Review of Child Development Research.* Vol. 5. Chicago: University of Chicago Press, 1975.

Guthrie, P. D. *Measures of Social Skills: An Annotated Bibliography.* Princeton, N.J.: Educational Testing Service, 1971.

Guttentag, M. "Evaluation of Social Intervention Programs." *Annals of the New York Academy of Sciences,* 1973, *218,* 3–15.

Guttentag, M. (Ed.). *Evaluation Studies: Review Annual.* Vol. 2. Beverly Hills, Calif.: Sage Publications, 1977.

Hagen, E. "Review of the Stanford Early School Achievement Test." In O. K. Buros (Ed.), *The Seventh Mental Measurements Yearbook.* Vol. 1. Highland Park, N.J.: Gryphon Press, 1972.

Hall, E. T. *The Silent Language.* New York: Doubleday, 1959.

Hall, M., and Keith, R. A. "Sex-Role Preference Among Children of Upper and Lower Social Class." *Journal of Social Psychology,* 1964, *62,* 101–110.

Hall, V. C., and Mery, M. "Review of the Concept Assessment Kit—Conservation." *Journal of Educational Measurement,* 1969, *6* (4), 266–269.

Hambleton, R. K., and others. "Criterion-Referenced Testing and Measurement: A Review of Technical Issues and Developments." *Review of Educational Research*, 1978, *48* (1), 1–47.

Hammond, R. L. "Evaluation at the Local Level." In B. R. Worthen and J. R. Sanders (Eds.), *Educational Evaluation: Theory and Practice*. Belmont, Calif.: Wadsworth, 1973.

Haney, W. *The Follow Through Planned Variation Experiment: A Technical History of the National Follow Through Evaluation*. Vol. 5. Cambridge, Mass.: Huron Institute, 1977.

Haney, W., and Cohen, D. K. "Testing the Tests." Staff Circular No. 1. Cambridge, Mass.: National Consortium on Testing Project, Huron Institute, 1978.

Harriman, P. L. "Review of the It Scale for Children." In O. K. Buros (Ed.), *The Sixth Mental Measurements Yearbook*. Highland Park, N.J.: Gryphon Press, 1965.

Harris, D. B. *Children's Drawings as Measures of Intellectual Maturity*. New York: Harcourt Brace Jovanovich, 1963.

Harrow, A. J. *A Taxonomy of the Psychomotor Domain: A Guide for Developing Behavioral Objectives*. New York: McKay, 1972.

Hartley, H. J. "PPBS and an Analysis of Cost Effectiveness." *Educational Administration Quarterly*, 1969, *5* (1), 65–80.

Hartup, W. W. "Early Education and Childhood Socialization." *Journal of Research and Development in Education*, 1968, *1* (3), 16–29.

Hartup, W. W., Glazer, J. A., and Charlesworth, R. "Peer Reinforcement and Sociometric Status." *Child Development*, 1967, *38*, 1017–1024.

Hartup, W. W., and Zook, E. A. "Sex-Role Preferences in Three- and Four-Year-Old Children." *Journal of Consulting Psychology*, 1960, *24*, 420–426.

Hayward, D. G., Rothenberg, M., and Beasley, R. *School-Aged Children in Three Urban Playgrounds*. New York: Environmental Psychology Program, City University of New York, 1973.

Haywood, H. C., and others. "Behavioral Assessment in Mental Retardation." In P. McReynolds (Ed.), *Advances in Psychological Assessment*. Vol. 3. San Francisco: Jossey-Bass, 1975.

Hedrick, D. L., Prather, E. M., and Tobin, A. R. *Sequenced Inventory of Communication Development*. Seattle: University of Washington Press, Undated.

Hein, G. E. *An Open Education Perspective on Evaluation*. Grand Forks: North Dakota Study Group on Evaluation, University of North Dakota, 1975.

Helmar, O. "Foreword." In H. A. Linstone and M. Turoff (Eds.), *The Delphi Method: Techniques and Applications*. Reading, Mass.: Addison-Wesley, 1975.

Henderson, E. H., Long, B. H., and Ziller, R. C. *Manual for the Self-Social Symbols Tasks and the Children's Self-Social Constructs Tests*. Charlottesville: Virginia Research Associates, Undated.

Henderson, S. E., and Stott, D. H. "Finding the Clumsy Child: Genesis of a Test of Motor Impairment." *Journal of Human Movement Studies*, 1977, *3*, 38–48.

Hendrick, J. *The Whole Child: New Trends in Early Education*. St. Louis: Mosby, 1975.

Hendricks, M., and Wortman, C. "Reactions to Random Assignment in an Ameliorative Social Program as a Function of Awareness of What Others Are Receiving and Outcome." Unpublished paper. Evanston, Ill.: Psychology Department, Northwestern University, 1975.

Henry, J. *Essays on Education.* Baltimore, Md.: Penguin, 1971.

Herbert, J. "Direct Observation as a Research Technique." *Psychology in the Schools,* 1970, *7,* 127–138.

Herron, R. E., and Sutton-Smith, B. (Eds.). *Child's Play.* New York: Wiley, 1971.

Hersen, M., and Barlow, D. H. *Single Case Experimental Designs: Strategies for Studying Behavior Change.* New York: Pergamon Press, 1976.

Hess, R. D., and Croft, D. J. *Teachers of Young Children.* Boston: Houghton Mifflin, 1972.

Hess, R. D., and Shipman, V. C. "Early Experience and the Socialization of Cognitive Modes in Children." *Child Development,* 1965, *36,* 869–886.

Hess, R. D., and others. *Techniques for Assessing Cognitive and Social Abilities of Children and Parents in Project Head Start.* Washington D.C.: Office of Economic Opportunity, 1966.

Heyneman, S. P., and Mintz, P. C. "The Frequency and Quality of Measures Utilized in Federally Sponsored Research on Children and Adolescents." *American Educational Research Journal,* 1977, *14,* 99–113.

High/Scope Educational Research Foundation. *The National Home Start Evaluation Interim Report IV: Summative Evaluation Results.* Washington, D.C.: Administration for Children, Youth, and Families, 1974.

High/Scope Educational Research Foundation. "Research Report: The Productive Language Assessment Tasks." *Bulletin of the High/Scope Foundation,* 1976, Winter (No. 3), 1–8.

Himelstein, P. "Review of the Slosson Intelligence Test." In O. K. Buros (Ed.), *The Seventh Mental Measurements Yearbook.* Vol. 1. Highland Park, N.J.: Gryphon Press, 1972.

Hobbs, N. *The Futures of Children: Recommendations of the Project on Classification of Exceptional Children.* San Francisco: Jossey-Bass, 1975.

Hobbs, N., and others (Eds.). *Issues in the Classification of Children: A Sourcebook on Categories, Labels, and Their Consequences.* Vols. 1 and 2. San Francisco: Jossey-Bass, 1975.

Hodges, W. L. "The Worth of the Follow Through Experience." *Harvard Educational Review,* 1978, *48* (2), 186–192.

Hoepfner, R. "Review of Torrance Tests of Creative Thinking." *Journal of Educational Measurement,* 1967, *4,* 191–192.

Hoepfner, R., and Fink, A. *Evaluation Study of the California State Preschool Program.* Los Angeles: Center for the Study of Evaluation, Graduate School of Education, University of California at Los Angeles, 1975.

Hoepfner, R., Stern, C., and Nummedal, S. G. *CSE-ECRC Preschool/Kindergarten Test Evaluations.* Los Angeles: Center for the Study of Evaluation and Early Childhood Research Center, Graduate School of Education, University of California at Los Angeles, 1971.

Hoepfner, R., and others. *CSE-RBS Test Evaluations: Tests of Higher-Order Cognitive, Affective, and Interpersonal Skills.* Los Angeles: Center for the Study of Evaluation, Graduate School of Education, University of California at Los Angeles, 1972.

Hoepfner, R., and others. *CSE Elementary School Test Evaluations.* Los Angeles: Center for the Study of Evaluation, Graduate School of Education, University of California at Los Angeles, 1976.

Holden, R. H. "Review of the Bayley Scales of Infant Development." In O. K. Buros (Ed.), *The Seventh Mental Measurements Yearbook.* Vol. 1. Highland Park, N.J.: Gryphon Press, 1972.

Holland, J. L. "Review of Torrance Tests of Creative Thinking." *Journal of Counseling Psychology,* 1968, *15,* 297–298.

Hollenbeck, G. P., and Kaufman, A. S. "Factor Analysis of the Wechsler Preschool and Primary Scale of Intelligence (WPPSI)." *Journal of Clinical Psychology,* 1973, *29,* 41–45.

Hollingshead, A. B., and Redlich, F. C. *Two-Factor Index of Social Position.* New Haven, Conn.: Department of Sociology, Yale University, 1957.

Hom, H. L., Jr., and Robinson, P. A. (Eds.). *Psychological Processes in Early Education.* New York: Academic Press, 1977.

Homans, G. C. "The Strategy of Industrial Sociology." *American Journal of Sociology,* 1949, *54* (4), 330–337.

Honig, A. S. "Issues in Staff Development: What You Need to Know to Select and Train Your Day Care Staff." Paper presented at the annual conference of day care center directors, Day Care and Child Development Council of America, Atlanta, March 1977.

Honig, A. S., and Lally, J. R. *Piagetian Infant Scales.* Syracuse, N.Y.: Syracuse University Children's Center, 1970.

Honig, A. S., and Lally, J. R. "Assessing Teacher Behaviors with Infants in Day Care." In B. Friedlander, G. Kirk, and G. Sterritt (Eds.), *Infant Assessment and Intervention.* New York: Brunner/Mazel, 1975.

Honzik, M. P. "The Development of Intelligence." In B. B. Wolman (Ed.), *Handbook of General Psychology.* Englewood Cliffs, N.J.: Prentice-Hall, 1973.

Hopkins, K. D., and Glass, G. V. *Basic Statistics for the Behavioral Sciences.* Englewood Cliffs, N.J.: Prentice-Hall, 1978.

Horner, R. D., and Keilitz, I. "Training Mentally Retarded Adolescents to Brush Their Teeth." *Journal of Applied Behavioral Analysis,* 1975, *8* (3), 301–309.

Horowitz, F. D., and Paden, L. Y. "The Effectiveness of Environmental Intervention Programs." In B. M. Caldwell and H. N. Ricciuti (Eds.), *Review of Child Development Research.* Vol. 3. Chicago: University of Chicago Press, 1973.

Horowitz, M. J., Duff, D. F., and Stratton, L. O. "Personal Space and the Body-Buffer Zone." In H. M. Proshansky, W. H. Ittelson, and L. G. Rivlin (Eds.), *Environmental Psychology: Man and His Physical Setting.* New York: Holt, Rinehart and Winston, 1970.

House, E. R. "The Conscience of Educational Evaluation." *Teachers College Record,* 1972, *73,* 405–414.

House, E. R. "Politics as Usual." In E. R. House (Ed.), *School Evaluation: The Politics and Process.* Berkeley, Calif.: McCutchan, 1973a.

House, E. R. "The Dominion of Economic Accountability." In E. R. House (Ed.), *School Evaluation: The Politics and Process.* Berkeley, Calif.: McCutchan, 1973b.

House, E. R. "Justice in Evaluation." In G. V. Glass (Ed.), *Evaluation Studies Review Annual.* Vol. 1. Beverly Hills, Calif.: Sage Publications, 1976.

House, E. R., and others. "No Simple Answer: Critique of the Follow Through Evaluation." *Harvard Educational Review,* 1978, *48* (2), 128–160.

Houston, T. R., Jr. "The Behavioral Sciences Impact Effectiveness Model." In P. H. Rossi and W. Williams (Eds.), *Evaluating Social Programs: Theory, Practice, and Politics.* New York: Seminar Press, 1972.

Houts, P. L. "Introduction: Standardized Testing in America." In P. L. Houts (Ed.), *The Myth of Measurability.* New York: Hart, 1977.

Hughes, J. E. *Hughes Basic Gross Motor Assessment.* Denver: Office of Special Education, Denver Public Schools, 1975.

Hunt, J. McV. *Intelligence and Experience.* New York: Ronald Press, 1961.

Hunt, J. McV. "Reflections on a Decade of Early Education." *Journal of Abnormal Child Psychology,* 1975, *3* (4), 275–330.

Hunt, J. V. "Review of the Slosson Intelligence Test." In O. K. Buros (Ed.), *The Seventh Mental Measurements Yearbook.* Vol. 1. Highland Park, N.J.: Gryphon Press, 1972.

Hunt, J. V. "Review of the Denver Developmental Screening Test." In W. K. Frankenburg and B. W. Camp (Eds.), *Pediatric Screening Tests.* Springfield, Ill.: Thomas, 1975a.

Hunt, J. V. "Review of the Peabody Picture Vocabulary Test." In W. K. Frankenburg and B. W. Camp (Eds.), *Pediatric Screening Tests.* Springfield, Ill.: Thomas, 1975b.

Hunt, J. V. "Review of the Developmental Profile." In O. K. Buros (Ed.), *The Eighth Mental Measurements Yearbook.* Vol. 1. Highland Park, N.J.: Gryphon Press, 1978a.

Hunt, J. V. "Review of the McCarthy Scales of Children's Abilities." In O. K. Buros (Ed.), *The Eighth Mental Measurements Yearbook.* Vol. 1. Highland Park, N.J.: Gryphon Press, 1978b.

Hutt, C., and Vaizey, M. J. "Differential Effects of Group Density on Social Behavior." *Nature,* 1966, *209,* 1371–1372.

Hutt, S. J., and Hutt, C. *Direct Observation and Measurement of Behavior.* Springfield, Ill.: Thomas, 1970.

Ilg, F. L., and Ames, L. B. *School Readiness: Behavior Tests Used at the Gesell Institute.* (New ed.) New York: Harper & Row, 1972.

Ittelson, W. H., Rivlin, L. G., and Proshansky, H. M. "The Use of Behavioral Maps in Environmental Psychology." In H. M. Proshansky, W. H. Ittelson, and L. G. Rivlin (Eds.), *Environmental Psychology: Man and His Physical Setting.* New York: Holt, Rinehart and Winston, 1970.

Ittelson, W. H., and others. *An Introduction to Environmental Psychology.* New York: Holt, Rinehart and Winston, 1974.

Jackson, P. W. *Life in Classrooms.* New York: Holt, Rinehart and Winston, 1968.

Jackson, P. W. "Naturalistic Studies of Schools and Classrooms: One Reader's Digest." In M. W. Apple, M. J. Subkoviak, and H. S. Lufler, Jr. (Eds.), *Educational Evaluation: Analysis and Evaluation.* Berkeley, Calif.: McCutchan, 1974.

Jamison, C. B. "Review of the Purdue Perceptual-Motor Survey." In O. K. Buros (Ed.), *The Seventh Mental Measurements Yearbook.* Vol. 2. Highland Park, N.J.: Gryphon Press, 1972.

Jecker, J. O., Maccoby, N., and Breitrose, H. S. "Improving Accuracy in Interpreting Non-verbal Cues of Comprehension." *Psychology in the Schools,* 1965, *2,* 239–244.

Jecker, J. O., and others. "Teacher Accuracy in Assessing Cognitive Visual Feedback from Students." *Journal of Applied Psychology,* 1964, *48,* 393–397.

Jensen, A. R. "How Much Can We Boost IQ and Scholastic Achievement?" *Harvard Educational Review,* 1969, *39,* 1–123.

Johnson, D. W. "Affective Outcomes." In H. J. Wahlberg (Ed.), *Evaluating Educational Performance: A Sourcebook of Methods, Instruments, and Examples.* Berkeley, Calif.: McCutchan, 1974.

Johnson, O. G. *Tests and Measurements in Child Development: Handbook II.* Vols. 1 and 2. San Francisco: Jossey-Bass, 1976.

Johnson, O. G., and Bommarito, J. W. *Tests and Measurements in Child Development: Handbook I.* San Francisco: Jossey-Bass, 1971.

Joint Committee on Standards for Educational Evaluation. *Standards for Evaluations of Educational Programs, Projects and Materials.* Draft Copy. Kalamazoo: The Evaluation Center, Western Michigan University, November 1978.

Jones, J. "ETS Considers Testing and the Public Interest." *APA Monitor,* 1976, *7* (12), 4, 13.

Jones, N. G. B. "Criteria for Use in Describing Facial Expressions of Children." *Human Biology,* 1971, *43* (3), 365–413.

Jones, N. G. B. "Characteristics of Ethological Studies of Human Behaviour." In N. G. B. Jones (Ed.), *Ethological Studies of Child Behaviour.* London, England: Cambridge University Press, 1972a.

Jones, N. G. B. (Ed.), *Ethological Studies of Child Behaviour.* London, England: Cambridge University Press, 1972b.

Jones, P., and Jones, S. *Parents Unite! The Complete Guide for Shaking Up Your Children's School.* New York: Wyden, 1976.

Jones, R., and Spolsky, B. *Testing Language Proficiency.* Arlington, Va.: Center for Applied Linguistics, 1975.

Jones, R. R., Reid, J. B., and Patterson, G. R. "Naturalistic Observation in Clinical Assessment." In P. McReynolds (Ed.), *Advances in Psychological Assessment.* Vol. 3. San Francisco: Jossey-Bass, 1975.

Jordan, W. C. "Mirror Image." *Grade Teacher,* 1971, *88* (5), 100–106.

Kagan, J. "Impulsive and Reflective Children: Significance of Conceptual Tempo." In J. D. Krumboltz (Ed.), *Learning and the Educational Process.* Skokie, Ill.: Rand McNally, 1965.

Kagan, J., and Kogan, N. "Individual Variation in Cognitive Processes." In P. H. Mussen (Ed.), *Carmichael's Manual of Child Psychology.* Vol. 1. (3rd ed.) New York: Wiley, 1970.

Kamii, C. K. "Evaluation of Learning in Preschool Education: Socioemotional, Perceptual-Motor, and Cognitive Development." In B. S. Bloom, J. T. Hastings, and G. F. Madaus (Eds.), *Handbook on Formative and Summative Evaluation of Student Learning.* New York: McGraw-Hill, 1971.

Kaplan, M. S. "Review of Children's Drawings as Measures of Intellectual Maturity." *Personnel and Guidance Journal,* 1965, *43,* 830–831.

Karnes, M. B., and Zehrbach, R. R. "Educational Intervention at Home." In M. C. Day and R. K. Parker (Eds.), *The Preschool in Action: Exploring Early Childhood Programs.* (2nd ed.) Boston: Allyn & Bacon, 1977.

Katkovsky, W., Preston, A., and Crandall, V. J. "Parents' Achievement Attitudes and Their Behavior with Their Children in Achievement Situations." *Journal of Genetic Psychology,* 1964, *104,* 105–121.

Katz, L. "Developmental Stages of Preschool Teachers." *Elementary School Journal,* 1972, *73* (1), 50–54.

Kaufman, A. S. "Factor Structure of the McCarthy Scales at Five Age Levels Between 2½ and 8½." *Educational and Psychological Measurement,* 1975, *35,* 641–656.

Kaufman, A. S., and Hollenbeck, G. P. "Factor Analysis of the Standardization Edition of the McCarthy Scales." *Journal of Clinical Psychology,* 1973, *29,* 358–362.

Kaufman, A. S., and Kaufman, N. L. *Clinical Evaluation of Young Children with the McCarthy Scales.* New York: Grune & Stratton, 1977.

Kelly, E. F. "Can Evaluation Be Used to Cut Costs?" In E. R. House (Ed.), *School Evaluation: The Politics and Process.* Berkeley, Calif.: McCutchan, 1973.

Kelly, J. G. "Naturalistic Observations in Contrasting Social Environments." In E. P. Willems and H. L. Raush (Eds.), *Naturalistic Viewpoints in Psychological Research.* New York: Holt, Rinehart and Winston, 1969.

Kent, R. N., and Foster, S. L. "Direct Observational Procedures: Methodological Issues in Naturalistic Settings." In A. R. Ciminero, K. S. Calhoun, and H. E. Adams (Eds.), *Handbook of Behavioral Assessment.* New York: Wiley, 1977.

Keogh, B. K. "Review of the Cognitive Skills Assessment Battery." In O. K. Buros (Ed.), *The Eighth Mental Measurements Yearbook.* Vol. 2. Highland Park, N.J.: Gryphon Press, 1978.

Keogh, B. K., and Becker, L. D. "Early Detection of Learning Problems: Questions, Cautions, and Guidelines." *Exceptional Children,* 1973, *40* (1), 5–11.

Kephart, N. C. "Review of the Southern California Kinesthesia and Tactile Perception Tests." In O. K. Buros (Ed.), *The Seventh Mental Measurements Yearbook.* Vol. 2. Highland Park, N.J.: Gryphon Press, 1972a.

Kephart, N. C. "Review of the Southern California Motor Accuracy Test." In O. K. Buros (Ed.), *The Seventh Mental Measurements Yearbook.* Vol. 2. Highland Park, N.J.: Gryphon Press, 1972b.

Kerlinger, F. N. *Foundations of Behavioral Research.* (2nd ed.) New York: Holt, Rinehart and Winston, 1973.

Kerr, W. A., and Remmers, H. H. *The American Home Scale.* Munster, Ind.: Psychometric Affiliates, 1942.

Khan, S. B., and Weiss, J. "The Teaching of Affective Responses." In R. M. W. Travers (Ed.), *Second Handbook of Research on Teaching.* Skokie, Ill.: Rand McNally, 1973.

Khatena, J., and Torrance, E. P. *Thinking Creatively with Sounds and Words: Norms—Technical Manual.* (Research ed.) Lexington, Mass.: Personnel Press, 1973.

King, E. W. *Educating Young Children . . . Sociological Interpretations.* Dubuque, Iowa: Wm. C. Brown, 1973.

King, E. W., and Kerber, A. *The Sociology of Early Childhood Education.* New York: American Elsevier, 1968.

Kirk, S. A., and Kirk, W. D. *Psycholinguistic Learning Disabilities: Diagnosis and Remediation.* Urbana: University of Illinois Press, 1971.

Kirk, S. A., McCarthy, J. J., and Kirk, W. D. *Illinois Test of Psycholinguistic Abilities.* (Revised ed.) Urbana: University of Illinois Press, 1968.

Kirschner Associates. *A National Survey of the Impacts of Head Start Centers on Community Institutions.* Washington, D.C.: Office of Child Development, 1970. (Also available in ERIC, ED 046516.)

Klett, C. J., and Pumroy, D. K. "Automated Procedures in Psychological Assessment." In P. McReynolds (Ed.), *Advances in Psychological Assessment.* Vol. 2. Palo Alto, Calif.: Science and Behavior Books, 1971.

Kogan, N. *Cognitive Styles in Infancy and Early Childhood Education.* Hillsdale, N.J.: Lawrence Erlbaum, 1976.

Kogan, N., and Pankove, E. "Long-term Predictive Validity of Divergent-Thinking Tests: Some Negative Evidence." *Journal of Educational Psychology,* 1974, *66,* 802–810.

Kohlberg, L. "Early Education: A Cognitive-Developmental View." *Child Development,* 1968, *39,* 1013–1062.

Kohlberg, L. "The Contribution of Developmental Psychology to Education—Examples from Moral Education." *Educational Psychologist,* 1973, *10,* 2–14.

Kohlberg, L. "Moral Stages and Moralization: The Cognitive-Developmental Approach." In T. Lickona (Ed.), *Moral Development and Behavior: Theory, Research, and Social Issues.* New York: Holt, Rinehart and Winston, 1976.

Kolstoe, O. P. "Review of the Measurement of Social Competence: A Manual for the Vineland Social Maturity Scale." *Exceptional Children,* 1954, *20,* 360f.

Kounin, J. S. *Discipline and Group Management in Classrooms.* New York: Holt, Rinehart and Winston, 1970.

Kourilsky, M. "An Adversary Model for Educational Evaluation." *Evaluation Comment,* 1973, *4* (2), 3–6.

Kraft, R. H. P. "Cost-Effectiveness Analysis in Vocational-Technical Education." In D. D. Sjogren (Ed.), *Four Evaluation Examples: Anthropological, Economic,*

Narrative, and Portrayal. AERA Monograph Series on Curriculum Evaluation No. 7. Skokie, Ill.: Rand McNally, 1974.

Krathwohl, D. R., Bloom, B. S., and Masia, B. B. *Taxonomy of Objectives: The Classification of Educational Goals. Handbook II: Affective Domain.* New York: McKay, 1964.

Krauskopf, C. J. "Review of the BITCH Test (Black Intelligence Test of Cultural Homogeneity)." In O. K. Buros (Ed.), *The Eighth Mental Measurements Yearbook.* Vol. 1. Highland Park, N.J.: Gryphon Press, 1978.

Krugman, M. "Review of the Vineland Social Maturity Scale." *Journal of Consulting Psychology,* 1956, *20,* 408–409.

Kuder, G. F., and Richardson, M. W. "The Theory of Estimation of Test Reliability." *Psychometrika,* 1937, *2,* 151–160.

LaCrosse, E. R., Jr. "Psychologist and Teacher: Cooperation or Conflict?" *Young Children,* 1970, *25,* 223–229.

LaCrosse, E. R., Jr. "Thoughts for New Administrators or What Nobody Ever Tells You about Administration Even When You Do Ask." Mimeo. Pasadena, Calif.: Pacific Oaks College, 1975.

Lake, D., Miles, M., and Earle, R., Jr. (Eds.). *Measuring Human Behavior.* New York: Teachers College Press, 1973.

Lally, J. R., and Honig, A. S. "The Family Development Research Program." In M. C. Day and R. K. Parker (Eds.), *The Preschool in Action: Exploring Early Childhood Programs.* (2nd ed.) Boston: Allyn & Bacon, 1977.

Landis, D. "Review of the Purdue Perceptual-Motor Survey." In O. K. Buros (Ed.), *The Seventh Mental Measurements Yearbook.* Vol. 2. Highland Park, N.J.: Gryphon Press, 1972a.

Landis, D. "Review of the Southern California Perceptual-Motor Tests." In O. K. Buros (Ed.), *The Seventh Mental Measurements Yearbook.* Vol. 2. Highland Park, N.J.: Gryphon Press, 1972b.

Laosa, L. M. "Nonbiased Assessment of Children's Abilities: Historical Antecedents and Current Issues." In T. Oakland (Ed.), *Psychological and Educational Assessment of Minority Children.* New York: Brunner/Mazel, 1977.

Laumann, E. O., and House, J. S. "Living Room Styles and Social Attributes: The Patterning of Material Artifacts in a Modern Urban Community." *Sociology and Social Research,* 1970, *54,* 321–342.

Laurendeau, M., and Pinard, A. *Causal Thinking in the Child.* New York: International Universities Press, 1962.

Laurendeau, M., and Pinard, A. *The Development of the Concept of Space in the Child.* New York: International Universities Press, 1970.

Law, A. I. "Evaluating Bilingual Programs." TM Report No. 61. Princeton, N.J.: Educational Testing Service ERIC Clearinghouse on Tests, Measurement, and Evaluation, 1977.

Lazar, I., and Darlington, R. B. *Lasting Effects after Preschool.* Denver: Education Commission of the States, 1978.

Lazar, I., and others. *The Persistence of Preschool Effects: A Long-term Follow-up of*

Fourteen Infant and Preschool Projects. Washington, D.C.: Administration for Children, Youth, and Families, 1977.

Lazar, J. B., and Chapman, J. E. *A Review of the Present Status and Future Research Needs of Programs to Develop Parenting Skills.* Washington, D.C.: Social Research Group, George Washington University, 1972.

Lee, L. L. *Developmental Sentence Analysis: A Grammatical Assessment Procedure for Speech and Language Clinicians.* Evanston, Ill.: Northwestern University Press, 1974.

Lefcourt, H. M. *Locus of Control: Current Trends in Theory and Research.* Hillsdale, N.J.: Lawrence Erlbaum, 1976.

Lefkowitz, M. M. "Some Relationships Between Sex-Role Preference in Children and Other Parent and Child Variables." *Psychological Reports,* 1962, *10,* 43–53.

Leiter, R. G. *Leiter International Performance Scale, Manual.* Parts I and II. Chicago: Stoelting, 1948 (I) and 1950 (II).

LeMay, D. C. *A Workshop in the Use of the Learning Accomplishment Profile, Diagnostic Edition (Revised).* Chapel Hill, N.C.: Chapel Hill Training-Outreach Project, 1977.

Lenneberg, E. H. *Biological Foundations of Language.* New York: Wiley, 1967.

Lerner, B. "The Supreme Court and the APA, AERA, NCME Test Standards: Past References and Future Possibilities." *American Psychologist,* 1978, *33* (10), 915–919.

Lesser, G. S. *Children and Television: Lessons from Sesame Street.* New York: Random House, 1974.

Lessinger, L. M. *Every Kid a Winner: Accountability in Education.* New York: Simon & Schuster, 1970.

Lessinger, L. M. "Accountability and Humanism: A Productive Educational Complementarity." In C. D. Sabine (Ed.), *Accountability: Systems Planning in Education.* Homewood, Ill.: ETC Publications, 1973.

Leton, D. A. "Review of the Developmental Test of Visual-Motor Integration." In O. K. Buros (Ed.), *The Eighth Mental Measurements Yearbook.* Vol. 2. Highland Park, N.J.: Gryphon Press, 1978.

Levenstein, P. "The Mother-Child Home Program." In M. C. Day and R. K. Parker (Eds.), *The Preschool in Action: Exploring Early Childhood Programs.* (2nd ed.) Boston: Allyn & Bacon, 1977.

Levine, E. L., Fineman, C. A., and Donlon, G. McG. *Prescriptive Profile Procedure for Children with Learning Disabilities.* Miami, Fla.: Dade County Public Schools, 1973. (Also available in ERIC, ED 074673.)

Levine, M. "Psychological Testing of Children." In L. W. Hoffman and M. L. Hoffman (Eds.), *Review of Child Development Research.* Vol. 2. New York: Russell Sage Foundation, 1966.

Levine, M. "Scientific Method and the Adversary Model: Some Preliminary Suggestions." *Evaluation Comment,* 1973, *4* (2), 1–3.

Levine, S., Elzey, F. F., and Lewis, M. *California Preschool Social Competency Scale Manual.* Palo Alto, Calif.: Consulting Psychologists Press, 1969.

LeVinson, B. M. "Parental Achievement Drives for Preschool Children, the Vineland Social Maturity Scale, and the Social Deviation Quotient." *Journal of Genetic Psychology,* 1961, *99,* 113–128.

Lewis, M. "Infant Intelligence Tests: Their Use and Misuse." *Human Development,* 1973, *16,* 108–118.

Lewis, M., and McGurk, H. "The Evaluation of Infant Intelligence: Infant Intelligence Scores—True or False?" *Research Bulletin 72–32.* Princeton, N.J.: Educational Testing Service, 1972.

Lewis, O. *Life in a Mexican Village: Tepoztlan Restudied.* Urbana: University of Illinois Press, 1951.

Liebert, R. M., Neale, J. M., and Davidson, E. S. *The Early Window: Effects of Television on Children and Youth.* New York: Pergamon Press, 1973.

Lin, N. *Foundations of Social Research.* New York: McGraw-Hill, 1976.

Lindberg, L., and Swedlow, R. *Early Childhood Education: A Guide for Observation and Participation.* Boston: Allyn & Bacon, 1976.

Linstone, H. A., and Turoff, M. (Ed.). *The Delphi Method: Techniques and Applications.* Reading, Mass.: Addison-Wesley, 1975.

Lipsitt, L. "Infant Learning: The Blooming, Buzzing, Confusion Revisited." In M. E. Meyer (Ed.), *Early Learning, The Second Western Symposium on Learning.* Bellingham: Western Washington State College, 1971.

Locks, N. A., Pletcher, B. A., and Reynolds, D. F. *Language Assessment Instruments for Limited-English-Speaking Students: A Needs Analysis.* Washington, D.C.: National Institute of Education, 1978.

Lofthouse, R. W. "The Effects of Spatial Density on Children's Interaction with Peers in a Public Kindergarten Classroom." Unpublished master's thesis, University of Colorado at Denver, 1978.

Long, B. H., and Henderson, E. H. "Self-Social Concepts of Disadvantaged School Beginners." *Journal of Genetic Psychology,* 1968, *113* (1), 41–51.

Long, B. H., and Henderson, E. H. "Social Schemata of School Beginners: Some Demographic Correlates." *Merrill-Palmer Quarterly,* 1970, *16,* 305–324.

Lott, D. F., and Sommer, R. "Seating Arrangements and Status." In R. Cochrane (Ed.), *Advances in Social Research.* London, England: Constable, 1973.

Love, J. M., and others. *National Home Start Evaluation: Final Report.* Ypsilanti, Mich.: High/Scope Educational Research Foundation, 1976.

Love, J. M., and others. *A Process Evaluation of Project Developmental Continuity: Draft Final Report of the PDC Feasibility Study, 1974–1977.* Ypsilanti, Mich.: High/Scope Educational Research Foundation, 1977.

Lumsden, J. "Review of the Illinois Test of Psycholinguistic Abilities, Revised Edition." In O. K. Buros (Ed.), *The Eighth Mental Measurements Yearbook.* Vol. 1. Highland Park, N.J.: Gryphon Press, 1978.

Lutz, F. W., and Ramsey, M. A. "The Use of Anthropological Field Methods in Education." *Educational Researcher,* 1974, *3,* 5–9.

Lynch, K. *The Image of the City.* Cambridge, Mass.: M.I.T. Press, 1960.

Lynch, K., and Rivkin, M. "A Walk Around the Block." In H. M. Proshansky,

W. H. Ittelson, and L. G. Rivlin (Eds.), *Environmental Psychology: Man and His Physical Setting.* New York: Holt, Rinehart and Winston, 1970.

Lytton, H. "Review of California Preschool Social Competency Scale." In O. K. Buros (Ed.), *The Eighth Mental Measurements Yearbook.* Vol. 1. Highland Park, N.J.: Gryphon Press, 1978.

McCall, G. J., and Simmons, J. L. (Eds.). *Issues in Participant Observation: Text and Reader.* Reading, Mass.: Addison-Wesley, 1969.

McCall, R. B., Applebaum, M. I., and Hogarty, P. S. "Developmental Changes in Mental Performance." *Monographs of the Society for Research in Child Development,* 1973, *38* (3, Serial No. 150).

McCall, R. B., Hogarty, P. S., and Hurlburt, N. "Transitions in Infant Sensorimotor Development and the Prediction of Childhood IQ." *American Psychologist,* 1972, *27,* 728–748.

McCandless, B. R. "Review of the Basic Concept Inventory." In O. K. Buros (Ed.), *The Seventh Mental Measurements Yearbook.* Vol. 2. Highland Park, N.J.: Gryphon Press, 1972.

McCarthy, D. "A Study of the Reliability of the Goodenough Drawing Test of Intelligence." *Journal of Psychology,* 1944, *18,* 201–206.

McCarthy, D. *Manual for the McCarthy Scales of Children's Abilities.* New York: Psychological Corporation, 1972.

McCarthy, J. J. "Review of the Basic Concept Inventory." In O. K. Buros (Ed.), *The Seventh Mental Measurements Yearbook.* Vol. 2. Highland Park, N.J.: Gryphon Press, 1972.

McCarthy, J. J. "Review of the Developmental Indicators for the Assessment of Learning." In O. K. Buros (Ed.), *The Eighth Mental Measurements Yearbook.* Vol. 1. Highland Park, N.J.: Gryphon Press, 1978.

Maccoby, E. E., and Zellner, M. *Experiments in Primary Education: Aspects of Project Follow Through.* New York: Harcourt Brace Jovanovich, 1970.

McCurdy, H. G. "Group and Individual Variability on the Goodenough Draw-a-Man Test." *Journal of Educational Psychology,* 1947, *38,* 428–436.

McDill, E. L., McDill, M. S., and Sprehe, J. T. "Evaluation in Practice: Compensatory Education." In P. H. Rossi and W. Williams (Eds.), *Evaluating Social Programs: Theory, Practice, and Politics.* New York: Seminar Press, 1972.

McDonald, F. J. "The Criteria for Accountability: Pupil or Professional Performance." *Evaluation Comment,* 1973, *4* (1), 6.

Macdonald, J. B. "An Evaluation of Evaluation." *Urban Review,* 1974, *7,* 3–14.

McGrew, W. C. "Interpersonal Spacing of Preschool Children." In K. Connolly and J. Bruner (Eds.), *The Growth of Competence.* New York: Academic Press, 1974.

McLean, L. D. "Judging the Quality of a School as a Place Where the Arts Might Thrive." In R. E. Stake (Ed.), *Evaluating the Arts in Education: A Responsive Approach.* Columbus, Ohio: Merrill, 1975.

McLean, L. D. "Evaluation of Early Childhood Education—No Simple Answer to the Right Question." Paper presented at the Nature and Nurture and

School Achievement Conference, York University, Toronto, Canada, May 1978.

McMurtry, C. A., and Williams, J. E. "The Evaluative Dimension of the Affective Meaning System of the Preschool Child." *Developmental Psychology*, 1972, *6*, 238–246.

McNeil, J. D., and Popham, W. J. "The Assessment of Teacher Competence." In R. M. W. Travers (Ed.), *Second Handbook of Research on Teaching*. Skokie, Ill.: Rand McNally, 1973.

McNemar, Q. *The Revision of the Stanford-Binet Scale: An Analysis of the Standardization Data*. Boston: Houghton Mifflin, 1942.

McReynolds, P. "An Introduction to Psychological Assessment." In P. McReynolds (Ed.), *Advances in Psychological Assessment*. Vol. 1. Palo Alto, Calif.: Science and Behavior Books, 1968.

McReynolds, P. "Introduction." In P. McReynolds (Ed.), *Advances in Psychological Assessment*. Vol. 2. Palo Alto, Calif.: Science and Behavior Books, 1971a.

McReynolds, P. "The Nature and Assessment of Intrinsic Motivation." In P. McReynolds (Ed.), *Advances in Psychological Assessment*. Vol. 2. Palo Alto, Calif.: Science and Behavior Books, 1971b.

McReynolds, P. "Historical Antecedents of Personality Assessment." In P. McReynolds (Ed.), *Advances in Psychological Assessment*. Vol. 3. San Francisco: Jossey-Bass, 1975a.

McReynolds, P. "Introduction." In P. McReynolds (Ed.), *Advances in Psychological Assessment*. Vol. 3. San Francisco: Jossey-Bass, 1975b.

Madden, R., and Gardner, E. F. *Stanford Early School Achievement Test: Directions for Administering*. Levels I and II. New York: Harcourt Brace Jovanovich, 1969 (Level I), 1971 (Level II).

Magnusson, D. *Test Theory*. Reading, Mass.: Addison-Wesley, 1967.

Magoon, A. J. "Constructivist Approaches in Educational Research." *Review of Educational Research*, 1977, *47* (4), 651–693.

Malinowski, B. *Argonauts of the Western Pacific*. New York: Dutton, 1961. (Originally published 1922.)

Malinowski, B. *Coral Gardens and Their Magic: Soil-Tilling and Agricultural Rites in the Trobriand Islands*. Vol. 1. Bloomington: Indiana University Press, 1965. (Originally published 1935.)

Mann, A. J., Harrell, A., and Hurt, M., Jr. *A Review of Head Start Research Since 1969*. Washington, D.C.: Social Research Group, George Washington University, 1976.

Mann. L. "Review of the Marianne Frostig Developmental Test of Visual Perception, Third Edition." In O. K. Buros (Ed.), *The Seventh Mental Measurements Yearbook*. Vol. 2. Highland Park, N.J.: Gryphon Press, 1972.

Mann, P. H. *Methods of Sociological Inquiry*. New York: Schocken, 1968.

Mardell, C. D., and Goldenberg, D. S. *Learning Disabilities/Early Childhood Research Project*. Springfield: Illinois State Office of the Superintendent of Public Instruction, 1972. (Also available in ERIC, ED 082408.)

Mardell, C. D., and Goldenberg, D. S. *DIAL—Developmental Indicators for the Assessment of Learning: Manual.* Highland Park, Ill.: DIAL, Inc., 1975.

Margolin, E. *Sociocultural Elements in Early Childhood Education.* New York: Macmillan, 1974.

Martuza, V. R. *Applying Norm-Referenced and Criterion-Referenced Measurement in Education.* Boston: Allyn & Bacon, 1977.

Mash, E. J., and McElwee, J. D. "Situational Effects on Observer Accuracy: Behavioral Predictability, Prior Experience, and Complexity of Coding Categories." *Child Development,* 1974, *45,* 367–377.

Maslow, A. H. *Motivation and Personality.* (2nd ed.) New York: Harper & Row, 1970.

Masonis, E. J. "Standardized, Objective Selection Procedures and the E.E.O.C. Guidelines: A Review of Some Problems and Solutions in Teacher Selection." Princeton, N.J.: Educational Testing Service, 1976.

Medinnus, G. R. *Child Study and Observation Guide.* New York: Wiley, 1976.

Medley, D. M. "Teacher-Made Tests." In D. W. Allen and E. Serfman (Eds.), *The Teacher's Handbook.* Glenview, Ill.: Scott, Foresman, 1971.

Medley, D. M., and Mitzel, H. E. "A Technique for Measuring Classroom Behavior." *Journal of Educational Psychology,* 1958, *49,* 86–92.

Medley, D. M., and Mitzel, H. E. "Measuring Classroom Behavior by Systematic Observation." In N. L. Gage (Ed.), *Handbook of Research on Teaching.* Skokie, Ill.: Rand McNally, 1963.

Mehrabian, A. *Public Places and Private Spaces.* New York: Basic Books, 1976.

Mehrens, W. A. "Review of the Stanford Early School Achievement Test." In O. K. Buros (Ed.), *The Seventh Mental Measurements Yearbook.* Vol. 1. Highland Park, N.J.: Gryphon Press, 1972.

Mehrens, W. A., and Lehmann, I. J. *Standardized Tests in Education.* New York: Holt, Rinehart and Winston, 1969.

Mehrens, W. A., and Lehmann, I. J. *Measurement and Evaluation in Education and Psychology.* (2nd ed.) New York: Holt, Rinehart and Winston, 1978.

Meier, J. H. "Screening, Assessment, and Intervention for Young Children at Developmental Risk." In N. Hobbs (Ed.), *Issues in the Classification of Children: A Sourcebook on Categories, Labels, and Their Consequences.* Vol. 2. San Francisco: Jossey-Bass, 1975.

Mercer, J. R. *Labeling the Mentally Retarded.* Berkeley: University of California Press, 1973.

Mercer, J. R. "A Policy Statement on Assessment Procedures and the Rights of Children." *Harvard Educational Review,* 1974, *44,* 125–141.

Mercer, J. R., and Lewis, J. F. *System of Multicultural Pluralistic Assessment (SOMPA).* New York: Psychological Corporation, 1977, 1978.

Merwin, J. C. "Historical Review of Changing Concepts of Evaluation." In R. W. Tyler (Ed.), *Educational Evaluation: New Roles, New Means,* 68th Yearbook, Part 2. National Society for the Study of Education. Chicago: University of Chicago Press, 1969.

Messick, S., and Anderson, S. "Educational Testing, Individual Development, and Social Responsibility." *The Counseling Psychologist,* 1970, *2,* 80–88.

Messick, S., and Barrows, T. S. "Strategies for Research and Evaluation in Early Childhood Education." In I. J. Gordon (Ed.), *Early Childhood Education,* 71st Yearbook, Part 2. National Society for the Study of Education. Chicago: University of Chicago Press, 1972.

Metfessel, N. S., and Michael, W. B. "A Paradigm Involving Multiple Criterion Measures for the Evaluation of the Effectiveness of School Programs." *Educational and Psychological Measurement,* 1967, *27,* 931–943.

Metropolitan Readiness Tests, Teacher's Manuals, Part II: Interpretation and Use of Test Results. Levels I and II. New York: Harcourt Brace Jovanovich, 1976.

Meyer, H. H., Kay, E., and French, J. R. P. "Split Roles in Performance Appraisal." *Harvard Business Review,* 1965, *43,* 123–129.

Milchus, N. J. "Research Studies Involving SCAMIN." Unpublished paper. Dearborn Heights, Mich.: Person-O-Metrics, 1977.

Milchus, N. J., Farrah, G. A., and Reitz, W. *The Self-Concept and Motivation Inventory: What Face Would You Wear? SCAMIN Manual of Interpretation.* Dearborn Heights, Mich.: Person-O-Metrics, 1968.

Milholland, J. E. "Review of the Culture Fair Intelligence Test." In O. K. Buros (Ed.), *The Sixth Mental Measurements Yearbook.* Highland Park, N.J.: Gryphon Press, 1965.

Miller, D. B. "Roles of Naturalistic Observation in Comparative Psychology." *American Psychologist,* 1977, *32,* 211–219.

Miller, L. B., and Dyer, J. L. "Four Preschool Programs: Their Dimensions and Effects." *Monographs of the Society for Research in Child Development,* 1975, *40* (5–6, Serial No. 162).

Miller, R. I. (Ed.). *Notes and Working Papers Concerning the Administration of Programs Authorized Under Title III, ESEA.* Washington, D.C.: U.S. Government Printing Office, 1967.

Millman, J. "Criterion-Referenced Measurement." In W. J. Popham (Ed.), *Evaluation in Education: Current Applications.* Berkeley, Calif.: McCutchan, 1974.

Mischel, W. *Personality and Assessment.* New York: Wiley, 1968.

Mischel, W., Zeiss, R., and Zeiss, A. "Internal-External Control and Persistence: Validation and Implications of the Stanford Preschool Internal-External Scale." *Journal of Personality and Social Psychology,* 1974, *29* (2), 265–278.

Moffett, J. *Teaching the Universe of Discourse.* Boston: Houghton Mifflin, 1968.

Montessori, M. *The Montessori Method.* New York: Schocken, 1964.

Moore, P. "Educational Testing Service Championed." *APA Monitor,* 1976a, 7 (11), 6–7.

Moore, P. "Nader Chides Researchers, Scores Testing," *APA Monitor,* 1976b, 7 (11), 1, 6–7, 18.

Moore, R. S., and Moore, D. N. *Better Late than Early: A New Approach to Your Child's Education.* New York: Reader's Digest Press, 1975.

Moore, S. G. "Correlates of Peer Acceptance in Nursery School Children." *Young Children,* 1967, *22,* 281–297.

Moore, S. G. "A Sociometric Status Test for Young Children: Manual of Instructions." Unpublished paper. Minneapolis: Institute of Child Development, University of Minnesota, 1973.

Moore, S. G., and Updegraff, R. "Sociometric Status of Preschool Children Related to Age, Sex, Nurturance-giving and Dependency." *Child Development,* 1964, *35,* 519–524.

Moos, R. H. "Conceptualizations of Human Environments." *American Psychologist,* 1973, *28,* 652–665.

Moos, R. H. "Assessment and Impact of Social Climate." In P. McReynolds (Ed.), *Advances in Psychological Assessment.* Vol. 3. San Francisco: Jossey-Bass, 1975a.

Moos, R. H. *Evaluating Correctional and Community Settings.* New York: Wiley, 1975b.

Moos, R. H. "A Typology of Junior High and High School Classrooms." *American Educational Research Journal,* 1978, *15* (1), 53–66.

Moos, R. H. *Evaluating Educational Environments: Procedures, Measures, Findings, and Policy Implications.* San Francisco: Jossey-Bass, 1979.

Moreno, J. L. *Who Shall Survive?* Washington, D.C.: Nervous and Mental Disease Publishing, 1934.

Morgan, G. A. V. "Review of the Bristol Social Adjustment Guides." In O. K. Buros (Ed.) *The Sixth Mental Measurements Yearbook.* Highland Park, N.J.: Gryphon Press, 1965.

Moriarty, A. E. *Constancy and IQ Change: A Clinical View of Relationships between Tested Intelligence and Personality.* Springfield, Ill.: Thomas, 1966.

Moriarty, A. E. "Review of the Denver Developmental Screening Test." In O. K. Buros (Ed.), *The Seventh Mental Measurements Yearbook.* Vol. 1. Highland Park, N.J.: Gryphon Press, 1972.

Moss, H. "Sex, Age, and State of Determinants of Mother-Infant Interaction." *Merrill-Palmer Quarterly,* 1967, *13,* 19–36.

Moss, M. H. *Tests of Basic Experiences: Examiner's Manual.* Levels K and L. Monterey, Calif.: CTB/McGraw-Hill, 1970–1971 (Level K); 1970, 1972 (Level L); and 1975 (Computer-Scored Version).

Moss, M. H. *Tests of Basic Experiences 2: Examiner's Manual.* Levels K and L. Monterey, Calif.: CTB/McGraw-Hill, 1978.

Mowrer, O. H. *Learning Theory and the Symbolic Processes.* New York: Wiley, 1960.

National Advisory Commission on Civil Disorders. *Report of the National Advisory Commission on Civil Disorders.* New York: Bantam, 1968.

National Council for Accreditation of Teacher Education. *Standards for Accreditation of Teacher Education.* Washington, D.C.: National Council for Accreditation of Teacher Education, 1970.

National Education Association. "Moratorium on Standardized Testing." *Today's Education, NEA Journal,* 1972, *61* (6), 41.

National Study of Secondary School Evaluation. *Evaluative Criteria.* (4th ed.) Washington, D.C.: National Study of Secondary School Evaluation, 1969.

Nedler, S. E., and McAfee, O. D. *Working with Parents: Guidelines for Early Childhood and Elementary Teachers.* Belmont, Calif.: Wadsworth, 1979.

Nelson, D., Fellner, M. J., and Norrell, C. L. *The Pictorial Test of Bilingualism and Language Dominance: Manual.* Chicago: Stoelting, 1975.

Newcomer, P. L. "Review of the Comprehensive Identification Process." In O. K. Buros (Ed.), *The Eighth Mental Measurements Yearbook.* Vol. 1. Highland Park, N.J.: Gryphon Press, 1978.

Nielsen, H. D., and Kirk, D. H. "Classroom Climates." In H. J. Walberg (Ed.), *Evaluating Educational Performance.* Berkeley, Calif.: McCutchan, 1974.

Nimnicht, G., Arango, M., and Adcock, D. "The Parent-Child Toy Library Program." In M. C. Day and R. K. Parker (Eds.), *The Preschool in Action: Exploring Early Childhood Programs.* (2nd ed.) Boston: Allyn & Bacon, 1977.

Nimnicht, G., and others. *A Guide to Securing and Installing the Parent-Child Toy-Lending Library.* Berkeley, Calif.: Far West Laboratory for Educational Research and Development, 1972.

Nitko, A. J. "Review of the Comprehensive Tests of Basic Skills." In O. K. Buros (Ed.), *The Eighth Mental Measurements Yearbook.* Vol. 1. Highland Park, N.J.: Gryphon Press, 1978.

Noll, V. H. "Review of the Boehm Test of Basic Concepts." *Journal of Educational Measurement,* 1970, *7,* 139–140.

Noll, V. H., and Scannell, D. P. *Introduction to Educational Measurement.* (3rd ed.) Boston: Houghton Mifflin, 1972.

Northway, M. L. "The Changing Pattern of Young Children's Social Relations." *Educational Research,* 1969a, *11,* 212–214.

Northway, M. L. "The Stability of Young Children's Social Relations." *Educational Research,* 1969b, *11,* 54–57.

Nowicki, S., Jr., and Duke, M. P. "A Preschool and Primary Internal-External Control Scale." *Developmental Psychology,* 1974, *10* (6), 874–880.

Nowicki, S., Jr., and Strickland, B. R. "A Locus of Control Scale for Children." *Journal of Consulting and Clinical Psychology,* 1973, *40* (1), 148–154.

Oakland, T. (Ed.). *Psychological and Educational Assessment of Minority Children.* New York: Brunner/Mazel, 1977.

Oakland, T. "Review of the Frostig Movement Skills Test Battery: Experimental Edition." In O. K. Buros (Ed.), *The Eighth Mental Measurements Yearbook.* Vol. 2. Highland Park, N.J.: Gryphon Press, 1978.

Oakland, T., De Luna, C., and Morgan, C. "Annotated Bibliography of Language Dominance Measures." In T. Oakland (Ed.), *Psychological and Educational Assessment of Minority Children.* New York: Brunner/Mazel, 1977.

Oakland, T., and Laosa, L. M. "Professional, Legislative, and Judicial Influences on Psychoeducational Assessment Practices in Schools." In T. Oakland (Ed.), *Psychological and Educational Assessment of Minority Children.* New York: Brunner/Mazel, 1977.

Oakland, T., and Matuszek, P. "Using Tests in Nondiscriminatory Assessment." In T. Oakland (Ed.), *Psychological and Educational Assessment of Minority Children.* New York: Brunner/Mazel, 1977.

Office of Economic Opportunity. *Rainbow Series, Project Head Start.* Washington, D.C.: Office of Economic Opportunity, 1965.

Oldham, N. B. *Citizens Advisory Committees.* Arlington, Va.: National School Public Relations Association, 1973.

O'Reilly, A. "Racial Attitudes of Negro Preschoolers." *California Journal of Educational Research,* 1971, *22,* 126–130.

Orne, M. T. "On the Social Psychology of the Psychological Experiment: With Particular Reference to Demand Characteristics and Their Implications." *American Psychologist,* 1962, *17,* 776–783.

Orpet, R. E. *Examiners Manual: Frostig Movement Test Battery.* (Experimental ed.) Palo Alto, Calif.: Consulting Psychologists Press, 1972.

Ortiz, C. C., and Ball, G. *The Enchilada Test.* Institute for Personal Effectiveness in Children, 1972.

Owens, T. R. "Educational Evaluation by Adversary Proceeding." In E. R. House (Ed.), *School Evaluation: The Politics and Process.* Berkeley, Calif.: McCutchan, 1973.

Palmer, J. O. *The Psychological Assessment of Children.* New York: Wiley, 1970.

Parlett, M., and Hamilton, D. "Evaluation as Illumination: A New Approach to the Study of Innovatory Programs." In G. V. Glass (Ed.), *Evaluation Studies Review Annual.* Vol. 1. Beverly Hills, Calif.: Sage Publications, 1976.

Patton, M. Q. *Alternative Evaluation Research Paradigm.* Grand Forks: North Dakota Study Group on Evaluation, University of North Dakota, 1975.

Pauker, J. D. "Review of the Test of Motor Impairment." In O. K. Buros (Ed.), *The Eighth Mental Measurements Yearbook.* Vol. 2. Highland Park, N.J.: Gryphon Press, 1978.

Payne, D. A. *The Assessment of Learning: Cognitive and Affective.* Lexington, Mass.: Heath, 1974.

Pedrini, D. T., and Pedrini, L. N. "The Vineland Social Maturity Scale: Recommendations for Administration, Scoring and Analysis." *Journal of School Psychology,* 1966, *5* (1), 14–20.

Perrone, V. "On Standardized Testing and Evaluation." In P. L. Houts (Ed.), *The Myth of Measurability.* New York: Hart, 1977.

Phi Delta Kappa Commission on Evaluation. *Educational Evaluation and Decision-Making.* Bloomington, Ind.: Phi Delta Kappa International, 1970.

Phillips, B. N. (Ed.). *Assessing Minority Group Children: A Special Issue of the Journal of School Psychology.* New York: Behavioral Publications, 1973.

Piaget, J. *The Moral Judgment of the Child.* New York: Free Press, 1965. (Originally published in 1932.)

Pickarts, E., and Fargo, J. *Parent Education: Toward Parental Competence.* New York: Appleton-Century-Crofts, 1971.

Piers, E. V. "Review of the Quick Test." In O. K. Buros (Ed.), *The Sixth Mental Measurements Yearbook.* Highland Park, N.J.: Gryphon Press, 1965.

Piers, E. V. and Harris, D. B. *Piers-Harris Children's Self-Concept Scale (The Way I Feel About Myself).* Nashville, Tenn.: Counselor Recordings and Tests, 1969.

Popham, W. J. *Educational Evaluation.* Englewood Cliffs, N.J.: Prentice-Hall, 1975.

Popham, W. J., and Carlson, D. "Deep Dark Deficits of the Adversary Evaluation Model." *Educational Researcher,* 1977, *6* (6), 3–6.

Posner, M. I., and Keele, S. W. "Skill Learning." In R. M. W. Travers (Ed.), *Second Handbook of Research on Teaching.* Skokie, Ill.: Rand McNally, 1973.

Prescott, E. "The Large Day Care Center as a Child-Rearing Environment." *Voice for Children,* 1970, *2* (4), 1–2.

Prescott, E., and Jones, E. *Group Day Care as a Child-Rearing Environment.* Washington, D.C.: Children's Bureau, Office of Child Development, 1967.

Prescott, E., and Jones, E. "Patterns of Teacher Behavior in Preschool Programs." Paper presented at annual meeting of the Society for Research in Child Development, Santa Monica, Calif., 1969.

Prescott, E., Jones, E., and Kritchevsky, S. *Assessment of Child-Rearing Environments: An Ecological Approach.* Washington, D.C.: Children's Bureau, Office of Child Development, 1971.

Prescott, E., and others. *Assessment of Child-Rearing Environments, An Ecological Approach: Part I, Who Thrives in Group Day Care; Part II, An Environmental Inventory.* Pasadena, Calif.: Pacific Oaks College, 1975.

Proger, B. B. "Review of the Southern California Perceptual-Motor Tests." *Journal of Special Education,* 1970, *4,* 117–120.

Proshansky, H. M., Ittelson, W. H., and Rivlin, L. G. (Eds.). *Environmental Psychology: Man and His Physical Setting.* New York: Holt, Rinehart and Winston, 1970.

Provus, M. M. "Evaluation of Ongoing Programs in the Public School System." In R. W. Tyler (Ed.), *Educational Evaluation: New Roles, New Means,* 68th Yearbook, Part 2. National Society for the Study of Education. Chicago: University of Chicago Press, 1969.

Provus, M. M. *Discrepancy Evaluation.* Berkeley, Calif.: McCutchan, 1971.

Provus, M. M. "The Discrepancy Evaluation Model." In P. A. Taylor and D. M. Cowley (Eds.), *Readings in Curriculum Evaluation.* Dubuque, Iowa: Wm. C. Brown, 1972.

Psychological Corporation. *Test Service Bulletin Number 48.* New York: Psychological Corporation, 1955.

Quilitch, H. R., Christophersen, E. R., and Risley, T. R. "The Evaluation of Children's Play Materials." *Journal of Applied Behavioral Analysis,* 1977, *10* (3), 501–502.

Raizen, S., and Bobrow, S. B. *Design for a National Evaluation of Social Competence in Head Start Children.* Santa Monica, Calif.: Rand, 1974.

Rao, C. R. *Linear Statistical Inference and Its Applications.* New York: Wiley, 1965.

Raths, J., and Katz, L. G. "Review of Circus: Comprehensive Program of Assessment Services for Pre-Primary Children." *Journal of Educational Measurement,* 1975, *12,* 144–147.

Raven, J. C. *Coloured Progressive Matrices.* New York: Psychological Corporation, 1947.

Razik, T. A. "Psychometric Measurement of Creativity." In R. L. Mooney and T. A. Razik (Eds.), *Explorations in Creativity.* New York: Harper & Row, 1967.

Reed, H. B. C., Jr. "Review of the Southern California Sensory Integration Tests." In O. K. Buros (Ed.), *The Eighth Mental Measurements Yearbook,* Vol. 2. Highland Park, N.J.: Gryphon Press, 1978.

Reid, J. B. "Reliability Assessment of Observation Data: A Possible Methodological Problem." *Child Development,* 1970, *41,* 1143–1150.

Remmers, H. H., Gage, N. L., and Rummel, J. F. *A Practical Introduction to Measurement and Evaluation.* (2nd ed.) New York: Harper & Row, 1965.

Resnick, L. B., Wang, M. C., and Rosner, J. "Adaptive Education for Young Children: The Primary Education Project." In M. C. Day and R. K. Parker (Eds.), *The Preschool in Action: Exploring Early Childhood Programs.* (2nd ed.) Boston: Allyn & Bacon, 1977.

Rest, J. R. "New Approaches in the Assessment of Moral Judgment." In T. Lickona (Ed.), *Moral Development and Behavior: Theory, Research, and Social Issues.* New York: Holt, Rinehart and Winston, 1976.

Rice, J. A. "Review of the Developmental Test of Visual-Motor Integration." In O. K. Buros (Ed.), *The Eighth Mental Measurements Yearbook.* Vol. 2. Highland Park, N.J.: Gryphon Press, 1978.

Rich, J. *Interviewing Children and Adolescents.* New York: St. Martin's, 1968.

Richardson, E. "The Physical Setting and Its Influence on Learning." In H. M. Proshansky, W. H. Ittelson, and L. G. Rivlin (Eds.), *Environmental Psychology: Man and His Physical Setting.* New York: Holt, Rinehart and Winston, 1970.

Riecken, H. W., and Boruch, R. F. (Eds.). *Social Experimentation: A Method for Planning and Evaluating Social Intervention.* New York: Academic Press, 1974.

Rimm, S., and Davis, G. A. "GIFT: An Instrument for the Identification of Creativity." *Journal of Creative Behavior,* 1976, *10,* 178–182.

Ringness, T. A. *The Affective Domain in Education.* Boston: Little, Brown, 1975.

Risley, T. R. "Living Environments Group Bibliography." Unpublished manuscript. Lawrence: Dept. of Human Development, University of Kansas, 1978.

Risley, T. R., and Baer, D. M. "Operant Behavior Modification: The Deliberate Development of Behavior." In B. M. Caldwell and H. N. Ricciuti (Eds.), *Review of Child Development Research.* Vol. 3. Chicago: University of Chicago Press, 1973.

Rivlin, A. M., and Timpane, P. M. *Planned Variation in Education.* Washington, D.C.: Brookings Institution, 1975.

Roach, E. G., and Kephart, N. C. *The Purdue Perceptual-Motor Survey.* Columbus, Ohio: Merrill, 1966.

Robin, S. S. "A Procedure for Securing Returns to Mail Questionnaires." In R. Cochrane (Ed.), *Advances in Social Research: A Book of Readings in Research Methods.* London, England: Constable, 1973.

Robinson, J. P., and Shaver, P. R. *Measures of Social Psychological Attitudes.* (Revised ed.) Ann Arbor: Institute for Social Research, University of Michigan, 1973.

Robison, H. F. *Exploring Teaching in Early Childhood Education.* Boston: Allyn & Bacon, 1977.

Rogers, D. D., and others. *A Cost Analysis of Follow Through Projects.* Bethesda, Md.: RMC Research Corporation, 1977.

Rohwer, W. D., Jr. "Prime Time for Education: Early Childhood or Adolescence?" *Harvard Educational Review*, 1971, *41*, 316–341.

Rosen, C. L. "Review of the Frostig Movement Skills Test Battery: Experimental Edition." In O. K. Buros (Ed.), *The Eighth Mental Measurements Yearbook*. Vol. 2. Highland Park, N.J.: Gryphon Press, 1978.

Rosen, P. (Ed.). "Tests for Spanish-Speaking Children." *Head Start Test Collection*. Princeton, N.J.: Educational Testing Service, 1977.

Rosenshine, B. "Teaching Behaviors Related to Pupil Achievement: A Review of Research." In I. Westbury and A. A. Bellack (Eds.), *Research Into Classroom Processes: Recent Developments and Next Steps*. New York: Teachers College Press, 1971.

Rosenshine, B., and McGaw, B. "Issues in Assessing Teacher Accountability in Public Education." *Phi Delta Kappan*, 1972, *53* (10), 640–643.

Rosenthal, R. *Experimenter Effects in Behavioral Research*. New York: Appleton-Century-Crofts, 1966.

Rosenthal, R., and Rosnow, R. L. *Artifact in Behavioral Research*. New York: Academic Press, 1969.

Rosner, J. "Review of Primary Academic Sentiment Scale." In O. K. Buros (Ed.), *The Seventh Mental Measurements Yearbook*. Vol. 2. Highland Park, N.J.: Gryphon Press, 1972.

Rotter, J. B. "Generalized Expectancies for Internal Versus External Control of Reinforcements." *Psychological Monographs*, 1966, *80* (1, Whole No. 609), 1–28.

Rowen, B. *The Children We See: An Observational Approach to Child Study*. New York: Holt, Rinehart and Winston, 1973.

Ryan, S. *A Report on Longitudinal Evaluations of Preschool Programs*. Vol. 1: *Longitudinal Evaluations*. Washington, D.C.: Department of Health, Education, and Welfare, 1974.

Ryans, D. G. *Characteristics of Teachers: Their Description, Comparison and Appraisal*. Washington, D.C.: American Council on Education, 1960.

Salomon, G., and McDonald, F. J. "Pretest and Posttest Reactions to Self-Viewing One's Teaching Performance on Video Tape." *Journal of Educational Psychology*, 1970, *61*, 280–286.

Samuda, R. J. *Psychological Testing of American Minorities*. New York: Harper & Row, 1975.

Sandler, L., and others. "Responses of Urban Preschool Children to a Developmental Screening Test." *Journal of Pediatrics*, 1970, *77* (5), 775–781.

Sanford, A. R. *A Manual for Use of the Learning Accomplishment Profile*. Winston-Salem, N.C.: Kaplan School Supply, 1974.

Sarason, S. B., and Gladwin, T. "Psychological and Cultural Problems in Mental Subnormality: A Review of Research." *Genetic Psychology Monographs*, 1958, *57*, 3–284.

Sattler, J. M. *Assessment of Children's Intelligence*. Philadelphia: Saunders, 1974.

Sattler, J. M. "Review of the McCarthy Scales of Children's Abilities." In O. K. Buros (Ed.), *The Eighth Mental Measurements Yearbook*. Vol. 1. Highland Park, N.J.: Gryphon Press, 1978.

Scarr-Salapatek, S. "Genetics and the Development of Intelligence." In F. D. Horowitz (Ed.), *Review of Child Development Research.* Vol. 4. Chicago: University of Chicago Press, 1975.

Schell, R. E., and Silber, J. W. "Sex-Role Discrimination Among Young Children." *Perceptual and Motor Skills,* 1968, *27,* 379–389.

Sciara, F. J., and Jantz, R. K. (Eds.). *Accountability in American Education.* Boston: Allyn & Bacon, 1972.

Science Research Associates. *DISTAR.* Chicago: Science Research Associates, 1972.

Scriven, M. "The Methodology of Evaluation." In R. E. Stake (Ed.), *Perspectives on Curriculum Evaluation.* AERA Monograph Series on Curriculum Evaluation No. 1. Skokie, Ill.: Rand McNally, 1967.

Scriven, M. "An Introduction to Meta-evaluation." *Educational Product Report,* 1969, *2* (5), 36–38.

Scriven, M. Remarks presented at an informal colloquium, University of California at Los Angeles, Spring 1972.

Scriven, M. "Goal-free Evaluation." In E. R. House (Ed.), *School Evaluation: The Politics and Process.* Berkeley, Calif.: McCutchan, 1973.

Scriven, M. "Evaluation Perspectives and Procedures." In W. J. Popham (Ed.), *Evaluation in Education: Current Applications.* Berkeley, Calif.: McCutchan, 1974.

Scriven, M. "Evaluation Bias and Its Control." In G. V. Glass (Ed.), *Evaluation Studies Review Annual.* Vol. 1. Beverly Hills, Calif.: Sage Publications, 1976.

Sechrest, L. "Nonreactive Assessment of Attitudes." In E. P. Willems and H. L. Raush (Eds.), *Naturalistic Viewpoints in Psychological Research.* New York: Holt, Rinehart and Winston, 1969.

Semeonoff, B. "Review of R. B. Ammons and C. H. Ammons, The Quick Test (QT)." *British Journal of Psychology,* 1964, *55,* 117.

Shaffer, L. F. "Review of The Measurement of Social Competence: A Manual for the Vineland Social Maturity Scale." *Journal of Consulting Psychology,* 1954, *18,* 74.

Shavelson, R. J., Hubner, J. J., and Stanton, G. C. "Self-Concept: Validation of Construct Interpretations." *Review of Educational Research,* 1976, *46* (3), 407–441.

Shaw, M. E., and Wright, J. M. *Scales for the Measurement of Attitudes.* New York: McGraw-Hill, 1967.

Shepard, L. A. "Review of The Self-Concept and Motivation Inventory (SCAMIN): What Face Would You Wear?" In O. K. Buros (Ed.), *The Eighth Mental Measurements Yearbook.* Vol. 1. Highland Park, N.J.: Gryphon Press, 1978.

Shipman, V. C. *Disadvantaged Children and Their First School Experiences: ETS–Head Start Longitudinal Study.* Vol. 1. Princeton, N.J.: Educational Testing Service, 1970.

Shipman, V. C., and others. *Disadvantaged Children and Their First School Experiences, ETS–Head Start Longitudinal Study: Notable Early Characteristics of High and Low Achieving Black Low-SES Children.* Princeton, N.J.: Educational Testing Service, 1976.

Shure, M.B. "Psychological Ecology of a Nursery School." *Child Development,* 1963, *34,* 979–992.

Siegel, A.W., and White, S.H. "The Development of Spatial Representations of Large-Scale Environments." In H.W. Reese (Ed.), *Advances in Child Development and Behavior.* Vol. 10. New York: Academic Press, 1975.

Siegel, P.M. "Prestige in the American Occupational Structure." Unpublished doctoral dissertation, University of Chicago, 1971.

Sigel, I.E. "Where Is Preschool Education Going: Or Are We Enroute Without a Map?" In *Assessment in a Pluralistic Society,* Proceedings of the 1972 Invitational Conference on Testing Problems. Princeton, N.J.: Educational Testing Service, 1973.

Silverman, R., Noa, J.K., and Russell, R.H. *Oral Language Tests for Bilingual Students: An Evaluation of Language Dominance and Proficiency Instruments.* Portland, Oreg.: Northwest Regional Educational Laboratory, 1976.

Silverstein, A.B. "Review of the McCarthy Scales of Children's Abilities." In O.K. Buros (Ed.), *The Eighth Mental Measurements Yearbook.* Vol. 1. Highland Park, N.J.: Gryphon Press, 1978.

Simon, A., and Boyer, E.G. (Eds.). *Mirrors for Behavior: An Anthology of Observation Instruments.* Philadelphia: Research for Better Schools, 1970.

Simpson, J.E. "A Method of Measuring the Social Weather of Children." In R.G. Barker (Ed.), *The Stream of Behavior.* New York: Appleton-Century-Crofts, 1963.

Sinclair, C.B. *Movement of the Young Child: Ages Two to Six.* Columbus, Ohio: Merrill, 1973.

Sinclair, R.L. "Elementary School Educational Environment: Measurement of Selected Variables of Environmental Press." Unpublished doctoral dissertation, University of Massachusetts, 1969.

Singer, R.N. *Motor Learning and Human Performance.* New York: Macmillan, 1968.

Singer, R.N. (Ed.). *Readings in Motor Learning.* Philadelphia: Lea and Febiger, 1972a.

Singer, R.N. (Ed.). *The Psychomotor Domain: Motor Behaviors.* Philadelphia: Lea and Febiger, 1972b.

Singer, R.N. *Motor Learning and Human Performance.* (2nd ed.) New York: Macmillan, 1975.

Sjogren, D.D. "Measurement Techniques in Evaluation." *Review of Educational Research,* 1970, *40* (2), 301–320.

Sjogren, D.D. "Introduction: Four Examples—Anthropology, Economic, Narrative, and Portrayal." In D.D. Sjogren (Ed.), *Four Evaluation Examples: Anthropological, Economic, Narrative, and Portrayal.* AERA Monograph Series on Curriculum Evaluation No. 7. Skokie, Ill.: Rand McNally, 1974.

Skinner, B.F. *Walden Two.* New York: Macmillan, 1948.

Skinner, B.F. *Science and Human Behavior.* New York: Macmillan, 1953.

Skinner, B.F. "The Science of Learning and the Art of Teaching." *Harvard Educational Review,* 1954, *24,* 86–97.

Skinner, B. F. *Verbal Behavior.* New York: Appleton-Century-Crofts, 1957.

Skinner, B. F. *The Technology of Teaching.* New York: Appleton-Century-Crofts, 1968.

Skinner, B. F. *Beyond Freedom and Dignity.* New York: Knopf, 1971.

Sloan, W. "The Lincoln-Oseretsky Motor Development Scale." *Genetic Psychology Monographs,* 1955, *51,* 183–252.

Slosson, R. L. *Slosson Intelligence Test.* East Aurora, N.Y.: Slosson Educational Publications, 1963.

Smith, E. R., and Tyler, R. W. *Appraising and Recording Student Progress.* New York: Harper & Row, 1942.

Smith, H. W. *Strategies of Social Research: The Methodological Imagination.* Englewood Cliffs, N.J.: Prentice-Hall, 1975.

Smith, L. M. "The Micro-ethnography of the Classroom." *Psychology in the Schools,* 1967, *4,* 216–221.

Smith, L. M., and Geoffrey, W. *The Complexities of an Urban Classroom: An Analysis toward a General Theory of Teaching.* New York: Holt, Rinehart and Winston, 1968.

Smith, L. M., and Pohland, P. A. "Education, Technology, and the Rural Highlands." In D. D. Sjogren (Ed.), *Four Evaluation Examples: Anthropological, Economic, Narrative, and Portrayal.* AERA Monograph Series on Curriculum Evaluation No. 7. Skokie, Ill.: Rand McNally, 1974.

Smith, M. S., and Bissell, J. S. "Report Analysis: The Impact of Head Start." *Harvard Educational Review,* 1970, *40* (1), 51–104.

Smith, R. M., Neisworth, J. T., and Greer, J. G. *Evaluating Educational Environments.* Columbus, Ohio: Merrill, 1978.

Smock, C. D. "Review of the Concept Assessment Kit—Conservation." *Professional Psychology,* 1970, *1* (5), 491–493.

Snapper, K. J., and others. *The Status of Children, 1975.* Washington, D.C.: Social Research Group, George Washington University, 1975.

Soar, R. S. *Final Report: Follow Through Classroom Process Measurement and Pupil Growth (1970–71).* Gainesville: College of Education, University of Florida, 1973.

Soar, R. S., Soar, R. M., and Ragosta, M. *Florida Climate and Control System.* Gainesville: Institute for Development of Human Resources, University of Florida, 1971.

Soares, A. T., and Soares, L. M. *Self-Perception Inventory Composite Manual.* Bridgeport, Conn.: University of Bridgeport, 1975.

Society for the Psychological Study of Social Issues. "Guidelines for Testing Minority Group Children." *Journal of Social Issues,* 1964, *20* (2), 127–145.

Sommer, R. "The Ecology of Privacy." In H. M. Proshansky, W. H. Ittelson, and L. G. Rivlin (Eds.), *Environmental Psychology: Man and His Physical Setting.* New York: Holt, Rinehart and Winston, 1970.

Sostek, A. M. "Review of the Brazelton Neonatal Behavioral Assessment Scale." In O. K. Buros (Ed.), *The Eighth Mental Measurements Yearbook.* Vol. 1. Highland Park, N.J.: Gryphon Press, 1978.

Spivack, G., and Swift, M. *Devereux Elementary School Behavior Rating Scale Manual*. Devon, Penn.: Devereux Foundation, 1967.

Spradley, J. P., and McCurdy, D. W. *Anthropology: The Cultural Perspective*. New York: Wiley, 1975.

Stake, R. E. "The Countenance of Educational Evaluation." *Teachers College Record*, 1967, *68* (7), 523–540.

Stake, R. E. "Objectives, Priorities, and Other Judgment Data." *Review of Educational Research*, 1970a, *40* (2), 181–212.

Stake, R. E. Personal communication, 1970b.

Stake, R. E. "School Accountability Laws." *Evaluation Comment*, 1973, *4* (1), 1–3.

Stake, R. E. "To Evaluate an Arts Program." In R. E. Stake (Ed.), *Evaluating the Arts in Education: A Responsive Approach*. Columbus, Ohio: Merrill, 1975.

Stake, R. E. "The Case Study Method in Social Inquiry." *Educational Researcher*, 1978, 7 (2), 5–8.

Stake, R. E., and Easley, J. A., Jr. *Case Studies in Science Education*. Champaign-Urbana: University of Illinois, 1978.

Stake, R. E., and Gjerde, C. L. "An Evaluation of TCITY, the Twin-City Institute for Talented Youth, 1971." In D. D. Sjogren (Ed.), Four Evaluation Examples: *Anthropological, Economic, Narrative, and Portrayal*. AERA Monograph Series on Curriculum Evaluation No. 7. Skokie, Ill.: Rand McNally, 1974.

Stake, R.·E., and Gooler, D. D. "Measuring Educational Priorities." *Educational Technology*, 1971, *11* (9), 44–48.

Stallings, J. A. "Implementation and Child Effects of Teaching Practices in Follow Through Classrooms." *Monographs of the Society for Research in Child Development*, 1975, *40* (7–8, Serial No. 163).

Stallings, J. A. *Learning to Look: A Handbook on Classroom Observation and Teaching Models*. Belmont, Calif.: Wadsworth, 1977.

Stallings, J. A., and Kaskowitz, D. H. *Follow Through Classroom Observation Evaluation 1972–1973*. Menlo Park, Calif.: Stanford Research Institute, 1974.

Stamp, I. M. *Psychologist's Manual: Stamp Behavior Study Technique*. Hawthorn, Victoria: Australian Council for Educational Research, 1972.

"Standardized Testing in America." *EDC News*, 1977, Issue No. 9, 1–3.

Stanford Research Institute. *Implementation of Planned Variation in Head Start: Preliminary Evaluations of Planned Variation in Head Start According to Follow Through Approaches (1969–1970)*. Menlo Park, Calif.: Stanford Research Institute, 1971. (Also available in ERIC, ED 052844.)

Stanford Research Institute. *Follow Through Program Sponsors*. Menlo Park, Calif.: Stanford Research Institute, 1972.

Stanley, J. C. "Controlled Field Experiments as a Model for Evaluation." In P. H. Rossi and W. Williams (Eds.), *Evaluating Social Programs: Theory, Practice, and Politics*. New York: Seminar Press, 1972a.

Stanley, J. C. (Ed.). *Preschool Programs for the Disadvantaged: Five Experimental Approaches to Early Childhood Education*. Baltimore: Johns Hopkins University Press, 1972b.

Stanley, J. C. (Ed.). *Compensatory Education for Children Ages Two to Eight: Recent*

Studies of Educational Intervention. Baltimore: Johns Hopkins University Press, 1973.

Stanley, J. C., and Hopkins, K. D. *Educational and Psychological Measurement and Evaluation.* (5th ed. of *Measurement in Today's Schools.*) Englewood Cliffs, N.J.: Prentice-Hall, 1972.

Starkweather, E. K. "Creativity Research Instruments Designed for Use with Preschool Children." *Journal of Creative Behavior,* 1971, *5,* 245–255.

Starkweather, E. K. *Starkweather Originality Test for Young Children.* Stillwater: Oklahoma State University, 1974.

Stebbins, L. B., and others. *Education as Experimentation: A Planned Variation Model.* Vols. IV A, B, C, D Cambridge, Mass.: Abt Associates, 1977. (Also issued by the U. S. Office of Education as *National Evaluation: Patterns of Effects,* Vols. II A, B, C, D of the Follow Through Planned Variation Experiment Series.)

Stedman, D. J. "Review of the Denver Developmental Screening Test." In W. K. Frankenburg and B. W. Camp (Eds.), *Pediatric Screening Tests.* Springfield, Ill.: Thomas, 1975.

Steele, J. M., House, E. R., and Kerins, T. "An Instrument for Assessing Instructional Climate through Low-Inference Student Judgments." *American Educational Research Journal,* 1971, *8* (3), 447–466.

Stein, A. H., and Friedrich, L. K. "Impact of Television on Children and Youth." In E. M. Hetherington (Ed.), *Review of Child Development Research.* Vol. 5. Chicago: University of Chicago Press, 1975.

Stephens, B., and others. "Factorial Structure of Selected Psycho-educational Measures and Piagetian Reasoning Assessments." *Developmental Psychology,* 1972, *6* (2), 343–348.

Stern, C. "Evaluating Language Curricula for Preschool Children." *Monographs of the Society for Research in Child Development,* 1968, *33* (8, Serial No. 124).

Stevens, J. J., Jr., and King, E. W. *Administering Early Childhood Education Programs.* Boston: Little, Brown, 1976.

Stolz, L. *Influences on Parent Behavior.* Stanford, Calif.: Stanford University Press, 1967.

Stone, L. J., Smith, H. T., and Murphy, L. B. (Eds.). *The Competent Infant: Research and Commentary.* New York: Basic Books, 1973.

Stott, D. H. *Bristol Social Adjustment Guides Manual.* San Diego, Calif.: Educational and Industrial Testing Service, 1972.

Stott, D. H., Moyes, F. A., and Henderson, F. A. *Test of Motor Impairment.* Guelph, Ontario, Canada: Brook Educational Publishers, 1972.

Stott, L. H., and Ball, R. S. "Infant and Preschool Mental Tests: Review and Evaluation." *Monographs of the Society for Research in Child Development,* 1965, *30* (3, Serial No. 101).

Straus, M. *Family Measurement Techniques: Abstracts of Published Instruments, 1935–1965.* Minneapolis: University of Minnesota Press, 1969.

Streissguth, A. P., and Bee, H. "Mother-Child Interactions and Cognitive Development in Children." In W. W. Hartup (Ed.), *The Young Child: Reviews of*

Research. Vol. 2. Washington, D. C.: National Association for the Education of Young Children, 1972.

Struthers, J., and De Avila, E. A. "Development of a Group Measure to Assess the Extent of Prelogical and Precausal Thinking in Primary Age Children." Paper presented at the convention of the National Science Teachers' Association, Detroit, 1967.

Stubbs, M., and Delamont, S. *Explorations in Classroom Observation.* New York: Wiley, 1976.

Stufflebeam, D. L. "Evaluation as Enlightenment for Decision-Making." Mimeo. Columbus: Evaluation Center, Ohio State University, 1968.

Stufflebeam, D. L. "The Relevance of the CIPP Evaluation Model for Educational Accountability." *Journal of Research and Development in Education,* 1971, *5* (1), 19–23.

Stufflebeam, D. L. "Alternative Approaches to Educational Evaluation: A Self-Study Guide for Educators." In W. J. Popham (Ed.), *Evaluation in Education: Current Applications.* Berkeley, Calif.: McCutchan, 1974a.

Stufflebeam, D. L. "Meta-evaluation." Mimeo. Kalamazoo: Evaluation Center, School of Education, Western Michigan University, 1974b.

Stufflebeam, D. L., and others. *Educational Evaluation and Decision-Making.* Itasca, Ill.: Peacock, 1971.

Summers, D. L., and Felker, D. W. "Use of the It Scale for Children in Assessing Sex-Role Preference in Negro Children." *Developmental Psychology,* 1970, *2,* 330–334.

Swift, M., and Spivack, G. "The Assessment of Achievement-Related Classroom Behavior." *Journal of Special Education,* 1968, *2* (2), 137–153.

System Development Corporation. *Effects of Different Head Start Program Approaches on Children of Different Characteristics: Reports on Analysis of Data from 1966–67, 1967–68, and 1968–69 National Evaluations.* Technical Memoranda No. 4862/001/00 and 4862/000/01. Santa Monica, Calif.: System Development Corporation, 1972. (Also available in ERIC, ED 072859 and ED 072860.)

Tannenbaum, A. J. "Review of the Culture Fair Intelligence Test." In O. K. Buros (Ed.), *The Sixth Mental Measurements Yearbook.* Highland Park, N.J.: Gryphon Press, 1965.

Taub, H. P., and others. *Accept My Profile: Perspectives for Head Start Profiles of Program Effects on Children.* Westport, Conn.: Mediax Associates, 1979.

Ten Brink, T. D. *Evaluation: A Practical Guide for Teachers.* New York: McGraw-Hill, 1974.

Terman, L. M., and Merrill, M. A. *Measuring Intelligence.* Boston: Houghton Mifflin, 1960.

Terman, L. M., and Merrill, M. A. *Stanford-Binet Intelligence Scale: 1972 Norms Edition.* Boston: Houghton Mifflin, 1973.

Thomas, H. "Psychological Assessment Instruments for Use with Human Infants." *Merrill-Palmer Quarterly,* 1970, *16,* 179–223.

Thomas, W. L. *The Thomas Self-Concept Test Manual.* Chicago: Achievement Motivation Program, W. Clement and Jessie V. Stone Foundation, 1972.

Thompson, G. R. *Primary Academic Sentiment Scale: Examiner's Manual.* Skokie, Ill.: Priority Innovations, 1968.

Thompson, N. L., and McCandless, B. "It Score Variations by Instructional Style." *Child Development,* 1970, *41* (2), 425–436.

Thorndike, E. L. "The Nature, Purposes, and General Methods of Measurements of Educational Products." In G. M. Whipple (Ed.), *The Measurement of Educational Products,* 17th Yearbook, Part 2. National Society for the Study of Education. Chicago: University of Chicago Press, 1918.

Thorndike, R. L. "Review of Torrance Tests of Creative Thinking." In O. K. Buros (Ed.), *The Seventh Mental Measurements Yearbook.* Vol. 1. Highland Park, N.J.: Gryphon Press, 1972.

Thorndike, R. L., and Hagen, E. P. *Measurement and Evaluation in Psychology and Education.* (4th ed.) New York: Wiley, 1977.

Thorpe, L. P., Clark, W. W., and Tiegs, E. W. *California Test of Personality Manual.* Monterey, Calif.: CTB/McGraw-Hill, 1953.

Thurstone, L. L. "Creative Talent." In *Proceedings of the 1950 Invitational Conference on Testing Problems.* Princeton, N.J.: Educational Testing Service, 1951.

Tinbergen, N. "Foreword." In N. G. B. Jones (Ed.), *Ethological Studies of Child Behaviour.* London, England: Cambridge University Press, 1972.

Tolman, E. C. "Cognitive Maps in Rats and Men." *Psychological Review,* 1948, *55,* 189–208.

Tomblin, E. A. R. *Effects of Participatory and Nonparticipatory Methods of Teacher Evaluation on Selected Teacher Variables.* Unpublished doctoral dissertation, University of Colorado, 1976.

Torgesen, J. "Problems and Prospects in the Study of Learning Disabilities." In E. M. Hetherington (Ed.), *Review of Child Development Research.* Vol. 5. Chicago: University of Chicago Press, 1975.

Torrance, E. P. *Guiding Creative Talent.* Englewood Cliffs, N.J.: Prentice-Hall, 1962.

Torrance, E. P. *Torrance Tests of Creative Thinking: Norms-Technical Manual.* (Research ed.) Lexington, Mass.: Personnel Press, 1966.

Torrance, E. P. "Predictive Validity of the Torrance Tests of Creative Thinking." *Journal of Creative Behavior,* 1972, *6,* 236–252.

Torrance, E. P. "Non-test Indicators of Creative Talent among Disadvantaged Children." *Gifted Child Quarterly,* 1973, *17,* 3–9.

Torrance, E. P. "Creativity Research in Education: Still Alive." In I. A. Taylor and J. W. Getzels (Eds.), *Perspectives in Creativity.* Chicago: Aldine, 1975.

Torrance, E. P., Khatena, J., and Cunnington, B. F. *Thinking Creatively with Sounds and Images: Direction Manual and Scoring Guide, Sounds and Images and Onomatopoeia and Images.* (Research ed.) Lexington, Mass.: Personnel Press, 1973.

Tractenberg, P. L. *Testing the Teacher: How Urban School Districts Select Their Teachers and Supervisors.* New York: Agathon Press, 1973.

Treffinger, D. J., and Poggio, J. P. "Needed Research on the Measurement of Creativity." *Journal of Creative Behavior,* 1972, *6,* 253–267.

Treiman, D. J. *Occupational Prestige in Comparative Perspective.* New York: Academic Press, 1977.

Trickett, E. J., and Moos, R. H. "Social Environment of Junior High and High School Classrooms." *Journal of Educational Psychology,* 1973, *65,* 93–102.

Tryk, H. E. "Assessment in the Study of Creativity." In P. McReynolds (Ed.), *Advances in Psychological Assessment.* Vol. l. Palo Alto, Calif.: Science and Behavior Books, 1968.

Tuckman, B. W. *Measuring Educational Outcomes: Fundamentals of Testing.* New York: Harcourt Brace Jovanovich, 1975.

Tyler, R. W. "General Statement on Evaluation." *Journal of Educational Research,* 1942, *35* (7), 492–501.

Tyler, R. W. "The Functions of Measurement in Improving Instruction." In E. F. Lindquist (Ed.), *Educational Measurement.* Washington, D.C.: American Council of Education, 1951.

Tyler, R. W. "The Evaluation of Teaching." In R. M. Cooper (Ed.), *The Two Ends of the Log: Learning and Teaching in Today's College.* Minneapolis: University of Minnesota Press, 1958.

Tyler, R. W. "Accountability in Education: The Shift in Criteria." In L. M. Lessinger and R. W. Tyler (Eds.), *Accountability in Education.* Worthington, Ohio: Charles A. Jones, 1971.

Tyler, R. W. "Introduction: A Perspective on the Issues." In R. W. Tyler and R. M. Wolf (Eds.), *Crucial Issues in Testing.* Berkeley, Calif.: McCutchan, 1974.

U.S. Bureau of the Census. *Statistical Abstract of the United States: 1977.* (98th ed.) Washington, D.C.: U.S. Bureau of the Census, 1977.

Uzgiris, I. C., and Hunt, J. McV. *Assessment in Infancy: Ordinal Scales of Psychological Development.* Urbana: University of Illinois Press, 1975.

Vandenberg, B. "Play and Development from an Ethological Perspective." *American Psychologist,* 1978, *33* (8), 724–738.

Van Lieshout, C. F. M. "Young Children's Reactions to Barriers Placed by Their Mothers." *Child Development,* 1975, *46,* 879–886.

Villaume, J., and Haney, W. *The Follow Through Planned Variation Experiment: Analysis of Interim Follow Through Evaluation Reports.* Vol. 5: *Appendix.* Cambridge, Mass.: Huron Institute, 1977.

Wachs, T. D. "Relation of Infants' Performance on Piaget Scales between Twelve and Twenty-four Months and Their Stanford-Binet Performance at Thirty-one Months." *Child Development,* 1975, *46,* 929–935.

Walberg, H. J. "Educational Process Evaluation." In M. W. Apple, M. J. Subkoviak, and H. S. Lufler, Jr. (Eds.), *Educational Evaluation: Analysis and Responsibility.* Berkeley, Calif.: McCutchan, 1974.

Walberg, H. J. "Psychology of Learning Environments: Behavioral, Structural, or Perceptual?" In L. S. Shulman (Ed.), *Review of Research in Education.* Vol. 4. Itasca, Ill.: Peacock, 1977.

Walberg, H. J., and Thomas, S. C. "Open Education: An Operational Definition and Validation in Great Britain and the United States." *American Educational Research Journal,* 1972, *9* (2), 197–208.

Walker, D. K. *Socioemotional Measures for Preschool and Kindergarten Children.* San Francisco: Jossey-Bass, 1973.

Walker, D. K., Bane, M. J., and Bryk, A. S. *The Quality of the Head Start Planned Variation Data.* Vols. 1 and 2. Cambridge, Mass.: Huron Institute, 1973. (Also available in ERIC, ED 082856 and ED 082857.)

Wallach, M. A. "Review of the Torrance Tests of Creativity." *American Educational Research Journal,* 1968, *5,* 272–281.

Wallach, M. A. "Creativity." In P. H. Mussen (Ed.), *Carmichael's Manual of Child Psychology.* Vol. 1. (3rd ed.) New York: Wiley, 1970.

Wallach, M. A., and Kogan, N. *Modes of Thinking in Young Children.* New York: Holt, Rinehart and Winston, 1965.

Warner, W. L., Meeker, M., and Eells, K. *Social Class in America: A Manual of Procedure for the Measurement of Social Status.* Chicago: Science Research Associates, 1949.

Waugh, R. P. "The ITPA: Ballast or Bonanza for the School Psychologist." *Journal of School Psychology,* 1975, *13* (3), 201–208f.

Webb, E. J., and others. *Unobtrusive Measures: Nonreactive Research in the Social Sciences.* Skokie, Ill.: Rand McNally, 1966.

Weber, E. *Early Childhood Education: Perspectives on Change.* Worthington, Ohio: Charles A. Jones, 1970.

Wechsler, D. *Wechsler Preschool and Primary Scale of Intelligence: Manual.* New York: Psychological Corporation, 1967.

Wechsler, D. *Wechsler Intelligence Scale for Children—Revised: Manual.* New York: Psychological Corporation, 1974.

Weick, K. E. "Systematic Observation Methods." In G. Lindzey and E. Aronson (Eds.), *The Handbook of Social Psychology: Research Methods.* Vol. 2. (2nd ed.) Reading, Mass.: Addison-Wesley, 1968.

Weinberg, R. A., and Moore, S. G. "Introduction." In R. A. Weinberg and S. G. Moore (Eds.), *Evaluation of Educational Programs for Young Children.* Washington, D.C.: Child Development Associate Consortium, 1975.

Weintraub, S. "Review of Animal Crackers." In O. K. Buros (Ed.), *The Eighth Mental Measurements Yearbook.* Vol. 1. Highland Park, N.J.: Gryphon Press, 1978.

Weisberg, H. I., and Haney, W. *Longitudinal Evaluation of Head Start Planned Variation and Follow Through.* Cambridge, Mass.: Huron Institute, 1977.

Wenar, C. "The Reliability of Mothers' Histories." *Child Development,* 1961, *32,* 491–500.

Wepman, J. M., and Hass, W. *A Spoken Word Count (Children—Ages 5, 6, and 7).* Chicago: Language Research Associates, 1969.

Werner, E. E. "Review of the Leiter International Performance Scale, Arthur Adaptation." In O. K. Buros (Ed.), *The Sixth Mental Measurements Yearbook.* Highland Park, N.J.: Gryphon Press, 1965.

Werner, E. E. "Review of the Denver Developmental Screening Test." In O. K. Buros (Ed.), *The Seventh Mental Measurements Yearbook.* Vol. 1. Highland Park, N.J.: Gryphon Press, 1972.

Westinghouse Learning Corporation/Ohio University. *The Impact of Head Start: An Evaluation of the Effects of Head Start on Children's Cognitive and Affective Development.* Vols. 1 and 2. Washington, D.C.: Office of Economic Opportunity, 1969. (Also available in ERIC, ED 036321.)

Westman, A. S. "Review of the Southern California Sensory Integration Tests." In O. K. Buros (Ed.), *The Eighth Mental Measurements Yearbook.* Vol. 2. Highland Park, N.J.: Gryphon Press, 1978.

White, B. L. *The First Three Years of Life.* Englewood Cliffs, N.J.: Prentice-Hall, 1975.

White, B. L., and Watts, J. C. *Experience and Environment: Major Influences on the Development of the Young Child.* Vol. 1. Englewood Cliffs, N.J.: Prentice-Hall, 1973.

White, L. E. "The Outdoor Play of Children Living in Flats: An Inquiry into the Use of Courtyards as Playgrounds." In H. M. Proshansky, W. H. Ittelson, and L. G. Rivlin (Eds.), *Environmental Psychology: Man and His Physical Setting.* New York: Holt, Rinehart and Winston, 1970.

White, S. H., and others. *Federal Programs for Young Children: Review and Recommendations.* Vol. 1: *Goals and Standards of Public Programs for Children.* Washington, D.C.: Department of Health, Education, and Welfare, 1973a.

White, S. H., and others. *Federal Programs for Young Children: Review and Recommendations.* Vol. 2: *Review of Evaluation Data for Federally Sponsored Projects for Children.* Washington, D.C.: Department of Health, Education, and Welfare, 1973b.

White, S. H., and others. *Federal Programs for Young Children: Review and Recommendations.* Vol. 3: *Recommendations for Federal Program Planning.* Washington, D.C.: Department of Health, Education, and Welfare, 1973c.

White, S. H., and others. *Federal Programs for Young Children: Review and Recommendations.* Vol. 4: *Summary.* Washington, D.C.: Department of Health, Education, and Welfare, 1973d.

Whitworth, R. H. "Review of the Wechsler Intelligence Scale for Children—Revised." In O. K. Buros (Ed.), *The Eighth Mental Measurements Yearbook.* Vol. 1. Highland Park, N.J.: Gryphon Press, 1978.

Wiederholt, J. L. "Review of the Illinois Test of Psycholinguistic Abilities, Revised Edition." In O. K. Buros (Ed.), *The Eighth Mental Measurements Yearbook.* Vol. 1. Highland Park, N.J.: Gryphon Press, 1978.

Wiegerink, R., and Weikart, D. P. "Measurement of Mother Teaching Styles." *Proceedings of the 75th Annual Convention of the American Psychological Association,* 1967, *2,* 333–334.

Willems, E. P. "Planning a Rationale for Naturalistic Research." In E. P. Willems and H. L. Raush (Eds.), *Naturalistic Viewpoints in Psychological Research.* New York: Holt, Rinehart and Winston, 1969.

Willems, E. P., and Raush, H. L. (Eds.), *Naturalistic Viewpoints in Psychological Research.* New York: Holt, Rinehart and Winston, 1969.

Williams, J. E., and Bennett, S. M. "The Definition of Sex Stereotypes Via the Adjective Check List." *Sex Roles,* 1975, *1,* 327–337.

Williams, J. E., Bennett, S. M., and Best, D. L. "Awareness and Expression of Sex

Stereotypes in Young Children." *Developmental Psychology,* 1975, *11,* 635–642.

Williams, J. E., and Best, D. L. "Sex Stereotypes and Trait Favorability on the Adjective Check List." *Educational and Psychological Measurement,* 1977, *37,* 101–110.

Williams, J. E., Best, D. L., and Associates. *Preschool Racial Attitude Measure II and Color Meaning Test II: General Information and Manuals of Direction.* Winston-Salem, N.C.: Department of Psychology, Wake Forest University, 1975.

Williams, J. E., Best, D. L., and Associates. *Sex Stereotype Measure II and Sex Attitude Measure: General Information and Manual of Directions.* Winston-Salem, N.C.: Department of Psychology, Wake Forest University, 1976.

Williams, J. E., Best, D. L., and Boswell, D. A. "Children's Racial Attitudes in the Early School Years." *Child Development,* 1975, *46,* 494–500.

Williams, J. E., Best, D. L., and Davis, S. W. *Sex Stereotype Measure II (SSM II): Technical Report.* Winston-Salem, N.C.: Department of Psychology, Wake Forest University, 1977.

Williams, J. E., and Edwards, C. D. "An Exploratory Study of the Modification of Color Concepts and Racial Attitudes in Preschool Children." *Child Development,* 1969, *40,* 737–750.

Williams, J. E., and Roberson, J. K. "A Method of Assessing Racial Attitudes in Preschool Children." *Educational and Psychological Measurement,* 1967, *27,* 671–689.

Williams, J. E., and others. "Preschool Racial Attitude Measure II." *Educational and Psychological Measurement,* 1975, *35,* 3–18.

Williams, R. L. "The BITCH-100: A Culture-Specific Test." Paper presented at the annual meeting of the American Psychological Association, Honolulu, September 1972.

Williams, W., and Evans, J. W. "The Politics of Evaluation: The Case of Head Start." In P. H. Rossi and W. Williams (Eds.), *Evaluating Social Programs: Theory, Practice, and Politics.* New York: Seminar Press, 1972.

Winkel, G. H., and Sasanoff, R. "An Approach to an Objective Analysis of Behavior in Architectural Space." In H. M. Proshansky, W. H. Ittelson, and L. G. Rivlin (Eds.), *Environmental Psychology: Man and His Physical Setting.* New York: Holt, Rinehart and Winston, 1970.

Wisler, C. E., Burns, G. P., Jr., and Iwamoto, D. "Follow Through Redux: A Response to the Critique by House, Glass, McLean, and Walker." *Harvard Educational Review,* 1978, *48* (2), 171–185.

Withall, J. "The Development of a Technique for the Measurement of Socioemotional Climate in Classrooms." *Journal of Experimental Education,* 1949, *17,* 347–361.

Wolcott, H. F. "Criteria for an Ethnographic Approach to Research in Schools." In J. T. Roberts and S. K. Akinsanya (Eds.), *Schooling in the Cultural Context.* New York: McKay, 1976.

Wolf, J. M., and others. *Compendium of Information Gathering Techniques Utilized in Previous Head Start Research Projects.* Westport, Conn.: Mediax Associates, 1978.

Wolf, R. "The Measurement of Environments." In A. Anastasi (Ed.), *Testing*

Problems in Perspective. Washington, D.C.: American Council on Education, 1966.

Wolf, R. L. "How Teachers Feel Toward Evaluation." In E. R. House (Ed.), *School Evaluation: The Politics and Process.* Berkeley, Calif.: McCutchan, 1973.

Wolf, R. L. "Trial by Jury: A New Evaluation Method. I. The Process." *Phi Delta Kappan,* 1975, *57* (3), 185–187.

Womer, F. B. *What Is National Assessment?* Ann Arbor, Mich.: National Assessment of Educational Progress, 1970.

Woolner, R. B. "Self-Concept—What Is It?" *Instructor,* 1971, *80* (7), 60.

Worthen, B. R., and Sanders, J. R. *Educational Evaluation: Theory and Practice.* Columbus, Ohio: Charles A. Jones, 1973.

Wright, H. F. "Observational Child Study." In P. H. Mussen (Ed.), *Handbook of Research Methods in Child Development.* New York: Wiley, 1960.

Wright, H. F. *Recording and Analyzing Child Behavior.* New York: Harper & Row, 1967.

Wright, J. C. *Kansas Reflection-Impulsivity Scale for Preschoolers (KRISP).* St. Louis: Central Midwest Regional Educational Laboratory, 1971.

Wylie, R. *The Self-Concept, Volume One: A Review of Methodological Considerations and Measuring Instruments.* (Revised ed.) Lincoln: University of Nebraska Press, 1974.

Yang, R. K., and Bell, R. Q. "Assessment of Infants." In P. McReynolds (Ed.), *Advances in Psychological Assessment.* Vol. 3. San Francisco: Jossey-Bass, 1975.

Yarger, S. J. "From Rock Through Melon to Mush: The Place of the Teaching Center in Research and Evaluation." In G. E. Dickson (Ed.), *Research and Evaluation in Operational Competency-Based Teacher Education Programs.* Toledo, Ohio: College of Education, University of Toledo, 1975.

Yarrow, M. R., Campbell, J. D., and Burton, R. V. *Child Rearing: An Inquiry into Research and Methods.* San Francisco: Jossey-Bass, 1968.

Yarrow, M. R., Campbell, J. D., and Burton, R. V. "Recollections of Childhood: A Study of the Retrospective Method." *Monographs of the Society for Research in Child Development,* 1970, *35* (5, Serial No. 138).

Zaner-Bloser. *Evaluation Scales for Handwriting.* Columbus, Ohio: Zaner-Bloser Handwriting, 1979.

Zegiob, L. E., Arnold, S., and Forehand, R. "An Examination of Observer Effects in Parent-Child Interactions." *Child Development,* 1975, *46,* 509–512.

Zehrbach, R. R. *Comprehensive Identification Process: Interviewer's Manual.* Bensenville, Ill.: Scholastic Testing Service, 1975a.

Zehrbach, R. R. *Comprehensive Identification Process: Screening Administrator's Manual.* Bensenville, Ill.: Scholastic Testing Service, 1975b.

Zehrbach, R. R. "Determining a Preschool Handicapped Population." *Exceptional Children,* 1975c, *42* (2), 76–83.

Zelniker, T., and Jeffrey, W. E. "Reflective and Impulsive Children: Strategies of Information Processing Underlying Differences in Problem Solving." *Monographs of the Society for Research in Child Development,* 1976, *41* (5, Serial No. 168).

Zettel, J. T., and Abeson, A. "The Right to a Free Appropriate Public Education."

In C. P. Hooker (Ed.), *The Courts and Education,* 77th Yearbook, Part 1. National Society for the Study of Education. Chicago: University of Chicago Press, 1978.

Zigler, E. F. "Raising the Quality of Children's Lives." *Children,* 1970, *17*, 166–170.

Zigler, E. F., and Hunsinger, S. "Bringing Up Day Care." *APA Monitor,* 1977, *8* (3), 1, 8–9.

Name Index

Subject Index